CHAPTER 1 POINTS AND LINES

LESSON 1-1 (pp. 2–7)

1. Georges Seurat
2. A pixel is a dot on a television screen or computer monitor; it is a combination of the words *picture* and *element*.
3. True; resolution is determined by the number of pixels per unit of area.
4. A dot-matrix printer prints using dots in a rectangular array (called a matrix).
5. False; provided that lines have to pass through the centers of the dots, several different lines cannot contain two given points.
6. A dot is a description of a point.
7. A discrete line is made up of points with space between their centers.
8. A discrete line may be horizontal, vertical, or oblique.
9. Points that lie on the same line are called collinear.
10. **a.** An IBM PC screen has 320 rows and 192 columns; $320 \times 192 = 61{,}440$ pixels.
    b. An Apple Macintosh screen has 512 rows and 342 columns; $512 \times 342 = 175{,}104$ pixels.
11. Sample:

12. Sample:

13. 200 rows $\times$ 300 columns = 60,000 pixels
    150 rows $\times$ 310 columns = 46,500 pixels
    If both screens have the same dimensions, the screen with 200 rows, 300 columns has better resolution.

14. Sample:

15. **a.** The background is white, so it seems that black squares were used.
    b. By clustering the black squares, some parts look darker.

16. Sample:

17. Sample:

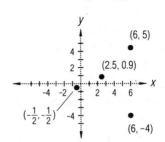

18. The Seurat painting is over 6 ft high and about 10 ft wide. The area is $\approx 6 \times 10 = 60$ sq ft.

19. Substitute 6 for y in
$$4x - 3y = 12:$$
$$4x - 3(6) = 12$$
$$4x - 18 = 12$$
$$4x = 30$$
$$x = 7.5$$

20.

21. **a.** $|{-23}| = 23$
    b. $|4 - 19| = |{-15}| = 15$
    c. $|19.3 - 11| = |8.3| = 8.3$
    d. $|7 - {-5}| = |7 + 5| = |12| = 12$

22. Answers will vary. The pictures in magazines and textbooks will have more dots per inch (dpi) than newspapers.

23. The light bulbs show the letters CAUT and AHE. A possible message is "CAUTION AHEAD."

24. Sample: Pointillism is a method of painting with tiny dots and no brush strokes.

LESSON 1–2 (pp. 8–13)

1. A point was an idealized dot with no size and no dimension.

2. The road mileage between New York and Los Angeles is 2786 miles.

3. The air distance is 2451 miles.

4. The distance between two points on a coordinatized line is the absolute value of the difference between the two coordinates.

5. The distance between A and B is written AB.

6. **a.** $|5 - 14| = |-9| = 9$
　　b. $|14 - 5| = |9| = 9$
　　c. $|-14 - (-5)| = |-14 + 5| = |-9| = 9$

7. $|-321 - 32| = |-353| = 353$

8. $|3 - (-4)| = |3 + 4| = |7| = 7$

9. $|x - y|$ or $|y - x|$

10. **a.** A point has zero dimensions.
　　b. A plane has two dimensions.
　　c. A line has one dimension.
　　d. Space has three dimensions.

11. A line is dense when there is no space between points on the line.

12. The measure is $|1 - 45| = |-44| = 44''$.

13. Samples: The mileage may be measured from different points in the cities, or along different roads.

14. Air mileage, measured along a straight line, is usually less than road mileage, because there may not be a straight road between the two points.

15. Cincinnati to Cleveland is 244 miles. Cincinnati to Toledo then Toledo to Cleveland is $200 + 111 = 311$ miles. The difference is $|311 - 244| = |67| = 67$ miles.

16.

a.

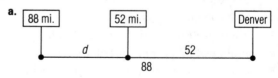

b.

17. **a.** $AB = |-50 - 100| = |-150| = 150$
　　　$BC = |100 - 325| = |-225| = 225$
　　　$AC = |-50 - 325| = |-375| = 375$
　　b. $AB + BC = 150 + 225 = 375 = AC$
　　　True; $AB + BC = AC$.

18. For point as dot:
　　True; a dot has size.
　　False; lines made of dots may cross with no points in common.
　　False; between two distinct dots on a line there is not necessarily another dot.
　　For point as location:
　　False; a location has no size.
　　True; if two coplanar lines are not parallel, then they have a point (of intersection) in common.
　　True; lines are dense.

19. $380 \times 192 = 72{,}960$ pixels

20. $380 \times 192 = 72{,}960$ pixels
　　$330 \times 154 = 50{,}820$ pixels
　　The screen with 380×192 pixels has better resolution because it has more pixels.

21. A discrete line is one made up of points with space between their centers.

22.

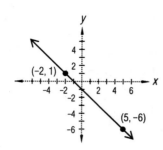

23. If $x - 3y = 5$, then
$$-3y = -x + 5$$
$$y = \frac{-x + 5}{-3} \text{ or }$$
$$y = \frac{x - 5}{3}.$$

For $x = 3$, $y = \frac{3 - 5}{3} = -\frac{2}{3}$.

For $x = -2$, $y = \frac{-2 - 5}{3} = -\frac{7}{3}$.

For $x = 5$, $y = \frac{5 - 5}{3} = 0$.

24. Space-time has four dimensions. Three of them are locations in space, the fourth represents a location in time.

25. Distances to the four cities will vary depending on your location.

LESSON 1-3 (pp. 14–18)

1. Three descriptions of point are dot, location, and ordered pair.

2. a., b. Pierre de Fermat and René Descartes developed the idea of using ordered pairs of numbers to represent points; that was around 1630, or about 360 years ago.

3. $x - 3y = 5$ is of the form $Ax + By = C$, neither A nor B is zero; the line is oblique.

4. $y = -1.234$ is of the form $Ax + By = C$ with $A = 0$; the line is horizontal.

5. $x = 8$ is of the form $Ax + By = C$ with $B = 0$; the line is vertical.

6. $14 - 9y = 32x$ can be rewritten as $32x + 9y = 14$, which is of the form $Ax + By = C$ with neither A nor B zero; the line is oblique.

7. a. Four characteristics of points and lines are: two points determine a line (uniqueness); points are without size, lines are without thickness, and planes have more than one line (dimension); lines can be coordinatized (number line); and distance between points is unique (distance).

b. Points as dots satisfy uniqueness (if lines have to go through the centers of the dots).

c. Points as ordered pairs satisfy all four characteristics.

8.

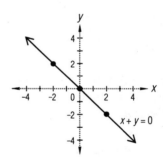

9.

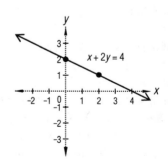

10.

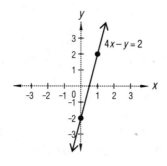

11.

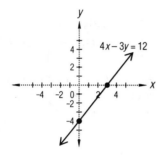

12. **a.** If (q, d) represents the number of dimes and quarters, then
$$10d + 25q = 1200,$$
$$10d = -25q + 1200$$
$$d = -2.5q + 120$$
Substitute values of q (for which $-2.5q$ is a whole number):

If $q = 0$, $d = 120$.
If $q = 2$, $d = -5 + 120 = 115$.
If $q = 4$, $d = -10 + 120 = 110$.
If $q = 6$, $d = -15 + 120 = 105$.
IF $q = 8$, $d = -20 + 120 = 100$.
These represent ordered pairs (0, 120), (2, 115), (4, 110), (6, 105), and (8, 100).
In general, if n is an even integer such that $0 \leq n \leq 48$, the ordered pair (q, d) is $\left(n, \dfrac{1200 - 25n}{10}\right)$.

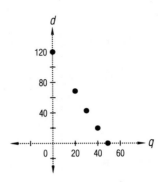

c. Yes. (The points are on the line with equation $10d + 25q = 2500$.)

13. The horizontal line through (0, -5) has a constant y-value; the equation is $y = -5$.

14. The vertical line through (7, -10) has a constant x-value; the equation is $x = 7$.

15. **a.–b.**

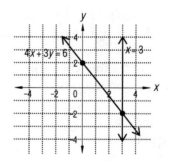

c. The lines intersect at $x = 3$. For
$$4x + 3y = 6,$$
$$4(3) + 3y = 6$$
$$12 + 3y = 6$$
$$3y = -6$$
$$y = -2$$
The intersection is (3, -2), which satisfies both equations.

16. $|1 - 10| = |-9| = 9$

17. The Hitachi resolution is greater than the IBM PC (about 660/square in.) but less than the Macintosh (about 1100/square in.)

18.

19. $AB = |7.7 - 9.5| = |-1.8| = 1.8$ cm

20. **a.** $CD = |-7 - (-211)| = |-7 + 211| = |204|$
$= 204$
b. $DC = |-211 - (-7)| = |-211 + 7| = |-204|$
$= 204$

21. **a.** Columbus to Savannah is 269 miles. Columbus to Atlanta, then Atlanta to Savannah, is $108 + 255 = 363$ miles. The difference is $|269 - 363| = |-94| = 94$ miles.
b. rate × time = distance
$(55 \text{ mph})t = 94$
$$t = \frac{94}{55} \approx 1.7 \text{ hours}$$

22. **a.** Rewrite $3x + 2y = 5$ as
$2y = -3x + 5$
$$y = \frac{-3x + 5}{2}$$
y is a whole number when x is odd, so any odd value of x will provide a lattice point.
If $x = 1, y = \frac{-3 + 5}{2} = \frac{2}{2} = 1$; a lattice point is $(1, 1)$.

b. Rewrite $4x - y = 8$ as
$-y = -4x + 8$
$y = 4x - 8$
Any integer value for x will give an integer value for y, so select any non-integer value for x:
If $x = \frac{1}{2}, y = 4(\frac{1}{2}) - 8 = 2 - 8 = -6$.
The point $(\frac{1}{2}, -6)$ is on the line $4x - y = 8$ but is not a lattice point.

23. Longitude and latitude values depend on your location.

LESSON 1–4 (pp. 19–24)

1. There are 7 bridges.
2. The Königsberg Bridge Problem: Is there a way to walk across all the bridges so that each bridge is crossed exactly once?
3. Leonhard Euler solved the problem in 1736.
4. The nodes represent land areas.
5. The arcs represent bridges.
6. A network is traversable when there is a path going over each arc exactly once without lifting the pencil off the paper.
7. A point is a node of a network.
8. A line is an arc of a network.
9. Euler noticed that odd vertices must be either a starting or finishing point of a traversable path.
10. **a.** Sample: **b.** Sample:

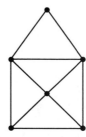

11.

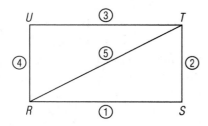

12. a.

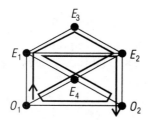

b. O_1 or O_2

c. O_2 or O_1

d. E's are even vertices; O's are odd vertices.

13. a. Start at A or B; then any direction yields a traversable path.

b. A or B

14. a. Start at any vertex. From L, J, H, or F, do outside or inside square first, then do other square. From K, M, G, or I, do $\frac{7}{8}$ of outside square, then do inside square, then finish outside square.

b. any vertex

15. a.

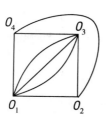

There are 4 odd vertices.

b. Not traversable; more than 2 odd vertices.

16. a.

5 even vertices

b. Yes; start at any vertex.

17. a.

b.

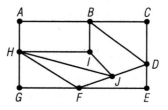

18. Yes

Start at middle of left hall or start in the middle of the figure.

19. For dots:

There is sometimes a point between two points on a line.

There are always infinitely many points on a line.

There is always exactly one line through the (centers of) two points.

For Ordered Pairs and Locations:

All six statements are always true.

For Nodes:

There is never a node between two nodes on an arc (that would make two arcs).

Never; an arc only contains 2 nodes.

There is sometimes an arc between two given nodes.

20. $4x - 3y = 6$

$$-3y = -4x + 6$$

$$y = \frac{4}{3}x - 2$$

x	-3	0	3	6
y	-6	-2	2	6

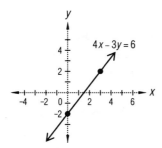

21.

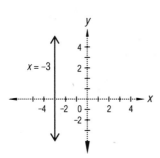

22. A horizontal line has a constant y-value, so the horizontal line through (-2, 5) is $y = 5$.

23. From the given information, a graph of A, B, and C is:

$$AB + BC = |\text{-}6 - 1| + |1 - 14|$$
$$= |\text{-}7| + |\text{-}13|$$
$$= 7 + 13$$
$$= 20$$

24. A laser beam is a model for a ray or line; it has one dimension.

25. $CD = |\text{-}2 - 3| = |\text{-}5| = 5$

26. **a.** **b.**

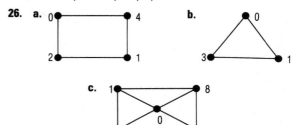

c.

LESSON 1-5 (pp. 25–29)

1. a. Yes; railroad tracks seem to meet in the distance in a perspective drawing.

b. No; railroad tracks are always parallel and do not meet.

2. A vanishing point is the point or points in a perspective drawing where parallel lines would seem to meet if extended.

3. Lines of sight are imaginary lines connecting the eye to points on an object.

4. a. Horizontal parallel lines would not intersect.

b. Vertical parallel lines would not intersect.

c. Oblique parallel lines are drawn to intersect (if extended).

5. In general, mathematicians do not use perspective in drawing.

6. In non-perspective drawings, hidden lines are shown as dotted lines.

7. **a.** Sample: **b.** Sample:

 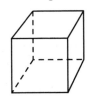

8. A vanishing point is best described as a location.

9. **a.** I and IV are drawn in perspective.
   b.

 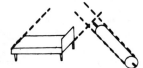

10. Sample:

11. Draw a two-dimensional, 6-sided model for the cube (this is called a *net* in Chapter 9).

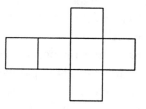

Use the three views of the cube to fill in the six faces.

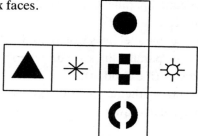

From this model, the opposite faces are

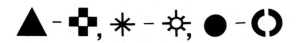

12. **a.** Opposite sides add to 7, so the sum of three pairs of opposite sides is 21. Showing are 8 dots, so $21 - 8 = 13$ dots are not showing.
    b. The bottom is 4 (because the top is 3); the back is 2 (because the front is 5); the sides are 1 and 6.

13. Not traversable; there are 4 odd vertices.

14. Traversable. Sample: P to Q to R to P to S to Q (bottom arc) to S (top arc) to R

15. **a.**

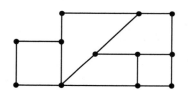

   b. No; there are 6 odd vertices.

16. A vertical line has a constant x-value; the vertical line through (-1, -6) is $x = -1$.

17. **a.**

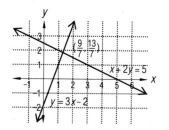

b. Answers may vary; the actual point of intersection is $(\frac{9}{7}, \frac{13}{7})$.

To find those values, substitute the expression for y from the first equation $(y = 3x - 2)$ into the second equation:
$$x + 2y = 5$$
$$x + 2(3x - 2) = 5$$
$$x + 6x - 4 = 5$$
$$7x = 9$$
$$x = \frac{9}{7}$$

$$y = 3x - 2$$
$$= 3(\tfrac{9}{7}) - 2$$
$$= \frac{27}{7} - \frac{14}{7}$$
$$= \frac{13}{7}$$

18. $AB = |461 - (-35)|$
$= |461 + 35|$
$= |496|$
$= 496$

19. $w = |17 - 73| = |{-56}| = 56$ cm

20. **a.** a man in a military uniform, with a little boy and a little girl

b. Sample: they were used as puzzles, to convey hidden political views, or to satirize.

LESSON 1-6 (pp. 30–34)

1. Space is the set of all points.

2. A figure is a set of points.

3. Plane geometry is the study of two-dimensional figures; solid geometry is the study of three-dimensional figures.

4. Samples: law, philosophy, economics, science, labor relations

5. circularity

6. point, line, plane

7. Samples: equation, number, variable, expression

8. Sample: Between two points on a line, there is always another point on that line.

9. Sample: concord, harmony, agreement, harmony; 3 words

10. Sample: inundate, flood, inundate; 2 words

11. Sample: satire, ridicule, derision, ridicule; 3 words

12. Sample: ability to do what you want to do

13. Sample: quantity

14. No; mathematicians usually use dashed or dotted lines to show depth.

15. **a.**   **b.**

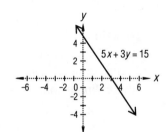

16.

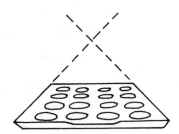

17.

18.

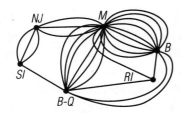

The network is traversable. The odd vertices, which are Manhatten and Randall's Island, must be the endpoints of the path.

19. $AB = |2.7 - 8| = |-5.3| = 5.3$

20.

	Location	O.P.	Node	Dot
i	A	A	S	S
ii	A	A	N	A
iii	A	A	A	N

21. **a.** A line has one dimension.
   b. A plane has two dimensions.
   c. A point has zero dimensions.
   d. Space has three dimensions.

22.

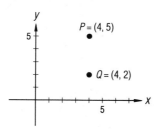

$PQ = |5 - 2| = 3$

23.

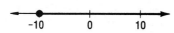

24.

25. **a.** Sample: In the Scott, Foresman Advanced Dictionary (1988), *point* has 29 meanings as a noun, 8 meanings as part of a phrase, 12 meanings as a transitive verb, and 5 meanings as an intransitive verb. The total is 54.

b. While not as many as "point," "number" has 27 meanings, "net" has 12, "do" has 29, and "set" has over 50.

LESSON 1–7 (pp. 35–39)

1. A postulate is an assumption.
2. Two purposes of postulates are to explain undefined terms and to serve as a starting point for logically deducing statements in geometry.
3. No; the unique line assumption does not hold for nodes.
4. Yes; the unique line assumption holds for locations.
5. Yes; the dimension assumption holds for ordered pairs.
6. No; the distance assumption does not hold for dots.
7. True; all parts of the Point-Line-Plane Postulate hold for points as locations.
8. Part (a), the unique line assumption, is violated by the figure.
9. The line through X and A is $\overleftrightarrow{XA}$ or $\overleftrightarrow{AX}$.
10. True, a line is parallel to itself.
11. The *Elements* is a set of books by Euclid that organized and presented postulates and theorems.
12. For Euclid, the Equation to Inequality Property was "The whole is greater than any of its parts."
13. Transitive Property of Equality
14. Commutative Property of Multiplication
15. Addition Property of Equality (Add -46 to each side.)
16. Addition Property of Inequality (Add -46 to each side.)
17. Equation to Inequality Property
18. Substitution Property of Equality
19. Distributive Property

20. a. Commutative Property of Multiplication
b. Distributive Property
c. Commutative Property of Multiplication

21. Addition Property of Equality

22.

There would be 999 dots between 0 and 1 (not including 0 or 1).

23. Sample: proboscis, snout, nose, smell, nose; 5 words

24. a. 5 nodes: A, B, C, D, E.
b. 10 arcs: $AB, AB, AC, AC, BC, BE, BD, CD, CE, DE$
c. It is not traversable because it has more than two odd vertices ($B, C, D,$ and E are odd vertices.)

25. a.

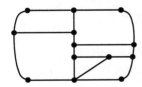

b. No; it has 8 odd vertices.

26. a.

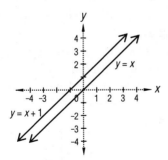

b. Both lines have slope 1; they are parallel.

27.

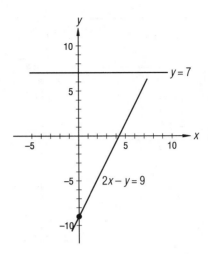

a. $y = 7$ is horizontal.
b. $2x - y = 9$ is oblique.

28. Samples: $>$, "is a subset of," "goes to the same school as," "is parallel to."

LESSON 1-8 (pp. 40–45)

1.

C is between A and B because $\sqrt{2}$ is between -2 and 2.

2. $\overline{AB}$ is the set with elements $A, B,$ and all points between A and B.

3. A laser beam is a model for a ray.

4. a. $\overline{AB}$ is a segment.
b. AB is a length.
c. $\overleftrightarrow{AB}$ is a line.
d. $\overrightarrow{AB}$ is a ray.

5. $\overrightarrow{MN}$ has endpoint M and contains a second point N.

6. If X is between Y and Z, then $YX + XZ = YZ$; that is choice (b).

7. If X is between Y and Z, then $YX + XZ = YZ$ and $YZ > XZ$; that is choice (d).

8.

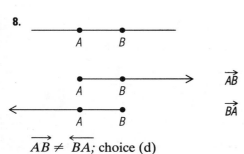

$\overrightarrow{AB} \neq \overleftarrow{BA}$; choice (d)

9.

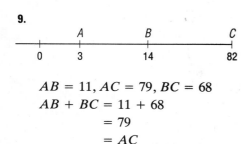

$AB = 11$, $AC = 79$, $BC = 68$
$AB + BC = 11 + 68$
$\qquad = 79$
$\qquad = AC$

10. **a.**

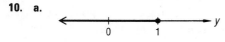

b. The graph is a ray.

11. **a.**

b. The graph is a segment.

12. $AC = AB + BC$
$100 = 21 + BC$
$BC = 79$
$\quad x = 17 + 79 = 96$

13. $AB = BC$
$\quad 21 = BC$
$\quad x = 17 + 21 = 38$

14.

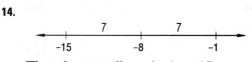

The other coordinate is -1 or -15.

15.

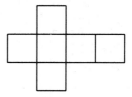

The two coordinates for R are -26 and 16.

16.

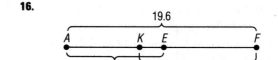

$AK = 19.6 - 12 = 7.6$
$EF = 19.6 - 10 = 9.6$
$KE = 19.6 - (7.6 + 9.6)$
$\quad = 19.6 - 17.2$
$\quad = 2.4$

17.

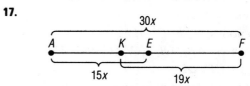

$AK = 30x - 19x = 11x$
$EF = 30x - 15x = 15x$
$KE = 30x - (11x + 15x)$
$\quad = 30x - 26x$
$\quad = 4x$

18. Distributive Property

19. Multiplication Property of Equality (Multiply both sides by $\frac{1}{5}$.)

20. Symmetric Property of Equality

21. **a.** True; a line is parallel to itself.

b. True; in a plane two lines either intersect or are parallel.

c. False; if two lines intersect in one point, they are not parallel.

22. Here is a "net" for the cube:

Opposite faces are U and M, G and S, P and C.

23.

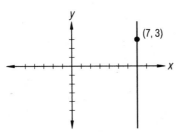

24.

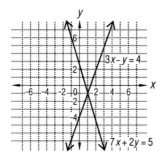

The equation is $x = 7$.

25. All longitude lines meet at two points (the poles); this would violate part (a), the unique line assumption.

26. **a.**

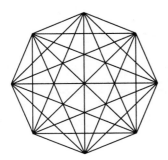

4 points yield 6 segments.

b.

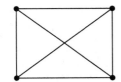

8 points yield 28 segments.

c. For n points, each can go to $n - 1$ other points, but this would count each segment twice. So the number of segments determined by n points is $\frac{1}{2}n(n - 1)$.

LESSON 1–9 (pp. 46–51)

1. The Triangle Inequality Postulate is that the sum of the lengths of two sides of any triangle is greater than the length of the third side.

2. For $\triangle ABC$:
$AB + BC > AC;$
$AC + CB > AB;$
$BA + AC > BC.$

3. (a) and (b) (For (c): $2 + 2 \not> 4$; For (d): $2 + 2 \not> 5$.)

4. (b) (For (a): $12 + 15 \not> 28$; For (c): $12 + 2 \not> 15$.)

5. (b) and (c) (For (a): $1 + 2 \not> 3$.)

6.

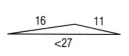

The third side is > 5 but < 27.

7.

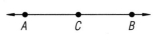

$BA + AC = BC$

8.

$AB = AC + CB$ by the Betweenness Theorem

$AB > AC$ by the Equation to Inequality Property

$AB + BC > AB$ by the Addition Property of Inequality

$AB + BC > AC$ by the Transitive Property of Inequality

9. For any three points A, B, and C, $AB + BC \geq AC$.

10.

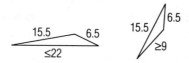 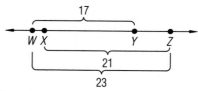

The distance is ≥ 9 and ≤ 22.

11.

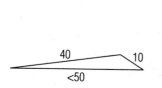

True, Q is between P and R.

12. **a.** $\frac{1}{2} = .5$, $\frac{1}{3} \approx .3$, $\frac{1}{4} = .25$

The sum of any two is greater than the third, so the lengths can be the sides of a triangle.

b. $\frac{1}{2} = .5$, $\frac{1}{3} \approx .33$, $\frac{1}{5} = .2$

The sum of any two is greater than the third, so the lengths can be the sides of a triangle.

c. $\frac{1}{2}, \frac{1}{2}, \frac{1}{4}$

The sum of any two is greater than the third, so the lengths can be the sides of a triangle.

13. **a.** Yes; the range for t, the third side, is $11 < t < 29$, so 9 cm is the shortest side.

b. No; the longest side can be up to 29 cm.

14.

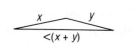 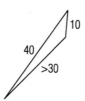

between 30 and 50 miles

15.

$|x - y| < z < x + y$

16. **a.**

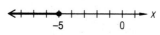

b. The graph is a ray.

17.

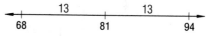

$WX = 23 - 21 = 2$
$XY = 17 - WX$
$= 17 - 2$
$= 15$

18.

The coordinates are 68 and 94.

19. Commutative Property of Addition

20. A postulate is an assumption.

21. **a.**

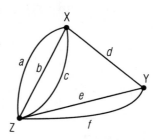

b. Yes, it is traversable because it has 2 odd vertices.

22.

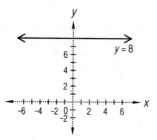

23. $|14 - x| = |14 - 42| = |-28| = 28$

24. The sum of any three lengths must be greater than the fourth length.

CHAPTER 1 PROGRESS SELF-TEST (p. 53)

1. $AB = |\text{-}8 - \text{-}4| = |\text{-}4| = 4$ units

2. **a.** sample:

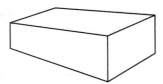

b. sample:

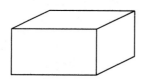

3.

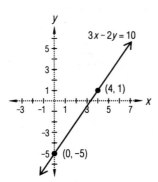

4. The Triangle Inequality Postulate states that the sum of two sides of a triangle must be longer than the third side. Since $4.8 + 3.7 = 8.5 < 9.2$, the three lengths cannot be the sides of a triangle.

5. Extremes;

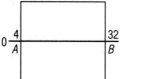

The distance d from Manila to Shanghai is less than or equal to $1115 + 1229$ and greater than or equal to $1229 - 1115$, or
$114 \le d \le 2344$.

6. "A line contains infinitely many points" is always true for dots, locations, and ordered pairs (because the lines have no ends) and is never true for nodes (an arc has only two nodes).

7. "A point has size" is always true for points as dots, and never true for locations, ordered pairs, and nodes.

8. Space has three dimensions: length, width, and depth.

9. Ignoring thickness, a sheet of paper is "flat," like a plane, so it has two dimensions.

10. If, in defining a word, you return to that original word, circularity has occurred.

11. **a.b.** The screen that is 180×310 pixels has 55,800 pixels; the screen that is 215×350 pixels has 75,250 pixels. The screen with more pixels per unit of area, which is the 215×350 screen, has better resolution.

12.

<table>
<tr><td>

4	32
A	B

</td><td>

$AB = |4 - 32|$
$= |\text{-}28|$
$= 28$ inches

</td></tr>
</table>

13. The distances are different because the air distance may be measured along a straight path, perhaps between airports, and the road distance may be measured along a path that follows highways, perhaps between two downtown locations.

14.

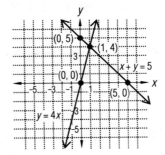

15

15. Two points on $x = \frac{3}{2}$ are $(\frac{3}{2}, 0)$ and $(\frac{3}{2}, 10)$; the line determined by these points is vertical.

16. Two points on $11x + y = 3$ are $(0, 3)$ and $(\frac{3}{11}, 0)$; the line determined by those points is oblique.

17. a. The network has no more than two odd vertices, so it is traversable.

    b. Sample: V to Z to T to V to W to Z to X to W

18. a.

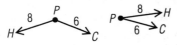

    b. The network has more than two odd vertices, so it is not traversable.

19. Extremes:

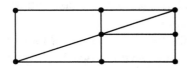

The time t needed to get from H to C is less than or equal to $8 + 6$ and more than or equal to $8 - 6$, so $2 \le t \le 14$.

20. If $3x > 11$, the Addition Property of Inequality lets you conclude that $3x + 6 > 17$.

21. If $AB + BC = 10$ and $AB = 7$, then Substitution lets you conclude that $7 + BC = 10$.

22.

The coordinate of a point 19 units from -42 is either $-42 - 19 = -61$ or $-42 + 19 = -23$.

23.

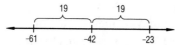

The set of points is a ray.

24. EF is a number; that is choice (a). $\overline{EF}$, $\overrightarrow{EF}$, and $\overleftrightarrow{EF}$ are sets of points.

16

CHAPTER 1 REVIEW (pp. 56–59)

1. a, b. of the 7 nodes, 5 are even and 2 are odd.

2. The network is traversable because it does not have more than two odd vertices.

3. a.–b. The network has 4 odd vertices, so it is not traversable.

4. a.

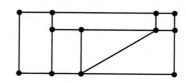

    b. The network has 6 odd vertices, so it is not traversable.

5. a.

    b.

6. a.

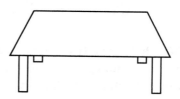

    b.

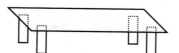

7. a. not drawn in perspective

8. **a.** drawn in perspective
   b.
   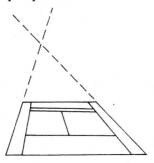

9. A mirror is a model for a plane; it has two dimensions.
10. A tightrope is a model for a segment, it has one dimension.
11. A point has zero dimensions.
12. A plane has two dimensions.
13. A line has one dimension.
14. Space has three dimensions.

	Dot	Location	O.P.	Node
15.	N	A	A	A
16.	A	A	A	N
17.	S	A	A	N
18.	S	A	A	S
19.	S	N	N	S

20. circularity
21. point, line, plane
22. Two major reasons for postulates are to explain undefined terms and to serve as a starting point for logically deducing geometric statements.
23. The Point-Line-Plane Postulate determines which description(s) of points, lines, and planes will be used.
24. Reflexive Property of Equality
25. Distributive Property
26. Multiplication Property of Inequality
27. Addition Property of Equality
28. Commutative Property of Addition
29. Addition Property of Inequality
30. Equation to Inequality Property
31. Transitive Property of Equality
32. Substitution Property
33. Multiplication Property of Equality

34.
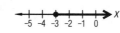

$$PQ + QR = PR$$

35. **a.**

   b. The graph is a ray.

36.
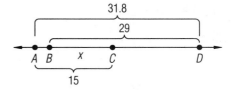

$$AB = 31.8 - 29$$
$$= 2.8$$

$$BC = AC - AB$$
$$= 15 - 2.8$$
$$= 12.2$$

37.
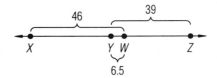

$$XW + YZ = XY + YW + YW + WZ$$
$$= (XY + YW + WZ) + YW$$
$$XW + YZ = XZ + YW$$
$$46 + 39 = XZ + 6.5$$
$$85 = XZ + 6.5$$
$$78.5 = XZ$$

38.

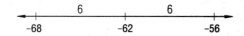

The coordinates are -68 or -56.

39.

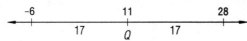

The coordinates are -6 or 28.

40.

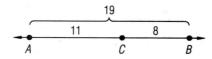

C is between A and B.

41.

$XZ = 10 + 6 = 16$

42. No; $14 + 15 \not> 30$.

43. No; $2 + 4 \not> 6$.

44. Yes; the sum of any two is greater than the third.

45. $\frac{1}{3} \approx .33, \frac{1}{4} = .25, \frac{1}{5} = .2$

Yes; the sum of any two is greater than the third.

46. No; $1.1 + 1.1 \not> 2.3$.

47. Yes, the sum of any two is greater than the third.

48.

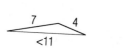

The third side is < 11 and > 3.

49. a.–b.

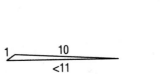

Yes; the third side is > 9 and < 11.

50. $|56 - 13| = |43| = 43$ cm

51. $|\text{-}6 - 2| = |\text{-}8| = 8°$ apart

52. The distances are different because they were measured between different locations and/or along different paths.

53. $JM = 356$ mi.

$JT + TM = 198 + 254 = 452$ mi.

The difference is $|356 - 452| = |\text{-}96| = 96$ mi.

54.

The distance is ≥ 138 miles and is ≤ 440 miles.

55.

The trip is ≥ 10 minutes and ≤ 40 minutes.

56.

The distance is ≥ 9 blocks and ≤ 15 blocks.

57.

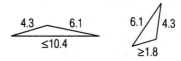

The distance is ≥ 1.8 light years and ≤ 10.4 light years.

58. $AB = |-4 - 2| = |-6| = 6$

59. $AB = |.5 - (-2)| = |2.5| = 2.5$

60. $|11 - c| = |11 - 15| = |-4| = 4$

61. $|11 - c| = |11 - (-31)| = |42| = 42$

62. $|2 - 9| = |-7| = 7$

63. $|-31 - 47| = |-78| = 78$

64. $|-14 - (-90)| = |-14 + 90| = |76| = 76$

65. $|x - y|$ or $|y - x|$

66.

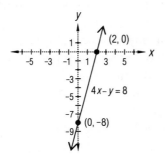

67.

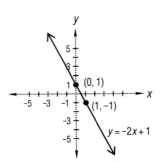

68.

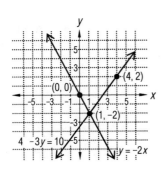

69.–72.

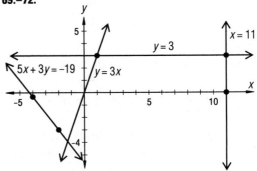

$5x + 3y = -19$ is oblique.

$x = 11$ is vertical.

$y = 3x$ is oblique

$y = 3$ is horizontal.

73.

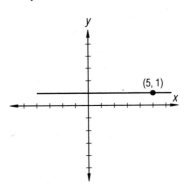

The equation is $y = 1$.

74.

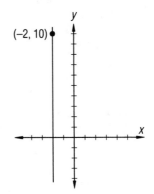

The equation is $x = -2$.

19

LESSON 2-1 (pp. 58-64)

1. The committee had trouble defining **terrorist**.

2. "Dual textured" means crispy on the outside and chewy on the inside.

3. The situation that led to a lawsuit was that several cookie companies were fighting over the recipe and patent rights for "dual textured cookies."

4. Some of the reasons to carefully define ideas are so that people have an initial point of agreement.

5. There are two triangles on p. 60 (one is the musical instrument), eight in rectangle (d) on p. 61, and one in the nonconvex set on p. 61, for a total of eleven triangles.

6. Sample

7. No; sample:

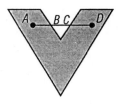

$\overline{BC}$ of $\overline{AD}$ is not on the set.

8. Yes, it is convex.

9. Yes, it is convex.

10. Sample:

11. Sample:

12. Choice (a) will fit the definition of midpoint.

13. **a.** Figures I, III, and IV are formed by four segments, but for Figures III and IV, the segments meet at other than the endpoints. So depending on the terms in the definition, Figure I is a quadrilateral and Figures III and IV may be.

    b. Figure II is not closed; Figure V is not formed by segments only.

14. Choice (a) is a circle (choice (b) is a ring, and choice (d) is a circular region).

15. Graph the points and connect them in the order given:

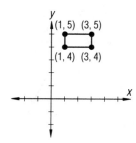

The resulting figure will fit our definition of rectangle (which is a quadrilateral with four right angles).

16. Assuming the orange is sphere-shaped, if the slice contains the center of the sphere then each piece is half an orange.

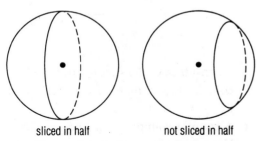

sliced in half   not sliced in half

17. Figure *ABCD*, a quadrilateral with four right angles, will fit our definition of rectangle.

18. Sample:

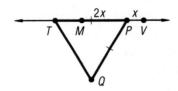

19. Substitute 10 for x and a for y into $3x + 4y = 6$ and solve for a:

$$3(10) + 4a = 6$$
$$30 + 4a = 6$$
$$4a = -24$$
$$a = -6$$

20. **a.** five ("penta" indicates 5)
   b. eight ("octa" indicates 8)
   c. ten ("deca" or "deci" indicates 10)
   d. three ("tri" indicates 3)
   e. seven ("hepta" indicates 7)
   f. four ("quadri" indicates 4)

21.
$$x - 23 = 180 - x$$
$$2x - 23 = 180$$
$$2x = 203$$
$$x = \frac{203}{2} = 101.5$$

22.
$$y = 6(90 - y)$$
$$y = 540 - 6y$$
$$7y = 540$$
$$y = \frac{540}{7} = 77\frac{1}{7}$$

23.
$$225z = 15\,\mathrm{m}$$
$$\frac{225z}{15} = \mathrm{m}$$
$$m = 15z$$

24. **a.** Sample: A cookie is a small, flat, sweet cake.
   b. Sample: A terrorist is a person who uses or favors deliberate violence against persons or groups by another group to achieve ends.

LESSON 2–2 (pp. 65–69)

1. Antecedent: a parallelogram has a right angle; consequent: it is a rectangle.

2. Antecedent: it (fruit kabob) is made with watermelon; consequent: fruit kabob is divine.

3. $s \Rightarrow p$ is the sentence, "If a figure is a square, then it is a polygon."

4. An *instance* of a sentence is a situation in which the sentence is **true**.

5. A counterexample to a conditional is an if-then statement for which the antecedent is true and the consequent is false.

6. A counterexample to $a \Rightarrow c$ is a situation for which a is true and c is false.

7. Goldbach's Conjecture: If n is an even number greater than 2, then there are always two primes whose sum is n.

8. a.–b.

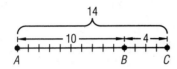

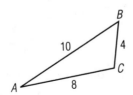

9. Only one counterexample is needed to show that a conditional is false.

10. To show that "If $x^2 = 16$, then $x = -4$" is false, let $x = 4$. Then the antecedent ($x^2 = 16$) is true and the consequent ($x = -4$) is false.

11. If a figure is a square, then it is a quadrilateral.

12. If an animal is an Irish setter, then it is a dog.

13. To satisfy Goldbach's Conjecture for $n = 40$, show that 40 is the sum of two primes: $40 = 3 + 37$ (or $11 + 29$ or $17 + 23$).

14. Choice (a) shows a hexagonal region (satisfying the antecedent) that is not convex (falsifying the consequent).

15. If $p \Rightarrow q$ is true, then it is not possible to have a counterexample to it.

16. **a.** An instance of the statement, "If you are in Toledo, then you are in the United States" is someone in Toledo, Ohio.

   b. A counterexample is someone in Toledo, Spain.

17.

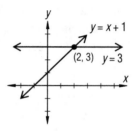

   a. An instance of the statement, "If a line contains (2, 3), then it is oblique" is the line $y = x + 1$.

   b. A counterexample is the line $y = 3$.

18. **a.** Not a triangle; it has an extra segment.

   b. Not a triangle; two "sides" are not segments.

   c. It is a triangle.

   d. Not a triangle; two segments do not intersect at endpoints.

19. **a.** nonconvex

   b. nonconvex

   c. convex

20. **a.** Sample:

   b. Sample:

21.

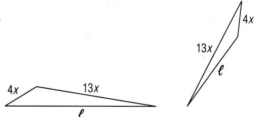

In order to form a triangle, l must be shorter than $4x + 13x = 17x$ and longer than $13x - 4x = 9x$.

22. $15x - 22 + 17x + 1 = 180$
$$32x - 21 = 180$$
$$32x = 201$$
$$x = \frac{201}{32}$$
$$x = 6\frac{9}{32}$$
$$x = 6.28125$$

23. $90 > 32 + z > 0$
$58 > z > -32$

24. a.

 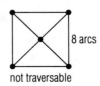

5 arcs — traversable   8 arcs — not traversable

If a network has 5 nodes, then it has at least 5 arcs.

b. If a network has 5 nodes, then it is not traversable.

25. a. If a person is 14 years old, then that person is a teenager.

b. If a person is 14 years old, then that person is a female.

26. "Ante" means "before" and "sequens" means "following." In an if-then sentence, the consequent usually follows the antecedent.

LESSON 2-3 (pp. 70–75)

1. If the antecedent is satisfied (or true), the program performs the instructions in the consequent.

2. If the antecedent is not satisfied (or false), the program ignores the instructions in the consequent and goes to the next-numbered line in the program.

3. The line numbers indicate the order of the instructions of the program.

4. For N = 1, the antecedent of line 40 is not satisfied, so the program ignores line 40 and goes to line 50, which ends the program.

5. For N = 100, the program prints "THE NUMBER OF DIAGONALS IS 4850".

6. For N = 3, the program prints "THE NUMBER OF DIAGONALS IS 0".

7. A polygon with 4 or fewer sides is an instance of a false antecedent; no conclusions are possible if the antecedent of a conditional is false.

8. a. The statement "If $1 = 2$, then $30 = 40$" is true, since any conditional with a false antecedent is considered to be true.

b. Starting with $1 = 2$, add 2 to each side to get $3 = 4$, then multiply each side by 10 to get $30 = 40$.

9. The antecedent, "Paris is in Germany," is false, so the conditional is considered to be true.

10. a. The ad said nothing about the result of not using Wonderlashes, so it did not lie.

b. By using Wonderlashes, Flora satisfied the antecedent. But the consequent did not result. So the ad lied.

11. a. Mr. Woodward wanted a cleaner house, so the antecedent was satisfied. Since he did not satisfy the consequent, the ad was false.

b. The change to "you might use Magikleen" makes the consequent always satisfied. So the ad is true.

12. a. For N = 400, the antecedent in line 30 is not satisfied. The program ignores the consequent in line 30 and goes to line 35, so it ends.

b. For N = 20, the antecedent in line 30 is satisfied, so the program prints "ORDER MORE ELECTRO-ROBOTS."

13. a. The formula in line 20 is $A = 3.14159r^2$ or $A = \pi r^2$, a formula for the area of a circle.

b. Nothing will be printed if the input value of R does not satisfy the antecedent in line 30. So nothing will be printed if $R \leq 0$.

14. If a polygon is a hexagon, then it has 9 diagonals.

15. If a figure is a cube with side s, then its volume is s^3.

16. If line is vertical, then it has an equation of the form $x = h$.

17. a. The antecedent for the conditional, "If $|x| = 10$, then $x = 10$" is $|x| = 10$.

b. A counterexample is $x = -10$, because it satisfies the antecedent ($|x| = 10$) but does not satisfy the consequent ($x \neq 10$).

18. a–b.

$$DY = XY - XD$$
$$= 26.7 - 11.2$$
$$= 15.5$$

19. The following networks are **counterexamples** because they are traversable (so they satisfy the antecedent) but they do not have exactly two odd nodes (so they do not satisfy the consequent).

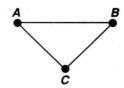

20. If $CD = x$, then $BC = 4x$ and so $BD = 5x$. If $BD = 12$, then $5x = 12$ and $x = \frac{12}{5}$. So $BC = 4x = 4(\frac{12}{5}) = \frac{48}{5} = 9.6$.

21. The third side must be less than $16 + 41 = 57$ and greater than $41 - 16 = 25$.

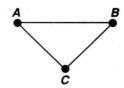

22.
$$50z + 3 = 67z + 1$$
$$50z + 2 = 67z$$
$$2 = 17z$$
$$z = \frac{2}{17}$$

23.
$$180 > q + 19 > 90$$
$$180 - 19 > q > 90 - 19$$
$$161 > q > 71$$

24. a. For $N = 3$: $d = \frac{N(N-3)}{2} = \frac{3(3-3)}{2}$
$$= \frac{3(0)}{2}$$
$$= 0$$

For $N = 4$: $d = \frac{N(N-3)}{2} = \frac{4(4-3)}{2}$
$$= \frac{4(1)}{2}$$
$$= 2$$

For $N = 5$: $d = \frac{N(N-3)}{2} = \frac{5(5-3)}{2}$
$$= \frac{5(2)}{2}$$
$$= 5$$

For $N = 6$: $d = \frac{N(N-3)}{2} = \frac{6(6-3)}{2}$
$$= \frac{6(3)}{2}$$
$$= 3(3)$$
$$= 9$$

For $N = 7$: $d = \frac{N(N-3)}{2} = \frac{7(7-3)}{2}$
$$= \frac{7(4)}{2}$$
$$= 7(2)$$
$$= 14$$

$$N = 8: d = \frac{N(N-3)}{2} = \frac{8(8-3)}{2}$$
$$= \frac{8(5)}{2}$$
$$= 4(5)$$
$$= 20$$

For $N = 9: d = \frac{N(N-3)}{2} = \frac{9(9-3)}{2}$
$$= \frac{9(6)}{2}$$
$$= 9(3)$$
$$= 27$$

For $N = 10: d = \frac{N(N-3)}{2} = \frac{10(10-3)}{2}$
$$= \frac{10(7)}{2}$$
$$= 5(7)$$
$$= 35$$

 b.

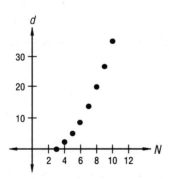

c. The points all lie on half of a parabola.

25. Line 20 should read: 20 for N = 3 to 50
The printout will read:
NUMBER OF DIAGONALS IN
POLYGONS
THE NUMBER OF SIDES IS 3
THE NUMBER OF DIAGONALS IS 0
THE NUMBER OF SIDES IS 4
THE NUMBER OF DIAGONALS IS 2
. . . and so on to
THE NUMBER OF SIDES IS 50
THE NUMBER OF DIAGONALS IS 1175

26. a. Lines 10 through 50 can remain the same.
Insert the following line:
45 IF N < 3 THEN PRINT "ERROR, A
POLYGON MUST HAVE AT LEAST 3
SIDES."

b. The printout will be:
COMPUTE NUMBER OF
DIAGONALS IN POLYGON
ENTER THE NUMBER OF SIDES
?2
ERROR, A POLYGON MUST HAVE
AT LEAST 3 SIDES.

LESSON 2–4 (pp. 76–80)

1. The converse of the conditional $p \Rightarrow q$ is the conditional $q \Rightarrow p$.

2. a. The converse is "If a line has an equation of the form $x = h$, then it is vertical."
b. The converse is true.

3. a. The converse is "If you are at least 13 years old, then you are a teenager."
b. The converse is false. A counterexample is a 25-year-old.

4.

	p	q	$p \Rightarrow q$	$q \Rightarrow p$
i	T	T	T	T
ii	T	F	F	T
iii	F	T	T	F
iv	F	F	T	T

In rows *i, iii,* and *iv,* the statement $p \Rightarrow q$ is true, but the converse $q \Rightarrow p$ may be true or false. The answer is choice (c).

5. a.

10 ft · 3 ft rectangle

perimeter = 26 ft, so p is true;
area = 30 ft², so q is false.
Thus $p \Rightarrow q$ is false.

b.

21 ft | 2 ft

area = 42 ft², so q is true;
perimeter = 46 ft, so p is false.
Thus $q \Rightarrow p$ is false.

6. If the consequent is true, that does not make the antecedent true. There is not enough information to tell.

7. **a.** $p \Rightarrow q$ is "If $2x + 31 = 4 - x$, then $x = -9$."
$q \Rightarrow p$ is "If $x = -9$, then $2x + 31 = 4 - x$."

b. If $\quad 2x + 31 = 4 - x$
then $\qquad 2x = -27 - x$
$\qquad\quad 3x = -27$
$\qquad\quad\; x = -9$
So $p \Rightarrow q$ is true.
If $\qquad x = -9$
then $\quad 3x = -27$
$\qquad\quad 2x = -27 - x$
$\quad 2x + 31 = 4 - x$
So $q \Rightarrow p$ is true.

8. **a.** $p \Rightarrow q$ is "If the perimeter of a square is 40 cm, then the area is 100 cm²."
$q \Rightarrow p$ is "If the area of a square is 100 cm², then the perimeter is 40 cm."

b. If perimeter is 40 cm, then $p = 4s$ so $s = 10$, and $A = s^2$ so $A = 100$ cm². So $p \Rightarrow q$ is true.
If area is 100 cm², then $A = s^2$ so $s = 10$, and $p = 4s$ so $p = 40$ cm. So $q \Rightarrow p$ is true.

9. **a.** $p \Rightarrow q$ is "If $AB + BC = AC$, then B is between A and C."
$q \Rightarrow p$ is "If B is between A and C, then $AB + BC = AC$."

b. That is the definition of betweenness, so both $p \Rightarrow q$ and $q \Rightarrow p$ are true.

10. **a.** $p \Rightarrow q$ is "If $s^2 = 40{,}000$, then $s = 200$."
$q \Rightarrow p$ is "If $s = 200$, then $s^2 = 40{,}000$."

b. A counterexample to $p \Rightarrow q$ is $s = -200$. Then p is true and q is false.
$q \Rightarrow p$ is true.

11. **a.** $p \Rightarrow q$ is "If B is between A and C, then A is between C and B."
$q \Rightarrow p$ is "If A is between C and B, then B is between A and C."

b. Both $p \Rightarrow q$ and $q \Rightarrow p$ are false, because for 3 collinear points, only one can be between the other two.

12.

ℓ

w

You need ℓ and w so that
$2(\ell + w) = 18$
$\ell w = 20$
So $\quad \ell + w = 9$
$\qquad\quad \ell = \dfrac{20}{w}.$

Then $\dfrac{20}{w} + w = 9$
$\qquad 20 + w^2 = 9w$
$\quad w^2 - 9w + 20 = 0$
$\quad (w - 5)(w - 4) = 0$
$\quad w - 5 = 0 \quad$ so $\quad w = 5 \quad$ or
$\quad w - 4 = 0 \quad$ so $\quad w = 4.$

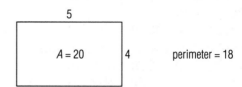

5

$A = 20$ | 4 | perimeter = 18

The dimensions are 5 ft by 4 ft.

13. Mr. Chu was assuming the conditional "If a country is communist, it has socialized medicine," but was arguing from its converse, "If a country has socialized medicine, then it has a communist government." Whether or not his first assumption is correct, reasoning from its converse is not correct (i.e., not valid).

14. a. The formula $d = \frac{n(n-3)}{2}$ gives the number of diagonals in a n-gon.

b. For $n = 8$: $d = \frac{8(8-3)}{2}$

$$= \frac{8(5)}{2}$$

$$= 4(5)$$

$$= 20$$

15. a. When N = 6, then the antecedent in line 30 is satisfied. So the program prints "THE SUM OF THE ANGLE MEASURES (IN DEGREES) IS 720"

b. When N = 1, the antecedent in line 30 is not satisfied. So the program ignores line 30, goes to line 40, and ends.

16. The word *whenever* is a synonym for *if:* If a figure is a square, then it is a quadrilateral.

17. The word *is* serves as the transition to the consequent. So in if-then form, the sentence is "If a person was born in New York City, then that person is a U.S. citizen."

18.

The graph is a ray.

19.

The graph is a segment.

20. Undefined terms are necessary to avoid circularity.

21. If the headquarters building is at Alpha, then the sum of the round trips is $0 + 2(21.2) + 2(28.3) = 99$; at Beta, the sum is $2(21.2) + 0 + 2(7.1) = 56.6$; at Gamma, the sum is $2(28.3) + 2(7.1) + 0 = 70.8$. It is most cost efficient to put the headquarters at Beta.

22. a. The mean is $\frac{10.3 + 31.5 + 38.6}{3} = \frac{80.4}{3} = 26.8$.

b. The median is 31.5.

c. The sum of the round trips at the median is 56.6 (from Question 21); at the mean, it is $2(16.5) + 2(4.7) + 2(11.8) = 66$; it is more efficient at the median.

23. Sample: "If you spend money, then you are buying a concert ticket" is false, but its converse is true: "If you are buying a concert ticket, then you are spending money."

LESSON 2–5 (pp. 81–86)

1. A good definition must:
  (i) include only words either commonly understood, defined earlier, or purposely undefined;
  (ii) accurately describe the idea being defined; and
  (iii) include no more information than is necessary.

2. A point M is the midpoint of a segment $\overline{AB}$ if and only if M is on $\overline{AB}$ and $AM = MB$.

3. The definition of the midpoint of a segment uses the two previously-defined ideas of segment and distance.

4. meaning: If a point M is the midpoint of a segment $\overline{AB}$, then M is on $\overline{AB}$ and $AM = MB$.
sufficient condition: If a point M is on a segment $\overline{AB}$ and $AM = MB$, then M is the midpoint of $\overline{AB}$.

5. $a \Rightarrow b$ and $b \Rightarrow a$ can be written as $a \Leftrightarrow b$.

6. The symbol $\Leftrightarrow$ is read "if and only if."

7.

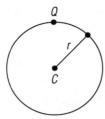

By the definition of circle (meaning), if Q is on $\odot C$ then $QC = r$.

8.

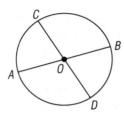

In $\odot O$, *diameter* may refer to a segment such as $\overline{AB}$ or $\overline{CD}$, or it may refer to the number equal to AB (or CD).

9.

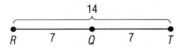

a. $RQ = \frac{1}{2}(RT) = \frac{1}{2}(14) = 7$

b. $TQ = RQ = 7$

c. $TQ = \frac{1}{2}(RT)$

d. $\frac{RQ}{RT} = \frac{7}{14} = \frac{1}{2}$

10. a. "goes around the center" is not clearly described.

   b. "sphere" is not previously defined, nor is it an undefined term.

   c. The distance from the certain point is not specifically stated as a "fixed" or constant distance.

11. Choice (d) of Question 14, Lesson 2–1, is not a circle because it includes the interior points; it is a circular region.

12. The defined term, *space,* is in the antecedent, so the statement is the meaning half.

13. sufficient condition—the defined term, opposite rays, is in the consequent.

14. sufficient condition—the defined term, collinear, is in the consequent.

15. meaning—the defined term, parallel, is in the antecedent.

16. $p \Rightarrow q$ is "the lawn mower needs gas if and only if the lawn mower doesn't start on 3 pulls."

17. A set is convex if and only if all segments connecting points in the set lie entirely in the set.

18. Choice (a) is not a good definition because "inside the circle" is not defined. Choice (b) is a good definition.

19. A plane, line, ray, or segment is a bisector of a given segment if and only if it contains the midpoint of the given segment and no other point of the given segment.

20. If M is equidistant from A and B, then $AM = MB$.

   So $\quad 4x + 10 = 5x - 7$
   $$4x + 17 = 5x$$
   $$17 = x.$$

21. a. converse: If $x^2 = \frac{4}{9}$, then $x = -\frac{2}{3}$.

   b. False; a counterexample is $x = \frac{2}{3}$.

22. a. converse: If you are studying geometry, then you are reading this book.

   b. False; a counterexample is if you are studying the geometry of any object other than this book.

23. a. converse: If A is between B and C, then $\overrightarrow{AB}$ and $\overrightarrow{AC}$ are opposite rays.

   b. True; it is the definition of opposite rays (sufficient condition).

24. a. If X = 20, then the antecedent is not satisfied and the program ignores line 30.

b–c. If X = 25 or X = 30, then the antecedent is satisfied and the program prints, for part (b), 3 * 25 − 75, which is zero, or, for part (c), prints 3 * 30 − 75, which is 15.

25.

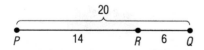

26. a. geology: The study of the composition of the crust of the earth.

b. geothermal: dealing with the internal heat of the earth.

c. geography: study of the earth's surface, climate, continents, countries, peoples, industries, and products.

d. geocentric: viewed or measured from the earth's center.

LESSON 2–6 (pp. 87–91)

1. A set is the union of two sets if and only if it contains the elements which are in either (or both) of the two sets.

2. A set is the intersection of two sets if and only if it contains the elements which are in both sets.

3.

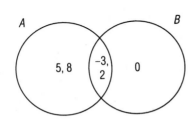

A = {-3, 2, 5, 8}
B = {-3, 0, 2}
A ∪ B = {5, 8, -3, 2, 0}
A ∩ B = {-3, 2}

4.

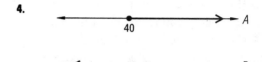

A ∪ B = {all real numbers}
A ∩ B = {x: $40 \leq x \leq 50$}

5. The Republic Airline route network is the **union** of the networks of **three** airlines.

6. W ∩ N indicates the routes covered by both Air West and North Central Airlines.

7. $m \cap n$, the points both on line m and circle n, are the two points of intersection, A and B, so $m \cap n = \{A, B\}$.

8. a. Segment $\overline{PE}$ is part of both $SPED$ and $PACE$, so $SPED \cap PACE = \overline{PE}$.

b. $SPED \cup PACE$ consists of rectangle $CASD$ and segment $\overline{PE}$.

9. A symbol for the null set is ∅ or { }.

10.

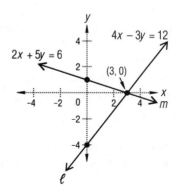

The intersection is around (3, 0). For an exact solution:

(1) $\quad 4x - 3y = 12$
(2) $\quad 2x + 5y = 6$
(3) $-4x - 10y = -12$ $\quad$ (-2 × Eq. 2)
$\quad\quad\quad -13y = 0$ $\quad\quad$ (Eq. 1 + Eq. 3)
$\quad\quad\quad\quad\quad y = 0$
$\quad 4x - 3(0) = 12$
$\quad\quad\quad\quad 4x = 12$
$\quad\quad\quad\quad\quad x = 3$

(3, 0) is an exact solution.

11. G ∪ H is all residents of Indonesia or of Jakarta, which is all residents of Indonesia. G ∩ H is all residents of Indonesia and of Jakarta, which is all residents of Jakarta.

12. G ∪ H is the ages of people who can drive or who can vote. Assuming you can drive earlier than you can vote, and there is no cut-off age for driving or voting, G ∩ H is the age of people who can drive and vote, or since voting age is older than driving age, those who can vote.

    G ∩ H is the age of people who can vote.

13. G ∪ H is students in some geometry course, which is the set of students taking geometry. G ∩ H = ∅ (unless there is a student who is in every geometry class)

14. *x* ∩ *y*, the intersection of Δ*GHI* and Δ*IJG*, is $\overline{GI}$.

15. *x* ∪ *y*, the union of the two triangles, is Δ*GHJ* and $\overline{GI}$, or {$\overline{GH}, \overline{HI}, \overline{IJ}, \overline{JG}, \overline{GI}$}.

16. **a.** There are 4 favorable outcomes (points *E*, *A*, *B*, *F*) out of 6 possible outcomes; that ratio is $\frac{4}{6} = \frac{2}{3}$.

    b. There are 4 favorable outcomes (points *A*, *D*, *B*, *C*) out of 6 possible outcomes; that ratio is $\frac{4}{6} = \frac{2}{3}$.

    c. There are 2 favorable outcomes (points *A*, *B*) out of 6 possible outcomes; that ratio is $\frac{2}{6} = \frac{1}{3}$.

17. **a.** "How fast you must go" is too vague.

    b. too much information

    c. involves terms not previously defined

18. If *P* is on ⊙*O* with radius *r*, then *PO* = *r*. If *PO* = *r*, then *P* is on ⊙*O* with radius *r*.

19. The term being defined, set intersection, is in the consequent, so the conditional is the sufficient condition half.

20.

21.

22. **a.** Converse: If *B* is not between *A* and *C*, and *AC* = *AB* − *BC*, then *B* is on $\overrightarrow{AC}$.

    b–c. The original statement can serve as a definition of $\overrightarrow{AC}$, so both it and its converse are true.

23. antecedent: You work more than 40 hours in a particular week.
    consequent: You receive time-and-a-half for overtime during that week.

24. $x = 2(180 - x)$
    $x = 360 - 2x$
    $3x = 360$
    $x = 120$
    Check: Does $120 = 2(180 - 120)$?
    Does $120 = 2(60)$? Yes

25.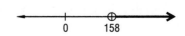

26.

LESSON 2–7 (pp. 92–97)

1. The segments intersect other than at the endpoints.
2. It is not closed (some segments do not intersect two others.)
3. Some segments intersect more than two others.
4. One of the "sides" is not a segment.
5. **a.** The vertices of $ABCDE$ are points A, B, C, D, and E.
   b. Pairs of consecutive sides are:
   $\overline{AB}$ and $\overline{BC}$,
   $\overline{BC}$ and $\overline{CD}$,
   $\overline{CD}$ and $\overline{DE}$,
   $\overline{DE}$ and $\overline{AE}$,
   $\overline{AE}$ and $\overline{AB}$.
   c. Consecutive vertices are:
   A and B,
   B and C,
   C and D,
   D and E,
   E and A.
6. **a.** An octagon ("octa") has 8 vertices.
   b. An n-gon has n vertices.
7. A polygonal region consists of the polygon along with its interior.
8. A polygon is convex if and only if its corresponding polygonal region is convex.
9. convex
10. nonconvex
11. convex

12. nonconvex
13. Choice (b) is not a quadrilateral, and choices (c) and (d) are convex; the only nonconvex quadrilateral is choice (a).
14.

15. most general:
    figure
    two-dimensional figure
    polygon
    triangle
    isosceles triangle
    equilateral triangle
    most specific
16.

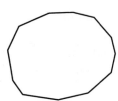

17.

18.

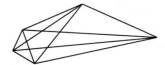

A pentagon has 5 diagonals.
19. The convex polygons are $ABCD$, $ABXE$, $AEYD$, and $EXCY$.
20. The convex polygons are $FGIJ$, $FGHK$, $KHIJ$ (rectangles); $FGHL$, $FGLK$ (trapezoids); FGL, LGH, FLK (triangles).

21. If a figure is a polygon, then it is the union of 3 or more segments in the same plane such that each segment intersects exactly two others, one at each endpoint.

22.

23.

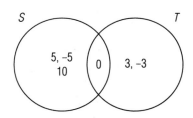

24. The given definition excludes triangles and quadrilaterals.

25. In the given definition, sides are parts of circles, not segments.

26.

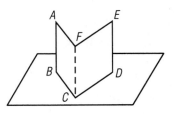

a. S ∪ T = {-5, -3, 0, 3, 5, 10}
b. S ∩ T = {0}
 Note {0} is not the same as { }.

27.

28. a.

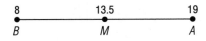

$AM = |13.5 - 19| = |\text{-}5.5| = 5.5$
$MB = |13.5 - 8| = |5.5| = 5.5$
So $AM = MB$.

b.

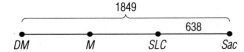

$BM = |39 - (\text{-}2)| = |39 + 2| = 41$
$MA = |\text{-}2 - (\text{-}43)| = |\text{-}2 + 43| = 41$
So $BM = MA$, and M is the midpoint of $\overline{AB}$ by the definition of midpoint (sufficient condition).

c. The midpoint of $\overline{AB}$ is the arithmetic mean of the coordinates for A and B; that is $\frac{x + y}{2}$.

29.

DM ———— M ———— SLC ———— Sac
  with 1849 from DM to SLC and 638 from SLC to Sac

a. If point M is halfway between Des Moines and Salt Lake City, then the distance from DM to M is $\frac{1}{2}(1849 - 638)$

$= \frac{1}{2}(1211)$

$= 605.5$ miles

b. The distance from M to Sacramento is $605.5 + 638 = 1243.5$ miles.

30. a. line through X and Y: $\overleftrightarrow{XY}$
 b. segment with end points X and Y: $\overline{XY}$
 c. distance between X and Y: XY

32

31. **a.** dodec: $2 + 10 = 12$
 b. duodec: $2 + 10 = 12$
 c. ennea: 9
 d. pentadec: $5 + 10 = 15$
 e. quad: 4
 f. tetra: 4
 g. tri: 3
 h. undec: $1 + 10 = 11$

CHAPTER 2 PROGRESS SELF-TEST (p. 99–100)

1. The "definition" contains too much information (not needed is $\frac{1}{2}AB = AM$, and $\frac{1}{2}AB = MB$"). That is a violation of the third listed property.

2. sample:

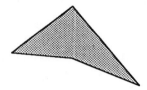

3. The antecedent is the "if clause" and the consequent is the "then clause": <u>Two angles have equal measure</u> if <u>they are vertical angles.</u>

4. In if-then form: If a figure is a trapezoid, then it is a quadrilateral.

5.
r ∪ t = $ABCD \cup \triangle ADC$
 $= \{\overline{AB}, \overline{BC}, \overline{CD}, \overline{DA},\} \cup \{\overline{AD}, \overline{DC}, \overline{AC},\}$
 $= \{\overline{AB}, \overline{BC}, \overline{CD}, \overline{DA}, \overline{AC}\}$

6.
So r ∪ t is the rectangle and its diagonal $\overline{AC}$.
r ∩ t = $\{\overline{AB}, \overline{BC}, \overline{CD}, \overline{DA},\} \cap \{\overline{AD}, \overline{DC}, \overline{AC},\}$
 $= \{\overline{AD}, \overline{DC}\}$
So r ∩ t consists of segments $\overline{AD}$ and $\overline{DC}$.

7. $p \Leftrightarrow q$: There are over 10 books on that shelf if and only if the shelf falls. In simpler language: The shelf will not hold more than 10 books.

8. **a.** Every triangle is a polygon, so the statement "If a figure is a triangle, then it is a polygon" is true.
 b. Converse: If a figure is a polygon, then it is a triangle.
 c. A counterexample to the converse is any quadrilateral, pentagon, or other polygon with more than three sides.

9. The statement is "If you do your homework every night, you will be guaranteed a passing grade." If you only know that the consequent is satisfied (Liane received a passing grade), it is impossible to tell if the antecedent (she did her homework every night) is true.

10. If 6 is entered for V, then the antecedent in line 20 is satisfied, so the computer prints 36 (which is V^2). The antecedent in line 30 is not satisfied, so the computer ignores line 30.

11. If 5 is entered for V, then the computer ignores line 20 because the antecedent is not satisfied. In line 30, the antecedent *is* satisfied, and the computer prints TOO SMALL (then the program ends).

12. In the statement, the defined term (convex set) is in the antecedent, so the statement is the sufficient condition half.

13. $AN = 20 + 10 = 30$

14. **a.** Hexagons have six sides; that is figure (iii).
 b. Quadrilaterals have four sides; that is figure (i).
 c. Octagons have eight sides; that is figure (iv).

15. A figure is an isosceles triangle if and only if it is a triangle with two (or more) sides of equal length.

16. sample:

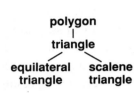

17.

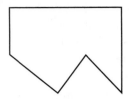

polygon
|
triangle

equilateral   scalene
triangle   triangle

18. The figure outlined has 18 sides, so it is an 18-gon.

CHAPTER 2 REVIEW (pp. 101–103)

1. nonconvex

2. convex

3. convex

4.

5.

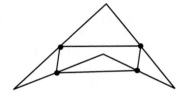

6. Sample:

7. Sample:

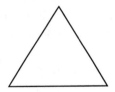

8. **a.** Drawing iv is a decagon (10 sides).
  b. Drawing ii is a pentagon (5 sides).
  c. Drawing i is a quadrilateral (4 sides).

9.

10. **a.** Converse: If $x^2 = 9$, then $x = 3$
  b. It is false; a counterexample is $x = -3$.

11. **a.** Converse: If M is the midpoint of $\overline{AB}$, then $AM = MB$.
  b. True; that is the definition of midpoint (meaning).

12. **a.** If you live in the U.S., then you are Hawaiian.
  b. False; a counterexample is any non-Hawaiian resident of the U.S.

13. Sample: It is important to define terms so that people can agree on what things mean.

14. A polygon is a union of three or more segments in the same plane such that each segment intersects exactly two others, one at each of its endpoints. The previously defined terms in that definition are union, segment, and endpoint.

15. The statement is inaccurate because it doesn't directly state that M is on $\overline{AB}$.

16. The statement uses terms that are not previously defined—"closed" and "path."

17. undefined terms: line, intersects, point; previously defined terms: circle, two.

18. Meaning half: If a line is a secant to a circle, then it intersects the circle in two points. Sufficient condition half: If a line intersects a circle in two points, then the line is a secant to the circle.

19. If a figure is a radius (of a circle), then it is a segment.

20. If a figure is a hexagon, then it has nine diagonals.

21. If $AB = 7$, then $BA = 7$.

22. A figure is a <u>rectangle</u> if <u>it is a square</u>.

23. If <u>p</u>, then <u>q</u>.

24.

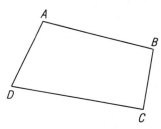

$ABCD$ is a figure which is the union of 4 segments *and* is a quadrilateral.

25.

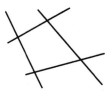

The figure is the union of 4 segments, but it is not a quadrilateral.

26.

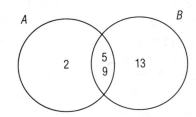

A = {2, 5, 9}, B = {5, 9, 13}.
A ∩ B = {5, 9}.

27.

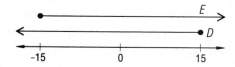

a. D ∩ E is the numbers in both sets D and E; that is all x such that $-15 \le x \le 15$.

b. D ∪ E is the numbers in set D or E (or both); that is the set of all real numbers.

28. a. The element in both $\triangle MNO$ and $\triangle MOP$ is segment $\overline{MO}$.

b. The elements in either $\triangle MNO$ or $\triangle MOP$ (or both) is the union of $\triangle MNP$ with segment $\overline{MO}$.

29. a. $q \Rightarrow p$: if $\triangle ABC$ has three 60° angles, then $\triangle ABC$ is equilateral.

b. $p \Leftrightarrow q$: $\triangle ABC$ is equilateral if and only if $\triangle ABC$ has three 60° angles.

30. No, $q \Rightarrow p$ need not be true. If $p \Rightarrow q$ is true, that *may* mean that p is false and q is true. If so, $q \Rightarrow p$ would be false.

31. A counterexample for $p \Rightarrow q$ is a situation in which p is true and q is false.

32. In if-then form, the sign states "If you litter, then you'll be fined $100." If the consequent is true, you cannot make any conclusion about the antecedent.

33. Since the antecedent is false (the moon is not made of green cheese), the conditional is true.

34. There are 12 segments making up the "top," so the figure is a 15-gon that is not convex.

35. The polygon has 5 sides, so it is a pentagon.

36. If N = 1, the computer prints "COMPUTE NUMBER OF DIAGONALS IN POLYGON" for line 10, then prints "?1" for line 20 and ignores line 30 because the antecedent is not satisfied.

37. If N = 20, the computer prints "COMPUTE NUMBER OF DIAGONALS IN POLYGON" for line 10, then prints "?20" for line 20. The antecedent in line 30 is satisfied, so it then prints "THE NUMBER OF DIAGONALS IS 170" for line 30 (because $20(20 - 3)/2 = 20(17)/2 = 170$).

38. If N = 3, the computer prints "COMPUTE NUMBER OF DIAGONALS IN POLYGON" for line 10, then "?3" for line 20. The antecedent in line 30 is satisfied, so the computer prints "THE NUMBER OF DIAGONALS IS 0" (because $3(3 - 3)/2 = 3(0)/2 = 0$).

39. If X = 0.4, then the antecedent in line 30 is satisfied (the antecedent in lines 20 and 40 are not satisfied, so those lines are ignored). The computer prints "0.8" because $2 * X = 2 * 0.4 = 2(0.4) = 0.8$.

40. If X = 20, then the antecedent in line 40 is satisfied (the antecedents in lines 20 and 30 are not satisfied, so those lines are ignored). The computer prints "20" because X = 20.

41.

```
            figure
              |
           triangle
           /      \
     isosceles    scalene
     triangle     triangle
```

42.

```
            polygon
            /      \
      hexagon      triangle
                      |
                  isosceles
                  triangle
                      |
                   scalene
                   triangle
```

LESSON 3-1   (pp. 104–112)

1. An angle is the **union** of two **rays** with the same **endpoint**.

2. The endpoints are not the same.

3. **a.** The vertex is P.
   b. The sides are $\overrightarrow{PR}$ (or $\overrightarrow{PT}$) and $\overrightarrow{PS}$ (or $\overrightarrow{PM}$ or $\overrightarrow{PN}$).
   c. The angle can be named:
   $\angle P$ $\angle TPM$ $\angle RPM$
   $\angle 1$ $\angle TPN$ $\angle RPN$
   $\angle TPS$ $\angle RPS$

4. Angles are measured in degrees (other units, not covered in this book, include radians, gradients, and revolutions).

5. $m\angle A$ is short for "The measure of angle A."

6. **a.** $\angle PQS \approx 58°$
   b. $\angle SQR \approx 122°$

7. **a.** $\angle SQT \approx 22°$
   b. $\angle TQR \approx 100°$

8. **a.** Two straight angles are $\angle AEC$ (or $\angle CEA$) and $\angle BED$ (or $\angle DEB$).
   b. Zero angles are $\angle AEA$, $\angle BEB$, $\angle CEC$, and $\angle DED$. (Other zero angles are $\angle EAE$, $\angle EAC$, $\angle EBE$, $\angle EBD$, and so on.)
   c–d. $m\angle 1 + m\angle 2 = 180$, so if $m\angle 1 = x$, then $m\angle 2 = 180 - x$.

9. **a–b.** By the Angle Addition Property,
   $m\angle FGH = m\angle 3 + m\angle 4$.
   So $m\angle FGH = 80 + 40 = 120$.

10. The measures of the three angles add to $360°$, so
   $x + 100 + 140 = 360$
   $x + 240 = 360$
   $x = 120$

11. **a.** The 3 angles with vertex A are $\angle CAB$ (or $\angle BAC$), $\angle BAD$, and $\angle DAC$.
   b. Each angle is one-third of $360°$, or $120°$.

12. **a–b.**

13. **a.**

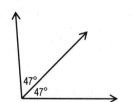

   b. Part **b** of the Angle Measure Postulate says you can draw an angle for a given measure between 0° and 180°; and you can draw that angle on either side of a given ray.

14. By the Angle Addition Property,
   $m\angle QNP = m\angle QNO + m\angle ONP$
   $83 = (9x - 2) + (4x + 7)$
   $83 = 13x + 5$
   $78 = 13x$
   $x = 6$
   So $M\angle QNO = 9x - 2 = 9(6) - 2 = 52$.
   $m\angle ONP = 4x + 7 = 4(6) + 7 = 31$.
   (To check, $52 + 31 = 83$)

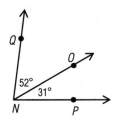

15. **a.** When your arm is "straight," the angle is just under a straight angle; its measure is about 175°.
   b. For very thin arms, the smallest angle could be between 20° and 30°; for muscular arms, the smallest angle could be 40° or greater.

16. **a–b.** Guesses may vary, but should be greater than 45° and less than 90°; the measure is 55°.

17. a–b. Guesses may vary, but should be greater than 0° and less than 45°; the measure is 35°.

18. a–b. Answers may vary, but should be between 135° and 180°; the measure is 155°.

19. a. Runway 32 represents a compass direction of 320°.

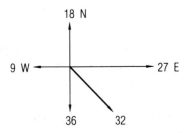

b. "Opposite" runways differ by 180°: 320° − 180° = 140°. So the number at the other end of runway 32 would be 14.

20. Draw a convex hexagon with unequal sides and angles, then draw the diagonals and count the points of intersection.

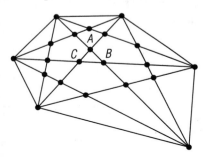

There are 15 points of intersection inside the hexagon and 6 on the hexagon, for a total of 21.

21. Draw a convex hexagon with equal sides and angles. (Some of the diagonals will be *concurrent.*)

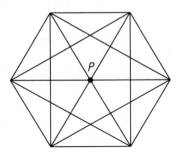

The only difference from the diagram in Question 20 is that point *P* represents points *A, B,* and *C.* So there are 2 fewer points of intersection, or 21 − 2 = 19 points of intersection.

22. There are many ways for two rays to intersect:

$\overrightarrow{AB} \cap \overrightarrow{AC} = \overrightarrow{AB}$ (ray)

$\overrightarrow{AB} \cap \overrightarrow{CD} = \overrightarrow{CD}$ (ray)

$\overrightarrow{AB} \cap \overrightarrow{CD} = \overline{AC}$ (segment)

$\overrightarrow{AB} \cap \overrightarrow{AC} = A$ (point)

$\overrightarrow{AB} \cap \overrightarrow{CD} = P$ (point)

$\overrightarrow{AB} \cap \overrightarrow{CD} = \{\}$

The possible intersections are a ray, a point, a segment, and the empty set.

23. a. Meaning half: If a line, ray, or segment is a bisector of $\overline{AB}$, then it contains the midpoint of $\overline{AB}$, and no other points of $\overline{AB}$.

b. Sufficient condition half: If a line, ray, or segment contains the midpoint of $\overline{AB}$ and no other points of $\overline{AB}$, then it is the bisector of $\overline{AB}$.

24. a. There are 60 minutes in one degree.

b. Not surprisingly, there are 60 seconds in one minute, so in one degree there are $(60)(60) = 3600$ seconds.

c. From horizon to horizon is 180°. To find the number of 30-minute angles that would fit across the sky, divide 30 minutes into 180°

$$\frac{180°}{30 \text{ min}} = \frac{180°}{30 \text{ min}} \cdot \frac{60 \text{ min}}{\text{degree}}$$
$$= (180)(2)°$$
$$= 360°.$$

LESSON 3–2 (pp. 113–119)

1. The five types of angles, classified by measure, are:

    zero   (zero degrees)
    acute   (between 0° and 90°)
    right   (90°)
   obtuse (between 90° and 180°)
  straight (180°).

2. Supplementary angles add to 180°.

$$x + 4x = 180$$
$$5x = 180$$
$$x = 36$$
$$4x = 144$$

The measure of the angle is 144°.
(To check, $144 + 36 = 180$.)

3. $\angle 6$ appears to be greater than 90°, so it is obtuse.

4. $\angle 5$ appears to be less than 90°, so it is acute.

5. $\angle 1$ and $\angle 3$ are **vertical** angles.

6. a. $m\angle 1 + m\angle 2 = 180$
$$121 + m\angle 2 = 180$$
$$m\angle 2 = 59$$

b. $m\angle 1 = m\angle 3$, so if $m\angle 1 = 121$, then $m\angle 3 = 121$.

c. $m\angle 4 = m\angle 2$, so from part **a**, $m\angle 4 = 59$

7. a. $m\angle 1 + m\angle 2 = 180$
$$x + m\angle 2 = 180$$
$$m\angle 2 = 180 - x$$

b. $m\angle 1 = m\angle 3$, so if $m\angle 1 = x$, then $m\angle 3 = x$

c. $m\angle 4 = m\angle 2$, so from part **a**, $m\angle 4 = 180 - x$.

8. a. If $\angle V$ and $\angle W$ are supplementary, then
$$m\angle V + m\angle W = 180$$
$$103 + m\angle W = 180$$
$$m\angle W = 77$$

b. $\angle V$ is greater than 90°, so it is obtuse.

c. $\angle W$ is less than 90°, so it is acute.

9.

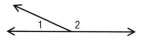

10.

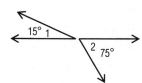

11.

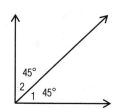

12. a. $\angle OPE$ forms a linear pair with $\angle OPA$, so $\angle OPE$ is supplementary to $\angle OPA$.

b. Another pair of supplementary angles are $\angle APT$ and $\angle TPE$.

13. **a.** The converse of the Linear Pair Theorem is "If two angles are supplementary, then they form a linear pair."

b.

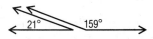

c. Since there is a counterexample to the conditional, the conditional is not true.

14. The complement to $m°$ is $(90 - m)°$. So an inequality is

$m < 90 - m$

$2m < 90$

$m < 45$

15. **a.** appears to be right (has a right angle)

b. is an acute triangle (has all acute angles)

c. is an obtuse triangle (has one obtuse angle)

16. If $\overrightarrow{BC}$ bisects $\angle ABD$, then

$3x = 5x - 10$

$-2x = -10$

$x = 5$

$3x = 3(5) = 15$

$5x - 10 = 5(5) - 10 = 15$

$m\angle ABD = 15 + 15 = 30$

17.

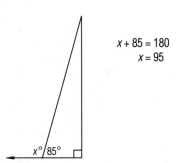

$x + 85 = 180$

$x = 95$

The largest angle the Tower makes with the ground is 95°.

18. $\angle D$ is about 60°.

19. $\angle Z$ is about 19°.

20. Due North is 90° north of East; the plane would have to turn another 80°.

21. **a.** 8 ("octa")

b. 6 ("hexa")

c. 5 ("penta")

d. 3 ("tri")

e. 4 ("quadri")

f. 7 ("hepta")

g. 9 ("nona")

h. 10 ("deca"; also "deci")

i. 35

j. n

22. Sample: Let A = {2, 4, 6} and B = {1, 2}. Then N(A) = 3, N(B) = 2, and N(A ∪ B) = N({1, 2, 4, 6}) = 4.

23. **a.** $p \cup q$ is the union of the front and bottom; it has 7 segments (4 for *ABEG,* and $\overline{BC}$, $\overline{CD}$, and $\overline{DA}$).

b. $p \cap q$ is segment $\overline{AB}$; that is just one segment.

24. **a.** The defined term, straight angle, is in the consequent, so it is the sufficient condition half.

b. The defined term, supplementary angles, is in the antecedent, so it is the meaning half.

c. The defined term, vertical angles, is in the antecedent, so it is the meaning half.

25. **a.** Meanings for *acute* are intense or having a sharp point.

b. Meanings for *obtuse* are lacking sharpness, dull, blunt.

So acute angles are more pointed, or sharper, than obtuse angles.

26. **a.** Sample: a *compliment* is an expression of admiration or praise.

b. Homonyms for *right* are rite, write, and wright.

c. Other mathematical terms that have homonyms are pi (pie), place (plaice), arc (ark), and disk (disc).

LESSON 3–3 (pp. 120–125)

1. In if-then form: If a sequence of justified conclusions is a proof of an if-then statement, then it leads from the antecedent to the conclusion.

2. The three kinds of justifications in a proof are definitions, postulates, and previously proved theorems.

3. Yes, a postulate from algebra (or other properties from algebra) can be used as a justification in a proof.

4. The justification is "If the measure of an angle is 90°, then it is a right angle" is the definition of right angle (sufficient condition). That is choice (d).

5. The justification is the Vertical Angle Theorem.

6. Theorem

7. Three reasons are:

   (1) What is obvious to one person may not be obvious to another person. Sometimes people disagree, and if two people accept a proof, they will have to agree with its conclusion.

   (2) If a statement cannot be proved after much effort, it is possible that it is not really true, or that it cannot be proved (or disproved) from the postulates assumed so far.

   (3) Unexpected results, once verified with a proof, must be accepted.

8. From $4x + 3 = 12$ to $4x = 9$, you have added -3 to each side of the equation. The justification is the Addition Property of Equality, which is choice (d).

9. **a–b.** If $4y = 32$, a conclusion could be $y = 8$. The justification would be the Multiplication Property of Equality.

10. **a–b.** From the given that I is between F and E, a conclusion could be $FI + IE = FE$. The justification would be the Betweenness Theorem.

11. $\angle 1$ and $\angle 2$ are adjacent angles, so you can find m$\angle FGH$, their sum, using the Angle Addition Property; that is choice (a).

12. The conditional, "If two angles form a linear pair, then they are supplementary," is the Linear Pair Theorem; that is choice (b).

13. The conditional, "If two angles are supplementary, then their sum is 180°," is the definition of supplementary angles (meaning).

14. The condition, "If a ray bisects an angle, then it forms two equal adjacent angles," is the definition of angle bisector (meaning).

15. The conditional, "If a ray forms two equal adjacent angles, then the ray is an angle bisector," is the definition of angle bisector (sufficient condition).

16. If an angle is acute, then its measure is between 0° and 90°.

17. If a set of points is a segment, then it consists of two points and all points between those two points.

18. If a set of points is a circle, it consists of all points in a plane that are a given distance (the radius) from a given point in the plane (the center).

19. Complementary angles sum to 90°, so
$$90 - m\angle T = 5m\angle T$$
$$-6m\angle T = -90$$
$$m\angle T = 15.$$

20. If $\overrightarrow{HF}$ and $\overrightarrow{HI}$ are opposite rays, then
$$m\angle FHG + m\angle GHI = 180$$
$$x + 5x = 180$$
$$6x = 180$$
$$x = 30$$
$$m\angle FHG = x = 30$$

21. Complementary angles sum to 90°, so

$$x = (90 - x) - 13$$
$$x = 77 - x$$
$$2x = 77$$
$$x = 38.5$$

The measure of the angle is 38.5°.

22.

23. If $\overrightarrow{XW}$ bisects $\angle YXZ$, and $\angle YXZ = 90°$, then $\angle YXW = 45°$.

24. Vertical angles have equal measure, so

$$12q = 4Z$$
$$q = \frac{Z}{3}.$$

25. $\text{m}\angle ABC = \text{m}\angle ABD + \text{m}\angle DBC$

$$101 = (2x) + (3x - 4)$$
$$101 = 5x - 4$$
$$105 = 5x$$
$$x = 21$$

$$\text{m}\angle DBC = 3x - 4$$
$$= 3(21) - 4$$
$$= 63 - 4$$
$$= 59$$

26. If a figure is a square, then it is a rectangle.

27. If X and Y are two angles, then X and Y cannot be both acute and supplementary.

28. **a–b.** Samples

(i) Tomorrow is Tuesday (100% sure).
Tomorrow is Wednesday (0% sure, or 100% sure it is false.)
Tomorrow will be rainy (perhaps 15% sure).

(ii) Last week the football team played its game (100% sure).
This week the team will win (perhaps 50% sure).

(iii) It will be "heads" on the tenth toss (50% sure).

LESSON 3–4 (pp. 126–131)

1. $\angle 5$ and $\angle 3$ are corresponding angles.

2. $\angle 1$ and $\angle 7$ are corresponding angles.

3. If $\text{m}\angle 4 = \text{m}\angle 6$, then by the Corresponding Angles Postulate (corr. $\angle$s = $\Rightarrow \parallel$ lines), the lines m and n should be drawn parallel.

4. $\angle ABE$ and $\angle DCB$ are corresponding angles, so by the Parallel Lines Postulate ($\parallel$ lines $\Rightarrow$ corr. $\angle$s =), $\text{m}\angle ABE = \text{m}\angle DCB = 80$.

5. $\angle ABC$ and $\angle FCD$ are corresponding angles. If they are equal, then $\overline{AB} \parallel \overline{CD}$ since corr. $\angle$s = $\Rightarrow \parallel$ lines. So the statement is true.

6. On the surface of the earth, longitude lines form equal corresponding angles with any latitude transversal, but the longitude lines are not parallel. So the Corresponding Angle Postulate is false on the surface of the earth.

7. slope $= \dfrac{y_2 - y_1}{x_2 - x_1}$

$$= \dfrac{2 - 4}{6 - 1}$$
$$= \dfrac{-2}{5}$$
$$= -\dfrac{2}{5}$$

8. slope $= \dfrac{y_2 - y_1}{x_2 - x_1}$

$$= \dfrac{3 - (-7)}{-7 - 3}$$
$$= \dfrac{10}{-10}$$
$$= -1$$

9. By the Parallel Lines and Slopes Theorem, if two nonvertical lines are parallel, then their slopes are equal.

10. Two points on $y = 4x - 5$ are (0, -5) and (1, -1), so slope $= \dfrac{y_2 - y_1}{x_2 - x_1}$

$$= \dfrac{-1 - (-5)}{1 - 0}$$
$$= \dfrac{-1 + 5}{1}$$
$$= 4$$

The slope of any line parallel to $y = 4x - 5$ will be 4.

11. Two points on $12x - 3y = 10$ are $(0, \frac{-10}{3})$ and $(\frac{5}{6}, 0)$, so

$$\text{slope} = \frac{y_2 - y_1}{x_2 - x_1}$$

$$= \frac{0 - (-\frac{10}{3})}{\frac{5}{6} - 0}$$

$$= \frac{\frac{10}{3}}{\frac{5}{6}}$$

$$= \frac{10}{3} \cdot \frac{6}{5}$$

$$= \frac{60}{15}$$

$$= 4$$

The slope of any line parallel to $12x - 3y = 10$ will be 4.

12. Slope is not defined for vertical lines, because the denominator, $x_2 - x_1$, would be zero.

13. The Transitivity of Parallelism Theorem

14. The diagram contains corresponding angles, vertical angles, and supplementary angles, so
$m\angle 1 = m\angle 7 = m\angle 4 = m\angle 6 = 122$
and
$m\angle 2 = m\angle 8 = m\angle 3 = m\angle 5 = 180 - 122 = 58$.

15. a. By corresponding angles and vertical angles, $\angle 6$ is equal to $\angle 4$, $\angle 1$ and $\angle 7$.
    b. The supplementary angles to $\angle 6$ (and $\angle 4$) are $\angle 5$, $\angle 8$, $\angle 3$, and $\angle 2$.

16. $\angle ABE$ is a corresponding angle with $\angle ACF$ (or $\angle BCF$, $\angle FCB$, $\angle FCA$) so $m\angle ACF = 106$.

17. The corresponding angle to $\angle EBC$ is $\angle FCD$ (or $\angle DCF$).

18. a. Line u has the largest slope (it has the greatest positive vertical change for a given positive horizontal change).
    b. Line w has negative slope (it has a negative vertical change for a positive horizontal change).

19. To calculate slope, it does not matter which point is considered first, so the statement is true.

20. It is generally easier to climb cliffs with lesser grades, so a 65°-grade would be easier to climb than an 80°-grade.

21. $\angle 1$ and $\angle 6$ are corresponding angles, so the justification is "corr. $\angle$s $=$ $\Rightarrow$ $\parallel$ lines."

22. $\angle 2$ and $\angle 3$ are vertical angles, so the justification is the Vertical Angle Theorem.

23.

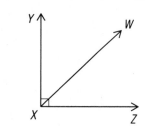

24. a.

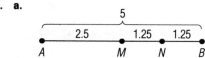

$MN = 1.25$

b. $AN = \frac{3}{4}AB$ since N is the midpoint of $\frac{1}{2}AB$. If $AN = x$, then $AB = \frac{4}{3}x$ and $NB = \frac{4}{3}x - x = \frac{x}{3}$.

25.

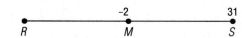

$MS = |-2 - 31| = |-33| = 33$
So the coordinate of R is $-2 - 33 = -35$.

26.

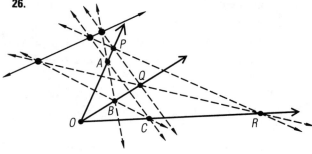

LESSON 3–5 (pp. 132–139)

1. a. Two lines are perpendicular if and only if they form a 90° angle.

   b. If two lines are perpendicular, then they form a 90° angle.

2.

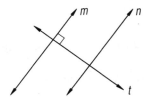

3. Two symbols for perpendicularity are ⊥ and ⌐.

4. a.

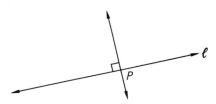

   b. By the Perpendicular to Parallels Theorem, if $m \parallel n$ and $t \perp m$, then $t \perp n$.

5. $\overline{AD}$ and $\overline{BC}$ are each perpendicular to $\overline{AB}$, so $\overline{AD} \parallel \overline{BC}$ by the Two Perpendiculars Theorem.

6. Line n is perpendicular to line m, one of two parallel lines, so it is also perpendicular to the other parallel line ℓ, by the Perpendicular to Parallels Theorem.

7. By the Perpendicular Lines and Slopes Theorem, the slope of a line perpendicular to one with slope $\frac{2}{3}$ is $-\frac{3}{2}$, since $(\frac{2}{3})(-\frac{3}{2}) = -1$.

8. By the Perpendicular Lines and Slopes Theorem, the slope of a line perpendicular to one with slope $x (x \neq 0)$ is $-\frac{1}{x}$, since $(x)(-\frac{1}{x}) = -1$. (If the slope x is zero, the slope of its perpendicular is not defined.)

9. If two nonvertical lines are perpendicular, the product of their slopes is -1. If the product of two slopes is -1, the two lines are perpendicular.

10.
$$\text{slope of line } t = \frac{y_2 - y_1}{x_2 - x_1}$$
$$= \frac{2 - 1}{2 - 0}$$
$$= \frac{1}{2}$$

So if $s \perp t$, the slope of s is -2, since $(-2)(\frac{1}{2}) = -1$.

11. a. $\overrightarrow{AD} \perp \overrightarrow{AC}$, so m$\angle DAC = 90$.

   b. m$\angle DAE$ + m$\angle DAC$ + m$\angle CAB = 180$
            m$\angle DAE$ + 90 + 40 = 180
                m$\angle DAE$ + 130 = 180
                      m$\angle DAE = 50$

12. Street intersections are perpendicular so no driver's head needs to turn more than 90° in each direction at the intersection to check for traffic from both directions.

13. a. $\angle S$ and $\angle PQR$ are corresponding angles for lines $\overleftrightarrow{SU}$ and $\overleftrightarrow{QR}$, so they are equal by $\parallel$ lines ⇒ corr. $\angle$s =.

   b. $\overline{QT}$ is perpendicular to $\overline{TU}$ (or $\overline{SU}$) one of two parallel lines, so it is perpendicular to $\overline{QR}$, the other parallel line, also, by the Perpendicular to Parallels Theorem.

   c. $\parallel$ lines ⇒ corr. $\angle$s = $\angle SQT$ and $\angle P$ are corresponding angles for $\overleftrightarrow{TQ}$ and $\overleftrightarrow{UP}$.

   d. $\ell \perp m$ ⇒ 90° angle $\overline{QT} \perp \overline{TU}$ and lines are perpendicular if and only if the lines containing them form a 90° angle.

14. a. $m\angle S = m\angle PQR$ by ∥ lines ⇒ corr. ∠s =, so if $m\angle PQR = 65$ then $m\angle S = 65$.

b. By 13b, $\overline{QT} \perp \overline{QR}$, so $\angle TQR = 90°$ by the definition of perpendicular lines (meaning)

c. $\angle TQS + \angle TQR + \angle RQP = 180°$
$$\angle TQS + 90° + 65° = 180°$$
$$\angle TQS + 155° = 180°$$
$$\angle TQS = 25°$$

d. $\overline{TQ} \parallel \overline{UP}$, so $\angle P = \angle SQT$ by ∥ lines ⇒ corr. ∠s =. Since $\angle SQT = 25°$ by part **c**, $\angle P = 25°$.

15. Two points on $9y + 2x = 180$ are $(0, 20)$ and $(90, 0)$, so

$$\text{slope} = \frac{y_2 - y_1}{x_2 - x_1}$$
$$= \frac{0 - 20}{90 - 0}$$
$$= \frac{-20}{90}$$
$$= -\frac{2}{9}.$$

For any line perpendicular to $9y + 2x = 180$, the slope will be $\frac{9}{2}$, since $(\frac{9}{2})(-\frac{2}{9}) = -1$.

16. a. By the Two Perpendiculars Theorem, coplanar lines $\overleftrightarrow{AB}$ and $\overleftrightarrow{CD}$, each perpendicular to $\overleftrightarrow{BC}$, must be parallel.

b. In space, lines $\overleftrightarrow{AB}$ and $\overleftrightarrow{CD}$ may be skew; they will not intersect. (On the surface of the earth, it is possible that $\overline{AB} \perp \overline{BC}$, $\overline{BC} \perp \overline{CD}$, and $\overline{AB} \perp \overline{CD}$.)

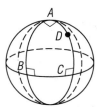

17. Since ∥ lines ⇒ corr. ∠s =, $m\angle 1 = m\angle 2 = 70$. By the Vertical Angle Theorem, $m\angle 1 = m\angle 4 = m\angle 7 = 70$.
By the Linear Pair Theorem, $\angle 3$, $\angle 5$, $\angle 6$, and $\angle 8$ are all supplementary to 70°, so each is 110°.

18. slope $= \dfrac{y_2 - y_1}{x_2 - x_1}$
$$= \frac{-9 - (-7)}{-10 - 4}$$
$$= \frac{-2}{-14}$$
$$= \frac{1}{7}$$

19. If $m\angle 3 = m\angle 8$, then $m \parallel n$ by corr. ∠s = ⇒ ∥ lines.

20. Since $\angle 7$ and $\angle 8$ are a linear pair, they are supplementary by the Linear Pair Theorem.

21. $m\angle 6$ is about 100.

22. The definition of perpendicular lines (meaning half) is $\ell \perp m \Rightarrow 90°$ angle.

23. The points on both circles are D and H, so $\odot A \cap \odot B = \{D, H\}$.

24.

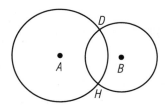

25.

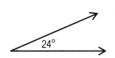

26. a.

b. Students' own mazes will vary. While every maze should have a unique starting and ending point, a maze can have more than one solution path.

7.

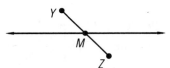

LESSON 3-6 (pp. 140–145)

1. In drawings, any tools may be used.
2. In constructions, the only permissible tools are a compass and unmarked straightedge.
3. The three rules of a construction are the Point Rule, Straightedge Rule, and Compass Rule.
4. The points that can be used are those that are given or are the intersections of figures that are constructed.
5. An **algorithm** is a sequence of steps leading to a desired end.
6. The **perpendicular bisector of a segment** is the line passing through the midpoint of a segment and perpendicular to it.

8.

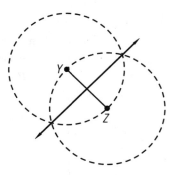

9.

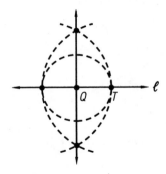

10. A **subroutine** is an algorithm you already know that you use in another algorithm.

11.

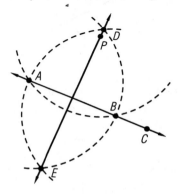

12. The justification for $\odot P$ containing A is the Compass Rule; the justification that $\odot P$ intersects $\overleftrightarrow{AC}$ at A and B is the Point Rule.

13.

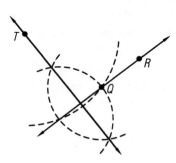

14.

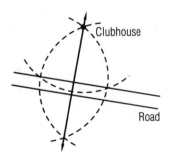

15.

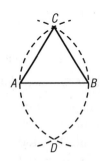

The construction is an equilateral triangle ABC.

16. **a.** $GH \approx 38$ mm
$GI \approx 31$ mm
$GJ \approx 27$ mm
$GK \approx 29$ mm
$GL \approx 33$ mm
$GM \approx 39$ mm

b. $\overline{GJ}$, which looks to be the perpendicular from G to $\overleftrightarrow{HM}$, is the shortest segment.

17. Meaning: If two lines are perpendicular, they form a 90° angle.

Sufficient condition: If two lines meet to form a 90° angle, they are perpendicular.

18. a. Two points on $x - 2y = 15$ are $(0, -\frac{15}{2})$ and $(15, 0)$, so

$$\text{slope} = \frac{y_2 - y_1}{x_2 - x_1}$$

$$= \frac{0 - (-\frac{15}{2})}{15 - 0}$$

$$= \frac{\frac{15}{2}}{15}$$

$$= \frac{15}{30}$$

$$= \frac{1}{2}.$$

b. The slope of any line perpendicular to

$x - 2y = 15$ is -2, since $(\frac{1}{2})(-2) = -1$.

19. $\angle 6$ and $\angle 1$ are supplementary, so

$$m\angle 6 + m\angle 1 = 180$$
$$(m\angle 1 + 12) + m\angle 1 = 180$$
$$2m\angle 1 + 12 = 180$$
$$2m\angle 1 = 168$$
$$m\angle 1 = 84.$$

20. If $\ell \parallel m$ and $m \parallel n$, then $\ell \parallel n$.

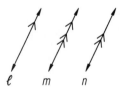

If $\ell \parallel m$ and $m \perp n$, then $\ell \perp n$.

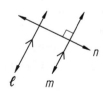

If $\ell \perp m$ and $m \parallel n$, then $\ell \perp n$.

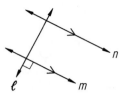

If $\ell \perp m$ and $m \perp n$, then $\ell \parallel n$.

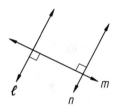

21. "Squaring the circle" is constructing a square whose area is equal to a given circle.

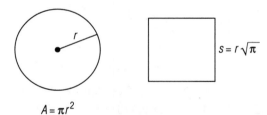

$A = \pi r^2$

It cannot be done as a construction because it is impossible to construct a segment with length $\sqrt{\pi}$ using only a compass and an unmarked straightedge.

"Duplicating the cube" means constructing (the side of) a cube whose volume is twice that of a given cube.

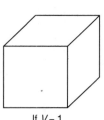

If $V = 1$,
then $e = 1$.

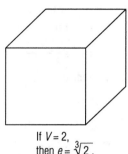

If $V = 2$,
then $e = \sqrt[3]{2}$.

It cannot be done as a construction because it is impossible to construct a segment with length $\sqrt[3]{2}$ with just a compass and an unmarked straightedge.

"Trisecting an angle" means constructing two rays that trisect a given angle.

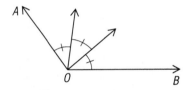

This construction is not possible using only a compass and unmarked straightedge (except for some special-case angles such as 45°, 90°, and 135°).

CHAPTER 3 PROGRESS SELF-TEST (p. 147–148)

1. sample:

2. $m\angle 3 = m\angle 4$ because of the Vertical Angle Theorem. So if $m\angle 3 = 77$, then $m\angle 4 = 77$ by the Transitive Property of Equality.

3. $\angle 3$ and $\angle 4$ are called Vertical Angles.

4. $\angle 3$ and $\angle 5$ form a linear pair, so $m\angle 3 + m\angle 5 = 180$. If $m\angle 3 = 2x$, then $m\angle 5 = 180 - 2x$ by the Addition Property of Equality.

5. From eye level (horizontal) to straight up (vertical) is 90°. So from 15° to 90° is $(90 - 15)° = 75°$.

6. If $\angle 1$ and $\angle 2$ are complementary, then $m\angle 1 + m\angle 2 = 90$ (definition of complementary (meaning)). Substituting $m\angle 1 = 5x - 7$ and $m\angle 2 = 4x + 16$, then $(5x - 7) + (4x + 16) = 90$, or $9x + 9 = 90$, so $9x = 81$ and $x = 9$. Finally, $m\angle 1 = 5x - 7 = 5(9) - 7 = 45 - 7 = 38$.

7.

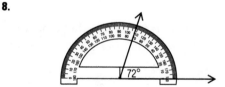

$m\angle A \approx 40$

8.

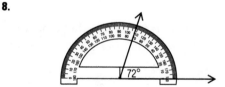

9.

$m\angle ABC = 110$, so $m\angle 1 + m\angle 2 = 110$.
$m\angle 2 = 4 \cdot m\angle 1$, so $m\angle 1 + 4m\angle 1 = 110$.
$$5m\angle 1 = 110$$
$$m\angle 1 = 22$$

10. For two adjacent angles, the statement that the sum of the measures of the two smaller angles equals the measure of the large angle is the Angle Addition Property; that is choice (d).

49

11. $\angle 1$ is acute, so $0 < 21 + x < 90$.
$$-21 < x < 69$$

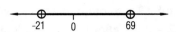

12. $\overrightarrow{BC}$ bisects $\angle ABD$, so m$\angle ABC = $ m$\angle CBD$ or $14y - 3 = 37 - y$. So $15y = 40$, and $y = \frac{40}{15} = \frac{8}{3}$.

13. Two lines (ℓ and m) perpendicular to the same line (n) are parallel to each other.

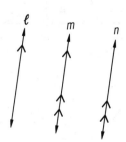

14. Two lines (ℓ and m) parallel to the same line (n) are parallel to each other.

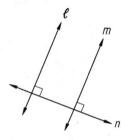

15. The slope of $\overline{AB}$ is $\frac{y_2 - y_1}{x_2 - x_1} = \frac{1 - 0}{4 - 0} = \frac{1}{4}$.

16. The slope of any line, segment, or ray perpendicular to $\overline{AB}$ is -4, because $(\frac{1}{4})(-4) = -1$.

17. Two points on $2x - y = 6$ are $(0, -6)$ and $(3, 0)$. The slope of the line through those points is $\frac{y_2 - y_1}{x_2 - x_1} = \frac{0 - -6}{3 - 0} = \frac{6}{3} = 2$.

18. The slope of any line perpendicular to $2x - y = 6$ is $-\frac{1}{2}$, because $(2)(-\frac{1}{2}) = -1$.

19. m$\angle 4 = $ m$\angle 3$ because $\parallel$ lines $\Rightarrow$ AIA $=$. $\angle 3$ is supplementary to a 40° angle, so m$\angle 4 = 140$ by the Transitive Property of Equality.

20. m$\angle 5 = 40$ because $\parallel$ lines $\Rightarrow$ AIA $=$.

21. The shortest path from point H to the street is the length of the $\perp$ segment from H to the street, or segment x; that is choice (b).

22.

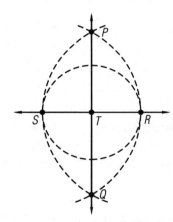

Step 1: $\odot T$, intersecting $\overleftrightarrow{TR}$
at A and B.   (Compass rule)
Step 2: $\odot A$ containing B, $\odot B$
containing A; they
intersect at P and Q. (Compass rule)
Step 3: $\overleftrightarrow{PQ}$ (Straightedge rule)

23. If Q is the midpoint of $\overline{QP}$, then $OQ = QP$; that is the definition of midpoint (meaning).

CHAPTER 3 REVIEW (pp. 149–153)

1. **a.** ∠LPO (or ∠OPL) and ∠NPM (or ∠MPN) are straight angles.

   b. Zero angles are ∠LPL, ∠MPM, ∠OPO, and ∠NPN. (Other zero angles are ∠PLP, ∠PLO, ∠OLP, etc.)

   c. Linear pairs are ∠LPM and ∠MPO, ∠MPO and ∠OPN, ∠OPN and ∠NPL, and ∠NPL and ∠LPM.

   d. Two other names for ∠1 are ∠LPM and ∠MPL.

2. ∠2 appears to be less than 90°, so it appears to be acute.

3.

4.

5. **a.** ∠1 and ∠2 are a linear pair, so $m\angle1 + m\angle2 = 180$ by the Linear Pair Theorem.
   So $m\angle1 + m\angle2 = 180$
   $m\angle1 + 78 = 180$
   $m\angle1 = 102$

   b. $m\angle1 = m\angle3$ by the Vertical Angle Theorem. So using the result of part a, $m\angle3 = 102$.

   c. $m\angle2 = m\angle4$ by the Vertical Angle Theorem, so $m\angle4 = 78$.

6. $m\angle1 = m\angle2 = 180$ by the Linear Pair Theorem, and $m\angle1 = m\angle3$, $m\angle2 = m\angle4$ by the Vertical Angle Theorem.

   a. If $m\angle2 = 3x$, then
   $m\angle1 + m\angle2 = 180$
   $m\angle1 + 3x = 180$
   $m\angle1 = 180 - 3x$.

   b. $m\angle3 = m\angle1 = 180 - 3x$

   c. $m\angle4 = m\angle2 = 3x$

7. $m\angle R \approx 52$

8. $m\angle Q \approx 147$

9.

10.

11.

12.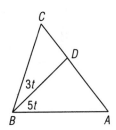

$72 = 3t + 5t$
$72 = 8t$
$t = 9$
To check, $5t = 45°$, $3t = 27°$, and $m\angle ABC = 5t + 3t = 8t = 72$.

13. If ∠3 is a straight angle, then
   $m\angle3 = 12 - x = 180$
   $-x = 168$
   $x = -168$.

14. If ∠4 is obtuse, then
   $90 < m\angle4 < 180$.
   So $90 < 31 + y < 180$
   $59 < y < 149$

15. $m\angle 1 + m\angle 2 = 180$ and $m\angle 2 = \frac{1}{4}m\angle 1$. So

$$m\angle 1 + \frac{1}{4}m\angle 1 = 180$$

$$\frac{5}{4}m\angle 1 = 180$$

$$m\angle 1 = 180(\frac{4}{5}) = 144$$

$$m\angle 2 = 180 - 144 = 36$$

16.
$$m\angle 1 + m\angle 2 = 180$$
$$(7x - 6) + (5x + 18) = 180$$
$$12x + 12 = 180$$
$$12x = 168$$
$$x = 14$$
$$m\angle 1 = 7x - 6 = 7(14) - 6 = 98 - 6 = 92$$
$$m\angle 2 = 5x + 18 = 5(14) + 18 =$$
$$70 + 18 = 88$$

17. If $m\angle PQS = 40$, then
$$(8x) + (9x - 7) = 40$$
$$17x - 7 = 40$$
$$17x = 47$$
$$x = \frac{47}{17}$$

18. If $\overrightarrow{QR}$ bisects $\angle PQS$, then
$$8x = 9x - 7$$
$$-x = -7$$
$$x = 7$$

19. By the Vertical Angle Theorem,
$$8y - 23 = 4y + 41$$
$$4y - 23 = 41$$
$$4y = 64$$
$$y = 16$$

20. Complementary angles add to 90°, so if the measure of the complement is x,
$$9x + x = 90$$
$$10x = 90$$
$$x = 9$$
$$9x = 81$$
The measure of an angle that is nine times its complement is 81° (the complement is 9°).

21. Supplementary angles add to 180°. If one angle has measure x, then its supplement is $180 - x$. The first angle is 42° less than its supplement, so
$$x = (180 - x) - 42$$
$$x = 180 - x - 42$$
$$2x = 138$$
$$x = 69.$$

22. If q is less than its supplement, then
$$q < 180 - q$$
$$2q < 180$$
$$q < 90.$$
So any acute angle has smaller measure than its supplement.

23. $\angle 5 = \angle 6$ by the Vertical Angle Theorem, so
$$17z = 2w$$
$$\frac{17z}{2} = w$$
or $\quad w = \frac{17}{2}z$

24. Because of parallel lines and vertical angles,
$m\angle 1 = m\angle 7 = m\angle 3 = m\angle 5 = 83$.
Because of linear pairs,
$$m\angle 2 = m\angle 8 = m\angle 6 = m\angle 4 = 180 - 83$$
$$= 97.$$

25.
$$m\angle 2 + m\angle 5 = 180$$
$$3(m\angle 5) + m\angle 5 = 180$$
$$4m\angle 5 = 180$$
$$m\angle 5 = 45$$
$$m\angle 2 = 180 - 45 = 135$$

26.

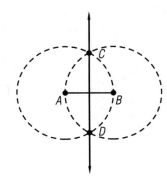

27.

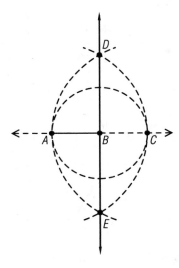

28.

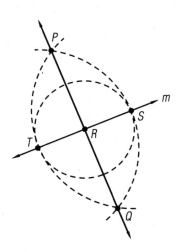

29.

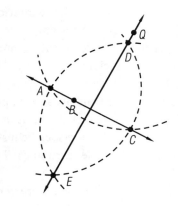

30.

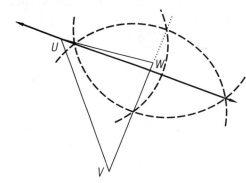

31. **a.** The size of the circle and the location of X, Y, and Z may vary.

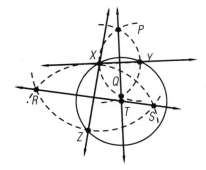

b. Point T is the center of the original circle.
c. The Straightedge Rule justifies steps 1, 3, and 5.

32. The conditional, "If a ray in the interior of an angle forms two equal, adjacent angles, then that ray bisects the angle" is the definition of angle bisector (sufficient condition). That is choice (c).

33. The conditional, "If (one of) a set of points is a given distance from a given point, then that set of points is a circle" is a specific instance of the definition of circle (meaning). That is choice (a).

34. The conditional, "If two angles are vertical angles, then they are equal" is the Vertical Angle Theorem. That is choice (d).

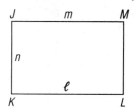

35. $\overline{MJ} \perp \overline{JK}$: write as $m \perp n$.
$\overline{MJ} \parallel \overline{KL}$: write as $m \parallel \ell$.
$\overline{KL} \perp \overline{JK}$: write as $\ell \perp n$.
The justification is "If $\ell \parallel m$ and $m \perp n$, then $\ell \perp n$." That is choice (a).

36. The justification is, "If $\ell \perp m$ and $m \perp n$, then $\ell \parallel n$." That is choice (b).

37. The conditional, "If two angles form a linear pair, then they are supplementary," is the Linear Pair Theorem.

38. The statement, "There is exactly one line through two distinct points" is part of the Point-Line-Plane Postulate.

39. The justification is the Angle Addition Property of the Angle Measure Postulate.

40.

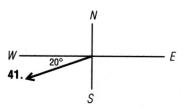

41.

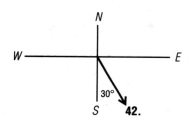

42.

43. The two angles formed by the nail are supplementary, so $180° - 45° = 135°$.

44.

45.

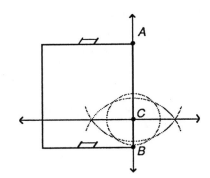

46. $\text{slope} = \dfrac{y_2 - y_1}{x_2 - x_1}$

$= \dfrac{1 - (-2)}{6 - (-5)}$

$= \dfrac{1 + 2}{6 + 5}$

$= \dfrac{3}{11}$

47. $\text{slope} = \dfrac{y_2 - y_1}{x_2 - x_1}$

$= \dfrac{4 - (-3)}{-3 - 4}$

$= \dfrac{4 + 3}{-7}$

$= \dfrac{7}{-7}$

$= -1$

48. Two points on $y = -\dfrac{3}{5}x + 11$ are $(0, 11)$ and $(5, 8)$.

$\text{slope} = \dfrac{y_2 - y_1}{x_2 - x_1}$

$= \dfrac{11 - 8}{0 - 5}$

$= \dfrac{3}{-5}$

$= -\dfrac{3}{5}$

49. Two points on $5x - 3y = 45$ are $(0, -15)$ and $(9, 0)$.

$\text{slope} = \dfrac{y_2 - y_1}{x_2 - x_1}$

$= \dfrac{-15 - 0}{0 - 9}$

$= \dfrac{-15}{-9}$

$= \dfrac{5}{3}$

50. The line which has a steeper climb, or which has a greater positive vertical change for a given positive horizontal change, is $2y = x + 1$.

51. Graph the two lines.

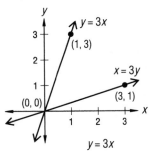

The line $y = 3x$ is steeper; it has greater slope.

52. If a line has slope 10, each line parallel to it has slope 10 (by the Parallel Lines and Slope Theorem), and each line perpendicular to it has slope $-\dfrac{1}{10}$ (by the Perpendicular Lines and Slopes Theorem).

53. If a line has slope $-\frac{2}{3}$, each line parallel to it

has slope $-\frac{2}{3}$ (by the Parallel Lines and Slope

Theorem), and each line perpendicular to it

has slope $\frac{3}{2}$ (by the Perpendicular Lines and

Slopes Theorem).

54. slope of $m = \dfrac{y_2 - y_1}{x_2 - x_1}$

$\qquad = \dfrac{-3 - (-1)}{-6 - 8}$

$\qquad = \dfrac{-3 + 1}{-14}$

$\qquad = \dfrac{-2}{-14}$

$\qquad = \dfrac{1}{7}$

The slope of n is -7, since $(\frac{1}{7})(-7) = -1$.

55. Graph the two lines.

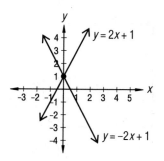

The two lines are neither parallel nor perpendicular (their slopes are 2 and -2); that is choice (c).

LESSON 4-1   (pp. 154–162)

1. A figure that is to be reflected is called the preimage.

2.
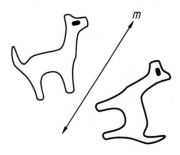

3.
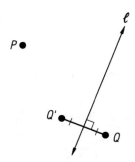

m is the ⊥ bisector of $\overline{AB}$.

4.

The reflection image of P over ℓ is P.

5. **a.**
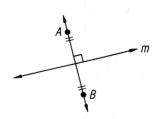

b.
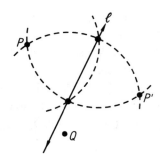

6. The justification for drawing $\odot S$ with radius SB is the Compass rule.

7. Use the letter "r" to denote a reflection.

8. **a.** $r(P)$ denotes "the reflection image of point P."

   b. $r_m(P)$ denotes "the reflection image of point P over line m."

9.
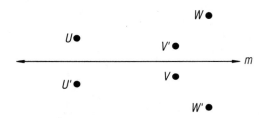

10.
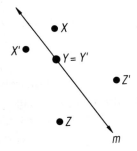

11. **a.** $r_x(x, y) = (x, -y)$, so
    $r_x(P) = r_x(3, 5) = (3, -5)$.

    b. $r_y(x, y) = (-x, y)$, so
    $r_y(3, 5) = (-3, 5)$.

12. **a.** $r_x(x, y) = (x, -y)$, so
    $r_x(-4, 1) = (-4, -1)$.

    b. $r_y(x, y) = (-x, y)$, so
    $r_y(-4, 1) = (4, 1)$.

13. a. $r_x(x, y) = (x, -y)$, so
$r_x(c, d) = (c, -d)$.
b. $r_y(x, y) = (-x, y)$, so
$r_y(c, d) = (-c, d)$.

14. a, b. ℓ is the $\perp$ bisector of $\overline{AB}$, so $r_\ell(A) = B$.
m is the $\perp$ bisector of $\overline{AC}$, so $r_m(A) = C$.
n is the $\perp$ bisector of $\overline{AD}$, so $r_n(A) = D$.

15.

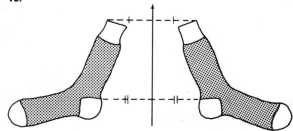

16.

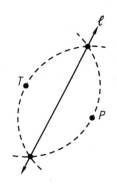

17. a. A mirror can help read the reflection (horizontally) of the message: HELP! I'M TRAPPED I𝖪SIDE THIS PAGE!
b. The letter "N" is oriented correctly in the message, so its reflection image will be oriented incorrectly.

18.

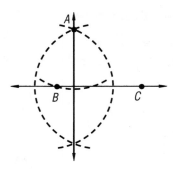

19.

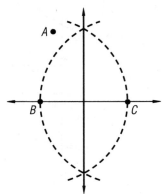

20. a. slope of $\ell = \dfrac{y_2 - y_1}{x_2 - x_1}$

$= \dfrac{1 - 0}{4 - 0}$

$= \dfrac{1}{4}$

slope of $m = \dfrac{y_2 - y_1}{x_2 - x_1}$

$= \dfrac{4 - 3}{3 - (-1)}$

$= \dfrac{1}{4}$

So $\ell \parallel m$ by the Parallel Lines and Slopes Theorem.

b. From part a, slope of $\ell = \dfrac{1}{4}$.

Slope of $n = \dfrac{y_2 - y_1}{x_2 - x_1}$

$= \dfrac{4 - 1}{3 - 4}$

$= \dfrac{3}{-1}$

$= -3$

The product of the two slopes is $(\frac{1}{4})(-3) =$ $-\frac{3}{4} \neq -1$, so ℓ and n are not perpendicular.

21. Two points on $x + 2y = 6$ are $(0, 3)$ and $(6, 0)$, so the slope is $\frac{0 - 3}{6 - 0} = \frac{-3}{6} = -\frac{1}{2}$.
    Two points on $2x - y = 8$ are $(0, -8)$ and $(4, 0)$, so the slope is $\frac{0 - (-8)}{4 - 0} = \frac{8}{4} = 2$.
    Since $(-\frac{1}{2})(2) = -1$, the lines are $\perp$ by the Perpendicular Lines and Slopes Theorem; that is choice (b).

22. **a.** $\angle VEO$ and $\angle GEO$ form a linear pair, so $m\angle VEO = 30$ by the Linear Pair Theorem.
    b. $\angle G$ and $\angle VEO$ are corresponding angles, and each has measure 30, so $\overline{EO} \parallel \overline{GL}$ because corr. $\angle$s $= \Rightarrow \parallel$ lines.

23. $a \parallel b$, so $3x = 75$ because $\parallel$ lines $\Rightarrow$ corr. $\angle$s $=$. So $x = 25$.

24. $r_\ell(A) = B$ and $r_\ell(C) = D$ means that ℓ is the $\perp$ bisector of $\overline{AB}$ and of $\overline{CD}$.

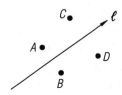

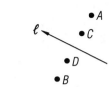

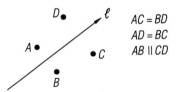

$AC = BD$
$AD = BC$
$AB \parallel CD$

Some consequents are:
$\overline{AB} \parallel \overline{CD}$ (since both are $\perp$ to line ℓ)
$AD = BC$, $AC = BD$
$m\angle CAD = m\angle CBD$
$m\angle ACB = m\angle ADB$
$m\angle ABC = m\angle BAD$
$m\angle ABD = m\angle BAC$

LESSON 4-2 (pp. 163–169)

1. Reflections preserve angle measure, betweenness, collinearity, and distance.

2. The reflection image of a point over a line is unique, so a point cannot have two different reflection images over the same line.

3. Since V is between A and Z, and reflections preserve betweenness, V' will be between A' and Z'.

4. The reflection image of $\overline{AC}$ over ℓ is $\overline{BD}$. Since reflections preserve distance, then $AC = BD$.

5. **a-b.** Reflections preserve angle measure, so $\angle DEF$ cannot be a reflection image of $\angle ABC$ because $m\angle DEF \neq m\angle ABC$.

6. Figure Reflection Theorem: If a figure is determined by certain points, then its reflection image is the corresponding figure determined by the reflection images of those points.

7. The image of X is Z, and the image of T is S, so $r_m(\overline{XT}) = \overline{ZS}$.

8. **a.**

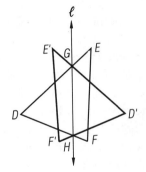

b. The measurements are:

$DE = D'F' \approx 1$ in. or 2.54 cm

$EF = E'F' \approx 1$ in. or 2.54 cm

$DF = D'F' \approx .75$ in. or 1.9 cm

9. a. Since $\overline{DE}$ and $\overline{DF}$ intersect the reflecting line, their images $\overline{D'E'}$ and $\overline{D'F'}$ will also intersect the reflecting line.

b. Since $r_\ell(G) = G$ and $r_\ell(H) = H$, since both points are on ℓ, $\overline{D'E'}$ and $\overline{D'F'}$ will interesect ℓ at G and H, respectively.

10. a.

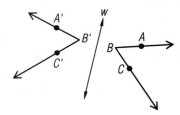

b. Using a protractor, $m\angle ABC = m\angle A'B'C' \approx 60$.

11.

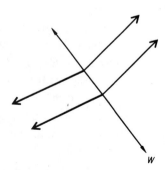

12. a. By the Figure Reflection Theorem, $A'B'C'D'E'$ is determined by the same number of points as $ABCDE;$ that is 5 points.

b. Since reflections preserve angle measure, $m\angle A'B'C' = m\angle ABC = 130$.

13. An angle is determined by 3 points—the vertex, and one non-endpoint on each of its two rays. By the Figure Reflection Theorem, the image of an angle is determined by the same number of points. So 3 image points are needed to draw the image of an angle.

14. Points S and Y are their own images over line w, so only one reflection point, P', is needed.

15. A circle is its own reflection over a line containing the diameter, so no additional points are needed.

16. a.

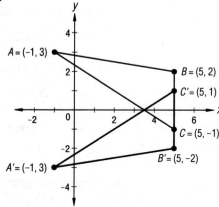

b. $r_x(x, y) = (x, -y)$, so
$A' = r_x(-1, 3) = (-1, -3)$,
$B' = r_x(5, 2) = (5, -2)$, and
$C' = r_x(5, -1) = (5, 1)$.

17. The image of $\overline{NO}$ is $\overline{RS}$, so $NO = RS$ because reflections preserve distance; that is choice (d).

18. The image of $\angle NMO$ is $\angle RQS$, so $m\angle NMO = m\angle RQS$ because reflections preserve angle measure; that is choice (a).

19. $r_\ell(M) = Q$, so $\ell \perp \overline{MQ}$ by the definition of reflection; that is choice (e).

20. $r_\ell(M) = Q$, so ℓ bisects $\overline{MQ}$ by the definition of reflection; that is choice (e).

21.

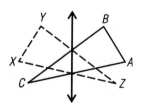

22.

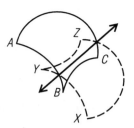

23.

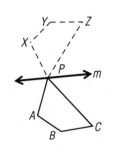

24.

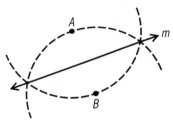

25.

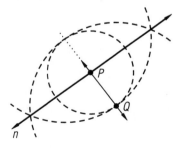

26. A line, segment, or ray is the ⊥ bisector of a segment if and only if it is ⊥ to the segment and contains the midpoint of the segment.

27. If a line has slope -3, each line parallel to it has slope -3 (by the Parallel Lines and Slopes Theorem) and each line perpendicular to it has slope $\frac{1}{3}$ (because of the Perpendicular Lines and Slopes Theorem).

28.

p	q	$p \Rightarrow q$
T	T	T
T	F	F
F	T	T
F	F	T

Lines 3 and 4 show that if $p \Rightarrow q$ is true and p is false, q may be true or false. So nothing more can be concluded.

29. The Transitive Property of Equality: If $a = b$ and $b = c$, then $a = c$.

30.

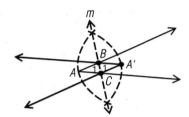

Since $r_m(A) = A'$, then $m \perp \overline{AA}'$ by the definition of reflection (meaning). Line m intersects the sides of $\angle 1$ in two points. Those two points and A' determine the image of $\angle 1$ by the Figure Reflection Theorem.

LESSON 4–3 (pp. 170–175)

1. An automatic drawer is any computer (or calculator) software that enables figures to be constructed.

2. Automatic drawers make drawing or constructing figures less time-consuming and difficult, they let you experiment with reflections and verify postulates or theorems, help you make or explore complicated drawings, and even print out the drawings you create.

3. **a.** $AB \approx \frac{13}{16}$ in. or 2.1 cm

$BC \approx \frac{5}{8}$ in. or 1.6 cm

$AD \approx \frac{13}{16}$ in. or 2.1 cm

$DC \approx \frac{5}{8}$ in. or 1.6 cm

b. The measurements verify that reflections preserve distance.

4. **a.**

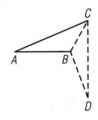

r $_{\overline{BC}}$ △*ABC* = △*DBC*

b.

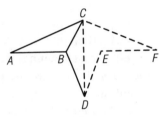

r $_{\overline{DC}}$ (*ABDC*) = (*FEDC*)

5. **a–b.** Since r(C) = D and r(F) = E, the lengths of $\overline{CF}$ and $\overline{DE}$ should be equal because reflections preserve distance.

6. **a–b.** Since r(F) = E and r(A) = A, the lengths of $\overline{AF}$ and $\overline{AE}$ should be equal because reflections preserve distance.

7. **a–b.** r(F) = E, r(D) = C, and r(B) = B. So ∠EDB is the reflection image of ∠FCB, and m∠EDB should equal m∠FCB because reflections preserve angle measure.

8. **a–b.**

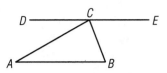

c. The measures of the angles will depend on the specific figure.

d. Since $\overleftrightarrow{DE} \parallel \overleftrightarrow{AB}$, m∠$DCA$ = m∠BAC and m∠ECB = m∠ABC because $\parallel$ lines ⇒ AIA = .

9. **a.** The measures of the angles will depend on the specific figure, but the pairs 1-2, 3-4, 5-6, and 7-8 should be supplementary.

b. Pairs of corresponding angles are:

1 and 3   8 and 6

2 and 4   7 and 5

c. Parts **a** and **b** verify that lines $\parallel$ ⇒ corr. ∠s = . (the Parallel Lines Postulate)

10. **a–b.** For any diagram, since m∠3 + m∠4 = 180 (by the Linear Pair Theorem) and m∠2 = m∠4 (since $\parallel$ lines ⇒ corr. ∠s =), then m∠2 + m∠3 = 180. Similarly, m∠6 + m∠7 = 180. So m∠2 + m∠3 + m∠6 + m∠7 = 360.

11. **a–b–c.**

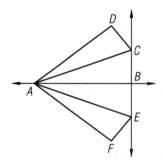

d. $\overline{EB}$ is the image of $\overline{BC}$. Also, $\overline{FE}$ is the image of $\overline{CD}$, which is the image of $\overline{BC}$. So $BC = DC = FE = EB$ because reflections preserve distance.

e. The right angles at F and D and the two right angles at B are all congruent. Also, the four small angles at A are congruent, and the four angles at E and at C are congruent.

12. Reflections preserve angle measure, betweenness, collinearity, and distance.

13.

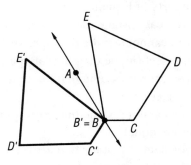

14.

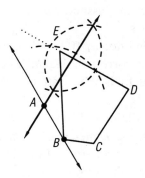

15. Since $r_y(x, y) = (-x, y)$, then
$P' = r_y(-2, 0) = (2, 0)$,
$Q' = r_y(-4, 3) = (4, 3)$, and
$R' = r_y(2, 7) = (-2, 7)$.

16. The slope of $\overleftrightarrow{PQ}$ is
$$\frac{y_2 - y_1}{x_2 - x_1} = \frac{3 - 0}{-4 - (-2)}$$
$$= \frac{3}{-2}$$
$$= -\frac{3}{2}.$$

The slope of $\overleftrightarrow{QR}$ is
$$\frac{y_2 - y_1}{x_2 - x_1} = \frac{7 - 3}{2 - (-4)}$$
$$= \frac{4}{6}$$
$$= \frac{2}{3}.$$
Since $(-\frac{3}{2})(\frac{2}{3}) = -1$, $\overleftrightarrow{PQ} \perp \overleftrightarrow{QR}$ by the Perpendicular Lines and Slopes Theorem, and $\angle PQR$ is a right angle by the definition of right angle (sufficient condition).

17.

18. **a.** acute means $0 < m < 90$, which is choice (vii).

b. complementary means $m_1 + m_2 = 90$, which is choice (i).

c. obtuse means $90 < m < 180$, which is choice (vi).

d. right means $m = 90$, which is choice (iv).

e. straight means $m = 180$, which is choice (v).

f. supplementary means $m_1 + m_2 = 180$, which is choice (ii).

g. zero means $m = 0$, which is choice (iii).

19. The angle can be named by its vertex ($\angle B$), by its interior ($\angle 1$), or by 3 points ($\angle ABC$ or $\angle CBA$).

20. **a** and **c** are convex, since every segment joining two points of the region lies completely within the region. Figure **b** is nonconvex because some segments joining two points of the region lie partially outside the region.

21. The letters common to {L, I, N, E, S} and {P, O, I, N, T, S} are I, N, and S, so A ∩ B = {I, N, S}.

22. Answers should have the same shape, but not necessarily the same size, as the figures in the text.

LESSON 4–4 (pp. 176–182)

1. If a figure is an equilateral triangle, then it is a triangle with all three sides having the same length.

2. **a.**

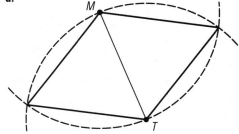

b. You could construct 2 triangles, one on each side of $\overleftrightarrow{MT}$.

3. The statement, "If a figure is a circle, then all its points are a given distance from the center" is the definition of circle (meaning).

4. People stopped using Euclid's *Elements* because developments in geometry ultimately made the *Elements* out-of-date.

5. **a.** ∠2 and ∠6 are corresponding angles, so m∠2 = m∠6 because ∥ lines ⇒ corr. ∠s =.

b. ∠6 and ∠8 are vertical angles so m∠6 = m∠8 by the Vertical Angle Theorem.

c. m∠2 = m∠6 and m∠6 = m∠8 from parts **a** and **b**, so m∠2 = m∠8 by the Transitive Property of Equality.

6. Yes, you can assume the intersection of lines.

7. No, you cannot assume that lines which do not intersect (in the diagram) are parallel.

8. No, you cannot assume that lines meet at right angles.

9. No, you cannot assume that corresponding angles are equal.

10. No, you cannot assume that a given point is equidistant from two other given points.

11. No, you cannot assume that lines meet at right angles.

12. **a.** The conditional, "If two lines are parallel, then the corresponding angles thus formed are equal." is abbreviated " ∥ lines ⇒ corr. ∠s =."

b. The conditional, "If m∠1 = m∠5 and m∠5 = m∠7, then m∠1 = m∠7" is the Transitive Property of Equality.

13. Statement 2 in Example 1 is m∠5 = m∠7 because of the Vertical Angle Theorem. You may assume from the diagram that ∠5 and ∠7 are vertical angles, and m ∥ n was also given in Example 1.

14.

conclusions	justifications
1. m∠4 = m∠2	∥ lines ⇒ corr. ∠s =
2. m∠2 = m∠8	Vertical Angle Theorem
3. m∠4 = m∠8	Transitive Property of Equality (steps 1 and 2)

15.

conclusions	justifications
1. m∠CBD = m∠D	given
2. m∠CBD = m∠ABE	Vertical Angle Theorem
3. m∠ABE = m∠D	Transitive Property of Equality (steps 1 and 2)

16.

conclusions	justifications
1. AB = BC BC = DC	definition of equilateral triangle (meaning)
2. AB = DC	Transitive Property of Equality (step 1)

17. a.

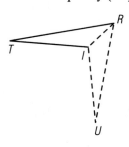

b. Since r $_{\overleftrightarrow{RI}}$(T) = U and r $_{\overleftrightarrow{RI}}$(I) = I, then the image of $\overline{TI}$ is $\overline{UI}$. So TI = UI because reflections preserve distance.

18. a.

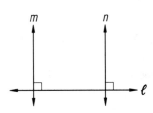

If two lines (m and n) are perpendicular to the same line (ℓ), then m and n are **parallel.**

b.

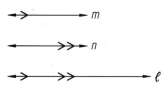

If two lines (m and n) are parallel to the same line (ℓ), then m and n are **parallel.**

19. ∠DCF and ∠ACF form a linear pair, so m∠ACF = 180 − 145 = 35. $\overline{BE} \parallel \overline{CF}$, so m∠ABE = m∠ACF because ∥ lines ⇒ corr. ∠s =. So m∠ABE = 35 by the Transitive Property of Equality.

20. ∠BEA and ∠AED form a linear pair. So if m∠BEA = 50, then m∠AED = 130 by the Linear Pair Theorem.

21. Adding -3x to each side of 3x − 4y = 5 results in -4y = -3x + 5; the justification is the Addition Property of Equality.

22. Multiplying both sides of -4y = -3x + 5 by $-\frac{1}{4}$ results in $y = \frac{-3x + 5}{-4}$; the justification is the Multiplication Property of Equality.

23.

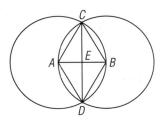

The angles of ΔACB and ΔABD are each 60°, and the sides all have the same length.

24.

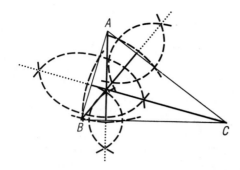

The three segments (altitudes for the triangle) meet at a single point (called the **orthocenter** of the triangle).

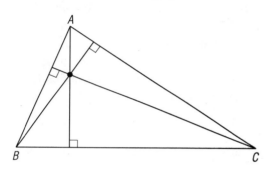

LESSON 4–5 (pp. 183–186)

1. **a.** $r_t(P) = P$ by the definition of reflection (meaning).

   b. $r_t(N) = M$ because t is the $\perp$ bisector of $\overline{MN}$ and by the definition of reflection (meaning).

   c. The images of P and M are P and N (by parts **a** and **b**), so the image of $\overline{PM}$ is $\overline{PN}$ and $PM = PN$ since reflections preserve distance.

2. Question 1 proves that if a point is on the $\perp$ bisector of a segment, then it is equidistant from the endpoints of the segment. That is the Perpendicular Bisector Theorem.

3. Any point on the $\perp$ **bisector** of a segment is equidistant from the **endpoints** of the segment.

4.

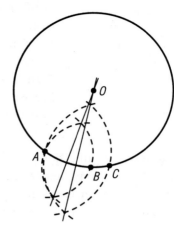

5.

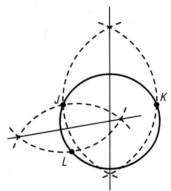

6.
conclusions	justifications
1. $CV = CW$	$\perp$ Bisector Theorem
2. $CW = CX$	$\perp$ Bisector Theorem
3. $VC = CX$	Transitive Property of Equality (steps 1 and 2)

7.
conclusions	justifications
1. $r_{\overleftrightarrow{QR}}(C) = D$	given
2. $\overleftrightarrow{QR}$ is the $\perp$ bisector of $\overline{CD}$.	definition of reflection (meaning)
3. $CQ = DQ$	$\perp$ Bisector Theorem

8. The tree is perpendicular to the segment joining the stakes, and bisects that segment. So the tree is the $\perp$ bisector of the segment, and the guy wires are equal by the $\perp$ Bisector Theorem.

9.

conclusions	justifications
1. $BC = AC$	definition of equilateral triangle (meaning)
2. $AC = CD$	definition of midpoint (meaning)
3. $BC = CD$	Transitive Property of Equality (steps 1 and 2)

10.

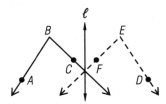

The justification is "Reflections preserve angle measure."

11. The reflection images are
Я, M, И, W, and X.
The letters **K** and **N** do *not* look like their reflection images over a vertical line.

12. If M is between A and B, then the reflection image M' is between A' and B'.

13. $m\angle 1 = m\angle 3$ and $m\angle 8 = m\angle 6$ by the Vertical Angle Theorem, and $m\angle 1 = m\angle 8$ because ∥ lines ⟹ corr. ∠s =. So $m\angle 1 = m\angle 3 = m\angle 8 = m\angle 6$. Similarly, $m\angle 2 = m\angle 4 = m\angle 5 = m\angle 7$.

14. a. There is 360° around the circle, so
$$3x + 2x + x + 4x = 360$$
$$10x = 360$$
$$x = 36$$
The four angles are:
$x = 36°$
$2x = 72°$
$3x = 108°$
$4x = 144°$.
The measure of the largest angle is 144°.

b. No pair of angles add to 90°, so no two angles are complementary.

c. Note that $2x + 3x = 5x = x + 4x$, so $2x + 3x = 180$ and $x + 4x = 180$. There are two pairs of supplementary angles: $2x + 3x$ (72° and 108°) and $x + 4x$ (36° and 144°).

15. a.

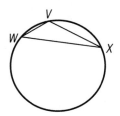

b. The center of the circle is **outside** the triangle.

c. The center of the circle will be inside, on, or outside the triangle as the triangle is acute, right, or obtuse, respectively.

LESSON 4-6 (pp. 187–191)

1.

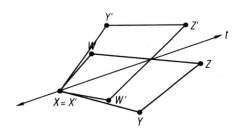

2. Sample:

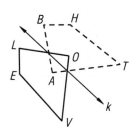

3. Sample:

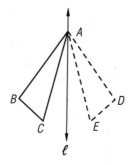

4. a–b. If $r_m(A) = C$, then $r_m(C) = A$ by the Flip-Flop Theorem.

5. a. If you "walk" from T to X to W to A to T, the interior is on your right, so the path $TXWA$ is **clockwise oriented.**

b. "Walking" from X to W to A to T, the interior is on your right, so the orientation is **clockwise.**

c. "Walking" from W to X to T to A, the interior is on your left, so the path is **counterclockwise.**

6. Reflections reverse orientation, so a figure and its reflection image have opposite orientations.

7. True; the orientation of a polygon depends on the order of the vertices.

8. If $T \rightarrow A \rightarrow B$ is clockwise, then so is $A \rightarrow B \rightarrow T$ and $B \rightarrow T \rightarrow A$ (part **d**). The other orientation is $B \rightarrow A \rightarrow T$ or $A \rightarrow T \rightarrow B$ or $T \rightarrow B \rightarrow A$, so parts **a, b,** and **c** are counterclockwise.

9. If $r(ONE) = SIX$, then the following pairs of points are reflections of each other:
O and S
N and I
E and X.

a. $r(N) = I$
b. $r(\angle EON) = \angle XSI$
c. $r(\overrightarrow{NO}) = \overrightarrow{IS}$
d. $r(\overline{EO}) = \overline{XS}$

10. If $ABCDXTZA$ is clockwise, then $AZTXDCBA$ is counterclockwise. Beginning with point D, that same counterclockwise path (back to D) is $DCBAZTXD$.

11. As you run around the bases, the infield is at your left hand, so the path is **counterclockwise.**

12. If $r(ABCD) = EFGH$, then $r(B) = F$ and $r(D) = H$. So if $BD = 12$ cm, then its image $\overline{FH}$ is also 12 cm, because reflections preserve distance.

13.

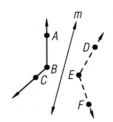

14.

conclusions	justifications
1. $r_\ell(A) = B$	definition of reflection (meaning)
2. $r_\ell(B) = A$	Flip-Flop Theorem
3. $r_\ell(\overline{AB}) = \overline{BA}$	Figure Reflection Theorem

15. a–b. $\overline{ZA} \perp \ell$ and ℓ bisects $\overline{ZA}$ because the reflecting line is the $\perp$ bisector of a segment joining a point and its image. That is the definition of reflection (meaning); that is choice (iii).

c. Since ℓ bisects $\overline{ZA}$, point M is the midpoint of $\overline{ZA}$ by the definition of bisector (meaning); that is choice (i).

d. Since M is the midpoint of $\overline{ZA}$, $AM = MZ$ by the definition of midpoint (meaning); that is choice (ii).

16.

conclusions	justifications
1. $AM = MB$	definition of midpoint (meaning)
2. $AM = AN$	given
3. $AN = MB$	Transitive Property of Equality (steps 1 and 2)

17.

conclusions	justifications
1. $\overline{WX} \perp m$	definition of reflection (meaning)
2. $\overline{YZ} \perp m$	definition of reflection (meaning)
3. $\overline{WX} \parallel \overline{YZ}$	Two Perpendiculars Theorem

18.

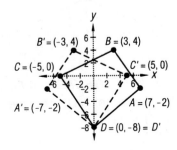

19. a. Using $A = (7, -2)$ and $B = (3, 4)$,

$$\text{slope} = \frac{y_2 - y_1}{x_2 - x_1}$$

$$= \frac{4 - (-2)}{3 - 7}$$

$$= \frac{6}{-4}$$

$$= -\frac{3}{2}$$

b. The slope of any line perpendicular to $\overleftrightarrow{AB}$ must be $\frac{2}{3}$, since $(-\frac{3}{2})(\frac{2}{3}) = -1$.

20.

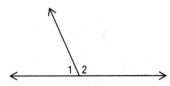

True. If $m\angle 1 + m\angle 2 = 180$, and $m\angle 1 < 90$ ($\angle 1$ is acute), then $m\angle 2 > 90$ (or $\angle 2$ is obtuse).

21.

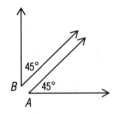

For a counterexample, let $x = m\angle A = m\angle B = 45$. Then $m\angle A$ and the measure of its complement are both x.

22. Samples: shoes, hands, scissors, school desks (with writing platforms attached to the chairs). Other samples are shirts or coats with button-buttonhole sides reversed, shoulder-mounted video cameras with viewfinders, and left- and right-hand-drive automobiles.

LESSON 4–7 (pp. 192–197)

1. A plane figure F is reflection-symmetric if and only if there is a line m such that $r_m(F) = F$.

2.

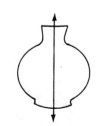

3.

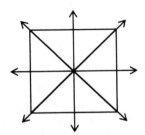

4.

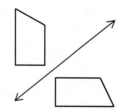

5.

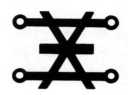

6. a. two

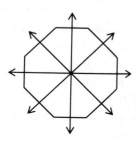

b. two

c. two

7.

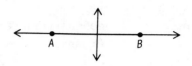

8.

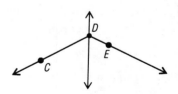

9. Since $\angle JFH = \angle GFH$, $\overrightarrow{FJ}$ and $\overrightarrow{FG}$ are reflection images of each other over $\overleftrightarrow{FH}$.
   a. $r_{\overleftrightarrow{FH}}(\overrightarrow{FJ}) = \overrightarrow{FG}$
   b. $r_{\overleftrightarrow{FH}}(\overrightarrow{FG}) = \overrightarrow{FJ}$
   c. $r_{\overleftrightarrow{FH}}(\angle JFG) = \angle GFJ$

10. If m is the bisector of $\angle ABC$, then $r_m(\overrightarrow{BA}) = \overrightarrow{BC}$.

11.

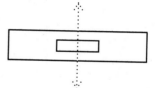

12.

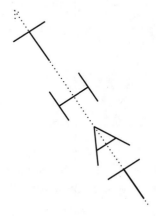

13.

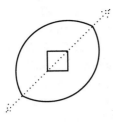

14. a. If ℓ is the $\perp$ bisector of $\overline{TU}$, then point V on ℓ is equidistant from T and U. So $UV = TV = 8$.

b. The images, over ℓ, of T, U, and V are U, T, and V, respectively, so $r_\ell(\triangle TUV) = \triangle UTV$.

15. a.

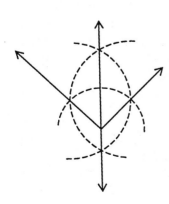

b. True; the figure has no symmetry lines. (For quadrilaterals; rectangles and rhombuses have two symmetry lines, isosceles trapezoids have one, and squares have four.)

16.

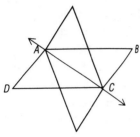

17.

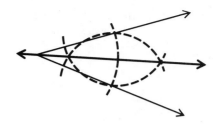

18.–19.

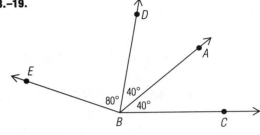

18. $m\angle EBC = 160$, which is choice (d).

19. $m\angle EBA = 120$, which is choice (d).

20. If $r(ABCD) = EFGH$, then pairs of corresponding points are:

A and E

B and F

C and G

D and H.

a. $r(EFGH) = ABCD$

b. $r(C) = G$

c. $r(\triangle ABD) = \triangle EFH$

d. $r(\angle GCH) = \angle CGD$

21.

conclusions	justifications
1. $m\angle AOB = m\angle BOC$	definition of angle bisector (meaning)
2. $m\angle BOC = m\angle COD$	definition of angle bisector (meaning)
3. $m\angle AOB = m\angle COD$	Transitive Property of Equality (steps 1 and 2)

22.

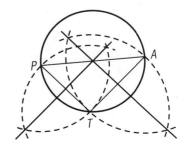

23. The slope of line m through $(3, -1)$ and $(-7, 4)$ is

$$\frac{y_2 - y_1}{x_2 - x_1} = \frac{4 - (-1)}{-7 - 3}$$

$$= \frac{5}{-10}$$

$$= -\frac{1}{2}$$

The slope of a line $\perp m$ is 2, since

$$\left(-\frac{1}{2}\right)(2) = -1.$$

24. **a.** The vertical angles to $\angle 1$ and $\angle 2$ are also 70°, so $\angle 4$ and $\angle 7$ are 70°.

b. Since $\angle 6$ and $\angle 2$ are a linear pair, they are supplementary. From part **a**, $\angle 2 = \angle 4$. So $m\angle 6 + m\angle 4 = 180$, and it is **false** that $\angle 4$ and $\angle 6$ are complementary.

25. Both a zero angle and a straight angle have two symmetry lines.

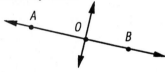

26. **a–b.**

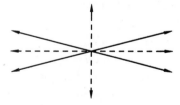

c. The two symmetry lines are perpendicular.

1. Point B is the reflection image of A, and point D is the reflection of C. So $\overline{BD}$ is the reflection image of $\overline{AC}$, and $AC = BD$ because reflections preserve distance.

2. Point B is the reflection image of A over line m, so $m \perp \overline{AB}$ by the definition of reflection (meaning).

3. The image of X is D, so $r_m(X) = D$.

4. The images of points A, B, and C are W, Z, and Y, respectively, so $r_m(\angle ABC) = \angle WZY$.

5. The orientation of $WXYZ$ is clockwise, so the orientation of the image of $WXYZ$ is counterclockwise.

6. Polygon $ABCD$ is symmetric across line n, so A and B are images of each other, and so are D and C. So $r_n(ABCD) = BADC$.

7. $r_n(\angle BDA) = \angle ACB$, so if $m\angle BDA = x$, then $m\angle ACB = x$, because reflections preserve angle measure.

8. m is the $\perp$ bisector of $\overline{WV}$.

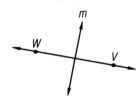

9. In general, a reflection over the x-axis of (x, y) is $(x, -y)$. So if $M = (2, 0)$, then $M' = (2, -0) = (2, 0)$; if $N = (5, -1)$, then $N' = (5, -(-1)) = (5, 1)$; if $P = (-3, 4)$, then $P' = (-3, -4)$.

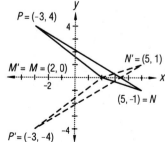

10. $\overleftrightarrow{MB}$ is the $\perp$ bisector of $\overline{PP'}$.

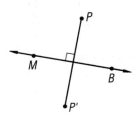

11. m is the $\perp$ bisector of $\overline{CC'}$, $\overline{EE'}$.

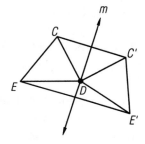

12. $\triangle FGH$ seems to be isosceles, with vertex $\angle H$. There is one line of symmetry, the $\perp$ bisector of base $\overline{FG}$.

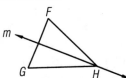

13. The figure appears to be a regular pentagon. That figure has 5 lines of symmetry, the $\perp$ bisectors of the sides.

14.

conclusions	justifications
1. m∠1 = m∠2	Given
2. m∠1 = m∠3	Vertical Angle Theorem
3. m∠3 = m∠2	Transitive Property of Equality (steps 1, 2)

15.

conclusions	justifications
1. $\ell \perp \overline{YZ}$	definition of reflection (meaning)
2. $\ell \perp \overline{WX}$	definition of reflection (meaning)
3. $\overline{WX} \parallel \overline{YZ}$	Two Perpendiculars Theorem

CHAPTER 4 REVIEW (pp. 200–203)

1.

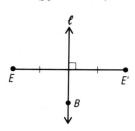

2.

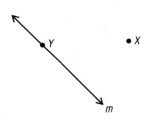

3.

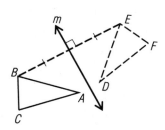

4.

73

5.

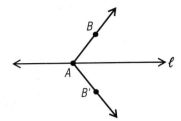

6.

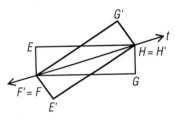

7.

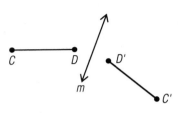

8.

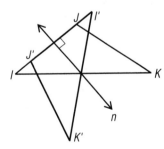

9.

10.

11.

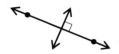

12. B is the reflection image of C over $\overleftrightarrow{AD}$, so $\overrightarrow{AD}$ bisects $\angle BAC$. If m$\angle BAD = 42$, then m$\angle CAD = 42$ and m$\angle BAC = 84$.

13. m$\angle B = $ m$\angle ACB$. Then, since m$\angle ACB +$ m$\angle ACE = 180$, if m$\angle B = x$ then m$\angle ACE = 180 - x$.

14. If $r_m(A) = B$, then the Flip-Flop Theorem states that $r_m(B) = A$.

15. If $r_\ell(A) = B$, then the definition of reflection (meaning) states that ℓ is the $\perp$ bisector of $\overline{AB}$.

16. If the points G, H, I, and J are images of C, D, E, and F, respectively, then $r(E) = I$ by the Figure Reflection Theorem.

17. $r(\angle EDF) = \angle IHJ$ by the Figure Reflection Theorem.

18. m$\angle EDF = $ m$\angle IHJ$ because reflections preserve angle measure.

19. The image of $\overline{FC}$ is $\overline{JG}$, so $FC = JG$ because reflections preserve distance.

20. If you "walk" from A to D to C to B to A, the interior of $ADCB$ is on your left, so the orientation of path $ADCB$ is **counterclockwise**.

21. Reflections reverse orientation, so the orientation of the image of $ADCB$ is **clockwise**.

22. If $\overleftrightarrow{XZ}$ is a symmetry line, then $\overleftrightarrow{XZ}$ is the $\perp$ bisector of $\overline{YW}$. So points on $\overleftrightarrow{XZ}$ are equidistant from the endpoints of $\overline{YW}$; specifically, $XY = XW$ and $ZY = ZW$. Congruent segments are $\overline{XY}$ and $\overline{XW}$, $\overline{ZY}$ and $\overline{ZW}$.

23. Because $\overleftrightarrow{XZ}$ is a symmetry line, it bisects the angles at X and Z, so m$\angle YXZ = $ m$\angle WXZ$, m$\angle YZX = $ m$\angle WZX$. Also, Y is the image of W, so m$\angle Y = $ m$\angle W$.

24. From Question 23, $m\angle WXZ = m\angle YXZ$, so if $m\angle WXZ = 35$, then $m\angle YXZ = 35$.

25. $r_m(A) = E$ and $r_m(B) = D$, so it is **true** that $FABCDE$ is symmetric to line m.

26. $r_m(D) = B$, so $\angle B$ has the same measure as $\angle D$ (because reflections preserve angle measure).

27. m is a symmetry line for $FABCDE$, so $r_m(\overrightarrow{FA}) = \overrightarrow{FE}$ and it is **true** that m bisects $\angle AFE$.

28. a–b. A segment $\overline{PQ}$ has two symmetry lines, the $\perp$ bisector of the segment and the line $\overleftrightarrow{PQ}$ containing the segment.

29. If $r_m(G) = H$, then $r_m(H) = G$ by the Flip-Flop Theorem.
Similarly, $r_m(F) = E$, and so $r_m(\overline{EH}) = \overline{FG}$. Then $EH = FG$ because reflections preserve distance.

30. I is on m, so $r_m(I) = I$ by the definition of reflection (meaning).
Then, since $r_m(\angle EGI) = \angle FHI$, $m\angle EGI = m\angle FHI$ because reflections preserve angle measure.

31.

conclusions	justifications
1. $m\angle 1 = m\angle 4$	$\parallel$ lines $\Rightarrow$ corr. $\angle$s $=$.
2. $m\angle 4 = m\angle 6$	Vertical Angle Theorem
3. $m\angle 1 = m\angle 6$	Transitive Property of Equality (steps 1 and 2)

32.

conclusions	justifications
1. $MP = MO$	definition of equilateral triangle (meaning)
2. $MO = MN$	given
3. $MP = MN$	Transitive Property of Equality (steps 1 and 2)

33.

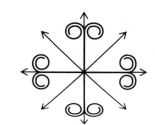

34.

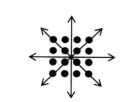

35.

36. The original message is a reflection over a vertical line. That reflection is "MATH Я WE."

37. $r_x(x, y) = (x, -y)$, so $r_x(3, 7) = (3, -7)$.

75

38. $r_y(x, y) = (-x, y)$, so
$A' = r_y(3, 7) = (-3, 7)$,
$B' = r_y(3, 1) = (-3, 1)$,
$C' = r_y(-2, 8) = (2, 8)$, and
$D' = r_y(0, 5) = (0, 5)$.

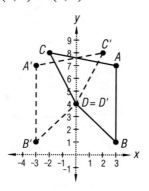

39. $r_y(x, y) = (-x, y)$, so
$r_y(a, b) = (-a, b)$.

40. $r_x(x, y) = (x, -y)$, so
$r_x(c, d) = (c, -d)$.

CHAPTER 5 POLYGONS

LESSON 5–1 (pp. 204–212)

1. **a.** The congruent sides are segments $\overline{IW}$ and $\overline{IN}$, so $\overline{WN}$ is the base.
   b. The vertex angle is $\angle I$.
   c. The base angles are $\angle W$ and $\angle N$.
   d. The angles of equal measure are the base angles, $\angle W$ and $\angle N$.

2. A symmetry line for $\triangle WIN$ is the bisector of $\angle I$ (it is also the line that contains the altitude to $\overline{WN}$, the median to $\overline{WN}$, or the $\perp$ bisector of $\overline{WN}$).

3. In an isosceles triangle, the line containing the vertex angle bisector is the same as the $\perp$ bisector of the base. Since a line is considered to be parallel to itself, the "two lines" satisfy choices (a)–(c); that is choice (d).

4. **a.** $\overline{EM}$, a segment from a vertex to the midpoint of the opposite side, is called a median.
   b. Since $\triangle DEF$ is isosceles, with $DE = EF$, then $\angle D$ and $\angle F$ are equal. Since $\overline{EM}$ is also the vertex angle bisector and perpendicular to the base, m$\angle MED$ = m$\angle MEF$ and m$\angle EMD$ = m$\angle EMF$.

5.
conclusions	justifications
1. m$\angle XWR$ = m$\angle 2$	Isosceles Triangle Theorem
2. m$\angle 1$ = m$\angle XWR$	Vertical Angle Theorem
3. m$\angle 1$ = m$\angle 2$	Transitive Property of Equality (steps 1, 2)

6. **a.** counterexample:

   $\triangle XYZ$ is isosceles but not equilateral, so the statement is false.

   b. If a triangle is equilateral, then any pair of sides have the same length, and the triangle must be isosceles; the statement is true.

7. **a.** equilateral triangle:

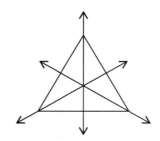

   3 symmetry lines; choice (iii)
   b. isosceles triangle:

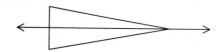

   1 symmetry line; choice (i)
   c. scalene triangle: If it had one symmetry line, the triangle would be isosceles. So it has no symmetry lines, that is choice (iv).

8. If $\overleftrightarrow{OE}$ is a symmetry line, then r$_{\overleftrightarrow{OE}}(H) = P$. So $\overline{EH} \cong \overline{EP}$ and $\overline{OH} \cong \overline{OP}$ because reflections preserve distance.

9. If $\overleftrightarrow{OE}$ is a symmetry line, then $\triangle HEP$ is isosceles and $\overrightarrow{EO}$ bisects $\angle HEP$. So m$\angle HEO$ = m$\angle PEO$ by the definition of angle bisector (meaning), and m$\angle H$ = m$\angle P$ by the Isosceles Triangle Theorem.

10. **a.** In $\odot H$, $HA = HM = HT$, and in $\odot A$, $AH = AM = AT$. So $AH = HM = MA$ by the Transitive Property of Equality, and $\triangle AHM$ is equilateral.
    b. m$\angle HMA$ = 60, since $\triangle AHM$ is equilateral. Other angles with the same measure are $\angle MHA$ and $\angle MAH$ in $\triangle AHM$ and, in $\triangle HAT$, $\angle HAT$, $\angle HTA$, and $\angle AHT$.

11. $\triangle ABC$ and $\triangle CDE$ are isosceles, so m$\angle B =$ m$\angle ACB$ and m$\angle DCE = $ m$\angle CED$. Also, m$\angle ACB = $ m$\angle DCE$ by the Vertical Angle Theorem. So m$\angle B = $ m$\angle CED$ by the Transitive Property of Equality.

12.

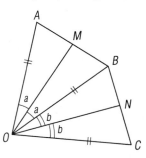

$\overrightarrow{OM}$ and $\overrightarrow{ON}$ are angle bisectors, and m$\angle AOC = 83$, so $2a + 2b = 83$. Then $a + b = 41.5$, so m$\angle MON = 41.5$.

13. $\triangle RTS$ is isosceles, so $\overline{TQ}$, the altitude to the base of an isosceles triangle, is the bisector of the vertex angle (choice a), the median to the base (choice b), and is $\perp$ to the base (choice c). Since all of (a)–(c) are true, the answer is choice (d).

14. **a.** For the symmetry line $\overleftrightarrow{AD}$,
  r(A) = A r(B) = F
  r(C) = E r(D) = D
  r(E) = C r(F) = B.
  So r($ABCDEF$) = $AFEDCB$.
  b. If $\overleftrightarrow{AD}$ is a symmetry line in hexagon $ABCDEF$, there will be three pairs of congruent sides: $\overline{AB} \cong \overline{AF}$, $\overline{BC} \cong \overline{FE}$, and $\overline{CD} \cong \overline{ED}$.
  c. $\overleftrightarrow{AD}$ bisects two angles, so m$\angle FAD = $ m$\angle BAD$ and m$\angle EDA = $ m$\angle CDA$. Also, reflections preserve angle measure, so m$\angle B = $ m$\angle F$ and m$\angle C = $ m$\angle E$.

15. By the Flip-Flop Theorem, if r$_m$(F) = G, then r$_m$(G) = F.

16.

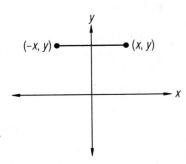

The reflection of (x, y) over the y-axis is $(-x, y)$.

17.

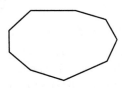

18.

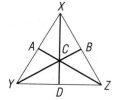

19. equilateral triangle (3 sides)
  rectangle   (4 sides)
  pentagon   (5 sides)
  7-gon   (7 sides)
  octagon   (8 sides)
  nonagon   (9 sides)

20. Other meanings of *median* include: having as many above as below; a strip of land between opposite lanes of traffic; relating to the Medes, inhabitants of Media (capitalized).

21. **a.**

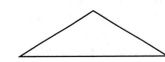

b.

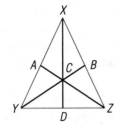

c.

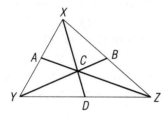

d. In any triangle, the three medians intersect at a single point (they are **concurrent**).

LESSON 5–2 (pp. 213–217)

1. a. Sufficient condition for a parallelogram: a quadrilateral with both pairs of opposite sides parallel.

b.

2. a. Sufficient condition for rhombus: a quadrilateral with four sides of equal length.

b.

3. a. Sufficient condition for a rectangle: a quadrilateral with four right angles.

b.

4. a. Sufficient condition for a square: a quadrilateral with four equal sides and four right angles.

b.

5. Sufficient condition for a kite: a quadrilateral with two distinct pairs of consecutive sides of the same length.

b.

6. a. Sufficient condition for a trapezoid: a quadrilateral with at least one pair of parallel sides.

b.

7. a. Sufficient condition for an isosceles trapezoid: a trapezoid with a pair of base angles equal in measure.

b.

8.

kite   parallelogram

rhombus   rectangle

square

9. A square is a special type of rhombus, so the statement is *true*.

10. Some rhombuses are not squares, so the statement is *false*.

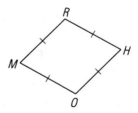

$RH = HO = OM = MR$, but no angle is a right angle.

11. A square is a special type of rhombus, and a rhombus is a special type of kite, so a square is a special type of kite; the statement is *true*.

12. Some kites are not rhombuses; the statement is *false*.

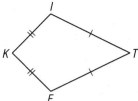

KI = KE, TI = TE, but KI ≠ TI.

13. Some trapezoids are not parallelograms; the statement is *false*.

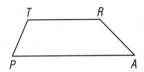

$\overline{TR} \parallel \overline{PA}$ but $\overline{TP}$ not $\parallel$ to $\overline{RA}$.

14. A square is a specific type of kite, so squares have certain properties that kites do not necessarily have. The statement is *false*.

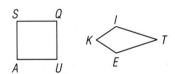

The angles of *KITE* are not necessarily right angles.

15. A parallelogram is a specific type of trapezoid. So any property of a trapezoid is also a property of a parallelogram, and the statement is *true*.

16. $\overline{ST} \parallel \overline{VU}$ and $\overline{SV} \parallel \overline{TU}$. So *STUV* is a parallelogram.

17. Angles *W, X, Y,* and *Z* are right angles, so *WXYZ* is a rectangle.

18. *AB = BC = CD = DA,* so *ABCD* is a rhombus. (*ABCD* is also a kite, but a rhombus is a specific kind of kite.)

19. *EF = FG = GH = HE* and angles *E, F, G* and *H* are right angles. So *EFGH* is a square.

20. *A* ∩ *B* is the set of all quadrilaterals that are both rhombuses (all 4 sides equal) and rectangles (4 right angles). That is the sufficient condition for a square, so *A* ∩ *B* is the set of all squares.

21. a. $\overline{QN}$ and $\overline{QP}$ are radii of ⊙*Q*, so *QN = QP* by the definition of circle (meaning).

b. Similarly in ⊙*O*, *ON = OP* by the definition of circle (meaning).

c. *NOPQ* is a kite by the definition of kite (sufficient condition).

22. A bedsheet is a rectangle; it is also a parallelogram, isosceles trapezoid, and trapezoid.

23. The warning sign is a square; it is also a rhombus, rectangle, parallelgram, isosceles trapezoid, kite, and trapezoid.

24. The top and bottom of the trough is a rectangle, so it is also a parallelogram, isosceles trapezoid, and trapezoid. Each side of the trough is an isosceles trapezoid, so it is also a parallelogram.

25. a. In isosceles $\triangle ABC$, m∠*B* = m∠*C*

so
$$4x - 7 = 2x + 13$$
$$2x - 7 = 13$$
$$2x = 20$$
$$x = 10.$$

b. m∠*B* = 4*x* − 7
$$= 4(10) - 7$$
$$= 40 - 7$$
$$= 33$$

26. *F* is the vertex angle of isosceles $\triangle DFE$, so *DF = FE,* and of isosceles $\triangle FEG$, so *FE = FG* (by the definition of isosceles triangle, meaning). Then *DF = FG* by the Transitive Property of Equality.

27.

28. A quadrilateral and a kite can be nonconvex. (The kite is sometimes called a **dart**.)

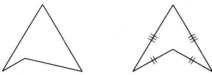

29.

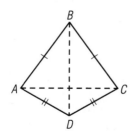

30. Other hierarchies outside mathematics are organizational structures in military and business, family trees, "feeder systems" of elementary and high schools. Other examples may be found by researching the term *taxonomy*.

LESSON 5-3 (pp. 218–222)

1. A conjecture is an educated guess or opinion.

2. To show a conjecture is true, a proof is needed.

3. To show a conjecture is not true, a counterexample is needed.

4. a.

b. Yes, the figure supports the conjecture that the diagonals of a kite are perpendicular.

c. The conjecture is true.

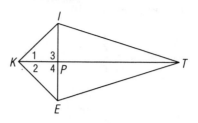

(You can prove that $\triangle KIT \cong \triangle KET$, so $\angle 1 \cong \angle 2$. Then $\triangle KIP \cong \triangle KEP$, so $\angle 3 \cong \angle 4$.)

5. a. *ABCD,* a rectangle, supports the conjecture that the diagonals have equal lengths.

b. *PQRS* is a counterexample to the conjecture.

6. *Refining a conjecture* means changing a false statement, slightly, so the new conjecture is not disproven by the counterexample that disproved the original conjecture.

7. A refinement of the conjecture "The diagonals of a parallelogram have equal length" is "The diagonals of a rectangle have equal length."

8. Counterexamples to the conjecture that "The diagonals of a rhombus are equal in length" are *ABCD* and *WXYV.*

9. In *ABCD,* the measures of the angles are about 60 or 30; in *JKLM,* the measures are each approximately 45; in *WXYV,* the measures are about 20 or 70.

10.

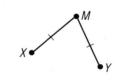

11.

12. A counterexample is that the square of the real number 0 is not positive.

13.

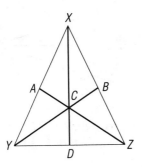

14. a.

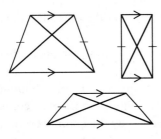

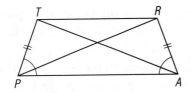

b. The conjecture is *true*.

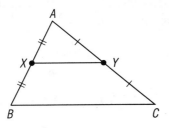

$TP = RA$, $\angle TPA \cong \angle RAP$, and $\overline{PA} \cong \overline{PA}$, so $\triangle TPA \cong \triangle RAP$ and $TA = PR$.

15.

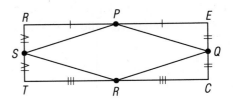

$AX = XB$, $AY = YC$. It is *true* that $\overline{XY} \parallel \overline{BC}$.

16.

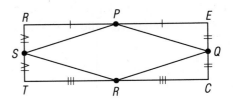

$SPQR$ is a rhombus, but it is not necessarily a rectangle.

17. The areas of the two shaded regions are equal. (First, show that Figure 1, with sides $\overline{PO}$, $\overline{RO}$, and one-quarter of $\odot O$ has the same area as Figure 2, which is the semicircle with center S. Then subtract the unshaded area with sides $\overline{PR}$ and $\widehat{PR}$. To show that the areas of Figure 1 and 2 are equal, let $OS = SP = x$. Then $OP = x\sqrt{2}$. The area of $\odot O$ is $\pi(x\sqrt{2})^2 = 2\pi x^2$, so the area of Figure 1 is $\frac{\pi x^2}{2}$. The area of $\odot S$ is πx^2, so the area of Figure 2 is $\frac{\pi x^2}{2}$.

18. A figure is a square if and only if it is a quadrilateral with 4 equal sides and 4 right angles.

19. A figure is a parallelogram if and only if it is a quadrilateral with both pairs of opposite sides parallel.

20. A figure is a rhombus if and only if it is a quadrilateral with 4 congruent sides.

21. A figure is an isosceles triangle if and only if it is a triangle with at least two congruent sides.

22. If $r_m(T) = U$, then $r_m(U) = T$ by the Flip-Flop Theorem. Then $RT = RU$ and $ST = SU$ since reflections preserve distances, and $RUST$ is a kite by the definition of kite (sufficient condition).

23. polygon
   quadrilateral
   kite
   rhombus
   square

24. C is the vertex angle in isosceles triangles ACB and BCD, so $AC = CB$ and $CB = CD$ by the definition of isosceles triangle (meaning). Then $AC = CD$ by the Transitive Property of Equality, and $\overline{BC}$ is a median by the definition of median (sufficient condition).

25. a. $r_\ell(F) = E$ (The reflection of point F over line ℓ is point E.)
   b. $r_\ell(E) = F$, $r_\ell(F) = E$, $r_\ell(G) = H$, and $r_\ell(H) = G$, so $r_\ell(EFGH) = FEHG$.
   c. $r_m(G) = F$, $r_m(E) = H$, and $r_m(F) = G$, so $r_m(\angle GEF) = \angle FHG$.

26. a.

   b.

   c.

LESSON 5-4 (pp. 223–227)

1. Every rectangle is a parallelogram, so the statement is *always true*.

2. Every square is a trapezoid, so the statement is *always true*.

3. Some rhombuses are not squares, so the statement is *sometimes true*.

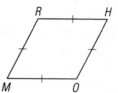

   $RHOM$ is a rhombus, but $RHOM$ is not a square.

4. For any quadrilateral in the hierarchy, its properties apply to the quadilaterals that are connected to and below it. So the result of the Kite Symmetry Theorem applies to kites, rhombuses, and squares.

5. a. The ends of the kite are the common vertices of the congruent sides. For $KITE$, the ends are points E and I.
   b. The symmetry line, which contains the ends, is line $\overleftrightarrow{EI}$.
   c. $\overleftrightarrow{EI}$ is a symmetry line, so $r_{\overleftrightarrow{EI}}(I) = I$, $r_{\overleftrightarrow{EI}}(K) = T$, and $r_{\overleftrightarrow{EI}}(E) = E$. So $r_{\overleftrightarrow{EI}}(\angle IKE) = \angle ITE$.

6. a. $RHOM$ is a quadrilateral with 4 equal sides, so it is a kite by the definition of kite (meaning).
   b. Each pair of opposite vertices are ends; the ends are R and O or H and M.
   c. $RHOM$ is a rhombus, so by the Rhombus Symmetry Theorem it has two lines of symmetry.

7. Points A and C are the ends of the kite, so $\overleftrightarrow{AC}$ is a symmetry line for the kite (by the Kite Symmetry Theorem) and bisects the angles at the ends of the kite (Kite Diagonal Theorem). So m$\angle DCE = 30$ and m$\angle BAE = 50$. Therefore, m$\angle BCD = 60$ and m$\angle BAD = 100$. $\overline{AC}$ is the $\perp$ bisector of $\overline{BD}$ (by the Kite Diagonal Theorem), so the 4 angles at E have measure 90; also, $ED = BE$ so $ED = 15$ and $BD = 30$. (With results from later in the text, $\triangle CEB$ and $\triangle CED$ are 30-60-90 right triangles, so m$\angle CBE =$ m$\angle CDE = 60$, $CB = CD = 30$, and $CE = 15\sqrt{3}$. Also, m$\angle ADE =$ m$\angle ABE = 40$, and $BA = DA = \dfrac{15}{\cos 40°}$, $AE = 15 \tan 40°$.)

8. $\overleftrightarrow{QS}$ bisects the congruent angles at ends Q and S, so m$\angle TQS =$ m$\angle TSQ =$ m$\angle RSQ = 51$, and m$\angle TQR =$ m$\angle TSR = 102$. Similarly, $\overleftrightarrow{RT}$ bisects the congruent angles at ends R and T, so m$\angle QRT =$ m$\angle SRT =$ m$\angle QTR =$ m$\angle STR = 39$, and m$\angle QTS = 78$. The 4 angles with vertex V have measure 90.

9. a. $\overline{BD}$ is a symmetry diagonal of $ABCD$ by the Kite Symmetry Theorem.
   b. $\overleftrightarrow{BD}$ is the $\perp$ bisector of $\overline{AC}$ by the Kite Diagonal Theorem.
   c. r$(A) = C$ and r$(C) = A$ by the definition of reflection (meaning).
   d. r$(B) = B$, r$(D) = D$ by the definition of reflection (meaning).
   e. r$(\angle BAD) = \angle BCD$ by the Figure Reflection Theorem.
   f. m$\angle BAD =$ m$\angle BCD$ because reflections preserve angle measure.

10. a. The reflection image of $\angle M$ over $\overleftrightarrow{RO}$ is $\angle H$, so m$\angle M =$ m$\angle H$ because reflections preserve angle measures.

b. Similarly, the reflection image of $\angle R$ over $\overleftrightarrow{MH}$ is $\angle O$, so m$\angle O =$ m$\angle R$.

11. a.

b, c. The proof for Question 9 does work for a nonconvex kite, so the Kite Diagonal Theorem is true for nonconvex kites.

12.

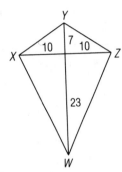

a. $XV = \frac{1}{2} XZ = \frac{1}{2}(20) = 10''$
b. $VZ = XV = 10''$
c. $WV = WY - VY = 30 - 7 = 23''$
d. m$\angle YVZ = 90$ by the Kite Diagonal Theorem.

13.

The figure is not a square.

14. The refined conjecture is *true*. The resulting figure is a rectangle, since (a) each pair of opposite sides is parallel to a diagonal, and the diagonals are $\perp$, and (b) each pair of opposite sides are congruent, since each is half the length of the diagonal to which it is parallel.

15. A figure is a trapezoid if and only if it is a quadrilateral with at least one pair of parallel sides.

16. A figure is an isosceles trapezoid if and only if it is a quadrilateral with one pair of parallel sides and a pair of congruent base angles.

17. The quadrilaterals that are isosceles trapezoids are rectangles, squares, and isosceles trapezoids.

18.

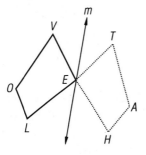

19.

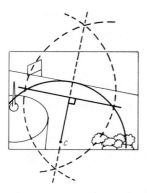

20. $m \parallel n$, so the corresponding angles are congruent.
$$7x + 10 = 6x + 31$$
$$x + 10 = 31$$
$$x = 21$$

21. $m\angle ABC = m\angle EBD$ by the Vertical Angle Theorem. So
$$8x - 7 = 3x + 68$$
$$5x - 7 = 68$$
$$5x = 75$$
$$x = 15$$

22. $m\angle ABC + m\angle CBD = 180$ by the Linear Pair Theorem, so
$$2y + 3 + 4y + 9 = 180$$
$$6y + 12 = 180$$
$$6y = 168$$
$$y = 28.$$
So $m\angle ABC = 2y + 3$
$$= 2(28) + 3$$
$$= 56 + 3$$
$$= 59.$$

23. Answers (and kites) will vary. Most "flat" kites are generally kite-shaped, in the mathematical sense, and the diagonal connecting the non-end vertices has a bend or arc in it.

LESSON 5–5 (pp. 228–233)

1. The Trapezoid Angle Theorem applies to trapezoids and to the quadrilaterals below it, which are parallelograms, isosceles trapezoids, rectangles, rhombuses, and squares.

2. The Isosceles Trapezoid Symmetry Theorem applies to isosceles trapezoids, rectangles, and squares.

3. The Rectangle Symmetry Theorem applies to rectangles and squares.

4. a. The bases of a trapezoid are the parallel sides. Since $\overleftrightarrow{ZD} \parallel \overleftrightarrow{OI}$, the bases are $\overline{ZD}$ and $\overline{OI}$.

   b. The base angles of a trapezoid share a common base. For base $\overline{ZD}$, the base angles are $\angle Z$ and $\angle D$; for base $\overline{OI}$, the base angles are $\angle O$ and $\angle I$.

   c. By the Trapezoid Angle Theorem, consecutive angles between a pair of parallel sides are supplementary. So $\angle Z$ and $\angle O$ are supplementary and $\angle D$ and $\angle I$ are supplementary. Since $m\angle Z = 68$, then $m\angle O = 112$; since $m\angle I = 95$, then $m\angle D = 85$.

5.

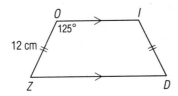

ZOID is an isosceles trapezoid, so $ID = ZO$ = 12 cm. By the Trapezoid Angle Theorem, $\angle O$ and $\angle Z$ are supplementary, so m$\angle Z$ = 55. Then, since both pairs of base angles in an Isosceles Triangle are equal in measure, m$\angle I$ = m$\angle O$ = 125 and m$\angle D$ and m$\angle Z$ = 55.

6.

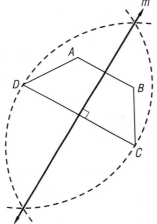

7. A statement is a corollary if and only if it is a theorem that is easily proved from another theorem.

8. a. $\overline{BC} \parallel \overline{DE}$, so m$\angle ABC$ = m$\angle D$ because $\parallel$ lines $\Rightarrow$ corr. $\angle$s =.

  b. m$\angle ABC$ + m$\angle CBD$ = 180 by the Linear Pair Theorem.

  c. m$\angle D$ + m$\angle CBD$ = 180 by substitution (m$\angle D$ for m$\angle ABC$).

9. a. $\overline{TF} \parallel \overline{SO}$, so *SOFT* is a trapezoid by the definition of trapezoid (sufficient condition).

  b. $IS = IO$, so m$\angle S$ = m$\angle O$ by the Isosceles Triangle Theorem.

c. m$\angle S$ = m$\angle O$, so *SOFT* is an isosceles trapezoid by the definition of isosceles trapezoid (sufficient condition).

10. Opposite angles of a parallelogram are congruent, so m$\angle P$ = m$\angle R$ = 27.3. Consecutive angles of a parallelogram are supplementary, so m$\angle L$ = m$\angle A$ = $180 - 27.3 = 152.7$.

11.

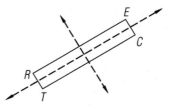

12. a. The $\perp$ bisector of $\overline{AB}$ is a symmetry line for *ABCD* (Isosceles Trapezoid Symmetry Theorem), so r(A) = B and r(C) = D. Then r($\overline{AC}$) = $\overline{BD}$, so $AC = BD$ because reflections preserve distance.

  b. The result in part **a** can be stated as the Isosceles Trapezoid Diagonal Theorem: The diagonals of an isosceles trapezoid are congruent.

13. a. *True* (The "theorem" proved in question 12 can be stated as the diagonals of an isosceles trapezoid are equal in measure.)

  b, c. *True*, because any property of an isosceles trapezoid must also hold for rectangles and squares, which are below isosceles trapezoids in the quadrilateral hierarchy.

14. a. Most beds are rectangles, and the Rectangle Symmetry Theorem states that every rectangle has two symmetry lines.

  b. Answers may vary; a sample answer is that rolling over in one's sleep is a left-right translation of a roughly-rectangular shape, so rectangles are the most efficient shapes for beds.

15. The ends of the kite are points I and E, so
$TI = KI = 4$ and $EK = ET = 8$. $\overline{EI}$ is the $\perp$
bisector of $\overline{KT}$, so $RT = 3$ and $KT = 6$. $\overline{EI}$
bisects the angles at the ends of the kite, so
$\text{m}\angle KIR = \text{m}\angle TIR = 49$ and $\text{m}\angle KER =$
$\text{m}\angle TER = \frac{1}{2}(44) = 22$. The 4 angles with
vertex R have measure 90.

    (In addition, $\text{m}\angle EKR = 180 - (90 + 22)$
$= 68$, so $\text{m}\angle ETR = 68$ also. Similarly,
$\text{m}\angle RKI = 180 - (90 + 49) = 41$, so also
$\text{m}\angle RTI = 41$. Finally, using the
Pythogorean Theorem, $ER = \sqrt{8^2 - 3^2} =$
$\sqrt{55}$ and $IR = \sqrt{4^2 - 3^2} = \sqrt{7}$.)

16. a. Line $\overleftrightarrow{IE}$, through the ends of the kite, is a
line of symmetry by the Kite Symmetry
Theorem.

  b. Line $\overleftrightarrow{IE}$, through the ends of the kite, is
the $\perp$ bisector of $\overline{KT}$ by the Kite-Diagonal
Theorem.

  c. $\overleftrightarrow{IE}$ is a symmetry line for the kite, so
$\text{r}_{\overleftrightarrow{IE}}(R) = R$ by the definition of reflection
(sufficient condition).

17. a. The ends of a kite are the common
endpoints of the congruent sides, so the
ends are points B and D.

  b–c. Using the results of questions 9–11 of
Lesson 5–4, a nonconvex kite does have a
symmetry line for kite $ABCD$, it is $\overleftrightarrow{BD}$),
and the Kite Diagonal Theorem does hold
for nonconvex kites.

18. a. $\triangle LOV$ is isosceles with vertex angle L, so
$\angle O = \angle V$ by the definition of isosceles
triangle (meaning).

  b. $LE = LE$ by the Reflexive Property of
Equality.

  c. $\overline{LE}$ is a median in $\triangle LOV$, so E is the
midpoint of $\overline{OV}$ by the definition of
median (meaning).

  d. E is the midpoint of $\overline{OV}$, so $EV = EO$ by
the definition of midpoint (meaning).

19. a. Four properties preserved by reflections
are angle measure, betweenness,
collinearity, and distance. (These
properties are often remembered by their
first letters: A-B-C-D.)

  b. A property not preserved by reflections is
the orientation of the figure.

20.

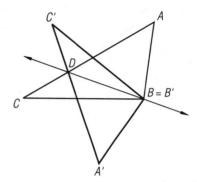

21. a. $\angle ADB$ and $\angle CDB$ form a linear pair, so
$\text{m}\angle ADB + \text{m}\angle CDB = 180$ by the Linear
Pair Theorem.

  So $\quad 3x - 2 + 9x - 10 = 180$
$$12x - 12 = 180$$
$$12x = 192$$
$$x = 16.$$

  b. $\text{m}\angle CDB = 9x - 10$
$$= 9(16) - 10$$
$$= 144 - 10$$
$$= 134$$

22. a. By the Vertical Angle Theorem, $3y = 57$
so $y = 19$.

  b. The corresponding angle for the angle with
measure 57 is $26 - y = 26 - 19 = 7$.
Since the corresponding angles are not
equal, lines m and n are not parallel.

23.

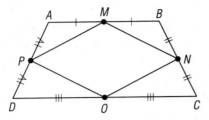

Using the result of question 12, $AC = BD$. Then, using the result that the segment connecting the midpoints of two sides of a triangle is half the length of the third side, $PM = MN = NO = OP$, because each is one-half of AC or BD. So $MNOP$ is a rhombus by the definition of rhombus (sufficient condition).

LESSON 5-6 (pp. 234–239)

1. **a.** The interior angles are between the (parallel) lines; they are $\angle 7$, $\angle 2$, $\angle 3$, and $\angle 6$.
   b. The alternate interior angles are between the (parallel) lines and on opposite sides of the transversal; they are the pair $\angle 7$ and $\angle 6$ and the pair $\angle 2$ and $\angle 3$.

2. If $\ell \parallel m$, then m$\angle 7$ = m$\angle 6$ by $\parallel$ lines $\Rightarrow$ AIA =, m$\angle 7$ = m$\angle 5$ by $\parallel$ lines $\Rightarrow$ corr. $\angle$s =, and m$\angle 7$ = m$\angle 8$ by the Vertical Angle Theorem.

3. $\angle 3$ is supplementary to $\angle 5$ and to $\angle 6$ by the Linear Pair Theorem. If $\ell \parallel m$, $\angle 3$ is supplementary to those angles equal in measure to $\angle 5$ or $\angle 6$; they are $\angle 7$ and $\angle 8$.

4. False; here is a counterexample:

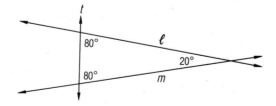

5. **a.** AIA $\Rightarrow \parallel$ Lines Theorem is an abbreviation for the statement that if two lines are cut by a transversal and form equal alternate interior angles, then the lines are parallel.
   b. $\parallel$ lines $\Rightarrow$ AIA = Theorem is an abbreviation for the statement that if two parallel lines are cut by a transversal, then alternate interior angles are equal in measure.
   c. The statement in part **a** is the converse of the statement in part **b**.

6. A parallelogram is not necessarily a kite. Here is a counterexample:

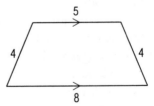

7. *True;* by the Quadrilateral Hierarchy Theorem, a rectangle has all the properties of a trapezoid.

8. An isosceles trapezoid is not necessarily a square; here is a counterexample:

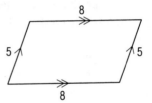

9. If $ABCD$ is a rhombus, then it is also a parallelogram. So $\overline{AD} \parallel \overline{BC}$ by the definition of parallelogram (meaning).

10. **a.** *Alternate exterior angles* refer to the angles outside the (parallel) lines, on opposite sides of the transversal; they are the pair $\angle 1$ and $\angle 4$ and the pair $\angle 8$ and $\angle 5$.

b. m∠1 = m∠2 and m∠4 = m∠3 by the Vertical Angle Theorem, and m∠2 = m∠3 by ∥ lines ⇒ AIA = . So m∠1 = m∠4 by the Transitive Property of Equality. A similar argument can show that m∠8 = m∠5. So if two lines are parallel, the alternate exterior angles are equal in measure.

11. a. m∠3 = m∠1 by the Vertical Angle Theorem.

b. m∠3 = m∠2 by the Transitive Property of Equality (step 1 and the given).

c. s ∥ t because corr. ∠s = ⇒ ∥ lines.

12. a. m∠1 + m∠2 + m∠3 = 180 by using the Linear Pair Theorem and the Angle Addition Property.

b. m∠1 = m∠5 by ∥ lines ⇒ AIA = . So if m∠1 = 35, then m∠5 = 35.

c. m∠3 is supplementary to m∠1 + m∠2 (from part **a**), so m∠3 = 35. Using m∠3 = m∠6, then m∠6 = 35 (by substitution). Then since ∠6 and ∠7 are supplementary (Linear Pair Theorem), m∠7 = 145.

13. m∠5 = 45, so m∠4 = 135 (Linear Pair Theorem) and m∠1 = 45 (∥ lines ⇒ AIA =). Similarly, m∠6 = 40 so m∠7 = 140 (Linear Pair Theorem) and m∠3 = 40 (∥ lines ⇒ AIA =). Finally,
m∠2 = 180 − (m∠1 + m∠3)
= 180 − (45 + 40)
= 180 − (85)
= 95.

14. ∠4 and ∠1 are supplementary (because m∠1 = m∠5, and ∠4 and ∠5 are supplementary). Also, (∠2 + ∠3) is supplementary to ∠1 (by the Linear Pair Theorem). So m∠1 = m∠2 + m∠3 and if m∠1 = x, then m∠2 + m∠3 = x; that is choice (a).

15. m∠*HGE* = m∠*GEB* (∥ lines ⇒ AIA =) and m∠*HGE* = m∠*DEC* (∥ lines ⇒ corr. ∠s =). So m∠*GEB* = m∠*DEC* = 57. By a similar argument with ∠*GHE*, m∠*HED* = m∠*AEB* = 43. ∠*FGE* and ∠*IHE* are supplementary to ∠*HGE* and ∠*GHE*, respectively, by the Linear Pair Theorem, so m∠*FGE* = 123 and m∠*IHE* = 137. Finally, m∠*GEH* = m∠*AEC* by the Vertical Angle Theorem, and ∠*GED* is supplementary to ∠*GEB*, where m∠*GEA* = m∠*GEB* + m∠*BEA* = 57 + 43 = 100, so m∠*GEH* = m∠*AEC* = 80.

16. a.

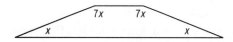

If the smaller base angles have measure x, then the larger base angles have measure $7x$. Then, by the Trapezoid Angle Theorem,
$x + 7x = 180$
$8x = 180$
$x = 22.5$.
The angles are 22.5°, 22.5°, 157.5° (= 7 · 22.5), and 157.5°.

b.

17. a.

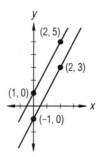

Two points on $y = 2x + 1$ are $(0, 1)$ and $(2, 5)$, so the slope is $\frac{5 - 1}{2 - 0} = 2$, and two points on $y = 2x - 1$ are $(0, -1)$ and $(2, 3)$, so the slope is $\frac{3 - (-1)}{2 - 0} = 2$. The lines are parallel.

b. Since the lines are parallel, they cannot be perpendicular.

18.

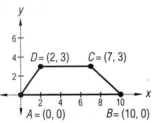

The figure is a trapezoid (it is not an isosceles trapezoid).

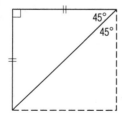

The resulting figure is an isosceles right triangle.

20. a. $r_{\overleftrightarrow{GH}}(A) = B$

b. For the reflecting line $\overleftrightarrow{EF}$, $r(A) = D$, $r(B) = C$, $r(C) = B$, and $r(D) = A$, so $r_{\overleftrightarrow{EF}}(ABCD) = DCBA$.

21. The base angles of an isosceles trapezoid are equal, by the definition of isosceles trapezoid (meaning), so $m\angle X = m\angle Y$.

So $-2q + 71 = -5q + 32$
$3q + 71 = 32$
$3q = -39$
$q = -13$.

Then $m\angle X = -2q + 71$
$= -2(-13) + 71$
$= 26 + 71$
$= 97$.

22. Using a protractor, approximate measurements are $m\angle T \approx 65$, $m\angle R \approx 55$, and $m\angle I \approx 60$.

23. Part of the Angle Measure Postulate is that every angle has a unique measure between 0 and 180.

24.

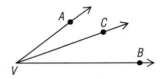

The Angle Addition Property states that if $\overrightarrow{VC}$ is in the interior of $\angle AVB$, then $m\angle AVC + m\angle CVB = m\angle AVB$.

25. A counterexample is any isosceles triangle with vertex angle greater than or equal to 90°. Sample:

26. a. Letters with alternate interior angles are:

A, H, I, M, N, and W.

b. Letters with corresponding angles are **E** and **F** (the letters **B**, **P**, and **R** could also be considered).

LESSON 5-7 (pp. 240–245)

1. **a.** $\ell \parallel \overline{AB}$, so m$\angle A$ = m$\angle 1$ by the $\parallel$ lines $\Rightarrow$ AIA = Theorem.
   b. Similarly, m$\angle B$ = m$\angle 3$ by the $\parallel$ lines $\Rightarrow$ AIA = Theorem.
   c. Since m$\angle 1$ + m$\angle 2$ + m$\angle 3$ = 180, then m$\angle A$ + m$\angle 2$ + m$\angle B$ = 180 by substitution.

2. m$\angle E$ + m$\angle F$ + m$\angle G$ = 180 by the Triangle-Sum Theorem, so m$\angle E$ = 180 − (m$\angle F$ + m$\angle G$) by the Addition Property of Equality and m$\angle E$ = 180 − (115 + 40) = 180 − (155) = 25.

3. The angles can be expressed as x, $3x$, and $5x$. Then, by the Triangle-Sum Theorem,
   $$x + 3x + 5x = 180$$
   $$9x = 180$$
   $$x = 20$$
   $$3x = 60$$
   $$5x = 100.$$
   The angles are 20°, 60°, and 100°.

4. **a.** $ABCD$ is a rectangle, so m$\angle 1$ = 90 by the definition of rectangle (meaning).
   b. $\overleftrightarrow{AB} \parallel \overleftrightarrow{DC}$, so m$\angle 2$ = m$\angle 5$ because $\parallel$ lines $\Rightarrow$ AIA = .
   c. m$\angle 2$ + m$\angle 6$ + m$\angle 1$ = 180 by the Triangle-Sum Theorem, and m$\angle 1$ = 90 (part **a**), so m$\angle 2$ + m$\angle 6$ = 90 by substitution and the Additional Property of Equality.
   d. Similarly to part **c**, m$\angle 3$ + m$\angle 5$ = 90.
   e. m$\angle 3$ + m$\angle 4$ + m$\angle 5$ = 180 by the Triangle-Sum Theorem.
   f. Since m$\angle 1$ + m$\angle 2$ + m$\angle 6$ = 180 and m$\angle 3$ + m$\angle 4$ + m$\angle 5$ = 180 by the Triangle-Sum Theorem. Then m$\angle 1$ + m$\angle 2$ + m$\angle 3$ + m$\angle 4$ + m$\angle 5$ + m$\angle 6$ = 360 by the Addition Property of Equality. (Another justification uses the Quadrilateral-Sum Theorem and the Angle Addition Property.)

5. The Quadrilateral-Sum Theorem is the statement that in a convex quadrilateral, the sum of the measures of the angles is 360.

6. The Polygon-Sum Theorem is the statement that the sum of the measures of the angles of a convex polygon of n sides is $(n - 2)180$.

7. **a.** If "lines" are circles on a sphere, then for a triangle formed by two longitudes and a latitude, the sum of the angles in the triangle is greater than 180°.

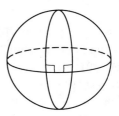

   b. These geometries are called non-Euclidean geometries. (There are also non-Euclidean geometries where the sum of the measures of the angles of a triangle is less than 180°. Consider a "plane" to be a given circular region, and "lines" to be circles which intersect the "plane" at right angles (more accurately, tangents to the "plane" and "line" are perpendicular).

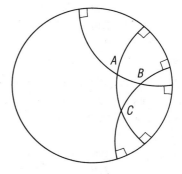

Then the sum of the angle measures of "$\triangle ABC$" is less than 180.

91

8. **a–b.** A convex kite is a convex quadrilateral, so the sum of its measures is 360 by the Quadrilateral-Sum Theorem (or the Polygon-Sum Theorem with $n = 4$).

9. **a–b.** An isosceles triangle is a triangle, so the sum of its measures is 180 by the Triangle-Sum Theorem (or the Polygon-Sum Theorem with $n = 3$).

10. **a–b.** The sum of the measures of a 10-gon is 1440 by the Polygon-Sum Theorem:
$(n - 2)(180) = (10 - 2)(180) = 8(180)$
$= 1440.$

11. **a–b.** The sum of the measures of a 20-gon is 3240 by the Polygon-Sum Theorem:
$(n - 2)(180) = (20 - 2)(180) =$
$18(180) = 3240.$

12. **a.** It is true that each side of the polygon that does not contain vertex A is part of exactly one triangle.
   b. The number of sides that do contain vertex A is 2, so the number of sides of the n-gon that do not contain vertex A is $n - 2$.
   c. The triangulated polygon has one triangle for each side that does not contain vertex A, so an n-gon triangulates into $n - 2$ triangles.

13. The sum of the three measurements is:

$$
\begin{array}{rr}
89° & 58' \\
106° & 12' \\
81° & 24' \\
\hline
276° & 94°
\end{array}
$$

Since $94' = 1°34'$, the sum of the three measurements is $277°34'$. The sum of the 4 angle measures is $360°$ or $359°60'$.
Subtracting:

$$
\begin{array}{rr}
359° & 60' \\
277° & 34' \\
\hline
82° & 26'
\end{array}
$$

So $x = 82°26'$.

14. By the Quadrilateral-Sum Theorem,
$$
\begin{aligned}
x + (x + 20) + (x - 50) + (x + 2) &= 360 \\
4x - 28 &= 360 \\
4x &= 388 \\
x &= 97
\end{aligned}
$$
So $m\angle P = x = 97$, $m\angle Q = x + 20 = 117$, $m\angle R = x - 50 = 47$, and $m\angle S = x + 2 = 99$. (To check, $97 + 117 + 47 + 99 = 360$.)

15. **a–b.** If the measure of each angle of an equilateral triangle is x, then $x + x + x = 180$ (by the Triangle-Sum Theorem) or $3x = 180$, so $x = 60$.

16. If the smallest angle is x, then the third angle is $3x$, and $x + 3x + 90 = 180$ (by the Triangle Sum Theorem), so $4x + 90 = 180$ or $4x = 90$ and $x = 22.5$. The three angles are $22.5, 67.5,$ and 90.

17.

If the 39° angle is the vertex angle, then the sum of the base angles is $180 - 39 = 141$, and each base angle has measured 70.5; the angles are $39°$, $70.5°$, and $70.5°$.

If the 39° angle is a base angle, then the sum of the two base angles is $78°$ and the vertex angle has measure $180 - 78 = 102$; the angles are $39°$, $39°$, and $102°$.

18.

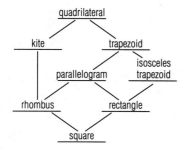

19. a. *ABED* is a trapezoid by the definition of trapezoid (sufficient condition), so m∠*A* = 180 − m∠*D* by the Trapezoid Angle Theorem. Also, m∠*ABE* = 180 − m∠*CBE* by the Linear Pair Theorem. It is given that m∠*D* = m∠*CBE*, so m∠*A* = m∠*ABE* by substitution and the Transitive Property of Equality. So *ABED* is an isosceles trapezoid by the definition of isosceles trapezoid (sufficient condition).

b. ∠*A* and ∠*D* are supplementary by the Trapezoid Angle Theorem.

20. A figure is a rhombus if and only if it is a quadrilateral with all 4 sides equal in length.

21. A figure is a trapezoid if and only if it is a quadrilateral with at least one pair of parallel sides.

22. In if-then form: the Isosceles Triangle Theorem states that if a triangle has two sides equal in length, then the angles opposite those sides are equal in measure.

23.

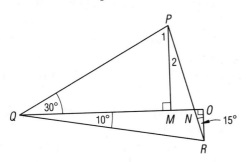

In Δ*PQM*, ∠1 is 60°, so the position of ship *Q* from ship *P* is 60° W of S or 30° S of W. In Δ*RON*, m∠*ONR* = 75, so in Δ*PMN*, m∠*PNM* = 75 and m∠2 = 15. So the position of ship *R* from ship *P* is 15° E of S or 75° S of E.

24. Answers may vary. By stretching string between each pair of cities (so that the string, if extended, would form a great circle around the globe), the three angle measures are approximately 80° (vertex at Los Angeles), 75° (vertex at London), and 115° (vertex at Rio de Janiero). The sum of the measures for that triangle is 270°.

CHAPTER 5 PROGRESS SELF-TEST (p. 249)

1. Squares are below rectangles in the Quadrilateral Hierarchy, so it is true that every square is a rectangle.

2.

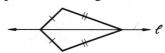

False; a kite has only one line of symmetry.

3. a. The sum of the three angle measures is 180, so $(5x) + (90 − x) + (x) = 180$, or $5x + 90 = 180$, so $5x = 90$ and $x = 18$.

b. m∠*A* = *x* = 18; m∠*B* = (90 − *x*) = 90 − 18 = 72; m∠*C* = 5*x* = 5(18) = 90. (To check: m∠*A* + m∠*B* + m∠*C* = 18 + 72 + 90 = 180.)

4.

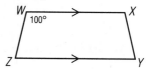

m∠*X* = 100 by the Isosceles Trapezoid Theorem. The sum of m∠*W* + m∠*X* + m∠*Y* + m∠*Z* = 360 because of the Quadrilateral Sum Theorem, so m∠*Y* + m∠*Z* = 160 by the Addition Property of Equality. By the Isosceles Trapezoid Theorem, m∠*Y* = m∠*Z*, so m∠*Y* = m∠*Z* = 80.

5.

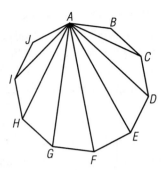

ABCDEFGHIJ, a convex decagon, can be triangulated into 8 triangles. The sum of the measures of the 8 triangles is 8(180) = 1440.

6. **a.** Δ*MNP* is equilateral, so it is also equilangular; m∠*M* = 60.

  b. The two acute angles at point *N*, ∠*MNP* and ∠*PNO*, are parts of equilateral triangles. So each angle has measure 60, and m∠*MNO* = 120.

7. Δ*MNO* is equilateral, so *MN* = *MP* = *NP*, and Δ*NOP* is equilateral so *NO* = *PO* = *NP*. By the Transitive Property of Equality, *MN* = *NO* = *OP* = *MP*. So *MNOP* is a rhombus (*True*) by the definition of rhombus (sufficient condition).

8.

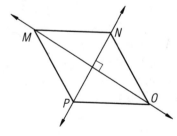

MNOP has two symmetry lines, $\overleftrightarrow{MO}$ and $\overleftrightarrow{NP}$.

9. **a.** *ABCD* is a parallelogram, so it is also a trapezoid. So m∠*A* + m∠*B* = 180 by the Trapezoid Angle Theorem.

  b. *ADCB* is a parallelogram, so $\overleftrightarrow{AD} \parallel \overleftrightarrow{BC}$. So m∠*D* = m∠*DCE* because ∥ lines ⇒ AIA =.

10.

conclusions	justifications
1. *AB* = *BC*	Given
2. m∠*A* = m∠*ACB*	Isosceles Triangle Theorem
3. m∠*ACB* = m∠*ECD*	Vertical Angle Theorem
4. m∠*A* = m∠*ECD*	Transitive Property of Equality (Steps 2 and 3)

11. **a.** ∠5 and ∠6 form a linear pair, so m∠5 + m∠6 = 180. Since ℓ ∥ *m*, ∠6 = ∠3 by ∥ lines ⇒ AIA =. So m∠5 + m∠3 = 180 or (9*z* − 52) + (2*z* + 45) = 180. Then 11*z* − 7 = 180 or 11*z* = 187, so *z* = 17.

  b. m∠3 = 2*z* + 45 = 2(17) + 45 = 34 + 45 = 79.

12. Sample:

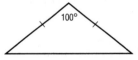

13. **a–b.** Counterexample:

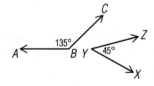

The counterexample shows that the conjecture is false. ∠1 and ∠2 are supplementary, but they do not form a linear pair.

14. **a.** For most briefcases, the top has the shape of a rectangle.

  b. Opinions may vary. One explanation is that the rectangular outline of the briefcase is convenient for carrying books and papers.

15.

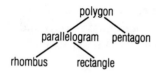

CHAPTER 5 REVIEW (pp. 249–251)

1.

2.

3.

4.

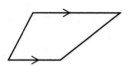

5. If $m\angle T = 2m\angle R$, then the angles can be expressed as x and $2x$. So $3x = 180$ by the Trapezoid Angle Theorem, and $x = 60$. So $m\angle R = 60$ and $m\angle T = 120$. (There are no restrictions on $m\angle A$ and $m\angle P$, except $m\angle A + m\angle P = 180$ by the Trapezoid Angle Theorem.)

6. $m\angle A + m\angle P = 180$ by the Trapezoid Angle Theorem, so
$$8x - 12 + 15x - 15 = 180$$
$$23x - 27 = 180$$
$$23x = 207$$
$$x = 9.$$
So $m\angle A = 8x - 12 = 8(9) - 12 = 72 - 12 = 60$.

7. **a.** *NICE* is an isosceles trapezoid, so $m\angle N = m\angle E$ by the definition of isosceles trapezoid (meaning). So
$$5x - 7 = 11x - 79$$
$$-6x = -72$$
$$x = 12.$$
So $\begin{aligned} m\angle E &= 11x - 79 \\ &= 11(12) - 79 \\ &= 132 - 79 \\ &= 53. \end{aligned}$

b. $m\angle E + m\angle C = 180$ by the Trapezoid Angle Theorem, so $53 + m\angle C = 180$ and $m\angle C = 180 - 53 = 127$.

8. By the Linear Pair Theorem $m\angle 1 + m\angle 2 + m\angle 3 = 180$. $\ell \parallel m$ so $m\angle 5 = m\angle 3$ because $\parallel$ lines $\Rightarrow$ AIA $=$. So $m\angle 1 + m\angle 2 + m\angle 5 = 180$ by substitution and $m\angle 2 = 180 - (m\angle 1 + m\angle 5)$ by the Addition Property of Equality. Given that $m\angle 1 + m\angle 5 = 140$, then $m\angle 2 = 180 - 140 = 40$.

9. $m\angle 3 + m\angle 2 = m\angle 7$ because $\parallel$ lines $\Rightarrow$ AIA $=$. Substituting, $60 + m\angle 2 = 117$ so $m\angle 2 = 117 - 60 = 57$.

10. If m∠5 = m∠6, then m∠4 = m∠7 because they are supplements to congruent angles. Also, m∠5 = m∠3 and m∠6 = m∠1 because ∥ lines ⇒ AIA = . So m∠1 = m∠3 = m∠5 = m∠6.

11. $s \parallel t$, so m∠3 = m∠6 because ∥ lines ⇒ AIA = . So
$$2x - 11 = -x + 46$$
$$3x - 11 = 46$$
$$3x = 57$$
$$x = 19.$$
$$m∠3 = 2x - 11$$
$$= 2(19) - 11$$
$$= 38 - 11$$
$$= 27.$$

12. m∠5 + m∠7 = 180 by the Linear Pair Theorem, and m∠5 = m∠1 by ∥ lines ⇒ corr. ∠s = . So by substitution,
$$m∠1 + m∠7 = 180$$
$$6x - 5 + 2x + 5 = 180$$
$$8x = 180$$
$$x = 22.5.$$
Then m∠1 = 6x - 5
$$= 6(22.5) - 5$$
$$= 135 - 5$$
$$= 130.$$

13. m∠ABC = 42, so m∠ACB = 42 by the Isosceles Triangle Theorem. m∠ACB = m∠GCF by the Vertical Angle Theorem, so m∠GCF = 42.

14. If m∠DBE = x, then m∠ABC = x (Vertical Angle Theorem) and m∠ACB = x (Isosceles Triangle Theorem). ∠ACG and ∠ACB are supplementary (Linear Pair Theorem), so m∠ACG = 180 − x.

15. If the measure of the third angle is x, then the Triangle Sum Theorem states that x + 43 + 91 = 180 so x = 180 − (43 + 91) = 180 − 134 = 46.

16. If the vertex angle has measure 72, then the sum of the other two angles is 108, so each one is 54; the three angles are 54°, 54°, and 72°. If the base angle is 72, then the other base angle is also 72, and the vertex angle has measure 180 − (72 + 72) = 180 − 144 = 36; the three angles are 72°, 72°, and 36°.

17. **a.** By the Triangle-Sum Theorem,
$$x + 2 + x + 3 + x + 1 = 180$$
$$3x + 6 = 180$$
$$3x = 174$$
$$x = 58.$$
b. So m∠D = x + 1 = 59, m∠E = x + 2 = 60, and m∠F = x + 3 = 61.

18. ∠UTS is supplementary to 140° (by the Linear Pair Theorem), so m∠UTS = 40. m∠TUR = 88 by the Vertical Angle Theorem. So, by the Quadrilateral-Sum Theorem,
$$88 + 40 + 3y + y = 360$$
$$4y + 128 = 360$$
$$4y = 232$$
$$y = 58.$$
So m∠R = 58, m∠S = 3(58) = 174, m∠STU = 40, and m∠TUR = 88. (As a check, 58 + 174 + 40 + 88 = 360.)

19. Using the Polygon-Sum Theorem with $n = 8$, the sum of the angles is
$$(n - 2)180 = (8 - 2)180 = 6(180) = 1080.$$

20. a.

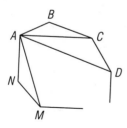

If $ABC \ldots MN$ is a convex polygon, and diagonals are drawn from vertex A, a diagonal can be drawn for every vertex except A, B, and N. So in an n-sided polygon, the number of diagonals that can be drawn is $n - 3$.

b. Except for the two sides which intersect at vertex A, each side of the polygon is in a separate triangle. So the number of triangular regions is $n - 2$.

c. For each of the $n - 2$ triangles, the sum of the measures of the angles is 180. So the sum of the measures for all the triangles, which is the sum for the polygon, is $(n - 2)180$.

21. From general to specific:
polygon (any number of sides)
quadrilateral (4 sides)
parallelogram (opposite sides parallel)
rhombus (parallelogram with 4 ≅ sides)
square (rhombus with right angles)

22. From least to greatest number of sides:

scalene triangle	(3 sides)
kite	(4 sides)
6-gon	(6 sides)
heptagon	(7 sides)
octagon	(8 sides)

23. The figure is a trapezoid with a pair of congruent base angles, so it is an isosceles trapezoid.

24. The figure is a quadrilateral with four sides equal in length, so it is a rhombus.

25. *True;* by the Quadrilateral Hierarchy Theorem, every square has all the properties of a parallelogram.

26. *False;* here is a counterexample.

27. $ABCD$ is a kite, so it has one symmetry line, $\overleftrightarrow{DB}$.

28. Since $\overleftrightarrow{DB}$ is a symmetry line, $m\angle A = m\angle C$ because reflections preserve angle measure.

29.

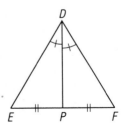

If $EP = PF$ and $m\angle EDP = m\angle PDF$, then $DE = DF$, so ΔDEF is isosceles; that is choice (c).

30.

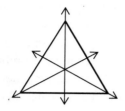

31. *False;* here is a counterexample.

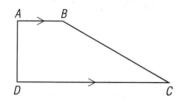

32. *True.* The Kite Diagonal Theorem states that one diagonal of a kite bisects the other, and in a rhombus each diagonal is a symmetry diagonal.

33. *True;* the Isosceles Trapezoid Symmetry Theorem states that the ⊥ bisector of one base is the ⊥ bisector of the other base.

34.

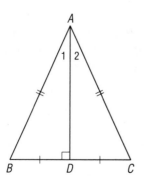

True; $\triangle ABD \cong \triangle ACD$, so m$\angle 1$ = m$\angle 2$ and $\overrightarrow{AD}$ bisects $\angle BAC$.

35. Answers may vary, but the conjecture is *false.* Here is a counterexample:

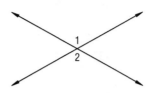

$\angle 1$ and $\angle 2$ are vertical angles, but $\angle 1$ and $\angle 2$ are obtuse.

36. Answers may vary, but the conjecture is *true.*

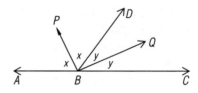

$\angle ABD$ and $\angle DBC$ form a linear pair, with bisectors $\overrightarrow{BP}$ and $\overrightarrow{BQ}$. then $x + x + y + y = 180$, or $2x + 2y = 180$, so $x + y = 90$ and $\angle PBQ$ is a right angle.

37. Answers may vary, but the conjecture is *true.* Here is a sample:

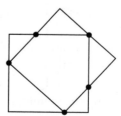

38. a. *True;* this is the definition of midpoint (meaning).

39. a. *False*

  b. Counterexample:

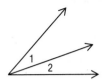

  ∠1 and ∠2 are adjacent, but they are not supplementary.

40. *ABCD* is a square, so *ABCD* is a parallelogram by the Quadrilateral Hierarchy Theorem. So $\overline{BC} \parallel \overline{AD}$ by the definition of parallelogram (meaning).

41. If m∠*F* = m∠*FHI*, then $\overline{EF} \parallel \overline{GH}$ because AIA = ⇒ ∥ lines. So *EFHG* is a trapezoid by the definition of trapezoid (sufficient condition).

42. The ⊥ bisector of either base is a symmetry line for *ABCD,* by the Isosceles Trapezoid Symmetry Theorem. For that symmetry line, r(*A*) = *B* and r(*C*) = *D*. So r($\overline{AC}$) = $\overline{BD}$, and *AC* = *BD* because reflections preserve distance.

43. Δ*ABC* is isosceles with vertex angle at *A,* and Δ*CAD* is isosceles with vertex angle at *C*. So *AB* = *AC* and *AC* = *CD* by the definition of isosceles triangle (meaning). So *AB* = *CD* by the Transitive Property of Equality.

44. a. $\overleftrightarrow{IE}$ connects the ends of kite *KITE*, so $\overleftrightarrow{IE}$ is the ⊥ bisector of $\overline{KT}$ by the Kite Diagonal Theorem.

  b. *X* is the midpoint of $\overline{KT}$ by the definition of bisector (meaning).

  c. *KX* = *TX* by the definition of midpoint (meaning).

45. In ⊙*P*, *PQ* = *PR*, and in ⊙*O*, *OQ* = *OR*, both by the definition of circle (meaning). So *OQPR* is a kite by the definition of kite (sufficient condition).

46. a. The polygon most like a piece of notebook paper is a rectangle.

  b. Answers will vary; one explanation is the ease of packaging packets of paper.

47. a. The 4 bases form a shape called a diamond. However, most diamonds are really rhombuses, while a "baseball diamond" is actually a square.

  b. The dimensions of a major league infield is 90 feet by 90 feet.

  c. Answers may vary; one explanation is that right-handed and left-handed batters have equal "sweeps" of field to hit to.

48. a. The stop sign has 8 sides; it is an octagon. The detour sign is a rectangle. The school crossing sign is a pentagon.

  b. Answers may vary; different shapes and colors are used so that certain shapes and colors are associated with specific types of information. For example, "information" signs (curve ahead, falling rocks) are squares "balanced" on a vertex, railroad warnings are circles, etc. Also, yellow signs indicate cautions, and so on.

49.

```
        parallelogram
   rectangle      rhombus
          square
```

50.

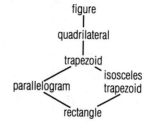

```
              figure
              |
          quadrilateral
              |
           trapezoid
                      isosceles
   parallelogram      trapezoid
           rectangle
```

CHAPTER 6 TRANSFORMATIONS AND CONGRUENCE

LESSON 6-1 (pp. 252–258)

1. A transformation is a correspondence between two sets of points such that (1) each point in the preimage set has a unique image, and (2) each point in the image set has exactly one preimage.

2. A transformation can be described by giving a rule which tells how to locate the image of any point.

3. *True;* the term "map" refers to a transformation from preimage to image.

4. *True;* by the definition of transformation (meaning), a preimage point has exactly one image.

5. *True;* by the definition of transformation (meaning), an image point has exactly one preimage.

6. *False;* a transformation can change the shape of a preimage, so the image of a triangle is not necessarily a triangle.

7. *False;* a transformation can split an image into parts or change its shape, so not every transformation is a reflection.

8. *False;* a transformation can distort a shape, so not every transformation preserves angle measure.

9. **a.** Transformation T maps (x, y) onto $(x - 8, y - 12)$. So T(M), the image of $(15, 12)$, is $(15 - 8, 12 - 12) = (7, 0)$.
   b. $K = (15, 15)$, so $K' = (15 - 8, 15 - 12) = (7, 3)$. Similarly, $L = (15, 9)$, so $L' = (15 - 8, 9 - 12) = (7, -3)$. The midpoint of $\overline{K'L'}$ is $= (7, 0)$. So M' is the midpoint of $\overline{K'L'}$.

10. Some of the early work in transformations was done to understand and describe perspective drawings.

11. **a.**

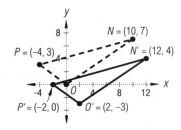

b. The image has been moved 2 units to the right and 3 units down; that is a slide.

12. Using the transformation S$(x, y) = (2x, x + y)$, then S$(5, 0) = (2 \cdot 5, 5 + 0) = (10, 5,)$; S$(5, 2) = (2 \cdot 5, 5 + 2) = (10, 7)$; S$(7, 2) = (2 \cdot 7, 2 + 7) = (14, 9)$; and S$(7, 0) = (2 \cdot 7, 7 + 0) = (14, 7)$.

13. From the graph, it is clear that images of right angles are no longer right angles, so angle measure is not preserved. From the defining transformation S$(x, y) = (2x, x + y)$, you can tell that the transformation does not preserve angle measure because the image of x and the image of y is not a simple addition or subtraction of a constant.

14. **a.**

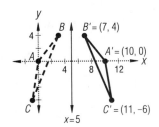

b. The transformation has the effect of a reflection of the image over the vertical line with equation $x = 5$.

15. **a–b.**

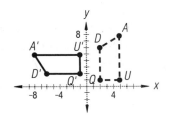

c. The transformation has the effect of turning the image in the counterclockwise direction by 90°.

16. a. There is one successful outcome (heads lands up) out of two possible outcomes (heads lands up or tails lands up). So P(heads on one toss) = $\frac{1}{2}$.

b. There are two successful outcomes (Saturday and Sunday) out of seven possible outcomes, so P(a selected day is a weekend day) = $\frac{2}{7}$.

17. For the three angles of any triangle, the sum of the angle measure is 180. If one of the angles is a right angle (measure 90), then the sum of the measures of the other two angles is 90. So each is acute and they are complementary; that is choice (b).

18. a. The number of even integers from 1 to 10 is five (2, 4, 6, 8, 10), so N(set of even numbers from 1 to 10) is 5.

b. Of the 100 numbers from 1 to 100, every other one is even, so N(set of even integers from 1 to 100) is 50.

19. a. Yes, a right triangle can be isosceles. Sample:

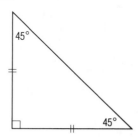

b. Similar to question 17, the right angle has measure 90 and the sum of other two measures is 90, so each of the acute angles has measure 45.

20. A rhombus is a trapezoid with either pair of opposite sides as bases, so by the Trapezoid Angle Theorem, the two angles adjacent to the 55 degree angle are supplementary to it and have measure 180 − 55 = 125. A rhombus is a trapezoid, so opposite angles have equal measure, and the measure of the angle opposite the 55 degree angle is also 55.

21.

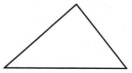

22. The distance between ℓ and m is the length of any perpendicular segment connecting them. $\overline{PR}$ seems to be perpendicular to ℓ and m, so the distance between ℓ and m seems to be PR; that is choice (b).

23. If m∠DAE = x, then m∠CAD = 2x. Ray $\overrightarrow{AC}$ bisects ∠BAD, so m∠BAC = m∠CAD = 2x. By the Angle Addition Property, m∠BAE = m∠BAC + m∠CAD + m∠DAE, so 2x + 2x + x = 80, or 5x = 80. So x = 16 and m∠DAE = x = 16.

24.

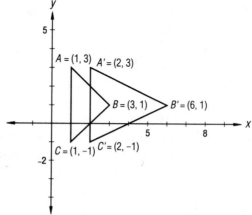

From the graphs, it seems that transformation T doubles the width of a figure while keeping its height constant. This

102

can also be seen from the transformation rule $T(x, y) = (2x, y)$—horizontal values are doubled and vertical values are not changed.

LESSON 6-2 (pp. 259–265)

1. A translation is the composite of two reflections over parallel lines.

2. You often see parallel mirrors in a barber shop, beauty salon or an exercise room. The parallel mirrors allow you to see the back of your head or body.

3. The first-applied transformation is written on the right, and each subsequently-applied transformation is written to the immediate left of the previous one. So first applying f, then s, is written as s ∘ f; that is choice (d).

4. **a.** The reflection of point F over line m is point C.
   b. The reflection of point F over line m is point C, and then the reflection of that point C over line ℓ is B.
   c. Part c is another way to write part b; the image point is point B.

5. **a.** The reflection image of point A over line ℓ is point D.
   b. The reflection image of point A over line ℓ is point D, and the reflection image of that point D over line m is point E.

6. By the Two Reflection Theorem for Translations, the transformation $r_\ell \circ r_m$ is a translation.

7. Five properties preserved under translations are angle measure, betweenness, collinearity, distance, and orientation.

8. A translation is a particular type of transformation (other types of transformations are reflections, glides, turns, size changes, and others), so transformation is a more general term than translation.

9. **a.** By the Two Reflection Theorem for Translations, the translation $r_\ell \circ r_m$ has magnitude two times the distance between ℓ and m, so it has magnitude 2 cm.
   b. The direction of the translation is from the line for the first-applied reflection to the line for the second-applied reflection, so the direction is from m to ℓ; that is vertically up.

10. **a–b–c.**

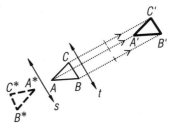

   d. In the drawings, $\overline{AA'}$, $\overline{BB'}$, and $\overline{CC'}$ appear to be parallel segments of the same length.
   e. By the Two Reflection Theorem for Translations, the length of $\overline{AA'}$, which is the distance between a preimage-image pair of points, is twice the distance between lines s and t; that is choice (ii).

11. For point A, the reflection across line m, any number of times, is point A. For point B, its reflection over line m is point C, and the reflection of that point C over line m is point B. So the reflection of $\overline{AB}$ over line m, then over line m again, is the original $\overline{AB}$.

12. In general, the composite transformation of a reflection with itself results in mapping a figure onto itself.

13. One method of translating an image 6 inches to the left is to use the translation $T(x, y) = (x - 6, y)$, where measurements are in inches.

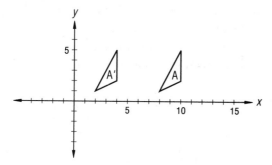

Another way is to draw any two vertical lines s and t that are 3 inches apart, with s to the right of t, and apply the composite $r_t \circ r_s$.

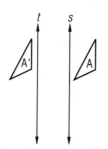

14.

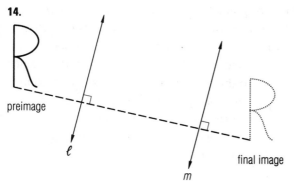

15.

From the hand mirror to her eyes is 1 foot, then to the back of her head is 8 inches, then to the wall mirror is 3 feet, then to the image of the back of her head is another 3 feet. One answer is that the distance from her eyes to the image of the back of her head is 8 inches + 3 feet + 3 feet = 6 feet, 8 inches. Another reasonable answer is that the light that travels from her eyes to the image of the back of her head travels 1 foot from her eyes to the hand mirror, 1 foot back to the location of her eyes, then the 6 feet, 8 inches to the image of the back of her head, for a total of 8 feet, 8 inches.

16. a.

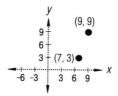

b. $T(7, 3) = (7 + 2, 3 + 6) = (9, 9)$, and the slope of the line through $(7, 3)$ and $(9, 9)$ is $\frac{9 - 3}{9 - 7} = \frac{6}{2} = 3$.

c. The effect of transformation T on a figure is to move it 2 units to the right and 6 units up. That can be seen from the transformation rule $T(x, y) = (x + 2, y + 6)$, which moves each point 2 units in the positive x-direction and 6 units in the positive y-direction.

17. a. The point that is 4 units to the right and 6 units down from (2, 5) is (2 + 4, 5 − 6) = (6, -1).

b. The point that is 4 units to the right and 6 units down from (*x, y*) is (*x* + 4, *y* − 6).

18. a. If S is the set of vertices of an octagon, an 8-sided figure, then S has 8 vertices. So N(S), the number of elements of set S, is 8.

b.

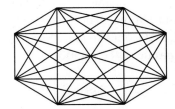

One method is to draw an octagon and all its diagonals, and count them—the number of diagonals is 20.
Another method: from each of the 8 vertices of the octagon you can draw 5 diagonals (you cannot draw a diagonal to the given vertex nor to either adjacent vertex). The product of 8 and 5 is 40, but each diagonal has been counted twice, so the number of diagonals is 20. In general, the number of diagonals in an *n*-gon is $\frac{n(n-3)}{2}$.

19. If T(*x, y*) = (*x* − 8, 3*y*), then T(-4, 5) = (-4 − 8, 3 · 5) = (-12, 15).

20. Lines ℓ and *m* are parallel, so m∠8 = m∠4 by // lines ⇒ corr. ∠s =. Also, m∠4 = m∠1 by the Vertical Angle Theorem, so m∠1 = m∠8 by the Transitive Property of Equality.

21. a. *True;* a rhombus is a special type of trapezoid, so if a figure is a rhombus it has all the properties of a trapezoid.

b. *False;* not all trapezoids are rhombuses. Sample:

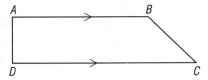

ABCD is a trapezoid, but *AB* ≠ *BC*.

22.

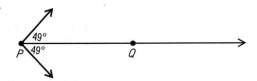

23. A figure is a circle if and only if it is a set of points in a plane that are a certain distance (its radius) from a given point (its center).

24. Using parallel mirrors, you view your image which is viewing its image (which you see), which is viewing its image (which you also see), and so on, and so on. The result is that you see many translation images, which are alternating views of your image (your back) and the image of your image (your front). Those alternating views appear in both directions.

LESSON 6–3 (pp. 266–272)

1. By the Two Reflection Theorem for Rotations, the composite of two reflections over two intersecting lines is a rotation.

2. The center of rotation in Question 1 (or in any composite of two reflections over intersecting lines) is the point of intersection of the reflecting lines.

3. If the magnitude of a rotation is expressed as a negative value, that is a convention that the direction of the rotation is clockwise; that is choice (a).

4. m∠POP' is twice the magnitude of the angle between lines ℓ and m, so m∠POP' = 2(37) = 74.

5. **a.** The reflection of point P over line ℓ is Q, and the reflection of point O over line ℓ is O, so the image of $\overline{OP}$ is $\overline{OQ}$, and OP = OQ because reflections preserve distance.

   b. Similarly, the reflection over line m of Q is P' and of O is O, so OQ = OP' because reflections preserve distance.

   c. So OP = OP' by the Transitive Property of Equality.

6. **a.** The reflections, over line ℓ, of points P, O, and D are points Q, O, and D, respectively, so the image of ∠POD is ∠QOD by the Figure Reflection Theorem.

   b. Since the image of ∠POD is ∠QOD, then m∠POD = m∠QOD because reflections preserve angle measure.

7. To rotate a figure -160°, you could reflect the figure over two lines where the acute angle between the lines has measure 80.

8. Intersecting mirrors can be found in barber shops and beauty salons, clothing stores, exercise rooms, and many bathrooms or dressing rooms; they are also found in kaleidoscopes.

9.

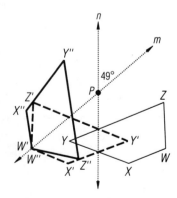

10. **a.**

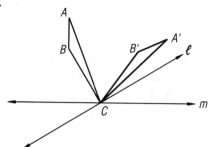

   b. The magniture of the rotation is twice the angle between lines ℓ and m. Since the measure of the angle from ℓ to m is about 32.5, and from ℓ to m is clockwise, the magnitude of the rotation is about -65.

11. **a.**

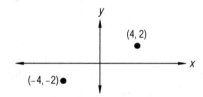

   The reflection of (a, b) over the x-axis is (a, -b) and the reflection of (p, q) over the y-axis is (-p, q). So the reflection over the x-axis of (4, 2) is (4, -2), and the reflection of that point over the y-axis is (-4, -2).

   b. In general, the reflection of a point (x, y) over the x-axis is (x, -y) and the reflection of that point over the y-axis is (-x, -y). So the result of the composite of reflections is a rotation with magnitude 180 degrees (or -180 degrees) and center at the origin.

12. Every rotation or series of rotations preserves all the properties on the list: angle measure, betweenness, collinearity, distance, and orientation.

13. By the Figure Reflection Theorem, the image of points M and N over line ℓ are points P and Q, and the image of points P and Q over line m are S and T. So the image of $\overline{MN}$, over a composite of reflections, is $\overline{ST}$, and $MN = ST$ because reflections preserve distance.

14. By the Figure Reflection Theorem, the image of $\angle MNL$ over line ℓ is $\angle PQO$, and the image of $\angle PQO$ over line m is $\angle STR$. So $\angle STR$ is the image of $\angle MNL$ over a composite of reflections, and $m\angle N = m\angle T$ because reflections preserve angle measure.

15. a. -172° (clockwise)

b. 172° (counterclockwise)

c. $\frac{1}{2}(172) = 86$

16. -120°

17. Translations preserve angle measure, collinearity, and orientation (and also betweenness and distance), so the answer is choice (d): All are preserved.

18.

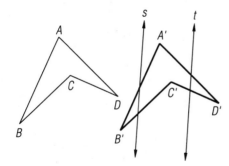

19. If $T(x, y) = (x + 43, y - 210)$, then $T(-30, -2) = (-30 + 43, -2 - 210) = (13, -212)$.

20. a. If one base angle of an isosceles triangle has measure 50, then the other base angle has measure 50, and the vertex angle has measure $180 - (50 + 50) = 180 - 100 = 80$.

b. If the vertex angle of an isosceles triangle has measure 50, then the sum of the two (equal-measure) base angles is $180 - 50 = 130$, so the measure of each base angle is 65.

21. If $ABCD$ is a rhombus, then it is also a parallelogram and $\angle A$ and $\angle B$ are supplementary. So

$$x + (3x + 3) = 180$$
$$4x + 3 = 180$$
$$4x = 177$$
$$x = 44.25$$

Opposite angles of $ABCD$ are congruent, so $m\angle D = m\angle B = 3x + 3 = 3(44.25) + 3 = 132.75 + 3 = 135.75$.

22. a. The sides are segments $\overline{AB}, \overline{BC}, \overline{CD}, \overline{DE}, \overline{EF}, \overline{FG}, \overline{GH}, \overline{HI}, \overline{IJ}, \overline{JK}, \overline{KL}$, and $\overline{LA}$; there are twelve sides, so $n = 12$. (Alternately, you can also count the number of vertices, which is also twelve.)

b. If you "walk" from A to B to C . . . to L and to A, the interior of the polygon is at your left. The convention is that when the interior is at your left, the orientation is counterclockwise.

23. a. In each hour, or 60 minutes, the minute hand makes one complete revolution of 360 degrees. So in 4 minutes, the minute hand makes $\frac{4}{60}$ or $\frac{1}{15}$ of 360 degrees.

$\frac{1}{15}(360) = 24$, so in 4 minutes the minute hand turns 24 degrees.

b. In twelve hours, the hour hand travels one revolution or 360 degrees, so in one hour, the hour hand travels $\frac{360}{12} = 30$ degrees.

Four minutes is $\frac{1}{15}$ of an hour, and in $\frac{1}{15}$ of an hour the hour hand travels $\frac{1}{15}$ of 30 degrees or 2 degrees.

24.

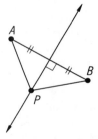

a–d. If point B is the image of A under a rotation, then consider point P to be the center of rotation. P is its own image under the rotation, so $PA = PB$ because reflections preserve distance. All the points P that satisfy the condition that $PA = PB$ lie on the perpendicular bisector of $\overline{AB}$.

LESSON 6–4 (pp. 273–278)

1.

2.

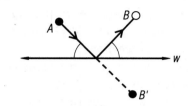

Aim the ball toward B', the reflection image of point B over the line w.

3.

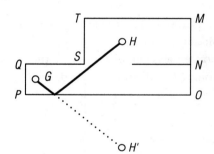

4.

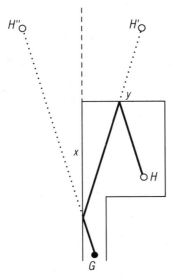

5.

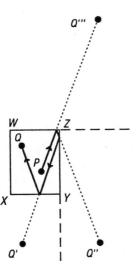

6.

Two angles have equal measures because of the Vertical Angle Theorem; two angles have equal measure because reflections preserve angle measure.

7.

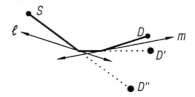

8.

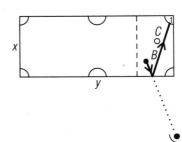

9.

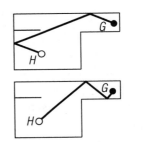

10.

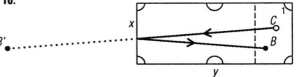

11.

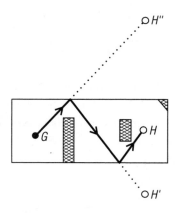

12.

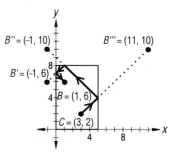

B', the image of B over side Y, is $(-1, 6)$. The image of $(-1, 6)$ over Z is $(-1, 10)$, and the image of $(-1, 10)$ over W is $(11, 10)$. So aim the cue ball toward $(11, 10)$.

13.

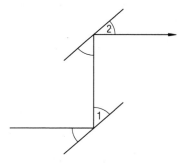

For angle 1, the measure of the preimage angle plus the measure of the image angle must be 90 so that the line of sight changes from horizontal to vertical. The two angles have equal measure, since reflections preserve angle measure, so the measure of

angle 1 is 45. A similar argument shows that $m\angle 2 = 45$ also.

14. If you "stand" at one of the acute angles, then for figures (b) and (c), the short side is on your right and the long side is on your left, while that is reversed for figure (a). So figure (a) is not a rotation image of the other two.

15.

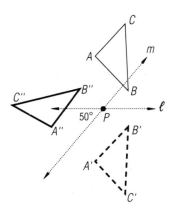

16. For equally likely outcomes, the probability of an event is the quotient of the number of favorable outcomes divided by the number of possible outcomes. For the given set of equally likely outcomes, there are 4 favorable outcomes (2, 4, 6, 8) and 7 possible outcomes, so $P(x$ is even$) = \frac{4}{7}$.

17. The center of the rotation is the intersection of lines ℓ and m, and the magnitude of the rotation is twice the measure of the angle between the lines, measured from m to ℓ. Since the intersection of the vertical line $x = 6$ and the horizontal line $y = 2$ is $(6, 2)$, the center of rotation is $(6, 2)$. And since m and ℓ are perpendicular, the magnitude of the rotation is 180 degrees (or -180 degrees).

18. The translation $r_n \circ r_m$ is the composite of first reflecting over line m, which is the horizontal line $y = 2$, and then reflecting over line n, which is the x-axis or the horizontal line $y = 0$. By the Two Reflection Theorem for Translations, the result is a translation twice the distance between the lines, or 4 units, in a direction from line m to line n, which is vertically down or in the negative y-direction.

19. a. If the measures of the angles are in the extended ratio 2:3:4, then the three angles can be expressed as $2x$, $3x$, and $4x$ and, by the Triangle-Sum Theorem, $2x + 3x + 4x = 180$. So $9x = 180$ and $x = 20$. So the measure of the largest angle is $4x = 4(20) = 80$.

   b. From part **a**, the largest angle has measure 80. So no angle has measure of 90 or greater, and the triangle must be acute.

20. Sample:

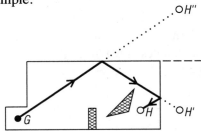

LESSON 6–5 (pp. 279–284)

1. Longer version: Two figures are congruent if and only if one is the image of the other under a translation, a reflection, a rotation or any composite of these. Shorter version: Two figures are congruent if and only if one is the image of the other under a reflection or composite of reflections.

2. If $\angle A$ is congruent to $\angle B$, then one is a composite of reflections of the other. Since reflections preserve angle measure, $m\angle A = m\angle B$; that is choice (c).

3. a. The reflection, over line m, of points B and C are G and H, respectively. So the image of $\overline{BC}$ is $\overline{GH}$ and, since reflections preserve distance, $BC = GH$ or $\overline{BC} \cong \overline{GH}$.

   b. The reflection, over line m, of points C, A, and B are H, F, and G, respectively. So the image of $\angle CAB$ is $\angle HFG$ and, since reflections preserve angle measure, $\angle CAB \cong \angle HFG$.

   c. The image of triangle BCD will be congruent to it; that image is triangle GHE.

4. If $\overline{AB} \cong \overline{CD}$ and $\overline{CD} \cong \overline{GF}$, then $\overline{AB} \cong \overline{GF}$ by the Transitive Property of Congruence.

5. If $\triangle MPQ \cong \triangle ABC$, then $\triangle ABC \cong \triangle MPQ$ by the Symmetric Property of Congruence.

6. $\angle QAM \cong \angle QAM$ by the Reflexive Property of Congruence.

7. a. r_p maps Figure 6 onto Figure 5, and r_n maps Figure 5 onto Figure 4, so the transformation that maps Figure 6 onto Figure 4 is $r_n \circ r_p$.

   b. r_n maps Figure 4 onto Figure 5, and r_p maps Figure 5 onto Figure 6, so the transformation that maps Figure 4 onto Figure 6 is $r_p \circ r_n$.

8. The transformation from Figure 1 to Figure 2 to Figure 3 to Figure 4 to Figure 5 is r_k then r_ℓ then r_m then r_n. So the composite transformation that maps Figure 1 onto Figure 5 is $r_n \circ r_m \circ r_\ell \circ r_k$.

9. Two synonyms for isometry are congruence transformation and composite of reflections.

10. Four properties preserved by isometries are angle measure, betweenness, collinearity, and distance.

11. Places outside of mathematics where congruent figures may be found include tool-and-die making, photocopying, assembly-line manufacturing, and making drop-forged parts.

12. The Segment Congruence Theorem states that two segments are congruent if and only if they have the same length, so if $AX = BY$, then $\overline{AX} \cong \overline{BY}$.

13. The Angle Congruence Theorem states that two angles are congruent if and only if they have the same measure, so if $\angle C \cong \angle T$, then $m\angle C = m\angle T$.

14. If $r(\triangle ABC) = \triangle DEF$, then $\triangle DEF$ is an image of $\triangle ABC$ under a composite of reflections, so the two triangles are congruent; that is choice (c).

15. Replace "sides of the same length" with "congruent sides"; the statement is "An isosceles triangle has two congruent sides."

16. Replace "angles have the same measure" with "angles are congruent"; the statement is "If two lines are cut by a transversal and alternate interior angles are congruent, then the lines are parallel."

17.

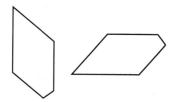

18.

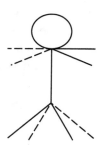

19. Yes; if two circles have different radii, then they are not congruent (although two circles are always similar to each other).

20. Using the results of question 7 as an example, if $r_\ell \circ r_m$ maps a point F onto point G, then the composite $r_m \circ r_\ell$ maps G onto F.

21. r_ℓ maps a figure onto its image, and r_ℓ maps that image back onto the original figure. So the composite $r_\ell \circ r_\ell$ maps a figure onto itself.

22. Any position of the minute hand is a rotation of any other position of the minute hand. Since a rotation is an isometry, which produces congruent figures, then any two positions of the minute hand are congruent.

23. **a.** $AB = AC$ in isosceles triangle ABC, and $AC = AD$ in isosceles triangle ADC. By the Transitive Property of Equality, $AB = AC = AD$, so $\overline{AB}$ is congruent to $\overline{AC}$ and $\overline{AD}$.

   b. Triangle ABC is isosceles, so $\angle B$ is congruent to $\angle ACB$. You know that $\angle ACD \cong \angle ADC$ since $\triangle CAD$ is isosceles, but there is no information relating the base angles in $\triangle ABC$ to the base angles in $\triangle ADC$.

24.

25.

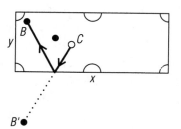

26.

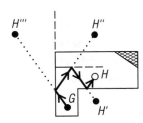

27. a. If all the triangles are equilateral, then also all the triangles are equiangular, and each of the 6 acute angles with vertex O has measure 60. Then the rotation that maps point B onto point C goes through 60 degrees; it is in the counterclockwise (or positive) direction, so its magnitude is 60 degrees.

  b. The rotation that maps point A onto point E is a rotation through two of the acute angles at O, or 120 degrees; it is in the clockwise (or negative) direction, so its magnitude is -120 degrees.

28. a, b. Each triple of lengths represents the three sides of an equilateral triangle, so the lengths are equal by the definition of equilateral triangle (meaning).

  c. The four lengths are equal by the Transitive Property of Equality (based on steps 1 and 2).

  d. Since the four sides of $OAFE$ are equal, $OAFE$ is a rhombus by the definition of rhombus (sufficient condition).

  e. Since $OAFE$ is a rhombus, it is also a parallelogram by the Quadrilateral Hierarchy Theorem.

29. a. By the Polygon-Sum Theorem, the sum of the measures of an octagon is $(n - 2)180$ for $n = 8$, or $6(180) = 1080$. If seven angles of an octagon have measure 150, the sum of those measures is $7(150) = 1050$. This is less than 1080, so such an octagon is possible.

  b. The measure of the eighth angle must be $1080 - 1050 = 30$.

30. Each reflection reverses the orientation of a figure, so a composite of an even number of reflections has the same orientation as the figure.

  a. A composite of 3 reflections (an odd number) will result in reversing the orientation of the figure; the image will have a counterclockwise orientation.

  b. A composite of 10 reflections (an even number) will have the same orientation as the figure; the image will have a clockwise orientation.

  c. F and G will have the same orientation for even numbers of reflections.

  d. F and G will have opposite orientations for odd numbers of reflections.

LESSON 6-6 (pp. 285–291)

1. When two congruent figures have the same orientation, at most 2 reflections are needed to map one onto the other.

2. When two congruent figures have different orientations at most 3 reflections are needed to map one onto the other.

3. A transformation is a glide reflection if and only if it is a composite of a reflection over a line m followed by a translation with nonzero magnitude and direction parallel to m. (Wordings may differ.)

4. The type of isometry that maps Figure A onto Figure B is a translation.

5. The type of isometry that maps Figure A onto Figure C is a glide reflection.

6. The type of isometry that maps Figure C onto Figure D is a glide reflection.

7.

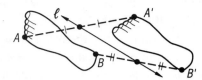

Figure I   Figure II

8.

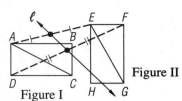

Figure II

Figure I

9.

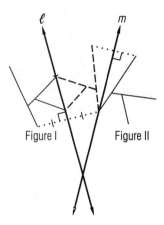

Figure I   Figure II

10.

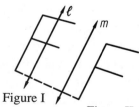

Figure I

Figure II

11. The four types of isometries are reflections, rotations, translations, and glide reflections.

12. *False;* if two figures are not congruent, then there is no isometry (i.e., no size-preserving transformation) mapping one onto the other.

13. a. Four properties preserved by glide reflections are the same as those preserved by reflections: angle measure, betweenness, collinearity, and distance.

    b. The property not preserved by glide reflections is the same as that not preserved by reflections: orientation.

14. a. $T(x, y) = (x + 6, -y)$, so if $A = (0, 6)$ then $A' = (0 + 6, -6) = (6, -6)$; if $B = (-5, 6)$ then $B' = (-5 + 6, -6) = (1, -6)$; and if $C = (-5, -2)$ then $C' = (-5 + 6, -(-2)) = (1, 2)$.

    b.

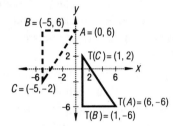

    c. The reflecting line is the horizontal x-axis.

    d. The translation has a magnitude of 6 units and the direction is that of the positive x-axis.

15. a.

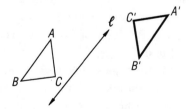

    b. The answer in part **a** is not unique, because the translation, parallel to ℓ can be in either of two directions.

16.

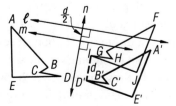

17. If the distances between two pairs of points are equal, then the segments determined by those pairs of points are congruent by the Segment Congruence Theorem.

18. If two angles are congruent, then the measures of those two angles are equal by the Angle Congruence Theorem.

19. Replace "angles of the same measure" with "congruent angles": The bisector of an angle splits it into two congruent angles.

20.

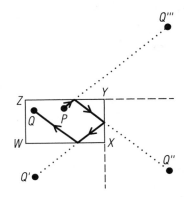

21. a. The ends are the vertices where the congruent sides meet. For *CHIP,* the ends are *C* and *I.*
    b. The symmetry line for a kite contains its ends. For *CHIP,* the symmetry line is $\overleftrightarrow{CI}$.
    c. The reflections across line $\overleftrightarrow{CI}$ of *C* and *I* are themselves, and the reflection of *P* is *H.* So the reflection of triangle *CIP* over line $\overleftrightarrow{CI}$ is triangle *CIH.*
    d. Since a triangle and its reflection image are congruent, the triangle congruent to $\triangle CIP$ is $\triangle CIH.$

22. m∠*CDG* = m∠*ADE* by the Vertical Angle Theorem, and m∠*ADE* = m∠*BEF* because ∥ lines ⇒ corr. ∠s =. So m∠*CDG* = m∠*BEF* by the Transitive Property of Equality.

23. a. If $9(m\angle T) > 801$, then $m\angle T > 89$ by the Multiplication Property of Equality. Since $m\angle T \le 180$, the possible values for $m\angle T$ are $89 < m\angle T \le 180$.
    b. Yes, ∠*T* can be an acute angle. (Possibilities for m∠*T* are 89.001, 89.5, 89.995, etc. The value must be greater than 89 and less than 90.)

24. If the area is less than 1000 square feet, and the dimensions are 50 feet and *x* feet, then
$$50x < 1000$$
$$x < 20.$$
Also, *x* must be positive, so the possible values for *x* are $0 < x < 20$.

25.

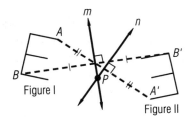

Figure I

Figure II

LESSON 6–7 (pp. 292–295)

1. By definition, two triangles (or any pair of figures) are congruent if and only if there is a composite of reflections (or a composite of translations, reflections, and rotations) such that one triangle is an image of the other.

2. Unless otherwise stated, corresponding parts refer to sides and angles. (Other "parts" of figures, not referred to in the CPCF Theorem, are medians, angle bisectors, etc.)

3. For congruent triangles, there are 6 pairs of corresponding parts (three pairs of sides, three pairs of angles).

4. "CPCF Theorem" is an abbreviation for the theorem that "If two figures are congruent, then any pair of corresponding parts is congruent."

5. In the statement that two specific triangles are congruent, the order of vertices tells you which points are images of which points. So, for the statement that $\triangle ATV \cong \triangle MCI$, then:
   a. the angle congruent to $\angle T$ is $\angle C$;
   b. the angle congruent to $\angle VAT$ is $\angle IMC$;
   c. the segment congruent to $\overline{IC}$ is $\overline{VT}$.

6. In the statement that two specific triangles are congruent, the order of vertices tells you which points are images of which points. So, for the statement that $\triangle ADE \cong \triangle BNO$:
   a. the sides that are congruent are $\overline{AD} \cong \overline{BN}$, $\overline{AE} \cong \overline{BO}$, and $\overline{DE} \cong \overline{NO}$;
   b. the angles that are congruent are $\angle A \cong \angle B$, $\angle D \cong \angle N$, and $\angle E \cong \angle O$.

7. In the statement that two specific figures are congruent, the order of vertices tells you which points are images of which points. So, for the statement that figure $ABCDEF \cong DEFABC$, then the segment congruent to $\overline{CD}$ is $\overline{FA}$.

8. If $\triangle ATV \cong \triangle MCI$, then the image of $\overline{AT}$ is $\overline{MC}$ and $AT = MC$. So if $AT = 5$ cm, then $MC = 5$ cm.

9. If $\triangle MCI \cong \triangle GTE$, then the image of $\angle ICM$ is $\angle ETG$ and $\angle ICM \cong \angle ETG$. So if $m\angle ICM = 94$, then $m\angle ETG = 94$.

10. a. $\triangle LXV \cong \triangle LWV$
   There are five other ways to write the same correspondence:
   $\triangle LVX \cong \triangle LVW$
   $\triangle XLV \cong \triangle WLV$ or $\triangle XVL \cong \triangle WVL$
   $\triangle VLX \cong \triangle VLW$ or $\triangle VXL \cong \triangle VWL$
   (By placing $\triangle LXV$ and its permutations on the right side, there are six more ways to write the correspondence.)

   b. The pairs of congruent angles are:
   $\angle LXV \cong \angle LWV$
   $\angle LVX \cong \angle LVW$
   $\angle XLV \cong \angle WLV$.
   (For each angle in each pair, the order of letters can be reversed, keeping the vertex in the middle, and the statement of congruence will still be true).
   The pairs of congruent sides are:
   $\overline{LX} \cong \overline{LW}$, $\overline{LV} \cong \overline{LV}$, and $\overline{XV} \cong \overline{WV}$.
   (For each segment in each pair, the order of letters can be reversed and the statement of congruence will still be true.)

11. a. $\triangle ABD \cong \triangle CBD$
   There are five other ways to write the same correspondence:
   $\triangle ADB \cong \triangle CDB$
   $\triangle BAD \cong \triangle BCD$ or $\triangle BDA \cong \triangle BDC$
   $\triangle DAB \cong \triangle DCB$ or $\triangle DBA \cong \triangle DBC$.
   (By placing $\triangle ABD$ and its permutations on the right side, there are six more ways to write the correspondence.)

   b. The pairs of congruent angles are:
   $\angle ABD \cong \angle CBD$
   $\angle ADB \cong \angle CDB$
   $\angle BAD \cong \angle BCD$.
   (For each angle in each pair, the order of letters can be reversed, keeping the vertex in the middle, and the statement of congruence will still be true.)
   The pairs of congruent sides are:
   $\overline{AB} \cong \overline{BC}$, $\overline{AD} \cong \overline{CD}$, and $\overline{DB} \cong \overline{DB}$.
   (For each segment in each pair, the order of letters can be reversed and the statement of congruence will still be true.)

12. a. $\triangle GLP \cong \triangle FDP$

There are five other ways to write the same correspondence:

$\triangle GPL \cong \triangle FPD$

$\triangle PGL \cong \triangle PFD$ or $\triangle PLG \cong \triangle PDF$

$\triangle LGP \cong \triangle DFP$ or $\triangle LPG \cong \triangle DPF$.

(By placing $\triangle GPL$ and its permutations on the right side, there are six more ways to write the correspondence.)

b. The pairs of congruent angles are:

$\angle PGL \cong \triangle PFD$ (or simply $\angle G \cong \angle F$)

$\angle GLP \cong \triangle FDP$ (or simply $\angle L \cong \angle D$)

$\angle GPL \cong \triangle FPD$.

(For each angle in each pair, the order of letters can be reversed, keeping the vertex in the middle, and the statement of congruence will still be true.)

The pairs of congruent sides are:

$\overline{GL} \cong \overline{FD}$, $\overline{GP} \cong \overline{FP}$, and $\overline{PL} \cong \overline{PD}$.

(For each segment in each pair, the order of letters can be reversed and the statement of congruence will still be true.)

13. a. $\triangle NOM \cong \triangle ONP$

There are 5 other ways to write the same correspondence:

$\triangle NMO \cong \triangle OPN$

$\triangle MNO \cong \triangle PON$ or $\triangle MON \cong \triangle PNO$

$\triangle OMN \cong \triangle NPO$ or $\triangle ONM \cong \triangle NOP$.

(By placing $\triangle NOM$ and its permutations on the right side, there are six more ways to write the correspondence.)

b. The pairs of congruent angles are:

$\angle NMO \cong \angle OPN$ (or simply $\angle M \cong \angle P$)

$\angle MNO \cong \angle PON$,

$\angle MON \cong \angle PNO$.

(For each angle in each pair, the order of letters can be reversed, keeping the vertex in the middle, and the statement of congruence will still be true.)

The pairs of congruent sides are:
$\overline{MN} \cong \overline{PO}$, $\overline{MO} \cong \overline{PN}$, and $\overline{NO} \cong \overline{ON}$.

(For each segment in each pair, the order of letters can be reversed and the statement of congruence will still be true.)

14. a. Yes; sorting records into 33 and 45 rpms involves sorting by size, and size is a congruence property.

b. Yes; fitting a window into its opening involves comparing sizes, and size is a congruence property.

c. Yes; constructing a given circle means matching the length of a segment, and matching segment lengths involves congruence.

d. No; "same liquid capacity" for different three-dimensional figures does not involve congruence.

e. Yes; comparison of two different shapes involves the idea of congruence.

f. Yes; fitting two jigsaw puzzles together involves the idea of congruence.

15.

16.

17. Four types of isometries (size-preserving transformations) are translations, reflections, rotations, and glide reflections.

18. Four properties preserved by isometries (size-preserving transformations) are angle measure, betweenness, collinearity, and distance. (A property not necessarily preserved is orientation.)

19. a. Here is a graph of the line with equation $y = 3x$ and a graph of that line under a -90 degree rotation with center $(0, 0)$.

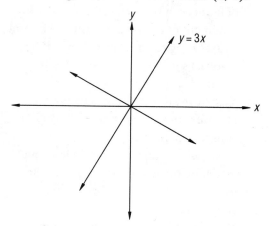

The slope of the line $y = 3x$ is 3 and the image is perpendicular to that line. So the slope of the image line is $-\frac{1}{3}$, by the Perpendicular Lines and Slopes Theorem.

b. Under any translation, the image of the line $y = 3x$ will be parallel to its preimage. So the slope of any image under a translation will be 3, by the Parallel Lines and Slopes Theorem.

20. The image (Figure II) has been rotated and its orientation has been reversed. That transformation can be described by a glide reflection.

21. The parts of the image (Figure II) are parallel to the corresponding parts of the preimage, and the orientation has not been changed. That transformation can be described by a translation.

22. The image (Figure II) has been rotated and its orientation has not been changed. That transformation can be described by a rotation.

23. The Isosceles Triangle Theorem states that "If two sides of a triangle have equal lengths, then the angles opposite those sides have equal measures." Using the word "congruent," that theorem can be restated as "If two sides of a triangle are congruent, then the angles opposite those sides are congruent." (Exact wordings may differ.)

24. If $\triangle D'E'F'$ is the image of $\triangle DEF$ under a translation, then:

a. $\angle FED \cong \angle F'E'D'$ because translations preserve angle measure.

b. $\overline{E'D'} \cong \overline{ED}$ because translations preserve distance.

c. If B is between E and D, then the image of B is between E' and D' because translations preserve betweenness.

25. The transformation $T(a, b) = (2a, 3b)$ multiplies the first component by 2 and the second component by 3. So $T(x, y) = (2x, 3y)$.

26. The first sentence translates to
$m\angle A > 3(180 - m\angle A)$. So
$m\angle A > 540 - 3m\angle A$
$4m\angle A > 540$
$m\angle A > 135$.
Also, for any angle, $m\angle A < 180$. So the measure of the angle must be greater than 135 and less than 180.

27. a. Some of the differences in Figure II from Figure I are: the paintbrush handle is longer; the legs on the right-hand side of the easel are longer; and the painter's left elbow has a smaller angle.

b. Answers will vary.

1. a.

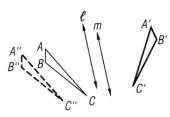

$$r_\ell \circ r_m(\Delta ABC) = r_\ell(\Delta A'B'C')$$
$$= \Delta A''B''C''$$

b. The transformation is a translation, in the direction $\perp$ to ℓ and m, in the direction from m to ℓ, with a distance twice that between ℓ and m.

2. The composition of two reflections is a rotation, so $r_\ell \circ r_m(\Delta ABC)$ is a rotation; that is choice (b).

3.

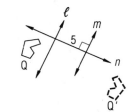

$$r_n \circ r_m(Q) = r_\ell(Q')$$
$$= Q''$$

The transformation is a translation, in the direction of line n, from m to ℓ, with a distance 10, which is twice the distance from m to ℓ.

4.

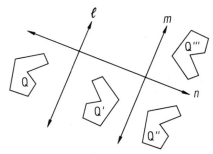

$$r_n \circ r_m \circ r_\ell(Q) = r_n \circ r_m(Q')$$
$$= r_n(Q'')$$
$$= Q'''$$

The transformation is a glide reflection, over the reflecting line n, at a distance twice that from ℓ to m, in the direction from ℓ to m.

5. The image of $\angle C$ is $\angle H$, and the image of $\angle H$ is $\angle L$. Because reflections preserve angle measure, the angle in ΔJKL with the same measure as $\angle C$ is $\angle L$.

6. $\overline{FG}$ is the image of $\overline{AB}$, and the image of $\overline{FG}$ is $\overline{KJ}$. Because reflections preserve length, the segments with the same length as $\overline{FG}$ are $\overline{AB}$ and $\overline{KJ}$.

7. $r_m(\Delta ABC) = \Delta FED$, and $r_\ell(\Delta FED) = \Delta HGI$. So $\Delta ABC \cong \Delta FED \cong \Delta HGI$.

8. According to the CPCF (Corresponding Parts of Congruent Figures) Theorem, if $\Delta ABC \cong \Delta DEF$, then all six pairs of corresponding parts are congruent: $\angle A \cong \angle D$, $\angle B \cong \angle E$, $\angle C \cong \angle F$, $\overline{AB} \cong \overline{DE}$, $\overline{AC} \cong \overline{DF}$, and $\overline{BC} \cong \overline{EF}$.

9. Five properties preserved by translations are angle measure, betweenness of points, collinearity of points, distances between points, and orientation.

10. Four kinds of isometries are slides, rotations, reflections, and glide reflections.

11. True. Since reflections are isometries, and isometries preserve congruence, then a series of reflections results in congruent figures.

12. a.

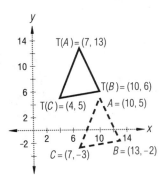

b. The transformation is a translation of 3 units to the left and 8 units up.

13. A hexagon has six sides and six vertices, so
V(hexagon) = 6.

14.

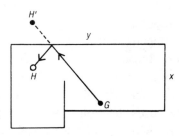

15.

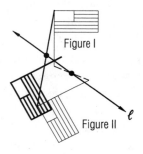

16.

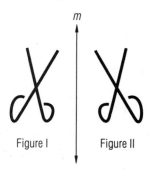

This isometry is a glide reflection: reflection over ℓ followed by a translation parallel to ℓ.

17.

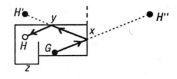

17. The isometry is a reflection across line *m*.

1.

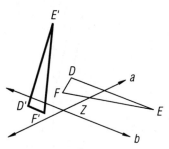

To find $r_a(r_b(\Delta DEF))$, first find $r_b(\Delta DEF)$, which is the reflection image over line *b* of ΔDEF. Then find the reflection, over line *a*, of that image.

2.

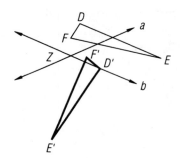

To find $r_b \circ r_a(\Delta DEF)$, first find $r_a(\Delta DEF)$, which is the reflection image over line *a* of ΔDEF. Then find the reflection, over line *b*, of that image.

3. a.

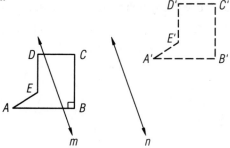

b. The transformation is a slide, in the direction perpendicular to *m* and *n,* of a distance twice that between *m* and *n,* in the direction from *m* (the first-applied reflection) to *n* (the second reflection).

4. a.

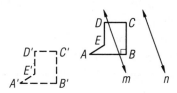

b. The transformation is a slide, in the direction perpendicular to *m* and *n,* of a distance twice that between *m* and *n,* in the direction from *n* (the first-applied reflection) to *m* (the second reflection).

5.

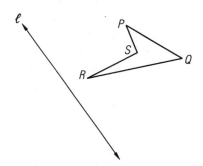

6. Rotations preserve all three choices (a) through (c): betweenness, distance, and orientation (and also angle measure and collinearity). So the answer is choice (d).

7. Both a rotation and a translation can be described as a composite of two reflections, so choices (b) and (c) are false. Moreover, since each reflection reverses orientation, the composite of two reflections must have a different orientation than the result of a single reflection. So a composite of two reflections can never be a reflection, and choice (a) is true.

8. The image of $\overline{BC}$ under r_m is $\overline{ED}$, and the image of $\overline{ED}$ under r_ℓ is $\overline{GI}$. Since reflections preserve distance, the side of $\triangle GHI$ that has the same length as $\overline{BC}$ is $\overline{GI}$.

9. The preimage of $\angle G$ under r_ℓ is $\angle E,$ and the preimage of $\angle E$ under r_m is $\angle B$. Since reflections preserve angle measure, the angle of $\triangle ABC$ that has the same measure as $\angle G$ is $\angle B$.

10.

 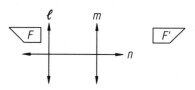

To find the result of the transformation $r_\ell \circ r_m(F)$, first find F', the reflection image of F over line $m,$ then find F'', the reflection image of F' over line ℓ. Another way to describe the result, since the transformation is a composite of reflections over parallel lines, is that $r_\ell \circ r_m$ is a translation of F in the direction perpendicular to ℓ and $m,$ at a distance twice that between ℓ and $m,$ in the direction from m (the first-applied reflection) to ℓ (the second reflection).

11.

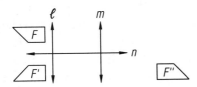

To find the result of the transformation $r_m \circ r_n(F)$, first find F', the reflection image of F over line n, then find F'', the reflection image of F' over line m. Another way to describe the result, since the transformation is a composite of reflections over intersecting lines, is that $r_m \circ r_n$ is a rotation of F at an angle twice that between m and n (in this case, at twice 90 or 180). (While not affecting this problem, the direction, from the first-applied reflection to the second, indicates that the rotation is in the counterclockwise direction, so the magnitude is $+180$ degrees.)

12.

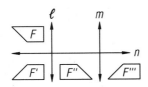

To find the result of $r_m \circ r_\ell \circ r_n(F)$, first find F', the reflection image of F over line n, then find F'', the reflection image of F' over line ℓ, then find F''', the reflection image of F'' over line m.

13. To rotate $\triangle MNO$ 30 degrees about a point C, you can reflect successively over two lines that form an angle of measure 15 (because the rotation is twice the measure of the angle) whose vertex is point C.

14. The preimage of segment $\overline{FE}$ for r_m is $\overline{AB}$, and the image of $\overline{FE}$ for r_ℓ is $\overline{HG}$. Since reflection images of segments are congruent to their preimages, the segments congruent to $\overline{FE}$ are $\overline{AB}$ and $\overline{HG}$.

15. The image of $\angle A$ for r_m is $\angle F$, and the image of F for r_ℓ is $\angle H$. Since reflection images of angles are congruent to their preimages, the angles congruent to $\angle A$ are $\angle F$ and $\angle H$.

16. Reflections preserve congruence, and reflections do not preserve orientation, so it is *false* that congruent figures must have the same orientation.

17. Glide reflections preserve congruence, so it is *true* that a figure and its glide reflection are always congruent.

18. Two figures are congruent if and only if one is the image of the other under a reflection or composite of reflections (or under a composite of translations, reflections, and/or rotations).

19. Four types of isometries (size-preserving transformations) are translations, reflections, rotations, and glide reflections.

20. The images of A, B, C, and D are E, H, G, and F, respectively, and their images are I, J, K, and L. Using that correspondence, $ABCD \cong EHGF \cong IJKL$.

21. The images of A, B, C, and D are E, H, G, and F, respectively, and their images are I, J, K, and L. Using that correspondence, $GFEH \cong CDAB \cong KLIJ$.

22. Since $ABCD \cong EHGF$ and $EHGF \cong IJKL$, then by the Transitive Property of Congruence, $ABCD \cong IJKL$.

23. From the figure, $r_s(\overline{AB}) = \overline{EH}$, and $r_t(\overline{EH}) = \overline{IJ}$. So $\overline{IJ}$ is the image of $\overline{AB}$ under a composite of reflections, and so $\overline{AB} \cong \overline{IJ}$ by the definition of congruence (sufficient condition).

24. $\angle K$ is the reflection image of $\angle C$ under the composite $r_t \circ r_s$, so $m\angle C = m\angle K$ because reflections (or composites of reflections) preserve angle measure.

25. For figure $ABCD$ (or any figure), $ABCD \cong$ $ABCD$ by the Reflexive Property of Congruence.

26. Triangles EDF and ABC have the same orientation, are congruent, and their corresponding sides are not parallel, so one can be mapped onto the other by a rotation.

27. Figures I and II have different orientations, and can be mapped onto each other by the composite of a reflection and a translation, so the type of isometry which maps one onto the other is a glide reflection.

28. Figures I and II have the same orientations (if you "stand" at an acute angle of each figure, the shorter side is to your left for Figure I and to your right for Figure II), and can be mapped onto each other by the composite of a reflection and a translation, so the type of isometry which maps one onto the other is a glide reflection.

29. Figures I and II have the same orientation and their corresponding linear parts are parallel, so one can be mapped onto the other by a translation.

30. Figures A and B have the same orientation and their corresponding parts are "parallel," so one can be mapped onto the other by a translation.

31. Figures B and C have different orientations and can be mapped onto each other by the composite of a reflection and a translation, so the type of isometry which maps one onto the other is a glide reflection.

32.

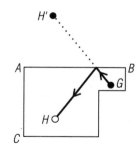

33.

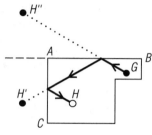

34.

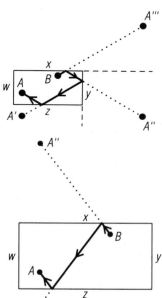

35.

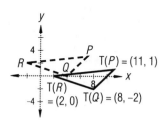

36. a.

If $T(x, y) = (x + 4, y - 2)$, then
$P' = T(P) = T(7, 3) =$
$(7 + 4, 3 - 2) = (11, 1)$;
$Q' = T(Q) = T(4, 0) =$
$(4 + 4, 0 - 2) = (8, -2)$;
$R' = T(R) = T(-2, 2) =$
$(-2 + 4, 2 - 2) = (2, 0)$.

b. Under T, the image of a point (or figure) is another point (or figure) that is 4 units to the right and 2 units below its preimage. This isometry is a translation.

37. a–b.

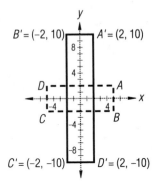

If $S(x, y) = (y, 2x)$, then
$A' = S(A) = S(5, 2) = (2, 10);$
$B' = S(B) = S(5, -2) = (-2, 10);$
$C' = S(C) = S(-5, -2) = (-2, -10);$
$D' = S(D) = S(-5, 2) = (2, -10).$

c. Under S, the image is the reflection over the line $y = x$ and its (new) vertical dimensions are doubled.

38. a–b.

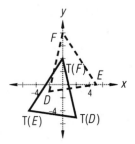

If $T(x, y) = (-x, y - 4)$, then
$D' = T(D) = T(-2, -1) =$
$(-(-2), -1 - 4) = (2, -5);$
$E' = T(E) = T(5, 0) =$
$(-(5), 0 - 4) = (-5, -4);$
$F' = T(F) = T(0, 8) =$
$(-(0), 8 - 4) = (0, 4).$

c. The transformation is a composite of a reflection over the y-axis and a translation of 4 units down, so it is a glide reflection.

39. There are four elements in set S, so $N(S) = 4.$

40. Of the six elements in the set, two of them are divisible by 4. So the probability, which is the number of favorable outcomes divided by the total number of outcomes, is $\frac{2}{6} = \frac{1}{3}.$

41. The result of transformation S is to rotate the figure by 180 degrees around the origin. This can also be described as the composite of a reflection over the x-axis and a reflection over the y-axis. So $S(x, y) = (-x, -y)$, which is choice (a).

42. The result of transformation T is to reduce the size of the figure to one-half in the x-direction and one-half in the y-direction. This can be described as $T(x, y) = (\frac{x}{2}, \frac{y}{2})$, which is choice (d).

CHAPTER 7   TRIANGLE CONGRUENCE

LESSON 7-1   (pp. 302–309)

1. A lean-to roof is a roof that has only one slanted side.

2. The Triangle Inequality is the statement that in any triangle, the sum of the lengths of two sides of the triangle must be greater than the length of the third side.

3.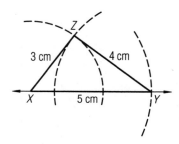

4.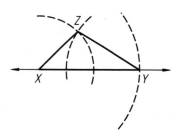

5. By the Triangle-Sum Theorem, the sum of the three angles of a triangle must be 180. So if two angles have measures x and y, then the measure of the third angle is $180 - (x + y)$ or $180 - x - y$.

6. In $\triangle ADC$ and $\triangle ABC$, $\overline{AC}$ is given as a bisector, so m$\angle DAC =$ m$\angle BAC$ and m$\angle DCA =$ m$\angle BCA$ by the definition of angle bisector (meaning). So $\angle B \cong \angle D$ because if two triangles have two pairs of angles congruent, then their third pair of angles is congruent.

7.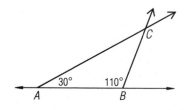

8.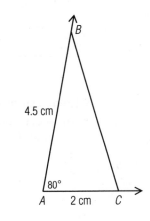

9.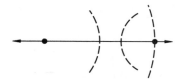

10.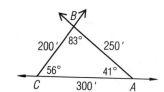

The sum of the two smaller lengths is not greater than the largest length, so these three lengths violate the Triangle Inequality and cannot be the lengths of three sides of a triangle.

125

11. a.

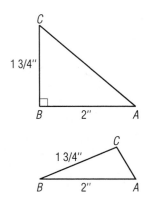

b. The SS condition is not a sufficient condition for congruence, so not all triangles will be congruent.

12. a.

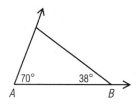

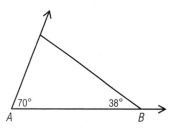

b. The AA condition is not a sufficient condition for congruence, so not all triangles will be congruent. However, AA is a sufficient condition for similarity, so all drawn triangles will have the same shape or be similar.

13. a.

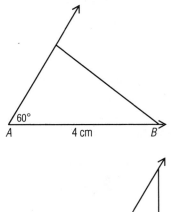

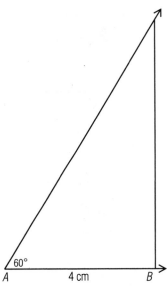

b. The SA condition is not a sufficient condition for congruence, so not all triangles will be congruent.

14. a.

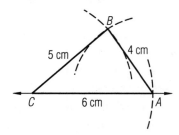

b. The SSS condition is a sufficient condition for congruence, so all triangles will be congruent.

15. a.

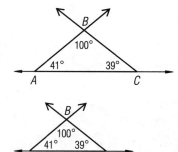

b. The AAA condition (like the AA condition) is not a sufficient condition for congruence (but is a sufficient condition for similarity). So not all triangles will have the same size (but they will have the same shape).

16. a.

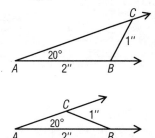

b. The SSA condition is not a sufficient condition for congruence, so not all triangles will be congruent.

17. a.

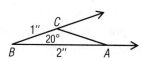

b. The SAS condition is a sufficient condition for congruence, so all triangles will be congruent.

18. a.

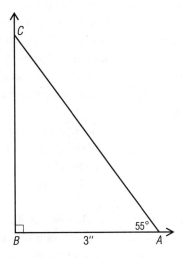

b. The ASA condition is a sufficient condition for congruence, so all triangles will be congruent.

19. a.

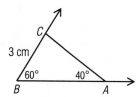

b. The AAS condition is a sufficient condition for congruence, so all triangles will be congruent.

20. If $\triangle QZP \cong \triangle KRA$, then three pairs of corresponding sides are congruent: $\overline{QZ} \cong \overline{KR}$, $\overline{QP} \cong \overline{KA}$, and $\overline{ZP} \cong \overline{RA}$ (in each pairing, the order of the letters for either or both segments can be switched, and the statements of congruence would still be true. For example, $\overline{QZ} \cong \overline{RK}$, $\overline{ZQ} \cong \overline{KR}$, and $\overline{ZQ} \cong \overline{RK}$). Also, three pairs of corresponding angles are congruent: $\angle Q \cong \angle K$, $\angle Z \cong \angle R$, and $\angle P \cong \angle A$. (Each angle can also be described using three letters, with the vertex as the middle letter.)

21. The composite of two reflections over parallel lines is a translation. (More specifically, it is a translation, in the direction perpendicular to the parallel lines, from the first-applied reflection to the second-applied reflection, at a distance twice that between the lines.)

22. By the Triangle-Sum Theorem, the sum of the three angles in $\triangle DEF$ is 180 degrees, so $4y + y + 72 = 180$. Then $5y = 108$ and $y = 21.6$. So m$\angle F = 21.6$ and m$\angle D = 4(21.6) = 86.4$.

23. The Kite Symmetry Theorem is the statement that the line containing the endpoints of a kite is a symmetry line for the kite.

24. The statement can be translated into the algebraic statement that m$\angle A > 90 - m\angle A$. From that it follows that 2m$\angle A > 90$ or m$\angle A > 45$. Also, since the angle has a complement, then its measure must be less than 90. So the measure must be greater than 45 and less than 90.

25.

The length of the third side must be less than the sum of the two given sides, and greater than their difference, so the length must be less than $91 + 38 = 129$ cm and greater than $91 - 38 = 53$ cm.

26.

"Hidden Pictures" puzzle by Christopher Wray from *Highlights for Children*, July-August, 1986.

LESSON 7–2 (pp. 310–316)

1. Four conditions that lead to triangle congruence are abbreviated SSS, SAS, ASA, and AAS.

2. **a.–b.** The phrase that appears in all the triangle congruence theorems ("then the two triangles are congruent") is the consequent; that is choice (b).

3. For the two triangles ABC and DOT, each side of one is congruent to a side of the other, so the triangles are congruent by the SSS Congruence Theorem.

4. The proof of the SSS Congruence Theorem uses the symmetry of a kite.

5. The proof of the SAS Congruence Theorem uses the Isosceles Triangle Symmetry Theorem, so it uses the symmetry of an isosceles triangle.

6. To have the SAS condition, the angle must be included by the two sides. So the additional information needed is that $\overline{BC} \cong \overline{DE}$; that is choice (a).

7. The ASA Congruence Theorem states that if, in two triangles, two angles and the included side of one are congruent to two angles and the included side of the other, then the triangles are congruent.

8. In triangle ACD, the two vertices for $\angle A$ and $\angle ADC$ are points A and D, so the side contained by those angles is segment $\overline{AD}$.

9. a. Line $\overleftrightarrow{FH}$ bisects $\angle EHG$, so the image of ray $\overrightarrow{HE}$ is ray $\overrightarrow{HG}$. So the image of E is on $\overleftrightarrow{HG}$ by the Side-Switching Theorem.

b. Line $\overleftrightarrow{FH}$ bisects $\angle EFG$, so the image of ray $\overrightarrow{FE}$ is ray $\overrightarrow{FG}$. So the image of E is on $\overleftrightarrow{FG}$ by the Side-Switching Theorem.

c. Because of the definition of congruence (that two figures are congruent if one is the result of a composite of reflections of the other), $\triangle EFH \cong \triangle GFH$.

10. Two sides and the included angle of one triangle are congruent to the corresponding parts of the other triangle. So the triangles are congruent by the SAS Congruence Theorem. To list the vertices in a correct order, note that $\angle B \cong \angle E$, and $\overline{BA} \cong \overline{EC}$, so $\triangle BAF \cong \triangle ECD$.

11. While two sides of one triangle are congruent to two sides of the other, and a pair of angles are congruent, the angles are not included by the two pairs of congruent sides. So this situation is **not** the ASA situation, and the triangles are not necessarily congruent. Here are triangles $JGK, HLI,$ and another triangle MNO to show that the triangles are not necessarily congruent.

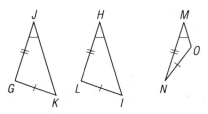

12. Two angles of one triangle are congruent to two angles of the other triangle (so then all three pairs of angles must be congruent), and one pair of sides is congruent. However, the congruent sides are not corresponding—they are opposite the non-corresponding angles in the two triangles. So this is **not** the AAS situation and the triangles are not necessarily congruent.

13. Two angles and the included side of one triangle are congruent to two angles and the included side of the other triangle, so the triangles are congruent by the ASA Congruence Theorem. To list the vertices in a correct order, note that vertex O in $\triangle NOY$ corresponds to vertex Y in $\triangle XYO$, and $\overline{OY} \cong \overline{YO}$. So the congruency can be stated as $\triangle OYN \cong \triangle YOX$.

14. The pair of congruent sides, $\overline{ET}$ and $\overline{TE}$, are opposite congruent angles, so the triangles are congruent by the AAS Congruence Theorem. Using the information that $\angle S$ and $\angle B$ are corresponding angles, and the two angles with vertex T are corresponding angles, a statement of the congruency is $\triangle STE \cong \triangle BTE$.

15. Two angles and the included side of one triangle are congruent to two angles and the included side of the other triangle, so the triangles are congruent by the ASA Congruence Theorem. Using the information that $\angle O$ and $\angle N$ are corresponding angles and that $\angle C$ and $\angle I$ are corresponding angles, a statement of the congruence is $\triangle OCG \cong \triangle NIP$.

16. a. The given segment congruencies indicate that point D corresponds with point J, point P with point K, and point O with point L. Moreover, points D, P, and O are in one triangle (and points J, K, and L in the other). So the statement of congruency is $\triangle DPO \cong \triangle JKL$.

b. If $OD = 5$ yards (and since $OD = LJ$), then $LJ = 5$ yards.

c. Since points O and L correspond, $\angle O \cong \angle L$.

d. If $m\angle P = 73$ (and since $m\angle P = m\angle K$), then $m\angle K = 73$.

17. a.

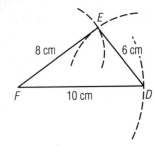

b. Yes, all accurately-drawn triangles should be congruent because of the SSS Congruence Theorem.

18. a. There are three possibilities:

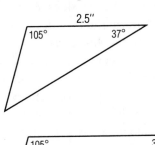

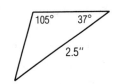

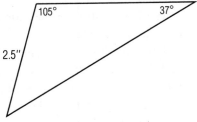

b. The triangles will not necessarily be congruent, because the given information of two pairs of angles and one pair of sides may not be either the AAS condition nor the ASA condition.

19. a.

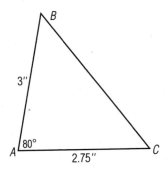

b. $\angle CAB$ is the angle included by the given sides $\overline{AB}$ and $\overline{CA}$. So all accurately-drawn triangles will be congruent to yours because of the SAS Congruence Theorem.

20. Side $\overline{BD}$ in each triangle is opposite the pair of congruent angles A and C. So $\triangle ABD \cong \triangle CBD$ by the AAS Congruence Theorem, so the left side ($\triangle ABD$) has the same "pattern outline" (same size and shape) as the right side ($\triangle CBD$).

21. Sally's construction determines two angles of the triangle and the included side. Anyone repeating her procedure should get a triangle congruent to hers because of the ASA Congruence Theorem.

22. In $\triangle ABC$, $m\angle A + m\angle B + m\angle C = 180$, by the Triangle-Sum Theorem, so $32 + 64 + m\angle C = 180$ by substitution, and $m\angle C = 180 - (32 + 64) = 84$. Then, since $m\angle F = m\angle C$ by the CPCF Theorem, $m\angle F = 84$ by the Transitive Property of Equality.

23. A square is a specific type of rhombus (it is a rhombus with right angles), a rhombus is a specific type of kite (it is a kite with both pairs of consecutive sides congruent), a kite is a specific type of quadrilateral, and a quadrilateral is a specific type of figure. So, from most general to most specific, the list is: figure, quadrilateral, kite, rhombus, square.

24. If $360 - 3x < 90$, then
$$270 - 3x < 0$$
$$270 < 3x$$
$$90 < x.$$
Since it is given that x is the measure of an angle, then x must be less than 180. Combining these conditions, $90 < x < 180$, so the angle is obtuse by the definition of obtuse angle (sufficient condition).

25.

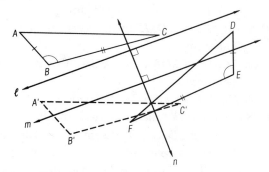

For lines m and ℓ, the effect of $r_m \circ r_\ell$ on $\triangle ABC$ is $\triangle A'B'C'$, so m and ℓ are parallel, the distance between them is half the distance between $\triangle ABC$ and $\triangle A'B'C'$, and ℓ (the first-applied line of reflection) is between $\triangle ABC$ and line m. Then line n is the perpendicular bisector of preimage-image pairs for $\triangle A'B'C'$ and $\triangle DEF$.

LESSON 7-3 (pp. 317–322)

1. a.

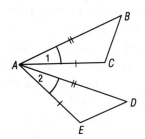

b. Two sides and the included angle of one triangle are congruent to two sides and the included angle of the other triangle, so the triangles are congruent by the SAS Congruence Theorem.

c. From the given, $\triangle ABC \cong \triangle ADE$ by the SAS Congruence Theorem. So $\angle B \cong \angle D$ by the CPCF Theorem.

131

2. a. $MC = MD$ and $ME = MF$ by the definition of midpoint (meaning).

b. $\angle CME \cong \angle DMF$ by the Vertical Angle Theorem.

c. $\triangle CME \cong \triangle DMF$ by the SAS Congruence Theorem.

d. $\overline{EC} \cong \overline{FD}$ by the CPCF Theorem.

3. Steps 1 and 2 of the proof, to show that $\triangle ABC \cong \triangle CDA$, are the same as in Example 3. The next step is that $\angle 2 \cong \angle 4$ because of the CPCF Theorem, and the last step is that $\overleftrightarrow{BC} \parallel \overleftrightarrow{AD}$ because of the AIA $= \Rightarrow \parallel$ Lines Theorem.

4. The converse of the Isosceles Triangle Theorem is that if two angles of a triangle are congruent, then the sides opposite those angles are congruent.

5. a. In the proof of the converse of the Isosceles Triangle Theorem, the justification for step 2, that $\overline{AD} \cong \overline{AD}$, is the Reflexive Property of Congruence.

b. The justification for step 4, that $\overline{AB} \cong \overline{AC}$, is the CPCF Theorem.

6. a-b. $\angle A$ and $\angle C$ have the same measure, so by the converse of the Isosceles Triangle Theorem, the sides opposite them are congruent, or $\overline{AB} \cong \overline{CB}$.

7. Draw $\overline{AC}$ (the justification for drawing it is the Point-Line-Plane Postulate). Then, since $AB = CD$ and $BC = AD$ from the given, and $\overline{AC} \cong \overline{AC}$ by the Reflexive Property of Congruence, $\triangle ABC \cong \triangle CDA$ by the SSS Congruence Theorem.

8. a. $\overline{AC} \cong \overline{AC}$ by the Reflexive Property of Congruence.

b. $\angle XCA \cong \angle YCA$ by the definition of angle bisector (meaning).

c. $\triangle ACX \cong \triangle ACY$ by the SAS Congruence Theorem.

d. $\angle X \cong \angle Y$ by the CPCF Theorem.

9. $\triangle ABC$ is isosceles, with vertex B, so $\overline{AB} \cong \overline{CB}$ by the definition of isosceles triangle (meaning). Then $\angle A \cong \angle C$ by the Isosceles Triangle Converse Theorem. Also, D is the midpoint of $\overline{AC}$, so $AD = CD$ by the definition of midpoint (meaning). So $\triangle ABD \cong \triangle CBD$ by the SAS Congruence Theorem. (There is another proof using $\overline{BD} \cong \overline{BD}$ and the SSS Congruence Theorem.)

10. a. There are four triangles with vertical angles: $\triangle DGJ$ and $\triangle DAB$, $\triangle DGA$ and $\triangle DJB$. There are two more triangles with base $\overline{GJ}$: $\triangle GJB$ and $\triangle GJA$; and there are two more triangles with base $\overline{AB}$: $\triangle ABG$ and $\triangle ABJ$.

b. There are three pairs of congruent triangles:
$\triangle AGD \cong \triangle BJD$
(by the SAS Congruence Theorem)
$\triangle AGJ \cong \triangle BJG$
(by the SSS Congruence Theorem)
$\triangle AGB \cong \triangle BJA$
(by the SSS Congruence Theorem).

11. a. *True*, the triangles must be congruent because of the SSS Congruence Theorem.

b. *False*, the triangles can have different orientation.

12. The SAS Congruence Theorem cannot be used to prove $\triangle ADC$ congruent to $\triangle ABC$ because the pair of congruent angles ($\angle DAC$ and $\angle BAC$) are not included by the pairs of congruent sides.

You can show that $\triangle ADC \cong \triangle ABC$. First, find P on $\overrightarrow{AC}$ so $CP = CA$. Then $ABPD$ is a parallelogram (Sufficient Conditions, part c) and all 4 angles formed by $\overline{PA}$ are congruent. Then both $\overline{AB}$ and $\overline{AD}$ are congruent to $\overline{PB}$, so $AD = AB$, and $\triangle ADC \cong \triangle ABC$ by SSS.

13. The pair of congruent angles, $\angle ACB$ and $\angle DCE$, are included by the two pairs of congruent sides ($AC = EC$ given, $BC = DC$ by the definition of midpoint, meaning), so the two triangles, $\triangle ABC$ and $\triangle EDC$, are congruent by the SAS Congruence Theorem.

14. Given that $HF = HJ$ and $HG = HI$, and since $\angle FHG \cong \angle JHI$ by the Vertical Angle Theorem, then $\triangle FGH \cong \triangle JIH$ by the SAS Congruence Theorem and $\overline{IJ} \cong \overline{GF}$ by the CPCF Theorem.

15.

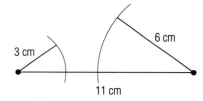

It is impossible for a triangle to have sides with lengths 3 cm, 6 cm and 11 cm, because that would violate the Triangle Inequality (the sum of the two shorter sides is not longer than the longest side).

16. If all five segments are congruent, then some of the conclusions are that triangles ABC and ADC are congruent, that each triangle is equilateral, that m$\angle D$ = m$\angle B$ = m$\angle DAC$ = m$\angle CAB$ = m$\angle ACB$ = m$\angle ACD$ = 60, that m$\angle DAB$ = m$\angle DCB$ = 120, and that $ABCD$ is a rhombus. Other conclusions can be the properties of a rhombus (for example, $\overleftrightarrow{AC}$ is a symmetry line, as line $\overleftrightarrow{DB}$ would be, and opposite sides are parallel).

17. If the perimeter of $ABCD$ is x, then the length of each of the five segments is one-fourth the perimeter, or $\frac{x}{4}$, and the length of segment AC is $\frac{x}{4}$.

18. By the Triangle-Sum Theorem, the sum of the measures of the three angles of any triangle is 180. For a right triangle, one of the angles has measure 90, so the sum of the other two angle measures (that is, the sum of the measures of the acute angles) is 90.

19. a.

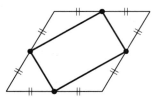

b. While opinions may vary, the figure thus formed is a rectangle but not necessarily a square and the conjecture is false.
By drawing the diagonals of the rhombus, and using the result that the sides of the new figure are parallel to the diagonals of the rhombus (which are perpendicular), it can be shown that the figure is a rectangle.

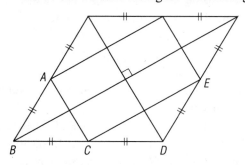

However, since $AB = BC = CD = DE$, if the new figure were a square, then $AC = CE$, and $\triangle ABE \cong \triangle CDE$ (by SSS) and $\angle ABC \cong \angle CDE$. But it is not necessary that $\angle ABC \cong \angle CDE$. So the new figure need not be a square. (It will only be a square if the original rhombus happened to be a square.)

133

20. **a.** An "SSSS condition for quadrilaterals" would be a statement that if, in two quadrilaterals, four sides of one are congruent respectively to four sides of the other, then the two quadrilaterals are congruent.

b.

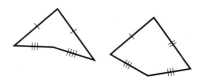

LESSON 7–4 (pp. 323–326)

1. **a.** There are 8 triangles: 4 with a vertex at S (triangles SQU, SDA, SDQ, and SUA); 2 more with common base $\overline{UA}$ (triangles UAD and UAQ); and 2 more with common base $\overline{QD}$ (triangles QDA and QDU).

b. $\triangle QUA$ might be congruent to $\triangle DAU$.

c. Another pair of overlapping triangles that might be congruent have common base $\overline{QD}$: triangles QDU and DQA.

2. **a.** $\angle A \cong \angle A$ by the Reflexive Property of Congruence.

b. $\triangle ADC \cong \triangle AEB$ by the SAS Congruence Theorem.

c. $\angle DCA \cong \angle EBA$ by the CPCF Theorem.

3. The first three steps of the proof, to show that $\triangle GHJ \cong \triangle GKI$, are the same as in Example 2. Then step 4 is that $\angle HGJ \cong \angle KGI$ by the CPCF Theorem.

4. Given that $\overline{QU} \cong \overline{AD}$ and $\overline{QA} \cong \overline{UD}$, then also $\overline{UA} \cong \overline{AU}$ by the Reflexive Property of Congruence. So $\triangle QUA \cong \triangle DAU$ by the SSS Congruence Theorem, and $\angle DUA \cong \angle QAU$ (that is, $\angle 1 \cong \angle 2$) by the CPCF Theorem.

5. Show that $\triangle AEB \cong \triangle ADC$: $AD = AE$ and $\text{m}\angle D = \text{m}\angle E$, given, and $\angle A \cong \angle A$ by the Reflexive Property of Congruence. So the two triangles are congruent by the ASA Congruence Theorem, and $EB = CD$ by the CPCF Theorem.

6. Show that $\triangle AEV \cong \triangle IVE$: $\overline{AE} \cong \overline{IV}$ and $\angle AEV \cong \angle EVI$, given, and $\overline{EV} \cong \overline{VE}$ by the Reflexive Property of Congruence. So the triangles are congruent by the SAS Congruence Theorem, and $\overline{AV} \cong \overline{IE}$ by the CPCF Theorem.

7. Show that $\triangle PRS \cong \triangle QSR$: $PR = QS$ and $PS = QR$, given, and $RS = SR$ by the Reflexive Property of Equality. So the triangles are congruent by the SSS Congruence Theorem, and $\text{m}\angle P = \text{m}\angle Q$ by the CPCF Theorem.

8. Triangle IGH is isosceles, so $\text{m}\angle G = \text{m}\angle H$ by the Isosceles Triangle Theorem. Then, with the given that $\overline{GJ} \cong \overline{HK}$ and $\overline{GI} \cong \overline{HI}$, $\triangle GJI \cong \triangle HKI$ by the SAS Congruence Theorem, and $\overline{JI} \cong \overline{KI}$ by the CPCF Theorem.

9. **a.** $\angle AEB \cong \angle FEG$ by the Vertical Angle Theorem.

b. $\triangle ABE \cong \triangle FGE$ by the SAS Congruence Theorem.

c. $\angle FGE \cong \angle ABE$ by the CPCF Theorem.

d. $\angle ABE \cong \angle DBC$ by the Vertical Angle Theorem.

e. $\angle FGE \cong \angle DBC$ by the Transitive Property of Congruence.

10. Since $\overline{RQ} \parallel \overline{UT}$, then $\text{m}\angle Q = \text{m}\angle U$ because $\parallel$ lines $\Rightarrow$ AIA =. $QS = US$ by the definition of midpoint (meaning), and $\text{m}\angle QSR = \text{m}\angle UST$ by the Vertical Angle Theorem. So $\triangle QSR \cong \triangle UST$ by the ASA Congruence Theorem, and $\overline{RS} \cong \overline{TS}$ by the CPCF Theorem. So S is the midpoint of $\overline{RT}$ by the definition of midpoint (sufficient condition).

11. Since $PC = PC$ (Reflexive Property of Equality), $m\angle PCA = m\angle PCB$ (since each equals 90), and $CA = CB$ (given), then $\triangle PCA \cong \triangle PCB$ by the SAS Congruence Theorem, and $PB = PA$ by the CPCF Theorem.

12. **a.**

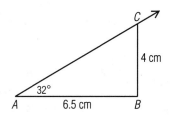

b. The given angle, $\angle A$, is not included by the given sides $\overline{AB}$ and $\overline{BC}$. So this is not the SAS condition. The two triangles in 12a are possible.

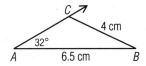

13. *True*; translations preserve congruence, so the two figures are congruent.

14. *True*; draw figure $MOSQ$. Then $\overline{QS}$ is the image of $\overline{MO}$, and they must be parallel and congruent by the definition of translation. So $MOSQ$ is a parallelogram by the Sufficient Conditions for a Parallelogram Theorem, and $MQ = OS$ by the Properties of a Parallelogram Theorem.

15. Given that $0 < 180 - 2y$, then
$$2y < 180 \text{ and}$$
$$y < 90.$$
Also, $y > 0$ since y is given to be the measure of an angle. So y, the measure of an angle, is between 0 and 90, so the angle is acute by the definition of acute angle (sufficient condition).

16. Using $WZ = WY + YZ$, you get $25 = 13 + YZ$, so $YZ = 12$. Then, using $XZ = XY + YZ$, you get $17 = XY + 12$, so $XY = 5$. Finally, using $WY = WX + XY$, you get $13 = WX + 5$, so $WX = 8$.

17. The question can be stated as follows: If, in two quadrilaterals, all four pairs of corresponding sides are congruent and one pair of corresponding angles is congruent, are the quadrilaterals necessarily congruent? The answer is no, the quadrilaterals are not necessarily congruent. Here is a counterexample—SSASS is satisfied, but the quadrilaterals are not congruent.

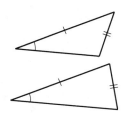

LESSON 7-5 (pp. 327–332)

1.

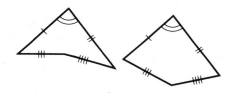

2. **a.** A triangle with sides represented by H and L is a right triangle.

   b. H represents the length of the hypotenuse (opposite the right angle), and L represents the length of a leg.

3. The proof of the HL Congruence Theorem uses the AAS Congruence Theorem, the Isosceles Triangle Theorem, and the Angle Addition Property. It does not use the Triangle-Sum Theorem, so the answer is choice (c).

4. The SSA condition leads to congruence if the corresponding, non-included angles are right angles or if the sides opposite the congruent angles are longer than the other congruent sides.

5. **a.** The two triangles are right triangles, with congruent hypotenuses and a pair of congruent legs; the theorem is the HL Congruence Theorem.

   b. $\angle B$ corresponds with $\angle E$, and $\overline{BA}$ corresponds with $\overline{EF}$, so $\triangle BAC \cong \triangle EFD$.

6. **a.** The two triangles are right triangles, and the right angles are included by the two pairs of congruent sides; the theorem is the SAS Congruence Theorem.

   b. $\angle G$ corresponds with $\angle K$, and leg $\overline{GI}$ corresponds with leg $\overline{KL}$, so $\triangle GIH \cong \triangle KLJ$.

7. **a.** The two triangles are right triangles, with congruent hypotenuses and a pair of congruent legs; the theorem is the HL Congruence Theorem.

   b. $\angle A$ corresponds with $\angle C$, and leg $\overline{AD}$ corresponds with leg $\overline{CD}$, so $\triangle ADB \cong \triangle CDB$.

8. **a-c.**

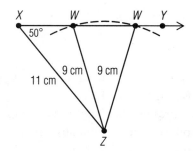

d. No, not all triangles will be congruent. The construction, which can be described as an SSA condition, allows for two different triangles.

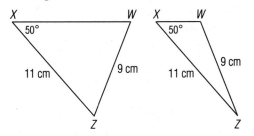

9. To show that $\triangle XZW \cong \triangle XYV$: both are right triangles, and it is given that hypotenuse $\overline{WZ} \cong$ hypotenuse $\overline{VY}$ and leg $\overline{ZX} \cong$ leg $\overline{YX}$, so the triangles are congruent by the HL Congruence Theorem. So $\angle W \cong \angle V$ by the CPCF Theorem.

10. **a.** To show that $\triangle PBA \cong \triangle RBA$: it is given that both are right triangles with a pair of congruent legs. Also, the hypotenuses are congruent by the Reflexive Property of Congruence. So the triangles are congruent by the HL Congruence Theorem.

   b. $PB = RB$ by the CPCF Theorem (and $PA = RA$, given), so $PBRA$ is a kite by the definition of kite (sufficient condition).

   c. Answers may vary. Some samples are that ray $\overrightarrow{AB}$ bisects $\angle PAR$ and $\angle PBR$ or that $\overleftrightarrow{AB}$ is the perpendicular bisector of $\overline{PR}$ (proofs may use the result that $\overline{AB}$ is the symmetry diagonal of the kite).

11. **a.** $OP = OA$ by the definition of circle (meaning).

   b. $OQ = OB$ by the definition of circle (meaning).

   c. $\triangle ABO \cong \triangle PQO$ by the SsA Congruence Theorem (from steps 1, 2, 3 and the given)

12. It is given that $\triangle ABD$ and $\triangle CBD$ are both right triangles with congruent hypotenuses, and $\overline{BD} \cong \overline{BD}$ by the Reflexive Property of Congruence. So $\triangle ABD \cong \triangle CBD$ by the HL Congruence Theorem.

13. June's hand and April's hand determine right triangles with the maypole, segments from their hands perpendicular to the maypole, and the streamers. The streamers (hypotenuses) are the same length, and the triangles involve the same part of the maypole, so the triangles are congruent by the HL Congruence Theorem.

14. a. Base angles WZY and XYZ are congruent by the definition of isosceles trapezoid (meaning).
    b. The non-parallel sides of the isosceles trapezoid, $\overline{WZ}$ and $\overline{XY}$, are congruent by the Isosceles Trapezoid Theorem.
    c. $\overline{ZY} \cong \overline{ZY}$ by the Reflexive Property of Congruence.
    d. In triangles WZY and XYZ, two sides and the included angle of one triangle are congruent to two sides and the included angle of the other triangle; that is the SAS Congruence Theorem (steps 1, 2, 3).
    e. $\overline{XZ} \cong \overline{WY}$ by the CPCF Theorem.

15. a. $BE = BD + DE$ and $DE + EC = DC$ by the definition of betweenness (meaning). Then, since $BD = EC$, $BD + DE = EC + DE$ (substitution), and $BE = DC$ by the Transitive Property of Equality. With $AB = AC$ and, in isosceles triangle ABC, $\angle B \cong \angle C$, then $\triangle ABE \cong \triangle ACD$ by the SAS Congruence Theorem. So $\angle ADE \cong \angle AED$ by the CPCF Theorem.

    b. In triangle ADE, $AD = AE$ because if two angles of a triangle are congruent, the sides opposite these angles are congruent. So $\triangle ADE$ is isosceles by the definition of isosceles triangle (sufficient condition). (It may be easier to prove part **b** first, by showing $\triangle ABD \cong \triangle ACE$ by SAS so that $AD = AE$. Then $\angle ADE \cong \angle AED$ by the Isosceles Triangle Theorem.)

16. Using $\overleftrightarrow{XY}$ as a symmetry line, a triangle congruent to $\triangle AGX$ is $\triangle DEX$. Then, using $\overleftrightarrow{AB}$ as a symmetry line, two more congruent triangles are $\triangle AGY$ and $\triangle DEY$.

17. a.
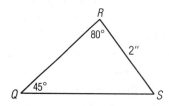

    b. Yes, all triangles will be congruent because this is the AAS condition.

18. a. The definition of congruence (if there is a composite of reflections mapping one figure onto another, then the figures are congruent) is a justification for the statement that $\triangle ABC \cong \triangle DEF$.

    b. The Flip-Flop Theorem (if a figure is an image of a second figure, then the second figure is an image of the first) is a justification for the statement that r$(\triangle DEF) = \triangle ABC$.

    c. The Figure Reflection Theorem is a justification for any of the following statements: r$(\overline{AB}) = \overline{DE}$, r$(\overline{BC}) = \overline{EF}$, r$(\overline{AC}) = \overline{DF}$, r$(\angle A) = \angle D$, r$(\angle B) = \angle E$, r$(\angle C) = \angle F$.

137

19. If two quadrilaterals each have opposite angles that are right angles, the quadrilaterals do not have to be congruent (they do not even have to have the same shape). Here is a counterexample:

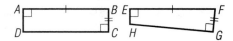

LESSON 7–6 (pp. 333–338)

1. Step 3: $\overline{PL} \parallel \overline{AR}$ by the definition of parallelogram (meaning).
Step 4: $\angle 5 \cong \angle 6$ because $\parallel$ lines $\Rightarrow$ AIA $=$.
Step 5: $\overline{PR} \cong \overline{RP}$ by the Reflexive Property of Congruence.
Step 6: The two triangles are congruent by the ASA Congruence Theorem.

2. a. In parallelogram $ABCD$, the congruent sides are the pairs of opposite sides: $\overline{AC} \cong \overline{BD}$ and $\overline{AB} \cong \overline{CD}$.
  b. The congruent angles are the pairs of opposite angles: $\angle A \cong \angle D$ and $\angle B \cong \angle C$.
  c. The midpoints of the diagonals, $\overline{AD}$ and $\overline{BC}$, are the same point.

3. a. If $ABDC$ is a rhombus, then all four sides are congruent, by the definition of rhombus (meaning).
  b-c. These answers are the same as in question 2—the opposite pairs of angles are congruent ($\angle A \cong \angle D$ and $\angle B \cong \angle C$), and the midpoints of the diagonals ($\overline{AD}$ and $\overline{BC}$) are the same point.

4. a-b. Since bases $\overline{ZO}$ and $\overline{ID}$ are parallel (by the definition of trapezoid—meaning), then the theorem stating that the distance between parallel lines is constant means that segments $\overline{RD}$ and $\overline{OP}$ are congruent.

5. A regular polygon with four sides is usually called a square.

6. a.

b.

7.

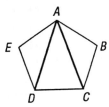

You can draw diagonals $\overline{AD}$ and $\overline{AC}$ in regular pentagon $ABCDE$ by the Point-Line-Plane Postulate. Then, by the definition of regular pentagon (meaning), $AB = AE$ and $BC = ED$, and also $\angle B \cong \angle E$. So $\triangle ABC \cong \triangle AED$ by the SAS Congruence Theorem, and $\overline{AC} \cong \overline{AD}$ by the CPCF Theorem.

8. a. There are 4 triangles with a vertex point T, 2 more (larger) triangles with $\overline{RH}$ as a base, and 2 more (large) triangles with $\overline{IG}$ as a base, so there are 8 triangles formed.

138

b. The 8 triangles form several sets of congruent triangles:

$\triangle RTH \cong \triangle ITG$

$\triangle RTI \cong \triangle HTG$.

The other 4 triangles are all congruent (they are listed here in the order "smaller acute angle, larger acute angle, right angle"): $\triangle RGH \cong \triangle HIR \cong \triangle IHG \cong \triangle GRI$. (It is also true that the triangles with a vertex at T are isosceles, so additional sets of congruent triangles could be $\triangle RTH \cong \triangle HTR$, $\triangle HTG \cong \triangle GTH$, and so on.)

9. If $OQ = PR = x$, that means the diagonals are congruent (and, incidently, the parallelogram is a rectangle). Since the diagonals intersect at their midpoints, then $OS = RS = QS = PS = \frac{x}{2}$.

10. If $m\angle POR = 102$, then since the angle opposite $\angle POR$ has the same measure, $m\angle PQR = 102$. Also, since consecutive angles of $PQRS$ are supplementary, $m\angle ORQ = m\angle OPQ = 180 - 102 = 78$.

11. a.

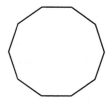

b. Using the result of the Polygon-Sum Theorem, $S = (n - 2)180$ where S is the sum of the measures of the angles, then $n = 10$ for a regular decagon and $S = 8(180) = 1440$.

c. For a regular decagon (or any regular polygon), the angles are all congruent. So if the sum of the measures of 10 congruent angles is 1440, then the measure of each angle is $\frac{1440}{10} = 144$.

12.

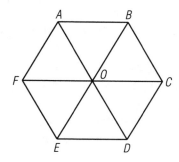

a-b. The six triangles are equilateral, so $AB = BC = CD = DE = EF = FA$ by the definition of equilateral triangle (meaning) and the Transitive Property of Equality. Also, the two angles with vertex A have measure 60 (since $\triangle AOB$ is equilateral) so $m\angle FAB = 120$; similarly, $m\angle ABC = m\angle BCD = m\angle CDE = m\angle DEF = mEFA = 120$. So $ABCDE$ is a hexagon with all sides congruent and all angles congruent, which means it is a regular hexagon by the definition of regular polygon (sufficient condition).

13. Triangles AEF and BDC are right triangles because perpendicular lines form right angles. Since it is given that $AF = BC$ and $AE = BD$, then $\triangle AEF \cong \triangle BDC$ by the HL Congruence Theorem, and $\angle F \cong \angle C$ by the CPCF Theorem.

14. The pair of congruent angles are not included by the pairs of congruent sides (in $\triangle ABC$), so this is not the SAS condition, and the pair of congruent sides is not the hypotenuse and leg (in $\triangle XYZ$), so this is not the HL condition. In short, the given information is not for corresponding parts in the two triangles, so you cannot conclude that the triangles are congruent.

15. X is the midpoint of $\overline{MN}$, so $MX = XN$ by the definition of midpoint (meaning). Then, in triangles MXZ and NXY, it is given that $\angle M \cong \angle N$ and $\angle MXZ \cong \angle NXY$. So $\triangle MXZ \cong \triangle NXY$ by the ASA Congruence Theorem, and $\angle Y \cong \angle Z$ by the CPCF Theorem.

16. Since $\triangle PTS$ is isosceles with vertex angle T, then $TP = TS$ by the definition of isosceles triangle (meaning) and so $\angle P \cong \angle S$ by the Isosceles Triangle Theorem. Since it is also given that m$\angle PTQ =$ m$\angle STR$, then $\triangle TPQ \cong \triangle TSR$ by the ASA Congruence Theorem. (**That is part a.**) Then $TQ = TR$ by the CPCF Theorem, and $\triangle TQR$ is isosceles by the definition of isosceles (sufficient condition). (**That is part b.**)

17. a.

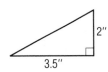

2″
3.5″

b. Since the given information is two sides and the angle included by them, this is the SAS condition, which is sufficient for congruency. So all correctly-drawn triangles will be congruent.

18. Lines $\overleftrightarrow{AB}$ and $\overleftrightarrow{CD}$ are two coplanar lines each perpendicular to the same line m, so $\overline{AB} \parallel \overline{CD}$ by the Two Perpendiculars Theorem.

19. The given information is a pair of congruent sides and a pair of congruent angles.
To have the ASA condition, you need another pair of congruent angles such that the pair of congruent sides is included by the two pairs of angles. That additional information must be $\angle B \cong \angle X$.
To have the AAS condition, you need another pair of congruent angles such that the pair of congruent sides is not included by the two pairs of angles. That additional information must be $\angle C \cong \angle Z$.
To have the SAS condition, you need another pair of congruent sides such that the pair of congruent angles is included by the two pairs of sides. That additional information must be $\overline{AC} \cong \overline{YZ}$.
(There is another possible answer. To have the SsA condition, which is that two sides and the angle opposite the longer of the two sides are congruent to corresponding parts in a second triangle. That additional information is either (1) $\overline{BC} \cong \overline{ZX}$, $BC > BA$, and m$\angle A >$ m$\angle C$ or (2) $\overline{AC} \cong \overline{YZ}$, $AC > AB$, and m$\angle B >$ m$\angle C$.)

20. There are many possible answers. Every instance of "reading up" and "reading down" on the Quadrilateral Hierarchy Theorem provides a sample:
True: If a figure is a square, then it is a rectangle.
False: If a figure is a rectangle, then it is a square.
True: If a figure is a rhombus, then it is a parallelogram.
False: If a figure is a parallelogram, then it is a rhombus.

21. a. Start with the diagonals. For diagonal $\overline{AC}$, it is in 2 triangles, $\triangle ACB$ and $\triangle ACV$. Similarly, each of the other 4 diagonals is in 2 triangles, so that accounts for 10 triangles.

Next, consider segment $\overline{AB}$. It is in 4 more triangles: $\triangle ABY$, $\triangle ABX$, $\triangle ABZ$, and $\triangle ABD$. Similarly, the other 4 sides of $ABCDE$ are each in 4 triangles. That accounts for 20 triangles.

Also, points A, B, C, D, and E are the vertex angles of small isosceles triangles AYZ, BXY, etc.; that is 5 more triangles. (The points are also the vertex angles of large triangles ACD etc., but they have already been counted.) So there are $10 + 20 + 5 = 35$ triangles in the drawing.

b. All the sets of congruent triangles are isosceles triangles.

One set involves the diagonals:
$\triangle ACB \cong \triangle BDC \cong \triangle CED \cong \triangle DAE \cong \triangle EBA \cong \triangle ACV \cong \triangle BDZ \cong \triangle CEY \cong \triangle DAX \cong \triangle EBW$

Two sets have as bases the sides of the regular pentagon:
$\triangle ABY \cong \triangle BCX \cong \triangle CDW \cong \triangle DEV \cong \triangle EAZ \cong \triangle ABD \cong \triangle BCE \cong \triangle CDA \cong \triangle DEB \cong \triangle EAC$.

Another set of congruent triangles are the small isosceles triangles with vertex angles at the vertices of the large pentagon:
$\triangle AYZ \cong \triangle BXY \cong \triangle CWX \cong \triangle DVW \cong \triangle EZV$.

Another set of congruent triangles, also isosceles, have the sides of the pentagon as their congruent sides and their vertex angles are acute:
$\triangle ABZ \cong \triangle ABX \cong \triangle BCY \cong \triangle BCW \cong \triangle CDX \cong \triangle CDV \cong \triangle DEZ \cong \triangle DEW \cong \triangle EAY \cong \triangle EAV$.

(Since all the triangles are isosceles, additional congruence statements can be made, like $\triangle YAB \cong \triangle YBA$, and so on.)

LESSON 7-7 (pp. 339–343)

1. Some of the properties of parallelograms are that opposite sides are parallel (definition), both pairs of opposite sides are congruent, both pairs of opposite angles are congruent, the diagonals bisect each other, and/or one pair of sides is parallel and congruent.

2. The definition of a parallelogram (sufficient condition) is that if a quadrilateral has two pairs of sides that are parallel, then the figure is a parallelogram.

3. Four sufficient conditions for a parallelogram are that opposite sides are parallel (definition), both pairs of opposite sides are congruent, both pairs of opposite angles are congruent, the diagonals bisect each other, and/or one pair of sides is parallel and congruent.

4. The following is a property of a rectangle: If a figure is a rectangle, then the diagonals are congruent. The converse (If the diagonals of a quadrilateral are congruent, then the figure is a rectangle) is false, as shown by these counterexamples:

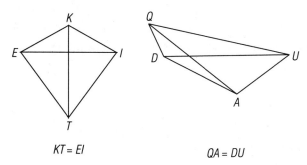

$KT = EI$ $QA = DU$

5. Step 6: the two triangles, *ABD* and *CDB,* are congruent, so ∠*ADB* ≅ ∠*CBD* by the CPCF Theorem.

Step 7: ∠*ADB* and ∠*CBD* are alternate interior angles for lines $\overleftrightarrow{AD}$ and $\overleftrightarrow{BC}$, so $\overleftrightarrow{AD}$ ∥ $\overleftrightarrow{BC}$ because AIA = ⇒ ∥ lines.

6. If diagonal $\overline{AC}$ is drawn instead of diagonal $\overline{BD}$, the "conclusions" for the proof are changed, but the "justifications" will stay the same. The "conclusions" are:

1. Draw $\overline{AC}$.
2. $\overline{AC} \cong \overline{AC}$
3. Δ*BAC* ≅ Δ*DCA*
4. ∠*BAC* ≅ ∠*DCA*
5. $\overline{AB} \parallel \overline{DC}$
6. ∠*BCA* ≅ ∠*DAC*
7. $\overline{BC} \parallel \overline{AD}$
8. *ABCD* is a parallelogram.

7. 1. You can draw $\overline{WY}$ by the Point-Line-Plane Postulate.

2. *WY* = *WY* by the Reflexive Property of Equality.

3. m∠*XWY* = m∠*ZYW* because ∥ lines ⇒ AIA = .

4. Δ*WZY* ≅ Δ*YXW* by the SAS Congruence Theorem.

5. m∠*ZWY* = m∠ *XYW* by the CPCF Theorem.

6. $\overline{WZ} \parallel \overline{XY}$ because AIA = ⇒ ∥ lines.

7. *WXYZ* is a parallelogram by the definition of parallelogram (sufficient condition).

8.

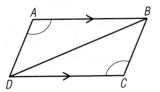

Draw diagonal $\overline{BD}$. Then $\overline{BD} \cong \overline{BD}$ (Reflexive Property of Congruence), ∠*A* ≅ ∠*C* (given), and ∠*ABD* ≅ ∠*CDB* (∥ lines ⇒ AIA = .) So Δ*ABD* ≅Δ*CDB* by the AAS Congruence Theorem.

There are many ways to finish the proof. One is to show that $\overline{AB} \cong \overline{CD}$ by the CPCF Theorem, and so *ABCD* is a parallelogram by the Sufficient Conditions for a Parallelogram Theorem (part d).

9. If the two meter sticks are joined together, and the two yardsticks are joined together, then the figure is a kite by the definition of kite (sufficient condition). If the meter sticks and yardsticks alternate, then the figure is a parallelogram by the Sufficient Conditions for a Parallelogram Theorem (part a).

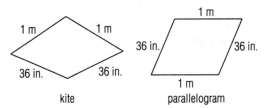

10. **a.** The sum of the measures of the two angles is 180 by the Linear Pair Theorem.

b. ∠*WXV* and ∠*W* are alternate interior angles for lines $\overleftrightarrow{WZ}$ and $\overleftrightarrow{XY}$, so $\overleftrightarrow{WZ} \parallel \overleftrightarrow{XY}$ because AIA = ⇒ ∥ lines.

c. ∠*WXV* and ∠*Y* are corresponding angles for lines $\overleftrightarrow{WX}$ and $\overleftrightarrow{ZY}$, so $\overleftrightarrow{WX} \parallel \overleftrightarrow{ZY}$ because corr. ∠s = ⇒ ∥ lines.

d. From steps 5 and 7, *WXYZ* is a parallelogram by the definition of parallelogram (sufficient condition).

11. Given that V, W, X, and Y are parallelograms, then each pair of "vertical" sides is parallel (by the definition of parallelogram—meaning), and congruent (Properties of a Parallelogram Theorem). So, by the Transitive Property of Parallels and the Transitive Property of Equality, the two "vertical" sides of figure Z are parallel and congruent. Hence Z is a parallelogram by the Sufficient Conditions for a Parallelogram Theorem (part d).

12. **a.** $\overline{AO} \cong \overline{OC}$ and $\overline{DO} \cong \overline{OB}$ by the definition of midpoint (meaning).

   b. $\angle AOD \cong \angle COB$ by the Vertical Angle Theorem.

   c. $\triangle AOD \cong \triangle COB$ by the SAS Congruence Theorem (steps 1 and 2).

   d. $\overline{AD} \cong \overline{BC}$ by the CPCF Theorem.

   e. $\angle ADO \cong \angle CBO$ by the CPCF Theorem.

   f. $\overline{AD} \parallel \overline{BC}$ because AIA = $\Rightarrow \parallel$ lines. $ABCD$ is a parallelogram by the Sufficient Conditions for a Parallelogram Theorem (part d).

13. If both pairs of opposite sides of a quadrilateral are congruent, then the figure is a parallelogram by the Sufficient Conditions for a Parallelogram Theorem (part a). So then the opposite angles of that quadrilateral are congruent by the Properties of a Parallelogram Theorem.

14. **a.** Use the formula $S = (n - 2)180$ from the Polygon-Sum Theorem where n is the number of sides and S is the sum of the measures of the angles. So, for an octagon, $n = 8$ and $S = (8 - 2)180 = 6(180) = 1080$.

b-c. From part **a**, the sum of the measures of the angles for any octagon is 1080. So for a regular octagon, the sum of the measures of the angles will still be 1080. Since all 8 angles of a regular octagon have the same measure (by the definition of regular polygon—meaning), then the measure of each angle of a regular octagon is $\frac{1080}{8} = 135$.

15.

$ABCD$ is a rectangle, so m$\angle ADC =$ m$\angle BCD = 90$ by the definition of rectangle (meaning) and the Transitive Property of Equality. $ABCD$ is also a parallelogram, by the Quadrilateral Hierarchy Theorem, so $AD = BC$ by the Properties of a Parallelogram Theorem. Then, since $DC = CD$ by the Reflexive Property of Equality, $\triangle ADC \cong \triangle BCD$ by the SAS Congruence Theorem, so $AC = BD$ by the CPCF Theorem.

16. The HL Congruence Theorem states that if, in two right triangles, the hypotenuse and leg of one are congruent to the hypotenuse and leg of the other, then the two triangles are congruent.

17. a.

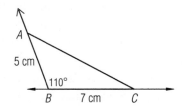

b–c. The given information is the SAS condition, which is sufficient for congruence. So all correctly-drawn triangles will be congruent.

18. a.

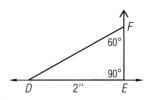

b–c. The given information is the AAS condition, which is sufficient for congruence. So all correctly-drawn triangles will be congruent.

19. a.

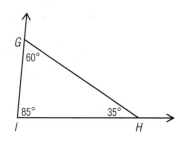

b–c. The given information is the AAA condition, which is not sufficient for congruence. (The triangles will, however, have the same shape so they are "similar.") So all correctly-drawn triangles will not necessarily be congruent.

20. If two quadrilaterals have a pair of opposite sides congruent and a pair of opposite angles congruent, the figure is not necessarily a parallelogram. Here is a counterexample:

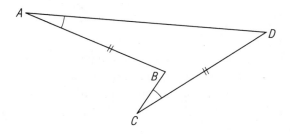

LESSON 7–8 (pp. 344–347)

1. According to the SAS Inequality Theorem, if two pairs of sides are congruent, then the order of lengths for the third pair of sides is the same as the order of angles measures for the angle included by the pairs of congruent sides. Since m∠A > m∠D, then BC, which is opposite ∠A, is greater than EF, which is opposite ∠D.

2. Some applications of the SAS Inequality Theorem are that the wider you open a door (or a lunchbox, or other such hinged openings), the wider the opening will be (up to a fixed limit).

3. The proof of the SAS Inequality Theorem uses the Betweenness Theorem (at the end of the proof, to show $XQ + QZ = XZ$) and uses the Isosceles Triangle Symmetry Theorem to state that m is the perpendicular bisector of $\overline{C'Z}$. It does not use the Isosceles Triangle Theorem; that is choice (c).

4. In the proof of the SAS Inequality Theorem, the Triangle Inequality is applied to $\Delta A'C'Q$.

5. a. The given information is the SAS condition, so the length AC is uniquely determined.

b. The branch of mathematics that studies the calculation of AC from the given measures of sides and angles is trigonometry.

6. a.

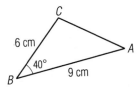

b.

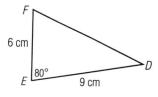

c. Using a ruler, $AC \approx 5.9$ cm and $DF \approx 9.9$ cm. (Using the "cosine law" from trigonometry, $b^2 = a^2 + c^2 - 2ac \cos b$, $AC \approx \sqrt{34.267} \approx 5.85$ and $DF \approx \sqrt{98.246} \approx 9.9119$.)

d. DF is greater than AC, so $\overline{DF}$ is longer than $\overline{AC}$.

e. The two triangles satisfy the antecedent of the SAS Inequality Theorem, since two sides of one are congruent to two sides of another, and the measures of the included angles are not equal. The consequent of the SAS Inequality Theorem is that the order of lengths of the third sides is the same as the order of lengths of the given pair of angles.

7. In triangles TRQ and TRS, two pairs of sides are congruent ($\overline{QT} \cong \overline{TS}$ and $\overline{TR} \cong \overline{TR}$). Also, m$\angle QTR = 75$, so m$\angle STR = 105$ because $\angle STQ$ is a straight angle. So triangles TRQ and TRS satisfy the antecedent of the SAS Inequality Theorem, and $RS > QR$ because RS is opposite $\angle STR$, which is larger than $\angle QTR$.

8.

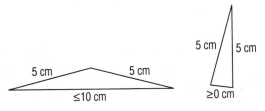

Assuming Percy's jaws can open to an angle of 180 degrees, the largest opening for $\overline{AC}$ is $BA + BC = 5 + 5 = 10$ cm. The smallest opening for $\overline{AC}$ occurs when Percy's mouth is shut; that opening is 0 cm.

9.

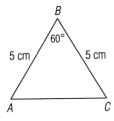

Since $\triangle ABC$ is isosceles, with vertex B, then m$\angle A = $ m$\angle C$. If m$\angle B = 60$, then m$\angle A + $ m$\angle C = 120$ because of the Triangle-Sum Theorem) and so m$\angle A = $ m$\angle C = 60$, and $\triangle ABC$ is equiangular and equilateral. So $AC = 5$ cm.

10. The before and after situations of "opening a lunchbox" satisfy the antecedent of the SAS Inequality Theorem because the lengths of the sides of the opening do not change as the angle increases. So the distance between the front of the top and the handle increases because of the SAS Inequality Theorem.

11.

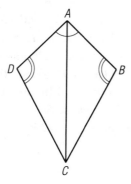

$\overline{AC}$ bisects $\angle BAD$, so $\angle BAC \cong \angle DAC$ by the definition of bisector (meaning). Also, $m\angle B = m\angle D$ (given) and $\overline{AC} \cong \overline{AC}$ (Reflexive Property of Congruence). So $\triangle BAC \cong \triangle DAC$ by the AAS Congruence Theorem, and $AB = AD$ and $BC = DC$ by the CPCF Theorem. So $ABCD$ is a kite by the definition of kite (sufficient condition).

12. It is given that $QT = RS$ and $TS = QR$, and $QS = SQ$ by the Reflexive Property of Equality. So $\triangle QTS \cong \triangle SRQ$ by the SSS Congruence Theorem. (**That is part a.**) Then $\angle TQS \cong \angle RSQ$ by the CPCF Theorem, and $\overline{QT} \parallel \overline{RS}$ because AIA $= \Rightarrow \parallel$ lines. (**That is part b.**)

13. No, the triangles are not necessarily congruent because the triangle on the right shows the ASA condition and the triangle on the left shows the AAS condition. So the pairs of congruent parts are not *corresponding* parts.

14. The congruent parts show the ASA condition, so the triangles are congruent by the ASA Congruence Theorem.

15. a.

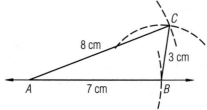

b.

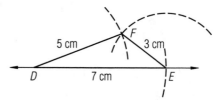

c. The two triangles can be redrawn as follows:

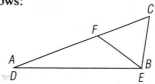

From this diagram, it is clear that one angle is in both triangles so the angles are congruent by the Reflexive Property of Congruence. Also, two angles form a linear pair, so the angles are supplementary by the Linear Pair Theorem.

(The law of cosines from trigonometry can also be used to calculate the measures of the angles to show that two angles are congruent and two angles are supplementary.)

16. The image of $\triangle GHI$ over line ℓ is $\triangle EFD$, and the image of $\triangle EFD$ over line m is $\triangle BAC$. Since reflections preserve congruence, $\triangle GHI \cong \triangle EFD \cong \triangle BAC$.

17. The result of two reflections over intersecting lines is a rotation, so $\triangle BAC$ is a rotation image of $\triangle GHI$.

18. Let the length of the second side be x. Then the first sentence says that the length of the first side is $2x$, and the second sentence says the length of the third side is $3x$. But the lengths x, $2x$, and $3x$ do not satisfy the Triangle Inequality, since it is not the case that $x + 2x > 3x$. So the lengths x, $2x$, and $3x$ cannot be the lengths of the sides of a triangle.

19. The examples of the SAS Inquality Theorem can be described as opening a door, a lunchbox, or other situations that act like a hinged opening. So the SAS Inequality Theorem is sometimes called the Hinge Theorem.

CHAPTER 7 PROGRESS SELF-TEST (p. 349)

1. a. Since $\angle 1 \cong \angle 3$ and $\angle 2 \cong \angle 4$ (given) and $\overline{AC} \cong \overline{AC}$ (Reflexive Property of Congruence), $\triangle ABC \cong \triangle CDA$.

b. The justification for the congruence is the ASA Congruence Theorem.

2. a. Since it is given that M is the midpoint of $\overline{AC}$, then $AM = MC$ by the definition of midpoint (meaning).

b. $\angle AMB \cong \angle CMD$ because of the Vertical Angle Theorem.

c. Since it is given that $\overleftrightarrow{AB} \parallel \overleftrightarrow{CD}$, then $\angle MBA \cong \angle MDC$ because $\parallel$ lines $\Rightarrow$ AIA $=$.

d. $\triangle MBA \cong \triangle MDC$ by the AAS Congruence Theorem (from parts **a, b, c**).

3. a.

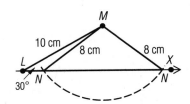

b-c. There are two possible triangles, so it is not necessarily so that everyone else's triangle will be congruent to yours.

4. a.

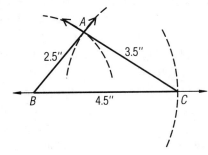

b-c. Given the lengths of 3 sides (and after checking that those three lengths can be the lengths of sides of a triangle), every triangle having sides with those lengths must be congruent, because of the SSS Congruence Theorem.

5. Each of the following conditions is sufficient for a quadrilateral to be a parallelogram: both pairs of opposite sides are parallel; both pairs of opposite angles are congruent; both pairs of opposite sides are congruent; one pair of opposite sides is parallel and congruent; two pairs of consecutive angles are supplementary.

6. If, in two triangles, two pairs of sides are congruent, then for the angles contained by those sides, the side opposite the greater angle has the greater length. (Exact wordings may differ.)

7.

	Conclusions	Justifications
a. 1.	$\overline{QP} = \overline{QP}$	Reflexive Property of Congruence
2.	$\triangle QPS \cong \triangle QPT$	HL Congruence Theorem (step 1 and given)
3.	$QS = QT$	CPCF Theorem
b. 4.	$\angle SQP \cong \angle TQP$	CPCF Theorem
5.	$\overrightarrow{QP}$ bisects $\angle SQT$.	definition of angle bisector (sufficient condition)

8. If $\overline{AB}$ and $\overline{CD}$ are both parallel and congruent, then $ABDC$ is a parallelogram by the Sufficient Conditions for a Parallelogram Theorem, part d.

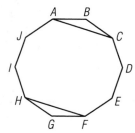

9.

	Conclusions	Justifications
1.	$\overline{AB} \cong \overline{FG}$, $\overline{BC} \cong \overline{GH}$, $\angle B \cong \angle G$	definition of regular polygon (meaning)
2.	$\triangle ABC \cong \triangle FGH$	SAS Congruence Theorem (step 1)
3.	$AC = FH$	CPCF Theorem

10.

	Conclusions	Justifications
1.	$\angle W \cong \angle W$	Reflexive Property of Congruence
2.	$\triangle WYU \cong \triangle WXV$	AAS Congruence Theorem
3.	$\overline{WU} \cong \overline{WV}$	CPCP Theorem
4.	$\triangle WUV$ is isosceles.	definition of isosceles triangle (sufficient condition)

11. In $\triangle ADB$ and $\triangle ADC$, $\overline{AD} \cong \overline{AD}$ (by the Reflexive Property of Equality), $\overline{BD} \cong \overline{CD}$ (given), and $\angle ADB \cong \angle ADC$ (they are both right angles). So $\triangle ADB \cong \triangle ADC$ by the SAS Congruence Theorem, and $AB = AC$ by the CPCF Theorem.

CHAPTER 7 REVIEW   (pp. 350–353)

1. a.

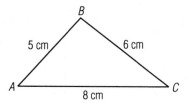

b-c. The given information is the SSS condition, so all correctly-drawn triangles will be congruent by the SSS Congruence Theorem.

2. a.

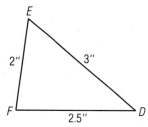

b-c. The given information is the SSS condition, so all correctly-drawn triangles will be congruent by the SSS Congruence Theorem.

3. a.

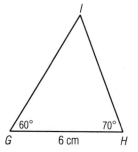

b-c. The given information is the ASA condition, so all correctly-drawn triangles will be congruent by the ASA Congruence Theorem.

4. a.

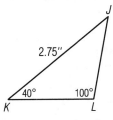

b-c. The given information is the AAS condition, so all correctly-drawn triangles will be congruent by the AAS Congruence Theorem.

5. a.

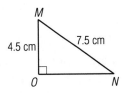

b-c. The given information is the HL condition, so all correctly-drawn triangles will be congruent by the HL Congruence Theorem.

6. a.

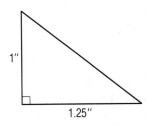

b-c. The given information is the SAS condition (since all right angles are congruent), so all correctly-drawn triangles will be congruent by the SAS Congruence Theorem.

7. a.

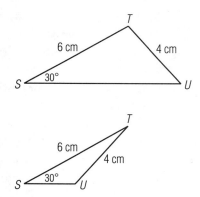

b-c. The given information is the SSA condition, which is not sufficient for congruency, so all correctly-drawn triangles will not necessarily be congruent.

8. a.

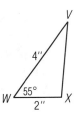

b-c. The given information is the SAS condition, so all correctly-drawn triangles will be congruent by the SAS Congruence Theorem.

9. a.

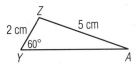

b-c. The given information is the SsA condition, so all correctly-drawn triangles will be congruent by the SsA Congruence Theorem.

10. **a.** Two pairs of corresponding sides and a pair of included angles are congruent, so $\triangle CAB \cong \triangle GFD$ by the SAS Congruence Theorem. (The order of vertices is "congruent angles, then segment with one tick mark, then third vertex.")

b. Using the correspondence from part **a** and the CPCF Theorem, $\overline{AB} \cong \overline{FD}$. (Or, $\overline{AB}$ and $\overline{FD}$ are the unmarked sides.)

c. Using the order of vertices from part **a** and the CPCF Theorem, $\angle A \cong \angle F$. (Or, $\angle A$ and $\angle F$ are included by the unmarked and one-tick sides.)

d. Using the order of vertices from part **a** and the CPCF Theorem, $\angle B \cong \angle D$. (Or, $\angle B$ and $\angle D$ are included by the unmarked and two-tick sides.)

11. **a.** In the two triangles, two pairs of angles are congruent as are a non-included pair of sides ($\overline{MP} \cong \overline{MP}$ by the Reflexive Property of Congruence), so the triangles are congruent by the AAS Congruence Theorem.

b. Using the order of vertices "two ticks, one tick, no ticks," the congruency is $\triangle NMP \cong \triangle OPM$.

12. **a-b.** Two pairs of sides are given congruent, and the third pairs of sides is congruent by the Reflexive Property of Congruence, so $\triangle CBD \cong \triangle ABD$ by the SSS Congruence Theorem.

13. **a-b.** Two pairs of sides are given congruent, and the two angles with vertex G are congruent by the Vertical Angle Theorem. Since those angles are included by the pairs of sides, then $\triangle GEF \cong \triangle GHI$ by the SAS Congruence Theorem.

14. **a-b.** The two triangles are given to be right triangles; it is also given that the hypotenuses are congruent. Also, a pair of legs is congruent by the Reflexive Property of Congruence, so $\triangle JKM \cong \triangle LKM$ by the HL Congruence Theorem.

15. **a-b.** Two pairs of angles and the included side of one triangle are congruent to the corresponding parts in another triangle, so $\triangle OPN \cong \triangle RQO$ by the ASA Congruence Theorem. (The order of vertices is "two-ticks, one tick, no ticks.")

16. **a.** $\overline{AC} \cong \overline{AC}$ by the Reflexive Property of Congruence.

b. $\triangle ADC \cong \triangle ABC$ by the ASA Congruence Theorem.

17. Given that $\overline{AD} \perp \overline{DC}$ and $\overline{AB} \perp \overline{BC}$, then $\angle D$ and $\angle B$ are right angles, and so $\triangle ABC$ and $\triangle ADC$ are right triangles (definition of right triangle—sufficient condition). Also, $\overline{AD} \cong \overline{AB}$ (given) and hypotenuse $\overline{AC} \cong \overline{AC}$ (Reflexive Property of Congruence). So $\triangle ADC \cong \triangle ABC$ by the HL Congruence Theorem.

18. $AP = BP$ in circle P and $AQ = BQ$ in circle Q by the definition of circle (meaning), and $PQ = PQ$ by the Reflexive Property of Equality. So $\triangle APQ \cong \triangle BPQ$ by the SSS Congruence Theorem.

19. $\overline{UW}$ bisects $\angle YUV$, so $\angle YUX \cong \angle WUV$ by the definition of angle bisector (meaning). Then, with the given that $\overline{UW} \cong \overline{UY}$ and $\angle V \cong \angle UXY$, it follows that $\triangle UVW \cong \triangle UXY$ by the AAS Congruence Theorem.

20. Given that $\overline{AB} \cong \overline{DC}$ and $\angle ABC \cong \angle DCB$, and since $\overline{BC} \cong \overline{CB}$ by the Reflexive Property of Congruence, then $\triangle ACB \cong \triangle DBC$ by the SAS Congruence Theorem.

21. **a.** $\overline{AD} \cong \overline{AD}$ by the Reflexive Property of Congruence.

   b. $\triangle ABD \cong \triangle ACD$ by the SSS Congruence Theorem.

   c. $\angle BAD \cong \angle CAD$ by the CPCF Theorem.

22. *ABCDEFGH* is a regular octagon, so $AB = BC$, $BC = CD$, and $m\angle ABC = m\angle BCD$ by the definition of regular polygon (meaning). Then $\triangle ABC \cong \triangle BCD$ by the SAS Congruence Theorem, and $\overline{AC} \cong \overline{BD}$ by the CPCF Theorem.

23. $\overline{JK}$ bisects $\angle MJL$, so $\angle MJK \cong \angle LJK$. Also, $\overline{MJ} \cong \overline{LJ}$ (given) and $\overline{JK} \cong \overline{JK}$ (Reflexive Property of Congruence), so $\triangle MJK \cong \triangle LJK$ by the SAS Congruence Theorem. Then $\angle M \cong \angle L$ by the CPCF Theorem.

24. *N* is the midpoint of $\overline{OE}$, so $ON = EN$ by the definition of midpoint (meaning). $\ell \parallel m$, so $\angle UON \cong \angle AEN$ because $\parallel$ lines $\Rightarrow$ AIA =. Also, $\angle UNO \cong \angle ANE$ by the Vertical Angle Theorem. So $\triangle UNO \cong \triangle ANE$ by the ASA Congruence Theorem, and $\overline{AE} \cong \overline{UO}$ by the CPCF Theorem.
   (Instead of using pair of vertical angles, two sets of AIA could be used, and the justification for the triangle congruence would be AAS.)

25. Given that $\angle ABC \cong \angle DCB$ and $\angle A \cong \angle D$, and since $\overline{BC} \cong \overline{CB}$ by the Reflexive Property of Congruence, then $\triangle ABC \cong \triangle DCB$ by the AAS Congruence Theorem, and $\overline{AC} \cong \overline{DB}$ by the CPCF Theorem.

26. By the Properties of a Parallelogram Theorem, the diagonals of a parallelogram intersect at their midpoints, so the diagonals bisect each other.

27. Opposite angles of a parallelogram are congruent. (Either diagonal forms two congruent triangles, and the opposite angles of the parallelogram will be corresponding sides in those triangles.)

28. If all pairs of consecutive angles in a trapezoid are supplementary, then the trapezoid is a parallelogram.
   (If consecutive angles are supplementary, then opposite angles are congruent, because they are supplementary to the same angle, and so the figure is a parallelogram by the Sufficient Conditions for a Parallelogram Theorem.)

29. By the Sufficient Conditions for a Parallelogram Theorem, a quadrilateral is a parallelogram if its diagonals bisect each other.

30. By the Sufficient Conditions for a Parallelogram Theorem, a quadrilateral is a parallelogram if one pair of opposite sides is both parallel and congruent.

31. $\overline{AB}$ and $\overline{DC}$ are the bases of trapezoid *ABCD*, so $\overline{AB} \parallel \overline{DC}$ by the definition of trapezoid (meaning). So $\angle ABD \cong \angle CDB$ because $\parallel$ lines $\Rightarrow$ AIA =. Also, it is given that $\angle A \cong \angle C$ (although they do not look congruent in the figure). $\overline{DB} \cong \overline{DB}$ by the Reflexive Property of Congruence, so $\triangle ABC \cong \triangle CDB$ by the AAS Congruence Theorem, and $\overline{AB} \cong \overline{CD}$. So $\overline{AB}$ and $\overline{CD}$ are both congruent and parallel, and *ABCD* is a parallelogram by the Sufficient Conditions for a Parallelogram Theorem (part d).

32.

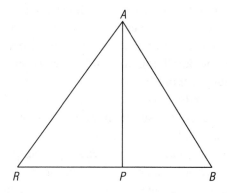

Triangles ABP and ARP are right triangles (because $\overline{AP} \perp \overline{BR}$) with congruent hypotenuses ($AB = AR$, given) and congruent legs ($AP = AP$ by the Reflexive Property of Equality). So $\triangle ABP \cong \triangle ARP$ by the HL Congruence Theorem, and $\overline{RP} \cong \overline{PB}$ by the CPCF Theorem. (Another proof: $\overline{AP}$ is the altitude in isosceles triangle ABR, so $\overline{AP}$ is the median by the Isosceles Triangle Bisector Theorem.)

33. Show that $\triangle XDB \cong \triangle XCB \cong \triangle XAB$: all the angles at B are right angles, so they are all congruent, and segment $\overline{XB}$ is in each triangle, and $m\angle D = m\angle C = m\angle A$, given. So the triangles are congruent by the AAS Congruence Theorem, and $BD = BC = BA$ by the CPCF Theorem.

34. The given information is the SSS condition, so the triangles are congruent by the SSS Congruence Theorem.

35. At each instant of opening the door (from closed to open at 90 degrees), the opening door forms a triangle with two pairs of sides congruent and the included angle increasing. So the side of the triangle opposite the "opening angle" gets larger and larger, by the SAS Inequality Theorem.

36. a-b. In triangles XPZ and XQR, $\angle P \cong \angle Q$ (they are both right angles), $XP = XQ$ (given), and $\angle PXZ \cong \angle QXR$ (Vertical Angle Theorem). So $\triangle XPZ \cong \triangle XQR$ by the ASA Congruence Theorem, and $\overline{ZP} \cong \overline{RQ}$.

37. Opposite sides of $ABCD$ are (approximately) equal, so by the Sufficient Conditions for a Parallelogram Theorem (part a), $ABCD$ is approximately in the shape of a parallelogram.

38. By the Sufficient Conditions for a Parallelogram Theorem (part c), a figure is a parallelogram if its diagonals bisect each other. So to be certain that $MPNQ$ is a parallelogram, attach $\overline{MN}$ and $\overline{PQ}$ so point O is the midpoint of $\overline{MN}$ and $\overline{QP}$.

CHAPTER 8 PERIMETER FORMULAS

LESSON 8-1 (pp. 354–361)

1. The notation "3:28" means it takes about 3 hours and 28 minutes to drive between Oklahoma City and Dallas.

2. A trucker with a perishable load would want the fastest (not necessarily the shortest) route from Chicago to Dallas. That would mean going to Springfield through Indianapolis and St. Louis (11.28 hours, rather than 11.73 hours through Indianapolis), and then going to Dallas through Akota 7.97 hours, as opposed to 8.22 hours through Tulsa and Oklahoma City).

3. **a.** In miles, the perimeter of *StICPHJS* is 246 + 185 + 170 + 143 + 108 + 137 + 210 = 1199 miles

   b. In hours and minutes, the perimeter of *StICPHJS* is 23:01.

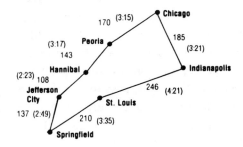

4. The perimeter can be expressed as:
   $a + a + b + b$
   $2a + 2b$
   $2(a + b)$.

5. Using the formula $p = 2(a + b)$ for the perimeter of a rectangle, the perimeter is $2(3.5 + .5) = 2(4) = 8$ miles.

6. Using the formula $p = ns$ for the perimeter of a regular polygon, with $n = 6$ and $s = 14$ mm, the perimeter is $p = 6(14) = 84$ mm.

7. Using the formula $p = ns$ for the perimeter of a regular polygon, with $n = 4$ and $s = t$, the perimeter is $p = 4t$.

8. Using the formula $p = ns$ for the perimeter of a regular polygon, with $n = 3$ and the side s, the perimeter is $p = 3s$.

9. Using the forumla $p = ns$ for the perimeter of a regular polygon, with $n = 7$ and $s = x + 1$, the perimeter is $p = 7(x + 1) = 7x + 7$.

10. Represent the lengths of the sides of the rectangle as x and $3x$. Then, using the formula $p = 2(\ell + w)$, $70 = 2(x + 3x)$ so $70 = 2(4x)$ or $70 = 8x$. So $x = 8.75$. The sides have length $x = 8.75$ units and $3x = 3(8.75) = 26.25$ units.

11. Represent the lengths of the sides of the poster as x and $1.5x$. Then, using the formula $p = 2(\ell + w)$ and given that the perimeter is 3 meters, $3 = 2(x + 1.5x)$ so $3 = 2(2.5x)$ or $3 = 5x$. So $x = 0.6$, and the sides are $x = 0.6$ meters and $1.5x = 0.9$ meters. So the width of the poster, the longer dimension, will be 0.9 meters.

12. **a-b.** A rhombus is an equilateral polygon (it is not, however, an equiangular polygon), so it is possible to use the formula $p = ns$ with $p = 12$ and $n = 4$ to find the length of a side. Then s, which represents the length of a side of the rhombus, is 3 feet.

13. Using the formula $p = ns$ with $p = 10$ feet and $n = 8$, then $s = \frac{10}{8} = 1.25$ feet or 1 foot 3 inches.

14. Using the formula $p = ns$ with $n = 3$, then $s = \frac{p}{3}$.

153

15. a. Using the diagram of the museum, it has 8 smallest sides, 18 middle sides, and 2 largest sides. So the perimeter can be expressed as $p = 8s + 18m + 2\ell$.

b. Using $s = 25$, $m = 50$, and $\ell = 100$, then $p = 8(25) + 18(50) + 2(100) = 200 + 900 + 200 = 1300$ meters.

c. For the surrounding rectangle, the shorter dimension is $\ell + 2m = 100 + 2(50) = 200$ meters. The longer dimension is about $8m = 8(50) = 400$ meters (this ratio agrees with the "1 block, 2 blocks" measurements). So the perimeter of the surrounding rectangle is twice the sum of the length and width, or $2(200 + 400) = 2(600) = 1200$ meters.

16. a. Answers may vary. Some of the situations in which people know distances in terms of time but not miles or kilometers are trips within their town (from home to a store, a school, a friend's house, the airport) or airplane or bus trips (trips between cities).

b. Sample situations in which travel time is more important than travel distance are if you have to get to a bus or airport terminal, or if you have to make a connecting bus or plane.

17.

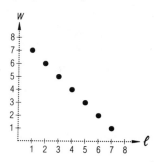

18. a. Use the formula from the Polygon-Sum Theorem, $S = (n - 2)180$, with $n = 10$: $S = (n - 2)180 = 8(180) = 1440$.

b. If the decagon is equiangular, then all 10 angles have the same measure and each measure is $\frac{1440}{10} = 144$.

c. Except for triangles, a polygon with equal sides need not have angles with equal measures. So no conclusion can be made about each angle of an equilateral decagon.

19. Using the formula from the Polygon-Sum Theorem, $S = (n - 2)180$. Then, if the polygon is equiangular, each angle measure is one-nth of the total. So the measure of each angle is $\frac{(n - 2)180}{n}$, which is choice (d).

20. The sum of the measures of the angles around point D is 360, since it is a full circle. Given that $m\angle ADC = 109$ and $m\angle ADB = 90$ (since it is a right angle), then $m\angle BDC = 360 - (109 + 90) = 360 - 199 = 161$.

21. Using the network on page 356, start at Springfield, trace one polygon, and then trace the other—it is easy to traverse the network. Analyzing the network, Springfield has 4 arcs, so it is an even node, and every other node is also even since each has two arcs. So there are not more than two odd nodes (there are none), and the network is traversable.

22. a. 1 yard = 3 feet

b. 1 kilometer = 1000 meters ("kilo" means "thousand")

c. 1 mile = 5280 feet

23. Using the ratio $\frac{1 \text{ inch}}{2.54 \text{ cm}} = \frac{x \text{ inches}}{2 \text{ cm}}$ then $2.54x = 2$, and $x = \frac{2}{2.54} \approx .7874 \approx \frac{3}{4}$ inch.

24. a. 3 feet   6 inches

  <u> 8 feet 11 inches</u>

   11 feet 17 inches

   or   11 feet (12 + 5) inches

   or   12 feet 5 inches

b. 8(2 feet, 3 inches) = 16 feet,

   24 inches = 18 feet

c. 2.4 meters + 62 centimeters =

   2.4 meters + 0.62 meters = 3.02 meters

   Another way:

   2.4 meters + 62 centimeters =

   240 centimeters + 62 centimeters =

   302 centimeters

25. Using $p = 2\ell + 2w$ with $\ell = 11$ and $p = 25$,

   then $25 = 2(11) + 2w$ or $25 = 22 + 2w$,

   so $3 = 2w$ and $w = 1.5$.

26. a. $5(3 + 2y) = 5(3) + 5(2y) = 15 + 10y$

b. One way to check is to assign a value to y,

   say $y = 4$. Then $5(3 + 2y) = 5(3 + 8) =$

   $5(11) = 55$. Also, $15 + 10y =$

   $15 + 10(4) = 15 + 40 = 55$. Since both

   results are the same, the multiplication has

   been checked.

27. Using the FOIL pattern,

   $(x + 1)(2x - 3) = 2x^2 - 3x + 2x - 3$

   $\qquad\qquad\qquad = 2x^2 - x - 3.$

   That is not the same as $2x^2 - 3$ (unless $x = 0$).

28. $(r + s)^2 = (r + s)(r + s)$

   $\qquad\quad = r^2 + rs + sr + s^2$

   $\qquad\quad = r^2 + 2rs + s^2.$

   That is choice (c).

29. a. The average speed from Dallas to

   Oklahoma City can be computed by

   dividing the distance by the time:

   $\dfrac{209}{3:28} \approx \dfrac{209}{3.47} = 60.29$ mph.

b. The average speed from Dallas to Atoka is

   also the distance divided by the time:

   $\dfrac{128}{2:31} \approx \dfrac{128}{2.52} = 50.86$ mph.

c. The condition that most likely accounts for
these different rates is that there are
different kinds of highways, with different
speed limits, between the pairs of cities.

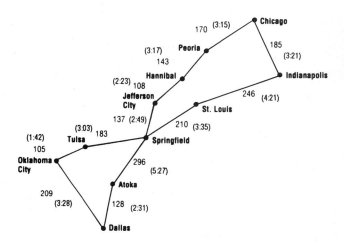

30. The difference in mileage between the cities
(from 289 miles to 294 miles) could indicate
that the mileage was being calculated using
different points, say, between city halls
rather than between airports, or even that
the mileage was measured along a different
highway route. The 1973 time, 5:15,
represents an average speed of 55 miles per
hour (55 mph × 5.25 hrs = 289 miles), while
the 1988 time, 6:45, represents an average
speed of 43.5 miles per hour (43.5 mph ×
6.75 hrs = 294 miles). The different average
speeds might be explained by different
highways or that the 1988 speed takes into
account constantly-heavy traffic conditions.

LESSON 8–2 (pp. 362–366)

1. A tessellation is a covering of a plane with
congruent copies of the same region, with no
holes and no overlaps.

2.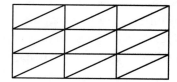

3.

4.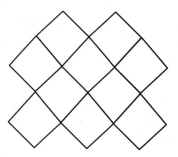

5. A museum where many tessellations can be found is the Alhambra in Grenada, Spain.

6. The key question concerning tessellations in this lesson is whether a given shape can be used as a fundamental region to cover the plane.

7. A new type of tessellating pentagon was discovered as recently as 1985 (by Rolf Stein, of the University of Dortmund in West Germany).

8. Samples: Floor or wall tiles, wallpaper patterns, parquet floors.

9.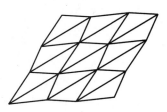

10.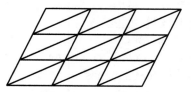

11.

12.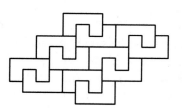

13. Around any vertex point in a tessellation, the sum of the angle measures must be 360. For the triangle, 6 regions must meet at that point (6 × 60 = 360); for the square, 4 regions must meet (4 × 90 = 360); and for the hexagon 3 regions must meet (3 × 120 = 360). But the measure of an angle of a regular pentagon is 144, which does not divide evenly into 360. So the regular pentagon cannot be a fundamental region for a tessellation; that is choice (c).

Examples:

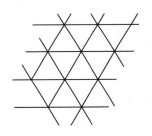

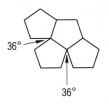

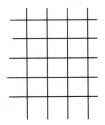

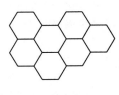

14. a.

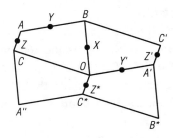

b. Around point O is each of the four angles of $ABOC$ and, by the Quadrilateral-Sum Theorem, the measures of the four angles of $ABOC$ add up to 360.

c. Continue the tessellation using copies of region $AC'B'A''$, as follows:

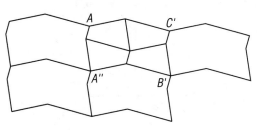

15. Using the formula for the perimeter of an equilateral polygon, $p = ns$, with $p = 13$ and $n = 5$, then $13 = 5s$ and the length of a side is $s = \dfrac{13}{5} = 2.6$ units.

16. Since opposite sides of a parallelogram are congruent, a formula for the perimeter of a parallelogram is $p = 2(a + b)$, where a and b are the lengths of adjacent sides. So $462 = 2(185 + b)$ or $231 = 185 + b$, so $b = 231 - 185 = 46$. The lengths of the sides are 185 cm, 46 cm, 185 cm, and 46 cm.

17. Using the Polygon-Sum Theorem, $S = (n - 2)180$, then for a pentagon the sum of the measures is $(5 - 2)180 = 3(180) = 540$. Since all 5 angles of a regular pentagon are congruent, the measure of each one must be $\dfrac{540}{5} = 108$.

18.

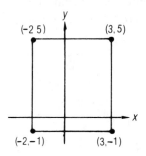

The length of the vertical sides is 6 and the length of the horizontal sides is 5. So the perimeter is 2(6 + 5) = 2(11) = 22 units.

19. It is given that m∠ABD = m∠BDC and m∠ADB = m∠DBC. Also, $\overline{BD} \cong \overline{BD}$ by the Reflexive Property of Congruence. So $\triangle ABD \cong \triangle CDB$ by the ASA Congruence Theorem, and AB = CD by the CPCF Theorem.

20. $(a + 5)^2 = (a + 5)(a + 5)$
$$= a^2 + 5a + 5a + 25$$
$$= a^2 + 10a + 25$$

21. If $2x^2 = 54$, then $x^2 = 27$ and $x = \pm\sqrt{27} = \pm\sqrt{(9)3} = \pm 3\sqrt{3}$.

22. $\sqrt{27} = \sqrt{(9)3} = 3\sqrt{3} = \pm 5.2$; that is choice (d).

23. a. The Moors were a people from North Africa who, for a time, controlled most of Spain.

b. The Moors were defeated in 1492.

24. a. Maurits C. Escher lived from 1898 to 1971.

b. Besides his tessellations, Escher is known for his fantasy pictures, such as the one showing water flowing continuously in a closed channel, staircases in different three-dimensional worlds, self-portrait reflections in a spherical mirror, and each of two hands drawing the other.

25.

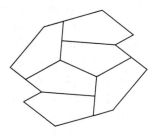

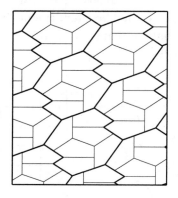

LESSON 8–3 (pp. 367–372)

1. a. Using unit A, the region is 3 units high and 9 units long, so its area is 27 square units.

b. Using unit B, the region is 5 units high and 15 units long, so its area is 75 square units.

2. a. The linear dimensions are measured in centimeters, so an appropriate unit for the area would be square centimeters.

b. Area(ABCD) = 8.3 × 11.4 = 94.62 ≈ 94.6 cm².

3. a. The perimeter of a rectangle with dimensions 3000 miles and 1600 miles is 2(3000 + 1600) = 2(4600) = 9200 miles.

b. The area of a rectangle with dimensions 3000 miles and 1600 miles is 3000 × 1600 = 4,800,000 square miles.

4. a. ABFG is a rectangle with dimensions 5 and 7; its area is 35 square units.

b. CDEF is a square with side 4; its area is 16 square units.

c. *ABCDEFG* is the union of *ABFG* and *CDEF*; by the Additive Property of the Area Postulate, its area is 35 + 16 = 51 square units.

5. The properties used in answering Question 4 are the Uniqueness Property, the Rectangle Formula of the Area Postulate (for parts **a** and **b**) and the Additive Property of the Area Postulate (for part **c**).

6. The area of the floor is the area of the figure with vertices (0, 0), (20, 0), (20, 20), and (0, 20) (so it is a square), with two rectangles taken away. The side of the square is 20, so its area is 400 square units. The small rectangle at the upper left has sides 7 and 5, so its area is 35 square units, and the small rectangle at the lower right has sides 5 and 10, so its area is 50 square units. So the area of the floor is 400 − (35 + 50) = 400 − 85 = 315 square units.

7. The area of the shaded region is 1935 square feet minus three rectangles: the one at the upper left has sides 43 − 28 = 15 and 8 − 0 = 8, so its area is (15)(8) = 120; the one at the upper right has sides 43 − 28 = 15 and 45 − 22 = 23, so its area is (15)(23) = 345; and the one at the lower right has sides 10 − 0 = 10 and 45 − 30 = 15, so its area is (10)(15) = 150. So the area of the shaded region is 1935 − (120 + 345 + 150) = 1935 − 615 = 1320 square feet; that checks.

8. Expressed in yards, 15 feet by 12 feet is 5 yards by 4 yards or 20 square yards. At $11.99 per square yard, the cost would be (20)($11.95) = $239.00.

9. a.

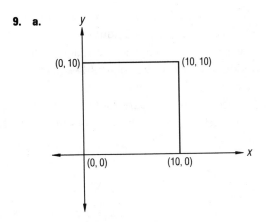

The figure is a square with side 10 units; its area is 100 square units.

b. The figure is a square with sides *k* units; its area is k^2 square units.

10. The area of *BCDNEM*, the shaded region, is the area of square *ABCD* minus the area of square *AMEN*. Since *AB* = 16 units (since *ABCE* is a square) and *M* is the midpoint of $\overline{AB}$, then the sides of *AMEN* are 8 units. So the area of the shaded region is (16)(16) − (8)(8) = 256 − 64 = 192 square units.

11. Using the formula for the area of a rectangle, $A = \ell w$, with $A = 50$ and $\ell = 100$, then $w = \frac{50}{100} = .5$; the width is $\frac{1}{2}$ yard (or 1.5 feet or 18 inches).

12. For any square, the length of each side (in linear units) is the square root of the measure of the area (given in square units).

a. $\sqrt{49} = 7$ units

b. $\sqrt{\frac{3}{4}} = \sqrt{.75} \approx .8666 \approx 1$ unit

c. $\sqrt{200} \approx 14.142 \approx 14$ units

d. $\sqrt{3141} \approx 56.0446 \approx 56$ units

13. a. The area is $(24'')(12'') = 288$ square inches.

b. The area is $(2')(1') = 2$ square feet.

c. Since 288 square inches = 2 square feet, divide both sides by 2 to get 144 square inches = 1 square foot.

(Another way: a square foot is 12 inches by 12 inches, or $(12)(12) = 144$ square inches.)

14. a. $MO = x + 5$

b. $MR = x + 3$

c. Area$(MOQR) = (x + 5)(x + 3)$
$$= x^2 + 3x + 5x + 15$$
$$= x^2 + 8x + 15$$

15. If the width is w and the length is $3w$, then the area is the product of those two measurements, or $3w^2$ square units.

16. The football field is 120 yd by 160 feet, or 360 ft by 160 ft; that area is $(360)(160) = 57{,}600$ ft². Each piece of sod is 3 ft by 1 ft = 3 ft². The number of pieces of sod needed is $\frac{57{,}600}{3} = 19{,}200$ pieces.

17.

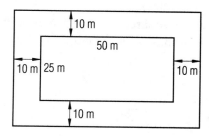

18. a.

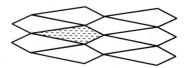

The dimensions of the fenced region are $50 + 2(10) = 70$ m and $25 + 2(10) = 45$ m, so the perimeter of the fenced region is $2(70 + 45) = 2(115) = 230$ m.

b. Let d represent the distance from the pool to the fence. Then the dimensions of the fenced region are $50 + 2d$ and $25 + 2d$. So the perimeter can be expressed as
$$200 = 2(50 + 2d + 25 + 2d), \text{ so}$$
$$200 = 2(75 + 4d)$$
$$200 = 150 + 8d$$
$$50 = 8d$$
$$d = 6.25.$$
The distance from the pool to the fence can be 6.25 m.

19. $x^2 = 16$
$x = 4$ or $x = -4$

20. $5y^2 = 240$
$y^2 = 48$
$y = \sqrt{48} = \sqrt{(16)(3)} = 4\sqrt{3}$
or $-4\sqrt{3}$ or $\approx \pm 6.93$

21. $\sqrt{75} = \sqrt{(25)(3)} = 5\sqrt{3}$; that is choice (b).

22. a. $\sqrt{2} \approx 1.41421 \approx 1.41$

b. $\sqrt{3} \approx 1.73205 \approx 1.73$

c. $\sqrt{4^2 + 3^2} = \sqrt{16 + 9} = \sqrt{25} = 5$; to the nearest hundredth, 5.00.

d. $\sqrt{\dfrac{25}{4}} = \dfrac{\sqrt{25}}{\sqrt{4}} = \dfrac{5}{2} = 2.50$

23. If the lengths of the three sides are expressed as x, $1.5x$, and $2x$, and the perimeter is 45 units, then
$$x + 1.5x + 2x = 45$$
$$4.5x = 45$$
$$x = 10.$$
So the three sides have lengths $x = 10$ units, $1.5x = 15$ units, and $2x = 20$ units.

24. $\frac{1}{2}ha + \frac{1}{2}hb = \frac{1}{2}h(a + b)$

25.

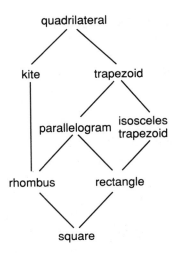

quadrilateral

kite   trapezoid

parallelogram   isosceles trapezoid

rhombus   rectangle

square

26. a-b. Answers will vary. A small bedroom, with measurements 11.25 feet and 9.75 feet would have area $(11.25)(9.75) = 109.6875 \approx 110$ ft^2; a large living room, with measurements 7.25 m and 4.5 m would have area $(7.25)(4.5) = 32.625 \approx 33$ m^2.

27. The primary factor in the increase of area was the acquisition of Alaska. It was purchased from Russia in 1867; the purchase price was $7.2 million.

LESSON 8–4 (pp. 373–377)

1. a. In the first grid, each square represents 1 square mile.

b. In the second grid, 4 miles is represented by the sides of 8 squares (and 3 miles is represented by the sides of 6 squares) so the side of each square is 0.5 miles and the area of each square is $0.5^2 = 0.25$ square miles.

c. In the finest grid, 4 miles is represented by the sides of 16 squares (and 3 miles is represented by the sides of 12 squares) so the side of each square is 0.25 miles and the area of each square is $0.25^2 = 0.0625$ square miles.

2. Some reasons for estimating the area of a lake might be to estimate the total amount of water in the lake, for zoning purposes, or to stock the lake with fish.

3. Using the formula from the lesson, $(I + \frac{1}{2}B)U$, then replacing I with E, B with P, and U with Q, the formula can be rewritten as $(E + \frac{1}{2}P)Q$ or $(E + \frac{P}{2})Q$; that is choice (b).

4. Using the estimate of the area $(I + \frac{1}{2}B)U$, where I is the number of squares inside the region, B is the number of squares containing part of the border, and U is the area of each square, then $I = 76$, $B = 58$, and, from Question 1c, $U = 0.0625$ square miles. So an estimate for the area is $(76 + \frac{58}{2})(.0625)$ $= (76 + 29)(.0625) = (105)(.0625) = 6.5625 \approx 6.6$ square miles.

5. a. Advantages to using grids are that the method works for any reasonably-smooth curve and that computers can be programmed to use the method.

b. A disadvantage to the method is that the decision as to whether or not a square is in the "I" category or the "B" category is sometimes arbitrary, so two people who use the same method may get different answers.

6. The area of a region is the limit of the estimates made using finer and finer grids.

7. A computer screen that is 5.5″ by 7.5″ has an area of $(5.5)(7.5) = 41.25$ square inches. If it contains 512 rows and 342 columns, then there are $(512)(342) = 175,104$ pixels. Dividing the number of pixels by the number of square inches, there are $\frac{175,104}{41.25}$ $= 4244.9454 \approx 4245$ pixels per square inch.

8. Use the estimate of the area $(I + \frac{1}{2}B)U$,

where I is the number of squares inside the region, B is the number of squares containing part of the border, and U is the area of each square.

a. For the grid at the left, $I = 3$, $B = 10$, and $U = (.25)^2 = .0625$ square inches. So the area is $(3 + 5)(.0625) = .5$ square inches.

b. For the grid at right, $I = 22$, $B = 20$ and $U = (.125)^2 = .015625$ square inches. So the area is $(22 + 10)(.0625) = (32)(.015625) = .5$ square inches.

9. Use the estimate of the area $(I + \frac{1}{2}B)U$,

where I is the number of squares inside the region, B is the number of squares containing part of the border, and U is the area of each square. For the lake, $I = 29$, $B = 53$, and $U = (0.5)^2 = 0.25$ sq km. So the area is

$(29 + \frac{53}{2})(0.25) = (29 + 26.5)(0.25)$

$= (55.5)(0.25) = 13.875 \approx 14$ sq km.

10. a. If a square (a square mile) has a side of 5280 feet, then its area is $(5280)^2 = 27{,}878{,}400$ square feet; there are $27{,}878{,}400$ square feet in a square mile.

b. Since 1 square mile equals 640 acres (given) and also equals $27{,}878{,}400$ square feet (part **a**), then 640 acres equals $27{,}878{,}400$ square feet (Transitive Property of Equality). Dividing both sides by 640, then 1 acre $= \frac{27{,}878{,}400}{640}$

$= 43{,}560$; there are 43,560 square feet in an acre (then, since $\sqrt{43{,}560} \approx 208.71$, a square field with a side of just over 200 feet covers 1 acre).

11. Set up and solve a proportion:

$\frac{\text{acres}}{\text{mile}} = \frac{640}{1} = \frac{215}{x}$.

Using the means-extremes product,

$640x = 215$

$x = \frac{215}{640}$

$x = 0.3359375$.

So 215 acres is about one-third of a square mile.

12. From Question 11b, 1 acre $= 43{,}560$ square feet, so half an acre is 21,780 square feet. If the lot is rectangular, then the product of the length and width is 21,780. The following graph of the equation $\ell w = 21{,}780$ shows possible values of ℓ and w.

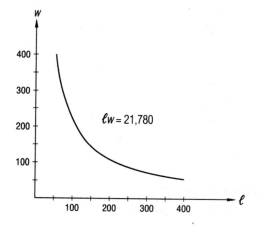

Some sample length-and-width pairs are (2178, 10), (1089, 20), (726, 30), (544.5, 40), (435.6, 50), (242, 90), and (145.2, 150).

13. Using 1 mi ≈ 1.6 km, then 1 mi$^2 \approx (1.6)^2 \approx 2.56$ km^2. So 20 square miles (the U.S. farm) is about $(20)(2.56) = 51.2$ km^2; that is bigger than the European farm, which is 30 km^2, so the U.S. farm is bigger.

14. The area of the larger square is x^2 and of the smaller square is y^2. So the shaded area is $x^2 - y^2$.

15. The expression $x^2 - y^2$ is called "the difference of two squares" and can be factored into conjugates.
So $x^2 - y^2 = (x + y)(x - y)$.
To confirm this, use the FOIL method to multiply the factors:
$(x + y)(x - y) = x^2 - xy + xy - y^2 = x^2 - y^2$.

16. The kitchen measures 10 feet by 12 feet, so in inches the measurements are $(10)(12) = 120$ and $(12)(12) = 144$. The area of the kitchen is $(120)(144) = 17{,}280$ square inches, and since each tile is 64 square inches, then $\frac{17{,}280}{64}$ = 270 tiles are needed. (Note: both measurements are divisible by 8 inches, so there would be no need to work with parts of tiles.)

17. Using the area formula $A = \ell w$ with $A = 96$ and $w = 4$, then $\ell = \frac{96}{4} = 24$ units. So the perimeter is $p = 2(\ell + w) = 2(24 + 4) = 2(28) = 56$ linear units.

18. If the unit of area for a figure is square kilometers, then the natural unit for the perimeter is (linear) kilometers.

19. In $\triangle PQA$ and $\triangle DRA$, it is given that two pairs of angles and a corresponding pair of non-included sides are congruent, so $\triangle PQA \cong \triangle DRA$ by the AAS Congruence Theorem. So $\overline{PA} \cong \overline{DA}$ by the CPCF Theorem, and $\triangle PAD$ is isosceles by the definition of isosceles triangle (sufficient condition).

20.

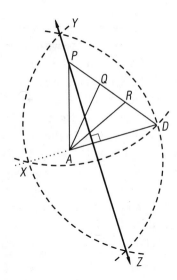

21. $x^2 + 9 = 25$
$\qquad x^2 = 16$
$\qquad x = 4 \quad$ or $\quad x = \text{-}4$

22. $y^2 + 10 = 90$
$\qquad y^2 = 80$
$\qquad y = \sqrt{80}$
$\qquad = \pm\sqrt{(16)(5)} = 4\sqrt{5} \quad$ or $\quad \text{-}4\sqrt{5}$
$\qquad \approx \pm 8.94$

23. It is possible to rewrite $\sqrt{48}$ as $\sqrt{(16)(3)} = 4\sqrt{3}$. So if $k\sqrt{3} = \sqrt{48} = 4\sqrt{3}$, then $k = 4$; that is choice (a).

24. First, calculate the area of the polygon: it can be enclosed by a rectangle with sides 3 and 2, so the area of the enclosing rectangle is 6 square units. There is an extra half-unit square at the lower left, and an extra one square unit at the upper right (it is half of a one-by-two rectangle). So the area of the polygon is $6 - (.5 + 1) = 6 - 1.5 = 4.5$ square units.

Second, count lattice points: there are 7 *on* the polygon, so $P = 7$, and there are 2 *inside* the polygon, so $I = 2$.

Then, calculate each value in the choices:

(a) $\frac{1}{2}P + I - 1 = 3.5 + 2 - 1 = 4.5$; that is a possibility.

(b) $\frac{1}{2}P + I = 3.5 + 2 = 5.5$; that is not correct.

(c) $\frac{1}{2}P + I + 1 = 3.5 + 2 + 1 = 6.5$; that is not correct.

(d) $\frac{1}{2}(P + I) = \frac{1}{2}(7 + 2) = 4.5$; that is a possibility.

To choose between the two possibilities, consider a two-by-two square. Its area is 4, $P = 8$, and $I = 1$. The value for choice (a) would be $\frac{1}{2}(8) + 1 - 1 = 4$, which checks, while the value for choice (d) would be $\frac{1}{2}(8 + 1) = 4.5$, which does not check. So the expression is the one given in choice (a).

25.

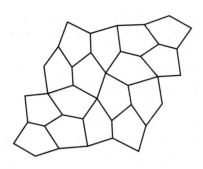

LESSON 8–5 (pp. 378–383)

1. A segment is an altitude of a triangle if and only if it is a segment from a vertex perpendicular to the line containing the opposite side.

2. **a.**

b.

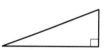

c.

3. A formula for the area A of a rectangle with length ℓ and width w is $A = \ell w$.

4. A formula for the area A of a right triangle with legs h and b is $A = \frac{1}{2}hb$.

5. A formula for the area A of a triangle with side b and altitude to that side h is $A = \frac{1}{2}hb$.

6. **a.** The area of $\triangle ABC$ is the difference between the areas of the two right triangles, or Area$(\triangle ABC) = $ Area$(\triangle ABD) - $ Area$(\triangle CBD)$.

b. Area$(\triangle ABD) = \frac{1}{2}(20)(7) = 70$ and

Area$(\triangle CBD) = \frac{1}{2}(5)(7) = 17.5$, so

Area$(\triangle ABC) = 70 - 17.5 = 52.5$ mm².

7. **a.** ΔEFH is a right triangle with legs 6 and 8, so its area is $\frac{1}{2}(6)(8) = 24$ square units.

b. ΔFGH is a right triangle with legs 15 and 8, so its area is $\frac{1}{2}(15)(8) = 60$ square units.

c. The area of ΔEGH can be calculated two ways. Its area is the sum of the areas of ΔEFH and ΔFGH, so the area of ΔEGH = 24 + 60 = 84 square units. Or, it has a side that is 21 units and the altitude to that side is 8, so its area is $\frac{1}{2}(21)(8) = 84$ square units.

8. The shaded region has a boundary that is a right triangle with legs 3 and 7, so its area is $\frac{1}{2}(3)(7) = 10.5$ square units.

9. The shaded region has a boundary that is a triangle with side 7.43 + 4.57 = 12 and altitude to that side of 2, so its area is $\frac{1}{2}(12)(2) = 12$ square units. (Another way: its area is the sum of the areas of two right triangles. One has legs 2 and 7.43, so the area is 7.43, the other has legs 4.57 and 2, so the area is 4.57. So the area of the larger triangle is 7.43 + 4.57 = 12 square units.

10. The shaded region has a boundary that is a right triangle with legs 1 and 2, so its area is $\frac{1}{2}(1)(2) = 1$ square unit.

11. **a.** For ΔPQR, the base $\overline{QR}$ has length 3 and the altitude $\overline{PT}$ to $\overline{QR}$ had length 6. So its area is $\frac{1}{2}(3)(6) = 9$ square units.

b. For ΔPRS, the base $\overline{RS}$ has length 5 and the altitude $\overline{PT}$ to $\overline{RS}$ has length 6. So its area is $\frac{1}{2}(5)(6) = 15$ square units.

c. For ΔPQS, the base $\overline{QS}$ has length 8 and the altitude $\overline{PT}$ to $\overline{QS}$ has length 6. So its area is $\frac{1}{2}(8)(6) = 24$ square units.

(Another way is to add the two areas found in parts **a** and **b** above, so the Area(ΔPQS) = 9 + 15 = 24 square units.)

12. Since east-west streets are perpendicular to north-south streets, the shaded region has a boundary that is a right triangle with legs 200 feet and 210 feet. So the area of the shaded triangle is $\frac{1}{2}(200)(210) = $ 21,000 square feet.

13. **a.**

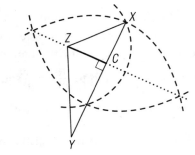

b. The length of $\overline{XY}$ is about 8.1 cm and the altitude to $\overline{XY}$ is about 2.3 cm, so the area of the triangle is $\frac{1}{2}(8.1)(2.3) = 9.315 \approx$ 9.3 cm².
(Using $\overline{XZ}$ as the leg, $\overline{XZ}$ is about 3.6 cm and the altitude to $\overline{XZ}$ is about 5.1 cm, so the area of the triangle is about $\frac{1}{2}(3.6)(5.1)$ = 9.18 $\approx$ 9.2 cm²).
(Using $\overline{YZ}$ as the leg, $\overline{YZ}$ is about 5.8 and the altitude to $\overline{YZ}$ is about 3.2 cm, so the area is about $\frac{1}{2}(5.8)(3.2) = 9.28 \approx$ 9.3 cm²).

14. a. The part of the roof has a boundary that is an isosceles triangle with leg 10 m and base 12 m, so the perimeter is $(10 + 10 + 12)$ $= 32$ m.

b. For the triangular boundary, a side is 12 and the altitude to that side is 8, so the area of the triangle is $\frac{1}{2}(12)(8) = 48$ m².

15. Calculating the area of $\triangle ABC$ using side $\overline{AB}$ having length 8 and $\overline{CF}$ (the altitude to $\overline{AB}$) having length 6, the area of the triangle is $\frac{1}{2}(8)(6) = 24$ square units. Calculating the area using side $\overline{CB}$ and its altitude $\overline{AW}$, which has length 7, then $24 = \frac{1}{2}(CB)(7)$. So $24 = 3.5(CB)$ and $CB \approx 6.86$ units.

16. Convert to inches (because it is easier to convert 1 linear foot to 12 inches than to convert 18 square inches to $\frac{18}{144} = \frac{1}{8}$ square foot). Using the formula $A = \frac{1}{2}hb$ with $A = 18$ and $h = 12$, then $18 = \frac{1}{2}(12)b$ so $18 = 6b$ and $b = 3$ inches.

17. To calculate the shaded area, subtract the areas of the four unshaded right triangles from the area of the grid, which is a square with side 7.

Upper left: $A = \frac{1}{2}(4)(5) = 10$.

Upper right: $A = \frac{1}{2}(3)(2) = 3$.

Lower right: $A = \frac{1}{2}(5)(4) = 10$.

Lower left: $A = \frac{1}{2}(3)(2) = 3$.

So the area of the shaded region is $49 - (10 + 3 + 10 + 3) = 49 - 26 = 23$ square units.
(Another way: use Pick's Theorem from Lesson 8–4, Question 24. P, the number of

lattice points on the polygon, is 4, and I, the number of lattice points inside the polygon, is 22. Then $\frac{1}{2}P + I - 1 = \frac{1}{2}(4) + 22 - 1 = 2 + 22 - 1 = 23$ square units.)

18.

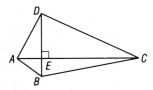

a. Area $(ADC) = \frac{1}{2}AC \cdot DE$;

Area $(ABC) = \frac{1}{2}AC \cdot EB$.

So Area $(ADCB)$
$= $ Area $(ADC) + $ Area (ABC)

$= \frac{1}{2}AC \cdot DE + \frac{1}{2}AC \cdot EB$

$= \frac{1}{2}AC(DE + EB)$

$= \frac{1}{2}AC \cdot BD$

b. kites, rhombuses, and squares have $\perp$ diagonals.

19. Use the estimate of the area $(I + \frac{1}{2}B)U$, where I is the number of squares inside the region, B is the number of squares containing part of the border, and U is the area of each square.

a. For the grid at the left, $I = 14$, $B = 31$, and $U = (96)^2 = 9216$ square miles. So an estimate for the area is $(14 + \frac{31}{2})(9216) = (14 + 15.5)(9216) = (29.5)(9216) = 271,872$ square miles.

b. For the grid at the left, $I = 89$, $B = 55$, and $U = (\frac{96}{2})^2 = (48)^2 = 2304$ square miles. So an estimate for the area is $(89 + \frac{55}{2})(2304) = (89 + 27.5)(2304) = (116.5)(2304) = 268,416$ square miles.

20. T is a midpoint, so $RV = 2x$ and the area of the large square is $(2x)^2 = 4x^2$. So the area of the shaded region is $4x^2 - x^2 = 3x^2$.

21.

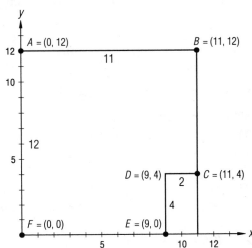

Area ($ABCDEF$) is the area of a rectangle with sides 12 and 11 reduced by a rectangle with sides 2 and 4. So Area($ABCDEF$) = $(12)(11) - (2)(4) = 132 - 8 = 124$ square units.

22. $\sqrt{18} = \sqrt{(9)(2)} = 3\sqrt{2}$

23. $\sqrt{45} = \sqrt{(9)(5)} = 3\sqrt{5}$

24. Two (or more) triangles have the same area if they have congruent bases and congruent altitudes. So the problem can be restated as finding all the triangles that have a base congruent to $\overline{LH}$ and an altitude congruent to $\overline{CJ}$. For base $\overline{LH}$, there are 4 other triangles with altitudes congruent to $\overline{CJ}$—they have their third vertex at A, B, D, or E. Now consider $\overline{AE}$ as a base, since it is congruent to $\overline{LH}$. There are 5 appropriate triangles—they have their third vertex at H, I, J, K, or L. So the number of triangles having the same area as $\triangle CLH$ is 9.

25. a.

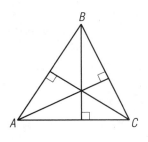

b.

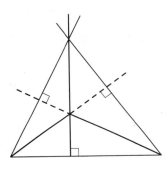

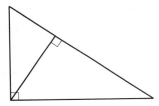

c. The altitudes of a triangle meet inside the triangle for an acute triangle, on the triangle for a right triangle, and outside the triangle for an obtuse triangle.

LESSON 8–6 (pp. 384–389)

1.

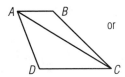 or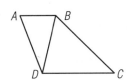

167

2. Step 1: Triangulate the polygon.
   Step 2: Get the area of each triangle by measuring lengths of sides and altitudes.
   Step 3: Add the areas to get the area of the polygon.

3. a. For trapezoid $EFGH$, the bases are the parallel sides $\overline{EF}$ and $\overline{HG}$, and the altitude is the distance between them, FI.

   b. Using the formula Area($EFGH$) = $\frac{1}{2}h(b_1 + b_2)$ with $h = 48$, $b_1 = 160$ and $b_2 = 120$, then Area($EFGH$) = $\frac{1}{2}(48)(160 + 120) = \frac{1}{2}(48)(280) =$ 6720 square units.

4. $EFIH$ is a trapezoid, so Area($EFIH$) = $\frac{1}{2}h(b_1 + b_2) = \frac{1}{2}(48)(160 + 180) =$ $\frac{1}{2}(48)(340) = 8160$ square units. (Another way: add the area of right triangle FIG to the area of $EFGH$, so Area($EFIH$) = $\frac{1}{2}(48)(60) + 6720 = 1440 + 6720 =$ 8160 square units.)

5. The formula for the area of any trapezoid is $A = \frac{1}{2}h(b_1 + b_2)$, where h is the altitude and b_1 and b_2 are the two bases.

6. To find the area of a trapezoid, you may either triangulate (because that will work for any polygon) or you may use the Trapezoid Area Formula; that is choice (c).

7. $\frac{1}{2}(b_1 + b_2)$ is the mean or average of b_1 and b_2.

8. Using the formula $A = \frac{1}{2}h(b_1 + b_2)$ with $h = 4$, $b_1 = 8$, and $b_2 = 15$, the area is $A = \frac{1}{2}(4)(8 + 15) = \frac{1}{2}(4)(23) =$ 46 square units.

9. Using the formula $A = \frac{1}{2}h(b_1 + b_2)$ with $h = 6$, $b_1 = 5$, and $b_2 = 14$, the area is $\frac{1}{2}(6)(5 + 14) = \frac{1}{2}(6)(19) = 57$ square units.

10. Using the formula $A = \frac{1}{2}h(b_1 + b_2)$ with $h = 7$, $b_1 = 19$, and $b_2 = 6$ (since b_2 is opposite the side of length 6 in a rectangle), the area is $\frac{1}{2}(7)(19 + 6) = \frac{1}{2}(7)(25) =$ 87.5 square units.

11. The area of any parallelogram is $A = hb$, where b is a base and h is the altitude to that base.

12. The given altitude has length 4, and the base for that altitude has length 9. Using $A = bh$ with $b = 9$, and $h = 4$, the area is $A = (9)(4) = 36$ square units.

13. The given altitude has length 120, and the base for that altitude has length 140. Using $A = bh$ with $b = 140$ and $h = 120$, the area is $A = (140)(120) = 16,800$ square units.

14. The vertical side of the trapezoid is an altitude, and its length is 7. The length of the "top" base is 4 [that is the distance between $(1, 7)$ and $(5, 7)$] and the length of the bottom base is 5. Using the formula $A = \frac{1}{2}h(b_1 + b_2)$, $A = \frac{1}{2}(7)(4 + 5) =$ $\frac{1}{2}(7)(9) = 31.5$ square units.

15. The vertical distance from the "top" base to the "bottom" base is b, the y-coordinate of the "top" base, and the lengths of the horizontal bases are $c - a$ [the distance between (c, b) and (a, b), with $c > a$) and a (the distance between $(a, 0)$ and $(0, 0)$]. Using the formula $A = \frac{1}{2}h(b_1 + b_2)$, the area is $A = \frac{1}{2}(b)(c - a + a) = \frac{1}{2}(b)(c) =$ $\frac{1}{2}bc$ square units.

16. Using the formula $A = \frac{1}{2}h(b_1 + b_2)$ with $A = 60$, $b_1 = 20$, and $b_2 = 15$, then $60 = \frac{1}{2}h(20 + 15)$ or $120 = 35h$.

So $h = \frac{120}{35} = \frac{24}{7}$ (linear) units.

17. $\triangle ABC$ is a right triangle, so its area is one-half the product of the legs or $\frac{1}{2}hx$ units^2; that is choice (d).

18. For $\triangle ABE$, the area is one-half the product of a side and the altitude to that side. Since altitude $\overline{AC}$ is given, use side $\overline{BE}$ and the area is $\frac{1}{2}(AC)(BE)$ or $\frac{1}{2}h(x + y + z)$ square units; that is choice (b).

19. To estimate the area of any region, you can use the method of Lesson 8-4. First, cover the region with a grid. Then use the approximation formula $A = (I + \frac{1}{2}B)U$, where I is the number of squares completely inside the region, B is the number of squares that contain the boundary of the region, and U is the area of each square in the grid. (At a store, of course, you would probably have to purchase at least the amount of fabric in a rectangle that encloses the region.)

20.

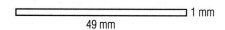

49 mm   1 mm

The sum of the length and width must be 50 mm so that the perimeter is 100 mm. If the sides of the rectangle are 49 mm and 1 mm, then the area is 49 mm^2 and the area condition is satisfied. But if the sides are 48 and 2, the area is 96 mm^2 and the area condition is not satisfied. Any pair of numbers (that add to 50) closer together than 49 and 1 will not satisfy the area condition. Actually, the exact values of the critical side lengths are $\frac{50 \pm \sqrt{2300}}{2} \approx 1.02$ and 48.98. (This is the solution to the equation $(50 - \ell)\ell = 50$ or $\ell^2 - 50\ell + 50 = 0$.)

21. In a circle, any diameter is twice as long as any radius, so if the length of a radius is $6x$, then the length of a diameter $2(6x) = 12x$ units.

22. The altitude to side $\overline{KM}$ is the easiest altitude to find. Using the formula $A = \frac{1}{2}hb$, the length b of side $\overline{KM}$ is 7 [the distance between (-2, 6) and (5, 6)] and the length of the altitude to side $\overline{KM}$ is 6, so $A = \frac{1}{2}(6)(7) = 21$ square units.

23. Using the FOIL pattern, $(a + b)(c + d) = ac + ad + bc + bd$.

24. $(e + f)^2 = (e + f)(e + f)$; using the FOIL pattern, that is $(e^2 + ef + fe + f^2 = e^2 + 2ef + f^2$.

25. a. For the area of the trapezoid that contains Nevada, use the formula $A = \frac{1}{2}h(b_1 + b_2)$ with $h = 310$, $b_1 = 210$, and $b_2 = 520$; the area is $A = \frac{1}{2}(310)(210 + 520) = \frac{1}{2}(310)(730) = 113,150$ square miles.

b. For the area of the trapezoid in southeast Nevada, use the formula $A = \frac{1}{2}h(b_1 + b_2)$ with $h = 30$, $b_1 = 80$, and $b_2 = 120$; the area is $A = \frac{1}{2}(30)(80 + 120) = \frac{1}{2}(30)(200) = 3000$ square miles.

c. The area of Nevada is approximately the difference between the areas in parts **a** and **b** above, so the area is $113{,}150 - 3{,}000 = 110{,}150$ square miles.

d. The actual area of Nevada is 109,895 square miles (Allstate Motor Club Almanac, 1988). The difference is $110{,}150 - 109{,}895 = 255$; that difference, $\frac{255}{109895}$, is 0.00232, which means the estimated area is less than one-quarter of one percent different from the actual area.

LESSON 8–7 (pp. 390–395)

1. A thousand years before Pythagoras was a thousand years before 550 B.C. (the sixth century B.C.), which was 1550 B.C. (the sixteenth century B.C.) or about 3600 years ago.

2. The (measure of a) side of a square is the square root of (the measure of) its area. If the area is 225 square meters, then the side is $\sqrt{225} = 15$ meters.

3. **a.** Each corner triangle is a right triangle with legs a and b, so the area of each corner triangle is $\frac{1}{2}ab$.

   b. The area of the large square is the square of the length of its side (which is $a + b$), so the area is $(a + b)^2$ or $a^2 + 2ab + b^2$.

c. The area of the tilted square is the area of the large square, less 4 times the area of each corner triangle. The side of the large square is $(a + b)$, so its area is $(a + b)^2$, and the area of each corner triangle (from part **a**) is $\frac{1}{2}ab$. So the area of the tilted square is $(a + b)^2 - 4(\frac{1}{2}ab) = a^2 + 2ab + b^2 - 2ab = a^2 + b^2$.

d. By equating two expressions for the area of the tilted square, $c^2 = a^2 + b^2$ so $c = \sqrt{a^2 + b^2}$.

4. Since the Pythagorean Theorem is the last step of the method from Question 3, it is shorter to apply the Pythagorean Theorem than to work through all four parts of the method in Question 3.

5. In this lesson, the Pythagorean Theorem is proved by finding two expressions for the area of a tilted square inside a larger square. That is the method of Question 3, which is choice (c).

6. The Pythagorean Theorem states that in any right triangle with legs a and b and hypotenuse c, then $a^2 + b^2 = c^2$. (In words: In a right triangle, the square of the hypotenuse is equal to the sum of the squares of the other two sides.)

7. Using $c^2 = a^2 + b^2$ with $a = 3$, and $b = 3$, then $c^2 = 3^2 + 3^2 = 9 + 9 = 18$. So $c^2 = 18$ and $c = \sqrt{18} = \sqrt{(9)(2)} = 3\sqrt{2} \approx 4.24$.

8. Using $c^2 = a^2 + b^2$ with $a = 9$ and $b = 40$, then $c^2 = 9^2 + 40^2 = 81 + 1600 = 1681$. So $c^2 = 1681$ and $c = \sqrt{1681} = 41$.

9. Using $c^2 = a^2 + b^2$ with $c = 13$ and $a = 5$, then $13^2 = 5^2 + b^2$ or $169 = 25 + b^2$. So $b^2 = 144$ and $b = \sqrt{144} = 12$.

10. Using $c^2 = a^2 + b^2$ with $c = 40$ and $a = 1$, then $40^2 = 1^2 + b^2$ or $1600 = 1 + b^2$. So $b^2 = 1599$ and $b = \sqrt{1599} \approx 39.987$.

11. In Example 2, if the track expanded $\frac{1}{2}''$ instead of $1''$, then AC would be 100 feet $\frac{1}{4}$ inch, which is $(100)(12) + .25 = 1200 + .25 = 1200.25$ inches. The solution would differ from the example starting in the second line of equations:
$$1200^2 + h^2 = 1200.25^2$$
$$1,440,000 + h^2 = 1,440,600.063$$
$$h^2 = 600.0625$$
$$h \approx 24.496 \text{ inches}$$
To the nearest inch, $h = 24$ inches.

12. In any Pythagorean Triple, the largest number must be the hypotenuse.
$3^2 + 4^2 = 9 + 16 = 25 = 5^2$, so $(3, 4, 5)$ is a Pythagorean Triple.

13. $24^2 + 70^2 = 576 + 4900 = 5476 = 74^2$, so $(70, 24, 74)$ is a Pythagorean Triple.

14. $10^2 + 24^2 = 100 + 576 = 676 = 26^2$, so $(10, 24, 26)$ is a Pythagorean Triple.

15. $8^2 + 14^2 = 64 + 196 = 260 \approx \sqrt{16.1245}^2 \neq 17^2$ ($17^2 = 289$), so $14, 8, 17$ is not a Pythagorean Triple.

16. $7^2 + 24^2 = 49 + 576 = 625 = 25^2$, so $(25, 24, 7)$ is a Pythagorean Triple.

17. $9^2 + 40^2 = 81 + 1600 = 1681 = 41^2$, so $(40, 9, 41)$ is a Pythagorean Triple.

18. $1.67^2 + 2.67^2 = 2.7889 + 7.1289 = 9.9178 \approx \sqrt{3.1493}^2 \neq 3.33^2$ ($3.33^2 = 11.0889$), so $1.67, 2.67, 3.33$ is not a Pythagorean Triple.

19. $1.5^2 + 3.6^2 = 2.25 + 12.96 = 15.21 = 3.9^2$, so $(1.5, 3.6, 3.9)$ is a Pythagorean Triple.

20. $2^2 + (\frac{8}{3})^2 = 4 + \frac{64}{9} = \frac{36}{9} + \frac{64}{9} = \frac{100}{9} = (\frac{10}{3})^2$, so $(2, 2\frac{2}{3}, 3\frac{1}{3})$ is a Pythagorean Triple.

21. If a square room has area 20 square feet, then the length of a wall is $\sqrt{20} \approx 4.4721$ feet $= (4.4721)(12) = 53.6652 \approx 54$ inches.

22.

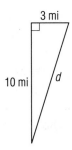

Using the Pythagorean Theorem,
$d^2 = 10^2 + 3^2 = 100 + 9 = 109$.
So $d^2 = 109$ and $d \approx 10.4403 \approx 10.4$ miles.

23.

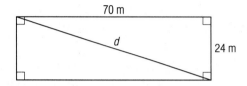

Using the Pythagorean Theorem,
$d^2 = \ell^2 + w^2$, so $d^2 = 24^2 + 70^2 = 576 + 4900 = 5476 = 74^2$. So $d = 74$ meters.

24.

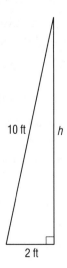

Using the Pythagorean Theorem,
$10^2 = 2^2 + h^2$ or $100 = 4 + h^2$, so $h^2 = 96$ and $h = \sqrt{96} \approx 9.797959 \approx 9.80$ feet.

25. If P is the foot of the perpendicular from Q to $\overline{TS}$, then $QP = 200$ (it is the same as RS) and $TP = 560 - 350 = 210$. So $TQ^2 = TP^2 + QP^2 = 210^2 + 200^2 = 44{,}100 + 40{,}000 = 84{,}100 = 290^2$, so $TQ = 290$ m.

The perimeter of the field is $290 + 350 + 200 + 560 = 1400$ m. At a rate of 90 meters per minute, the time needed would be $\frac{1400}{90} \approx 15.56$ minutes.

26. Using c to represent the hypotenuse, $c^2 = x^2 + (2x)^2 = x^2 + 4x^2 = 5x^2$, so $c = x\sqrt{5}$. Equating $x\sqrt{5}$ with kx or (xk), $k = \sqrt{5} \approx 2.2$.

27. The area of region $FNDCG$ is the sum of the areas of two trapezoids, $FNBG$ and $NDCB$; use the formula for the area of a trapezoid, $A = \frac{1}{2}h(b_1 + b_2)$. For trapezoid $FNBG$, the altitude is 250 and the bases are 160 and 200, so the area is $\frac{1}{2}(250)(160+200) = \frac{1}{2}(250)(360) = 45{,}000$ square units. For trapezoid $NDCB$, the altitude is 66 and the bases are 200 and 80, so the area is $\frac{1}{2}(66)(200 + 80) = \frac{1}{2}(66)(280) = 9240$. The area of $FNDCG = $ the sum of these two areas; $45{,}000 + 9{,}240 = 54{,}240$ square units. Now find the area of trapezoid $FDCG$. Its altitude GC is $250 + 66 = 316$ and its bases are 160 and 80, so its area is $\frac{1}{2}(316)(160 + 80) = \frac{1}{2}(316)(240) = 37{,}920$ square units. So the area of the shaded triangle is $54{,}240 - 37{,}920 = 16{,}320$ square units.

28. The formula for the area of a trapezoid is $A = \frac{1}{2}h(b_1 + b_2)$. In a parallelogram, $b_1 = b_2 = b$, so the formula can be rewritten as $A = \frac{1}{2}h(b + b) = \frac{1}{2}h(2b) = hb$.

29. The triangle in Question 7 is a right triangle, so its area is half the product of the legs; $A = \frac{1}{2}(3)(3) = 4.5$ square units.

30.

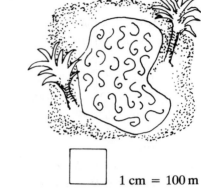

$1 \text{ cm} = 100 \text{ m}$

Use the approximation formula $A = (I + \frac{B}{2})U$, where I is the number of squares inside the region, B is the number of squares that contain part of the boundary, and U is the area of each square (100^2 m or $10{,}000$ m²). The area is about 70,000 square meters.

31. If the perimeter is 26, then $2(\ell + w) = 26$ or $\ell + w = 13$. What pair of numbers has sum 13 and product 12? Try 10 and 3: no, the product is 30, too high. Try 11 and 2: no, the product is 22, still too high (but closer). Try 12 and 1: the product is 12. The two numbers are 12 and 1.

Algebraic solution: the two numbers are w and $13 - w$, since their sum is 13.
So $w(13 - w) = 12$
$$13w - w^2 = 12$$
$$0 = w^2 - 13w + 12$$
$$0 = (w - 12)(w - 1)$$

and $w = 12$ or $w = 1$. Therefore, $\ell = 1$ or $\ell = 12$; the width is 1 unit and the length is 12 units.

32. Some samples:
For $x = 10$ and $y = 9$,
$x^2 - y^2 = 19, 2xy = 180$,
and $x^2 + y^2 = 181$.
To check, $19^2 + 180^2 = 361 + 32{,}400 = 32{,}761 = 181^2$, so $(19, 180, 181)$ is a Pythagorean Triple.
For $x = 15$ and $y = 2$,
$x^2 - y^2 = 221, 2xy = 60$,
and $x^2 + y^2 = 229$.
To check, $221^2 + 60^2 = 48{,}841 + 3{,}600 = 52{,}441 = 229^2$, so $(221, 60, 229)$ is a Pythagorean Triple.
In general, note that
$(x^2 - y^2)^2 + (2xy)^2$
$= (x^4 - 2x^2y^2 + y^4) + (4x^2y^2)$
$= x^4 + 2x^2y^2 + y^4$
$= (x^2 + y^2)^2$,
so the three expressions form a Pythagorean Triple.

LESSON 8-8 (pp. 396–401)

1. The minor arcs are $\overset{\frown}{RQ}$ and $\overset{\frown}{PQ}$ (or $\overset{\frown}{QR}$, $\overset{\frown}{QP}$); also $\overset{\frown}{RS}$, $\overset{\frown}{SP}$, and $\overset{\frown}{SQ}$.

2. **a.** $\overset{\frown}{PQ}$ has the same measure as its central angle, so m $\overset{\frown}{PQ}$ = 30°.
b. m $\overset{\frown}{PSQ}$ + m $\overset{\frown}{PQ}$ = 360°, so m $\overset{\frown}{PSQ}$ = 330°.

3. **a.** $\overline{PR}$ is a diameter, so m $\overset{\frown}{PSR}$ = 180°.
b. $\overline{PR}$ is a diameter, so m $\overset{\frown}{PQR}$ = 180°.
c. m $\overset{\frown}{PQ}$ + m $\overset{\frown}{QR}$ = 180°, and m $\overset{\frown}{PQ}$ = 30°, so m $\overset{\frown}{QR}$ = 150°.

4. P and Q, the points on the circle, are the endpoints of $\overset{\frown}{PQ}$.

5. $\angle ROQ$ is a central angle of $\odot O$.

6. $\overline{PR}$ is a diameter, so $\overset{\frown}{PSR}$ is a semicircle.

7. Arc length is a linear distance, and arc measure is an amount of a turn.

8. Circumference is a synonym for perimeter.

9. Circumference is a distance, so circumference is not an arc measure; it is an arc length.

10. π is $\frac{C}{d}$, the ratio of the circumference of a circle to the length of its diameter.

11. π is often approximated by the fraction $\frac{22}{7}$ or the decimals 3.14159, 3.1416, or 3.14.

12. **a.** Three radii are shown: $\overline{FC}$, $\overline{FD}$, and $\overline{FA}$.
b. One diameter is shown: $\overline{AC}$.
c. If $CF = 7$, then FD, which is also a radius, is 7 units.
d. If $CA = 28$, then FD, which is half of CA, is 14 units.
e. If $CA = 6x$, then FC, which is a radius, is half of CA, so $FC = 3x$.

13. **a.** If $CA = 8$, then the diameter is 8 units and the circumference is $\pi d = 8\pi$.
b. Substituting $\pi = 3.1416$ into 8π, $C = (3.1416)(8) = 25.1328 \approx 25.1$ units.

14. In Example 2, the bike travels 69.08 inches each revolution. If it makes 210 revolutions per minute, then in 5 minutes it makes $(5)(210) = 1050$ revolutions. So it would travel $(1050)(69.08) = 72{,}534$ inches or $\frac{72{,}534}{12} = 6044.5$ feet or $\frac{6044.5}{5280} = 1.14$ miles.

15. **a.** The circumference of circle O is $2\pi r = (2\pi)(5) = 10\pi$. The central angle for $\overset{\frown}{AB}$ is 30°, so $\overset{\frown}{AB}$ is $\frac{30}{360} = \frac{1}{12}$ of the circumference. So $\overset{\frown}{AB}$ is $\frac{10\pi}{12} = \frac{5\pi}{6}$ units.
b. Substituting 3.1416 for π, $\overset{\frown}{AB} = \frac{(5)(3.1416)}{6} = 2.618 \approx 2.62$ units.

16. The side of the square is 10 m, so the diameter of the pond is also 10 m. Using the formula $C = \pi d$ with $d = 10$, $C = 10\pi \approx 31.4$ m.

17. **a.** In each rotation, the tip of the minute hand travels 360 degrees. In one day, the minute hand travels $(24)(360) = 8640$ degrees (24 rotations per day, 360° per rotation).

    b. In each rotation, the tip of the minute hand travels the circumference of a 20-foot-radius circle. Using the formula $C = 2\pi r$ with $r = 20$, then $C = 2\pi(20) = 40\pi$ feet. In a day, the minute hand travels 24 revolutions (from part **a**), so the tip of the minute hand travels $(40\pi)(24) = 960\pi \approx 3016$ feet.

18. Using the formula $C = 3.1416d$, with $C = 110$, then $d = \dfrac{110}{3.1416} = 35.014 = 35$ seconds.

19. E, F, G, and H are midpoints, so $AE = 4$ and $AH = 3$. So all the corner triangles are right triangles with legs 3 and 4, so the hypotenuses are all 5 (because $3^2 + 4^2 = 5^2$) and the perimeter of $EFGH$ is $(4)(5) = 20$ units.

20. **a.** $\triangle PON$ is equilateral, and $PO = 2$, so $NO = 2$ and $MO = 1$. So $PM^2 + 1^2 = 2^2$, or $PM^2 + 1 = 4 = 5$. So $PM^2 = 3$, and $PM = \sqrt{3}$ units.

    b. The area of $\triangle PON$ is one-half the length of the base $\overline{NO}$ times the length of the altitude $\overline{PM}$, so the area is $\frac{1}{2}(2)(\sqrt{3}) = \sqrt{3} \approx 1.7$ square units.

21. A formula for the area of a trapezoid with bases b_1 and b_2 and altitude h is $A = \frac{1}{2}h(b_1 + b_2)$.

22. A formula for the area of a rectangle with length ℓ and width w is $A = \ell w$.

23. A formula for the perimeter of a square with side s is $p = 4s$.

24. A formula for the perimeter of a kite with sides a, a, b, and b is $p = 2(a + b)$.

25. To derive a formula for the measure of an angle in a regular n-gon, start with the formula for the sum of the measures of angles in an n-gon (from the Polygon-Sum Theorem), $S = (n - 2)(180)$. Then since the angles have equal measures, divide by the number of angles to get $\dfrac{(n - 2)(180)}{n}$. (Another way: the measure of each exterior angle of an n-gon has measure $\dfrac{360}{n}$, and each interior angle is the supplement of that angle, or $180 - \dfrac{360}{n}$. Remove parentheses in the first method to show that both answers are the same:

$$\frac{(n - 2)(180)}{n} = \frac{(180n - 360)}{n}$$
$$= \frac{180n}{n} - \frac{360}{n}$$
$$= 180 - \frac{360}{n}$$

26. The formula for the area of a triangle with base b and altitude to that side h is $A = \frac{1}{2}bh$.

27. $\triangle XYZ$ and $\triangle XYW$ have the same base, $\overline{XY}$, and the same altitude, the distance between parallel lines ℓ and m. So the two triangles have the same area; that is choice (b).

28. $q = XY + XZ + ZY$
    $r = XY + YW + XW$
    Then, since $XY = XY$ (Reflexive Property of Equality) and $XZ = YW$ ($XYWZ$ is a parallelogram), then the total lengths for q and r are in the same order as the lengths ZY and XW. Since $\angle ZXY$ is acute, then $ZY < XW$ by the SAS Inequality Theorem. So $q < r$, choice (c).

29. In Example 2, the rider traveled about 1727 feet per minute. Dividing by 5280 (because there are 5280 feet per mile) and then multiplying by 60 (because there are 60 minutes in an hour), the rider traveled $\frac{(1727)(60)}{(5280)} = 19.625 \approx 20$ miles per hour.

30. **a.** Answers may vary. Sample measurements for the circumference of the neck may be 14 inches to 18 inches.

b. Using the formula $C = 2\pi r \approx 6.28r$, divide the circumference by 6.28 to get an approximation for the radius. For $C = 14$, $r = \frac{14}{6.28} \approx 2.2$ inches; for $C = 18$, $r \approx 2.9$ inches.

c. Another way to get the radius would be to measure the diameter (for example, by measuring the distance between two parallel straightedges, one touching each side of the neck), and then dividing by 2.

LESSON 8–9 (pp. 402–406)

1. **a.** The height of the "parallelogram" is the radius of the circle, which is 10 units.

b. The base of the "parallelogram" is one-half the circumference of the circle, which is $\frac{1}{2}(2\pi r) = \frac{1}{2}(2\pi(10)) = 10\pi \approx 31.42$ units.

c. The area of the "parallelogram" is the product of the height and base, which is $(10)(10\pi) = 100\pi \approx 314.2$ units^2.

2. An exact value for the area of a circle with radius r is the formula $A = \pi r^2$.

3. To find an exact value for the area of a circle with radius $70''$, use the formula $A = \pi r^2$ with $r = 70$. The area is $A = \pi(70)^2 = 4900\pi$ square inches.

4. To find an exact value for the area of a circle with diameter 10 inches, first find the length of the radius, which is 5 inches, and then use the formula $A = \pi r^2$ with $r = 5$. The area is $A = \pi(5)^2 = 25\pi$ square inches.

5. Using the value $A = 4900\pi$ square inches from Question 3, $A = (4900)(3.1416) = 15,393.84 \approx 15,394$ square inches.

6. **a.** As in Example 2, the probability that the dart lands in the square equals

$$\frac{\text{area of square}}{\text{area of circle}}.$$

If the side of the square is 9 cm, then the area of the square is 81 cm^2. Then to find the area of the circle, you need r^2. Since $r^2 + r^2 = 9^2$, then $2r^2 = 81$ and $r^2 = \frac{81}{2}$.

So the area of the circle is $\pi r^2 = \pi(\frac{81}{2}) = \frac{81\pi}{2}$ cm^2.

Thus the probability is $\frac{81}{\frac{81\pi}{2}} = \frac{2}{\pi}$

which is the same value as in Example 2. So the probability is about 64%. (Note: this problem indicates that the probability of landing in the square is independent from the actual size of the square, and will be the same for any square drawn in a circle.)

b. The area of the shaded region between the circle and the square is $\frac{81\pi}{2} - 81 \approx 127.2345 - 81 = 46.2345 \approx 46.2$ cm^2.

7. **a.** Using the formula for the area of a circle, $A = \pi r^2$ with $r = 60$ m, $A = \pi(60)^2 = 3600\pi \approx 11,310$ m^2.

b. Using the formula for the circumference of a circle, $C = 2\pi r$ with $r = 60$ m, $C = 2\pi(60) = 120\pi \approx 377$ m.

8. a. Using the formula $A = \pi r^2$ with $A = 144\pi$, then $144\pi = \pi r^2$ so $r^2 = 144$ and $r = 12$ units.

  b. From part **a**, the radius of the circle is 12 units, so the diameter is 24 units.

  c. Using the formula $C = \pi d$ with $d = 24$, the circumference is $24\pi \approx 75.4$ units.

9. a. The area of the shaded region is the area of the square minus one-half the area of the circle. First, the area of the square: it is $8^2 = 64$ square units. Next, the area of the circle: the radius is 4 units, so the area is $\pi 4^2 = 16\pi$ square units and one-half the area is 8π square units. So the area of the shaded region is $64 - 8\pi \approx 64 - 25.133 = 38.867$ square units.

  b. The perimeter of the shaded region consists of 3 sides of the square and a semicircle. A side of the square is 8 units, so 3 sides is 24 units. The circumference of the circle is $\pi d = \pi \cdot 8$ units, so the circumference of the semicircle is 4π units, and the perimeter of the shaded region is $24 + 4\pi \approx 24 + 12.566 \approx 36.57$ units.

10. a. On a 10″ pizza, the part of the pizza that measures 10″ is the diameter of the pizza.

  b. The area of an 18″ pizza is $\pi(9)^2 = 81\pi$ square inches and the area of a 10″ pizza is $\pi(5)^2 = 25\pi$ square inches. The ratio of those areas is $\frac{81\pi}{25\pi} = \frac{81}{25} = 3.24$. So there are 3.24 times more ingredients in an 18″ pizza than in a 10″ pizza.

11. a. The probability that if a dart lands on the target, it will land inside the smaller circle is the ratio

  $\dfrac{\text{area of bull's eye}}{\text{area of large circle}}$.

The area of the bull's eye is πx^2, and the area of the large circle is $\pi(4x)^2 = \pi 16x^2$. So the probability is

$\dfrac{\pi x^2}{\pi 16 x^2} = \dfrac{1}{16} = 0.0625 = 6.25\%.$

  b. The probability that if a dart lands on the target, it will land **outside** the smaller circle is the ratio

  $\dfrac{\text{area of the region outside the bull's eye}}{\text{area of large circle}}$.

The area of the region outside the bull's eye is the area of the large circle minus the area of the bull's eye, or $\pi 16x^2 - \pi x^2 = \pi 15x^2$. So the probability is $\dfrac{\pi 15 x^2}{\pi 16 x^2} = \dfrac{15}{16} \approx 0.9375 = 93.75\%.$

(Another way: The dart must land either inside the bull's eye or outside the bull's eye, so the probability for outside the bull's eye is $1 - 0.0625 = 0.9375 = 93.75\%$.)

12. a. The total amount of metal in the rectangular sheet is $(12)(24) = 288$ cm². Each circle has radius 3 cm (since 4 radii add up to 12 cm), so the area of each circle is $\pi 3^2 = 9\pi$ cm² and the area of all 8 circles is 72π cm². So the amount of wasted metal is $288 - 72\pi \approx 288 - 226.2 \approx 61.8$ cm².

  b. Using 288 cm² as the "base amount" of metal, the percent wasted is $\dfrac{61.8}{288} \approx 0.215 = 21.5\%$. A slightly different answer is obtained if the "base amount" is considered to be the amount of material used, which is 72π. Then the percent wasted is $\dfrac{61.8}{72\pi} \approx \dfrac{61.8}{226.2} \approx 0.273 = 27.3\%$.

13. a. The central angle for arc $\overset{\frown}{AB}$ is $72°$, so $m\,\overset{\frown}{AB} = 72°$.

b. The central angle for arc $\overset{\frown}{AB}$ is $\frac{72}{360} = \frac{1}{5}$ of the circle, so the length of arc $\overset{\frown}{AB}$ is $\frac{1}{5}$ of the circumference. Using the formula $C = 2\pi r$ with $r = 15$, then $C = 30\pi$. So the length of arc $\overset{\frown}{AB}$ is $\frac{1}{5}(30\pi) = 6\pi \approx$ 18.8 units.

14. In each revolution the tip of the blade travels the circumference of a 12-meter-radius circle, which is $2\pi(12) = 24\pi$ meters. If it makes 15 revolutions in one minute, then it makes $(15)(60) = 900$ revolutions in one hour. So it travels $(900)(24\pi) = 21,600\pi \approx$ 67,858 meters.

15. The side of the square is 90, so the diameter of the circle is also 90. Using the formula $C = \pi d$, the circumference of the circle is 90π ≈ 282.74 units.

16. a.

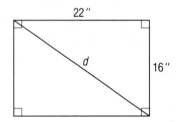

The diagonal is the hypotenuse of a right triangle with legs 16″ and 22″.
So $d^2 = 16^2 + 22^2 = 256 + 484 = 740$ and $d = \sqrt{740} \approx 27.2″$.

b. The rectangle has dimensions $\ell = 22$ and $w = 16$, so the perimeter is $2(\ell + w) = 2(22 + 16) = 2(38) = 76″$.

17. a. The area of a right triangle is one-half the product of the legs, so the area of the right triangle is $\frac{1}{2}(4x)(9x) = \frac{1}{2}(36x^2) = 18x^2$ square units.

b. First, use the Pythagorean Theorem to find the length of the hypotenuse of the triangle:
$c^2 = (4x)^2 + (9x)^2 = 16x^2 + 81x^2 = 97x^2$
so $c = x\sqrt{97}$. The perimeter of the triangle is $4x + 9x + x\sqrt{97} = x(13 + \sqrt{97}) \approx x(13 + 9.85) =$ $22.85x$ units.

18. To see if 13, 84, and 85 can be the lengths of sides of a right triangle, check them to see if they form a Pythagorean Triple.
$13^2 + 84^2 = 169 + 7056 = 7225 = 85^2$,
so the three numbers **can** be the lengths of sides of a right triangle.

19. Estimate the area using the approximation formula $(I + \frac{B}{2})U$, where I is the number of squares inside the region, B is the number of squares that contain boundary, and U is the area of each square in the grid.

a. For the grid at the left, $I = 0$, $B = 16$, and $U = 55^2 = 3025$ (the sides of 6 squares make up 330 miles, and $\frac{330}{6} = 55$). So the area is approximately $(0 + 8)(3025) =$ 24,200 square miles.

b. For the grid at the right, $I = 12$, $B = 35$, and $U = (\frac{330}{12})^2 = 27.5^2 = 756.25$. So the area is approximately $(12 + 17.5)(756.25)$ $= (29.5)(756.25) = 22,309.375 \approx 22,300$ square miles.

20.

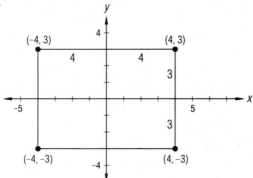

The polygon is a rectangle with horizontal dimension 8 and vertical dimension 6, so its area is $(6)(8) = 48$ square units.

21. In a parallelogram, opposite angles are congruent and consecutive angles are supplementary. So $m\angle E = 130$ and $m\angle D = m\angle F = 180 - 130 = 50$.

22.

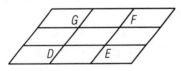

23. a. 1 centimeter $= \frac{1}{100}$ meter

(The prefix "centi" means "one hundredth.")

b. 1 yard = 36 inches

c. 1 mile = 1760 yards

(1 mile = 5280 feet, and $\frac{5280}{3} = 1760$)

24. a. Answers may vary. For a soft drink can, the diameter is about $2\frac{9}{16}$ inches.

b. Answers may vary. For a soft drink can, the circumference is about $8\frac{1}{4}$ inches. (For any cylinder, the circumference is about π times the diameter.)

c. Answers may vary slightly; the ratio of the two numbers in parts **a** and **b** should be close to 3.14.

d. The value from part **c** should approximate π.

e. The value from part **c** is based on measurements, so the numbers will be affected by the precision of the measuring instrument, irregularities in the actual object measured, and the skill of the measurer, so the value from part **c** is unlikely to be exactly π.

CHAPTER 8 PROGRESS SELF-TEST (p. 408–409)

1. Sample:

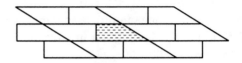

2. Using the formula $A = \ell \times w$, Area = 200 m² and length = 25 m.
$200 = 25 \times w$, so $w = 8$ m.

3. In a regular polygon, all sides have the same length. So if a regular hexagon has a perimeter q, then each of its 6 sides has length one-sixth of the perimeter, or $\frac{q}{6}$.

4. Using the formula $A = \frac{1}{2}bh$ with $b = 210$ units and $h = 80$ units, $A = \frac{1}{2}(210)(80)$
$= (105)(80) = 8400$ units².

5. Using the formula $A = bh$ with $b = 40$ units and $h = 11$ units, $A = (40)(11) = 440$ units².

6. Using the formula $A = \frac{1}{2}h(b_1 + b_2)$ with height h and bases a and c, $A = \frac{1}{2}h(a + c)$.

7.

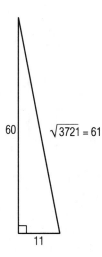

$c^2 = 11^2 + 60^2$
$\quad = 121 + 3600$
$\quad = 3721$
$\quad c = 61$

The perimeter of the triangle is $60 + 11 + 61 = 132$ units.

8.

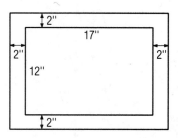

The outside dimensions are $12 + 4$ and $17 + 4$, or $16''$ and $21''$. The outside perimeter is $2(16 + 21) = 2(37) = 74''$.

9. The perimeter of the square is $p = 4s = 4(10) = 40$ units. The circumference of the circle is $C = 2\pi r = 2\pi(5) = 10\pi$. The difference is $p - C = 40 - 10\pi \approx 8.6$ units.

10. The area of the circle is $A = \pi r^2 = \pi(5)^2 = 25\pi$. The area of the square is $A = s^2 = 10^2 = 100$. The probability that a point inside the square is also inside the circle is $\frac{25\pi}{100} = \frac{\pi}{4} \approx .785$, or 7.85%.

11. The entire circumference is $C = 2\pi r = 2\pi 20 = 40\pi$. $\overset{\frown}{CD}$ represents $45°$ or $\frac{1}{8}$ of the circle, so the length of $\overset{\frown}{CD}$ is $\frac{40\pi}{8} = 5\pi \approx 15.7$ units.

12. $m\overset{\frown}{CBD} = 360° - m\overset{\frown}{CD}$. Since $\overset{\frown}{CD}$ is $\frac{1}{8}$ of the circle, or $45°$, then $m\overset{\frown}{CBD} = 360° - 45° = 315°$.

13. There seem to be 29 unit squares inside the island and 36 unit squares on the island's boundary, and each unit square represents $10^2 = 100$ miles^2. Adding half the number of boundary squares to the number of squares inside the island, and multiplying by 100, the area can be approximated as 4700 square miles. (Answers may vary.)

14.

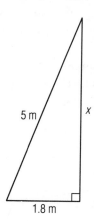

$x^2 + 1.8^2 = 5^2$
$\quad x^2 = 25 - 3.24$
$\quad\quad = 21.76$
$\quad x \approx 4.66476$
$\quad\quad \approx 4.7$ meters

15. Using the formula $A = \pi r^2$ with $r = 80$ miles, $A = \pi(80)^2 = 6400\pi \approx 20,100$ miles^2.

16. In yards, 9 ft by 15 ft is 3 yds by 5 yds; that product is 15 yds^2.

17. If the perimeter of a square is 2640 ft, then each side has length $\frac{2640}{4} = 660$ ft. The area of a square with side 660 ft is $660^2 = 435{,}600$ ft^2.

18.

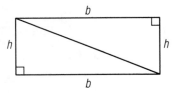

The area of a rectangle with height h and base b is $A = bh$. Two right triangles, each with base b and height h, make up that rectangle, so a formula for the area of either right triangle is $A = \frac{1}{2}bh$.

19. a. $11^2 + 60^2 = 121 + 3600 = 3721 = 61^2$. Since $a^2 + b^2 = c^2$, the three lengths (11, 60, 61) can be the lengths of sides of a right triangle.

b. The statement, if $a^2 + b^2 = c^2$, then a, b, and c can be the lengths of sides of a right triangle, is the Pythagorean Converse Theorem.

20.

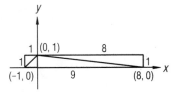

The horizontal base has length 9, and the height is 1, so the area of the triangle is
$A = \frac{1}{2}bh = \frac{1}{2}(9)(1) = 4.5$ units^2.

21.

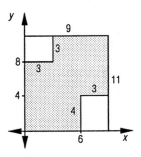

The area of the shaded octagon is the area of the large rectangle ($\ell = 9$, $w = 11$, $A = \ell \times w = 99$), less the area of the small rectangle at the upper left ($\ell = 3$, $w = 3$, $A = \ell \times w = 9$), then less the area of the small rectangle at the lower right ($\ell = 3$, $w = 4$, $A = \ell \times w = 12$). So the area of the octagon is $99 - 9 - 12 = 78$ units^2.

CHAPTER 8 REVIEW (pp. 410–413)

1.

2.

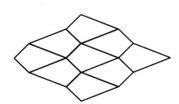

3.

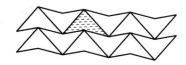

4. Use the approximation formula $(I + \frac{B}{2})U$ where I is the number of squares inside the region, B is the number of squares containing border of the region, and U is the area of each grid unit. For the given grid, $I = 9$, $B = 28$, and $U = 100^2 = 10,000$ ft^2. So an approximation for the area is $(9 + 14)(10,000) = (23)(10,000) = 230,000$ ft^2.

5. Use the approximation formula $(I + \frac{B}{2})U$ where I is the number of squares inside the region, B is the number of squares containing border of the region, and U is the area of each grid unit. For the given grid, $I = 62$, $B = 60$, and $U = 50^2 = 2500$ ft^2 (the side of each square is half the length of the side of the grid at the left). So an approximation for the area is $(62 + 30)(2500) = 92 \cdot 2500 = 230,000$ ft^2.

6. Impose a grid over the piece of metal. Then use the approximation formula $(I + \frac{B}{2})U$ where I is the number of squares inside the region, B is the number of squares containing border of the region, and U is the area of each grid unit.

7. For a kite with sides 10, 10, 6, and 6 (since a kite has two pairs of congruent sides), the perimeter of the kite is $(10 + 10 + 6 + 6) = 32$ units.

8. A rhombus has 4 congruent sides, so the perimeter of a rhombus with side t has perimeter $4t$.

9. A regular pentagon has 5 congruent sides, so the perimeter of a regular pentagon with side 47 meters is $(5)(47) = 235$ meters.

10. The side of a square with area 324 square feet is $\sqrt{324} = 18$ feet. So the perimeter of the square is $(4)(18) = 72$ feet.

11. Use the formula for the perimeter of a rectangle $p = 2(\ell + w)$ with $p = 28$ and $\ell = 4$. Then $28 = 2(4 + w)$ or $14 = 4 + w$ so $w = 10$. The other side has length 10 cm.

12. An equilateral triangle has 3 congruent sides. If the perimeter is P, then the length of each side is $\frac{P}{3}$ units.

13. The parallelogram has sides x and $2x$, so its perimeter is $2(x + 2x) = 2(3x) = 6x$ units. If the perimeter is given to be 75, then $6x = 75$ and $x = 12.5$. So the sides are $x = 12.5$ units and $2x = 25$ units.

14. An equilateral hexagon has 6 congruent sides. If the perimeter is 1, then the length of each side is $\frac{1}{6}$ unit.

15. If the perimeter of a square is 100 ft, then the length of each side is 25 ft, and its area is $25^2 = 625$ ft^2.

16. The area of a rectangle is the product of its length and width, so the area of the rectangle is $(3.5)(1.3) = 4.55$ cm^2.

17. The area of a triangle is one-half the product of a side and an altitude to that side. Using side $\overline{GE}$, the area of the triangle is $\frac{1}{2}(GE)(FH) = \frac{1}{2}(36x)(16x) = 288x^2$ units ^{2}.

18. A formula for the area of a trapezoid is $A = \frac{1}{2}h(b_1 + b_2)$. For $h = 6, b_1 = 11$, and $b_2 = 13$, then $A = \frac{1}{2}(6)(11 + 13) = \frac{1}{2}(6)(24) = 72$ square units.

19. A formula for the area of a triangle is $A = \frac{1}{2}bh$, where b is a base and h is the altitude to that base. For $b = 14$ and $h = 12$, then $A = \frac{1}{2}(14)(12) = 84$ square units.

20.

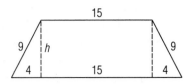

A formula for the area of a trapezoid is

$A = \frac{1}{2}h(b_1 + b_2)$. For the given isosceles

trapezoid, the bottom base is made up of
segments with length 4, 15, and 4 units. Use
the Pythagorean Theorem to find the altitude
of the trapezoid:

$4^2 + h^2 = 9^2$

$16 + h^2 = 81$

$h^2 = 65$

$h = \sqrt{65}$

So the area of the trapezoid is

$A = \frac{1}{2}(\sqrt{65})(15 + 23) = \frac{1}{2}(\sqrt{65})(38) =$

$19\sqrt{65} \approx 153.18$ square units.

21. The area of a right triangle is one-half the

product of the legs. So if $60 = \frac{1}{2}(6)(s)$, then

$120 = 6s$ and $s = 20$; the other leg has length
20 millimeters.

22. Using the formula for the area of a trapezoid

$A = \frac{1}{2}h(b_1 + b_2)$ with $A = 800$, $b_1 = 20$,

and $b_2 = 30$, then $800 = \frac{1}{2}h(20 + 30)$ or

$1600 = 50h$. So $h = 32$ feet.

23. The measure of the side of a square is the
square root of the measure of its area. If the
area is $12.25s^2$, then a side is $\sqrt{12.25s^2}$
$= 3.5s$

24. Using the formula for the area of a rectangle
$A = \ell w$ with $A = 20$ and $\ell = 21$, then

$20 = 21w$ and $w = \frac{20}{21} \approx 0.95$ units.

length = 21

$\frac{20}{21}$ = width

25. Using the formulas $C = 2\pi r$ and $A = \pi r^2$
with $r = 10$, then:
   a. $C = 2\pi(10)$ and $A = \pi(10)^2 = 100\pi$;
   b. $C = 20\pi \approx 62.8318 \approx 62.83$ units and
   $A = 100\pi \approx 314.159 \approx 314.16$ square units.

26. Using the formulas $C = 2\pi r$ and $A = \pi r^2$
with $d = 6$ cm, then $r = 3$ cm and:
   a. $C = 2\pi(3) = 6\pi$ and $A = \pi(3)^2 = 9\pi$;
   b. $C = 6\pi \approx 18.8$ cm and $A = 9\pi \approx$
   28.3 cm^2.

27. Using the formula $A = \pi r^2$ with $A = 144\pi$,
then $144\pi = \pi r^2$ and $r = 12$. So the diameter
is 24 units.

28. Using the formula $C = 2\pi r$ with $C = 40x$
meters, then $40x = 2\pi r$ or $20x = \pi r$. So

$r = \frac{20x}{\pi} \approx 6.4x$ meters.

29. **a.** The measure of arc $\overset{\frown}{AD}$ is the same as its
   central angle. Since m$\angle AOD = 20$, then
   m $\overset{\frown}{AD} = 20°$.
   b. $\overline{DB}$ is a diameter, so $\overset{\frown}{DAB}$ is a semicircle
   with measure 180°. So m $\overset{\frown}{AB} =$
   $180 -$ m $\overset{\frown}{AD} = 180° - 20° = 160°$.
   c. m$\overset{\frown}{ADB}$ = m $\overset{\frown}{AD}$ + m $\overset{\frown}{DB}$ = 20° + 180°
   = 200°.

30.

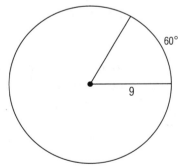

A circle with radius 9 has circumference
$C = 2\pi r = 2\pi(9) = 18\pi$. The length of a 60°

arc is $\frac{60}{360} = \frac{1}{6}$ of the entire circumference, or

$\frac{18\pi}{6} = 3\pi$ units. That is approximately

9.4248 or 9.4 units.

31. Using the Pythagorean Theorem, $1^2 + 2^2 = x^2$ or $1 + 4 = x^2$ or $x^2 = 5$ and so $x = \sqrt{5} \approx 2.24$ units.

32. Using the Pythagorean Theorem, $y^2 + 20^2 = 29^2$ or $y^2 + 400 = 841$. So $y^2 = 441$ and $y = 21$ units.

33. Using the Pythagorean Theorem to find the length c of the hypotenuse, $c^2 = (6x)^2 + (7x)^2 = 36x^2 + 49x^2 = 85x^2$. So $c = x\sqrt{85}$, and the perimeter of the triangle is $6x + 7x + x\sqrt{85} = (13 + \sqrt{85})x \approx (13 + 9.2)x = 22.2x$ units.

34. First, use the Pythagorean Theorem to find the length ℓ of the other leg of the right triangle: $\ell^2 + 40^2 = 50^2$ or $\ell^2 + 1600 = 2500$, so $\ell^2 = 900$ and $\ell = 30$. (Note that this is a 30-40-50 right triangle; the side lengths are a multiple of the side lengths of a 3-4-5 right triangle.)

    Then, find the area of the right triangle by finding one-half the product of the legs:

    $\frac{1}{2}(30)(40) = 600$ square units.

35. Use the Pythagorean Theorem to find the hypotenuse c of a right triangle with legs 60 cm and 45 cm: $c^2 = (60)^2 + (45)^2 = 3600 + 2025 = 5625$, so $c = 75$ cm. [Note that this right triangle is a multiple of a 3-4-5 right triangle, because the side lengths can be expressed as 3(15), 4(15), and 5(15).]

36. Does $a^2 + b^2 = c^2$?
    $8^2 + 31^2 = 64 + 961 = 1025 \approx (32.0156)^2 \neq 32^2$
    So the numbers are not the lengths of sides of a right triangle.

37. Does $a^2 + b^2 = c^2$?
    $16^2 + 30^2 = 256 + 900 = 1156 = 34^2$
    So the numbers can be the lengths of sides of a right triangle.

38. Does $a^2 + b^2 = c^2$?
    $1^2 + \sqrt{3}^2 = 1 + 3 = 4 = 2^2$
    So the numbers can be the lengths of sides of a right triangle. (Note that the largest number of the three is 2, so it is checked for the length of the hypotenuse.)

39. The three numbers, 2, 4, and 20, do not satisfy the Triangle Inequality because $2 + 4 < 20$. So the three numbers cannot be lengths of the sides of **any** triangle.

40. The formula for the area of a trapezoid is derived by triangulating a trapezoid (dividing it into triangles). Then the formula for the area of a triangle is applied to each triangle.

41. A parallelogram is a trapezoid with two congruent bases. In the Trapezoid Area Formula, b_1 and b_2 are replaced with b, and the result is the formula for the area of a parallelogram.

42. Some samples of a rectangle with perimeter 200 ft and area less than 100 ft^2 are a 99-by-1 rectangle, a $99\frac{1}{2}$-by-$\frac{1}{2}$ rectangle, and a $99\frac{3}{4}$-by-$\frac{1}{4}$ rectangle.

99×1

$99\frac{1}{2} \times \frac{1}{2}$

$99\frac{3}{4} \times \frac{1}{4}$

The exact cut-off value for the length is the solution to the two equations:
$\ell + w = 100$
$\ell w < 100$
These equations lead to the quadratic equation $\ell^2 - 100\ell + 100 = 0$, for which the solution is $\ell = \dfrac{100 \pm \sqrt{9600}}{2}$ or the approximate values 98.9898 or 1.0102.

43. The area of a triangle is one-half the base times the altitude. Since $\triangle ABC$ and $\triangle ABD$ have the same base, (segment $\overline{AB}$) and the same altitude (the distance between parallel lines ℓ and m), the two triangles have the same area; that is choice (b).

44. Using the formula for the area of a circle $A = \pi r^2$, the radius of the larger circle is $2x$, so its area is $\pi(2x)^2 = 4x^2\pi$, and the radius of the smaller circle is x, so its area is πx^2. The area of the shaded region is the difference in these measurements, or $4x^2\pi - \pi x^2 = \pi(4x^2 - x^2) = \pi(3x^2) = 3x^2\pi$ units^2.

45. The side of the large square $WXYZ$ is $3s$, so its area is $(3s)^2 = 9s^2$. The side of the small square is s, so its area is s^2. The area of the shaded region is the difference in these measurements, or $9s^2 - s^2 = 8s^2$ units^2.

46. If the unit of the perimeter is given in millimeters, then a natural unit for the area of the figure is square millimeters.

47. The horizontal measurement of the outside of the frame is 3 cm + 20 cm + 3 cm = 26 cm, and the vertical measurement of the outside of the frame is 3 cm + 8 cm + 3 cm = 14 cm. So the perimeter of the outside of the frame is $2(\ell + w) = 2(26 + 14) = 2(40) = 80$ cm.

48. The perimeter of a regular octagon is $p = 8s$, where s is the length of a side. So if $s = k$ units, the perimeter of the octagon is $8k$ units.

49. The perimeter of a room with dimensions 9′ and 11′ is $2(9 + 11) = 2(20) = 40′$. If a baseboard is needed all around the perimeter except for 3′, then the amount of baseboard needed is $40 - 3 = 37′$.

50.

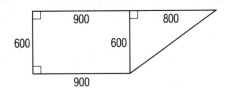

The two legs of the right triangle are 600′ and 800′, so the length of its hypotenuse is 1000′ (this is a 3-4-5 right triangle, with each side multiplied by 200). So the total perimeter of the trapezoid is $1700 + 1000 + 900 + 600 = 4200′$. At a rate of 300′ per minute, the number of minutes needed to walk the perimeter is $\frac{4200}{300} = \frac{42}{3} = 14$ minutes.

51.

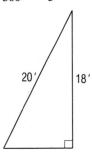

Use the Pythagorean Theorem to find the distance d:
$d^2 + 18^2 = 20^2$, so $d^2 + 324 = 400$ and $d^2 = 76$. So $d = \sqrt{76} \approx 8.7178 \approx 8.7$ feet.

52. Use the Pythagorean Theorem to find the hypotenuse c of a right triangle with legs 100 m and 200 m:
$100^2 + 200^2 = c^2$, so $c^2 = 10,000 + 40,000 = 50,000$ and $c = \sqrt{50,000} \approx 223.60679 \approx 224$ m.

53. Using the formula for the area of a square $A = s^2$ with $s = 210$ meters, $A = (210)^2 = 44,100$ square meters.

54. A rectangular room 6′ by 4′ is 72″ by 48″, which is $(72)(48) = 3456$ square inches. The room would need 3456 1-inch-square tiles.

55. Using the formula for the area of a trapezoid $A = \frac{1}{2}h(b_1 + b_2)$ with $h = 600'$, $b_1 = 1700'$, and $b_2 = 900'$, then the area is

$\frac{1}{2}(600)(1700 + 900) = \frac{1}{2}(600)(2600)$

$= 780,000$ ft^2.

56.

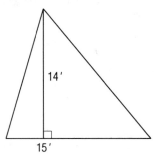

14'

15'

Using the formula $A = \frac{1}{2}bh$ with $b = 15'$ and

$h = 14'$, then $A = \frac{1}{2}(15)(14) = 105$ ft^2.

57. The probability of landing on the smaller square is the ratio of the area of the small square to the area of the large square. From Question 45, those areas were s^2 and $9s^2$, so the probability is $\frac{s^2}{9s^2} = \frac{1}{9} \approx .11$ or 11.1%.

58. The question calls for the area of a circle with radius 3 km. Using the formula $A = \pi r^2$ with $r = 3$, then $A = \pi 3^2 = 9\pi \approx 28.3$ km^2.

59. A side of the park is 600 feet, so the diameter of the circle is also 600 feet. Using the formula for the circumference of a circle $C = \pi d$ with $d = 600$, the circumference is 600π feet $\approx 1884.954 \approx 1885$ feet.

60. In each revolution, the car travels the length of the tire's circumference, which is 2π feet. Dividing this distance into the total distance of 5280 feet, the number of revolutions the tire makes is $\frac{5280}{2\pi} \approx 840.3380$ or just over 840 revolutions.

61. Using the formula for the circumference of a circle $C = \pi d$, and given that $C = 100$ feet, then $d = \frac{100}{\pi} \approx 31.83$ or about 31.8 feet, which is about 31 feet $9\frac{1}{2}$ inches.

62. The questions calls for the ratio of the area of the small circle to the area of the large circle. Using the results from Question 44, the area of the small circle is πx^2 and the area of the large circle is $\pi 4x^2$, so the ratio of the area is $\frac{\pi x^2}{\pi 4x^2} = \frac{1}{4}$, so the probability is .25 or 25%.

63.

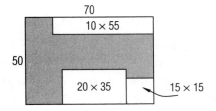

The area of the shaded decagon is the area of a rectangle with dimensions 50 and 70, minus the rectangular region at the upper right (which has dimensions 10 and 55), then minus the rectangular region at the lower right corner (dimensions 15 and 15), and minus the rectangular region at the middle bottom (dimensions 20 and 35). So the area of the shaded region is

$(50)(70) - (10)(55) - (15)(15) - (20)(35)$
$= 3500 - 550 - 225 - 700 = 2025$ square units.

64.

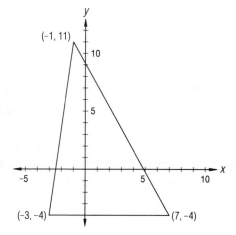

Using the formula $A = \frac{1}{2}bh$ for the area of a triangle, and using the side joining (-3, -4) and (7, -4) as the base, then $b = 10$. The altitude is the distance from (-1, 11) to the line $y = -4$, which is 15. So the area of the triangle is $\frac{1}{2}(10)(15) = 75$ square units.

65. The area of the shaded quadrilateral is the area of the entire grid (dimensions 10 and 6) less the areas of the four right triangles in the corners of the grid (starting from the upper left corner and moving clockwise, the lengths of the legs are 3 and 4, 6 and 1, 5 and 4, and 6 and 3. So the area of the shaded quadrilateral is

$(10)(6) - [\frac{1}{2}(3)(4) + \frac{1}{2}(6)(1) + \frac{1}{2}(5)(4) + \frac{1}{2}(6)(3)]$

$= 60 - (6 + 3 + 10 + 9)$

$= 60 - 28$

$= 32$ square units.

(Another method: use Pick's Theorem (page 377) that the area is $\frac{1}{2}P + I - 1$, where P is the number of lattice points **on** the polygon and I is the number of lattice points **inside** the polygon. For this figure, $P = 6$ and

$I = 30$, so the area is $\frac{1}{2}(6) + 30 - 1$

$= 3 + 30 - 1 = 32$ square units.)

66. The figure is a trapezoid with $h = a$, $b_1 = b$, and $b_2 = b - c$. Substituting these variables into the formula $A = \frac{1}{2}h(b_1 + b_2)$, the area

is $\frac{1}{2}(a)(b + b - c) = \frac{1}{2}(a)(2b - c) =$

$\frac{1}{2}a(2b^2 - c) = ab - \frac{1}{2}ac.$

CHAPTER 9 THREE-DIMENSIONAL FIGURES

LESSON 9-1 (pp. 414–420)

1. The higher dimensional counterparts for a line (a one-dimensional "expanse") are a plane (a two-dimensional expanse) and space (the three-dimensional expanse).

2. The higher dimensional counterparts for polygons (closed figures in 2-space, the sides are parts of lines) are polyhedra (closed figures in 3-space, the sides are parts of planes).

3. A higher dimensional counterpart for the circle is the sphere.

4. A higher dimensional counterpart for collinear (in or on the same line) is coplanar (on the same plane).

5. A higher dimensional counterpart for perpendicular lines is a line perpendicular to a plane or perpendicular planes.

6. A higher dimensional counterpart for the statement "If two lines in a plane are perpendicular to the same line, then they are parallel" is the statement "If two planes (in space) are perpendicular to the same plane, then they are parallel."

7.

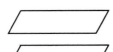

8.

9.

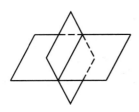

10.

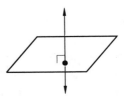

11. **a.** A three-legged stool will always rest solidly on rough ground (assuming the center of gravity of the stool is directly above the horizontal triangular region formed by the tips of the legs) because the three tips of the legs conform to the plane determined by those tips.

    b. A four-legged stool will rest solidly on level ground if the four tips of the legs determine a single plane.

    c. The answers to parts *a* and *b* are related to part *f* of the Point-Line-Plane Postulate.

12. **a.** A line and a point not on the line determine a plane (Point-Line-Plane Postulate, part f, because two of the three points determine a line, which lies in the plane by part e), which means they can be contained by exactly one plane.

    b. For two lines ℓ and m that intersect at point A, consider line ℓ and a point B that is on m but not on ℓ. Line ℓ and point B determine a plane (from part *a* of this question). Then because points A and B are both in the plane, all of line m is in the plane (by the Point-Line-Plane Postulate, part e). So two intersecting lines determine a plane, which means they can be contained in exactly one plane.

    c. Part f of the Point-Line-Plane Postulate states that three noncollinear points determine a plane, so they can be contained by exactly one plane.

d. The three vertices of a triangle determine a plane (by part f of the Point-Line-Plane Postulate), and the sides of the triangle must be in that plane by part e of the Point-Line-Plane Postulate. So a triangle can be contained by exactly one plane.

13. The front and back walls of most classrooms are parallel, and the distance between them can be measured by any line perpendicular to them. The line segment where the floor meets either side wall will serve as the distance between the front and back walls.

14. Assuming the floor is horizontal, the distance from the upper right-hand corner of this page to the floor would be measured along a vertical line from the upper right-hand corner of the page down to the floor.

15. Two perpendicular planes are illustrated where either the floor or ceiling meets one of the west, east, north, or south walls, or where the north or south wall meets either the east or west wall. So there are 12 illustrations of two perpendicular planes, 4 with a pair of vertical walls, 4 with the ceiling, and 4 with the floor.

16. An illustration of three planes each perpendicular to the other two is at any of the 4 ceiling corners or any of the 4 floor corners. In each case, two vertical planes are perpendicular, and they meet a horizontal plane which is perpendicular to both vertical planes.

17. An illustration of a line perpendicular to a plane is any of the 8 places where the floor or ceiling meets a wall or any of the 4 places where two walls meet. The line is the meeting of two of the surfaces, and it is perpendicular to the third surface.

18.

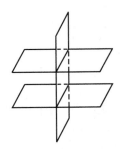

or

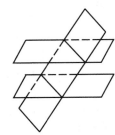

19.

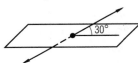

20.

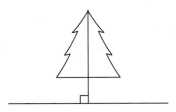

When any vertical tree falls to a horizontal position, it falls through an angle of 90 degrees.

21. a.

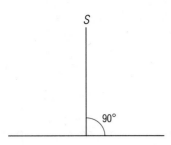

The largest possible angle of inclination occurs when the object S is directly above the viewer. This angle, from the horizontal to the vertical, is 90 degrees.

b. A star that is $\frac{1}{3}$ the way from the horizon to directly overhead is $\frac{1}{3}(90) = 30$ degrees from the horizontal, so its angle of inclination is 30°.

22. A figure is a segment if and only if it consists of two distinct points and all points between those two points.

23. A figure is a polygon if and only if it is the union of three or more segments in the same plane such that each segment intersects exactly two others, one at each of its endpoints.

24. A figure is a quadrilateral if and only if it is a polygon with 4 sides.

25. A figure is a rectangle if and only if it is a quadrilateral with 4 right angles.

26. M is the midpoint of $\overline{BC}$ and $\overline{AD}$, so $\overline{BC}$ and $\overline{AD}$ bisect each other by the definition of bisect (sufficient condition). So $ABCD$ is a parallelogram by the Sufficient Conditions for a Parallelogram Theorem (part c).

27. By the Vertical Angle Theorem, $5x - 2y = y$, so $5x = 3y$, and $y = \frac{5x}{3}$. Then, by the Linear Pair Theorem, $5x - 2y + x = 180$ or $6x - 2y = 180$. Multiply both sides of the equation by .5 to get $3x - y = 90$. Substituting for y, you can write $3x - \frac{5}{3}x = 90$ so $\frac{4}{3}x = 90$. So $x = \frac{3}{4}(90) = 67.5$, and $y = \frac{5}{3}x = \frac{5}{3}(67.5) = 112.5$.

28.

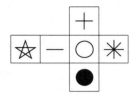

The pairs of symbols on opposite faces are:

 and ◯, — and ✳, + and ●

29. a-b. The bottoms of most chair legs are slightly further apart than their tops. This has to do with the stability of the chair, because people often brush against a chair or sit with their weight to one side.

LESSON 9–2 (pp. 421–426)

1. The distinction between a solid and a surface is that a surface is the boundary of a three-dimensional figure, while a solid is the union of the boundary and the region of space enclosed by the surface.

2. a. **b.**

3. **a.** A segment connecting two vertices is an edge (or a diagonal).

b. The box has a top, bottom, and 4 sides, so it has 6 faces.

c. Pairs of parallel faces are:
top and bottom—*ABCD* and *GHEF*;
front and back—*CDFE* and *BAGH*; and
right and left—*ADFG* and *BCEH*.

d. The box has 4 edges on the top ($\overline{AB}$, $\overline{BC}$, $\overline{CD}$, and $\overline{DA}$), 4 edges on the bottom ($\overline{GH}$, $\overline{HE}$, $\overline{EF}$, and $\overline{FG}$), and 4 edges on the sides ($\overline{AG}$, $\overline{BH}$, $\overline{CE}$, $\overline{DF}$), for a total of 12 edges.

e. Pairs of parallel edges not on the same face are:
$\overline{AG}$ and $\overline{CE}$, $\overline{BH}$ and $\overline{DF}$, $\overline{AD}$ and $\overline{HE}$, or $\overline{GF}$ and $\overline{BC}$.

4. **a.** The special name for the surface of a cylindric solid if its base is a hexagon is a hexagonal prism.

b. The special name for the surface of a cylindric solid if its base is a circle is a cylinder.

5.

6.

7.

8.

9. Another name for *rectangular parallelepiped* is box.

10. The three-dimensional object which most resembles a phonograph record (ignoring the center hole) is a solid right cylinder (another common name is "disk").

11. The three-dimensional object which most resembles an unsharpened pencil without an eraser is a solid hexagonal right prism (if the pencil has a hexagonal crosssection) or a solid right cylinder (if the pencil has a circular crosssection).

12.

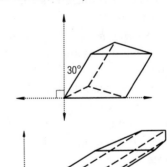

13.

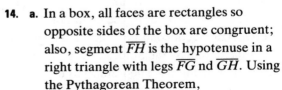

14. **a.** In a box, all faces are rectangles so opposite sides of the box are congruent; also, segment $\overline{FH}$ is the hypotenuse in a right triangle with legs $\overline{FG}$ nd $\overline{GH}$. Using the Pythagorean Theorem,
$FH^2 = FG^2 + GH^2 = 4^2 + 12^2$
$= 16 + 144 = 160$, so $FH = \sqrt{160} = \sqrt{(16)(10)} = 4\sqrt{10} \approx (4)(3.1623) \approx 12.649$ units.

b. Segment $\overline{BH}$ is the hypotenuse of a right triangle with legs $\overline{FH}$ and $\overline{BF}$. Using the Pythagorean Theorem,
$BH^2 = FH^2 + BF^2 = 160 + 3^2 = 169$
(note that the value of FH^2 was found in part a). So $BH = \sqrt{169} = 13$ units.

c. $\triangle BFH$ is a right triangle, so its area is one-half the product of its legs. Using the length of $\overline{FH}$ found in part a, and the given length of $\overline{BF}$, the area is $\frac{1}{2}(3)\sqrt{160} \approx$ 18.97 square units.

15. a. The height of the cylinder is given by segment $\overline{BC}$. Using the Pythagorean Theorem, $17^2 = 8^2 + BC^2$ or $289 = 64 + BC^2$. So $BC^2 = 225$ and $BC = 15$ units. (Note: The lengths of the sides of the triangle are the Pythagorean Triple 8, 15, 17.)

b. The lower base is a circle with radius 6, so its area is $\pi(6)^2 = 36\pi \approx 113$ square units.

16. a. The cube has 12 edges (4 horizontal on the top face, 4 horizontal on the bottom face, and 4 vertical on the sides). If the length of each edge is 5, then the total length of the 12 edges is $(12)(5) = 60$ units.

b. Every cube has 12 edges, so if the length of each edge is n units, the total length of the 12 edges is $12n$ units.

17.

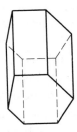

18. First, use the coordinates of points B and D to find that $G = (60, 50)$.
Next, compare the coordinates of point $B = (60, 0)$ and point $C = (85, 20)$: to get from B to C, the point is moved 25 units on the x-axis and 20 units on the y-axis. Similar moves result in the following:
from point A to point H means that
$H = (0+25, 0+20) = (25, 20)$;
from point D to point E means that
$E = (0+25, 50+20) = (25, 70)$;
from point G to point F means that
$F = (60+25, 50+20) = (85, 70)$.

19. Three-dimensional counterparts of intersecting lines (which meet at a single point) are either two intersecting planes (which meet in a line) or three intersecting planes (which meet in a point).

20.

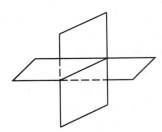

21. Two given (distinct) points determine a single line, and an unlimited number of planes contain that line. So an infinite number of planes contain two given points.

22. The area of the shaded portion of the diagram is the difference between the area of a quarter of the circle and the isosceles right triangle AOB. The area of the circle is $\pi 2^2 = 4\pi$ cm^2, so one quarter of that is π cm^2, and the area of the right triangle is one-half the product of the legs, or $\frac{1}{2}(2)(2) = 2$ cm^2. So the area of the shaded region is $\pi - 2 \approx 1.14$ cm^2.

23.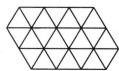

24. a. Coplanar means "can be contained by a single plane." A more detailed definition is the following: Given a set of points, lines (or segments or rays), planes or plane figures (such as angles, polygons, circles, or other curves), that set of figures is coplanar if and only if there is a single plane that contains all the elements in that set.

b. Collinear means "can be contained by a single line." A more detailed definition is the following: Given a set of points, lines, segments, rays, or any combination of those figures, that set of figures is collinear if and only if there is a single line which contains all the elements in that set.

25. $2\ell w + 2wh = 2w(\ell + h)$

26. $\pi r^2 + \pi h^2 = \pi(r^2 + h^2)$

27. $\pi r^2 + 2\pi rh = \pi r(r + 2h)$

28. For some prisms, if you shine a beam of light through the prism, the light is "refracted" or broken into its component colors, red, orange, yellow, green, blue, indigo, and violet.

29. One explanation is that the hexagon is the most "efficient" shape for tessellating the plane because it results in the smallest perimeter for a given region of the plane.

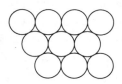

Another explanation is that the bees form circular cells, as shown above, but the "corners" between cells fill in, resulting in hexagonal cells.

LESSON 9-3 (pp. 427–432)

1. a. The base of the square pyramid is a square; that is the figure $ABDE$.

b. The vertex of the figure is the labelled point not on the base; that is point C.

c. A lateral edge is a segment connecting the vertex of the pyramid to a vertex of the base. There are 4 lateral edges for the given figure: $\overline{CA}$, $\overline{CB}$, $\overline{CD}$ and $\overline{CE}$.

d. A lateral face is determined by the vertex and a segment of the base. There are 4 lateral faces: $\triangle CBD$, $\triangle CDE$, $\triangle CEA$, and $\triangle CAB$.

2.

3. a. The name of the surface that is a conic solid with a circular base and axis $\perp$ to the base is a right cone.

b. The axis of a cone is the line through the vertex and the center of the base; that is $\overleftrightarrow{MO}$.

c. A lateral edge is a segment connecting the vertex to a point on the base. Two lateral edges are labelled in the figure: $\overline{ML}$ and $\overline{MN}$.

d. The vertex of a cone is the point where the lateral edges meet; that is point M.

e. The base of a cone is the surface opposite the vertex; that is circle O. (Note: the base of a cone, whether is is a right cone or an oblique cone, is always a circle.)

f. The height of a cone is the distance from the vertex to the plane of the base. Since this is a right cone, segment $\overline{MO}$ is perpendicular to the base, and the height is MO.

g. The slant height of a cone is the length of a lateral edge. For this cone, the slant height is ML or MN.

4. The figure is a pyramid with a 5-sided base, so it is a pentagonal pyramid. (Further, it seems to be a regular pentagonal pyramid.)

5. The figure is a pyramid with a 6-sided base, so it is a hexagonal pyramid. (Further, it seems to be a regular hexagonal pyramid.)

6. The figure has a circular base, so it is a cone, and the axis is not perpendicular to the base, so it is an oblique cone.

7.

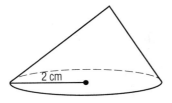

8. **a-b.**

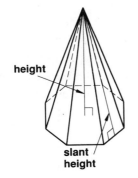

9. **a.** The height is the distance from the vertex P to the (shaded) pentagonal base, which is given as 10 units.

   b. The slant height is PR, which can be found using the Pythagorean Theorem in $\triangle PRQ$: $PR^2 = PQ^2 + QR^2 = 10^2 + 4^2 = 100 + 16 = 116$. So $PR = \sqrt{116} = \sqrt{(4)(29)} = 2\sqrt{29} \approx (2)(5.385) = 10.770 \approx 10.8$ units.

10. **a.** A pyramid has one face for each segment of the base. So if the base is an n-gon, then the pyramid will have n faces and a base, for $n + 1$ faces.

   b. The edges of a pyramid are the lateral edges (joining the vertex of the pyramid and each vertex of the base) and the segments of the base. In an n-gon, there are n lateral edges and n segments at the base, so there are $2n$ edges.

11. **a.**

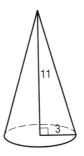

   b. The slant height h is the hypotenuse of a right triangle with legs 3 and 11, so $h^2 = 3^2 + 11^2 = 9 + 121 = 130$, so $h = \sqrt{130} \approx 11.4$ cm.

   c. The area of the base is the area of a circle with radius 3 cm, which is $\pi(3)^2 = 9\pi \approx 28.27$ cm^2.

12. In a circus, an elephant often stands or even sits on an object that is a (strong!) truncated cone.

13.

14. **a.** The circumference of the base of the cone is the length of $\overset{\frown}{BC}$, which is one quarter of the circumference of a circle with radius 4″. The circumference of that circle is $C = 2\pi r = 2\pi(4) = 8\pi$ inches, so one quarter of that circumference is $\frac{8\pi}{4} = 2\pi \approx 6.28$ inches.

b. The circumference of the base of the cone is 2π inches, so using the formula $C = 2\pi r$ with $C = 2\pi$, then $2\pi = 2\pi r$ and so $r = 1$ inch.

15. a. The view is from directly above.

b. The view is from the side, level with the base of the pyramid (so the entire base is at eye level), and not directly in front of one of the lateral edges of the pyramid.

c. The view is from the side, level with the base of the pyramid (so the entire base is at eye level), and directly in front of one of the lateral edges of the pyramid.

16. A figure is a cylindric solid if and only if it is the set of points between a region and its translation image in space, including the region and its image.

17. The difference between a right cylinder and an oblique cylinder can be described in terms of the relation between a lateral edge of the cylinder and either base. If the lateral edge is perpendicular to a base, it is a right cylinder; if the lateral edge is not perpendicular to a base, it is an oblique cylinder.

18. a. Three noncollinear points determine a plane (Point-Line-Plane Postulate, part f), so they are contained by exactly one plane.

b. The three vertices of a triangle determine a plane (part f of the Point-Line-Plane Postulate), and every point on each segment of the triangle lies in that plane (part e of the Point-Line-Plane Postulate). So the number of planes containing a given triangle is exactly one.

c. A given line is contained by an infinite number of planes. (Consider the line as the central axis of a revolving door. Then for the door you push, every position represents a plane containing the given line.)

19. a. The justification that $m\angle C = 90$ is the Triangle-Sum Theorem, which states that the sum of the measures of the angles of a triangle is 180. (The Addition Property of Equality is also used.)

b. From the information that $m\angle C = 90$, the justification that $\overline{BC} \perp \overline{CA}$ is the definition of perpendicular (sufficient condition).

c. The justification that $\triangle ABC$ is a right triangle is the definition of right triangle (sufficient condition).

d. From the information that $\triangle ABC$ is a right triangle (and, since C is a right angle, $\overline{AB}$ is the hypotenuse), the justification that $AC^2 + BC^2 = AB^2$ is the Pythagorean Theorem.

20. a. The figure is a cube, so all edges have the same length; that length is given as 5 units. Segment $\overline{AB}$ is an edge, so $AB = 5$ units.

b. $\overline{EA}$ is the hypotenuse of a right triangle whose legs are edges of the cube. So $EA^2 = 5^2 + 5^2 = 25 + 25 = 50$, and $EA = \sqrt{50} = \sqrt{(25)(2)} = 5\sqrt{2} \approx 7.07$ units.

c. $\overline{ET}$ is the hypotenuse of right triangle TEA, so $ET^2 = TA^2 + EA^2 = 5^2 + 50 = 25 + 50 = 75$, and $TA = \sqrt{75} = \sqrt{(25)(3)} = 5\sqrt{3} \approx 8.66$ units. (Note that part c called for a value of EA^2, and that value was available from part b.)

21. Call the dimensions of the first rectangle ℓ and w, so its area is ℓw. Then the length of the second rectangle is 2ℓ and its width is $3w$, so its area is $(2\ell)(3w) = 6\ell w$. That is 6 times the area of the first rectangle.

22. $\pi r \ell + 2\pi r = \pi r(\ell + 2)$

23. $\ell h + wh = h(\ell + w)$

24. a. The other six are the Hanging Gardens of Babylon, the statue of Zeus at Olympia, the temple of Artemis at Ephesus, the Mausoleum at Halicarnassus, the Colossos at Rhodes, and the Pharos of Alexandria.

b. Sample: The Brooklyn Bridge or the Hoover Dam.

LESSON 9–4 (pp. 433–438)

1. A figure is a sphere if and only if it is the set of points in space at a fixed distance (its radius) from a point (its center).

2. The definition of circle refers to a set of points in a plane, while the definition of sphere refers to a set of points in space.

3. The intersection of a plane and a sphere is either a single point (if the plane just touches the sphere) or a circle (if the plane cuts the sphere). (Another possible "intersection" is the empty set, if the plane and sphere have no points in common.)

4. "Great circle" is defined for a set of points on a sphere: A figure is a great circle (of a sphere) if and only if it is the intersection of (that) sphere and a plane that contains the center of the sphere.

5. "Small circle" is defined for a set of points on a sphere: A figure is a small circle (of a sphere) if and only if it is the intersection of (that) sphere and a plane that does not contain the center of the sphere.

6. A plane section of a three-dimensional figure is the intersection of a plane with that figure.

7. a.

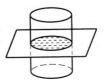

b. The section and the base are congruent.

8. a.

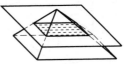

b. The section and the base are similar. The plane section is smaller than the base.

9. The conic sections are curves that are formed by the intersection of a plane and a double cone; the conic sections are circles, ellipses, parabolas, and hyperbolas. (Three other conic sections can be described: by intersecting the plane at the common vertex of the cones, a point is determined; by intersecting the plane through the axis, two intersecting lines are determined; and by "resting" the plane on the cone, a line is determined. These three figures are sometimes called "degenerate" conic sections.)

10. The equator is the intersection of the (spherical) earth and a plane through the center of the earth. That is the sufficient condition for a great circle, which is choice (c).

11. Some examples of fields which use plane sections of objects are architecture (plans and elevations of buildings or other structures), biology and medicine (microscope slides and scans), and geology (illustrations of rock strata).

12. a. At the equator, the radius of the earth is about 6378 kilometers or 3963 miles, so the diameter is about $(2)(6378) = 12{,}756$ kilometers or $(2)(3963) = 7926$ miles.

b. At the poles, the radius of the earth is about 6357 kilometers or 3950 miles, so the diameter is about $(2)(6357) = 12{,}714$ kilometers or $(2)(3950) = 7900$ miles.

13. **a–b.**

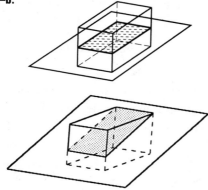

c. rectangles

14. **a–b.**

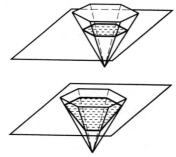

c. regular hexagon and hexagon

15. **a–b.**

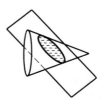

c. circle and ellipse

16.

17.

18. A blown-up balloon resembles a surface that is round and three dimensional; that is a sphere.

19. A golf ball resembles a solid that is round and three dimensional; that is a solid sphere.

20. **a-d. Proof:**
    Let P be the foot of the $\perp$ from point O to plane M. Let A be a fixed point and X be any other point on the intersection. Then $\overline{OP} \perp \overline{PA}$ and $\overline{OP} \perp \overline{PX}$ because **(a) any line in M through P is perpendicular to $\overleftrightarrow{OP}$.** $\overline{OP} \cong \overline{OP}$ because of the **(b) Reflexive Property of Congruence** and $\overline{OA} \cong \overline{OX}$ because of **(c) the definition of sphere (meaning)**. So $\triangle OPX \cong \triangle OPA$ by **(d) the HL Congruence Theorem.** Thus, due to **(e) the CPCF Theorem,** $PX = PA$. Thus any point X on the intersection lies at the same distance from P as A does. So by the definition of circle (sufficient condition), the intersection of sphere O and plane M is the circle with center P and radius PA.

21.

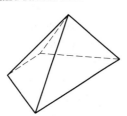

22.

23. The figure is a box, so all faces are rectangles, all angles are right angles, and opposite sides of each face are congruent.
    a. $CD = AB$, so $CD = 10$ units.
    b. $\overline{DE}$ is the hypotenuse of a right triangle with legs 6 and 8, so $DE^2 = 6^2 + 8^2 = 36 + 64 = 100$ and $DE = 10$ units. (Note that legs with lengths 6 and 8 mean the triangle is a 6–8–10 right triangle.)

c. $\overline{CE}$ is the hypotenuse of $\triangle CED$, so $CE^2 = ED^2 + DC^2 = 10^2 + 10^2 = 100 + 100 = 200$. So $DC = \sqrt{200} = \sqrt{(100)(2)} = 10\sqrt{2} \approx 14.14$ units.

24. **a.** Using the formula for the circumference of a circle $C = 2\pi r$ and the information that $r = 3963$ miles at the equator, then $C = 2\pi(3963) = 7926\pi \approx 24{,}900$ miles.
    b. Using the formula for the circumference of a circle $C = 2\pi r$ and the information that $r = 6378$ kilometers at the equator, then $C = 2\pi(6378) = 12{,}756\pi \approx 40{,}074 \approx 40{,}100$ kilometers.

25. **a.**

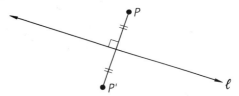

The reflection image of a point P over a line ℓ when P is not on ℓ is the point P' such that ℓ is the perpendicular bisector of segment $\overline{PP'}$.
    b. A plane figure F is a reflection-symmetric figure if and only if there is a line m such that $r_m(F) = F$.

26. The information about the radius of the earth implies that 6378 km is equal to 3963 mi (or 6357 km equals 3950 mi). Dividing the number of kilometers by the number of miles, there $\frac{6378}{3963} = 1.6094$ or 1.6 km in a mile ($\frac{6357}{3950}$ also equals $1.6094 \approx 1.6$).

27. **a.** The prime meridian passes through England, the European countries of France and Spain, the African countries of Algeria, Mali, Upper Volta, Ghana, and Togo, and Antarctica.

b. The International Date Line crosses the Pacific Ocean (the "Line" juts and bends around countries, so it passes over water only, not land (other than Antarctica).

c. The prime meridian is used for measuring latitude on the earth; it is the "zero position" for indicating east-west locations on the earth. (As you travel around the earth latitudinally, you have to change your watch (at the equator, about every thousand miles); the International Date Line is the place where you adjust for these 24 possible time changes.)

28. a. Yes

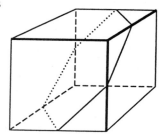

b. Yes

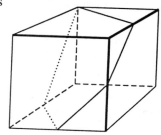

c. Yes

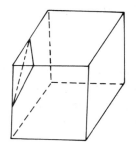

d. Yes. The plane section can be a trapezoid.

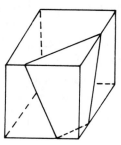

LESSON 9–5 (pp. 439–443)

1. a-b. A right circular cylinder has many symmetry planes, so it has bilateral symmetry. There is one symmetry plane that is perpendicular to the axis, bisecting it, and there are infinitely many more symmetry planes that contain the axis (each intersects the bases of the cylinder at a diameter).

2. a-b. A regular square pyramid has four symmetry planes, so it has bilateral symmetry. All 4 symmetry planes are perpendicular to the base of the pyramid and contain the vertex; two symmetry planes contain the vertices of the base, and two symmetry planes bisect opposite sides of the base.

3. a-b. A top has many symmetry planes, so it has bilateral symmetry. There are an infinite number of symmetry planes, each one containing the axis of the cone and cylinder, intersecting the circular bases of the cone and cylinder at diameters of those bases.

4. **a-b.** All faces of a parallelepiped are parallelograms, so it has no symmetry planes and does not have bilateral symmetry.

5. **a-b.** A right cone has many symmetry lines, so it has bilateral symmetry. There are an infinite number of symmetry lines, each one containing the axis of the cone and intersecting the base of the cone at a diameter.

6. **a-b.** An oblique circular cone has one symmetry plane, so it has bilateral symmetry. The symmetry plane contains the altitude of the cylinder and the segment from the base of the altitude to the center of the base of the cylinder.

7. A box has three symmetry planes. Each one bisects two pairs of faces and is parallel to the third pair of faces.

8. If a human stands upright, the symmetry plane is perpendicular to the ground, midway between the ears or halfway between the right and left sides; that is choice (c).

9. A property of a figure not preserved by reflections in space (similar to a property not preserved by reflections in a plane) is orientation. (So when you wave your right hand in front of a mirror, the image seems to be waving its left hand.)

10.

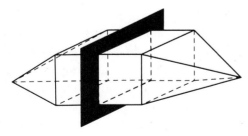

11. A cube has 9 symmetry planes. Three are the same as those of a box (each one bisects two pairs of faces and is parallel to the third pair of faces), and then there are six more that intersect faces at the diagonals, 2 for each pair of opposite faces.

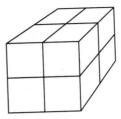 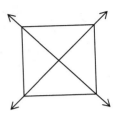

3 planes parallel to opposite faces

2 planes through diagonals for each pair of opposite faces

12.

13.

14. Yes, a prism can have just one line of symmetry. Similar to the oblique circular cylinder in Question 6, many oblique prisms can have just one line of symmetry. It would have to contain the altitude of the prism and the center of the base and the base must have a line of symmetry.

199

15. **a-b.**

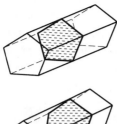

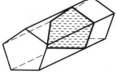

c. The section in part **a** is a pentagon that is congruent to the bases, and the section in part **b** is a pentagon that is not congruent to the bases.

16. **a-b.**

c. The section in part *a* is a hexagon that is congruent to the bases, and the section in part *b* is a hexagon that is not congruent to the bases.

17. A penny resembles a solid right cylinder.

18. A desk drawer resembles a box without its top (it can also be described as a rectangular parallelepiped less one face).

19. **a.** The figure *Z-FOUR* is a square pyramid. (If the foot of the perpendicular from *Z* to the base is at the intersection of the diagonals of the base, then it would be a regular square pyramid.)

b. The base of the figure is the square, *FOUR*.

c. The vertex of the figure is the point not in the plane of *FOUR*, which is point *Z*.

d. The lateral edges are the segments connecting the vertex *Z* to the vertices of the base *FOUR*; they are $\overline{ZF}$, $\overline{ZO}$, $\overline{ZU}$, and $\overline{ZR}$.

e. The faces of the figure are the base and the triangles formed by the vertex of the figure and segments of the base; they are quadrilateral *FOUR*, $\triangle ZFO$, $\triangle ZOU$, $\triangle ZUR$, and $\triangle ZRF$.

20. **a.** The bases of the parallelepiped are the parallelograms *HIJK* and *DEFG*. Each has height 3 (it is given for segment $\overline{IY}$) for the base whose length is 13. Using the formula for the area of a parallelogram $A = bh$, then $A = (13)(3) = 39$ units^2.

b. The perimeter of a base is the perimeter of a parallelogram whose opposite sides are 5 and 13 units; the perimeter is $2(5 + 13) = 2(18) = 36$ units.

c. The height of the parallelepiped is the length of the altitude $\overline{KX}$; that is given as $KX = 9$ units.

21. **a.**

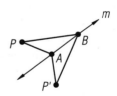

b. P' is the reflection of P over line $\overleftrightarrow{AB}$, so $PA = P'A$ and $PB = P'B$ because A and B are their own images for a reflection over $\overleftrightarrow{AB}$ and reflections preserve distance. So $PBP'A$ has two pairs of consecutive sides congruent, and it is a kite by the definition of kite (sufficient condition).

22. **a.** 1 square yard = (1 yard)(1 yard)
   = (3 feet)(3 feet)
   = 9 square feet

b. 1 square mile = (1 mile)(1 mile)

   = (1760 yards)(1760 yards)

   = 3,097,600 square yards

(Note: it is not necessary to remember that there are 1760 yards in a mile. If you know that there are 5280 feet in a mile, divide by three to derive the number of yards in a mile.)

c. 1 square mile = 640 acres (This is given on page 376.)

23. $x^2y - 4x = x(xy - 4)$

24. $2\ell h + 2\ell w + 2wh = 2(\ell h + \ell w + wh)$

25.

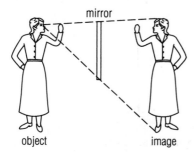

object   image

From your eyes, the image of the bottom of your feet appears at the same height as the bottoms of your feet. The line of sight from your eyes to the image intersects the mirror at the halfway point from your eyes to that image, so the mirror only has to extend down to that point. Similarly, from the level of your eyes upward, the mirror has to extend only halfway to the top of your head. In sum, the mirror can be as short as half your total height if it is correctly positioned on the wall.

26. Most people's faces do not have exact bilateral symmetry. That is why a photograph of your face may look slightly strange to you: the image you see in the mirror reverses the orientation, while a photograph preserves orientation.

LESSON 9-6   (pp. 444–448)

1. To an architect, elevations are views of what a house or other structure looks like from the front, side, rear, or other viewing position.

2. a-c.

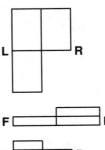

3. a-c.

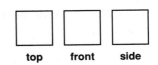

top   front   side

4. a-c.

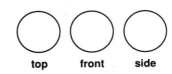

top   front   side

5. a-c.

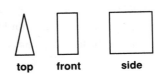

top   front   side

6. a-c.

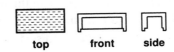

top   front   side

7. a-c.

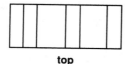

top

front

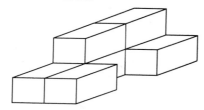

side

8. Here is a possible drawing of the building based on the views:

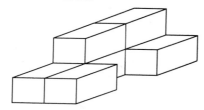

  a. Either the front view or the side view shows the height of the building; it is 2 stories tall.

  b. Either the side view or the top view shows the length of the building from front to back; it is 3 sections long from front to back.

  c. The front view indicates that the tallest part is on the left, and the side view indicates the tallest part is in the middle or back. So the tallest parts are the back left section and the middle left section.

9.

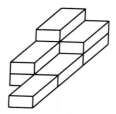

10. Applying the scale to the front elevation, the width of the house seems to be about 46 feet.

11. Applying the scale to the side or front elevation, the height of the building seems to be about 28 feet.

12.

The solid that has the given views is a solid right cylinder.

13. A cube has nine symmetry planes. (For each pair of opposite faces, the plane parallel to and halfway between those two faces is a symmetry plane; there are three such planes. Also for each pair of opposite faces, the plane that contains parallel diagonals is a symmetry plane; there are two such planes for each pair of faces, or six such planes.)

14. a. A right circular cone has an infinite number of symmetry planes. Each one contains the vertex of the cone and a diameter of the base of the cone.

  b.

c.

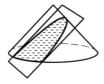

d. Part b: The plane section parallel to the base is a circle. (If the plane intersects the vertex of the cone, the plane section would be a point; if the plane is "above" the vertex, the section would be the empty set.)

Part **c:** The plane section parallel to an edge would be a parabola. (If the plane "just rested on" the cone, the intersection would be a line; if the plane was outside the cone, the section would be the empty set.)

15.

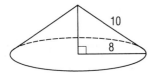

The height of the cone is a leg of a right triangle whose hypotenuse is the slant height (10 units) and whose other leg is the radius of the base (8 units). So the right triangle is a 6-8-10 right triangle ($6^2 + 8^2 = 10^2$) and the height of the cone is 6 units.

16. Every great circle lies on a plane that contains the center of the earth. If that great circle is to contain a point in New York and a point in Tokyo, then those three points determine a single plane, and the intersection of a single plane with a sphere is (at most) a single circle. So the number of great circles that contain a given point in New York and a given point in Tokyo is exactly one.

17. The solid formed has two parallel, regular heptagonal (7-sided) bases, so it is a regular heptagonal prism. (If the direction of translation is perpendicular to the base, it would be a right heptagonal prism.)

18. a. The radius of a sphere is half the diameter, so the radius would be $\frac{1}{2}(2160) =$ 1080 miles.

b. The question asks for the length of half the circumference of a sphere. Using $\frac{1}{2}C = \frac{1}{2}(2\pi r)$ with $r = 1080$, the distance is $\frac{1}{2}(2)\pi(1080) = 1080\pi \approx 3392.9 \approx$ 3400 miles.

19. a. Using $A = s^2$ with $A = 11$, then $s = \sqrt{11} \approx 3.317 \approx 3.3$ units.

b. The diagonal d is the hypotenuse of an isosceles right triangle with legs $= \sqrt{11}$. So $d^2 = (\sqrt{11})^2 + (\sqrt{11})^2 = 11 + 11 = 22$, and $d = \sqrt{22} \approx 4.6904 \approx 4.7$ units.

20. a. To find Area ($\triangle ABC$), first find AD; it is the length of a leg in right triangle ABD. Using the Pythagorean Theorem,

$$AD^2 + 52^2 = 65^2$$
$$AD^2 + 2704 = 4225$$
$$AD^2 = 1521$$
$$AD = 39$$

So Area ($\triangle ABC$) $= \frac{1}{2}(BC)(AD)$

$$= \frac{1}{2}(52 + 30)(39)$$

$$= \frac{1}{2}(82)(39)$$

$$= 1599 \text{ square units}$$

b. $\overline{AC}$ is the hypotenuse in right triangle
ADC. Using the Pythagorean Theorem,
$$AC^2 = AD^2 + DC^2$$
$$= 1521 + 30^2$$
$$= 1521 + 900$$
$$= 2421$$
So $AC = \sqrt{2421} \approx 49.20366 \approx$
49.20 units.

21. $ABCD$ is a parallelogram, so $AB = CD$
(opposite sides of a parallelogram are
congruent, from the Properties of a
Parallelogram Theorem), and Q is the
midpoint of $\overline{AC}$ and $\overline{BD}$ (also from the
Properties of a Parallelogram Theorem). So
$AQ = CQ$ and $BQ = DQ$ from the
definition of midpoint (meaning), and $\triangle AQB$
$\cong \triangle CQD$ by the SSS Congruence Theorem.
(Other proofs can use the vertical angles at Q
and the alternate interior angles for
transversals $\overleftrightarrow{AC}$ and $\overleftrightarrow{BD}$.)

22. $x^2y^2 + 4x^2y + 6xy = xy(xy + 4x + 6)$
23. $\pi r^2 + 2\pi rh - \pi h = \pi(r^2 + 2rh - h)$
24. Answers will vary. Some checks for accuracy
are that the front and side views should have
the same height, the side and top views
should have the same front-to-back length,
and the front and top views should have the
same right-to-left length.

LESSON 9–7 (pp. 449–454)

1. An object is a polyhedron if and only if it is a
3-dimensional surface which is the union of
polygonal regions and which has no holes.
2. **a.** A cone is not a polyhedron because the
curved part of the surface is not a polygon.
b. A cube is a polyhedron (all six faces are
squares).
c. A cylinder is not a polyhedron because the
curved part of the surface is not a polygon.

d. A prism is a polyhedron because the
lateral faces are rectangles and the bases
are polygons.
e. A pyramid is a polyhedron because the
lateral faces are triangles and the bases are
polygons.
f. A sphere is not a polyhedron because the
curved surface is not a polygon.
3. **a.** There are six vertices: A, B, C, D, E,
and F.
b. The edges are:
in face ABC—$\overline{AB}, \overline{BC}, \overline{AC}$;
in face ABF—$\overline{BF}, \overline{AF}, (\overline{AB}$ is already
listed);
in face ACE—$\overline{AE}, \overline{CE}$ ($\overline{AC}$ is already
listed);
in face AEF—$\overline{EF}$ ($\overline{AF}$, and $\overline{AE}$ are already
listed);
in face BCD—$\overline{CD}, \overline{BD}$ ($\overline{BC}$ is already
listed);
in face BDF—$\overline{DF}$ ($\overline{BD}$ and $\overline{BF}$ are already
listed);
in face CDE—$\overline{ED}$ ($\overline{CD}$ and $\overline{CE}$ are
already listed);
in face DEF—($\overline{DE}, \overline{EF}$, and $\overline{DF}$ are
already listed);
There are 12 edges.
c. The faces are listed in part **b** (in
alphabetical order).
4. A hexahedron ("six faces") is shown on
page 449.
a. A hexahedron has 4 vertices on the "top"
face and 4 more on the "bottom" face, for
8 vertices.
b. A hexhedron has 4 edges on each of the
top and bottom faces, and 4 "vertical"
edges, for a total of 12 edges.
c. A hexahedron, by definition, has 6 faces.
(They can be described as the top, bottom,
left side, right side, front, and back.)

5. Face **a** is opposite F, so it is the back face; face **b** is opposite D, so it is the up face; and face **c** is opposite R, so it is the left side.

6.

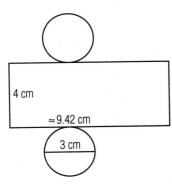

7.

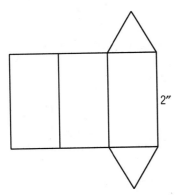

4 cm

≈9.42 cm

3 cm

8.

2″

9. **a.** The figure will be a cone without a base.

b.

10.

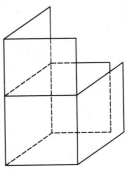

Choice (d) folds up to a box with "two tops and no bottom"; so choice (d) is not a net for a cube.

11.

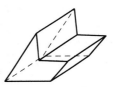

12.

figure	(any geometric set of points)
surface	(any "connected" 3-dimensional set of points)
polyhedron	(a surface that is the union of polygons)
pyramid	(a polygon with a vertex and a polygonal base)
pentagonal pyramid	(a pyramid with a 5-sided base)
regular pentagonal pyramid	(a special type of pentagonal pyramid)

13. a. A pyramid whose base in an octagon has a pyramid vertex and 8 vertices at the base, or 9 vertices.

b. It has 8 lateral edges connecting the pyramid vertex to the vertices of the base, and 8 edges around the base, or 16 edges.

c. It has 8 lateral faces (one for the pyramid vertex with each segment of the base) and the base, for 9 faces.

14. a. A prism whose base is an n-gon has n vertices on the top base and n vertices on the bottom base, for $2n$ vertices.

b. It has n edges on each of the top and bottom bases, and n lateral edges, for $3n$ edges.

c. It has n lateral sides, a top, and a bottom, for $n + 2$ faces.

15.

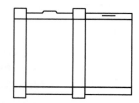

16. Here are some data:

figure:	box	square pyramid	hexagonal prism
Vertices:	8	5	12
Edges:	12	8	18
Faces:	6	5	8

Test each choice:

(a) $V + E - F = 8 + 12 - 6 = 14$ (box);
$= 5 + 8 - 5 = 8$ (sq pyramid);
$= 12 + 18 - 8 = 22$ (hex prism);

(b) $F + E - V = 6 + 12 - 8 = 10$ (box);
$= 5 + 8 - 5 = 8$ (sq pyramid);
$= 8 + 18 - 12 = 14$ (hex prism);

(c) $F + V - E = 6 + 8 - 12 = 2$ (box);
$= 5 + 5 - 8 = 2$ (sq pyramid);
$= 8 + 12 - 18 = 2$ (hex prism);

(d) $E + F - V = 12 + 6 - 8 = 10$ (box);
$= 8 + 5 - 5 = 8$ (sq pyramid);
$= 18 + 8 - 12 = 14$ (hex prism);

The relationship for these data is $F + V - E = 2$; that is choice (c).

17.

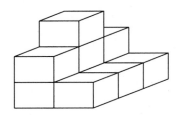

a. The height is shown in the front and right side views; the height is 3 stories.

b. The length from front to back is shown in the top and right side views; the length from front to back is 3 sections.

c. The front shows the tallest part on the left, and the right side shows the tallest place in the middle; so the tallest place is the middle section of the left side.

18.

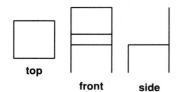

19. a-b. The prism in Example 2 has bases that are scalene triangles, so there are no vertical planes of symmetry. The prism is a right prism, so there is a horizontal plane of symmetry parallel to and halfway between the faces. Since the prism has a plane of symmetry, the figure is reflection-symmetric.

20. A bass drum is a surface with two circular parallel bases, so it is a cylindric surface; that is choice (b).

21. a. If $x = 6$, then $\triangle TQS$ is a 6-8-10 right triangle and $QS = 8$. So y is half of 8, or $y = 4$.

b. If $x = 8$, then again $\triangle TQS$ is a 6-8-10 right triangle and $QS = 6$. So y is half of 6, or $y = 3$.

c. If $x = 8$, then $y = 3$, and $\triangle TQR$ is a right triangle so its area is half the product of the legs. So Area($\triangle TQR$) $= \frac{1}{2}xy =$ $\frac{1}{2}(8)(3) = 12$ units^2.

22. IN $\triangle CAE$ and $\triangle CDB$, there is a pair of right angles and $\angle C$ is in both triangles. So the third pair of angles must also have the same measure, or m$\angle CBD$ = m$\angle E$. So m$\angle CBD$ − m$\angle E$ = 0, and the statement is *true*.

23. If all four sides of a quadrilateral are congruent, then the quadrilateral is a rhombus by the definition of rhombus (sufficient condition).

24. To state that angles 1 and 2 are supplementary means that m$\angle 1$ + m$\angle 2$ = 180. Substituting m$\angle 1$ = t and m$\angle 2$ = $t - 10$, then:
$$t + (t - 10) = 180$$
$$2t - 10 = 180$$
$$2t = 190$$
$$t = 95$$

25. a. A tetrahedron has 3 vertices on the "bottom" face and one more vertex, for 4 vertices.

Another way: there are 4 faces. Each face has 3 vertices, so multiply the number of faces by 3. But 3 faces meet at each vertex (which means each vertex will have been counted 3 times), so divide by 3. Thus the number of vertices is $\frac{(4)(3)}{3} = 4$.

A hexahedron has 6 faces. Each face has 4 vertices, so multiply by 4, and 3 faces meet at each vertex, so divide by 3. Thus the number of vertices is $\frac{(6)(4)}{3} = 8$.

An octahedron has 8 faces. Each face has 3 vertices, so multiply by 3, and 4 faces meet at each vertex, so divide by 4. Thus the number of vertices is $\frac{(8)(3)}{4} = 6$.

A dodecahedron has 12 faces. Each face has 5 vertices, so multiply by 5, and 3 faces meet at each vertex, so divide by 3. Thus the number of vertices is $\frac{(12)(5)}{3} = 20$.

An icosahedron has 20 faces. Each face has 3 vertices, and 5 faces meet at each vertex, so divide by 5. Thus the number of vertices is $\frac{(20)(3)}{5} = 12$.

b. To find the number of edges, multiply the number of faces by the number of edges on each face. Then, since 2 faces meet at each edge (for any polyhedron), divide by 2.
Tetrahedron:
$$\frac{(4 \text{ faces})(3 \text{ edges per face})}{2} = 6 \text{ edges}$$
Hexahedron:
$$\frac{(6 \text{ faces})(4 \text{ edges per face})}{2} = 12 \text{ edges}$$
Octahedron:
$$\frac{(8 \text{ faces})(3 \text{ edges per face})}{2} = 12 \text{ edges}$$
Dodecahedron:
$$\frac{(12 \text{ faces})(5 \text{ edges per face})}{2} = 30 \text{ edges}$$
Icosahedron:
$$\frac{(20 \text{ faces})(3 \text{ edges per face})}{2} = 30 \text{ edges}$$

26.

27.

28.

29.

30.

LESSON 9-8 (pp. 455–459)

1. The Four-Color Conjecture was first stated by Thomas Guthrie, in 1852.

2. **a.** The Four-Color Theorem: Suppose regions which share a border of some length must have different colors. Then any map or regions on a plane or a sphere can be colored in such a way that only four colors are needed.

   b. The Four-Color Theorem was proved by Wolfgang Haken and Kenneth Appel, in 1976.

3. The conjecture was stated in 1852 and proved in 1976; that is an elapsed time of 1976 − 1852 = 124 years.

4.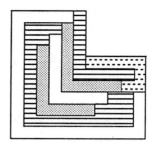

5. sample: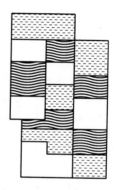

6. Elizabeth Wilmer is a person who won second prize in the nation in the Westinghouse Science Talent Search for her work on a three-color problem; she won the prize in 1987, when she was a student at Stuyvesant High School in New York City.

7. Any map on a torus can be colored with no more than 7 colors.

8.

9.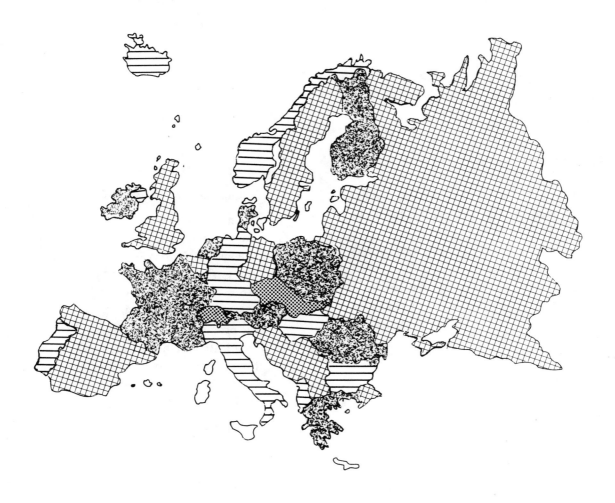

Color 1:	**Color 2:**	**Color 3:**	**Color 4:**
1. Luxembourg	11. Spain	21. Portugal	31. Ireland
2. Switzerland	12. Britain	22. Iceland	32. France
3. Czechoslovakia	13. Belgium	23. Northern Ireland	33. Denmark
	14. Yugoslavia	24. Norway	34. Poland
	15. East Germany	25. West Germany	35. Austria
	16. Turkey (in part)	26. Italy	36. Rumania
	17. USSR	27. Hungary	37. Greece
	18. Sweden	28. Albania	38. Netherlands
		29. Bulgaria	39. Finland

10.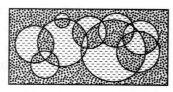

No more than two colors are needed to color this map.

11.

12.

13. From most general to most specific, the terms are:

surface	(any three-dimensional figure)
polyhedron	(any solid with polygons for faces)
prism	(a polyhedron with parallel bases)
right prism	(a prism whose bases are perpendicular to its axis)
box	(a right prism with rectangular bases)

14. **a.**

b.   **c.**

15.

16.

17.

18.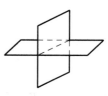

19. **a.** $A\text{-}BCDE$ is a regular pyramid, so $BCDE$ is a square and $OF = \frac{1}{2}(ED)$, so $OF = 6$. Then segment $\overline{AF}$, whose length is the slant height, is the hypotenuse of right triangle AOF, so $AF^2 = AO^2 + OF^2 = 10^2 + 6^2 = 100 + 36 = 136$. Then $AF = \sqrt{136} \approx 11.6619 \approx 11.7$.

b. $\triangle AOD$ is a right triangle, so its area is half the product of its legs. One leg, $\overline{AO}$, has length 10, and the other leg, $\overline{OD}$, is the hypotenuse in right triangle ODF. Then $OD^2 = 6^2 + 6^2 = 36 + 36 = 72$ and $OD = \sqrt{72} = \sqrt{(36)(2)} = 6\sqrt{2}$. So the area of $\triangle AOD$ is $\frac{1}{2}(10)(6\sqrt{2}) = 30\sqrt{2} \approx 42.43$.

20. a. $\overset{\frown}{RTS}$ is $\frac{290}{360} = \frac{29}{36}$ of the circumference of the circle, and the circumference is $2\pi r = 2\pi(30) = 60\pi$. So the length of $\overset{\frown}{RTS}$ is $\frac{29}{36}(60\pi) = \frac{1740\pi}{36} \approx 151.8$ cm.

b. To find the area of the circle, use $A = \pi r^2$ with $r = 30$ cm: $A = \pi(30)^2 = 900\pi \approx 2827.4$ cm^2.

c. The fraction of the circle that is in sector RSQ is $\frac{70}{360} = .194444 \approx 19\%$.

21. If $x = 4$, then
$$2x^3 - 7x^2 - x + 11 = 2(4)^3 - 7(4)^2 - (4) + 11$$
$$= 2(64) - 7(16) - 4 + 11$$
$$= 128 - 112 - 4 + 11$$
$$= 23$$

22. The names of the countries are listed in the answer to Question 9 of this lesson.

23. a. Oregon, Arizona, Colorado, S. Dakota, Missouri, Mississippi, Ohio, Virginia, New Jersey, Rhode Island

b. Nevada, Wyoming, Oklahoma, Louisiana, Iowa, Kentucky, Georgia, Maryland, Massachusetts

c. Idaho, New Mexico, Nebraska, N. Dakota, Arkansas, Wisconsin, Indiana, Alabama, N. Carolina, W. Virginia, New York, New Hampshire, Delaware

d. Washington, California, Utah, Montana, Kansas, Texas, Minnesota, Illinois, Michigan, Tennessee, Pennsylvania, Florida, S. Carolina, Vermont, Maine.

e. Hawaii, Alaska

24. a. Sample: Some Rand McNally globes use 6 colors.

b. Sample: areas are colored according to elevation or features such as mountains and bodies of water.

CHAPTER 9 PROGRESS SELF-TEST (p. 461)

1. The figure is a prism, since it has parallel bases. Moreover, the bases are triangles, and are ⊥ to the planes of the sides. So the figure is a right triangular prism.

2. The edges are $\overline{AD}$, $\overline{BE}$, $\overline{CF}$, $\overline{AB}$, $\overline{BC}$, $\overline{AC}$, $\overline{DE}$, $\overline{EF}$, and $\overline{DF}$; there are 9 edges.

3. The faces are ABC, DEF, $ABED$, $BCFE$, and $ACFD$; there are 5 faces.

4. The vertices are A, B, C, D, E, and F; there are 6 vertices.

5. A solid is the union of a surface and all the points in the interior of the surface.

6. sample:

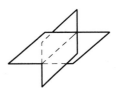

7. sample:

8. sample:

9. sample:

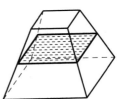

10. view from above:

top view

There are 4 symmetry planes. Each is ⊥ to the bases of the pyramid. Two planes bisect opposite pairs of angles of the bases, and two planes bisect opposite pairs of sides of the bases.

11. a. There are four lateral edges; $\overline{GI}$, $\overline{GJ}$, $\overline{GK}$, and $\overline{GH}$.
  b. The vertex is point G.

12.

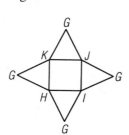

GO is the height of the pyramid and GL is the slant height.

13.

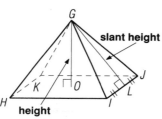

14.

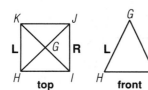

15. The intersection of sphere O and plane m containing O is called a great circle of sphere O.

16. samples:

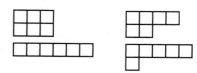

17. a. The height of the cone is represented by segment $\overline{AD}$.
  b. The base of the cone is a circle with radius $OB = 10$ cm. The area of the base is $A = \pi r^2 = \pi(10)^2 = 100\pi \approx 314.16$ cm².

18. a. $FIHG$ is a rectangle with height 22″. The length is the leg of a right triangle with hypotenuse 9″ and leg 4″, or $\sqrt{9^2 - 4^2} = \sqrt{81 - 16} = \sqrt{65}$ inches. So Area($FIHG$) $= 22\sqrt{65} \approx 177.4$ inches².
  b. The area of right triangle EFG is one-half the product of the legs, or $\frac{1}{2}(4)(\sqrt{65}) = 2\sqrt{65} \approx 16.12$ inches².

19. A box is a hexahedron, which is a prism, which is a polyhedron. A box is not a pyramid; that is choice (b).

20.

The figure is a solid right square prism.

21. $\pi r^2 + 2\pi rh = \pi r(r + 2h)$

22. sample:

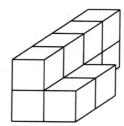

  a. The building is two stories tall.
  b. It is 4 sections from front to back.
  c. The tallest parts are all the sections on the left side.

23. sample:

1.

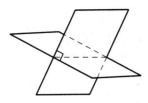

2.

3.

4.

5.

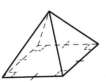

6.

7. a.

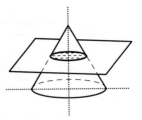

b.

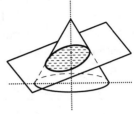

c. The plane section parallel to the base is a circle, and the plane section not parallel to and not intersecting the base is an ellipse.

8. a.

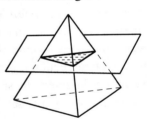

b.

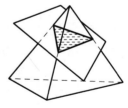

c. The plane section parallel to the base is a triangle (similar to the base), and the plane section not parallel to and not intersecting the base is also a triangle (not similar to the base).

9. a.

b.

c. The plane section parallel to the bases is a parallelogram congruent to the bases, and the plane section not parallel to and not intersecting the bases is a parallelogram not congruent to the bases.

10. a.

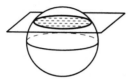

b. The plane section of a sphere that does not contain the center is a small circle of the sphere. (If the plane is tangent to the sphere, the plane section is a point; if the plane does not intersect the sphere, the plane section is the empty set.)

11. a.

b.

c.

12. a-c.

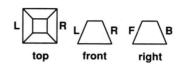

13. a-c.

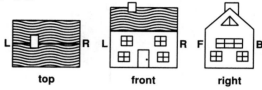

14.

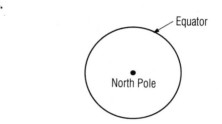

15. The nets can be folded into the following shapes:

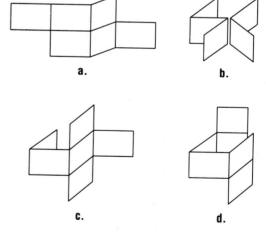

The nets for cubes are choices (c) and (d).

16.

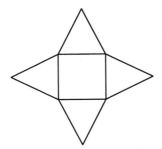

17.

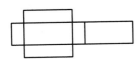

18.

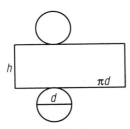

19. a. The base of the regular triangular pyramid is an equilateral triangle with side 12.

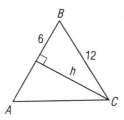

The altitude for that equilateral triangle is the leg h of a right triangle with hypotenuse 12 and other leg 6:
$$h^2 + 6^2 = 12^2$$
$$h^2 + 36 = 144$$
$$h^2 = 108$$
$$h = \sqrt{108} = \sqrt{(36)(3)} = 6\sqrt{3}$$

So the area of the base is $\frac{1}{2}bh =$
$$\frac{1}{2}(12)(6\sqrt{3}) = 36\sqrt{3} \approx (36)(1.732) \approx$$
62.4 square units.

b. The slant height, DE, is the leg of a right triangle with hypotenuse $DA = 10$ and other leg $AE = 6$:
$$DE^2 + 6^2 = 10^2$$
$$DE^2 + 36 = 100$$
$$DE^2 = 64$$
$$DE = 8$$
(Note: ΔDAE is a 6-8-10 right triangle.)

20. a. The height of the oblique square prism is represented by $\overline{LN}$.

b. Segment $\overline{LG}$ is the hypotenuse of a right triangle whose legs are 15 and 40, so
$$LG^2 = 15^2 + 40^2 = 225 + 1600 = 1825,$$
so $LG = \sqrt{1825} = \sqrt{(25)(73)} =$
$5\sqrt{73} \approx 42.72$ units.

c. The base is a square, so if its perimeter is 52 units, then the length of a side is $\frac{52}{4} =$
13 units. So $KLGF$ is a parallelogram with base $KL = 13$ and height $LM = 40$, and the area of $KLGF = bh = (13)(40) =$
520 units².

21. a. The base of the cylinder is a circle with radius $CD = 3$ cm, so the area of the base is $\pi r^2 = \pi(3)^2 = 9\pi \approx 28.27$ cm²

b. The heighth of the cylinder is the leg of a right triangle with hypotenuse 9 and other leg $10 - 3 = 7$ cm.
So $h^2 + 7^2 = 9^2$
$$h^2 + 49 = 81$$
$$h^2 = 32$$
So $h = \sqrt{32} = \sqrt{(16)(2)} =$
$4\sqrt{2} \approx 5.66$ cm².

22. The radius of a great circle will be the same as the radius of the sphere, so the area of the great circle is $A = \pi r^2 = \pi(12)^2 = 144\pi \approx$ 452.39 square inches.

23. a.

25 mm

24 mm

b. The radius of the base is the leg ℓ of a right triangle with hypotenuse 25 and other leg 24. So:
$$\ell^2 + 24^2 = 25^2$$
$$\ell^2 + 576 = 625$$
$$\ell^2 = 49$$
$$\ell = 7$$
Then, using a value of 7 mm for the radius of the base, the area of the base is $\pi(7)^2 = 49\pi \approx 153.9$ mm^2.

24. a. The front and side views show the height of the building; it is two stories high.

b. The side and top views show the length of the building from front to back; it is two sections from front to back.

c. The front view shows the tallest part is on the right, and the side view shows the tallest part is at the back, so the tallest part is the back, right part of the building.

25. a. The front and side views show the height of the building; it is two stories high.

b. The side and top views show the length of the building from front to back; it is three sections from front to back.

c. The front view shows the tallest part is the middle section, and the side view shows the tallest part is at the back, so the tallest part is the back middle section of the building.

26. a.

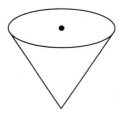

The solid that has the given views is a right cone (with the circular base at the top).

27. a. Some names for the figure are a hexahedron (six-sided solid), a parallelepiped (all faces are parallelograms), a square prism (assuming faces $ABCD$ and $HEFG$ are squares), a rectangular prism (using any opposite pair of faces as the bases), or a box.

b. Consider any pair of opposite faces as the bases. The figure has 4 edges on each base, and 4 edges connecting those bases, for a total of 12 edges.

c. There are 16 pairs of edges that are not coplanar:
either $\overline{HE}$ or $\overline{AB}$ with either $\overline{GD}$ or $\overline{FC}$;
either $\overline{EF}$ or $\overline{BC}$ with either $\overline{HA}$ or $\overline{GD}$;
either $\overline{GF}$ or $\overline{DC}$ with either $\overline{HA}$ or $\overline{EB}$;
either $\overline{GH}$ or $\overline{AD}$ with either $\overline{EB}$ or $\overline{FC}$.

28. a. The figure has a circular base and a vertex, so it is a cone. (If $\overline{QP}$ is perpendicular to $\overline{RS}$, the cone would be a right cone; otherwise, it would be an oblique cone.)

b. Two lateral edges are labeled: $\overline{QR}$ and $\overline{QS}$.

c. The vertex is the point where the lateral edges meet; that is point Q.

d. The base is circle P.

e. The axis is the line through the vertex and the center of the base; that is $\overleftrightarrow{QP}$.

29. a. The vertices are points A, B, C, D, E, F, and G; there are 7 vertices.

b. The edges are $\overline{AB}$, $\overline{BC}$, $\overline{CD}$, $\overline{DA}$, $\overline{AE}$, $\overline{DE}$, $\overline{BG}$, $\overline{CG}$, $\overline{CE}$, $\overline{CF}$, $\overline{EG}$, $\overline{EF}$, and $\overline{FG}$; there are 13 edges.

c. 2 faces are quadrilaterals *ABCD* and *ABGE*.

d. The polyhedron has 8 faces (*ABCD, ABGE, ADE, BCG, DEC, EFC, CFG,* and *EGF*), so it is an octahedron.

30.

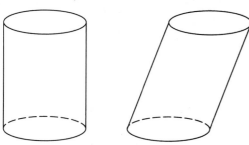

In a right cylinder, the base is perpendicular to the lateral edges and the axis; in an oblique cylinder, the base is not perpendicular to the lateral edges and axis.

31.

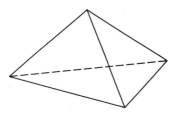

Yes, for a triangular pyramid (or tetrahedron), any face can be considered as the base and the figure is still a pyramid.

32. From most general to most specific:

polyhedron	(any figure with polygons as faces)
prism	(special polyhedron)
square prism	(prism with square base)
cube	(square prism with height equal to edge of base)

33. In general, the type of figure whose bases are congruent figures in parallel planes is a prism. If the figure contains all the points between the bases, it is a solid, and if the base is also a pentagon, then the figure is a solid pentagonal prism.

34. The three-dimensional figure most resembling a phonograph record (with no middle hole) is a solid right cylinder.

35. The three-dimensional figure most resembling a bubble is a sphere.

36. The three-dimensional figure most resembling the moon is a (presumably) solid sphere.

37. The three-dimensional figure most resembling a sheet of notebook paper is a solid rectangular prism. (Alternatively, it may be considered as an illustration of a portion of a plane.)

38. **a-b.** The figure has 5 symmetry planes, each containing the vertex of the pyramid and an angle bisector of the base, so it has bilateral symmetry.

39. **a-b.** The figure has an infinite number of symmetry planes, so the figure has bilateral symmetry. Each symmetry plane contains parallel diameters of the bases of the cylinder (and also is concurrent with the "longitude lines" of the hemisphere).

40. A box has 3 symmetry planes. For each of the three pairs of opposite faces, there is a symmetry plane parallel to and midway between them.

41.

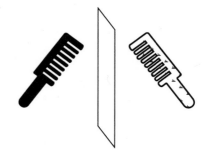

42. $ph - \frac{1}{2}\ell p = p(h - \frac{1}{2}\ell)$

43. $\ell w h + 2\ell w = \ell w(h + 2)$

44. $x^2 y + 2xy + xy^2 = xy(x + 2 + y)$

45. $4\pi r^2 + \pi r^3 = \pi r^2(4 + r)$

46. The Four-Color Conjecture was first stated by Thomas Guthrie.

47. The Four-Color Conjecture dealt with maps on planes and spheres.

48. A proof of the Four-Color Theorem was found in 1976.

49.

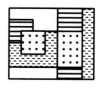

50.

218

CHAPTER 10 SURFACE AREAS AND VOLUMES

LESSON 10-1 (pp. 466–472)

1. The term that indicates the boundary of a three-dimensional figure is *surface area* (the term *volume* refers to the space "inside" the figure).

2. **a.** The lateral area of a solid is the sum of the areas of the lateral sides (those are the surfaces other than the base(s)).

   b. A formula for the lateral area of a right prism is L.A. = ph, where p is the perimeter of the base and h is the height of the prism.

3. The lateral area has perimeter $2(8 + 15) = 2(23) = 46$ cm, and the height is 20 cm, so L.A. = $ph = (46)(20) = 920$ cm². Also, the base has area $(15)(8) = 120$ cm². Since the surface area is the lateral area plus the area of the base, S.A. = L.A. + B = 920 + 120 = 1040 cm².

4. In a prism or cylinder, the surface area is the sum of the lateral area plus the area of the two bases, or S.A. = L.A. + $2B$.

5. **a.** The surface is a cube (or regular hexahedron).

   b. The lateral surface is in grey; its perimeter is $(5)(4) = 20$ units and its height is 5 units, so L.A. = ph = $(20)(5)$ = 100 units².
   Alternatively, each grey square has area 25, so all four grey squares represents an area of 100 units².)

   c. Each base has area 25 units², so S.A. = L.A. + $2B$ = 100 + 2(25) = 100 + 50 = 150 units².

6. **a.** The surface is a right prism whose base is a right triangle.

   b. The lateral surface is in grey; its perimeter is $(5 + 3 + 4) = 12$ cm and its height is 9 cm, so L.A. = $(12)(9)$ = 108 cm². (Alternatively, the grey rectangles have areas $(5)(9) = 45$, $(3)(9) = 27$, and $(4)(9) = 36$, so the lateral area is 45 + 27 + 36 = 108 cm².)

   c. Each base is a right triangle, so the area of each base is half the product of the legs, or $\frac{1}{2}(3)(4) = 6$ cm². So the S.A. = L.A. + $2B$ = 108 + 2(6) = 108 + 12 = 120 cm².

7. **a.** The surface is a right cylinder.

   b. The lateral surface is grey; it is a rectangle whose horizontal measurement is the circumference of a circle with radius 1.5—that is $C = 2\pi r = 2\pi(1.5) = 3\pi$—and whose vertical measurement is 5. So the lateral area is $(3\pi)(5) = 15\pi \approx 47.12$ units².

   c. Each base is a circle with radius 1.5 units, so the area of each base is $A = \pi r^2 = \pi(1.5)^2 = 2.25\pi$. So the S.A. = L.A. + $2B$ = $15\pi + 2(2.25\pi) = 15\pi + 4.5\pi = 19.5\pi \approx 61.26$ units².

8. The lateral area of a right cylinder is the height of the cylinder multiplied by the circumference of the base.

9. **a.** If the base of the right cylinder has radius r, then the area of either base is the area of a circle with radius r—that is πr^2.

   b. The lateral area of the right cylinder is the product of the height of the cylinder and the circumference of the base. The height is given as h, and the circumference of the base is $C = 2\pi r$. So the lateral area is $(h)(2\pi r)$ or $2\pi rh$.

c. The surface area of the right cylinder is the sum of the lateral area and twice the area of the base. The area of the base is $A = \pi r^2$, so the surface area is $2\pi rh + 2\pi r^2$, or $2\pi r(h + r)$.

10. The circumference is $C = 2\pi r = 2\pi(2) = 4\pi$ cm, and the height is 7 cm, so the lateral area is $(4\pi)(7) = 28\pi \approx 87.96$ cm². The surface area is the lateral area plus the area of the two bases, and the area of each base is $A = \pi r^2 = \pi(2)^2 = 4\pi$. So the surface area is $28\pi + 2(4\pi) = 36\pi \approx 113.10$ cm².

11. The bases are right triangles with legs of 4 inches and 5 inches, so the hypotenuse is $\sqrt{41}$ inches and the perimeter of the base is $4 + 5 + \sqrt{41} = 9 + \sqrt{41}$ inches. So the lateral area, the product of the perimeter and height, is $(9 + \sqrt{41})(10) \approx 154$ square inches. The surface area is the lateral area plus the area of the two bases, and the area of each right-triangular base is one-half the product of the legs, or $\frac{1}{2}(5)(4) = 10$ square inches. So the surface area is L.A. $+ 2B \approx 154 + 20 = 174$ square inches.

12. The amount that a railroad box car will hold is a measure of its "capacity" or volume.

13. The amount of metal needed to build a box car is related to the two-dimensional measurements of the sides and bottom, which is its surface area.

14. The amount that you weigh is related to your mass, or volume (and your "density.")

15. The amount that you sweat due to exercise is related to the amount of skin you have, which is your surface area.

16.

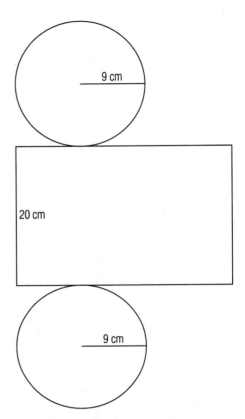

The radius of the base of the can is 9 cm, so the circumference is $C = 2\pi r = 2\pi(9) = 18\pi$ cm and the area of the base is $A = \pi r^2 = \pi 9^2 = 81\pi$ cm². So the lateral area, the product of the circumference and height, is $(18\pi)(20) = 360\pi$ cm², and the surface area is S.A. $=$ L.A. $+ 2B = 360\pi + 2(81\pi) = 360\pi + 162\pi = 522\pi \approx 1639.91 \approx 1640$ cm².

17. Suppose the box is oriented so the base has dimensions 9 cm and 10 cm, and the height is 11 cm.

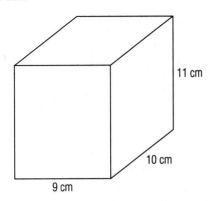

Then the perimeter of the box is $2(9 + 10) = 2(19) = 38$ cm, and the lateral area is $(38)(11) = 418$ cm^2. The area of each base is $(9)(10) = 90$ cm^2, so the S.A. = L.A. + $2B$ = $418 + 2(90) = 418 + 180 = 598$ cm^2.

(Another way: each pair of dimensions is the area of a face of the box, and each face appears twice. So the total area is $2[(9)(10) + (9)(11) + (10)(11)] = 2(90 + 99 + 110) = 2(299) = 598$ cm^2.

18.

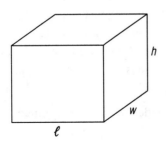

The perimeter of the box is $p = 2(\ell + w) = 2\ell + 2w$, the area of the base (top or bottom) is ℓw, and the height is h. So S.A. = L.A. + $2B = ph + 2B = (2\ell + 2w)h + 2(\ell w) = 2\ell h + 2wh + 2\ell w$. (Another way: each pair of dimensions is the area of a face of the box, and each face appears twice. So the total area is $2(\ell h + wh + \ell w)$.)

19. A cube has 6 faces. If the edge of a cube has length s units, then each face of the cube has area s^2 square units, and the surface area is $6s^2$ square units.

20. In Question 17, the edges of a box were 9 cm, 10 cm, and 11 cm, and the surface area was 598 cm^2. Doubling those edges (that is, multiplying each edge by 2), a new box has edges 18 cm, 20 cm, and 22 cm; its surface area is $2[(18)(20) + (20)(22) + (18)(22)] = 2(360 + 440 + 396) = 2(1196) = 2392 = 4(598)$; the surface area has been multiplied by 4 (which is 2 squared).

Another example (and the general case): In Question 18, the edges were ℓ, w, and h, and the total area was $2\ell h + 2wh + 2\ell w$. Doubling each edge, the new dimensions are (2ℓ), $(2w)$, and $(2h)$, and the surface area is $2[(2\ell)(2h) + (2w)(2h) + (2\ell)(2w)] = 2(4\ell h + 4wh + 4\ell w) = 8(\ell h + wh + \ell w)$. Again, the new surface area is 4 times the old surface area.

21. The first step is to find the area of the side and top of the storage tank:

radius of top: one-half diameter, or 25 m

area of top: $A = \pi r^2 = \pi(25)^2 = 625\pi$ m²

circumference of tank: $C = \pi d = 50\pi$ m

lateral area $= Ch = (50\pi)(75) = 3750\pi$ m²

So the area of the top and side is

$625\pi + 3750\pi = 4375\pi$ m².

For each coat of paint, one gallon covers 45 m², so the number of gallons needed for

4375π m² is $\frac{4375\pi}{45} \approx 97.222\pi$ gallons.

Multiplying that by 2 (for two coats of paint), the amount of paint needed is $194.444\pi \approx 610.87 \approx 611$ gallons of paint.

22.

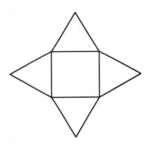

23. A regular polygon has a center; it is the point which is equidistant from all its vertices.

24. If you start with $(2\ell + 2w)h$ and conclude $2\ell h + 2wh$, the justification for that conclusion is the Distributive Property. (More rigorously, because the Distributive Property is stated as $a(b + c) = ab + ac$, you have also applied the Commutative Property to change $(2\ell + 2w)h$ to $h(2\ell + 2w)$.)

25. The cube of $\frac{2}{3}$ is $(\frac{2}{3})^3 = \frac{2^3}{3^3} = \frac{8}{27}$

26. a. Sample: $7'' \times 11\frac{3}{4}'' \times 17''$

b. $(7)(11.75) + 2(17)(7) + 2(17)(11.75) \approx$ 719.75 in.²

c.

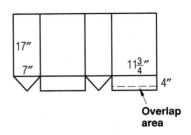

d. Sample: 789 in.²

27. Here are two possible sets of measurements: If the base is a 2 inch-by-2 inch square, then the perimeter of the base is 8 inches and the base uses 4 square inches. The remaining 96 square inches of cardboard will allow the

lateral sides to be $\frac{96}{8} = 12$ inches tall.

If the base is a 4 inch-by-4 inch square, then the perimeter of the base is 16 inches and the base uses 16 square inches. The remaining 84 square inches of cardboard will allow the

lateral sides to be $\frac{84}{16} = 5.25$ inches tall.

In general, if the base has dimensions ℓ and w (and $\ell w < 100$ because you have only 100 square inches of cardboard), then the perimeter of the base is $2\ell + 2w$ and the area of the base is ℓw. The remaining $100 - \ell w$ square inches of cardboard will allow the

lateral sides to be $\frac{100 - \ell w}{2\ell + 2w}$ inches tall.

LESSON 10–2   (pp. 473–477)

1.

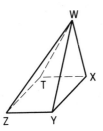

2.

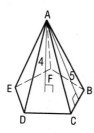

3.

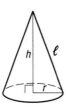

4. Each lateral face of a regular pyramid is an isosceles triangle.

5. For the formula for the lateral area of a pyramid, L.A. = $\frac{1}{2}\ell p$, ℓ stands for the slant height of the pyramid (which is the altitude to the base of the isosceles triangles that form the faces) and p stands for the perimeter of the base (which is the product of the number of sides of the base and the length of each of those sides).

6. For the formula for the lateral area of a cone, L.A. = $\frac{1}{2}\ell p$, ℓ stands for the slant height of the cone and p is the circumference of the base of the cone (which is $2\pi r$, where r is the radius of the base).

7. A right cone is the limit of regular pyramids as the number of sides of the base increases without bound.

8. Using the formula L.A. = $\frac{1}{2}\ell p$, ℓ is given as 10 and p is 36 (because the base is an equilateral triangle with side 12). So L.A. = $\frac{1}{2}(10)(36) = 180$ square units.

9. The perpendicular from the vertex of a regular pyramid intersects the base at the center of the regular polygon that forms the base.

10. From Example 1, the lateral area of the pyramid of Khufu is about 86,400 m², while the area of a football field is less than 5400 m². Since $\frac{86,400}{5400} = 16$, the lateral area of the pyramid is more than 16 times larger than the area of a football field.

11. a.

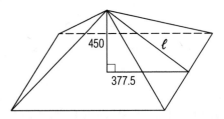

The slant height ℓ is the hypotenuse of a right triangle with legs 450 and $\frac{755}{2} = 377.5$. Using the Pythagorean Theorem:
$\ell^2 = 450^2 + 377.5^2$
$= 202,500 + 142,506.25$
$= 345,006.25$
So $\ell \approx 587.4$ feet.

b. Using the formula L.A. = $\frac{1}{2}\ell p$ with $\ell = 587.4$ and $p = 4(755) = 3020$, then L.A. = $\frac{1}{2}(587.4)(3020) = 886,974$ ft².

12. a. The slant height ℓ is the hypotenuse of a right triangle with legs 11 and 3. Using the Pythagorean Theorem,
$\ell^2 = 11^2 + 3^2 = 121 + 9 = 130.$
So $\ell = \sqrt{130} \approx 11.4$ units.

b. Using the formula L.A. $= \frac{1}{2}\ell p$ with
$\ell = \sqrt{130}$ and $p = 2\pi r = 2\pi(3) = 6\pi$,
then L.A. $= \frac{1}{2}(\sqrt{130})(6\pi) = 3\pi\sqrt{130} \approx$
$(3)(3.1416)(11.4) \approx 107.5$ square units.

c. Adding the area of the base, 9π, to the lateral area, the surface area is
$(3\pi\sqrt{130}) + 9\pi \approx 135.7$ square units.

13. Consider the Triangle Inequality Theorem: it states that the sum of the lengths of two sides of a triangle is greater than the length of the third side. This can also be described by considering two points A and B and another point C not on segment $\overline{AB}$:

Then the distance directly from A to B (along line $\overleftrightarrow{AB}$) must be less than the distance from A to B through C (that is, if you leave line $\overleftrightarrow{AB}$). Here is an analogy (similar situation) in space:

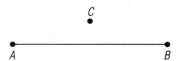

The amount of area inside the circle (staying in the plane of the circle) must be less than the amount of surface area if you leave the plane.
So for a given cone, the area of the base is always less than the lateral area of the cone; that is choice (a).

14. a-b. In a pyramid, the height, slant height, and a segment half the length of a side form a right triangle. The hypotenuse of a right triangle is the longest side of the triangle, so the slant height is always greater than the height.

15. a.

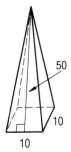

b. Using the formula L.A. $= \frac{1}{2}\ell p$, the slant height ℓ is given to be 50 and the perimeter is given to be 40. So L.A. $= \frac{1}{2}(50)(40) = 1000$ square units.

c. The base is a square and its perimeter is 40, so each side is 10 and the area of the base is 100. So the surface area, the sum of the lateral area and the base, is $1000 + 100 = 1100$ square units.

16. a.

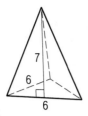

b. Using the formula L.A. $= \frac{1}{2}\ell p$, the slant height ℓ is given to be 7 and the perimeter is 18 (because the base is an equilateral triangle with side 6). So L.A. $= \frac{1}{2}(7)(18)$ = 63 square units.

c. The base is a triangle with area $9\sqrt{3}$. So the surface area, the sum of the lateral area and the base, is $63 + 9\sqrt{3} \approx$ $63 + 15.59 = 78.59$ square units.

17. a.

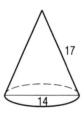

b. Using the formula L.A. $= \frac{1}{2}\ell p$, the slant height is 17 and the circumference of the base is 14π (because the diameter of the base is given as 14). So L.A. $= \frac{1}{2}(17)(14\pi)$ = $119\pi \approx 373.85$ square units.

c. The base is a circle with diameter 14, so the radius is 7 and the area of the base is $A = \pi r^2 = \pi(7)^2 = 49\pi$. So the surface area, the sum of the lateral area and the base, is $119\pi + 49\pi = 168\pi \approx 527.79$ square units.

18. The faces of the box are rectangles, and each rectangle is counted twice. Converting to measurement having the same units, the measurements are 12″, 15″, and 18″ and the surface area is
$2[(12)(15) + (12)(18) + (15)(18)]$
$= 2(180 + 216 + 270) = 2(666) =$
1332 square inches.
In terms of feet, the dimensions are 1, 1.25, and 1.5, and the surface area is
$2[(1)(1.25) + (1)(1.5) + (1.25)(1.5)]$
$= 2(1.25 + 1.5 + 1.875)$
$= 2(4.625) = 9.25$ square feet.
To check, there are 144 square inches in a square foot, so 9.25 square feet equals $(9.25)(144) = 1332$ square inches.

19. a. Metal is needed for the two circular bases. The area of each base is $A = \pi r^2 =$ $\pi(2.75)^2 = 7.5625\pi$, so the area of both bases is $2(7.5625\pi) = 15.125\pi \approx$ 47.5 cm².

b. Cardboard is needed for the lateral area; when opened up, the lateral side is a rectangle with height 9.5 cm and base equal to the circumference of the base. Since $C = \pi d$, the circumference is $\pi(5.5) = 5.5\pi$. So the lateral area is $(5.5\pi)(9.5) = 52.25\pi \approx 164.1$ cm².

20.

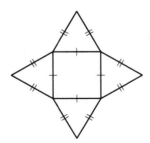

21. For the pyramid in Question 8, the triangle formed by the slant height, half an edge of the base, and the lateral edge, is a right triangle with legs 10 and 6. Using the Pythagorean Theorem to find the hypotenuse h,

$$h^2 = 6^2 + 10^2$$
$$h^2 = 36 + 100$$
$$h^2 = 136$$

So $h = \sqrt{136} = \sqrt{(4)(34)} = 2\sqrt{34} \approx 11.66$ cm.

22. The four assumed properties of area are: the Uniqueness Property—Given a unit region, every polygonal region has a unique area.
the Rectangle Formula—The area of a rectangle with dimensions ℓ and w is ℓw.
the Congruence Property—Congruent figures have the same area.
the Additive Property—The area of the union of two nonoverlapping regions is the sum of the areas of the regions.

23. a.

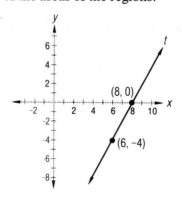

b. Using the definition of slope, $\frac{y_2 - y_1}{x_2 - x_1}$, the

slope is $\frac{-4 - 0}{6 - 8} = \frac{-4}{-2} = 2$.

c. By the Perpendicular Lines and Slopes Theorem, the slope of any line

perpendicular to t will be $-\frac{1}{2}$, because

$(-\frac{1}{2})(2) = -1$.

24. a. Subtract 3 from each side of the equation $x + 3 = 64$ to get $x = 61$.

b. Divide each side of the equation

$y \cdot 3 = 64$ by 3 to get $y = \frac{64}{3}$.

c. The equation $z^3 = 64$ states that the cube of a number is 64. Check some small numbers: $2^3 = 4 \cdot 2 = 8$, $3^3 = 9 \cdot 3 = 27$, $4^3 = 16 \cdot 4 = 64$. So $z = 4$.

25. When the cone is formed, the lateral edge of the cone is the length of segment $\overline{AB}$ or segment $\overline{BC}$; depending on your initial choice, that is 4″ or 10 cm. The

circumference of the base of the cone is $\frac{3}{4}$ of

the circumference of the original disk. The original disk has circumference $C = 2\pi r = 2\pi(4) = 8\pi''$ (or 20π cm), so the circumference of the base of the cone is

$\frac{3}{4}(8\pi) = 6\pi$ (or $\frac{3}{4}(20\pi) = 15\pi$). Using the

formula L.A. $= \frac{1}{2}\ell p$, the lateral area of the

cone is $\frac{1}{2}(4)(6\pi) = 12\pi \approx 37.70$ in.^{2}

(or $\frac{1}{2}(10)(15\pi) = 75\pi \approx 235.6$ cm^2).

LESSON 10-3 (pp. 478–482)

1. The volume of a box with dimensions 30 cm, 70 cm, and 84 cm is $(30)(70)(84) = 176,400$ cm^3.

2. The volume of a cube with edge 1 cm is 1 cubic centimeter or 1 cm^3.

3. No, two solids with the same surface area do not necessarily have the same volume. Consider a cube with side 5 cm. Its surface area consists of 6 faces, each with area 25 cm^2, so its surface area is 150 cm^2, and its volume is $5^3 = 125$ cm^3. Next consider a box with dimensions $1 \times 1 \times 37$. If the 1×1 squares are the bases, then the perimeter of the base is 4, so the lateral area is $(4)(37) = 148$. Add to that the area of each base, and the surface area is $148 + 1 + 1 = 150$ cm^2. The volume is $(1)(1)(37) = 37$ cm^2.

4. If two cubes have the same surface area, then the face of each cube has the same area, and so each cube has the same edge. So the two cubes will have the same volume.

5. x is a cube root of y if and only if $x^3 = y$.

6. **a.** The cube of 8 is $(8)(8)(8) = (64)(8) = 512$.
   b. Because $(2)(2)(2) = (4)(2) = 8$, the cube root of 8 is 2.

7. The exact cube root of 50 is written $\sqrt[3]{50}$.

8. Using a calculator, the cube root of 100 can be found using the following keystrokes: 100 $\boxed{y^x}$ $= 3$ $\boxed{1/x}$$\boxed{=}$4.6415888 ≈ 4.64

9. **a.** The top of the bag in Example 1 has dimensions 7″ and 12″, so its area is $(7)(12) = 84$ in.^{2}; the surface area of the bag is increased by 84 in^2.
   b. Putting a top on the bag does not change the dimensions of the bag, so it does not affect the bag's volume.

10. **a.** In the volume formula $V = Bh$ for the volume of a box, B stands for the area of the base.
    b. Since $B = \ell w$, substituting ℓw for B in the formula results in $V = (\ell w)h$, the formula for the volume of a box.

11. Using the formula $V = Bh$ for the volume of a box with $V = 576$ in.^{3} and $B = 48$ in.^{2}, then $576 = 48h$ and $h = \frac{576}{48} = 12$ in.

12. If a cube has volume 29,791 cm^3, then the side of the cube is $\sqrt[3]{29{,}791} = 31$ cm (to check: $(31)(31)(31) = (961)(31) = 29{,}791$). So the area of a face of the cube is $31^2 = 961$, and the area of all six faces of the cube is $(961)(6) = 5766$ cm^2.

13. Using a calculator, $\sqrt[3]{25} \approx 2.9240$ and $\sqrt[3]{100} \approx 4.6416$, so $\sqrt[3]{25} + \sqrt[3]{100} \approx 2.9240 + 4.6416 = 7.5656 \approx 7.57$.

14. **a.** The faces of the two cubes have measurements x^2 and $(3x)^2 = 9x^2$, so the surface areas of the two cubes are $6x^2$ and $6(9x^2) = 54x^2$. The ratio of the total surface areas is $\frac{6x^2}{54x^2} = \frac{6}{54} = \frac{1}{9}$, (which is the square of the ratios of the sides).
    b. The volume of the cubes are x^3 and $(3x)^3 = 27x^3$, so the ratio of the volumes is $\frac{x^3}{27x^3} = \frac{1}{27}$ (which is the cube of the ratio of the sides).

15. **a.** 1 yard = 3 feet
    b. 1 square yard = (1 yard)(1 yard)
    $\qquad\qquad\qquad = $ (3 feet)(3 feet)
    $\qquad\qquad\qquad = $ 9 square feet
    c. 1 cubic yard = (1 yard)(1 yard)(1 yard)
    $\qquad\qquad\qquad = $ (3 feet)(3 feet)(3 feet)
    $\qquad\qquad\qquad = $ 27 cubic feet

16. a. 10 PRINT "GIVE DIMENSIONS OF
BOX"
20 INPUT L, W, H
30 PRINT "THE VOLUME IS" L*W*H
"CUBIC UNITS."
40 PRINT "THE SURFACE AREA IS"
2*(L*W + W*H + L*H) "SQUARE
UNITS."
50 END
(Note the expression in line 30 is how a
computer calculates the product of ℓ, w,
and h. The expression in line 40 is the
computer expression for
$2(\ell w + wh + \ell h)$.

b. For $L = 7$, $W = 12$, and $H = 17$, the
printout should look like:
RUN
?7, 12, 17
THE VOLUME IS 1428 CUBIC UNITS.
THE SURFACE AREA IS 814 SQUARE
UNITS.
The volume of 1428 in.^{3} agrees with the
results in Example 1 of Lesson 10-3. The
surface area of the paper bag in Example 1
of Lesson 10-1 was 730 in.^{2}; add the area
of the top of the bag (which is $7 \times 12 =$
84 in.^{2}) to get $730 + 84 = 814$ in.^{2}.

17. a.

b. Using the formula L.A. $= \frac{1}{2}\ell p$ with ℓ, the
slant height, given as 12 and p, the
circumference, found by $C = 2\pi r = 2\pi(4)$
$= 8\pi$, then L.A. $= \frac{1}{2}(12)(8\pi) = 48\pi \approx$
150.8 units^2.

18. For the regular square pyramid, the slant
height is ℓ, the perimeter is $4s$, and the area
of the base is s^2, so using the formulas
S.A. $=$ L.A. $+ B$ and L.A. $= \frac{1}{2}\ell p$, then
S.A. $= \frac{1}{2}\ell(4s) + s^2 = 2\ell s + s^2$.

19. a. For the cylinder, each base has radius
$\frac{12}{2} = 6$, and so the area of each base is
$A = \pi r^2 = \pi(6)^2 = 36\pi$. The
circumference of the base is
$C = \pi d = 12\pi$, and the height is 7, so the
lateral area is $Ch = (12\pi)(7) = 84\pi$.
Using the formula S.A. $=$ L.A. $+ 2B$, the
surface area is $84\pi + 2(36\pi) =$
$84\pi + 72\pi = 156\pi \approx 490.088$ in.^{2}.

b. To find the number of square feet of
paper, first calculate the number of square
inches in a square foot:
1 ft$^2 = (1$ ft$)(1$ ft$) = (12$ in.$)(12$ in.$) =$
144 in.^{2}.
Dividing 490.088 in.^{2} by 144, the number
of square feet is $\frac{490.088}{144} \approx 3.40$. Assuming
you have to buy an integral number of
square feet, you would need 4 square feet
of wrapping paper to cover the cylinder.

20. a. The area of $\triangle GHI$ is the product of the measures of base $\overline{HI}$ and its altitude $\overline{GJ}$. To find $\overline{HI}$, note that segment $\overline{HJ}$ is a leg of a right triangle with hypotenuse 6 and other leg 5, so

$HJ^2 + 5^2 = 6^2$

$HJ^2 + 25 = 36$

$HJ^2 = 11$

So $HJ = \sqrt{11}$.

$\triangle GHI$ is isosceles, so altitude $\overline{GJ}$ bisects base $\overline{HI}$, and so $HI = 2\sqrt{11}$. Then the area of $\triangle GHI$ is $\frac{1}{2}(HI)(GJ) = \frac{1}{2}(2\sqrt{11})(5)$

$= 5\sqrt{11} \approx 16.58$ ft^2.

b. The surface area of the tent consists of the two triangular bases of the prism (each with area $5\sqrt{11}$) and the two "pitched" rectangles, each with dimensions 6' and 7' (there is no "bottom" for the tent; the sides rest on the ground). So the surface area of the tent is $2(5\sqrt{11}) + 2(6)(7) = 10\sqrt{11} + 84 \approx 33.166 + 84 = 117.166 \approx 117$ square feet.

21. a. The singular for polyhedra is polyhedron.

b. The singular for radii is radius.

c. The singular for vertices is vertex.

22. Some examples of long thin containers are perfume bottles and champagne glasses.

23. a. Samples:

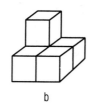

a

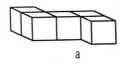

b

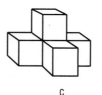

c

b. Arrangements a and c have surface area 22 units^2; this is the maximum surface area.

c. Arrangement b has surface area 20 units^2; this is the minimum surface area.

LESSON 10-4 (pp. 483–487)

1.

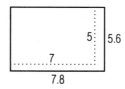

$5.6 \cdot 7.8 = (5+.6)(7+.8)$

$\qquad = (5)(7)+(5)(.8)+(7)(.6)+(.6)(.8)$

This shows (geometrically and algebraically), that $(5.6)(7.8)$ equals $(5)(7)$ plus some positive amount. So $(5.6)(7.8)$ is greater than $(5)(7)$.

2. $ab = ba$ is a statement of the Cummutative Property of Multiplication.

3. $xyz = zyx$ is a statement of the Commutative Property of Multiplication (and also the Associative Property of Multiplication).

4. Expressing the same area in two different ways (as $(x + 3)(x + 1)$ and as $x^2 + x + 3x + 3$) is a statement of the pattern referred to as the FOIL pattern or FOIL property (or distributive property).

5. Expressing the same area in two different ways (as $(a + b + c)(d + e)$ and as $ad + ae + bd + be + cd + ce$) is an illustration of how to find the product of a trinomial and a binomial (or distributive property).

6. Expressing the same volume in two different ways (as $(x + w)(y + z)(u + v)$ and as $xyv + xyu + wyv + wyu + xzv + xzu + wzv + wzu$) is an illustration of how to find the product of three binomials (or the distributive property).

7. Use FOIL:
$$(x + 9)(2x + 3) = 2x^2 + 3x + 18x + 27$$
$$= 2x^2 + 21x + 27$$

8. Use FOIL:
$$(3a + 5)(7a + 6) = 21a^2 + 18a + 35a + 30$$
$$= 21a^2 + 53a + 30$$

9. First find the product of two binomials:
$$(a+1)(a+2)(a+3) = (a+1)(a^2+2a+3a+6)$$
$$= (a+1)(a^2+5a+6)$$
Next multiply each term in the trinomial by each term in the binomial:
$$(a+1)(a^2+5a+6) = a^3+5a^2+6a$$
$$+a^2+5a+6$$
$$= a^3+6a^2+11a+6$$

10. Multiply each term in the trinomial by each term in the binomial:
$$(a+b+2)(3a+8b)$$
$$= (a+b+2)(3a)+(a+b+2)(8b)$$
$$= 3a^2+3ab+6a+8ab+8b^2+16b$$
$$= 3a^2+6a+11ab+16b+8b^2$$

11. If the original volume is ℓwh, then the new volume is $(3\ell)wh = 3(\ell wh)$; the volume is multiplied by 3 (which is the multiplier of the length).

12. If the original volume is ℓwh, then the new volume is $(3\ell)(3w)(3h) = 27\ell wh$; the volume is multiplied by 27 (which is the product of the three multipliers of the length, width, and height).

13. If the original volume is ℓwh, the new volume is $(\ell + 6)wh = \ell wh + 6wh$; the new volume is increased by six times the product of the width and height.

14. The lead forms a shell that is the difference in two volumes. The volume of the outside of the shell is $(28.2 \text{ cm})(20.2 \text{ cm})(14.2 \text{ cm}) = 8088.888 \text{ cm}^3$, and the volume of the inside of the shell is $(28 \text{ cm})(20 \text{ cm})(14 \text{ cm}) = 7840 \text{ cm}^3$. The difference in those two volumes is the amount of lead, which is $8088.888 - 7840 = 248.888 \approx 249 \text{ cm}^3$.

15. a. Bag Y has dimensions h, w, and d, so its volume is hwd. Bag X has dimensions $1.4h$, $1.2w$, and $1.2d$, so its volume is $(1.4h)(1.2w)(1.2d) = 2.016hwd$. So bag X holds 2.016 times as much as bag Y.

   b. Assuming that the costs of the bags of rice depend mainly on the cost of the rice, bag X, which holds over twice as much as bag Y, should cost about twice as much as bag Y.

16. $(x-1)(2x-5) = 2x^2-5x-2x+5$
$$= 2x^2-7x+5$$

17. $(y-x)(y+x) = y^2+xy-xy-x^2$
$$= y^2-x^2$$

18. $(3a + 2)(b - 6)(a - b)$
$$= (3a + 2)(ab - b^2 - 6a + 6b)$$
$$= (3a)(ab - b^2 - 6a + 6b) +$$
$$2(ab - b^2 - 6a + 6b)$$
$$= 3a^2b - 3ab^2 - 18a^2 + 18ab +$$
$$2ab - 2b^2 - 12a + 12b$$
$$= 3a^2b - 3ab^2 - 18a^2 + 20ab -$$
$$2b^2 - 12a + 12b$$

19. $(a+b+c)^2 = (a+b+c)(a+b+c)$
$= a(a+b+c)+b(a+b+c)+c(a+b+c)$
$= a^2+ab+ac+ab+b^2+bc+ac+bc+c^2$
$= a^2+b^2+c^2+2(ab+bc+ac)$

20. a. one meter $= 100$ centimeters

    b. 1 square meter $= $ (1 meter)(1 meter)
$= $ (100 cm)(100 cm)
$= 10,000$ square centimeters

    c. 1 cubic meter $= $ (1 m)(1 m)(1 m)
$= $ (100 cm)(100 cm)(100 cm)
$= 1,000,000$ cubic centimeters

21. Using a calculator, the cube root of π is
$\boxed{\pi}\ \boxed{y^x}\ 3\ \boxed{1/x}\ \boxed{=}\,1.46459189 \approx 1.46$.
To check: Which is closer to π, 1.46^3 or
1.47^3? $\pi - 1.46^3 = 3.14159 - 3.112136 = $
$.029454$, while $1.47^3 - \pi = $
$3.176523 - 3.14159 = .034933$.
So 1.46 is the cube root of π to the nearest
hundredth.

22. If a cube has volume 27 in.^{3}, then its edge is
$\sqrt[3]{27\text{ in.}^3} = 3$ in. So the area of each face is
9 in.^{2}, and the surface area is 6×9 in.$^2 = $
54 in.^{2}.

23. The height of 72 cards is 2.7 cm, which
means the height of each card is $\frac{2.7}{72} = $
$.0375$ cm. So the dimensions of a single card
are 5.6 cm, 8.7 cm, and .0375 cm, and the
volume of the card is $(5.6)(8.7)(.0375) = $
1.827 cm^3.

24. a.

b. Each face of the lateral surface is an
isosceles triangle with base 18 and leg 41,
so the altitude ℓ of the triangle (which is
the slant height of the pyramid) is the leg
of a right triangle with hypotenuse 41 and
other leg 9. Using the Pythagorean
Theorem,
$\ell^2 + 9^2 = 41^2$
$\ell^2 + 81 = 1681$
$\ell^2 = 1600$
$\ell = 40$

Using the formula for the lateral area of a
prism, L.A. $= \frac{1}{2}\ell p$, the slant height is 40
and the perimeter is $(5)(18) = 90$, so
L.A. $= \frac{1}{2}(40)(90) = 1800$ units^2.

25. $\pi r^2 = 10$
$r^2 = \dfrac{10}{\pi}$
$r = \pm\sqrt{\dfrac{10}{\pi}} \approx \pm\sqrt{3.183} \approx \pm1.78$

26.

$(a + b)^3$ represents a cube where each side is
expressed as $(a + b)$. That cube can be
expressed as 8 volumes:
$a^3 + a^2b + a^2b + a^2b + ab^2 + ab^2 + ab^2 + b^3$
$= a^3 + 3a^2b + 3ab^2 + b^3$
So $(a + b)^3 = a^3 + 3a^2b + 3ab^2 + b^3$.

LESSON 10-5 (pp. 488–493)

1. A cubic foot of liquid is about 7.48 gallons.

2. The diameter of the tank is 120 ft, so the radius is 60 ft and the area of the base is $A = \pi r^2 = \pi(60)^2 = 3600\pi$ ft^2. So the volume of the tank is $V = Bh = (3600\pi)(60) = 216{,}000\pi$ ft^3; multiplying that by 7.48 gallons per ft^3, the number of gallons in the tank is $(216{,}000\pi)(7.48) = 1{,}615{,}680\pi \approx 5{,}075{,}808.4$ gallons.

3. A deck of cards is used to illustrate that an oblique prism and a right prism can have the same volume (choice b), and thus the volume of an oblique prism is Bh (choice c), and, in general, this leads to Cavalieri's Principle (choice a). It is not used to show that a cylinder and a prism have the same volume formula; that is choice (d).

4. Francesco Bonaventura Cavalieri, who was born in 1598 and died in 1647, lived most of his life in the 1600s, which is the 17th century. He was an Italian mathematician.

5. Cavalieri's Principle is part e of the Volume Postulate: Let I and II be two solids included between parallel planes. If every plane P parallel to the given planes intersects I and II in sections with the same area, then Volume (I) = Volume (II).

6. A formula for the volume of an oblique cylinder is $V = Bh = \pi r^2 h$, where B is the area of the base (or r is the radius of the base), and h is the height of the cylinder.

7. The radius of the base is 5, so the area of the base is $A = \pi r^2 = 25\pi$; the height h is 9, so the volume of the oblique cylinder is $V = Bh = (25\pi)(9) = 225\pi \approx 706.86$ units^3.

8. The base is a right triangle with legs 3 and 4, so the area of the base is one-half the product of the legs or $\frac{1}{2}(3)(4) = 6$ units^2. So the volume is $V = Bh = (6)(12) = 72$ units^3.

9. The edge of the square base is 5 m, so the area of the base is 25 m^2; using the volume formula $V = Bh$ with $b = 25$ m^2 and $h = 20$ m, then $V = (25)(20) = 500$ m^3.

10. The volume of the parallelopiped is the product of the shaded base and the height ZY. Find the area of the shaded parallelogram using its side $\overline{VX}$ and altitude to that side $\overline{UW}$. Find the height $\overline{ZY}$ using the right triangle ZYX.

The shaded parallelopiped has base 8. To find the altitude to that base, note that the altitude $\overline{UW}$ is a leg in right triangle VUW with hypotenuse 13 and other leg 5. Using the Pythagorean Theorem:
$$UW^2 + 5^2 = 13^2$$
$$UW^2 + 25 = 169$$
$$UW^2 = 144$$
$$UW = 12.$$
So the area of the base is $(8)(12) = 96$ units^2. Next, use the Pythagorean Theorem in right triangle ZYX:
$$ZY^2 + 15^2 = 22^2$$
$$ZY^2 + 225 = 484$$
$$ZY^2 = 259$$
$$ZY = \sqrt{259}$$
So the volume of the parallelepiped is $V = Bh = (96)(\sqrt{259}) \approx (96)(16.09) = 1544.64 \approx 1555$ units^3.

11. The base is a rectangle, so its area is $(3)(7) = 21$ ft^2, and the height is 10 ft, so the volume is $V = Bh = (21)(10) = 210$ ft^3.

12. A sewer pipe is a right cylinder. The radius of the pipe is 2 ft, so the area of the base is $A = \pi r^2 = \pi(2)^2 = 4\pi$ ft^2. Using the formula $V = Bh$ with $B = 4\pi$ ft^2 and $h = 200$ ft, then $V = (4\pi)(200) = 800\pi \approx 2513.274 \approx 2513$ ft^3.

13.

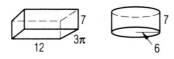

14. Using the formula $V = Bh$ with $V = 38$ m³ and $h = 4$ m, then $38 = 4B$ and $B = \frac{38}{4} = 9.5$ m².

15. Using the formula for the volume of a prism $V = Bh$ with $B = 21$ m² and $h = 9$ m, then $V = (21)(9) = 189$ m³.

16. a. If the diameters are 2.3 in. and 3.3 in., then the radii are 1.15 in. and 1.65 in., and the areas of the bases are $\pi(1.15)^2 = 1.3225\pi$ and $\pi(1.65)^2 = 2.7225\pi$. The height of each glass is h, so the volumes are $1.3225\pi h$ and $2.7225\pi h$, and the ratio of the second glass's capacity to the first glass's capacity is $\frac{2.7225\pi h}{1.3225\pi h} = 2.0586$. So the second glass holds just over twice as much as the first glass.

b. If you multiply the diameter of a glass by a factor t, then that factor is squared when you find the area of the base of the glass. If the heights of the two glasses are the same, then the capacity is changed just by t^2. If you wanted to double the capacity of the glass, then $t^2 = 2$ and $t = \sqrt{2} \approx 1.414$. Since the factor involved in the problem is $\frac{3.3}{2.3} = 1.435$, which is greater than $\sqrt{2}$, the capacity is more than doubled.

17. Cavalieri's Principle applies to solids such that each has two congruent bases, such as cylinders and prisms. A cone does not have two congruent bases, so Cavalieri's Principle cannot be applied to a cylinder and a cone.

18. A cylinder with height h and radius r has volume $V = Bh = \pi r^2 h$, and another cylinder with same height h and half the radius has volume $V = Bh = \pi\left(\frac{r}{2}\right)^2 h = \frac{1}{4}\pi r^2 h$. So the volume is changed by a factor of one-fourth. In general, if two cylinders have the same height and the radius is changed by a factor of t, then the volume is changed by a factor of t^2.

19. A cylinder with base B and height h has volume $V = Bh$, and another cylinder with the same base B and height $2h$ has volume $V = B(2h) = 2Bh$. In general, if two cylinders have the same base and the height is changed by a factor of w, then the volume is changed by that same factor w.

20. The base of the cylinder has radius 3 cm, so the area of the base is $A = \pi r^2 = \pi(3)^2 = 9\pi$ cm². The height of the cylinder is 15 cm, so its volume is $V = Bh = (9\pi)(15) = 135\pi$ cm³. The cylinder is filled with water, so each cm³ (that is, each cubic centimeter) has a mass of 1 g, so 135π cm³ has a mass of $135\pi \approx 424.115 \approx 424$ g.

21. $(4x - 5y)(x + 2y + 7)$
$= (4x)(x + 2y + 7) - (5y)(x + 2y + 7)$
$= 4x^2 + 8xy + 28x - (5xy + 10y^2 + 35y)$
$= 4x^2 + 8xy + 28x - 5xy - 10y^2 - 35y$
$= 4x^2 + 3xy + 28x - 10y^2 - 35y$

22. If the dimensions of a box are h, ℓ, and w, then the volume is $V = h\ell w$. The dimensions of the second box are $(4h)$, (5ℓ), and $(5w)$, so its volume is $(4h)(5\ell)(5w) = 100h\ell w$. So the volume of the box has been multiplied by 100 (which is the product of the multiples of the sides).

23. The amount of lead used is the volume of the "shell." The volume of the outside of the shell is $V = (4)(3.5)(2.5) = 35$ cm^3, and the volume of the inside of the shell is $V = (3)(2.5)(2) = 15$ cm^3. The amount of lead is the difference in volumes: $35 - 15 = 20$ cm^3.

24. The prism in Question 8 has bases that are right triangles, so the area of each base is one-half the product of the legs, or $\frac{1}{2}(3)(4) = 6$ units^2. Using the formula L.A. $= ph$ where p, the perimeter of the base, is $3 + 4 + 5 = 12$ units and h, the height, also happens to be 12 units, L.A. $= (12)(12) = 144$ units^2. So S.A. $=$ L.A. $+ 2b = 144 + 2(6) = 144 + 12 = 156$ units^2.

25. In Example 2 on page 491, $MTSN$ is a parallelogram with base $MN = 9$ and the altitude to that base is the length of segment $\overline{RS}$. That length was found in Example 2: $RS = 12$ units. So the area of $MTSN$ is the product of a base and the altitude to that base, or $(9)(12) = 108$ units^2.

26. From most general to most specific, the formulas are:

$A = \frac{1}{2}h(b_1 + b_2)$ (the area of a trapezoid)

$A = hb$ (the area of a parallelogram)

$A = \ell w$ (the area of a rectangle)

$A = s^2$ (the area of a square)

27. $\overline{CD}$ and $\overline{EF}$ are parallel and congruent, so $CDEF$ is a parallelogram by the Sufficient Conditions for a Parallelogram (part d). Then $\overline{CF} \parallel \overline{DE}$ by the definition of a parallelogram (meaning), and $\angle FCE \cong \angle DEC$ because $\parallel$ lines $\Rightarrow$ AIA $=$.

28. a. Sample: A 12-ounze can has a radius of $1\frac{1}{4}''$ and a height of $5''$. That is a volume of $\pi(1.25)^2(5) \approx 24.5$ in.^{3}

b. There are $\frac{24.5}{12} \approx 2$ cubic inches per fluid ounce.

LESSON 10–6   (pp. 494–498)

1. The best formulas to remember are the ones which apply to the most figures.

2. The formula S.A. $=$ L.A. $+ 2B$ applies to cylindric solids with 2 bases; these are boxes, cylinders, and prisms.

3. The formula S.A. $=$ L.A. $+ B$ applies to cylindric solids with 1 base; these are cones and pyramids.

4. a-b. There are 7 basic formulas to learn in this chapter. Up to this lesson, 4 have been seen:

L.A. $= \ell p$ (lateral area of a prism or cylinder)

L.A. $= \frac{1}{2}\ell p$ (lateral area of a cone or pyramid)

$V = Bh$ (volume of a prism or cylinder)

$V = \ell wh$ (volume of a box)

5. In the formula L.A. $= ph$ for the lateral area of a prism or cylinder, p represents the perimeter or circumference of the prism or cylinder and h represents its height.

6. The process for obtaining special formulas for cones and cylinders is to substitute the circle formulas $B = \pi r^2$ and $p = 2\pi r$ into the corresponding formulas for pyramids and prisms.

7. Starting with the formula for the lateral area of a prism, L.A. $= ph$, and substituting $p = 2\pi r$ for the circumference of the base, the result is L.A. $= 2\pi rh$.

8. Starting with the formula for the volume of a prism, $V = Bh$, and substituting $B = \pi r^2$ for the area of the base, the result is $V = \pi r^2 h$.

9. Mathematicians recall many of the formulas they have to use by remembering simpler formulas, and deriving the one(s) they need from those simpler formulas.

10. Starting with the formula for the surface area of a prism or cylinder, S.A. = L.A. + 2B, and substituting L.A. = ph = $2\pi rh$ and $B = \pi r^2$, then S.A. = $2\pi rh + 2\pi r^2$.

11. **a.** Starting with the formula for the lateral area of a cone, L.A. = $\frac{1}{2}p\ell$, and substituting $p = 2\pi r$, then

    L.A. = $\frac{1}{2}(2\pi r)\ell = \pi r \ell$.

    b. Starting with the formula for the surface area of a cone, S.A. = L.A. + B, and substituting L.A. = $\pi r \ell$ (from part a) and $B = \pi r^2$, then S.A. = $\pi r \ell + \pi r^2$.

12. **a.**

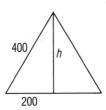

The height of the equilateral triangle is the leg of a right triangle with hypotenuse 400 and other leg 200. Using the Pythagorean Theorem,

$$h^2 + 200^2 = 400^2$$
$$h^2 + 40,000 = 160,000$$
$$h^2 = 120,000.$$

So $h = \sqrt{120,000} = \sqrt{(40,000)(3)} = 200\sqrt{3}$, and the area of the triangle is

$$\frac{1}{2}bh = \frac{1}{2}(400)(200\sqrt{3}) = 40,000\sqrt{3} \approx$$

$69282.03 \approx 69282$ units².

b.

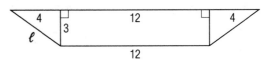

The height h of the equilateral triangle is the leg of a right triangle with hypotenuse s and other leg $\frac{s}{2}$. Using the Pythagorean Theorem,

$$h^2 + \left(\frac{s}{2}\right)^2 = s^2$$
$$h^2 + \frac{s^2}{4} = s^2$$
$$h^2 = \frac{3s^2}{4}$$

So $h = \frac{s\sqrt{3}}{2}$ and the area of the triangle is

$$\frac{1}{2}bh = \left(\frac{1}{2}s\right)\left(\frac{s\sqrt{3}}{2}\right) = \frac{s^2\sqrt{3}}{4}$$

13. **a.** Using the formula $A = \sqrt{s(s-a)(s-b)(s-c)}$ with $a = 9$, $b = 12$, and $c = 15$, then $s = \frac{9 + 12 + 15}{2}$

$$= \frac{36}{2} = 18 \text{ and}$$

$$A = \sqrt{(18)(18 - 9)(18 - 12)(18 - 15)}$$
$$= \sqrt{(18)(9)(6)(3)} = \sqrt{2916} \approx 54 \text{ units}^2.$$

b. Note that $9^2 + 12^2 = 81 + 144 = 225 = 15^2$, so the 9-12-15 triangle is a right triangle. (Another way to know that the three sides form a right triangle is that 9, 12, and 15 are the same multiple of 3, 4, and 5, so again the triangle is a right triangle.) The area of a right triangle is one-half the product of the legs, so the area is $\frac{1}{2}(9)(12) = \frac{1}{2}(108) = 54$ units².

(Another method would be to draw an accurate model of the triangle, measure one of the altitudes, and use those measurements to calculate the area.)

14. Using the formula $A =$ $\sqrt{s(s-a)(s-b)(s-c)}$ with $a = 10$, $b = 17$, and $c = 21$, then $s = \dfrac{10 + 17 + 21}{2}$

$= \dfrac{48}{2} = 24$ and

$A = \sqrt{(24)(24-10)(24-17)(24-21)} =$ $\sqrt{(24)(14)(7)(3)} = \sqrt{7056} = 84$ units^2.

15. Using the formula $A =$ $\sqrt{s(s-a)(s-b)(s-c)}$ with $a = b = c =$ 400, then $s = \dfrac{400 + 400 + 400}{2} = \dfrac{1200}{2} = 600$

and $A =$

$\sqrt{(600)(600-400)(600-400)(600-400)}$ $= \sqrt{(600)(200)(200)(200)} =$ $\sqrt{(48)(100,000,000)} =$ $\sqrt{(3)(16)(100,000,000)} = 40,000\sqrt{3} \approx$ $69,282$ units^2, which is the same value as in Question 12a.

16. **a.** Using the formula for the area of a trapezoid, $A = \frac{1}{2}h(b_1 + b_2)$ with $h = 3$ (here, h represents the altitude of the trapezoidal base), $b_1 = 12$, and $b_2 = 20$, the area of the base is $A = \frac{1}{2}(3)(12 + 20)$

$= \frac{1}{2}(3)(32) = 48$. So the volume of the prism is $V = Bh$ (here, h represents the height of the prism) $= (48)(10) =$ 480 units^3.

b. The formula for the lateral area of a prism is L.A. $= ph$, where p is the perimeter of the base and h is the height of the prism.

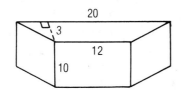

To find the length ℓ of the leg of the prism, note it can be broken down into a rectangle and two congruent right triangles, so ℓ is the hypotenuse of a right triangle with legs 3 and 4, and its length is 5 units (it is a 3-4-5- right triangle). So the perimeter of the trapezoidal base is $(20 + 5 + 12 + 5) = 42$ units, and L.A. $= ph = (42)(10) = 420$ units^2.

c. Using the formula for the surface area of a prism, S.A. $=$ L.A. $+ 2B$ with L.A. $=$ 420 units^2 (from part b) and $B = 48$ units^2 (from part a), then S.A. $= 420 + 2(48) =$ $420 + 96 = 516$ units^2.

17. If the radius of the base of a cylinder is 27, then the area of the base is $B = \pi r^2 =$ $\pi(27)^2 = 729\pi$. The height of the cylinder is the length of the diameter, so $h = 2(27) =$ 54, and the volume is $V = Bh = (729\pi)(54)$ $= 39366\pi \approx 123,671.93 \approx 123,672$ units^3.

18. $(x + y)(x + y) = x^2 + xy + xy + y^2$
$\qquad\qquad\qquad\quad = x^2 + 2xy + y^2$

19. If a cube has side 8, then its volume is $V = 8^3$ $= 512$ cubic units. If another solid has dimensions $(8 + a)$, $(8 - a)$ and 8, then its volume is $V = \ell wh = (8 + a)(8 - a)8 =$ $(64 - a^2)(8) = 512 - 8a^2$ units^3. The volume of the new box is smaller than the volume of the old cube by the factor $8a^2$ units^3.

20. **a.**

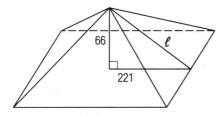

The slant height of the pyramid is the hypotenuse ℓ in a right triangle with legs 66 m and 221 m. Using the Pythagorean Theorem,

$\ell^2 = 66^2 + 221^2$

$\ell^2 = 4356 + 48,841$

$\ell^2 = 53,197.$

So $\ell = \sqrt{53,197} \approx 231$ m. Using the formula for the lateral area of a pyramid,

L.A. $= \frac{1}{2}\ell p$ with $\ell = \sqrt{53,197}$ m and

$p = 4(442) = 1768$ m, then L.A. $=$

$\frac{1}{2}(\sqrt{53,197})(1768) \approx 203,900$ m².

b. In Example 1 of Lesson 10-2, the lateral area of the Pyramid of Khufu was calculated as 86,400 m². So the lateral area of Teotihuacan is $\frac{204,000}{86,400} \approx 2.36$ or about 2 and a third times greater than the lateral area of the Pyramid of Khufu.

21. **a.**

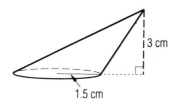

1.5 cm

b. The radius of the base is 1.5 cm, so its area is $B = \pi r^2 = \pi(1.5)^2 = 2.25\pi$ cm².
Adding this to the given measure of the lateral area of the cone, the surface area is
S.A. $=$ L.A. $+ B = 16 + 2.25\pi \approx$
$16 + 7.07 = 23.07 \approx 23$ cm².

22. The area of the ring is the difference between the areas of the two circles. The area of the larger circle is πr^2 and the area of the smaller circle is πh^2, so the area of the ring is $\pi r^2 - \pi h^2$ or $\pi(r^2 - h^2)$.

23. Using the definition of slope,
$$m = \frac{y_2 - y_1}{x_2 - x_1} = \frac{0 - b}{a - 0} = \frac{-b}{a} = -\frac{b}{a}.$$

24. Some points on the line $y = -\frac{1}{2}x + 3$ are
$(0, 3)$, $(2, 2)$, and $(-2, 4)$.

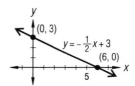

25. Answers may vary.
a. Sample:

4.5   8

b. Sample:

15

5

LESSON 10-7 (pp. 499–504)

1. According to Cavalieri's Principle, two pyramids with congruent bases and heights have equal volumes.

2. The volume of pyramid A-$BCDE$ is $\frac{1}{3}Bh$, which is one-third the volume of the box.

3. The volume V of a pyramid with height 6 and base area 57 is $V = \frac{1}{3}Bh = \frac{1}{3}(57)(6)$
$= 114$ units^3.

4. A formula for the volume of a cone is
$V = \frac{1}{3}Bh$ or $V = \frac{1}{3}\pi r^2 h$.

5. If the base of a cone in 2 ft, then its base has area $B = \pi r^2 = \pi 2^2 = 4\pi$ ft^2, and the volume is $V = \frac{1}{3}Bh = \frac{1}{3}(4\pi)(8) = \frac{32\pi}{3} \approx$ 33.5 ft^3.

6. The base is a right triangle, so its area is one-half the product of the legs or $\frac{1}{2}(5)(6) =$ 15 units^2, and $V = \frac{1}{3}Bh = \frac{1}{3}(15)(8) =$ 40 units^3.

7. The area of the base is $B = \frac{1}{2}h(b_1 + b_2) =$ $\frac{1}{2}(2)(5 + 9) = 14$ units.
So the volume of the pyramid is $V = \frac{1}{3}Bh =$ $\frac{1}{3}(14)(12) = 56$ units^2.

8. The diameter of the base is 18, so the radius is 9 and the area of the base is $B = \pi r^2 =$ $\pi(9)^2 = 81\pi$ units^2. So the volume is $V = \frac{1}{3}Bh = \frac{1}{3}(81\pi)(27) = 729\pi \approx 2290.22$ ≈ 2290 units^3.

9. Using $V = \frac{1}{3}Bh$ with $V = 40$ cm^3 and $h = 5$ cm, then $40 = \frac{1}{3}B(5)$ and

$B = \frac{120}{5} = 24$. So $B = \pi r^2 = 24$, and $r^2 = \frac{24}{\pi}$, so $r = \sqrt{\frac{24}{\pi}} \approx 2.76$.

10. If a cone and a cylinder have identical bases and equal heights, then the volume of the cone is $\frac{1}{3}$ the volume of the cylinder. So if the volume of the cylinder is V, the volume of the cone is $\frac{1}{3}V$.

11. Using the formula $V = \frac{1}{3}Bh$, then $B =$
45 acres $= (45$ acres$)(43{,}560 \frac{\text{ft}^2}{\text{acre}}) =$
$1{,}960{,}200$ ft^2 and $h = 177$ ft, so $V =$ $\frac{1}{3}(1{,}960{,}200)(177) = 115{,}651{,}800$ ft^3 or $\approx$ $116{,}000{,}000$ ft^3.

12. **a.** Using the formula $V = \frac{1}{3}Bh$ with $B = \pi r^2$ $= \pi(4)^2 = 16\pi$ and $h = 10$, then $V = \frac{1}{3}(16\pi)(10) = \frac{160\pi}{3} \approx 167.55$ cm^3.

   b. To find out the number of cupfuls needed to fill a liter jug, divide the volume of the cup into a liter. That is $\dfrac{1000}{\frac{160\pi}{3}} = \dfrac{3000}{160\pi} = \dfrac{75}{4\pi}$
$\approx 5.968 \approx 6$ cupfuls.

   c. The formula for the lateral area of a cone is L.A. $= \frac{1}{2}p\ell$, and the perimeter is $p = 2\pi r = 2\pi(4) = 8\pi$. To find the slant height ℓ, note that ℓ is the hypotenuse of a right triangle with legs 4 and 10, so:
$\ell^2 = 4^2 + 10^2$
$\ell^2 = 16 + 100 = 116$
So $\ell = \sqrt{116} = \sqrt{(4)(29)} = 2\sqrt{29}$.
So the lateral area is $\frac{1}{2}(8\pi)(2\sqrt{29}) =$ $8\pi\sqrt{29} \approx (8)(3.1416)(5.385) = 135.350 \approx$ 135 cm^2.

13. The formula for the volume of a cone is $V = \frac{1}{3}Bh = \frac{1}{3}\pi r^2 h$. If the height is kept the same and the radius is multiplied by 7, then the volume is changed by a factor of 7^2 or 49; the volume will be 49 times as great.

14. In the formula for the volume of a pyramid, the height appears with an exponent of one. So if the height is multiplied by 31.8, then the volume is multiplied by that same factor, 31.8.

15. a. The height of the cone is the length of $\overline{AB}$. Since $\triangle ABC$ is a 6-8-10 right triangle, $AB = 6$ units.

   b. Using the formula for the volume of a cone, $V = \frac{1}{3}Bh$, then $B = \pi r^2 = \pi(8)^2 = 64\pi$ and $h = 6$, so $V = \frac{1}{3}(64\pi)(6) = 128\pi$ $\approx 402.124 \approx 402$ units^3.

16. A formula for the surface area of a box with dimensions ℓ, w, and h is $2(\ell w + wh + \ell h)$, so the amount of paper needed to cover a box with those dimensions (in inches) is $2(\ell w + wh + \ell h)$ in.^{2}

17. Using the formula L.A. $= \frac{1}{2}p\ell$, then $p = 4s$ and L.A. $= \frac{1}{2}(4s)(\ell) = 2s\ell$.

18. The bases of the prism are right triangles with legs 6 and 9, so the area of the base is one-half the product of the legs or $\frac{1}{2}(6)(9) = 27$ units^2. So the volume is $V = Bh = (27)(8) = 216$ units^3.
To find the surface area, first find the hypotenuse h of the base:
$h^2 = 6^2 + 9^2$
$h^2 = 36 + 81 = 117$
So $h = \sqrt{117}$.
Then the surface area of the prism is

S.A. $=$ L.A. $+ 2B = ph + 2B$
$= (6 + 9 + \sqrt{117})(8) + 2(27)$
$= (15 + \sqrt{117})(8) + 54$
$= 120 + 8\sqrt{117} + 54$
$= 174 + 8\sqrt{117}$
$= 260.53$ units^2.

19. The area of the large rectangle can be expressed in two ways. One is as the product of two lengths, $(x + z)(y + 8)$, and the other is as the sum of four areas,
$xy + 8x + yz + 8z$.

20.

The area of a cross section of the wood before planing is $(2)(4) = 8$ in.^{2}, and the area of a cross section after planing is
$\left(1\frac{5}{8}\right)\left(3\frac{5}{8}\right) = (1.625)(3.625) = 5.890625$ in.^{2}
So the cross section (and thus the entire k-foot piece of lumber) has lost 2.109375 in.^{2}, and $\frac{2.109375}{8} = 0.263672 \approx 26\%$

21. The box-shaped tank has dimensions 20 in., 12 in. (convert it from 1 foot), and 10.5 in., so its volume is $(20)(12)(10.5) = 2520$ in.^{3}
Dividing that volume by 168 in.^{3}, the number of guppies the tank could accommodate is
$\frac{2520}{168} = 15$ guppies.

22. a.  **b.**

c. If a cone and a cylinder have the same height and same base, the volume of the cylinder should be 3 times the volume of the cone. So you should have to empty the cone into the cylinder 3 times to fill the cylinder.

23. a.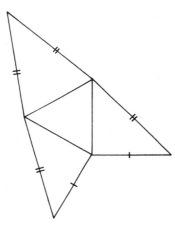

b.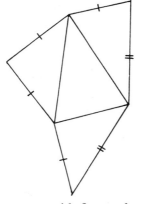

c. The three pyramids fit together to form a right triangular pyramid, so you have shown that the volume of a pyramid is one-third the volume of a prism with the same base and same height.

LESSON 10-8 (pp. 505–509)

1. a. To find the radius of a section of the sphere, use the Pythagorean Theorem (note: the formula for the area of a circle calls for r^2, so it is not necessary to find r):
$4^2 + r^2 = 6^2$
$r^2 = 36 - 16 = 20$
So the area of a section of the sphere is $A = \pi r^2 = 20\pi$.

b. The area of the ring is the difference between the area of the base of the cylinder, which is 36π, and the area of the small circle is 16π. So the area of the ring is $36\pi - 16\pi = 20\pi$.

2. a. To find the volume of the cylinder, use the formula $V = Bh = \pi r^2 h = \pi(6^2)(12) = \pi(36)(12) = 432\pi$ units^3.

b. The volume of each cone is $V = \frac{1}{3}Bh = \frac{1}{3}(36\pi)(6) = 72\pi$, so the volume of the two cones is 144π units^3.

c. The volume of solid region between the cylinder and the two cones is the difference in those volumes, or $432\pi - 144\pi = 288\pi$ units^3.

d. Using the formula for the volume of a sphere, $V = \frac{4}{3}\pi r^3 = \frac{4}{3}\pi(6)^3 = \frac{4}{3}\pi(216) = \frac{864\pi}{3} = 288\pi$ units^3.

3. By applying Cavalieri's Principle, the equal answers to parts **a** and **b** of Question 1 lead to equal answers to parts **c** and **d** of Question 2.

4. a.

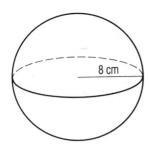

8 cm

b. Using the formula $V = \frac{4}{3}\pi r^3$ with $r = 8$,

then $V = \frac{4}{3}\pi(8)^3 = \frac{4}{3}\pi(512) =$

$\frac{2048\pi}{3}$ cm^3.

5. In Example 2, it was found that a standard bowling ball has about 333 cubic inches of material. This is between 300 and 400 cubic inches, which is choice (d).

6. The volume of the box is $V = s^3 = (9.5)^3 = 857.375$ in.^{3}, and the radius of the basketball is $\frac{9.5}{2} = 4.75$ in., so its volume is $V = \frac{4}{3}\pi r^3$

$= \frac{4}{3}\pi(4.75)^3 = 142.8958\pi \approx 448.92$ in.^{3} So

the percent of the box filled by the basketball

is $\frac{448.92}{857.375} \approx 0.5236 \approx 52\%$.

7. Using the formula $V = \frac{4}{3}\pi r^3$ with

$V = 268$ m^3, then $268 = \frac{4}{3}\pi r^3$ and $\pi r^3 =$

$(268)\left(\frac{3}{4}\right) = 201$, so $r^3 = \frac{201}{\pi} \approx 63.98$ and

$r = \sqrt[3]{63.98} \approx 3.99958 \approx 4.0$ m.

8. The volume of the ice cream is the volume of a cone plus the volume of a hemisphere.

For the cone, $V = \frac{1}{3}Bh = \frac{1}{3}(\pi 3^2)(10) =$

$\frac{1}{3}(9\pi)(10) = 30\pi$ cm^3.

For the hemisphere, $V = \frac{1}{2}\left(\frac{4}{3}\pi r^3\right) = \frac{2}{3}\pi r^3 =$

$\frac{2}{3}\pi(3^3) = \frac{2}{3}\pi(27) = 18\pi$ cm^3.

So the volume of ice cream is $30\pi + 18\pi = 48\pi \approx 150.8$ cm^3.

9. The radius of the spherical water tank is

$\frac{16}{2} = 8$ m, so its volume is $V = \frac{4}{3}\pi r^3 =$

$\frac{4}{3}\pi(8)^3 = \frac{4}{3}\pi(512) = \frac{2048\pi}{3} \approx 2144.66$ cm^3.

a. If the town uses 500 m^3 each day and puts back 300 m^3 each day, then the tank loses 200 m^3 each day. The number of days it can continue doing this is $\frac{2144.66}{200} =$ 10.7233 or 10 days (it will run out of water on the eleventh day).

b. If no water is available to put back into the tank, then the number of days the tank can be depleted by 500 m^3 is $\frac{2144.66}{500} =$ 4.28932, or just over 4 days.

10. If a sphere has diameter d, then its radius is $\frac{d}{2}$, so its volume is $V = \frac{4}{3}\pi r^3 = \frac{4}{3}\pi\left(\frac{d}{2}\right)^3 =$

$\frac{4}{3}\pi\left(\frac{d^3}{8}\right) = \frac{4\pi d^3}{24} = \frac{1}{6}\pi d^3$.

11. Each cone has radius 5 and height 10, so the volume of each cone is $V = \frac{1}{3}Bh =$

$\frac{1}{3}(\pi 5^2)(10) = \frac{1}{3}(25\pi)(10) = \frac{250\pi}{3}$. So the

volume of the union of the two cones is

$2\left(\frac{250\pi}{3}\right) = \frac{500\pi}{3} \approx 523.60$ units^3.

12. The volume of the cube is $V = s^3 = 7^3 = 343$ units^3. The volume of the regular

pyramid atop the cube is $V = \frac{1}{3}Bh =$

$\frac{1}{3}(7^2)(6.5) = \frac{1}{3}(49)(6.5) \approx 106.167$ units^3. So

the total volume is $343 + 106.167 = 449.167$ units^3.

13. Questions 11 and 12 apply the Additive Property of the Volume Postulate: The volume of the union of two non-overlapping solids is the sum of the volumes of the solids.

14. a. If the surface area of a cube is 96 m^2, then the area of one of its six faces is $\frac{96}{6} =$ 16 m^2, and each edge of the cube is 4 m. So the volume of the cube is $V = s^3 = 4^3 = 64$ m^3.

b. If the surface area of a cube is x units^2, then the area of each face is $\frac{x}{6}$ units^2 and each edge of the cube has length $\sqrt{\frac{x}{6}}$ units. So the volume of the cube is $V = s^3 =$ $\left(\sqrt{\frac{x}{6}}\right)\left(\sqrt{\frac{x}{6}}\right)\left(\sqrt{\frac{x}{6}}\right) = \frac{x}{6}\sqrt{\frac{x}{6}}$ units^3.

15. The formula $V = Bh$ applies to cylindric solids, which include boxes, cylinders, and prisms.

16. The formula L.A. $= \frac{1}{2}\ell p$ applies to figures with one base, which are cones and pyramids.

17. a. The volume of a prism is the product of its base area and height. If two prisms have congruent bases and equal heights, then they must have the same volume, so the statement is *true*.

b. The surface area of a prism is the lateral area plus two times the base area, and the lateral area is the perimeter times the slant height. If the bases of two solids are congruent, then their bases have the same area and the same perimeter. However, if they can have equal heights they can still have unequal slant heights, so their lateral areas are not necessarily equal. Thus two prisms with congruent bases and equal heights do not necessarily have the same surface area; the statement is *false*.

18. $(x+3)(2y)(z+4) = (2y)(x+3)(z+4)$
$$= (2y)(xz+4x+3z+12)$$
$$= 2xyz+8xy+6yz+24y$$

19. a. A box with dimensions ℓ, w, and h has surface area $2(\ell w + \ell h + wh)$ and a box with dimensions (3ℓ), $(3w)$, and $(3h)$ has surface area
$2[(3\ell)(3w) + (3\ell)(3h) + (3w)(3h)]$
$= 2(9\ell w + 9\ell h + 9wh)$
$= 2[(9)(\ell w + \ell h + wh)]$
$= (9)(2(\ell w + \ell h + wh))$.
So the new surface area is 9 times the original surface area. (Note: when the linear dimensions were multiplied by a number, the area was multiplied by the square of that number.)

b. A box with dimensions ℓ, w, and h has volume ℓwh, and a box with dimensions (3ℓ), $(3w)$, and $(3h)$ has volume $(3\ell)(3w)(3h) = 27\ell wh$. So the new volume is 27 times the original volume. (Note, when the linear dimensions were multiplied by a number, the volume was multiplied by the cube of that number.)

20. To the nearest tenth,
$\sqrt[3]{85} - \sqrt[3]{5} \approx 4.3968 - 1.7100 =$ $2.6868 \approx 2.7$.

21. a. To find the surface area of the cube with a hole:
the lateral area of the outside is $(4)(9) = 36$ squares;
the area of the top face is 8 squares;
the area of the bottom face is 8 squares;
the hole exposes 4 columns of 3 squares each, which is 12 squares.
So the surface area is
$(36 + 8 + 8 + 12) = 64$ squares.

b. On the top face, all 8 cubes are painted on exactly three faces (the 4 corner cubes have all their painted faces on the outside of the cube, and the other 4 cubes have two faces painted on the outside and one face painted "in the hole"). The bottom face also has all 8 cubes painted on exactly three faces. For the middle layer, all the cubes are painted on exactly two faces, so none is painted on three faces. So the number of cubes painted on exactly three faces is 16 cubes.

c. From part **b**, all 8 cubes in the middle layer are painted on exactly two faces. (Four are painted on the two outside faces, and four are painted on one outside face and one face "in the hole.") So the number of cubes painted on exactly two faces is 8.

d. Of the 24 cubes, 16 are painted on exactly three faces and 8 are painted on exactly two faces, so none is painted on exactly one face.

e. Of the 24 cubes, 16 are painted on exactly three faces and 8 are painted on exactly two faces, so none aren't painted.

22. $\triangle ABD$ is isosceles with vertex $\angle A$, so $AB = AC$ by the definition of isosceles triangle (meaning). $\overline{AD}$ bisects $\angle BAC$, so $\angle BAD \cong \angle CAD$ by the definition of angle bisector (meaning). Also, $\overline{AD} \cong \overline{AD}$ by the Reflexive Property of Congruence, so $\triangle ADB \cong \triangle ADC$ by the SAS Congruence Theorem, and $\overline{BD} \cong \overline{CD}$ by the CPCF Theorem. So $\triangle BCD$ is isosceles by the definition of isosceles triangle (sufficient condition).

23. $\dfrac{3}{r} \cdot \dfrac{1}{3} \cdot r \cdot x = \dfrac{3}{3} \cdot \dfrac{r}{r} \cdot x = x$

24. $\dfrac{3}{r} \cdot \dfrac{4}{3}\pi r^3 = \dfrac{3}{3} \cdot \dfrac{r}{r} \cdot 4\pi r^2 = 4\pi r^2$

25. The projection is from a point of the center of the earth through the surface of the globe onto a cylinder that touches the earth around the equator. That cylinder is then cut vertically and flattened.

LESSON 10-9 (pp. 510–513)

1. A sphere can be imagined as the union of "almost pyramids" whose base areas add up to the surface area of the sphere.

2. The Sphere Surface Area Formula states that the surface area of a sphere with radius r is four times the area of a great circle of the sphere, or S.A. $= 4\pi r^2$.

3. The surface area of a sphere is 4 times the area of a great circle (of that sphere).

4. **a.** The surface area of a sphere with radius 6 is S.A. $= 4\pi r^2 = 4\pi(6^2) = 4\pi(36) = 144\pi$ units^2.
   b. $144\pi = 452.389 \approx 452$ units^2.

5. **a.** A sphere with diameter 100 in. has a radius of 50 in., so its S.A. $= 4\pi r^2 = 4\pi(50)^2 = 4\pi(2500) = 10,000\pi$ in.^{2}
   b. $10,000\pi \approx 31415.9265 \approx 31,416$ in.^{3}

6. The no-base figure is the sphere; the one-base figures are the cone and pyramid; and the two-base figures are the prisms and cylinders (the prisms include boxes and cubes).

7. The area of the earth is S.A. $= 4\pi r^2 = 4\pi(3950)^2 = 4\pi(15,602,500) = 62,410,000\pi \approx 196,066,797.5$ mi^2. The percent of that area represented by the United States is $\dfrac{3,600,000}{196,066,797.5} \approx 0.018361 \approx 1.84\%$.

8. If the diameter of a sphere is d, then its radius is $\dfrac{d}{2}$, and its surface area is S.A. $= 4\pi r^2 = 4\pi\left(\dfrac{d}{2}\right)^2 = 4\pi\left(\dfrac{d^2}{4}\right) = \pi d^2$ units^2.

9. Using the result from Question 8, that S.A. $= \pi d^2$, then the area of an entire sphere with diameter 35 m is $\pi(35)^2 = 1225\pi \approx$ 3848.45 m². At a cost of \$3.20 per m², the cost of covering the entire sphere would be $(3848.45)(3.2) = 12,315.04$ or about \$12,315. (The illustration shows that the dome is about three-fourths of a sphere, so the cost would be about $(12,315)(.75) = 9236.25$ or over \$9200.)

10. **a.** The circumference of a great circle is 9.1 in., so using the formula $C = 2\pi r$, then $9.1 = 2\pi r$ and $r = \dfrac{4.55}{\pi}$ in. So the volume of the baseball is $V = \frac{4}{3}\pi r^3 =$ $\frac{4}{3}\pi\left(\dfrac{4.55}{\pi}\right)^3 = \dfrac{(4)(4.55)^2}{(3)\pi^2} \approx 12.72 \approx 12.7$ in.³

    b. Using the formula S.A. $= 4\pi r^2$ with $r = 1.45$ in., then S.A. $= 4\pi(1.45)^2 = 4\pi(2.1025) = 8.41\pi \approx 26.42 \approx 26.4$ in.²

11. **a.** If the radius of the earth is r, then the surface area of the earth is $4\pi r^2$. If the moon's diameter is one-fourth that of the earth's, then its radius is also one-fourth that of the earth's, and the surface area of the moon is $4\pi\left(\dfrac{r}{4}\right)^2 = 4\pi\left(\dfrac{r^2}{16}\right) = \frac{1}{4}\pi r^2$. So the surface area of the moon is one-sixteenth that of the earth.

    (Another way: the surface area of a sphere changes with the square of the change of a linear dimension. If a linear dimension is divided by 4, then the surface area will be divided by $4^2 = 16$.)

    b. If the radius of the earth is r, then the volume of the earth is $\frac{4}{3}\pi r^3$. The moon's radius is about $\dfrac{r}{4}$, so its volume is $\frac{4}{3}\pi\left(\dfrac{r}{4}\right)^3$ $= \frac{4}{3}\pi\left(\dfrac{r^3}{64}\right) = \dfrac{1}{64}\left(\dfrac{4}{3}\pi r^3\right)$. So the volume of the moon is one-sixty-fourth that of the earth.

    (Another way: the volume of a sphere changes with the cube of the change of a linear dimension. If a linear dimension is divided by 4, then the volume will be divided by $4^3 = 64$.)

12. Using the formula for the volume of a sphere, $V = \frac{4}{3}\pi r^3$ with $V = 36\pi$, then $36\pi = \frac{4}{3}\pi r^3$ so $36 = \frac{4}{3}r^3$ and $r^3 = (36)\left(\dfrac{3}{4}\right) = 27$. So $r = \sqrt[3]{27} = 3$ m. Then using the formula S.A. $= 4\pi r^2$, the surface area of the sphere is $4\pi(3)^2 = 4\pi(9) = 36\pi \approx 113.1$ m².

13. The surface area of the sphere is $4\pi r^2$, and the lateral area of the cylinder can be found using the formula L.A. $= ph$ where the perimeter p is $2\pi r$ and the height h is $2r$. So the lateral area of the cylinder is $(2\pi r)(2r) = 4\pi r^2$. So the surface area of the sphere is the same as the lateral area of the cylinder.

14. To find the volume of the earth, use the formula $V = \frac{4}{3}\pi r^3$ with $r = 3950$ mi: $V = \frac{4}{3}\pi(3950)^3 = \frac{4}{3}\pi(61629875000) \approx$ 258.10 mi³.

15. a.

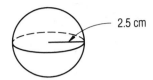

2.5 cm

b. The volume is $V = \frac{4}{3}\pi r^3 = \frac{4}{3}\pi(2.5)^3 =$

$\frac{4}{3}\pi(15.625) \approx 20.833\pi \approx 65.45$ cm³.

16.

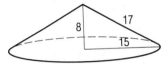

The height h of the cone is the leg of a right triangle with hypotenuse 17 and other leg 15. Using the Pythagorean Theorem,

$h^2 + 15^2 = 17^2$

$h^2 + 225 = 289$

$h^2 = 64$

$h = 8.$

Using the formula for the volume of a cone,

$V = \frac{1}{3}Bh = \frac{1}{3}(\pi r^2)h$ with $r = 15$ and $h = 8$,

the volume is $\frac{1}{3}(\pi 15^2)(8) = \frac{1}{3}(225\pi)(8) =$

$600\pi \approx 1884.955 \approx 1885$ units³.

17. If the radius and height of the taller, skinny jar are r and h, then the volume of that jar is $V = Bh = \pi r^2 h$. For the short, wider jar, the radius is $2r$ and the height is $\frac{h}{2}$, so the volume is $V = \pi(2r)^2\left(\frac{h}{2}\right) = \pi(4r^2)\left(\frac{h}{2}\right) = 2\pi r^2 h$. So the volume of the short, wider jar is twice that of the taller, skinny jar.

(Another way: in the formula for the volume of a cylinder, the height appears with the exponent one and the radius (or diameter) appears with the exponent two. So halving the height halves the volume, but then doubling the radius quadruples the volume. The end result is to double the volume.)

18. a.

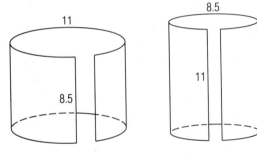

For one cylinder, the circumference of the base is 8.5" and the height is 11", and for the other cylinder the circumference is 11" and the height is 8.5". Both cylinders will have the same lateral area of $(11)(8.5) = 93.5$ in.²

b. If the circumference is 8.5″, then 8.5 = $2\pi r$ and $r = \dfrac{4.25}{\pi} \approx 1.353″$; that cylinder will have height 11″ and so its volume is $V = Bh = \pi r^2 h = \pi(1.353)^2(11) \approx 63.26$ in.^{3}

For the other cylinder with circumference 11″, $11 = 2\pi r$ and $r = \dfrac{5.5}{\pi} \approx 1.75″$; that cylinder has height 8.5″ and so its volume is $V = Bh = \pi(1.75)^2(8.5) \approx 81.78$ in.^{3} The cylinder with the greater volume is the one that uses the longer side of the piece of paper as the circumference of the base.

19. The edges of the first cube have length 13, so its volume is $V = s^3 = 13^3 = 2197$ units^3. The second cube has 5 times that volume, so its volume is $(2197)(5) = 10{,}985$ units^3. The length of a side of the larger cube is $\sqrt[3]{10{,}985} \approx 22.2297 \approx 22.2$ units.

(Another way: if the second cube has 5 times the volume, then each side of the second cube is $\sqrt[3]{5}$ times the side of the first: $(13)(\sqrt[3]{5}) \approx (13)(1.709976) \approx 22.22969 \approx 22.2$ units.

20. Both parts **a** and **b** calculate the amount of foil that will be touching the block(s) of cheese rather than the amount needed to securely wrap the block(s).

a. The surface area of a box with dimensions ℓ, w, and h is $2(\ell w + wh + \ell h)$, so the surface area of a box with dimensions 30 cm, 15 cm, and 15 cm is
$2[(30)(15) + (15)(15) + (30)(15)]$
  $= 2(450 + 225 + 450)$
  $= 2(1125)$
  $= 2250$ cm^2.

b.

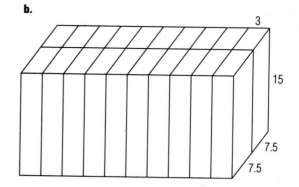

One way that the large block may have been cut is that it was sliced nine times through the top from front to back and then once more through the top from side to side. In any case, the result is 20 smaller blocks, each with dimensions 15 cm, 7.5 cm, and 3 cm.

For each small block, the surface area is
$2[(15)(7.5) + (15)(3) + (7.5)(3)]$
  $= 2(112.5 + 45 + 22.5)$
  $= 2(180)$
  $= 360$ cm^2.

For all 20 blocks, the total surface area is
$(20)(360) = 7200$ cm^2.

21. For the transformation $T(x, y) = (3x, 3y)$,
$A' = T(2, 1) = (6, 3)$,
$B' = T(-1, -1) = (-3, -3)$, and
$C' = T(0, -3) = (0, -9)$.

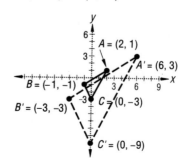

22. Canada ($\approx 1.96\%$), China ($\approx 1.88\%$), Soviet Union ($\approx 4.39\%$)

23. **a.** 32.5%
b. 16.2%
c. 64.3%

CHAPTER 10 PROGRESS SELF-TEST (p. 515)

1. **a.** sample

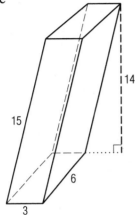

The formula for the volume of a prism is $V = Bh$.

b. Using $V = Bh$ with $B = (6))(3) = 18$ and $h = 14$, $V = (18)(14) = 252$ cm³.

2. **a.**

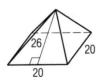

The formula for the lateral area of a regular prism is L.A. $= \frac{1}{2}p\ell$.

b. Using L.A. $= \frac{1}{2}p\ell$ with $p = 4(20) = 80$ and $\ell = 26$, L.A. $= \frac{1}{2}(80)(26) = 1040$ units².

3. Using $V = \frac{4}{3}\pi r^3$ with $r = \frac{1}{2}(620) = 310$ mi,

$$V = \frac{4}{3}\pi(310)^3 = \frac{119{,}164{,}000\pi}{3} \approx 124{,}788{,}249$$

$\approx 1.25 \times 10^8$ mi³.

4.

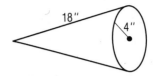

Using L.A. $= \frac{1}{2}C\ell$, with $C = 2\pi r = 8\pi$ and

$\ell = 18$, L.A. $= \frac{1}{2}(8\pi)(18) = 72\pi \approx 226$ in².

5. The figure is a right cylinder with radius 3″ and height 20″. Using $V = Bh$, $V = \pi(3^2)(20) = 180\pi \approx 565.5$ in.³

6. Using $V = \frac{1}{3}Bh = \frac{1}{3}\pi r^2 h$ with $r = 8$ and $h = 15$, $V = \frac{1}{3}\pi(8)^2(15) = 320\pi \approx 1005.3$ units³.

7.

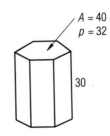

Using L.A. $= ph$ with $p = 32$ and $h = 30$, L.A. $= (32)(30) = 960$ units².

8. Using $V = Bh$ with $B = 40$ and $h = 30$, $V = (40)(30) = 1200$ units³.

9.

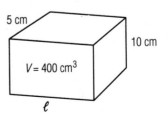

Using $V = \ell wh$, $400 = \ell(5)(10)$ so $400 = 50\ell$ and $\ell = 8$ cm.

10. Using the figure from Question 9,
$$\text{S.A.} = 2B + ph$$
$$= 2(5 \times 8) + 2(5 + 8)(10)$$
$$= 80 + 260$$
$$= 340 \text{ cm}^2$$

11. Using S.A. $= 4\pi r^2$ with S.A. $= 100\pi$,
$100\pi = 4\pi r^2$ so $25 = r^2$ and $r = 5$ units.

12. $\sqrt[3]{400} = 400 \boxed{y^x} 3 \boxed{1/x} \boxed{=} 7.368063 \approx 7$.

13. Cavalieri's Principle: Let I and II be two solids included between parallel planes. If every plane P parallel to the given planes intersects I and II in sections with same area, then Volume (I) = Volume (II).

14.

By the Pyramid-Cone Volume Formula, the volume of the pyramid is one-third the volume of the prism.

15. The ratio of surface areas is the square of the ratio of similitude, so Jupiter's surface area is 11^2 or 121 times as large as the earth's.

16. S.A. = L.A. + B is the formula for a figure with one base, so it is the formula for pyramids and cones.

17. L.A. = ph is the formula for right cylindric solids, so it is the formula for prisms (including boxes and cubes) and right cylinders.

18. The volume can be expressed as a product of its three dimensions or as a sum of the volumes of the eight small boxes. So $V = (x + 1)(y + 2)(z + 6) = xyz + yz + 2z + 2xz + 6xy + 6y + 12 + 12x$.

CHAPTER 10 REVIEW (pp. 516–519)

1.

2.

3.

4.

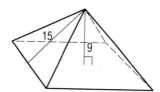

5. **a.** Using the formula L.A. $= ph$ with $p = 2\pi r = 2\pi(4) = 8\pi$ and $h = 9$, then L.A. $= ph = (8\pi)(9) = 72\pi \approx 226.19$ units^2.
   b. Using the formula S.A. = L.A. + $2B$ with $B = \pi r^2 = \pi(4)^2 = 16\pi$, then S.A. $= 72\pi + 2(16\pi) = 72\pi + 32\pi = 104\pi \approx 326.73$ units^2.
   c. Using the formula $V = Bh$, then $B = 16\pi$ from part **b** and $V = (16\pi)(9) = 144\pi \approx 452.39$ units^3.

6. a. Using the formula $V = Bh$ with $B = s^2 = 3^2 = 9$ and $h = 10$, then $V = (9)(10) = 90$ units^3.

b. Using the formula L.A. $= ph$ with $p = 4(3) = 12$ and $h = 10$, then L.A. $= (12)(10) = 120$ units^2. Then, using the formula S.A. $=$ L.A. $+ 2B$, the surface area is $120 + 2(3^2) = 120 + 2(9) = 120 + 18 = 138$ units^2.

7. The base of the prism is a right triangle with legs 5 and 12, so its area is one-half the product of the legs or $\frac{1}{2}(5)(12) = 30$ units^2. Then, using the formula for the volume of a prism $V = Bh$, the volume is $(30)(24) = 720$ units^3.

8. Using the formula for the volume of a cylinder, $V = Bh = \pi r^2 h$ with $V = 30\pi$ and $r = 3$, then $30\pi = \pi(3)^2h$ so $30 = 9h$ and $h = \frac{30}{9} = \frac{10}{3}$ units.

9. Using the formula for the volume of a cube, $V = s^3$, with $V = 125$ units^3, then $125 = s^3$ and $s = 5$ units. The surface area of a cube with side s is S.A. $= 6s^2$, so a cube with side 5 has surface area $(6)(5^2) = (6)(25) = 150$ units^2.

10.

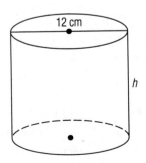

12 cm

h

To use the formula for the volume of a right cylinder, $V = Bh = \pi r^2 h$, you need the radius and the height of the cylinder. The diameter is given as 12 cm, so the radius is 6 cm. To find the height, use the formula for the lateral area of a cylinder, L.A. $= ph = 2\pi rh$ with L.A. $= 60\pi$ and $r = 6$:
$$60\pi = 2\pi(6)h$$
$$60 = 12h$$
$$h = 5$$
So $V = \pi r^2 h = \pi(6^2)(5) = \pi(36)(5) = 180\pi \approx 565.5$ cm^3.

11. The formula for the surface area of a cone is S.A. $=$ L.A. $+ B$. To find the lateral area, note that the diameter of the base of the cone is 7 units so its radius is 3.5 units, and the perimeter or circumference of the base is $p = 2\pi r = 2\pi(3.5) = 7\pi$ units. The slant height ℓ is the hypotenuse of a right triangle with legs 3.5 and 10, so:
$$\ell^2 = 3.5^2 + 10^2$$
$$\ell^2 = 12.25 + 100 = 112.25.$$
So S.A. $=$ L.A. $+ B$
$$= \tfrac{1}{2}p\ell + \pi r^2$$
$$= \tfrac{1}{2}(2\pi r)\ell + \pi r^2$$
$$= \tfrac{1}{2}(2\pi)(3.5)(\sqrt{112.25}) + \pi(3.5)^2$$
$$\approx 116.50 + 38.48$$
$$\approx 155 \text{ units}^2$$
To find the volume of the cone,
$$V = \tfrac{1}{3}Bh = \tfrac{1}{3}\pi r^2 h = \tfrac{1}{3}\pi(12.25)(10) =$$
$$\tfrac{1}{3}\pi(122.5) \approx 128.28 \text{ units}^3.$$

12. Using the formula $V = \tfrac{1}{3}Bh = \tfrac{1}{3}(s^2)h$, then the volume is $\tfrac{1}{3}(80^2)(30) = \tfrac{1}{3}(6400)(30) = 64{,}000$ units^3.

13. a. The slant height is the hypotenuse of a right triangle with legs 30 and 40; so the slant height is 50 units (right triangle is a multiple of the 3-4-5 right triangle).

b. Using the formula for the lateral area of a pyramid, L.A. $= \frac{1}{2}p\ell$ with $p = 4(80) = 320$ and $\ell = 50$, the lateral area is $\frac{1}{2}(320)(50) = 8000$ units².

c. Using the formula for the total surface area of a pyramid, S.A. $=$ L.A. $+ B$, then the surface area is $8000 + (80)(80) = 8000 + 6400 = 14,400$ units².

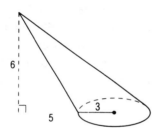

14. Using the formula for the volume of a cone, $V = \frac{1}{3}Bh = \frac{1}{3}\pi r^2 h$ with $r = 3$ and $h = 6$,

then the volume is $\frac{1}{3}\pi(3^2)(6) = \frac{1}{3}\pi(9)(6) = 18\pi \approx 56.55$ units³.

15. Using the formula for the lateral area of a pyramid L.A. $= \frac{1}{2}p\ell$ with the perimeter $p = 20$ and the slant height $\ell = 20$, the lateral area is $\frac{1}{2}(20)(20) = 200$ units².

16. Using the formula for the volume of a pyramid $V = \frac{1}{3}Bh$ with $V = 75$ and $B = 5$,

then $75 = \frac{1}{3}(5h)$ and $5h = 225$ so $h = 45$ cm.

17. If a sphere has radius 72, then its surface area is S.A. $= 4\pi r^2 = 4\pi(72)^2 = 4\pi(5184) = 20,736\pi \approx 65,144$ units².

The volume of the sphere is $V = \frac{4}{3}\pi r^3 = \frac{4}{3}\pi(72)^3 = \frac{4}{3}\pi(373,248) = 497,664\pi \approx 1,563,458$ units³.

18. If a sphere has diameter 3 mm, then its radius is 1.5 mm. So its surface area is S.A. $= 4\pi r^2 = 4\pi(1.5)^2 = 4\pi(2.25) = 9\pi \approx 28.27$ mm².

The volume of the sphere is $V = \frac{4}{3}\pi r^3 = \frac{4}{3}\pi(1.5)^3 = \frac{4}{3}\pi(3.375) = 4.5\pi \approx 14.14$ mm³.

19. Using the formula for the volume of a sphere, $V = \frac{4}{3}\pi r^3$ with $V = 288\pi$, then $288\pi = \frac{4}{3}\pi r^3$ and $288 = \frac{4}{3}r^3$. So $r^3 = (288)\left(\frac{3}{4}\right) = 216$ and $r = \sqrt[3]{216} = 6$ units.

20. Using the formula for the volume of a sphere, $V = \frac{4}{3}\pi r^3$, with $V = 40\pi$, then $40\pi = \frac{4}{3}\pi r^3$ so $40 = \frac{4}{3}r^3$ and $r^3 = (40)\left(\frac{3}{4}\right) = 30$. Thus $r = \sqrt[3]{30}$. Then, using the formula for the surface area of a sphere, S.A. $= 4\pi r^2$ with $r = \sqrt[3]{30}$, the surface area is $4\pi(\sqrt[3]{30})(\sqrt[3]{30}) = 4\pi(\sqrt[3]{900}) \approx (4)(3.1416)(9.655) \approx 121.33$ units².

21. The cube root of 27,000 is $\sqrt[3]{27,000} = \sqrt[3]{(27)(1000)} = (\sqrt[3]{27})(\sqrt[3]{1000}) = (3)(10) = 30$.

22. Using a calculator, find the the cube root of 50 by using the following keystrokes: 50 $\boxed{y^x}$ 3 $\boxed{1/x}$ $\boxed{=}$ 3.68403 ≈ 3.7.
To check: $3.7^3 = 50.653$ and $3.6^3 = 46.656$, so 3.7^3 is closer to 50 than 3.6^3. So the cube root of 50, to the nearest tenth, is 3.7.

23. The cube with side 4 has volume $V = s^3 = 4^3 = 64$ units^3. The second cube has twice that volume, so its volume is $(2)(64) = 128$ units^3. The side of the second cube is $\sqrt[3]{128} \approx 5.039868 \approx 5.04$ units.

(Another way: The volume is to be doubled, so the side must be multiplied by the factor $\sqrt[3]{2}$. So the side of the second cube is $(4)(\sqrt[3]{2}) \approx (4)(1.25992) \approx 5.03968 \approx 5.04$ units.)

24. $\sqrt[3]{15} + \sqrt[3]{21} \approx 2.47 + 2.76 = 5.23$

25. Starting with the general formula for the surface area of a pyramid,

S.A. = L.A. + B, and substituting

L.A. $= \frac{1}{2}p\ell = \frac{1}{2}(4s)\ell = 2s\ell$ and $B = s^2$,

then the formula is S.A. $= 2s\ell + s^2$.

26. The height h of the cone is the leg of a right triangle with hypotenuse ℓ and other leg r. Using the Pythagorean Theorem:

$h^2 + r^2 = \ell^2$

$h^2 = \ell^2 - r^2$.

So $h = \sqrt{\ell^2 - r^2}$. Substituting this value into the formula for the volume of a cone

$V = \frac{1}{3}Bh = \frac{1}{3}(\pi r^2)h$, the formula becomes

$V = \frac{1}{3}(\pi r^2)(\sqrt{\ell^2 - r^2})$.

27. **a.** If the dimensions of a box are ℓ, w, and h, then its surface area is $2(\ell w + \ell h + wh)$. If another box has triple those dimensions, its measurements are 3ℓ, $3w$, and $3h$, so its surface area is

$2[(3\ell)(3w) + (3\ell)(3h) + (3w)(3h)]$
$= 2(9\ell w + 9\ell h + 9wh)$
$= 2[(9)(\ell w + \ell h + wh)]$
$= (9)(2)(\ell w + \ell h + wh)$.

So if the dimensions of a box are tripled, the surface area of the box is multiplied by 9.

(Another way: if all the linear dimensions of a figure are multiplied by 3, the measure of the area is multiplied by the square of that number, or 9.)

b. If the dimensions of a box are ℓ, w, and h, then its volume is $V = \ell wh$. If another box has triple those dimensions, its measurements are 3ℓ, $3w$, and $3h$, so its volume is $V = (3\ell)(3w)(3h) = 27\ell wh$. So if the dimensions of a box are tripled, the volume of the box is multiplied by 27.

(Another way: if all the linear dimensions of a figure are multiplied by 3, the measure of the volume is multiplied by the cube of that number, or 27.)

28. If the original cube has side s, then its volume is s^3. The second cube, with sides $9s$, has volume $(9s)^3 = 729s^3$. So the volume of the second cube is 729 times the volume of the first cube.

(Another way: if all the linear dimensions of a figure are all multiplied by 9, then the volume of that figure is multiplied by the cube of 9, or 729.)

29. The volume of a cylinder (such as a pizza) changes according to the square of the diameter (or radius, or circumference) and the first power of the thickness or height. If the height is kept the same and the diameter is doubled, the volume of the cylinder will be quadrupled (multiplied by 4).

30. If the diameter of a sphere (or its radius or circumference) is multiplied by a number, then its volume is multiplied by the cube of that number. So if the diameter of the sun is 109 times that of the earth, then the volume of the sun is $109^3 = 1,295,029$ times that of earth.

31. Cavalieri's Principle applies to solids whose bases are included between parallel planes (which is satisfied by the prism and pyramid) and for which every plane parallel to the bases intersects the solids in sections with the same area. For the prism and pyramid, the plane sections other than at one base do not have the same areas, so Cavalieri's Principle does not apply.

32. In deriving the formula for the volume of a sphere, a plane section of a sphere was shown to be equal to the difference between the plane sections of a cylinder and a pair of cones.

33. **a.** The formula for the volume of a cylindric solid is $V = Bh$. If two cylindric solids have congruent (hence equal-area) bases and equal heights, they must have the same volume, so the statement is *true*.

b.

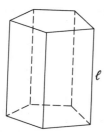 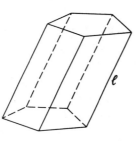

A formula for the surface area of a cylindric solid is S.A. = L.A. + $2B = p\ell + 2B$, where p is the perimeter (circumference) of the base, ℓ is the slant height, and B is the area of the base. The two cylindric solids have congruent bases, so the areas of the bases are equal and the perimeters are also equal. However, the slant heights of the two solids are not equal, so the lateral areas (and hence the surface areas) are not equal; the statement is *false*.

34. Using the formula for the surface area of a sphere, S.A. = $4\pi r^2$ with $r = 6000$ km, the surface area of Venus is $4\pi(6000)^2 = 4\pi(36,000,000) = 144,000,000\pi \approx 452,389,342$ km^2.

35. Using the formula for the circumference of sphere, $C = 2\pi r$ with $C = 5$ feet, then $5 = 2\pi r$ and $r = \frac{2.5}{\pi}$. So the surface area of that sphere is S.A. $= 4\pi r^2 = 4\pi\left(\frac{2.5}{\pi}\right)^2 = 4\pi\left(\frac{6.25}{\pi^2}\right) = \frac{25}{\pi} \approx 7.96$ ft^2 or about 8 ft^2.

36.

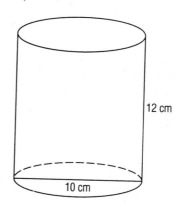

12 cm

10 cm

For a cylinder without the top base,
$$\begin{aligned}
\text{S.A.} &= \text{L.A.} + B \\
&= 2\pi rh + \pi r^2 \\
&= 2\pi(5)(12) + \pi(5)^2 \\
&= 120\pi + 25\pi \\
&= 145\pi \\
&\approx 455.53 \text{ cm}^2
\end{aligned}$$

37.

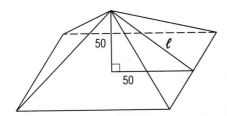

The slant height ℓ of the pyramid is the hypotenuse of a right triangle with legs 50 cubits and 50 cubits, so $\ell^2 = 50^2 + 50^2 = 2500 + 2500 = 5000$ and $\ell = \sqrt{5000} = \sqrt{(2500)(2)} = 50\sqrt{2}$. So the lateral area of the pyramid is L.A. $= \frac{1}{2}p\ell = \frac{1}{2}(400)(50\sqrt{2}) = 10,000\sqrt{2} \approx 14,142$ cubits^2.

38. The diameter of the base of the cylinder is 6 m, so its radius is 3 m and the area of the base is $B = \pi r^2 = \pi(3)^2 = 9\pi$ m^2. Then, using the formula for the volume of a cylinder, $V = Bh$, the volume is $(9\pi)(10) = 90\pi \approx 282.7$ m^3.

39. The diameter of the base of the cup is 10 cm, so its radius is 5 cm and the area of the base is $B = \pi r^2 = 25\pi$. The volume of the cup is
$V = Bh = \pi r^2 h = \pi(5)^2(12)$
$= 300\pi \approx 942.5$ cm^3.

40. The volume of a cube 2.5 in. on a side is $2.5^3 = 15.625$ in.^{3}

41. Using the formula for the volume of a pyramid $V = \frac{1}{3}Bh$ with $B = 100^2 = 10,000$ and $h = 50$, the volume is $\frac{1}{3}(10,000)(50) = \frac{500,000}{3} \approx 166,667$ cubits^3.

42. The volume of a suitcase 3 feet by 1 foot by 2 feet is, in cubic inches, $(36)(12)(24) = 10,368$ in.^{3}

The volume of a single dollar bill is $(6.125)(2.562)(.004) = .062769$ in.^{3}, so the volume of one million of them is $(.062769)(1,000,000) = 62,769$ in.^{3} So one suitcase would not hold all the dollars; over 6 suitcases would be needed.

43. $(5x+2)(4y+3) = (5x)(4y+3) + (2)(4y+3)$
$= 20xy + 15x + 8y + 6$

44. $(a + 6)(2a + 1)(a + 8)$
$= (a + 6)(2a^2 + 16a + a + 8)$
$= (a + 6)(2a^2 + 17a + 8)$
$= a(2a^2 + 17a + 8) + 6(2a^2 + 17a + 8)$
$= 2a^3 + 17a^2 + 8a + 12a^2 + 102a + 48$
$= 2a^3 + 29a^2 + 110a + 48$

45. The area can be expressed as the product of two lengths, $(2x + 7)(x + 12)$, or as the sum of four areas, $2x^2 + 24x + 7x + 84$.

46. The volume can be expressed as the product of three lengths:
$(a + 15)(b + 9)(c + 8)$
or as the sum of 8 volumes:
$abc + 8ab + 9ac + 15bc + 72a + 120b + 135c + 1080$.

LESSON 11–1   (pp. 520–526)

1. **a.** The mathematician associated with the invention of algebra is Francois Vieté.

   b. The mathematicians associated with the invention of analytic geometry are Rene Descartes and Pierre Fermat.

2. Descartes' dream was that mathematics and logic could provide the means whereby any problem in *any* field of endeavor could be solved.

3. Another name for analytic geometry is coordinate geometry.

4. The Parallel Lines and Slopes Theorem states that two nonvertical lines are parallel if and only if they have the same slope.

5. The Perpendicular Lines and Slopes Theorem states that two nonvertical lines are perpendicular if and only if the product of their slopes is -1.

6. **a.** The justification that the slope of $\overline{AD}$ is $\frac{1}{3}$ is the definition of slope (meaning).

   b. The slope of $\overline{BC}$ is $\frac{1-0}{9-6} = \frac{1}{3}$.

   c. The slope of $\overline{AB}$ is $\frac{0-0}{6-0} = \frac{0}{6} = 0$.

   d. The slope of $\overline{DC}$ is $\frac{1-1}{9-3} = \frac{0}{6} = 0$.

   e. The justification that $\overline{AB} \parallel \overline{DC}$ and $\overline{AD} \parallel \overline{BC}$ is the Parallel Lines and Slopes Theorem.

   f. The conclusion justified by the definition of parallelogram (sufficient condition) is that $ABCD$ is a parallelogram.

7. The slope of $\overline{XY}$ is $\frac{7-3}{3-11} = \frac{4}{-8} = -\frac{1}{2}$; the slope of $\overline{XZ}$ is $\frac{7-9}{3-4} = \frac{-2}{-1} = 2$; and the slope of $\overline{YZ}$ is $\frac{3-9}{11-4} = \frac{-6}{7} = -\frac{6}{7}$. The product of the slopes of $\overline{XY}$ and $\overline{XZ}$ is -1, so $\overline{XY} \perp \overline{XZ}$ by the Perpendicular Lines and Slopes Theorem, and $\triangle XYZ$ is a right triangle by the definition of right triangle (sufficient condition).

8. Figures graphed on coordinate systems are computer graphics, television and film cartoons, video games, models of objects, and designs of automobiles, furniture, clothes, and buildings.

9. The slope of $\overline{EF} = \frac{2-0}{0--2} = \frac{2}{2} = 1$; the slope of $\overline{GH} = \frac{-3--5}{5-3} = \frac{2}{2} = 1$; the slope of $\overline{EH} = \frac{2--3}{0-5} = \frac{5}{-5} = -1$. The slope of $\overline{FG} = \frac{0--5}{-2-3} = \frac{5}{-5} = -1$. So $\overline{EF} \perp \overline{EH}$, $\overline{EF} \perp \overline{FG}$, $\overline{HG} \perp \overline{FG}$ and $\overline{HG} \perp \overline{EH}$ by the Perpendicular Lines and Slopes Theorem, and $EFGH$ is a rectangle by the definition of rectangle (sufficient condition).

10. The slope of $\overline{EG} = \frac{2--5}{0-3} = \frac{7}{-3} = -\frac{7}{3}$, and the slope of $\overline{FH} = \frac{0--3}{-2-5} = \frac{3}{-7} = -\frac{3}{7}$. Since $\left(-\frac{7}{3}\right)\left(-\frac{3}{7}\right) = 1$, the product of the two slopes is not negative one, and so segments $\overline{EG}$ and $\overline{FH}$ are not perpendicular.

11. To show that $WXYZ$ is a parallelogram, calculate the slopes of the opposite pairs of sides and show that the opposite sides are parallel (use the name of the quadrilateral, $WXYZ$, to identify that $\overline{WX}$ and $\overline{YZ}$ are one pair of opposite sides, and $\overline{XY}$ and $\overline{ZW}$ are the other pair of opposite sides:

the slope of $\overline{WX} = \dfrac{0 - 0}{0 - a} = \dfrac{0}{-a} = 0$;

the slope of $\overline{YZ} = \dfrac{c - c}{(a + b) - b} = \dfrac{0}{a} = 0$;

the slope of $\overline{XY} = \dfrac{0 - c}{a - (a + b)} = \dfrac{-c}{-b} = \dfrac{c}{b}$;

the slope of $\overline{ZW} = \dfrac{c - 0}{b - 0} = \dfrac{c}{b}$.

So $\overline{WX} \parallel \overline{YZ}$ and $\overline{XY} \parallel \overline{ZW}$ by the Parallel Lines and Slopes Theorem, and $WXYZ$ is a parallelogram by the definition of parallelogram (sufficient condition).

12. a.

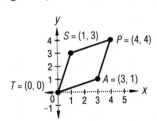

b. The slope of $\overline{SA} = \dfrac{3 - 1}{1 - 3} = \dfrac{2}{-2} = -1$, and

the slope of $\overline{PT} = \dfrac{4 - 0}{4 - 0} = \dfrac{4}{4} = 1$. Since

the product of the slopes of $\overline{SA}$ and $\overline{PT}$ is -1, then $\overline{SA} \perp \overline{PT}$ by the Perpendicular Lines and Slopes Theorem.

13. a.

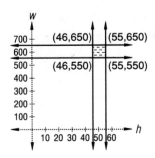

b. The graph is a rectangle along with the interior of that rectangle; the vertices of the rectangle are (46, 550), (55, 550), (55, 650), and (46, 650).

14. The coefficients of y are opposites, so add the two equations:

$$3x + y = 7$$
$$\underline{x - y = 1}$$
$$4x \quad\quad = 8$$
$$x = 2$$

Substituting $x = 2$ into the first equation,

$$3(2) + y = 7$$
$$6 + y = 7$$
$$y = 1$$

The point of intersection is (2, 1).

To check:

In the first equation, does $3(2) + 1 = 7$? Yes.

In the second equation, does $2 - 1 = 1$? Yes.

15. The signs of the y-variables are opposites, so multiply the second equation by 5 and add the equations:

$$2x - 5y = 20$$
$$4x + y = 18$$

$$2x - 5y = 20$$
$$\underline{20x + 5y = 90}$$
$$22x \quad\quad = 110$$
$$x = 5$$

Substituting $x = 5$ into the second equation (because it has a coefficient of 1 for the y-variable),

$$4(5) + y = 18$$
$$20 + y = 18$$
$$y = -2$$

The point of intersection is (5, -2).

To check:

In the first equation, does $2(5) - 5(-2) = 20$? That is, does $10 - -10 = 20$? Yes.

In the second equation, does $4(5) + -2 = 18$? Yes.

16. Multiply the first equation by -4 (that will make the x-coefficients opposites) and add the equations:

$$y = \tfrac{1}{2}x$$
$$y = 2x - 5$$

$$-4y = -2x$$
$$\underline{y = 2x - 5}$$
$$-3y = -5$$
$$y = \tfrac{-5}{-3} = \tfrac{5}{3}$$

Substitute $y = \tfrac{5}{3}$ into the first equation:

$$\tfrac{5}{3} = \tfrac{1}{2}x$$
$$\tfrac{10}{3} = x$$

So the point of intersection is $\left(\tfrac{10}{3}, \tfrac{5}{3}\right)$.

To check:

In the first equation, does $\tfrac{5}{3} = \left(\tfrac{1}{2}\right)\left(\tfrac{10}{3}\right)$?
Yes.

In the second equation, does $\tfrac{5}{3} = 2\left(\tfrac{10}{3}\right) - 5$? That is, does $\tfrac{5}{3} = \tfrac{20}{3} - \tfrac{15}{3}$? **Yes.**

17. a. Using the formula for the lateral area of a cylinder, L.A. $= ph = 2\pi rh$ with $r = 5'$ (because the diameter is $10'$) and $h = 20'$, the lateral area is $2\pi(5)(20) = 200\pi \approx 628.3$ ft^2.

b. First, find the volume of the cylinder using the formula $V = Bh = \pi r^2 h$; the volume is $\pi(5)^2(20) = 500\pi$ ft^3. Then since 1.25 ft^3 is needed for each bushel, the number of bushels is $\tfrac{500\pi}{1.25} = 400\pi \approx 1256.64 \approx$ 1256 bushels (the result is rounded down, or "truncated," to find the number of full bushels).

18. An octahedron, by definition, has 8 faces, each of which is a triangle.
The number of vertices is the number of faces (8), times the number of vertices per face (3), divided by the number of faces that come together at each vertex (4), so the number of vertices is $\tfrac{8 \cdot 3}{4} = 6$.

The number of faces is 8 (by definition of octahedron, meaning part).
The number of edges is the number of faces (8), times the number of edges per face (3), divided by the number of faces that come together at each edge (2), so the number of edges is $\tfrac{8 \cdot 3}{2} = 12$.

19. From the statement that ABC is a right triangle with hypotenuse $\overline{AB}$, the justification that AB^2 = AC^2 + CB^2 is the Pythagorean Theorem.

20. From the statement that $\odot P$ contains Q and R, the justification that $PQ = PR$ is the definition of a circle (meaning).

21. a. The distance between two points on a number line with coordinates 50 and 500 is the absolute value of the difference between those coordinates:
$|500 - 50| = |450| = 450$ units or
$|50 - 500| = |-450| = 450$ units.

b. The points (50, 100) and (500, 100) are both on the vertical line $y = 100$. Using that line as a number line, the distance between the points is the same as that found in part **a**, or 450 units.

22. a.

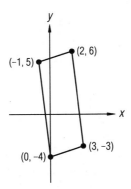

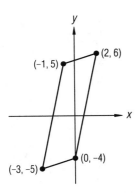

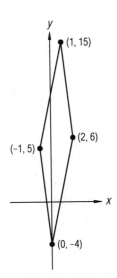

For the parallelogram at the left, the movement from (-1, 5) to (2, 6) is to the right 3 and up 1. That same movement from (0, -4) results in (3, -3).

For the parallelogram in the middle, the movement from (2, 6) to (-1, 5) is to the left 3 and down 1. That same movement from (0, -4) results in (-3, -5).

For the parallelogram at the right, the movement from (0, -4) to (2, 6) is to the right 2 and up 10. That same movement from (-1, 5) results in (1, 15).

b. There are exactly three possible locations for the fourth vertex. One explanation is that the 3 given points determine exactly 3 segments. Each segment must be one diagonal of the parallelogram, so there are exactly 3 possible parallelograms.

LESSON 11–2 (pp. 527–531)

1. The distance between A and B is

$$\sqrt{(x_2 - x_1)^2 + (y_2 - y_1)^2}$$
$$= \sqrt{(6 - -5)^2 + (2 - 2)^2}$$
$$= \sqrt{11^2 + 0^2}$$
$$= \sqrt{121}$$
$$= 11 \text{ units.}$$

(Another way: A and B are on the horizontal line $y = 2$, so the distance between them is $|6 - -5| = |11| = 11$.)

2. The distance between B and C is

$$\sqrt{(x_2 - x_1)^2 + (y_2 - y_1)^2}$$
$$= \sqrt{(6 - 6)^2 + (7 - 2)^2}$$
$$= \sqrt{0^2 + 5^2}$$
$$= \sqrt{25}$$
$$= 5 \text{ units.}$$

(Another way: B and C are on the vertical line $x = 6$, so the distance between them is $|2 - 7| = |-5| = 5$.)

3. The distance between A and C is
$$\sqrt{(x_2 - x_1)^2 + (y_2 - y_1)^2}$$
$$= \sqrt{(6 - \text{-}5)^2 + (7 - 2)^2}$$
$$= \sqrt{11^2 + 5^2}$$
$$= \sqrt{121 + 25}$$
$$= \sqrt{146}$$
$$\approx 12.083 \text{ units.}$$

4. The distance between A and the origin is
$$\sqrt{(x_2 - x_1)^2 + (y_2 - y_1)^2}$$
$$= \sqrt{(\text{-}5 - 0)^2 + (2 - 0)^2}$$
$$= \sqrt{(\text{-}5)^2 + 2^2}$$
$$= \sqrt{25 + 4}$$
$$= \sqrt{29}$$
$$\approx 5.385 \text{ units.}$$

5. The distance between B and D is
$$\sqrt{(x_2 - x_1)^2 + (y_2 - y_1)^2}$$
$$= \sqrt{(2 - 6)^2 + (\text{-}4 - 2)^2}$$
$$= \sqrt{(\text{-}4)^2 + (\text{-}6)^2}$$
$$= \sqrt{16 + 36}$$
$$= \sqrt{52}$$
$$\approx 7.21 \text{ units.}$$

6. The distance between (x_1, y_1) and (x_2, y_2) is $\sqrt{(x_2 - x_1)^2 + (y_2 - y_1)^2}$.

7.

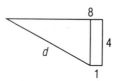

The distance d is the hypotenuse of a right triangle whose horizontal leg d is $8 - 1 = 7$ miles and whose vertical leg is 4 miles. Using the Pythagorean Theorem:
$d^2 = 7^2 + 4^2 = 49 + 16 = 65$, so
$d = \sqrt{65} \approx 8.06$ miles.

Another way: If the coordinates of the starting point are (0, 0), then the point 8 miles east is (8, 0); 4 miles south of that is (8, -4); and 1 mile west of that is (7, -4). The

distance between (0, 0) and (7, -4) is
$$\sqrt{(x_2 - x_1)^2 + (y_2 - y_1)^2}$$
$$= \sqrt{(7 - 0)^2 + (\text{-}4 - 0)^2}$$
$$= \sqrt{7^2 + (\text{-}4)^2}$$
$$= \sqrt{49 + 16}$$
$$= \sqrt{65}$$
$$\approx 8.06 \text{ miles.}$$

8. a. The first step is to find the lengths of the three sides of the triangle.
JK is the distance between (-5, 0) and (5, 8)
$$= \sqrt{(x_2 - x_1)^2 + (y_2 - y_1)^2}$$
$$= \sqrt{(5 - \text{-}5)^2 + (8 - 0)^2}$$
$$= \sqrt{10^2 + 8^2}$$
$$= \sqrt{100 + 64}$$
$$= \sqrt{164}.$$
KL is the distance between (5, 8) and (4, -1)
$$= \sqrt{(x_2 - x_1)^2 + (y_2 - y_1)^2}$$
$$= \sqrt{(4 - 5)^2 + (\text{-}1 - 8)^2}$$
$$= \sqrt{(\text{-}1)^2 + (\text{-}9)^2}$$
$$= \sqrt{1 + 81}$$
$$= \sqrt{82}.$$
And JL is the distance between (-5, 0) and (4, -1)
$$= \sqrt{(x_2 - x_1)^2 + (y_2 - y_1)^2}$$
$$= \sqrt{(4 - \text{-}5)^2 + (\text{-}1 - 0)^2}$$
$$= \sqrt{9^2 + (\text{-}1)^2}$$
$$= \sqrt{81 + 1}$$
$$= \sqrt{82}.$$
So $KL = JL$ by the Transitive Property of Equality, and $\triangle JKL$ is isosceles by the definition of isosceles triangle (sufficient condition).

b. $JK \neq JL$, so $\triangle JKL$ is not equilateral. (Note, however, that $JK^2 = KL^2 + JL^2$, so $\triangle JKL$ is a right triangle.)

9.

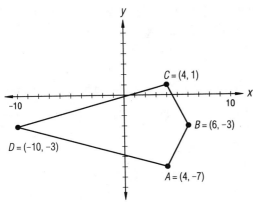

$BC = \sqrt{(x_2 - x_1)^2 + (y_2 - y_1)^2}$
$= \sqrt{(4 - 6)^2 + (1 - -3)^2}$
$= \sqrt{(-2)^2 + 4^2}$
$= \sqrt{4 + 16}$
$= \sqrt{20} = \sqrt{(4)(5)} = 2\sqrt{5}$

$BA = \sqrt{(x_2 - x_1)^2 + (y_2 - y_1)^2}$
$= \sqrt{(4 - 6)^2 + (-7 - 3)^2}$
$= \sqrt{(-2)^2 + (-4)^2}$
$= \sqrt{4 + 16}$
$= \sqrt{20} = \sqrt{(4)(5)} = 2\sqrt{5}$

$DC = \sqrt{(x_2 - x_1)^2 + (y_2 - y_1)^2}$
$= \sqrt{(4 - -10)^2 + (1 - -3)^2}$
$= \sqrt{14^2 + 4^2}$
$= \sqrt{196 + 16}$
$= \sqrt{212} = \sqrt{(4)(53)} = 2\sqrt{53}$

$DA = \sqrt{(x_2 - x_1)^2 + (y_2 - y_1)^2}$
$= \sqrt{(4 - -10)^2 + (-7 - 3)^2}$
$= \sqrt{14^2 + (-4)^2}$
$= \sqrt{196 + 16}$
$= \sqrt{212} = \sqrt{(4)(53)} = 2\sqrt{53}$

So $BC = BA$ and $DC = DA$, so $ABCD$ is a kite by the definition of kite (sufficient condition).

10. Placing the school at the origin, the coordinates for Charles are (1, -1.5) and the coordinates for Cynthia are (-2, -.8). The distance between those two points is

$\sqrt{(x_2 - x_1)^2 + (y_2 - y_1)^2}$
$= \sqrt{(-2 - 1)^2 + (-.8 - -1.5)^2}$
$= \sqrt{(-3)^2 + .7^2}$
$= \sqrt{9 + .49}$
$= \sqrt{9.49}$
≈ 3.08 miles.

11. a. Any values with $x_2 < x_1$ is a counterexample showing that the statement is *false*. For example, let $x_2 = 10$ and $x_1 = 17$. Then $|x_2 - x_1| = |10 - 17| = |-7| = 7$, and $(x_2 - x_1) = (10 - 17) = -7$. So $|x_2 - x_1| \neq (x_2 - x_1)$.

b. $|x_2 - x_1|^2$ is the square of the distance between x_2 and x_1, and $(x_2 - x_1)^2$ is the square of the difference between x_2 and x_1. Since both squares are positive, the values are equal and $|x_2 - x_1|^2 = (x_2 - x_1)^2$; the statement is *true*.

c. $|x_2 - x_1|$ is the distance between x_2 and x_1, and $|x_1 - x_2|$ is the distance between x_1 and x_2. Since those two numbers represent the same distance, $|x_2 - x_1| = |x_1 - x_2|$; the statement is *true*.

d. $(x_1 - x_2)^2 = x_1^2 - 2x_1x_2 + x_2^2$
$= x_2^2 - 2x_2x_1 + x_1^2$
$= (x_2 - x_1)^2;$
so the statement is *true*.

12. a. The distance between (1, 2) and (3, 4)
$= \sqrt{(x_2 - x_1)^2 + (y_2 - y_1)^2}$
$= \sqrt{(3 - 1)^2 + (4 - 2)^2}$
$= \sqrt{2^2 + 2^2}$
$= \sqrt{4 + 4}$
$= \sqrt{8}$
≈ 2.83 units.

b. The distance between (3, 4) and (1, 2) is the same as the distance between (1, 2) and (3, 4) because they represent the endpoints of a single segment, and a segment has a unique length.

c. In general, the distance between (x_1, y_1) and (x_2, y_2) is the same as the distance between (x_2, y_2) and (x_1, y_1).

13. The length of the radius $\overline{BA}$ is the distance
$$\sqrt{(x_2 - x_1)^2 + (y_2 - y_1)^2}$$
$$= \sqrt{(-1 - 11)^2 + (3 - 2)^2}$$
$$= \sqrt{(-12)^2 + 1^2}$$
$$= \sqrt{144 + 1}$$
$$= \sqrt{145}.$$

The distance CB is the distance
$$\sqrt{(x_2 - x_1)^2 + (y_2 - y_1)^2}$$
$$= \sqrt{(11 - 3)^2 + (2 - -7)^2}$$
$$= \sqrt{8^2 + 9^2}$$
$$= \sqrt{64 + 81}$$
$$= \sqrt{145}$$

So A and C are the same distance from B, and so C is on the circle with center B and radius $\overline{BA}$ by the definition of circle and radius (sufficient condition).

14. The slope of $\overline{AD}$ is the slope between points $A = (0, 0)$ and $D = (3, 3) = \dfrac{3 - 0}{3 - 0} = \dfrac{3}{3} = 1$, and the slope of $\overline{BC}$ is the slope between points $B = (4, 0)$ and $C = (5, 1) = \dfrac{1 - 0}{5 - 4} = \dfrac{1}{1} = 1$. The slopes are the same, and so $\overline{AD} \parallel \overline{BC}$ by the Parallel Lines and Slopes Theorem, and so $ABCD$ is a trapezoid by the definition of trapezoid (sufficient condition).

15. The slope of $\overline{PQ}$ is the slope between points $P = (3z, 4z)$ and $Q = (7z, 2z) = \dfrac{2z - 4z}{7z - 3z} = \dfrac{-2z}{4z} = -\dfrac{1}{2}$.

The slope of $\overline{PR}$ is the slope between points $P = (3z, 4z)$ and $R = (2z, -8z) = \dfrac{-8z - 4z}{2z - 3z}$
$$= \dfrac{-12z}{-z} = 12.$$

The slope of $\overline{QR}$ is the slope between points $Q = (7z, 2z)$ and $R = (2z, -8z) = \dfrac{-8z - 2z}{2z - 7z}$
$$= \dfrac{-10z}{-5z} = 2.$$

Since the product of the slopes of $\overline{PQ}$ and $\overline{QR}$ is $\left(-\dfrac{1}{2}\right)(2) = -1$, then $\overline{PQ} \perp \overline{QR}$ by the Perpendicular Lines and Slopes Theorem, and $\triangle PQR$ is a right triangle by the definition of right triangle (sufficient condition).

(Another way: Show that the lengths of the three sides are:
$$PQ = \sqrt{16z^2 + 4z^2} = \sqrt{20z^2}$$
$$PR = \sqrt{z^2 + 144z^2} = \sqrt{145z^2}$$
$$QR = \sqrt{25z^2 + 100z^2} = \sqrt{125z^2}$$
and then show that $PR^2 = PQ^2 + QR^2$ so that $\triangle PQR$ is a right triangle by the Converse of the Pythagorean Theorem.)

16. Multiply the first equation by -2 and then add the equations:

$$-2x + y = 11$$
$$x + 2y = 6$$

$$4x - 2y = -22$$
$$\underline{x + 2y = 6}$$
$$5x = -16$$
$$x = -3.2$$

Then substitute $x = -3.2$ into the first equation:

$$-2(-3.2) + y = 11$$
$$6.4 + y = 11$$
$$y = 4.6$$

The solution is $(-3.2, 4.6)$.
To check:
In the first equation, is $-2(-3.2) + 4.6 = 11$?
That is, is $6.4 + 4.6 = 11$? Yes.
In the second equation, is $-3.2 + 2(4.6) = 6$?
That is, is $-3.2 + 9.2 = 6$? Yes.

17. Multiply the first equation by 3 and then add the equations:

$$y = 13$$
$$4x - 3y = 10$$

$$3y = 39$$
$$\underline{4x - 3y = 10}$$
$$4x = 49$$
$$x = 12.25$$

The value for y is already given, so the solution is $(12.25, 13)$.
To check:
In the first equation, is $13 = 13$? Yes.
In the second equation, is $4(12.25) - 3(13) = 10$? That is, is $49 - 39 = 10$? Yes.

18. **a.** The diagonal d of the square is the hypotenuse of an isosceles right triangle with legs 100. Using the Pythagorean Theorem:
$$d^2 = 100^2 + 100^2 = 10{,}000 + 10{,}000 = 20{,}000 \text{ so } d = \sqrt{20{,}000} = \sqrt{(10{,}000)(2)}$$
$$= 100\sqrt{2} \text{ units.}$$

b. In general, the diagonal d of a square with sides x is the hypotenuse of a right isosceles triangle with legs x. Using the Pythagorean Theorem:
$$d^2 = x^2 + x^2 = 2x^2, \text{ so } d = \sqrt{2x^2} = x\sqrt{2} \text{ units.}$$

19. If the base has length b and the altitude has length h, then the area of the parallelogram is $A = bh$ and the area of the triangle is $A = \frac{1}{2}hb$. So the area of the parallelogram is twice the area of the triangle.

20. **a-b.** If the three angles are in a right triangle, and one acute angle is 45° more than the other, then the measures of the three angles are 90 (for the right angle), x, and $x + 45$. By the Triangle-Sum Theorem:
$$90 + x + x + 45 = 180$$
$$2x + 135 = 180$$
$$2x = 45$$
$$x = 22.5.$$

So the measure of the other acute angle is $22.5 + 45 = 67.5$; the three angle measures are $22.5, 67.5,$ and 90.

21. The mean of a set of scores is the total number of points divided by the number of tests. For the 3 tests with scores 92, 83, and 95, the mean is $\frac{92 + 83 + 95}{3} = \frac{270}{3} = 90.$

22. **a.** The distance between $(10, 23)$ and $(2, 8)$ is
$$\sqrt{(x_2 - x_1)^2 + (y_2 - y_1)^2}$$
$$= \sqrt{(2 - 10)^2 + (8 - 23)^2}$$
$$= \sqrt{(-8)^2 + (-15)^2}$$
$$= \sqrt{64 + 225}$$
$$= \sqrt{289}$$
$$= 17,$$

so X could be $(10, 23)$ because that point is the proper distance from $(2, 8)$.

b. All the points that are 17 units from (2, 8) lie in a circle with center (2, 8) and radius 17:

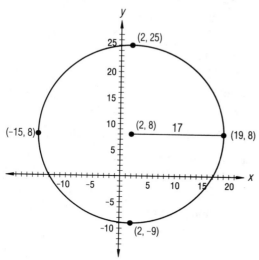

Four points can be found on the circle by moving 17 units from (2, 8) to the right, up, to the left, and down; those points are (19, 8), (2, 25), (-15, 8), and (2, -9), respectively.

Other points can be found using the Pythagorean Triple 8-15-17. To find these points, any point 8 units vertically and 15 units horizontally (or 15 units horizontally and 8 units vertically) will be 17 units from the center, so it will be on the circle.

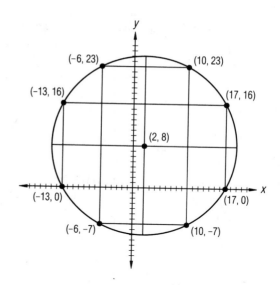

These points, counterclockwise from the positive x-axis, are: (17, 16), (10, 23), (-6, 23), (-13, 16), (-13, 0), (-6, -7), (10, -7), and (17, 0).

LESSON 11–3 (pp. 532–536)

1. Check whether or not the given point (x, y) is on the circle $(x - 3)^2 + (y - 2)^2 = 10^2$:
   a. For (13, 2), is $(13 - 3)^2 + (2 - 2)^2 = 100$? That is, is $10^2 + 0^2 = 100$? Yes, so (13, 2) is on the circle.
   b. For (3, -8), is $(3 - 3)^2 + (-8 - 2)^2 = 100$? That is, is $0^2 + (-10)^2 = 100$? Yes, so (3, -8) is on the circle.
   c. For (8, 7), is $(8 - 3)^2 + (7 - 2)^2 = 100$? That is, is $5^2 + 5^2 = 100$? No, $5^2 + 5^2 = 25 + 25 = 50$, so (8, 7) is not on the circle.
   d. For (9, -6), is $(9 - 3)^2 + (-6 - 2)^2 = 100$? That is, is $6^2 + (-8)^2 = 100$? Yes, $36 + 64 = 100$, so (9, -6) is on the circle.

2. **a.** Using the general formula $(x - h)^2 + (y - k)^2 = r^2$ with $(h, k) = (-3, 5)$ and $r = 1$, the formula for the circle is $(x - -3)^2 + (y - 5)^2 = 1^2$ or $(x + 3)^2 + (y - 5)^2 = 1$.

b. For 4 points on the circle, move one unit to the right, up, to the left, and down from the center (-3, 5); those points are (-2, 5), (-3, 6), (-4, 5), and (-3, 4), respectively.

3. a. The distance between (x, y) and (7, 1) is
$$\sqrt{(x_2 - x_1)^2 + (y_2 - y_1)^2}$$
$$= \sqrt{(x - 7)^2 + (y - 1)^2}$$

b. Using the general formula $(x - h)^2 + (y - k)^2 = r^2$ with $(h, k) = (7, 1)$ and $r = 5$, a formula for the circle is $(x - 7)^2 + (y - 1)^2 = 25$.

c.

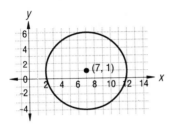

d. For 4 points on the circle, move 5 units to the right, up, to the left, and down from the center (7, 1); these points are (12, 1), (7, 6), (2, 1), and (7, -4), respectively.

4. The point on the circle, (3, 0), is 3 units from the center, so the radius is 3. Using the general formula $(x - h)^2 + (y - k)^2 = r^2$, with $(h, k) = (0, 0)$ and $r = 3$, then the formula is $(x - 0)^2 + (y - 0)^2 = 3^2$ or $x^2 + y^2 = 9$.

5. The proof of the equation for a circle relies on the distance formula
$$\sqrt{(x - h)^2 + (y - k)^2} = r,\text{ which is a form}$$
of the Pythagorean Theorem.

6. a-b. Comparing the equation
$(x - 5)^2 + (y - 11)^2 = 81$ with the formula $(x - h)^2 + (y - k)^2 = r^2$, then the center is $(h, k) = (5, 11)$ and $r = 9$.

c. Some other points on the circle are 9 units horizontally or vertically from the center (5, 11); they are (14, 11), (5, 20), (-4, 11), and (5, 2).

7. a-b. Rewriting the equation $(x + 1)^2 + y^2 = 2$ as $(x - -1)^2 + (y - 0)^2 = (\sqrt{2})^2$ and comparing that with the general equation $(x - h)^2 + (y - k)^2 = r^2$, then the center is $(h, k) = (-1, 0)$ and the radius is $\sqrt{2}$.

c. Some other points on the circle are $\sqrt{2}$ units horizontally or vertically from the center (-1, 0); they are $(-1 + \sqrt{2}, 0)$, $(-1, \sqrt{2})$, $(-1 - \sqrt{2}, 0)$, and $(-1, -\sqrt{2})$.

8. a-b. Rewriting the equation $x^2 + y^2 = 25$ as $(x - 0)^2 + (y - 0)^2 = 5^2$ and comparing that with the general equation $(x - h)^2 + (y - k)^2 = r^2$, then the center is $(h, k) = (0, 0)$ and the radius is 5.

c. Some other points on the circle are 5 units horizontally or vertically from the center (0, 0); they are (5, 0), (0, 5), (-5, 0), and (0, -5).

[Some other lattice points on the circle have horizontal and vertical distances 3 and 4 units; those points, counterclockwise from the positive x-axis, are (4, 3), (3, 4), (-3, 4), (-4, 3), (-4, -3), (-3, -4), (3, -4), and (4, -3).]

9. a-b. Rewriting the equation $(x + 6)^2 + (y + 2)^2 = 1$ as $(x - -6)^2 + (y - -2)^2 = 1^2$ and comparing that with the general equation $(x - h)^2 + (y - k)^2 = r^2$, then the center of the circle is $(h, k) = (-6, -2)$ and the radius is 1.

c. Some other points are 1 unit horizontally or vertically from the center (-6, -2); they are (-5, -2), (-6, -1), (-7, -2), and (-6, -3).

10. a.

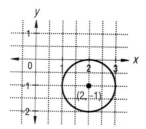

b. The point of tangency is directly above the center; that point is (2, 0).

c. Using the general formula $(x - h)^2 + (y - k)^2 = r^2$ with $(h, k) = (2, -1)$ and $r = 1$, the equation is
$(x - 2)^2 + (y - -1)^2 = 1^2$ or
$(x - 2)^2 + (y + 1)^2 = 1$.

d. Using the formula $A = \pi r^2$ for the area of a circle, $A = \pi(1)^2 = \pi$. So the area of the circle is π square units or about 3.14 square units.

11.

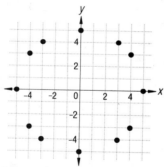

Four of the points are 5 units horizontally or vertically from the center (0, 0); they are (5, 0), (0, 5), (-5, 0), and (0, -5). Eight other lattice points have horizontal and vertical distances of 3 and 4 from the center. Counterclockwise from the positive x-axis, these points are (4, 3), (3, 4), (-3, 4), (-4, 3), (-4, -3), (-3, -4), (3, -4) and (4, -3).

12.

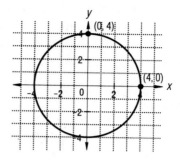

13.

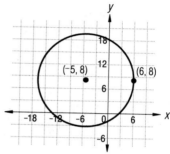

14. Using the general expression for the distance, $d = \sqrt{(x_2 - x_1)^2 + (y_2 - y_1)^2}$, with the two points (4, -7) and (-1, 5), the distance is
$$d = \sqrt{(-1 - 4)^2 + (5 - -7)^2}$$
$$= \sqrt{(-5)^2 + 12^2}$$
$$= \sqrt{25 + 144}$$
$$= \sqrt{169}$$
$$= 13 \text{ units.}$$

15. Using the general expression for distance, $d = \sqrt{(x_2 - x_1)^2 + (y_2 - y_1)^2}$, with the two points $(9x, -40x)$ and (0, 0), the distance is
$$d = \sqrt{(9x - 0)^2 + (-40x - 0)^2}$$
$$= \sqrt{(9x)^2 + (-40x)^2}$$
$$= \sqrt{81x^2 + 1600x^2}$$
$$= \sqrt{1681x^2}$$
$$= 41x \text{ units.}$$

16. If the park has coordinates (0, 0), then Nancy lives at (-6, 3) and Domaso lives at (0, -5). The distance between these points is
$$d = \sqrt{(x_2 - x_1)^2 + (y_2 - y_1)^2}$$
$$= \sqrt{(0 - -6)^2 + (-5 - 3)^2}$$

$$= \sqrt{6^2 + (-8)^2}$$
$$= \sqrt{36 + 64}$$
$$= \sqrt{100}$$
$$= 10 \text{ blocks.}$$

17. Find the slopes of the four sides.

For $Q = (9a, 4b)$ and $R = (6a, 2b)$, the slope of

$$\overline{QR} = \frac{y_2 - y_1}{x_2 - x_1}$$
$$= \frac{2b - 4b}{6a - 9a}$$
$$= \frac{-2b}{-3a}$$
$$= \frac{2b}{3a}.$$

For $R = (6a, 2b)$ and $S = (a, -7b)$, the slope of

$$\overline{RS} = \frac{y_2 - y_1}{x_2 - x_1}$$
$$= \frac{-7b - 2b}{a - 6a}$$
$$= \frac{-9b}{-5a}$$
$$= \frac{9b}{5a}.$$

For $S = (a, -7b)$ and $T = (-a, -14b)$, the slope of

$$\overline{ST} = \frac{y_2 - y_1}{x_2 - x_1}$$
$$= \frac{-14b - -7b}{-a - a}$$
$$= \frac{-7b}{-2a}$$
$$= \frac{7b}{2a}.$$

For $T = (-a, -14b)$ and $Q = (9a, 4b)$, the slope of

$$\overline{TQ} = \frac{y_2 - y_1}{x_2 - x_1}$$
$$= \frac{4b - -14b}{9a - -a}$$
$$= \frac{18b}{10a}$$
$$= \frac{9b}{5a}.$$

$\overline{RS}$ and $\overline{TQ}$ have equal slopes, so $\overline{RS} \parallel \overline{TQ}$ by the Parallel Lines and Slopes Theorem, so $QRST$ is a trapezoid by the definition of trapezoid (sufficient condition).

18. Multiply the first equation by -4 and add the equations:
$$x - 7y = 15$$
$$4x + 5y = -6$$

$$-4x + 28y = -60$$
$$\underline{4x + 5y = -6}$$
$$33y = -66$$
$$y = -2$$

Substitute $y = -2$ into the first equation:
$$x - 7(-2) = 15$$
$$x + 14 = 15$$
$$x = 1$$

The point of intersection is $(1, -2)$.
To check:
In the first equation, is $1 - 7(-2) = 15$?
That is, is $1 + 14 = 15$? Yes.
In the second equation, is $4(1) + 5(-2) = -6$?
That is, is $4 + -10 = -6$? Yes.

19. If lines $\overleftrightarrow{AB}$ and $\overleftrightarrow{BC}$ have the same slope, then they are parallel by the Parallel Lines and Slopes Theorem. And, since they contain the same point B, then they are the same line (the justification for that conclusion is proved in this text on page 660: it is called the Uniqueness of Parallels Theorem).

20.

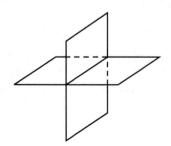

21.

22. $\triangle XYZ$ is isosceles with vertex angle X, so $XY = XZ$ by the definition of isosceles triangle (meaning). V and W are midpoints, so $XV = \frac{1}{2}XY$ and $XW = \frac{1}{2}XZ$ by the definition of midpoint (meaning). So $XV = XW$ by substitution and then the Transitive Property of Equality, and $\triangle XVW$ is isosceles (with vertex angle X) by the definition of isosceles triangle (sufficient condition).

23. The center of the circle cannot be a lattice point, because then the interior of the circle would have to contain that lattice point. If the center is not a lattice point, such as (3, 4.8), then the radius must be less than the distance to the nearest lattice point (3, 5)—the radius must be less than .2. So a sample equation is $(x - 3)^2 + (y - 4.8)^2 = (.1)^2$. If the center is a point such as (1.4, 2.7), then it is closest to the lattice point (1, 3), and the radius must be less than the distance between (1.4, 2.7) and (1, 3), which is $\sqrt{.4^2 + .3^2} = \sqrt{.16 + .09} = \sqrt{.25} = .5$.

LESSON 11-4 (pp. 537–543)

1. The mean of a set of numbers is the sum of the numbers divided by the number of numbers, so the mean of 100, 50, and 200 is $\frac{100 + 50 + 200}{3} = \frac{350}{3} = 116\frac{2}{3}$.

2. The mean of a set of numbers is the sum of the numbers divided by the number of numbers, so the mean of -1, -3, -5, and -7 is $\frac{-1 + -3 + -5 + -7}{4} = \frac{-16}{4} = -4$.

3. The mean of a set of numbers is the sum of the numbers divided by the number of numbers, so the mean of 1492 and 1776 is $\frac{1492 + 1776}{2} = \frac{3268}{2} = 1634$.

4. The balancing point will be the mean of -81 and 47, which is $\frac{-81 + 47}{2} = \frac{-34}{2} = -17$.

5. The x-coordinate of the center of gravity is the mean of the x-coordinates, and the y-coordinate of the center of gravity is the mean of the y-coordinates. So the center of gravity is $\left(\frac{0 + 10 + 12 + 0}{4}, \frac{0 + 0 + 13 + 7}{4}\right)$

$= \left(\frac{22}{4}, \frac{20}{4}\right)$

$= (5.5, 5)$.

6. Using the formula that the midpoint of the segment with endpoints (a, b) and (c, d) is $\left(\frac{a + c}{2}, \frac{b + d}{2}\right)$, and the two points are (x_1, y_1) and (x_2, y_2), the coordinates of the midpoint are $\left(\frac{x_1 + x_2}{2}, \frac{y_1 + y_2}{2}\right)$.

7. a. Using the formula that the midpoint of the segment with endpoints (a, b) and (c, d) is $\left(\frac{a + c}{2}, \frac{b + d}{2}\right)$, and the two points are (12, -4) and (-2, -8), the coordinates of the midpoint are $\left(\frac{12 + -2}{2}, \frac{-4 + -8}{2}\right) = \left(\frac{10}{2}, \frac{-12}{2}\right) = (5, -6)$.

b. Use slope to show that the three points with coordinates $(12, -4)$, $(5, -6)$, and $(-2, -8)$ are collinear:

The slope of the line through $(12, -4)$ and $(5, -6)$ is $\frac{y_2 - y_1}{x_2 - x_1} = \frac{-6 - -4}{5 - 12} = \frac{-2}{-7} = \frac{2}{7}$;

and the slope of the line through $(5, -6)$ and $(-2, -8)$ is $\frac{y_2 - y_1}{x_2 - x_1} = \frac{-8 - -6}{-2 - 5} = \frac{-2}{-7} = \frac{2}{7}$.

So the two lines are parallel (by the Parallel Lines and Slopes Theorem), and since they contain the same point $(5, -6)$, they must be collinear.

Now use the distance formula to show that the two segments have the same length. The length of the segment between $(12, -4)$ and $(5, -6)$

$$= \sqrt{(x_2 - x_1)^2 + (y_2 - y_1)^2}$$
$$= \sqrt{(5 - 12)^2 + (-6 - -4)^2}$$
$$= \sqrt{(-7)^2 + (-2)^2}$$
$$= \sqrt{49 + 4}$$
$$= \sqrt{53}.$$

The length of the segment between $(5, -6)$ and $(-2, -8)$

$$= \sqrt{(x_2 - x_1)^2 + (y_2 - y_1)^2}$$
$$= \sqrt{(-2 - 5)^2 + (-8 - -6)^2}$$
$$= \sqrt{(-7)^2 + (-2)^2}$$
$$= \sqrt{49 + 4}$$
$$= \sqrt{53}.$$

So the segments have the same length, and $(5, -6)$ is the midpoint of $(12, -4)$ and $(-2, -8)$ by the definition of midpoint (sufficient condition).

8. Using the formula that the midpoint of the segment with endpoints (a, b) and (c, d) is $\left(\frac{a + c}{2}, \frac{b + d}{2}\right)$, and the two points are (a, b) and $(0, 0)$, the midpoint is $\left(\frac{a + 0}{2}, \frac{b + 0}{2}\right) = \left(\frac{a}{2}, \frac{b}{2}\right)$.

9. a. L is midway between $(0, 0)$ and $(13, 0)$, so
$$L = \left(\frac{0 + 13}{2}, \frac{0 + 0}{2}\right) = (6.5, 0).$$
M is midway between $(3, 12)$ and $(13, 0)$, so $M = \left(\frac{3 + 13}{2}, \frac{12 + 0}{2}\right) = \left(\frac{16}{2}, \frac{12}{2}\right) = (8, 6)$.
N is midway between $(0, 0)$ and $(3, 12)$ so
$$N = \left(\frac{0 + 3}{2}, \frac{0 + 12}{2}\right) = (1.5, 6).$$

b. Two points on $\overline{LM}$ are $L = (6.5, 0)$ and $M = (8, 6)$, so the slope of $\overline{LM}$ is $\frac{y_2 - y_1}{x_2 - x_1}$
$$= \frac{6 - 0}{8 - 6.5} = \frac{6}{1.5} = 4.$$
Two points on $\overline{DE}$ are $D = (3, 12)$ and $E = (0, 0)$, so the slope of $\overline{DE}$ is $\frac{y_2 - y_1}{x_2 - x_1}$
$$= \frac{0 - 12}{0 - 3} = \frac{-12}{-3} = 4.$$
So $\overline{LM}$ and $\overline{DE}$ have the same slope, and $\overline{LM} \parallel \overline{DE}$ by the Parallel Lines and Slopes Theorem.

c. Two points on $\overline{MN}$ are $M = (8, 6)$ and $N = (1.5, 6)$. M and N have the same y-coordinate, so $\overline{MN}$ is horizontal and has slope 0. Segment $\overline{EF}$ is on the x-axis, so its slope is 0. Thus $\overline{MN} \parallel \overline{EF}$ by the Parallel Lines and Slopes Theorem.

d. Use the distance formula to find the distance between $M = (8, 6)$ and $N = (1.5, 6)$:
$$d = \sqrt{(x_2 - x_1)^2 + (y_2 - y_1)^2}$$
$$= \sqrt{(1.5 - 8)^2 + (6 - 6)^2}$$
$$= \sqrt{(-6.5)^2 + 0^2}$$
$$= 6.5 \text{ units.}$$
To find the distance between E and F, note that they are on the horizontal line $y = 0$, so their distance apart is the absolute value of the difference of their x-coordinates, or $|0 - 13| = |-13| = 13$ units. So $MN = 6.5$
$$= \tfrac{1}{2}(13) = \tfrac{1}{2}EF.$$

10. Use the distance formula to find the distance between $M = (1, 4)$ and $N = (4, 11)$ in Example 2:
$$d = \sqrt{(x_2 - x_1)^2 + (y_2 - y_1)^2}$$
$$= \sqrt{(4 - 1)^2 + (11 - 4)^2}$$
$$= \sqrt{3^2 + 7^2}$$
$$= \sqrt{9 + 49}$$
$$= \sqrt{58}.$$
Then use the distance formula to find the distance between $B = (2, -4)$ and $C = (8, 10)$:
$$d = \sqrt{(x_2 - x_1)^2 + (y_2 - y_1)^2}$$
$$= \sqrt{(8 - 2)^2 + (10 - -4)^2}$$
$$= \sqrt{6^2 + 14^2}$$
$$= \sqrt{36 + 196}$$
$$= \sqrt{232}$$
$$= \sqrt{(4)(58)}$$
$$= 2\sqrt{58}.$$
So $MN = \sqrt{58} = \tfrac{1}{2}(2\sqrt{58}) = \tfrac{1}{2}BC.$

11. $\dfrac{a + c}{2} - a = \dfrac{a + c}{2} - \dfrac{2a}{2}$
$$= \dfrac{a + c - 2a}{2} = \dfrac{c - a}{2}$$

12. $c - \dfrac{a + c}{2} = \dfrac{2c}{2} - \dfrac{a + c}{2}$
$$= \dfrac{2c - a - c}{2} = \dfrac{c - a}{2}$$

13. $\dfrac{d - \dfrac{b + d}{2}}{c - \dfrac{a + c}{2}} = \dfrac{\dfrac{2d}{2} - \dfrac{b + d}{2}}{\dfrac{2c}{2} - \dfrac{a + c}{2}} =$

$$\dfrac{\dfrac{2d - b - d}{2}}{\dfrac{2c - a - c}{2}} = \dfrac{\dfrac{d - b}{2}}{\dfrac{c - a}{2}} = \dfrac{d - b}{c - a}$$

14. a. The midpoint of the segment with endpoints $P = (1980, 7.6)$ and $Q = (1986, 8.8)$ is
$$\left(\dfrac{1980 + 1986}{2}, \dfrac{7.6 + 8.8}{2} \right)$$
$$= \left(1983, \dfrac{16.4}{2} \right)$$
$$= (1983, 8.2).$$
(Note that it was easier to find the mean of 1980 and 1986 as a mental calculation ("halfway between 80 and 86"), than as a pencil-and-paper or calculator problem.)

b. An interpretation of the coordinates (1983, 8.2) is that in 1983 there were approximately 8.2 million families in the United States that the census department classified as nonwhite.

15. The midpoint of the segment with endpoints $(14, -11)$ and $(-4, -35)$ is $\left(\dfrac{14 + -4}{2}, \dfrac{-11 + -35}{2} \right)$
$$= \left(\dfrac{10}{2}, \dfrac{-46}{2} \right) = (5, -23).$$
The slope of the segment connecting $(5, -23)$ and $(0, 0)$ is $\dfrac{-23 - 0}{5 - 0} = \dfrac{-23}{5} = -4.6.$

16. The midpoint of the segment connecting $A = (5, 7)$ and $C = (-13, 11)$ is
$$\left(\frac{5 + -13}{2}, \frac{7 + 11}{2}\right) = \left(\frac{-8}{2}, \frac{18}{2}\right) = (-4, 9).$$
Then, the length of the segment connecting $(-4, 9)$ with $B = (-2, 0)$ is
$$\sqrt{(-2 - -4)^2 + (0 - 9)^2} = \sqrt{2^2 + (-9)^2} =$$
$$\sqrt{4 + 81} = \sqrt{85} \approx 9.22 \text{ units.}$$

17. If the new endpoints of the stick are 12 and 80, then the reading at the midpoint of the stick is $\frac{12 + 80}{2} = \frac{92}{2} = 46$. If the pieces were cut from the other ends, then the new endpoints of the stick are 20 and 88, and the reading at the midpoint is
$$\frac{20 + 88}{2} = \frac{108}{2} = 54.$$

18. **a.** First, find the coordinates of M, N, P, and Q:
$$M = \left(\frac{3 + 20}{2}, \frac{15 + 4}{2}\right) = \left(\frac{23}{2}, \frac{19}{2}\right)$$
$$= (11.5, 9.5);$$
$$N = \left(\frac{20 + 20}{2}, \frac{20 + 4}{2}\right) = \left(\frac{40}{2}, \frac{24}{2}\right)$$
$$= (20, 12);$$
$$P = \left(\frac{9 + 20}{2}, \frac{25 + 20}{2}\right) = \left(\frac{29}{2}, \frac{45}{2}\right)$$
$$= (14.5, 22.5);$$
$$Q = \left(\frac{3 + 9}{2}, \frac{15 + 25}{2}\right) = \left(\frac{12}{2}, \frac{40}{2}\right)$$
$$= (6, 20).$$
So $MN = \sqrt{(11.5 - 20)^2 + (9.5 - 12)^2}$
$$= \sqrt{(-8.5)^2 + (-2.5)^2}$$
$$= \sqrt{72.25 + 6.25}$$
$$= \sqrt{78.5},$$
and $PQ = \sqrt{(14.5 - 6)^2 + (22.5 - 20)^2}$
$$= \sqrt{8.5^2 + 2.5^2}$$
$$= \sqrt{72.25 + 6.25}$$
$$= \sqrt{78.5}.$$
So $MN = PQ$.

b. The slope of $\overline{MN}$ is
$$\frac{y_2 - y_1}{x_2 - x_1} = \frac{12 - 9.5}{20 - 11.5}$$
$$= \frac{2.5}{8.5} = \frac{25}{85} = \frac{5}{17},$$
and the slope of $\overline{PQ}$ is
$$\frac{y_2 - y_1}{x_2 - x_1} = \frac{22.5 - 20}{14.5 - 6}$$
$$= \frac{2.5}{8.5} = \frac{5}{17}.$$
So $\overline{MN} \parallel \overline{QP}$ by the Parallel Lines and Slopes Theorem.
(A shorter, simpler, and more elegant proof for parts **a** and **b** is that $\overline{MN}$ and $\overline{QP}$ are both parallel to and half the length of $\overline{AC}$, by a generalization of Example 2 and Question 10 (which is proved as the Midpoint Connector Theorem in the next lesson). So $\overline{MN} \parallel \overline{QP}$ by the Transitivity of Parallels Theorem, and $MN = QP$ by the Transitive Property of Equality.)

c. $\overline{MN}$ and $\overline{PQ}$ are congruent and parallel, so $MNPQ$ is a parallelogram by the Sufficient Conditions for a Parallelogram Theorem (part d).

19. Rewriting the equation as
$(x - 0)^2 + (y - 0)^2 = (\sqrt{75})^2$, and comparing that to the general equation
$(x - h)^2 + (y - k)^2 = r^2$, then:
a. The center of the circle is $(h, k) = (0, 0)$;
b. The radius is $\sqrt{75} = \sqrt{(25)(3)} = 5\sqrt{3} \approx 8.66$ units.
c. Four points on the circle can be found by moving horizontally or vertically a distance of $5\sqrt{3}$ units from the center $(0, 0)$; those points are $(5\sqrt{3}, 0)$, $(0, 5\sqrt{3})$, $(-5\sqrt{3}, 0)$, and $(0, -5\sqrt{3})$.
d. Using the formula for the area of a circle $A = \pi r^2$ with $r = \sqrt{75}$, then
$A = \pi(\sqrt{75})^2 = 75\pi \approx 235.62$ units.

20.

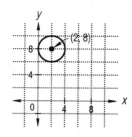

21. Multiply the second equation by 2 and then add them:

$5x - 2y = 25$
$3x + y = 4$

$\begin{array}{r} 5x - 2y = 25 \\ 6x + 2y = 8 \\ \hline 11x = 33 \\ x = 3 \end{array}$

Substituting $x = 3$ into the second equation:

$3(3) + y = 4$
$9 + y = 4$
$y = -5$.

The point of intersection is (3, -5).
To check:
In the first equation, is $5(3) - 2(-5) = 25$?
That is, is $15 - -10 = 25$? Yes.
In the second equation, is $3(3) + -5 = 4$?
That is, is $9 + -5 = 4$? Yes.

22. Rewrite the first equation in the form $ax + by = c$, multiply the first equation by -2, and then add the equations:

$x = 14y - 13$
$2x + 3y = 36$

$\begin{array}{r} x - 14y = -13 \\ 2x + 3y = 36 \end{array}$

$\begin{array}{r} -2x + 28y = 26 \\ 2x + 3y = 36 \\ \hline 31y = 62 \\ y = 2 \end{array}$

Substitute $y = 2$ into the first equation:
$x = 14(2) - 13 = 28 - 13 = 15$.
The solution is (15, 2).
To check:
In the first equation, is $15 = 14(2) - 13$?
Yes.
In the second equation, is $2(15) + 3(2) = 36$? That is, is $30 + 6 = 36$? Yes.

23. a. The perimeter of the square base is 64 cm, so its side is 16 cm. A formula for the volume of the pyramid is $V = \frac{1}{3}Bh = \frac{1}{3}(s^2)(h) = \frac{1}{3}(16^2)(30) = \frac{1}{3}(256)(30) = 2560$ cm^3.

b.

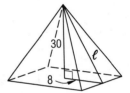

The slant height ℓ of the pyramid is the hypotenuse of a right triangle with legs 8 and 30, so $\ell^2 = 8^2 + 30^2 = 64 + 900 = 964$, so $\ell = \sqrt{964} = \sqrt{(4)(241)} = 2\sqrt{241}$. A formula for the surface area of a regular pyramid is S.A. = L.A. + B. Using L.A. $= \frac{1}{2}\ell p$, the lateral area is $\frac{1}{2}(2\sqrt{241})(64) = 64\sqrt{241}$ and the surface area is $64\sqrt{241} + 256 \approx 993.5 + 256 = 1249.5$ cm^2.

24. Using the slope formula $\frac{y_2 - y_1}{x_2 - x_1}$, the slope of the line connecting $(a, 0)$ and $(0, -a)$ is $\frac{-a - 0}{0 - a} = \frac{-a}{-a} = 1$.

25. a. $\sqrt{x^2} = x$

b. $\sqrt{4x^2} = \sqrt{(2x)(2x)} = 2x$

c. $\sqrt{5x^2} = \sqrt{(x^2)(5)} = x\sqrt{5}$

26. a-b .The polygonal shapes of students' regions will vary. The algebraic value of the center of gravity (the x-coordinate is the mean of the x-coordinates of the vertices, and the y-coordinate is the mean of the y-coordinates of the vertices) should be close to the coordinates found using the trial and error method.

LESSON 11–5 (pp. 544–549)

1. If $LN = 12$, the other lengths that can be found are $LA = AN = BC = 6$ units.

2. If $AB = 5.2$, the other lengths that can be found are $NC = CM = 5.2$ units and $NM = 10.4$ units.

3. The Midpoint Connector Theorem is that the segment connecting the midpoints of two sides of a triangle is parallel to and half the length of the third side.

4.

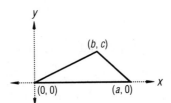

5.

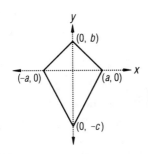

6.

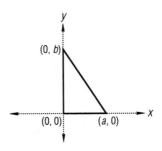

7.

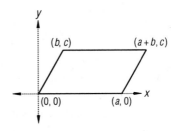

8. The coordinates of D, the midpoint of the segment connecting $(0, 5)$ and $(7, 0)$, is
$$\left(\frac{0+7}{2}, \frac{5+0}{2}\right) = \left(\frac{7}{2}, \frac{5}{2}\right) = (3.5, 2.5).$$ So the length of the segment connecting $D = (3.5, 2.5)$ and $A = (0, 0)$ is
$$\sqrt{(3.5 - 0)^2 + (2.5 - 0)^2} = \sqrt{12.25 + 6.25}$$
$$= \sqrt{18.5} \approx 4.3 \text{ units.}$$

9. $\sqrt{4a^2 + 4b^2} = \sqrt{4(a^2 + b^2)}$
$$= \sqrt{4} \cdot \sqrt{a^2 + b^2}$$
$$= 2\sqrt{a^2 + b^2}$$

10.

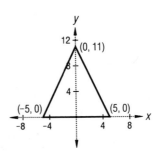

271

11.

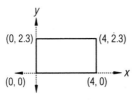

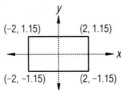

12. a. The justification that $\overline{BC} \parallel \overline{LN}$ and $\overline{AB} \parallel \overline{MN}$ is the Midpoint Connector Theorem.

b. The justification that $ABCN$ is a parallelogram is the definition of parallelogram (sufficient condition).

13. If the sides of the large triangle are $DE = 20$, $EF = 16$, and $DF = 24$, then by the Midpoint Connector Theorem the sides of the small triangle are $NM = 10$, $LN = 8$, and $LM = 12$, so the perimeter of $\triangle LMN$ is $10 + 8 + 12 = 30$ units.

14. Segment $\overline{YD}$ connects the midpoints of two sides of $\triangle REC$, so $\overline{YD} \parallel \overline{RC}$ by the Midpoint Connector Theorem. Thus $YDCR$ is a trapezoid by the definition of trapezoid (sufficient condition).

15. If $RC = 58$, then by the Midpoint Connector Theorem, $YD = 29$. If $ED = 20$, then $DC = 20$ by the definition of midpoint (meaning), and so $EC = 40$ and also $RT = 40$ by the Properties of a Parallelogram Theorem. In right triangle REC,
$$RE^2 + EC^2 = RC^2$$
$$RE^2 + 40^2 = 58^2$$
$$RE^2 = 58^2 - 40^2 = 3364 - 1600 = 1764.$$
So $RE = \sqrt{1764} = 42$, and also $TC = 42$ (by the Properties of a Parallelogram Theorem). Finally, $RY = YE = 21$ by the definition of midpoint (meaning).

16.

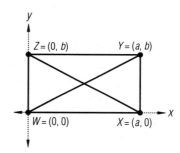

The diagonal with endpoints $(0, 0)$ and (a, b) has midpoint $\left(\frac{0 + a}{2}, \frac{0 + b}{2}\right) = \left(\frac{a}{2}, \frac{b}{2}\right)$. The diagonal with endpoints $(a, 0)$ and $(0, b)$ has midpoint $\left(\frac{a + 0}{2}, \frac{0 + b}{2}\right) = \left(\frac{a}{2}, \frac{b}{2}\right)$. So the diagonals of a rectangle have the same midpoint. (Another way to state this is that the diagonals of a rectangle bisect each other.)

17. The x- and y-values of its center of gravity are the means of the x- and y-coordinates, respectively. So the x-value of the center of gravity is $\frac{-1 + 8 + 9 + 3.5 + -3.5}{5} = \frac{16}{5} = 3.2$, and the y-value of the center of gravity is $\frac{0 + 0 + 3 + 6 + 6}{5} = \frac{15}{5} = 3$.

18. The x- and y-values of its center of gravity are the means of the x- and y-coordinates, respectively. So the center of gravity has

coordinates $\left(\dfrac{a + 0 + \text{-}a + 0}{4}, \dfrac{0 + b + 0 + \text{-}c}{4}\right)$

$= \left(\dfrac{0}{4}, \dfrac{b - c}{4}\right)$

$= \left(0, \dfrac{b - c}{4}\right)$.

19. a. VL is the distance between points $(11, 21)$ and $(6, 33)$

$= \sqrt{(11 - 6)^2 + (21 - 33)^2}$

$= \sqrt{5^2 + (\text{-}12)^2}$

$= \sqrt{25 + 144}$

$= \sqrt{169} = 13$ units.

b. The slope of $\overline{VL}$ is

$\dfrac{y_2 - y_1}{x_2 - x_1} = \dfrac{33 - 21}{6 - 11}$

$= \dfrac{12}{\text{-}5}$

$= \dfrac{\text{-}12}{5}$ or $\text{-}2.4$.

c. The midpoint of $\overline{VL}$ has coordinates

$\left(\dfrac{11 + 6}{2}, \dfrac{21 + 33}{2}\right) = \left(\dfrac{17}{2}, \dfrac{54}{2}\right) = (8.5, 27)$.

20. a. VL is the distance between points (a, b) and $(c, d) = \sqrt{(a - c)^2 + (b - d)^2}$.

b. The slope of $\overline{VL}$ is $\dfrac{d - b}{c - a}$ or $\dfrac{b - d}{a - c}$.

c. The midpoint of $\overline{VL}$ has coordinates $\left(\dfrac{a + c}{2}, \dfrac{b + d}{2}\right)$.

21. The center of the circle is $(\text{-}2, 0)$, and its radius is the distance from the point to $(3, 0)$, which is 5 units (that is, $|\text{-}2 - 3| = |\text{-}5| = 5$). Substituting these values into the general equation for a circle, $(x - h)^2 + (y - k)^2 = r^2$, an equation for the given circle is $(x - \text{-}2)^2 + (y - 0)^2 = 5^2$, or $(x + 2)^2 + y^2 = 25$.

22. If the two numbers are x and y, the two sentences can be translated into the following equations:

$2x + 3y = 462$

$x + y = 254$.

Multiply the second equation by -2 and add the equations:

$2x + 3y = 462$

$\underline{\text{-}2x + \text{-}2y = \text{-}508}$

$y = \text{-}46$

Substitute $y = \text{-}46$ into the second equation:

$x + \text{-}46 = 254$

$x = 300$.

The point of intersection is $(300, \text{-}46)$.

To check:

In the first equation, is $2(300) + 3(\text{-}46) = 462$? That is, is $600 - 138 = 462$? Yes.

In the second equation, is $300 + \text{-}46 = 254$? Yes.

23.

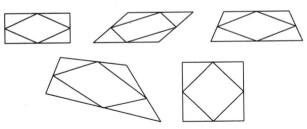

Consider either pair of opposite sides of a quadrilateral formed by connecting the midpoints of sides: the two sides of that smaller quadrilateral are each parallel to, and half the length of, a diagonal of the original quadrilateral. So the sides of that smaller quadrilateral are parallel to each other (Transitivity of Parallels Theorem) and congruent to each other (Transitive Property of Equality) and so the smaller quadrilateral is a parallelogram by the Sufficient Conditions of a Parallelogram Theorem, part d.

LESSON 11-6 (pp. 550–556)

1. Any point in three dimensions can be located with an ordered triple.

2. The location in a room where two walls and the floor meet is an illustration of three walls each perpendicular to the other two, so it can represent the origin of a coordinate system in three dimensions; the statement is *true*.

3.

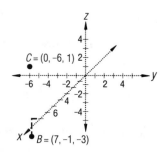

4. Using the distance formula in three dimensions, $d =$
$\sqrt{(x_2 - x_1)^2 + (y_2 - y_1)^2 + (z_2 - z_1)^2}$ with the points $P = (3, 7, -2)$ and $Q = (5, -11, 0)$, the distance is
$\sqrt{(5 - 3)^2 + (-11 - 7)^2 + (0 - -2)^2}$
$= \sqrt{2^2 + (-18)^2 + 2^2}$
$= \sqrt{4 + 324 + 4}$
$= \sqrt{332}$
≈ 18.22 units.

5. CF is the length of the diagonal of a box with dimensions 5, 11, and 9. Using the Diagonal of a Box Formula, that distance is
$\sqrt{5^2 + 11^2 + 9^2}$
$= \sqrt{25 + 121 + 81}$
$= \sqrt{227}$
≈ 15.07 units.

6. Using the general equation of a sphere,
$(x - h)^2 + (y - k)^2 + (z - j)^2 = r^2$, with center $(h, k, j) = (-5, 3, -10)$ and $r = 13$, the equation is
$(x - -5)^2 + (y - 3)^2 + (z - -10)^2 = 13^2$ or
$(x + 5)^2 + (y - 3)^2 + (z + 10)^2 = 169$.

7. The midpoint of the segment connecting $P = (3, 7, -2)$ and $Q = (5, -11, 0)$ is
$\left(\dfrac{3 + 5}{2}, \dfrac{7 + -11}{2}, \dfrac{-2 + 0}{2}\right) = \left(\dfrac{8}{2}, \dfrac{-4}{2}, \dfrac{-2}{2}\right) =$
$(4, -2, -1)$.

8. **a-b.** Comparing the general equation of a sphere,
$(x - h)^2 + (y - k)^2 + (z - j)^2 = r^2$,
with the given equation,
$(x - 18)^2 + (y - 5)^2 + (z + 11)^2 = 36$,
then the center is $(h, k, j) = (18, 5, -11)$ and the radius is $\sqrt{36} = 6$.

   c. To find the coordinates of some points, move 6 units (the length of the radius) from the center, in the positive or negative direction, parallel to one of the axes. So some points are:
   (24, 5, -11) or (12, 5, -11),
   (18, 11, -11) or (18, -1, -11), and
   (18, 5, -5) or (18, 5, -17).

9. **a.**

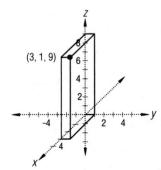

   b. The dimensions of the box are 3, 1, and 9, so the volume of the box is $V = \ell w h =$
   $(3)(1)(9) = 27$ units^3.

274

10. **a.** Point $D = (10, 1, 2)$, so:

$A = (10, 0, 2)$ (it differs from A only in its y-value)

$B = (0, 0, 2)$ (it has the same z-value as A)

$C = (0, 1, 2)$ (it has the same y-value as D and the same z-value as A)

$E = (10, 0, 0)$ (it has the same x-value as A)

$G = (0, 1, 0)$ (it has the same y-value as D)

$H = (10, 1, 0)$ (it differs from D only it its z-value).

b. The dimensions of the box are 10 (in the x-direction), 1 (in the y-direction), and 2 (in the z-direction), so its volume is $V = \ell wh = (10)(1)(2) = 20$ units^3.

c. The surface are of a box with dimensions ℓ, w, and h is $2(\ell w + wh + \ell h)$, so the surface area of this box is
$2[(10)(1) + (1)(2) + (10)(2)] =$
$2(10 + 2 + 20) = 2(32) = 64$ units^2.

11. AB is the distance between $A = (2, -1, 7)$ and $B = (4, 0, -5)$ so
$$AB = \sqrt{(2 - 4)^2 + (-1 - 0)^2 + (7 - -5)^2}$$
$$= \sqrt{(-2)^2 + (-1)^2 + 12^2}$$
$$= \sqrt{4 + 1 + 144}$$
$$= \sqrt{149}.$$
BC is the distance between $B = (4, 0, -5)$ and $C = (-11, 8, 2)$ so
$$BC = \sqrt{(4 - -11)^2 + (0 - 8)^2 + (-5 - 2)^2}$$
$$= \sqrt{15^2 + (-8)^2 + (-7)^2}$$
$$= \sqrt{225 + 64 + 49}$$
$$= \sqrt{338}.$$
AC is the distance between $A = (2, -1, 7)$ and $C = (-11, 8, 2)$ so
$$AC = \sqrt{(2 - -11)^2 + (-1 - 8)^2 + (7 - 2)^2}$$
$$= \sqrt{13^2 + (-9)^2 + 5^2}$$
$$= \sqrt{169 + 81 + 25}$$
$$= \sqrt{275}.$$
So the perimeter of $\triangle ABC$ is $\sqrt{149} + \sqrt{338}$ $+ \sqrt{275} \approx 12.21 + 18.38 + 16.58 =$ 47.17 units.

12. The midpoint of $\overline{AB}$ is the midpoint of the segment with coordinates $A = (2, -1, 7)$ and $B = (4, 0, -5)$; that midpoint is
$\left(\dfrac{2 + 4}{2}, \dfrac{-1 + 0}{2}, \dfrac{7 + -5}{2}\right) = \left(\dfrac{6}{2}, \dfrac{-1}{2}, \dfrac{2}{2}\right) =$
$(3, -.5, 1)$.
The midpoint of $\overline{BC}$ is the midpoint of the segment with coordinates $B = (4, 0, -5)$ and $C = (-11, 8, 2)$; that midpoint is
$\left(\dfrac{4 + -11}{2}, \dfrac{0 + 8}{2}, \dfrac{-5 + 2}{2}\right) = \left(\dfrac{-7}{2}, \dfrac{8}{2}, \dfrac{-3}{2}\right) =$
$(-3.5, 4, -1.5)$.
The midpoint of $\overline{AC}$ is the midpoint of the segment with coordinates $A = (2, -1, 7)$ and $C = (-11, 8, 2)$; that midpoint is
$\left(\dfrac{2 + -11}{2}, \dfrac{-1 + 8}{2}, \dfrac{7 + 2}{2}\right) = \left(\dfrac{-9}{2}, \dfrac{7}{2}, \dfrac{9}{2}\right) =$
$(-4.5, 3.5, 4.5)$.

13. The length of the diagonal of a box with dimensions 20″, 40″, and 5″ is
$$d = \sqrt{20^2 + 40^2 + 5^2}$$
$$= \sqrt{400 + 1600 + 25}$$
$$= \sqrt{2025}$$
$$= 45''.$$

14. The center of the sphere is $(0, 0, 0)$ and the radius is 5. Substituting those values into the general equation for a sphere,
$(x - h)^2 + (y - k)^2 + (z - j)^2 = r^2$, the equation is
$(x - 0)^2 + (y - 0)^2 + (z - 0)^2 = 5^2$ or
$x^2 + y^2 + z^2 = 25$.

15. Place the right triangle so the legs are on the positive x- and y-axes. There are two possibilities:

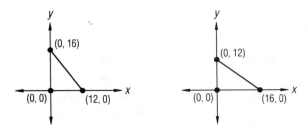

275

16. a. The figure shown has two sides parallel, and the other two sides are not necessarily congruent, so the figure is a trapezoid.

b. The statement is: The segment joining the midpoints of the non-base sides of a trapezoid is parallel to the bases.

For a proof, note that for the segment joining the midpoints of the non-base sides, the y-coordinates are equal, so the line is horizontal and the slope is zero. This is also true for the bases of the trapezoid (their slope is zero), so the segment is parallel to the bases by the Parallel Lines and Slopes Theorem.

17. P and L are midpoints, so $\overline{PL} \parallel \overline{MN}$ by the Midpoint Connector Theorem. Then $\angle QLP \approx \angle QNM$ because $\parallel$ lines $\Rightarrow$ corr. $\angle$s $=$.

18. L is a midpoint, so $QN = 2(3x)$ by the definition of midpoint (meaning).
L and P are midpoints, so $MN = 2(2x + 1)$ by the Midpoint Connector Theorem.
Finally, QM is given to be $4x$.
So the perimeter of
$\Delta QMN = 2(3x) + 2(2x + 1) + 4x = 6x + 4x + 2 + 4x = 14x + 2$.

19. a. D is the midpoint of $B = (5, 7)$ and $C = (23, 3)$, so $D = \left(\dfrac{5 + 23}{2}, \dfrac{7 + 3}{2}\right) = \left(\dfrac{28}{2}, \dfrac{10}{2}\right) = (14, 5)$.

b. AD is the length of the segment from $A = (11, 15)$ to $D = (14, 5)$, so
$$AD = \sqrt{(14 - 11)^2 + (5 - 15)^2}$$
$$= \sqrt{3^2 + (-10)^2}$$
$$= \sqrt{9 + 100}$$
$$= \sqrt{109}$$
$$\approx 10.44.$$

c. The center of gravity of a triangular region is at the point of intersection of the three medians. $\overline{AD}$ is a median, so the center of gravity of triangular region ABC will be on $\overline{AD}$; the statement is *true*.

20. The length of the segment joining $(4, -7)$ and $(-12, 5)$ is $\sqrt{(4 - -12)^2 + (-7 - 5)^2}$
$$= \sqrt{16^2 + (-12)^2}$$
$$= \sqrt{256 + 144}$$
$$= \sqrt{400}$$
$$= 20.$$
The length of the segment joining $(-12, 5)$ and $(9, -7)$ is $\sqrt{(-12 - 9)^2 + (5 - -7)^2}$
$$= \sqrt{(-21)^2 + 12^2}$$
$$= \sqrt{441 + 144}$$
$$= \sqrt{585}$$
$$= \sqrt{9} \cdot \sqrt{65}$$
$$= 3\sqrt{65}.$$
The length of the segment joining $(4, -7)$ and $(9, -7)$ is 5 (since they are both on the horizontal line $y = -7$).
So the perimeter of the triangle is
$20 + 3\sqrt{65} + 5 \approx 20 + 24.19 + 5 = 25 + 3\sqrt{65} \approx 49.19$ units.

21. For the two equations
$5x - 2y = 15$ and
$\qquad y = 6$,
substitute the value $y = 6$ into the first equation:
$5x - 2(6) = 15$
$5x - \quad 12 = 15$
$5x \qquad = 27$
$$x = \frac{27}{5} = 5.4.$$
The point of intersection is $(5.4, 6)$.
To check:
In the first equation, is $5(5.4) - 2(6) = 15$? That is, is $27 - 12 = 15$? Yes.
In the second equation, is $6 = 6$? Yes.

22. When students set up a coordinate system in their bedroom or classroom, the floor should represent the xy-plane, and the line where the walls meet should represent the z-axis.

276

23. A hypersphere is a four-dimensional analog for a sphere, so it is the set of points in 4-space that are a given distance (the radius) from a point in 4-space (the center). If the four dimensions are x, y, z, and w, the center is at the 4-tuple (h, k, j, g), and the radius is r, then an equation for the hypersphere is $(x-h)^2 + (y-k)^2 + (z-j)^2 + (w-g)^2 = r^2$. A hypercube is a four-dimensional analog for a cube; it may be described as a four-dimensional figure each of whose sides is a cube.

CHAPTER 11 PROGRESS SELF-TEST   (p. 558)

1. $\overline{FD}$ connects the midpoints of $\overline{BC}$ and $\overline{AC}$, so $\overline{FD} \parallel \overline{AB}$ and $FD = \frac{1}{2}AB$ by the Midpoint Connector Theorem. $EB = \frac{1}{2}AB$ by the definition of midpoint (meaning), so $FD = EB$ by the Transitive Property of Equality. Then $EBDF$ is a parallelogram by the Sufficient Conditions for a Parallelogram Theorem, part d.

2. If $AB = 11$ and $BC = 22.3$, then $AE = EB = 5.5$ and $BD = DC = 11.15$ by the definition of midpoint (meaning), and $FD = 5.5$ and $ED = 11.15$ by the Midpoint Connector Theorem (while the lengths $AF = FC = ED$ and $AC = 2AF$ are not known, a restriction is that $11.15 - 5.5 = 5.65 < AC < 11.15 + 5.5 = 16.65$.)

3.

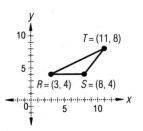

$RS = |3 - 8| = |\text{-}5| = 5$

$ST = \sqrt{(x_2 - x_1)^2 + (y_2 - y_1)^2}$
$\quad = \sqrt{(11 - 8)^2 + (8 - 4)^2}$
$\quad = \sqrt{3^2 + 4^2}$
$\quad = 5$

$RT = \sqrt{(x_2 - x_1)^2 + (y_2 - y_1)^2}$
$\quad = \sqrt{(11 - 3)^2 + (8 - 4)^2}$
$\quad = \sqrt{8^2 + 4^2}$
$\quad = \sqrt{64 + 16}$
$\quad = \sqrt{80}$

The perimeter is $5 + 5 + \sqrt{80} = 10 + \sqrt{80}$ ≈ 18.94 units.

4. The coordinates of the center of gravity are the means of the x- and y-coordinates:
$$\left(\frac{\text{-}5 + 6 + 9 + 6 + \text{-}8}{5}, \frac{4 + 4 + 0 + \text{-}4 + \text{-}4}{5} \right) =$$
$$\left(\frac{8}{5}, \frac{0}{5} \right) = (1.6, 0).$$

5. **a–b.** Comparing $(x + 1)^2 + (y - 9)^2 = 25$ with the general equation $(x - h)^2 + (y - k)^2 = r^2$, where (h, k) is the center and r is the radius, the center is $(\text{-}1, 9)$ and the radius is 5.

   c. Four points on the circle can be found by moving 5 units from the center; those four points are $(\text{-}6, 9)$, $(4, 9)$, $(\text{-}1, 14)$, and $(\text{-}1, 4)$.

6.

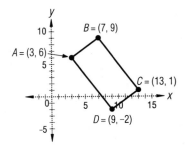

The slope of $\overline{AB} = \dfrac{y_2 - y_1}{x_2 - x_1} = \dfrac{9 - 6}{7 - 3} = \dfrac{3}{4}$.

The slope of $\overline{BC} = \dfrac{y_2 - y_1}{x_2 - x_1} = \dfrac{1 - 9}{13 - 7} = \dfrac{-8}{6} =$

$\dfrac{-4}{3} = -\dfrac{4}{3}$.

The slope of $\overline{CD} = \dfrac{y_2 - y_1}{x_2 - x_1} = \dfrac{-2 - 1}{9 - 13} =$

$\dfrac{-3}{-4} = \dfrac{3}{4}$.

The slope of $\overline{DA} = \dfrac{y_2 - y_1}{x_2 - x_1} = \dfrac{6 - -2}{3 - 9} = \dfrac{8}{-6} =$

$\dfrac{4}{-3} = -\dfrac{4}{3}$.

Since opposite sides are parallel (by the Parallel Lines and Slopes Theorem), $ABCD$ is a parallelogram. Since adjacent sides are $\perp$ (by the Perpendicular Lines and Slopes Theorem), $ABCD$ is a rectangle. The answer is choice (a).

7.

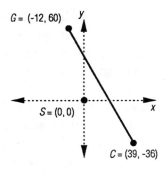

7. Place Selkirk at $(0,0)$. Then $G = (-12, 60)$ and $C = (39, -36)$.

The distance $GC = \sqrt{(x_2 - x_1)^2 + (y_2 - y_1)^2}$

$= \sqrt{(39 - -12)^2 + (-36 - 60)^2)} =$

$\sqrt{51^2 + (-96)^2} = \sqrt{2601 + 9216} =$

$\sqrt{11{,}817} \approx 108.7$ miles.

8.

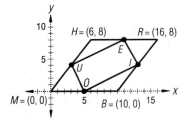

E is the midpoint of $\overline{HR}$; its coordinates are $\left(\dfrac{6 + 16}{2}, \dfrac{8 + 8}{2}\right) = \left(\dfrac{22}{2}, \dfrac{16}{2}\right) = (11, 8)$. I is the midpoint of $\overline{RB}$; its coordinates are $\left(\dfrac{10 + 16}{2}, \dfrac{0 + 8}{2}\right) = \left(\dfrac{26}{2}, \dfrac{8}{2}\right) = (13, 4)$. O is the midpoint of MB; its coordinates are $\left(\dfrac{0 + 10}{2}, \dfrac{0 + 0}{2}\right) = (5, 0)$. U is the midpoint of $\overline{MH}$; its coordinates are $\left(\dfrac{0 + 6}{2}, \dfrac{0 + 8}{2}\right) = (3, 4)$.

9. Here is one proof (of many possible) that *EIOU* is a rectangle: First, $EI = UO$ and $UE = OI$ (by drawing $\overline{HB}$ and $\overline{MR}$, and using the Midpoint Connector Theorem). So *EIOU* is a parallelogram by the Sufficient Conditions for a Parallelogram Theorem. The slope of $\overline{UO}$ is $\frac{y_2 - y_1}{x_2 - x_1} = \frac{0 - 4}{5 - 3} = \frac{-4}{2} = -2$ and the slope of $\overline{OI}$ is $\frac{y_2 - y_1}{x_2 - x_1} = \frac{4 - 0}{13 - 5} = \frac{4}{8} = \frac{1}{2}$. Then $\overline{UO} \perp \overline{OI}$ by the Perpendicular Lines and Slopes Theorem, so *EIOU* is a rectangle by the definition of rectangle (sufficient condition).

10.

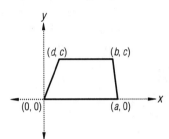

11. For $P = (3, -1, 8)$ and $Q = (-4, 9, 0)$, $\overline{PQ} = \sqrt{(x_2 - x_1)^2 + (y_2 - y_1)^2 + (z_2 - z_1)^2}$
$= \sqrt{(-4 - 3)^2 + (9 - -1)^2 + (0 - 8)^2} = \sqrt{(-7)^2 + (10)^2 + (-8)^2} = \sqrt{49 + 100 + 64} = \sqrt{213} \approx 14.59$ units.

12. Using the formula $(x - h)^2 + (y - k)^2 + (z - j)^2 = r^2$ with $(h, k, j) = (0, -19, 4)$ and $r = 6$, the equation is $(x - 0)^2 + (y - -19)^2 + (z - 4)^2 = 6^2$ or $x^2 + (y + 19)^2 + (z - 4)^2 = 36$.

13. $2x - 3y = 8$
$4x - 5y = 20$
Multiply the first equation by -2 to eliminate the *x*-variable:
$-4x + 6y = -16$
$\underline{4x - 5y = 20}$
$y = 4$
$2x - 3(4) = 8$
$2x - 12 = 8$
$2x = 20$
$x = 10$
The solution is $(10, 4)$.

14. The midpoint of $\overline{WY}$ is $\left(\frac{0 + (2a + 2b)}{2}, \frac{0 + (2c)}{2}\right) = (a + b, c)$, and the midpoint of $\overline{XZ}$ is $\left(\frac{2b + 2a}{2}, \frac{2c + 0}{2}\right) = (a + b, c)$. So $\overline{WY}$ and $\overline{XZ}$ have the same midpoint.

CHAPTER 11 REVIEW (pp. 559–561)

1.

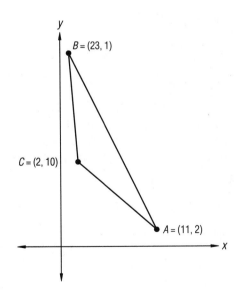

Find the lengths of the three sides of the triangle using the distance formula:

$$AB = \sqrt{(23 - 11)^2 + (1 - 2)^2}$$
$$= \sqrt{12^2 + (\text{-}1)^2}$$
$$= \sqrt{144 + 1}$$
$$= \sqrt{145};$$
$$BC = \sqrt{(23 - 2)^2 + (1 - 10)^2}$$
$$= \sqrt{21^2 + (\text{-}9)^2}$$
$$= \sqrt{441 + 81}$$
$$= \sqrt{522};$$
$$CA = \sqrt{(11 - 2)^2 + (2 - 10)^2}$$
$$= \sqrt{9^2 + (\text{-}8)^2}$$
$$= \sqrt{81 + 64}$$
$$= \sqrt{145}.$$

So $AB = CA$ by the Transitive Property of Equality, and $\triangle ABC$ is an isosceles triangle by the definition of isosceles triangle (sufficient condition).

2. Find the slopes of the three sides using the slope formula:

the slope of $\overline{XY}$ is $\dfrac{q - 0}{0 - q} = \dfrac{q}{\text{-}q} = \text{-}1$;

the slope of $\overline{YZ}$ is $\dfrac{3q - q}{2q - 0} = \dfrac{2q}{2q} = 1$;

the slope of $\overline{XZ}$ is $\dfrac{3q - 0}{2q - q} = \dfrac{3q}{q} = 3$.

The product of the slopes $\overline{XY}$ and $\overline{YZ}$ is -1, so $\overline{XY} \perp \overline{YZ}$ by the Perpendicular Lines and Slopes Theorem, and $\triangle XYZ$ is a right triangle by the definition of right triangle (sufficient condition).

3.

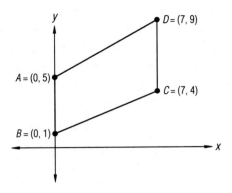

Sides $\overline{AB}$ and $\overline{CD}$ are parallel, since each is on a vertical line. Also, the length of $\overline{AB}$ is 4 units and the length of $\overline{CD}$ is 5 units. Find the lengths of the other two sides of the quadrilateral:

$$AD = \sqrt{(7 - 0)^2 + (9 - 5)^2}$$
$$= \sqrt{7^2 + 4^2}$$
$$= \sqrt{49 + 16}$$
$$= \sqrt{65}.$$
$$BC = \sqrt{(7 - 0)^2 + (4 - 1)^2}$$
$$= \sqrt{7^2 + 3^2}$$
$$= \sqrt{49 + 9}$$
$$= \sqrt{58}.$$

So two sides of the quadrilateral are parallel, and no pairs of consecutive sides are congruent. So the quadrilateral is **not** a kite and it **is** a trapezoid.

4.

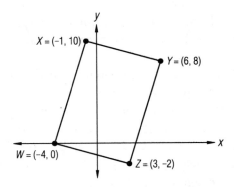

Find the slopes of the four sides:

the slope of $\overline{XY}$ is $\dfrac{10 - 8}{-1 - 6} = \dfrac{2}{-7} = -\dfrac{2}{7}$;

the slope of $\overline{YZ}$ is $\dfrac{8 - \text{-}2}{6 - 3} = \dfrac{10}{3}$;

the slope of $\overline{WZ} = \dfrac{\text{-}2 - 0}{3 - \text{-}4} = \dfrac{\text{-}2}{7} = -\dfrac{2}{7}$;

the slope of $\overline{XW} = \dfrac{10 - 0}{-1 - \text{-}4} = \dfrac{10}{3}$.

So opposite sides are parallel by the Parallel Lines and Slopes Theorem, and the figure is a parallelogram by the definition of parallelogram (sufficient condition). (Some alternative proofs, using the Sufficient Conditions for a Parallelogram Theorem, would be to show that both pairs of opposite sides are congruent, or that the diagonals bisect each other, or that one pair of sides is congruent and parallel.)

5. One way to prove that the segments joining consecutive midpoints are congruent is to use the midpoint formula and find the coordinates of the midpoints, then use the distance formula and find the lengths of those segments:

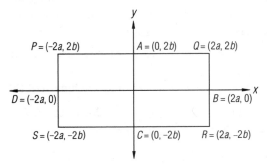

The midpoints of the horizontal segments have the same y-value as the endpoints and 0 for an x-value, and the midpoints of the vertical segments have the same x-value as the endpoints and 0 for a y-value, so $A = (0, 2b)$, $B = (2a, 0)$, $C = (0, \text{-}2b)$, and $D = (\text{-}2a, 0)$. Then:

$$AB = \sqrt{(0 - 2a)^2 + (2b - 0)^2}$$
$$= \sqrt{(\text{-}2a)^2 + (2b)^2}$$
$$= \sqrt{4a^2 + 4b^2}$$

Performing similar operations for the other segments, $BC = CD = DA = \sqrt{4a^2 + 4b^2}$, and all the segments have the same length. For another proof, note that each triangle PAD, QAB, RCB, and SCD is a right triangle with legs of lengths $2a$ and $2b$, so all four triangles are congruent by the SAS Congruent Theorem, and the hypotenuses are congruent by the CPCF Theorem.

6. The lengths of the two horizontal sides are $DC = (a + b) - b = a$ and $AB = a - 0 = a$, so $\overline{AB}$ and $\overline{DC}$ have the same length. $AD = \sqrt{(b - 0)^2 + (c - 0)^2} = \sqrt{b^2 + c^2}$, and $BC = \sqrt{(a + b - a)^2 + (c - 0)^2} = \sqrt{b^2 + c^2}$, so $\overline{AD}$ and $\overline{BC}$ have the same length.

7. The slope of diagonal $\overline{XZ}$ is $\frac{s-0}{0-s} = \frac{s}{-s} = -1$, and the slope of the diagonal $\overline{YW}$ is $\frac{s-0}{s-0} = \frac{s}{s} = 1$.

Since the product of those two slopes is -1, the two diagonals are perpendicular by the Perpendicular Lines and Slopes Theorem.

8. Triangle LNM is isosceles with vertex angle L. The midpoint of $\overline{LM}$ is $\left(\frac{0 + 2a}{2}, \frac{2b + 0}{2}\right)$ $= \left(\frac{2a}{2}, \frac{2b}{2}\right) = (a, b)$, and the length of the median connecting $N = (-2a, 0)$ to (a, b) is
$$\sqrt{(-2a - a)^2 + (0 - b)^2}$$
$$= \sqrt{(-3a)^2 + (-b)^2}$$
$$= \sqrt{9a^2 + b^2}.$$
Also, the midpoint of $\overline{LN}$ is $\left(\frac{0 + -2a}{2}, \frac{2b + 0}{2}\right) = \left(\frac{-2a}{2}, \frac{2b}{2}\right) = (-a, b)$, and the length of the median connecting $M = (2a, 0)$ to $(-a, b)$ is
$$\sqrt{(2a - -a)^2 + (0 - b)^2}$$
$$= \sqrt{(3a)^2 + (-b)^2}$$
$$= \sqrt{9a^2 + b^2}.$$
So the two medians have the same length. Since LNM represents any isosceles triangle, then in any isosceles triangle, the two medians from the base angles to the midpoints of the congruent sides have the same length.

9. If W is the midpoint of $\overline{VX}$ and $VW = 41$, then $WX = 41$ by the definition of midpoint (meaning), and $VX = 82$ by addition (or by the Betweenness Property, since $VW + WX = VX$). Points Y and W are midpoints and $YW = 40$, so $ZV = 80$ by the Midpoint Connector Theorem. ZX is less than $80 + 82$ and is greater than $82 - 80$, by the Triangle Inequality, so ZX is between 162 and 2, and each of ZY and YX is half that value by the definition of midpoint (meaning).

10. Points Y and W are midpoints, so $\overline{YW} \parallel \overline{ZV}$ by the Midpoint Connector Theorem, and so $m\angle XWY = m\angle XVZ$ because $\parallel$ lines $\Rightarrow$ corr. $\angle$s $=$.

11. Points E and F are midpoints, so $\overline{EF} \parallel \overline{DB}$ by the Midpoint Connector Theorem, and $BDEF$ is a trapezoid by the definition of trapezoid (sufficient condition). (Also, the sides $\overline{CB}$ and $\overline{CD}$ of the rhombus are congruent, so the "half-sides" $\overline{BF}$ and $\overline{DE}$ are congruent, and $BDEF$ is an isosceles trapezoid.)

12. If $BC = 6$, then $AB = AD = DC = 6$ by the definition of rhombus (meaning), and $BF = FC = DE = EC = 3$ by the definition of midpoint (meaning). And since $BD = 10$, then $EF = 5$ by the Midpoint Connector Theorem.

13. The x-value of the balance point (center of gravity) is the mean of the x-values of the vertices, and the y-value of the balance point is the mean of the y-values of the vertices. So the balance point is
$$\left(\frac{0 + 4 + 4 + -4 + -4}{5}, \frac{-6 + -3 + 3 + 3 + -3}{5}\right)$$
$$= \left(\frac{0}{5}, \frac{-6}{5}\right)$$
$$= (0, -1.2).$$

14. The x-value of the center of gravity is the mean of the x-values of the vertices, and the y-value of the balance point is the mean of the y-values of the vertices. So the center of gravity is
$$\left(\frac{0 + 4 + 0}{3}, \frac{0 + 0 + 3}{3}\right) = \left(\frac{4}{3}, \frac{3}{3}\right) = \left(\frac{4}{3}, 1\right).$$

15. A segment has two "vertices" or endpoints, so the center of gravity of a segment is the midpoint of that segment.

16. If 8 cm is cut from the "zero" end and 3 cm is cut from the "hundred" end, the two endpoints will read 8 and 97, and the balance point of that stick will read $\frac{8 + 97}{2} = \frac{105}{2} =$ 52.5 cm. Or, if 8 cm is cut from the "hundred" end and 3 cm is cut from the "zero" end, the two endpoints will read 3 and 92 and the balance point will read $\frac{3 + 92}{2} = \frac{95}{2} = 47.5$ cm.

17. The total trip is $5 + 6 = 11$ miles north and $2 + 3 = 5$ miles east. The hypotenuse of a right triangle with legs 11 and 5 is $\sqrt{11^2 + 5^2}$ $= \sqrt{121 + 25} = \sqrt{146} \approx 12.08$ miles.

18. a.

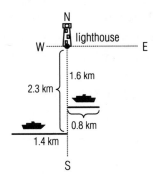

b. If the coordinates of the lighthouse are (0, 0), then the two ships have coordinates (-1.4, -2.3) and (.8, -1.6). The distance between these two points is
$$\sqrt{(-1.4 - .8)^2 + (-2.3 - -1.6)^2}$$
$$= \sqrt{(-2.2)^2 + (-7)^2}$$
$$= \sqrt{4.84 + 49}$$
$$= \sqrt{5.33}$$
$$\approx 2.3 \text{ km.}$$

19. Using the formula for the diagonal of a box, the length of the longest dowel is $\sqrt{8^2 + 12^2 + 24^2} = \sqrt{64 + 144 + 576} = \sqrt{784} = 28$ inches.

20. Using the formula for the diagonal of a box, the length of the longest straw that will fit in the crate is $\sqrt{45^2 + 30^2 + 80^2} =$ $\sqrt{2025 + 900 + 6400} = \sqrt{9325} \approx 96.566 \approx$ 96.6 mm.

21. The distance between (3, 5) and (-7, -1) is
$$\sqrt{(3 - -7)^2 + (5 - -1)^2}$$
$$= \sqrt{10^2 + 6^2}$$
$$= \sqrt{100 + 36}$$
$$= \sqrt{136}$$
$$\approx 11.66 \text{ units.}$$

22. The distance between (a, b) and the origin is the hypotenuse of a right triangle with legs a and b; that is $\sqrt{a^2 + b^2}$.

23. The length of the side connecting (3, 2) and (3, 7) is 5 units.
The length of the side connecting (3, 2) and (6, 11) is $\sqrt{(3 - 6)^2 + (2 - 11)^2}$
$$= \sqrt{(-3)^2 + (-9)^2}$$
$$= \sqrt{9 + 81}$$
$$= \sqrt{90}.$$
The length of the side connecting (3, 7) and (6, 11) is $\sqrt{(3 - 6)^2 + (7 - 11)^2}$
$$= \sqrt{(-3)^2 + (-4)^2}$$
$$= 5 \text{ (it is a 3-4-5- right triangle).}$$
So the perimeter of the triangle is
$5 + \sqrt{90} + 5 = 10 + \sqrt{90} \approx 10 + 9.49$
$= 19.49.$

24.

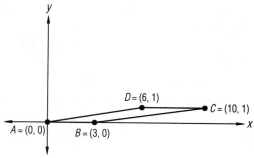

The two oblique sides are longer than the two horizontal sides.

$AD = \sqrt{6^2 + 1^2} = \sqrt{36 + 1} = \sqrt{37}$, and

$BC = \sqrt{(10 - 3)^2 + (1 - 0)^2}$
$= \sqrt{7^2 + 1^2}$
$= \sqrt{49 + 1}$
$= \sqrt{50}$.

So $\overline{BC}$ is the longest side of trapezoid $ABCD$.

25. Using the general equation for a circle, $(x - h)^2 + (y - k)^2 = r^2$, with $(h, k) = (8, -1)$ and $r = 15$, the equation is
$(x - 8)^2 + (y - -1)^2 = 15^2$ or
$(x - 8)^2 + (y + 1)^2 = 225$.

26. Using the general equation for a circle, $(x - h)^2 + (y - k)^2 = r^2$, with $(h, k) = (0, 6)$ and $r = 4$, the equation is $(x - 0)^2 + (y - 6)^2 = 4^2$ or $x^2 + (y - 6)^2 = 16$.

27. a-b. Rewriting the equation of the circle, $(x - 6)^2 + (y + 3)^2 = 169$ as $(x - 6)^2 + (y - -3)^2 = 13^2$ and comparing that with the general equation for a circle, $(x - h)^2 + (y - k)^2 = r^2$, then the center is (6, -3) and the radius is 13.

c. You can find four points on the circle by moving 13 units horizontally or vertically from the center (6, -3). Those four points are (19, -3), (6, 10), (-7, -3), and (6, -16).
[Other points are 5 and 12 units vertically or horizontally from the center, because 5, 12, 13 is a Pythagorean Triple. Those points are (18, 2), (11, 9), (1, 9), (-6, 2), (-6, -8), (1, -15), and (11, -15).]

28. a-b. Rewriting the equation of the circle, $x^2 + y^2 = 50$ as $(x - 0)^2 + (y - 0)^2 = (\sqrt{50})^2$, and comparing that with $(x - h)^2 + (y - k)^2 = r^2$, then the center is (0, 0) and the radius is $\sqrt{50} = 5\sqrt{2}$.

c. Four points on the circle are $\sqrt{50}$ units from the center, horizontally or vertically. Those points are $(\sqrt{50}, 0)$, $(0, \sqrt{50})$, $(-\sqrt{50}, 0)$, $(0, -\sqrt{50})$.

29.

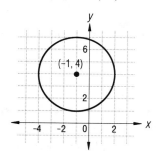

30.

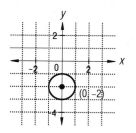

31. The midpoint of the segment joining (3, 2)
and (6, -2) is $\left(\frac{3+6}{2}, \frac{2+-2}{2}\right) = \left(\frac{9}{2}, \frac{0}{2}\right) =$
(4.5, 0).

32. The midpoint of the segment joining (2a, 2b)
and (0, 2c) is $\left(\frac{2a+0}{2}, \frac{2b+2c}{2}\right) =$
(a, b + c).

33. The midpoint of the segment connecting
(50, -10) and (60, 70) is $\left(\frac{50+60}{2}, \frac{-10+70}{2}\right)$
$= \left(\frac{110}{2}, \frac{60}{2}\right) = (55, 30)$. Then the slope of
the line through (0, 0) and (55, 30) is $\frac{30-0}{55-0}$
$= \frac{30}{55} = \frac{6}{11} \approx 0.55$.

34. The midpoint of $\overline{AC}$ is $\left(\frac{3+9}{2}, \frac{0+8}{2}\right) =$
$\left(\frac{12}{2}, \frac{8}{2}\right) = (6, 4)$, and the length of the
segment connecting (4, 5) to (6, 4) is
$\sqrt{(4-6)^2 + (5-4)^2}$
$= \sqrt{(-2)^2 + 1^2}$
$= \sqrt{4+1}$
$= \sqrt{5}$
≈ 2.24 units.

35.

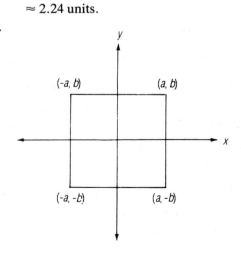

36.

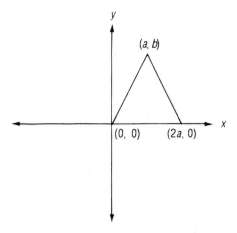

37.

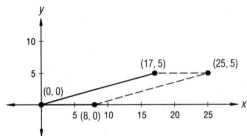

The movement from (0, 0) to (17, 5) is 17
units to the right and 5 units up. A similar
movement from (8, 0) is (8 + 17, 0 + 5) =
(25, 5).

38.

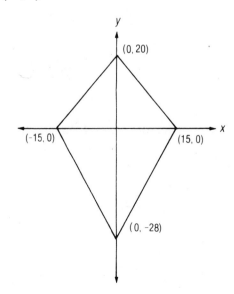

39. a.

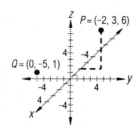

b. The midpoint of $(-2, 3, 6)$ and $(0, -5, 1)$ is

$$\left(\frac{-2 + 0}{2}, \frac{3 + -5}{2}, \frac{6 + 1}{2}\right)$$

$$= \left(\frac{-2}{2}, \frac{-2}{2}, \frac{7}{2}\right)$$

$$= (-1, -1, 3.5).$$

c. The distance between $(-2, 3, 6)$ and $(0, -5, 1)$ is

$$\sqrt{(-2 - 0)^2 + (3 - -5)^2 + (6 - 1)^2}$$

$$= \sqrt{(-2)^2 + 8^2 + 5^2}$$

$$= \sqrt{4 + 64 + 25}$$

$$= \sqrt{93}$$

$$\approx 9.64 \text{ units.}$$

40. a.

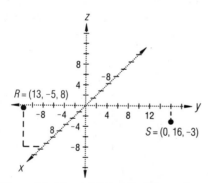

b. The midpoint of $(13, -5, 8)$ and $(0, 16, -3)$

is $\left(\frac{13 + 0}{2}, \frac{-5 + 16}{2}, \frac{8 + -3}{2}\right)$

$$= \left(\frac{13}{2}, \frac{11}{2}, \frac{5}{2}\right)$$

$$= (6.5, 5.5, 2.5).$$

c. The distance between $(13, -5, 8)$ and $(0, 16, -3)$ is

$$\sqrt{(13 - 0)^2 + (-5 - 16)^2 + (8 - -3)^2}$$

$$= \sqrt{13^2 + (-21)^2 + 11^2}$$

$$= \sqrt{169 + 441 + 121}$$

$$= \sqrt{731}$$

$$\approx 27.04 \text{ units.}$$

41. Using the general equation of a sphere, $(x - h)^2 + (y - k)^2 + (z - j)^2 = r^2$ with $(h, k, j) = (4, -3, 0)$ and $r = 10$, then the equation is
$(x - 4)^2 + (y - -3)^2 + (z - 0)^2 = 10^2$ or
$(x - 4)^2 + (y + 3)^2 + z^2 = 100$.

42. Rewriting the equation
$(x - 1)^2 + (y + 2)^2 + (z - 5)^2 = 4$ as
$(x - 1)^2 + (y - -2)^2 + (z - 5)^2 = 2^2$ and
comparing that with the general equation,
$(x - h)^2 + (y - k)^2 + (z - j)^2 = r^2$, the
center is $(1, -2, 5)$ and the radius is 2.

43. Multiply the second equation by 2 and add them:

$$2x + y = 5$$
$$-x - 5y = 11$$

$$\begin{array}{r} 2x + y = 5 \\ -2x - 10y = 22 \\ \hline -9y = 27 \\ y = -3. \end{array}$$

Substituting $y = -3$ into the first equation,
$$2x + -3 = 5$$
$$2x = 8$$
$$x = 4.$$

The solution is $(4, -3)$.
To check:
In the first equation, is $2(4) + -3 = 5$? Yes.
In the second equation, is $-4 - 5(-3) = 11$?
That is, is $-4 + 15 = 11$? Yes.

44. Add the equations:
$$x + y = 180$$
$$\underline{x - y = 25}$$
$$2x = 205$$
$$x = 102.5.$$
Substitute $x = 102.5$ into the first equation:
$$102.5 + y = 180$$
$$y = 77.5$$
The solution is $(102.5, 77.5)$.
To check:
In the first equation, is $102.5 + 77.5 = 180$?
Yes.
In the second equation,
is $102.5 - 77.5 = 25$? Yes.

45. Substituting the value of x in the second equation into the first equation:
$$y - 3x = 8$$
$$x = 7$$
$$y - 3(7) = 8$$
$$y - 21 = 8$$
$$y = 29.$$
The solution is $(7, 29)$.
To check:
In the first equation, is $29 - 3(7) = 8$?
That is, is $29 - 21 = 8$? Yes.
In the second equation, is $7 = 7$? Yes.

LESSON 12–1   (pp. 562–568)

1. Occupations which use scale models include clothes designers, city planners, scientists, automobile designers, and model car, plane, or train enthusiasts.

2. For $B' = (-10, -4)$ and $C' = (0, 2)$, the slope of $\overline{B'C'}$ is $\frac{y_2 - y_1}{x_2 - x_1} = \frac{2 - -4}{0 - -10} = \frac{6}{10} = \frac{3}{5}$. Then, for $B = (-15, -6)$ and $C = (0, 3)$, the slope of $\overline{BC}$ is $\frac{y_2 - y_1}{x_2 - x_1} = \frac{3 - -6}{0 - -15} = \frac{9}{15} = \frac{3}{5}$. So $\overline{B'C'}$ and $\overline{BC}$ have the same slope, and $\overline{B'C'} \parallel \overline{BC}$ by the Parallel Lines and Slopes Theorem.

3. For $B' = (-10, -4)$ and $C' = (0, 2)$,
$$B'C' = \sqrt{(x_1 - x_2)^2 + (y_1 - y_2)^2}$$
$$= \sqrt{(-10 - 0)^2 + (-4 - 2)^2}$$
$$= \sqrt{(-10)^2 + (-6)^2}$$
$$= \sqrt{100 + 36}$$
$$= \sqrt{136}$$
$$= \sqrt{(4)(34)}$$
$$= 2\sqrt{34}.$$
For $B = (-15, -6)$ and $C = (0, 3)$,
$$BC = \sqrt{(x_1 - x_2)^2 + (y_1 - y_2)^2}$$
$$= \sqrt{(-15 - 0)^2 + (-6 - 3)^2}$$
$$= \sqrt{(-15)^2 + (-9)^2}$$
$$= \sqrt{225 + 81}$$
$$= \sqrt{306}$$
$$= \sqrt{(9)(34)}$$
$$= 3\sqrt{34}.$$
So $B'C' = \frac{2}{3}BC$.

4. **a.** S_k is the tranformation which maps (x, y) onto (kx, ky).
   b. The number k is the magnitude of S_k.

5. **a.**

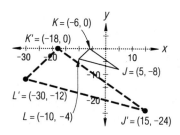

   b. The image of $\triangle JKL$ has sides with lengths three times the length of the sides of $\triangle JKL$. The angles of the two triangles are congruent.

6. **a.** $P' = S_7(P) = S_7(-2, 11) = [(7)(-2), (7)(11)] = (-14, 77).$
   $Q' = S_7(Q) = S_7(3, -5) = [(7)(3), (7)(-5)] = (21, -35).$
   b. The slope of $\overline{QP} = \frac{-5 - 11}{3 - -2} = \frac{-16}{5}.$
   The slope of $\overline{Q'P'} = \frac{-35 - 77}{21 - -14} = \frac{-112}{35} = \frac{-16}{5}.$
   So the slopes of $\overline{QP}$ and $\overline{Q'P'}$ are equal.
   c. $Q'P' = \sqrt{(-14 - 21)^2 + (77 - -35)^2}$
   $$= \sqrt{(-35)^2 + 112^2}$$
   $$= \sqrt{1225 + 12,544}$$
   $$= \sqrt{13,769}$$
   $$= \sqrt{(49)(281)}$$
   $$= 7\sqrt{281}$$
   $QP = \sqrt{(-2 - 3)^2 + (11 - -5)^2}$
   $$= \sqrt{(-5)^2 + 16^2}$$
   $$= \sqrt{25 + 256}$$
   $$= \sqrt{281}$$
   So $Q'P' = 7 \cdot QP.$

7. Property 3 is that the image of a point is between the preimage and the origin.

$$OA' = \sqrt{(-6)^2 + 10^2}$$
$$= \sqrt{36 + 100}$$
$$= \sqrt{136}$$
$$= 2\sqrt{34}$$

$$OA = \sqrt{(-9)^2 + 15^2}$$
$$= \sqrt{81 + 225}$$
$$= \sqrt{306}$$
$$= 3\sqrt{34}$$

$$AA' = \sqrt{(-9 - -6)^2 + (15 - 10)^2}$$
$$= \sqrt{(-3)^2 + 5^2}$$
$$= \sqrt{9 + 25}$$
$$= \sqrt{34}$$

Since $AA' + OA' = OA$, then A' is between O and A.

8.

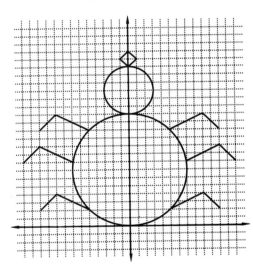

9. a. $S_1(x, y) = (1x, 1y) = (x, y)$, so the image of (x, y) under S_1 is the same point (x, y).

b. S_1 is the identity size transformation, because it maps a point onto itself.

10. The height of the cabin is represented by the point $(0, 12)$. Since each unit on the paper is one quarter inch, the point $(0, 12)$ is 3 inches from the floor of the cabin. The actual height is 48 times that, so the height of the cabin is $(3)(48) = 144$ inches $= 12$ feet.

11. a. $P' = S_5(P) = S_5(-3, 12, 4)$
$$= [(5)(-3), (5)(12), (5)(4)]$$
$$= (-15, 60, 20).$$

b. $Q' = S_5(Q) = S_5(2, -8, 0)$
$$= [(5)(2), (5)(-8), (5)(0)]$$
$$= (10, -40, 0).$$

c. $QP = \sqrt{(-3-2)^2 + (12--8)^2 + (4-0)^2}$
$$= \sqrt{(-5)^2 + 20^2 + 4^2}$$
$$= \sqrt{25 + 400 + 16}$$
$$= \sqrt{441}$$
$$= 21$$

$Q'P' = \sqrt{(-15-10)^2 + (60--40)^2 + (20-0)^2}$
$$= \sqrt{(-25)^2 + 100^2 + 20^2}$$
$$= \sqrt{625 + 10,000 + 400}$$
$$= \sqrt{11,025}$$
$$= 105$$

So $Q'P' = 5 \cdot QP$.

12. a. $\overleftrightarrow{LK} \parallel \overleftrightarrow{FG}$, so m$\angle L$ = m$\angle F$, and m$\angle K$ = m$\angle G$ because $\parallel$ lines $\Rightarrow$ AIA $=$. Also, $LM = MF$ by the definition of midpoint (meaning). So $\triangle KLM \cong \triangle GFM$ by the AAS Congruence Theorem.
(A similar proof uses the vertical angles at M and either the ASA or AAS Congruence Theorem.)

b. Using the congruence in part a, $MG = MK$ by the CPCF Theorem.

13. The Figure Reflection Theorem states that if a figure is determined by certain points, then its reflection image is the corresponding figure determined by the reflection images of those points.

14.

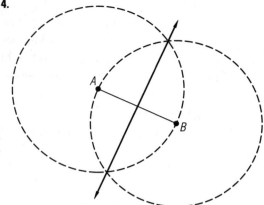

15. If $\frac{2}{9} = \frac{3}{x}$, then by the means-extremes product, $2x = 27$. So $x = 13.5$ by the Multiplication Property of Equality.

16. If $\frac{2y - 5}{5} = \frac{3y + 14}{8}$

then $(8)(2y - 5) = (5)(3y + 14)$.

So $16y - 40 = 15y + 70$

$y - 40 = 70$

$y = 110$.

17. *A* and *B* are points, so *AB* represents a number.

$AB - 9 = \frac{3}{4}AB$

$\frac{1}{4}AB - 9 = 0$

$\frac{1}{4}AB = 9$

$AB = 36$

18. a. The vertices of $\triangle JKL$ are $J = (5, -8)$, $K = (-6, 0)$, and $L = (-10, -4)$. Multiplying the coordinates by -3, the new coordinates are:

$[(-3)(5), (-3)(-8)] = (-15, 24)$;

$[((-3)(-6), (-3)(0)] = (18, 0)$;

$[(-3)(-10), (-3)(-4)] = (30, 12)$.

b. The figure formed by these new coordinates is a triangle whose sides have three times the length of the sides of the original triangle and whose angles are congruent to the angles of the original triangle. It is rotated 180° about the origin.

c. In general, the result of multiplying the coordinates of the vertices of a triangle (or other figure) by a negative constant is to determine the vertices of another figure similar to the first figure. Also, each figure is a size change image of the other and is rotated 180° about the origin.

LESSON 12-2 (pp. 569–574)

1. In the expansion of the face in this lesson, the center is the point *O* and the magnitude is the number 2.5.

2. In the contraction of the face in this lesson, the center is the point *O* and the magnitude is the number $\frac{1}{3}$.

3.

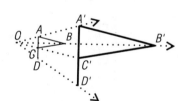

4.

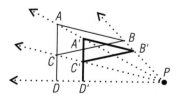

5. If S is a size transformation with scale factor 6 and center *O*, and if *A* is any point, then S(*A*) is 6 times as far from *O* as *A* is.

6. a. $A'B'C'D'$ is farther from O than $ABCD$ is and the sides of $A'B'C'D'$ are longer than the sides of $ABCD$. So the size change from $ABCD$ to $A'B'C'D'$ is an expansion.

b. If $OA = 10$ and $AA' = 4$, then, since A', A, and O are collinear, $OA' = 14$ so $\frac{OA'}{OA} = \frac{14}{10} = 1.4$; the magnitude of the size change is 1.4.

7. If k is the scale factor of an expansion, then $k > 1$.

8. If k is the scale factor of a contraction, then $0 < k < 1$.

9. In order to show that the transformation S_k is a size change of magnitude k with center O, the two statements that must be proved for the preimage point $P = (a, b)$ and its image point $P' = (ka, kb)$ are:
(1) P' lies on ray $\overrightarrow{OP}$;
(2) $OP' = k \cdot OP$.

10. If $k = \frac{2}{3}$, then the distance from the center O to the image points is $\frac{2}{3}$ the distance from the center O to the preimage points. So if $OA = 9$, then OA' is $\frac{2}{3}(9) = 6$. Also, since $OA' + AA' = OA$ by the definition of betweenness, then $6 + AA' = 9$, so $AA' = 3$.

11. For center O, preimage point B, and image point B', $OB' = k \cdot OB$ so $k = \frac{OB'}{OB}$. Using $OB = 5$ and $OB' = 3$, then $k = \frac{3}{5}$.

12. For center O, preimage point C, and image point C', $OC' = k \cdot OC$. If it is given that $OC' = 2 \cdot OC$, then $k = 2$.

13. From $\frac{OB}{OB'} = \frac{4}{3}$, form the equivalent proportion $\frac{OB'}{OB} = \frac{3}{4}$. Then multiply both sides of the equation by OB to get $OB' = \frac{3}{4} \cdot OB$. This is of the form $OB' = k \cdot OB$, so $k = \frac{3}{4}$.

14.

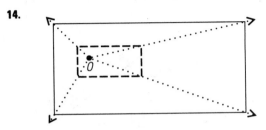

15.

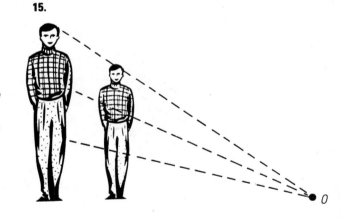

16.

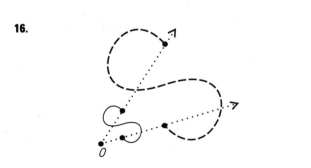

17.

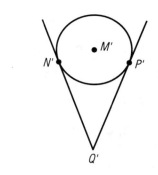

18.

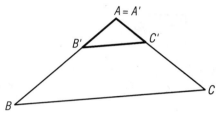

19.

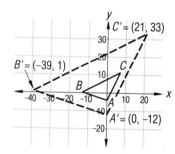

$A' = S_3(A) = S_3(0, -4)$

$$= [(3)(0), (3)(-4)]$$
$$= (0, -12)$$

$B' = S_3(B) = S_3\left(-13, \frac{1}{3}\right)$

$$= [(3)(-13), (3)\left(\frac{1}{3}\right)]$$
$$= (-39, 1)$$

$C' = S_3(C) = S_3(7, 11)$

$$= [(3)(7), (3)(11)]$$
$$= (21, 33)$$

20. a. The slope of $\overleftrightarrow{PQ}$ is $\frac{y_2 - y_1}{x_2 - x_1} = \frac{8 - 2}{-4 - 9} = \frac{6}{-13}$;

the slope of $\overleftrightarrow{PR}$ is $\frac{y_2 - y_1}{x_2 - x_1} = \frac{-10 - 2}{35 - 9} = \frac{-12}{26}$

$$= -\frac{6}{13}.$$

Since both lines have the same slope and contain point P, the lines coincide; P, Q, and R are collinear.

b. $QP = \sqrt{(9 - -4)^2 + (2 - 8)^2} =$

$\sqrt{13^2 + (-6)^2} = \sqrt{169 + 36} = \sqrt{205}$

$PR = \sqrt{(9 - 35)^2 + (2 - -10)^2} =$

$\sqrt{(-26)^2 + 12^2} = \sqrt{676 + 144} = \sqrt{820} =$

$2\sqrt{205}$

$QR = \sqrt{(-4 - 35)^2 + (8 - -10)^2} =$

$\sqrt{(-39)^2 + 18^2} = \sqrt{1521 + 324} =$

$\sqrt{1845} = 3\sqrt{205}$

Since $QP + PR = QR$, then P is between Q and R.

c. $P' = S_4(P) = S_4(9, 2)$

$$= [(4)(9), (4)(2)]$$
$$= (36, 8)$$

$Q' = S_4(Q) = S_4(-4, 8)$

$$= [(4)(-4), (4)(8)]$$
$$= (-16, 32)$$

$R' = S_4(R) = S_4(35, -10)$

$$= [(4)(35), (4)(-10)]$$
$$= (140, -40)$$

d. The slope of $\overleftrightarrow{P'Q'}$ is $\frac{y_2 - y_1}{x_2 - x_1} = \frac{32 - 8}{-16 - 36} =$

$\frac{24}{-52} = -\frac{6}{13}.$

The slope of $\overleftrightarrow{P'R'}$ is $\frac{y_2 - y_1}{x_2 - x_1} = \frac{-40 - 8}{140 - 36} =$

$\frac{-48}{104} = -\frac{6}{13}.$

Since both lines have the same slope, and both contain point P', the lines coincide; P', Q', and R' are collinear.

e. $P'R' = \sqrt{(140 - 36)^2 + (-40 - 8)^2} =$
$\sqrt{104^2 + (-48)^2} = \sqrt{10,816 + 2304} =$
$\sqrt{13,120} = \sqrt{(64)(205)} = 8\sqrt{205}$
$P'Q' = \sqrt{(-16 - 36)^2 + (32 - 8)^2} =$
$\sqrt{(-52)^2 + 24^2} = \sqrt{2704 + 576} =$
$\sqrt{3280} = 4\sqrt{205}$
$Q'R' = \sqrt{(140 - \text{-}16)^2 + (-40 - 32)^2} =$
$\sqrt{156^2 + (-72)^2} = \sqrt{24,336 + 5184} =$
$\sqrt{29,520} = \sqrt{(9)(3280)} = 3\sqrt{3280} =$
$3\sqrt{(16)(205)} = 12\sqrt{205}$
Since $Q'P' + P'R' = Q'R'$, then P' is between Q' and R'.

21. Using the Pythagorean Theorem,
$AC^2 = AB^2 + BC^2$
$\quad = 300^2 + 400^2$
$\quad = 90,000 + 160,000$
$\quad = 250,000$
So $AC = \sqrt{250,000} = \sqrt{(500)(500)} = 500$.
(Note that $\triangle ABC$ is a 3-4-5 right triangle.)
So the perimeter of $\triangle ABC$ is $300' + 400' + 500' = 1200'$.

22. The figure of Question 21 has 2 even vertices (B and D) and 2 odd vertices (A and C). Since it has no more than 2 odd vertices, it is traversable.
Start at either odd vertex:

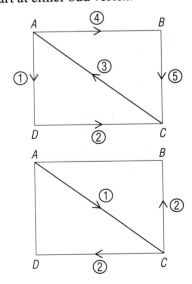

23. a. 1 mile = 5280 feet, and 1 foot = 12 inches, so
1 mile = (5280)(12) = 63,360 inches.
b. 1 kilometer = 1000 meters, and
1 meter = 1000 millimeters, so
1 kilometer = (1000)(1000)
$\qquad\qquad$ = 1,000,000 millimeters.

24. a. $\dfrac{z + 1}{2} = \dfrac{30}{40}$
$\quad (40)(z + 1) = (2)(30)$
$\quad\quad 40z + 40 = 60$
$\quad\quad\quad\quad 40z = 20$
$\quad\quad\quad\quad\quad z = \dfrac{20}{40} = \dfrac{1}{2}$

b. $\dfrac{M}{5} = \dfrac{6}{M}$
$M^2 = 30$
$M = \pm\sqrt{30} \approx \pm 5.477 \approx \pm 5.5$

25.

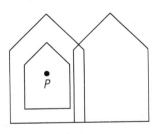

The images are congruent to each other and similar to the original pentagon.

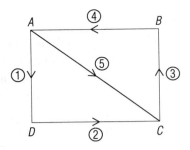

LESSON 12-3 (pp. 575–580)

1. The Size Change Distance Theorem states that the distance between any two image points is k times the distance between their preimages. That can be restated: k is the distance between two image points divided by the distance between two corresponding preimage points. So if you know the lengths of a segment and its image under a size change, you can find the magnitude of the size change by dividing the image distance by the preimage distance.

2. The Size Change Distance Theorem, which states that the distance between any two image points is k times the distance between their preimages, does not mention the location of the center of the size change. So it is *false* that the length of the image depends on the location of the center of the size change.

3. Under a size tranformation, the size of an image segment is not necessarily the same as the size of its preimage segment. So it is *false* that size transformations preserve distance.

4. If image distances are k times actual size, then the actual-size measurements are $\frac{1}{k}$ times the measurements of the image. If a leg in the image is 3 cm, then the actual leg is $\frac{3}{k}$ cm.

5. The Size Change Theorem states that size transformations preserve angle measure, betweenness, and collinearity. (Also, lines and their images are parallel.)

6. Size tranformations preserve angle measures, and $\angle TJK$ corresponds with $\angle T'J'K'$. So given that $m\angle T'J'K' = 43$, then $m\angle TJK = 43$.

7. If $\overleftrightarrow{CD}$ is the image of $\overleftrightarrow{AB}$ under a size transformation, then $\overleftrightarrow{CD} \parallel \overleftrightarrow{AB}$ by the Size Change Theorem.

8. The images of points B, C, and D are T, E, and J, respectively, so $S(\angle BCD) = \angle TEJ$ by the Figure Size Change Theorem.

9. By the Figure Size Change Theorem, the image of $\angle BAD$ is $\angle TXJ$, so if $m\angle BAD = 73$, then $m\angle TXJ = 73$ by the Size Change Theorem.

10. If $S(TINY) = HUGE$, then in particular $S(N) = G$.

11. **a.** By the Size Change Distance Theorem, EF is k times BC. Given that $EF = 20$ and $BC = 8$, then $20 = k(8)$ or $k = \frac{20}{8} = 2.5$.

   b. By the Size Change Distance Theorem, $DE = k \cdot AB = (2.5)(6) = 15$.

   c. By the Size Change Distance Theorem, $DF = k \cdot AC$, so $AC = \frac{DF}{k} = \frac{30}{2.5} = 12$.

12. **a.** By the Size Change Distance Theorem, MO is k times MS, or $10 = k(16)$, so $k = \frac{10}{16} = \frac{5}{8} = 0.625$.

   b. $T(M) = M$, so M is the center of T.

   c. By the Size Change Distance Theorem, $OR = k \cdot SA = \frac{5}{8}(12) = \frac{60}{8} = 7.5$ units.

   d. By the Size Change Distance Theorem, $MI = k \cdot ME$, so $ME = \frac{MI}{k} = \frac{13}{.625} = 20.8$ units.

13.

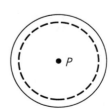

14.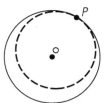

15.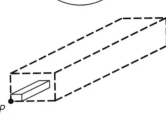

16. **a.** By the Size Change Distance Theorem, the width of the image, 7 cm, is k times the width of the preimage, 5 cm, or $7 = 5k$, so $k = \frac{7}{5} = 1.4$.

b. By the Size Change Distance Theorem, the length ℓ of the image is k times the length 12 cm of the preimage, so $\ell = (1.4)(12) = 16.8$ cm.

c. The measurements of the preimage are 5 cm and 12 cm, so its area is $(5)(12) = 60$ cm^2.
The measurements of the image are 7 cm and 16.8 cm, so its area is $(7)(16.8) = 117.6$ cm^2.

d. The area of the enlargement is $\frac{117.6}{60} = 1.96$ times the area of the original. (Note: $1.96 = 1.4^2$, so the ratio of the areas is the square of the ratio of the sides.)

e. The perimeter of the enlargement is $2(7 + 16.8) = 2(23.8) = 47.6$ cm, and the perimeter of the original is $2(5 + 12) = 2(17) = 34$ cm. So the perimeter of the enlargement is $\frac{47.6}{34} = 1.4$ times the perimeter of the original. (Note: the ratio of the perimeters is the same as the ratio of the sides.)

17. By the Size Change Distance Theorem, $OB = k \cdot OA$, so $7 = k \cdot 6$, and $k = \frac{7}{6}$. Also by the Size Change Distance Theorem, $OD = k \cdot OC$ and $BD = k \cdot AC$, so:
$OD = \frac{7}{6}(6.1) = \frac{42.7}{6} = \frac{427}{60} \approx 7.117$;
$AC = \frac{BD}{k} = \frac{4}{\frac{7}{6}} = \frac{24}{7} \approx 3.43$;
$OB = OA + AB = 6 + 1 = 7$;
$CD = OD - OC \approx 7.117 - 6.1 = 1.017$.

18. $k = 2$

Figure A   Figure B

19. By the Size Change Distance Theorem, 1 cm (the distance on the image) is k times 1 km (the distance on the preimage). Since 1 cm is $\frac{1}{100}$ of a meter, and 1 meter is $\frac{1}{1000}$ of a kilometer, then 1 cm is $\frac{1}{100,000}$ of 1 km, and the scale of the map is $\frac{1}{100,000}$ or 1:100,000.

20. From $P = (4, -6)$ and $P' = (2, -3)$, it can be seen that $k = \frac{1}{2}$. So:
$Q' = k(Q) = k(-9, 12) = (-4.5, 6)$;
$T' = k(T) = k(0, -8) = (0, -4)$;
$R' = k(R)$, so $(5, 13) = \frac{1}{2}(R)$ and
$R = (10, 26)$.

21. The anchor line is the hypotenuse of a right triangle with legs 9′ and 15′. So the hypotenuse is $\sqrt{9^2 + 15^2} = \sqrt{306} \approx 17.5$ feet. The anchor line should be about $17\frac{1}{2}$ feet long.

22.

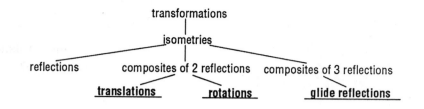

transformations
|
isometries
|
reflections — composites of 2 reflections — composites of 3 reflections
| | |
translations   **rotations**   **glide reflections**

23. $\dfrac{2x}{k} = \dfrac{b}{y}$

If $x = 9$, $b = 7$, and $y = 50$, then $\dfrac{2(9)}{k} = \dfrac{7}{50}$.

So $2(9)(50) = 7k$

$900 = 7k$

$k = \dfrac{900}{7} \approx 128.57$

24. $\dfrac{2x}{k} = \dfrac{b}{y}$

If $x = 1$ and $y = 1$, then

$\dfrac{2(1)}{k} = \dfrac{b}{1}$

$2 = kb$

$k = \dfrac{2}{b}$

25.

$\dfrac{t + 3}{100} = \dfrac{t - 5}{200}$

$200(t + 3) = 100(t - 5)$

$200t + 600 = 100t - 500$

$100t + 600 = -500$

$100t = -1100$

$t = -11$

26. a. The definition of size change uses points and positive real numbers; the same definition will work for size changes in three dimensions.

b. Properties preserved under size changes in three dimensions would be that angle measures would be preserved, betweenness would be preserved, collinearity would be preserved, and lines and their images would be parallel (and planes and their images would also be parallel).

27. a.

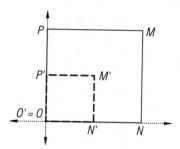

b. The original figure is a square, so its four sides are congruent and its four angles are right angles by the definition of a square (meaning). If each side of the preimage has length s, then for the image each side is ks, so the four sides are congruent. Also, size changes preserve angle measure, so the four angles are still right angles. So the image is a square by the definition of square (sufficient condition).

LESSON 12-4 (pp. 581-585)

1. Three ways of writing the ratio of 7 to 9 are
   $7:9$, $7/9$, and $\frac{7}{9}$; an expression that does not
   mean the ratio 7 to 9 is 7.9; that is choice (d).

2. A ratio is a quotient of two numbers.

3. A proportion is a statement that two ratios
   are equal.

4. a. The extremes are the first and fourth
   terms, 7 and y.
   b. The means are the second and third terms,
   x and 11.
   c. The first term is 7.
   d. The 4th term is y.
   e. The 3rd term is 11.
   f. The 2nd term is x.

5. a. A conclusion based on the Means-
   Extremes Property is that $ru = st$.
   b. A conclusion based on the Means
   Exchange Property is that $\frac{r}{t} = \frac{s}{u}$.
   c. A conclusion based on the Reciprocals
   Property is that $\frac{s}{r} = \frac{u}{t}$.

6. Three true proportions using the numbers 2,
   93, 62, and 3 are $\frac{2}{3} = \frac{62}{93}$, $\frac{2}{62} = \frac{3}{93}$, $\frac{3}{2} = \frac{93}{62}$.

7. The numbers 2, 4, 6, and 8 are not
   proportional because no true proportions can
   be written using those four numbers:
   $\frac{2}{4} \neq \frac{6}{8}$; $\frac{2}{6} \neq \frac{4}{8}$; $\frac{2}{8} \neq \frac{4}{6}$.

8. Segments $\overline{AB}$ and $\overline{FG}$ correspond, and the
   segment that corresponds with $\overline{AD}$ is $\overline{FE}$, so
   the proportion is $\frac{AB}{FG} = \frac{AD}{FE}$.

9. Using the proportion $\frac{AB}{FG} = \frac{BC}{GH}$, then
   $\frac{12}{10} = \frac{15}{GH}$ so $12 \cdot GH = 150$ and
   $GH = \frac{150}{12} = 12.5$.

10. a. The equation that results if both sides of
    the equation $ad = bc$ are divided by bd is
    $\frac{ad}{bd} = \frac{bc}{bd}$ or $\frac{a}{b} = \frac{c}{d}$.
    b. The equation that results if both sides of
    the equation $ad = bc$ are divided by ac is
    $\frac{ad}{ac} = \frac{bc}{ac}$ or $\frac{d}{c} = \frac{b}{a}$.

11. From the expression $\frac{u}{v} = \frac{w}{x} = \frac{y}{z}$, then
    $\frac{u}{w} = \frac{v}{x}$, $\frac{u}{y} = \frac{v}{z}$, $\frac{w}{y} = \frac{x}{z}$, etc.

12. If $\frac{a}{x} = \frac{b}{c}$, then $bx = ac$ and $x = \frac{ac}{b}$.

13. a. The proportion $\frac{GJ}{GH} = \frac{GK}{GI}$ is the
    proportion of "long sides to corresponding
    short sides"; the proportion is *true*.
    b. The proportion $\frac{GH}{GJ} = \frac{GI}{GK}$ is the
    proportion "short sides to corresponding
    long sides"; the proportion is *true*.
    c. The ratio $\frac{JK}{HI}$ is "long side to short side"
    while the ratio $\frac{GI}{GK}$ is "short side to long
    side." So the equation $\frac{JK}{HI} = \frac{GI}{GK}$ is not a
    true proportion; the statement is *false*.

14. Using the proportion $\frac{GH}{GJ} = \frac{HI}{JK}$, then
    $\frac{100}{130} = \frac{120}{JK}$ so $JK(100) = (120)(130) =$
    15,600, so $JK = 156$.

15. Set up and solve a proportion:
    $$\frac{2.3}{4} = \frac{1.05}{x}$$
    $2.3x = 4.20$
    $$x = \frac{4.20}{2.3} \approx 1.826$$
    4 pounds of fruit should cost about $1.83.

16. a. Set up and solve a proportion:

$$\frac{13}{x} = \frac{1.5}{2.5}$$

$$1.5x = (13)(2.5) = 32.5$$

$$x = 21.667$$

You could bike about 21 or 22 miles in two and a half hours.

b. Set up and solve a proportion:

$$\frac{m}{x} = \frac{h}{r}$$

$$xh = mr$$

$$x = \frac{mr}{h}$$

17. If $wx = yz$, then some true proportions using w, x, y, and z are $\frac{w}{y} = \frac{z}{x}$, $\frac{w}{z} = \frac{y}{x}$, $\frac{z}{w} = \frac{x}{y}$, etc.

18. $\angle VXY$ corresponds to $\angle BDE$, so m$\angle VXY$ = 47 by the Size Change Theorem. Also by that theorem, since $\overline{UY}$ corresponds to $\overline{AE}$, then $UY = (1.5)(30) = 45$ units.

19. S$(A) = (\frac{16}{2}, \frac{-6}{2}) = (8, -3)$ and S$(B) =$ $(\frac{10}{2}, \frac{8}{2}) = (5, 4)$; the distance between them is $\sqrt{(8 - 5)^2 + (-3 - 4)^2} = \sqrt{3^2 + (-7)^2} = \sqrt{9 + 49} = \sqrt{58}$.
$AB = \sqrt{(16 - 10)^2 + (-6 - 8)^2} = \sqrt{6^2 + (-14)^2} = \sqrt{36 + 196} = \sqrt{232} = \sqrt{(4)(58)} = 2\sqrt{58}$.
So the distance between S(A) and S(B) is half AB.

20.

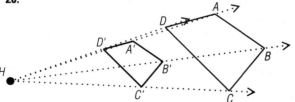

21. For the image to be 5 times as large (in linear dimensions) as the original, the photo paper must be five times as far from the lens as the negative. The negative is 2 inches from the lens, so the photo paper must be $(5)(2) = 10$ inches from the lens.

22. Two figures α and β are congruent, written $\alpha \cong \beta$, if and only if α is the image of β under a translation, a reflection, a rotation, or any composite of these. (In a shorter form, α is the image of β under a reflection or composite of reflections.)

23. a. The three figures are regular polygons, so all the segments in the diagram are congruent, by the definition of regular polygon (meaning) and the Transitive Property of Congruence. Then $\triangle FGL \cong \triangle HIJ$ by the SSS Congruence Theorem.

b. m$\angle GHI$ = m$\angle GHJ$ + m$\angle JHI$ by the Angle Addition Property of the Angle Measure Postulate. $\angle JHI$ is in equilateral triangle JHI, so its measure is 60.
There are two ways to find m$\angle GHJ$. One way is to first find an exterior angle of a regular pentagon—it is $\frac{360}{5}$ = 72—and then find the supplement of that angle: $180 - 72 = 108$.
The other way to find m$\angle GHJ$ is to first find the sum of the measures of a pentagon—it is $3(180) = 540$—and then find one-fifth of that: $\frac{540}{5} = 108$.
So m$\angle GHI = 108 + 60 = 168$.

24. a. Triangles that are size transformations of each other are similar triangles, and there are three sets of similar triangles.
One set consists of the lengths {3, 4, 5}, {5, 4, 3}, and {1.8, 2.4, 3}. (Note that multiplying 3, 4, and 5 by .6 results in 1.8, 2.4, and 3.)
A second set of similar triangles consists of {8, 6, 12} and {9, 12, 18}. (Multiplying 8, 6, and 12 by 1.5 results in 12, 9, and 18.)
The third set of similar triangles is {2, 4.5, 4} and {8, 16, 18}. (Multiplying 2, 4.5, and 4 by 4 results in 8, 18, and 16.)

b. The scale factors are 1, .6, and $\frac{1}{.6} = \frac{5}{3}$ for the first set, 1.5 and $\frac{1}{1.5} = \frac{2}{3}$ for the second set, and 4 and $\frac{1}{4}$ for the third set.

c. There can be more than one scale factor for a pair, depending on which is the preimage and which is the image. For example, in the third set, the scale factor is either 4 or $\frac{1}{4}$.

LESSON 12–5 (pp. 586–592)

1. The transformation $S \circ r_\ell$ is a composite of a size change and a reflection, so it is a similarity transformation.
2. Figures I and III are the same shape but different sizes, so they are similar.
3. Figures I and II are the same shape and the same size, so they are both similar and congruent.
4. The symbol "~" is read "is similar to."
5. Two figures F and G are similar, written F ~ G, if and only if there is a similarity transformation mapping one onto the other.
6. Every similarity transformation *does* preserve betweenness. (If B is between A and C, then the image of B is between the images of A and C.)
7. Every similarity transformation *does* preserve angle measure.
8. Every similarity transformation does *not* preserve orientation.
9. Every similarity transformation does *not* preserve distance. (The image of $\overline{AB}$ does not necessarily have the same length as $\overline{AB}$.)
10. Every similarity transformation does not preserve "tilt".
11. A reflection is the composite of S_1 and a reflection, so it is a similarity transformation by the definition of similarity transformation (sufficient condition).
12. A size change with magnitude $\frac{1}{3}$ is the composite of $S_{\frac{1}{3}}$ and two reflections over the same line, so it is a similarity transformation by definition of similarity transformation (sufficient condition).
13. A translation is a composite of S_1 and a composite of reflections, so it is a similarity transformation by the definition of similarity transformation (sufficient condition).
14. The composite of a rotation and a size change is the composite of reflections (equivalent to the rotation) and the size change, so it is a similarity transformation by the definition of similarity transformation (sufficient condition).

15. If the two figures are similar, then corresponding angles are congruent by the definition of similar figures (meaning). So the statement that $m\angle I = \frac{4}{7} \cdot m\angle D$ is *false*.

16. a-b. Corresponding side lengths are in the ratio $\frac{4}{7}$, so set up and solve the following proportion:

$$\frac{FJ}{AE} = \frac{4}{7}$$
$$\frac{10}{AE} = \frac{4}{7}$$
$$4 \cdot AE = 70$$
$$AE = 17.5 \text{ units}$$

The length that corresponds to segment $\overline{FJ}$ can be found; that length is $AE = 17.5$ units.

17. Set up and solve a proportion involving the corresponding sides $\overline{DE}$ and $\overline{IJ}$:

$$\frac{IJ}{DE} = \frac{4}{7}$$
$$\frac{IJ}{x} = \frac{4}{7}$$
$$7 \cdot IJ = 4x$$
$$IJ = \frac{4x}{7}$$

18. Set up and solve a proportion:

$$\frac{\text{longer side}}{\text{shorter side}} = \frac{40}{30} = \frac{150}{x}$$
$$40x = (30)(150) = 4500$$
$$x = \frac{4500}{40} = 112.5 \text{ mm}$$

19. a.

b. The intermediate image has lengths that are twice as long as the original, and the final image has lengths that are 1.5 times as long as the intermediate image. So the final image has lengths that are $(2)(1.5) = 3$ times as long as the original.

20. The size of the final image would have lengths that are $(4)\left(\frac{1}{5}\right) = \frac{4}{5}$ times the lengths of the original logo. Also, the use of different centers would mean that the original and final image were not "concentric."

21. The width of the folded card is 4 cm. Set up and solve the following proportion:

$$\frac{\text{length}}{\text{width}} = \frac{8}{w} = \frac{w}{4}$$
$$w^2 = 32$$
$$w = \sqrt{32} = \sqrt{(16)(2)} = 4\sqrt{2} \approx 5.66 \text{ cm}$$

22. a. Segments $\overline{MZ}$ and $\overline{SQ}$ are corresponding parts, so the ratio of similitude is
$$\frac{MZ}{SQ} = \frac{5}{10} = \frac{1}{2}.$$

b. If $ST = 6$, then the corresponding radius of the smaller cone is 3, so $LM = 3$.

23. Set up and solve the following proportion:

$$\frac{BC}{EF} = \frac{AB}{DE}$$
$$\frac{12}{16} = \frac{AB}{8}$$
$$16 \cdot AB = (8)(12) = 96$$
$$AB = \frac{96}{16} = 6 \text{ units}$$

24. a. A similarity transformation is the composite of a size transformation and reflections. Since a reflection does not necessarily preserve the "tilt" of a line, then the image of a line under a similarity transformation is not necessarily parallel to the preimage. So the statement $S(\ell) \parallel \ell$ is *false*.

b. If $\ell \parallel m$, then any transversal to ℓ and m forms corresponding angles that are congruent. The similarity transformation S will perserve those angles, so the images of ℓ, m, and the transversal will have corresponding angles that are congruent, and S(ℓ) and S(m) will be parallel. So the statement "If $\ell \parallel m$, then S(ℓ) $\parallel$ S(m)" is *true*.

25. Set up and solve the following proportion:

$$\frac{\text{number of cans}}{\text{cost}} = \frac{3}{2.00} = \frac{5}{x}$$

$3x = 10.00$

$x = 3.34$; so 5 cans of tuna would cost about $3.34.

26. a. Applying the Means Exchange Property to $\frac{a}{b} = \frac{c}{d}$ results in $\frac{a}{c} = \frac{b}{d}$. So the proportion is a true one.

b. Add 1 to each side of the proportion:

$$\frac{a}{b} = \frac{c}{d}$$

$$\frac{a}{b} + 1 = \frac{c}{d} + 1$$

$$\frac{a}{b} + \frac{b}{b} = \frac{c}{d} + \frac{d}{d}$$

$$\frac{a+b}{b} = \frac{c+d}{d}$$

So the proportion is a true one.

c. False; for example:

$\frac{2}{3} = \frac{4}{6}$, but $\frac{2}{6} \neq \frac{4}{3}$.

27. a. Since the size transformation preserves angle measures, $m\angle BDE = m\angle BAC$, so $\overline{DE} \parallel \overline{AC}$ because corr. $\angle$s $\Rightarrow \parallel$ lines. So the statement is *true*.

b. Setting up a proportion,

$$\frac{\text{smaller triangle}}{\text{larger triangle}} = \frac{BD}{AB} = \frac{ED}{AC},$$

so the proportion is a true one.

c. Using the proportion in part b, where $x = BD$:

$$\frac{x}{AB} = \frac{ED}{AC}$$

$$\frac{x}{x+5} = \frac{12}{16}$$

$$16x = 12(x+5)$$

$$16x = 12x + 60$$

$$4x = 60$$

$$x = 15.$$

28.

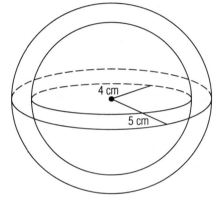

The volume of rubber can be computed by subtracting the volume of the core from the volume of the ball:

$$\frac{4}{3}\pi(5)^3 - \frac{4}{3}\pi(4)^3 = \frac{4}{3}\pi(125) - \frac{4}{3}\pi(64)$$

$$= \frac{500}{3}\pi - \frac{256}{3}\pi$$

$$\approx 523.599 - 268.083$$

$$\approx 255.516 \text{ cm}^3$$

29. a-b. If three angles of one triangle are congruent to three angles of another, the triangles are similar but not necessarily congruent. As an example, consider the triangle with sides 3 cm, 4 cm, and 5 cm and the triangle with sides 3 in., 4 in., and 5 in. There are 3 pairs of congruent angles, but the triangles are not congruent.

30. a-b. Answers will vary depending on the size of the objects and their models.

31. The "Law of Cosines" is a mathematical formula for finding the length of one side of a triangle when two sides and one angle are known.

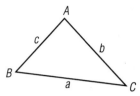

The law of cosines states that
$c^2 = a^2 + b^2 - 2ab \cos C$.

LESSON 12-6 (pp. 593–598)

1. a. The ratio of any two corresponding lengths is the same as the ratio of similitude, which is $\frac{15}{21}$ or $\frac{5}{7}$.

b. The ratio of the areas of the largest faces is the square of the ratio of similitude, or $\left(\frac{5}{7}\right)^2 = \frac{25}{49}$.

c. The ratio of the volumes of the boxes is the cube of the ratio of similitude, or $\left(\frac{5}{7}\right)^3 = \frac{125}{343}$.

2. Area is the product of two lengths.

3. Volume is the product of three lengths.

4. a. The ratio of perimeters is the same as the ratio of similitude, or $\frac{5}{3}$.

b. The ratio of areas is the square of the ratio of similitude, or $\left(\frac{5}{3}\right)^2 = \frac{25}{9}$.

c. The ratio of volumes is the cube of the ratio of similitude, or $\left(\frac{5}{3}\right)^3 = \frac{125}{27}$.

d. The ratio of the lengths of corresponding sides is the same as the ratio of similitude, or $\frac{5}{3}$.

5. The ratio of volumes is the cube of the ratio of similitude, so Volume $(R') = k^3 \cdot$ Volume (R) $= 4^3(34) = (64)(34) = 2176$ cubic units.

6. The ratio of areas is the square of the ratio of similitude, so Area $(G') = k^2 \cdot$ Area $(G) =$ $\left(\frac{2}{3}\right)^2 72 = \left(\frac{4}{9}\right)(72) = 32$ square meters.

7. The sides are 5 in. and 13 in., so the ratio of similitude is $\frac{5}{13}$. The ratio of perimeters is the same as the ratio of similitude, or $\frac{5}{13}$.

8. a. Using the formula $A = \frac{1}{2}bh$, the area is $\frac{1}{2}(10)(6) = 30$ units^2.

b. The ratio of areas is the square of the ratio of similitude, so Area $(EFG) = k^2 \cdot$ Area $(ABC) =$ $5^2(30) = (25)(30) = 750$ units^2.

9. a. $\overline{AC}$ is the hypotenuse of a right triangle with legs 6 and 8; its length is 10 (it is a 3-4-5 right triangle). $\overline{AB}$ is the hypotenuse of a right triangle with legs 2 and 6, its length is $\sqrt{4 + 36} = \sqrt{40}$. So the perimeter of $\triangle ABC$ is $10 + 10 + \sqrt{40} = 20 + \sqrt{40} \approx$ 26.325 units.

b. The ratio of similitude is 5, so the perimeter of $\triangle EFG$ is 5 times the perimeter of $\triangle ABC$: $5(20 + \sqrt{40}) = 100 + 5\sqrt{40} \approx$ $100 + (5)(6.325) = 131.625$ units.

10. a. Using the volume formula $V = Bh =$ $\pi r^2 h$, the volume is $\pi (11)^2(25) = 3025\pi \approx$ 9503 units^3. The surface area is $2\pi rh + 2B$ $= 2\pi rh + 2\pi r^2 = 2\pi(11)(25) + 2\pi (11)^2$ $= 550\pi + 242\pi = 792\pi \approx 2488$ units^2.

b. According to the Fundamental Theorem of Similarity, if R is the image of Q under a size change of magnitude 3, then R will have 3^3 or 27 times the volume of Q and 3^2 or 9 times the surface area.

c. The volume of cylinder R is k^3 times the volume of cylinder Q, and the surface area of cylinder R is k^2 times the surface area of cylinder Q.

So the volume of cylinder R is $(3025\pi)(3^3) = (3025\pi)(27) = 81{,}675\pi \approx 256{,}590$ units^3.

The surface area of cylinder R is $(792\pi)(3^2) = (792\pi)(9) = 7128\pi \approx 22{,}393$ units^2.

11. a. Consider the transformation as being from the known pyramid (the smaller one) to the unknown pyramid (the larger one). The volume of the larger solid is the cube of the ratio of similitude times the volume of the smaller solid. The ratio of similitude is $\frac{12}{8} = \frac{3}{2}$ and the volume of the smaller solid is 100 in.^{3}, so the volume of the larger solid is $(100)\left(\frac{3}{2}\right)^3 = (100)\left(\frac{27}{8}\right) = \frac{2700}{8} = 337.5$ in.^{3}.

b. Consider the transformation as being from the larger pyramid to the smaller one. The volume of the smaller solid is the cube of the ratio of similitude times the volume of the larger solid. The ratio of similitude is $\frac{8}{12} = \frac{2}{3}$ and the volume of the larger solid is 100 in.^{3}, so the volume of the smaller solid is $(100)\left(\frac{2}{3}\right)^3 = (100)\left(\frac{8}{27}\right) = \frac{800}{27} \approx 29.63$ in.^{3}.

12. The ratio of perimeters is the same as the ratio of similitude, so the ratio of similitude is $\frac{20}{28} = \frac{5}{7}$. That is the same as the ratio of corresponding lengths, so the ratio of corresponding lengths is $\frac{5}{7}$.

13. a. The ratio of similitude is $\frac{3}{5} = .6$, so the base area of the smaller statue is $(.6)^2$ times the base area of the larger statue. So the base area of the smaller statue is $(.6)^2(50) = (.36)(50) = 18$ cm^2.

b. The ratio of the volumes of brass is the cube of the ratio of similitude. So if the smaller statue used 216 cm^3 of brass, the larger statue used $(216)\left(\frac{5}{3}\right)^3 = (216)\left(\frac{125}{27}\right) = \left(\frac{216}{27}\right)(125) = (8)(125) = 1000$ cm^3 of brass.

14. a. The ratio of volumes is $\frac{288}{7776} = \frac{1}{27}$, so the ratio of similitude is the cube root of $\frac{1}{27}$, or $\frac{1}{3}$.

b. The ratio of surface areas is the square of the ratio of similitude, or $\left(\frac{1}{3}\right)^2 = \frac{1}{9}$.

15. Each prism is the product of its base and its height. The area of the larger base is $1.5^2 = 2.25$ times the area of the smaller base. After multiplying each base by the same number, the ratio of volumes will still be 2.25; that is choice (b).

16. Take any pair of corresponding sides to find the ratio of similitude:
$\frac{10}{15} = \frac{10}{15} = \frac{12}{18} = \frac{2}{3}$.
(One way to tell that the sides with lengths 10 and 15 correspond is to select the pair of sides opposite the curved part of each figure.) If the mapping is from the smaller figure to the larger, then the ratio of similitude is $\frac{3}{2}$.

17. If $AB = 3$, then the corresponding side to $\overline{AB}$ is k times the length of $\overline{AB}$, or
$DE = (2.5)(3) = 7.5$ units.
If BC is 5, then the corresponding side to $\overline{BC}$ is k times the length of $\overline{BC}$, or
$EF = (2.5)(5) = 12.5$ units.
If $m\angle B = 135$, then the angle that corresponds to $\angle B$ has the same measure, or $m\angle E = 135$.

18. Set up and solve a proportion:
$$\frac{\text{smaller side}}{\text{longer side}} = \frac{2}{6} = \frac{.5}{x}$$
$$2x = (6)(.5) = 3$$
$$x = 1.5 \text{ inches}$$

19. If $\frac{x}{10} = \frac{11}{y}$, then also $\frac{x}{11} = \frac{10}{y}, \frac{y}{11} = \frac{10}{x}$, and $\frac{y}{10} = \frac{11}{x}$.

20. Set up and solve a proportion:
$$\frac{\text{vertical}}{\text{horizontal}} = \frac{3}{8} = \frac{x}{20}$$
$$8x = 60$$
$$x = 7.5 \text{ m}$$
The height of the goalpost is 7.5 meters.

21. If r is the radius of the can, then the height of the can is $6r$ and the volume of the can is
$V = Bh = \pi r^2 h = \pi r^2(6r) = 6\pi r^3$.
The volume of the three balls is
$(3)\left(\frac{4}{3}\right)\pi r^3 = 4\pi r^3$.

The difference in volumes is the amount of the can's volume outside the balls, or
$6\pi r^3 - 4\pi r^3 = 2\pi r^3$.
So the percent of volume outside the balls is
$\frac{2\pi r^3}{6\pi r^3} = \frac{1}{3} = 33\frac{1}{3}\%$.

22. Answers will vary. The actual weight of the object should be approximated by the product of the weight of the model and the cube of the ratio of similitude.

LESSON 12-7 (pp. 599–603)

1. Brobdingnagians are 12 times the height of Gulliver, and weigh $12^3 = 1728$ times as much.

2. Lilliputians are $\frac{1}{12}$ times the height of Gulliver and weigh $\left(\frac{1}{12}\right)^3 = \frac{1}{1728}$ ($\approx .0005787$) times as much.

3. Brobdingnagians are $(12)(12) = 144$ times the height of Lilliputians and weigh $144^3 = 2{,}985{,}984$ times as much.

4. Robert Wadlow was the tallest man whose height was recorded; he was about 8 feet, 11.1 inches tall.

5. The ratio of similitude is 5, so her weight would be $5^3 = 125$ times the weight of an average woman.

6. The ratio of similitude is 5, so her nose length (a linear measurement) would be 5 times that of an average woman.

7. The ratio of similitude is 5, so the area of the bottom of her foot would be $5^2 = 25$ times that of an average woman.

8. The ratio of similitude is 5, so her wrist circumference (a linear measurement) would be 5 times that of an average woman.

9. Champion weightlifters rarely lift more than twice their body weight, so the statement is *false*.

10. Prices of pizza depend on the area of the pizza, which is proportional to the square of the ratio of the diameters, so the statement is *false*.

11. The weight of an animal increases with the cube of the increase in linear dimensions, so an elephant needs thicker legs (proportionally) than a mosquito because the legs are holding up much more weight (proportionally).

12. If the ratio of similitude (the scale) is $\frac{1}{15}$, then the weight of the model will be $\left(\frac{1}{15}\right)^3 = \frac{1}{3375}$ the weight of the object and the amount of paint needed will be $\left(\frac{1}{15}\right)^2 = \frac{1}{225}$ of the amount needed for the object.

13. The figurines are similar, so the ratio of similitude is the same as the ratio of heights: $\frac{50}{40} = \frac{5}{4}$. The weight of the taller one is the cube of the ratio of similitude times the weight of the smaller one:
$$\left(\frac{5}{4}\right)^3(8) = \left(\frac{125}{64}\right)(8) = \frac{125}{8} = 15.625 \text{ kg.}$$

14. The cost of the pizza should vary with the ratio of the squares of the diameters:
$$\frac{16^2}{12^2} = \frac{1.50}{x}$$
$$256x = (144)(1.50) = 216$$
$$x = \frac{216}{256} = .84375 \approx .85$$
The ingredients should cost about 85 cents.

15. a. The boxes are not similar (the sides of the bases have ratio of similitude 1, but the heights have ratio of similitude 2).
    b. Two of the smaller boxes are equivalent to the larger box, so the ratio of volumes is $\frac{1}{2}$.

c. The surface area of the smaller box consists of 2 bases and the lateral area, while the surface of the larger box consists of 2 bases (the same as the smaller box) and a lateral area that is twice that of the smaller box.
If the dimensions of the smaller box are ℓ, w, and h, then its surface area is
$2(\ell w) + (2\ell + 2w)h =$
$2\ell w + 2\ell h + 2wh.$
The dimensions of the larger box are ℓ, w, and $2h$, so its surface area is
$2(\ell w) + (2\ell + 2w)(2h) =$
$2\ell w + 4\ell h + 4wh.$
While there is no simple relationship between the two surface areas, the surface area of the larger box is less than twice that of the smaller box.

16. The ratio of similitude is $\frac{7}{6}$, so the weight of the taller player would be
$$(200)\left(\frac{7}{6}\right)^3 = (200)\left(\frac{343}{216}\right) = \frac{68,600}{216} \approx 317.6 \text{ lb.}$$

17. a. The ratio of surface areas is the square of the ratio of similitude, so the ratio of radii would be about $\sqrt{13} \approx 3.6$.
    b. The ratio of volumes would be the cube of the ratio of similitude, so the ratio of volumes would be $(\sqrt{13})^3 \approx 3.6^3 \approx 47$.

18. The area of the image would be the area of the original times the square of the size change (the ratio of similitude), so the area of the image would be
$$(70)\left(\frac{2}{5}\right)^2 = (70)\left(\frac{4}{25}\right) = \frac{280}{25} = 11.2 \text{ units}^2.$$

19. For the angles:
$m\angle M = m\angle P = 95; m\angle S = m\angle Q = 43;$
$m\angle R = m\angle T = 180 - (95 + 43)$
$= 180 - 138 = 42.$
For the sides, set up and solve proportions:
$$\frac{PQ}{MS} = \frac{PR}{MT} = \frac{QR}{ST}$$
$$\frac{20}{12} = \frac{20.4}{MT} = \frac{QR}{17.9}$$
Using the first two ratios:
$20 \cdot MT = (12)(20.4) = 244.8$
$\quad MT = 12.24$
Using the first and third ratios:
$12 \cdot QR = (20)(17.9) = 358$
$\quad QR = 29.833$

20. Two figures F and G are similar, written
F ~ G, if and only if there is a similarity
transformation mapping one onto the other.

21.

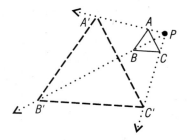

22. K is the midpoint of $\overline{FJ}$, so $JK = KF$ by the
definition of midpoint (meaning). Parallel
lines are given, so $m\angle F = m\angle JKI$ and
$m\angle GKF = m\angle J$ because $\parallel$ lines $\Rightarrow$
corr. $\angle$s $=$. So $\triangle FGK \cong \triangle KIJ$ by the ASA
Congruence Theorem.

23. **a.** The following are the ratios of weight
lifted to the maximum weight for that class
(the open-ended weight class is
not included):
$$\frac{153.0}{52.0} = 2.942$$
$$\frac{171.0}{56.0} = 3.054$$
$$\frac{190.0}{60.0} = 3.167$$
$$\frac{200.5}{67.0} = 2.993$$
$$\frac{215.5}{75.0} = 2.873$$
$$\frac{225.0}{82.5} = 2.727$$
$$\frac{235.0}{90.0} = 2.611$$
$$\frac{241.5}{100.0} = 2.415$$
$$\frac{250.5}{110.0} = 2.277$$

b. The trend seems to be that the ratio is
getting smaller as the weight classes
increase.

c. An explanation is that the strength of a
weightlifter increases more slowly than the
weight of the weightlifter.

24. **a-c.** Answers will vary.

d. The costs in making a pizza are the cost of
ingredients, payroll, and fuel for the oven;
other costs include rent, insurance, taxes,
water bills, etc.; paying for the cooking
and serving utensils, and supplying a profit
for the owners.

LESSON 12-8 (pp. 604–608)

1. **a.** Using the markings in the angles, the
corresponding vertices are W and F, V and
E, and U and D.

b. Using sides $\overline{UW}$ and $\overline{DF}$, a ratio of
similitude is $\frac{10}{33}$.

c. No angle measures are given, so no angle measures can be found.

To find the lengths of the sides, set up and solve proportions:

$$\frac{VW}{EF} = \frac{UW}{DF} = \frac{UV}{DE}$$

$$\frac{VW}{32} = \frac{10}{33} = \frac{UV}{25}$$

Using the first two ratios,
$$33 \cdot VW = 320$$
$$VW = \frac{320}{33} \approx 9.697$$

Using the second and third ratios,
$$33 \cdot UV = 250$$
$$UV = \frac{250}{33} \approx 7.576$$

2. a. $\overline{ON}$ is parallel to $\overline{QP}$, so the corresponding vertices are M and M, Q and O, and P and N.

b. The ratio of similitude is $\frac{OM}{QM} = \frac{3}{9} = \frac{1}{3}$.

c. No angle measures are given, so no angle measures can be found.
$QM = 6 + 3 = 9$, and $MP = 2 + 4 = 6$. The lengths of the sides of the large triangle are 3 times the lengths of corresponding sides of the small triangle. So $QP = 3 \cdot ON = (3)(4) = 12$.

3. Setting up proportions using corresponding sides, $\frac{RS}{UV} = \frac{RT}{UW}$ and $\frac{RS}{UV} = \frac{ST}{VW}$.

4. One way to prove $\triangle ABC \sim \triangle DEF$ is to find a size change image of $\triangle ABC$ that is congruent to $\triangle DEF$.

5. The SSS Similarity Theorem states that if the three sides of one triangle are proportional to the three sides of a second triangle, then the triangles are similar.

6. Multiply each side of the 5, 12, 13 triangle by 5 to get $(5)(5) = 25$, $(5)(12) = 60$, and $(5)(13) = 65$. So the statement that the 5, 12, 13 triangle is similar to the 60, 65, 25 triangle is *true*.

7. The ratio of the shortest sides of the two triangles is $\frac{20}{9} \approx 2.22$, and the ratio of the longest sides of the two triangles is $\frac{29}{41} \approx .71$ (and the ratio for the two middle sides is $\frac{21}{40}$ $= .525$). These ratios are not equal, so the statement that the triangles are similar is *false*.

8. a-b. In $\triangle FED$, $FD = \sqrt{40^2 - 24^2} = \sqrt{1600 - 576} = \sqrt{1024} = 32$, and in $\triangle ABC$, $AB = \sqrt{65^2 - 52^2} = \sqrt{4225 - 2704} = \sqrt{1521} = 39$.

Setting up the ratios of sides as shortest-to-shortest, and so on, the ratios are $\frac{24}{39}$, $\frac{32}{52}$, $\frac{40}{65}$; each ratio equals $0.61538\ldots$, so the triangles are similar.

9. a. The two vertices where the shortest pairs of sides meet are Q and V, and the vertices where the longest pairs of sides meet are P and T; the third pair of vertices is R and U. So the similarity is $\triangle QPR \sim \triangle VTU$.

b. Sample: Apply the size change with magnitude 3, center Q to $\triangle PQR$. Take the image and reflect over the perpendicular bisector of $\overline{P'T}$. Then rotate with center T magnitude $m\angle Q''TV$.

10.

Conclusions	Justifications
1. $WX = \frac{1}{2}WY$, $WV = \frac{1}{2}WZ$	def. of midpoint (meaning)
2. $XV = \frac{1}{2}YZ$	Midpoint Connector Thm.
3. $\frac{WX}{WY} = \frac{1}{2}$, $\frac{WV}{WZ} = \frac{1}{2}$, $\frac{XV}{YZ} = \frac{1}{2}$	Mult. Prop. of Eq.
4. $\frac{WX}{WY} = \frac{WV}{WZ} = \frac{XV}{YZ}$	Trans. Prop. of Eq.
5. $\triangle WXV \sim \triangle WYZ$	SSS Similarity Thm. (step 4)

11.

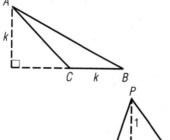

Here is a counterexample. The altitude of $\triangle ABC$ is 3 times the altitude of $\triangle PQR$, and the base of $\triangle ABC$ is also 3 times the base of $\triangle PQR$. However, the triangles are not similar.

12. If there were a person $\frac{1}{6}$ as tall as you, with your physique, then the ratio of similitude would be $\frac{1}{6}$, and that person would weigh $\left(\frac{1}{6}\right)^3 = \frac{1}{216}$ as much as you (the ratio of weights is the cube of the ratio of similitude). This weight would be supported by $\left(\frac{1}{6}\right)^2 = \frac{1}{36}$ times the area that supports you (the ratio of areas is the square of the ratio of similitude).

13. The ratio of similitude is the same as the ratio of linear measurements, so it is $\frac{13}{10} = 1.3$. The weight of the larger box would be $(1.3)^3$ times the weight of the smaller box, so the weight of the larger box would be $(1.3)^3(20) = (2.197)(20) = 43.94 \approx 44$ lb.

14. The ratio of areas is $\frac{120}{30} = 4$, so the ratio of similitude is $\sqrt{4} = 2$. So the length of the hypotenuse of the larger triangle is 2 times the length of the hypotenuse of the smaller one.

15. The volume of the new sphere is the volume of the old sphere times the cube of the ratio of similitude. So the volume of the new sphere is $(36\pi)(3^3) = (36\pi)(27) = 972\pi \approx 3054$ units^3.

16. If the larger triangle is the result of a size change of magnitude 5, then the linear dimensions of the smaller triangle are $\frac{1}{5}$ those of the larger one.

17. a. The formula $V = \frac{1}{3}Bh$ gives the volume of a pyramid or cone with base area B and height h.

b. The formula S.A. $= 2\ell w + 2wh + 2\ell h$ gives the surface area of a box with dimensions ℓ, w, and h.

c. The formula $p = a + b + c$ gives the perimeter of a triangle with sides a, b, and c.

d. The formula $V = \pi r^2 h$ gives the volume of a cylinder with radius r and height h.

e. The formula L.A. $= \pi r \ell$ gives the lateral area of a cone with radius r and slant height ℓ.

18. $\frac{2x + 10}{2} = \frac{2x}{2} + \frac{10}{2}$
$= x + 5$,
which is choice (b).

19. There is no SSSS Similarity Theorem for quadrilaterals. Here is a counterexample—the four pairs of sides are proportional, but the quadrilaterals have different shapes.

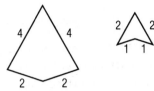

LESSON 12-9   (pp. 609–614)

1. a. Using the order, "vertex opposite longest side, then shortest side, then other side," the correspondence is $\Delta CBA \sim \Delta ZXY$.

b. The ratio of similitude is
$$\frac{6}{3} = \frac{5.9}{2.95} = \frac{5.8}{2.9} = 2.$$

c. The only angle measure that can be found is for the angle that corresponds with $\angle A$—m$\angle Y = 60$.

2. a. Using the order, "24 degree angle, 115 degree angle, other angle," the correspondence is $\Delta HGK \sim \Delta HIJ$.

b. The ratio of similitude is $\frac{GK}{IJ} = \frac{90}{50} = \frac{9}{5}$.

c. The length of HG is $\frac{9}{5}$ of the length of HI,

so $HG = \frac{9}{5}(80) = (9)(16) = 144$ units.

Also, m$\angle K =$ m$\angle HJI =$
$180 - (115 + 24) = 180 - 139 = 41$.

Also, $HK = HJ + 89$, so
$$\frac{HJ}{HJ + 89} = \frac{5}{9}$$
$$9 \cdot HJ = 5 \cdot HJ + 445$$
$$4 \cdot HJ = 445$$
$$HJ = 111.25$$
and $HK = 200.25$.

3. The AA Similarity Theorem states that if two triangles have two angles of one congruent to two angles of the other, then the triangles are similar.

4. a. The corresponding triangle congruence theorem for the SSS Similarity Theorem is the SSS Congruence Theorem.

b. The corresponding triangle congruence theorem(s) for the AA Similarity Theorem are the ASA Congruence Theorem and the AAS Congruence Theorem.

c. The corresponding triangle congruence theorem for the SAS Similarity Theorem is the SAS Congruence Theorem.

5. a-b. In the large triangle, the sum of the measures is 180, so $2x = 110$ and $x = 55$. So the large triangle has angle measures of 70, 55, and 55. The smaller triangle has two angles of measure 55, so the two triangles are similar by the AA Similarity Theorem.

6. a-b. The ratio of the two longer legs is $\frac{1}{2}$, and

the ratio of the two shorter legs is $\frac{5}{7}$.

These ratios are not equal, so the two triangles are not similar.

7. a-b. The two triangles have one angle in common, and two pairs of sides are in proportion $\left(\frac{4}{6} = \frac{8}{12}\right)$, so the triangles are similar by the SAS Similarity Theorem.

8. a-b. The triangles each have a right angle and another pair of congruent angles, so the triangles are similar by the AA Similarity Theorem.

9. a-b. The ratio for each pair of sides is $\frac{2}{1}$, so the triangles are similar by the SSS Similarity Theorem.

10. a. The ratios $\frac{48}{20}$ and $\frac{36}{15}$ are each equal to $\frac{12}{5}$ or 2.4; a size change of magnitude 2.4 would make the image of $\triangle PQR$ congruent to $\triangle XYZ$.

b. Under the size change, $\angle P$ would still be congruent to $\angle X$, and the two pairs of sides would be congruent. So the triangles would be congruent by the SAS Congruence Theorem.

11.

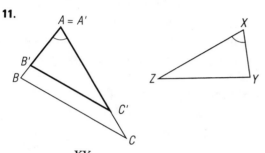

Let $k = \frac{XY}{AB}$ be the magnitude of a size transformation applied to $\triangle ABC$. Then $A'B' = k \cdot AB$ and $A'C' = k \cdot AC$. Also, since $m\angle A = m\angle A'$, then $\triangle A'B'C' \cong \triangle XYZ$ by the SAS Congruence Theorem. Thus $\triangle ABC$ can be mapped onto $\triangle XYZ$ by a composite of size changes and reflections, so $\triangle ABC \sim \triangle XYZ$.

12. $\overleftrightarrow{AB} \parallel \overleftrightarrow{DE}$, so $m\angle A = m\angle E$ and $m\angle B = m\angle D$ because $\parallel$ lines $\Rightarrow$ AIA $=$. So $\triangle ABC \sim \triangle EDC$ by the AA Similarity Theorem.

13. From the given, $\frac{WY}{VY} = 3$ and $\frac{XY}{YZ} = 3$.

Also, $\angle WYX \cong \angle VYZ$ by the Vertical Angle Theorem. So $\triangle WXY \cong \triangle VZY$ by the SAS Similarity Theorem.

14. Set up and solve a proportion:

$$\frac{\text{vertical distance}}{\text{horizontal distance}} = \frac{g}{5} = \frac{1}{1.2}$$
$$1.2g = 5$$
$$g = \frac{5}{1.2} \approx 4.167 \text{ m}$$

The height of the garage is about 4.167 m.

15. a-b. The ratio of the shortest sides of the triangles is $\frac{12}{8} = 1.5$, the ratio of the longest sides of the triangles is $\frac{20}{16} = 1.25$, and the ratio of the other two sides is $\frac{16}{12} = 1.333$. Since the ratios are different, the sides are not in proportion and the triangles are not similar.

16. a. The ratio of the surface areas is the square of the ratio of linear dimensions. So the ratio of surface areas is $\left(\frac{865,400}{88,000}\right)^2 \approx (9.834)^2 \approx 96.71 \approx 97$.

b. The ratio of the volumes is the cube of the ratio of linear dimensions. So the ratio of volumes is $\left(\frac{865,400}{88,000}\right)^3 \approx (9.834)^3 \approx 951$.

17.

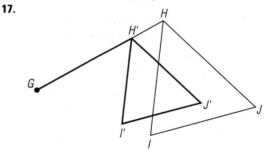

18.
$$\frac{x^2}{90} = \frac{3}{10}$$
$$10x^2 = 270$$
$$x^2 = 27$$
$$x = \sqrt{27} \text{ or } -\sqrt{27}, \text{ or } x = \pm 5.196.$$

19. Yes, there is an HL Similarity Theorem and an SsA Similarity Theorem; they are the similarity-theorem counterparts for the HL Congruence Theorem and SsA Congruence Theorem.

1. a. $\dfrac{AC}{AX} = \dfrac{AB}{AY} = \dfrac{BC}{YX}$

b. $\dfrac{AB}{BY} = \dfrac{AC}{CX}$

2. Set up and solve a proportion:

$\dfrac{2}{5} = \dfrac{3}{CE}$

$2 \cdot CE = 15$

$CE = 7.5$

3. Set up and solve a proportion:

$\dfrac{8}{32} = \dfrac{6}{FJ}$

$8 \cdot FJ = 192$

$FJ = 24$

4. a. $\dfrac{NQ}{ON} = \dfrac{5}{30} = \dfrac{1}{6}$

b. $\dfrac{MP}{MO} = \dfrac{NQ}{ON} = \dfrac{5}{30} = \dfrac{1}{6}$

c. $MO = 6 \cdot MP$ (from part b)

$= (6)(6)$

$= 36$

d. $OP = OM + MP$

$= 36 + 6$

$= 42$

e. $\dfrac{ON}{OQ} = \dfrac{30}{35} = \dfrac{6}{7}$

f. $\dfrac{OM}{OP} = \dfrac{36}{42} = \dfrac{6}{7}$

g. $\dfrac{MN}{PQ} = \dfrac{OM}{OP} = \dfrac{6}{7}$

h. $6 \cdot PQ = 7 \cdot MN$ (from part g)

$PQ = \dfrac{(7)(14)}{6} = \dfrac{(7)(7)}{3} = \dfrac{49}{3} = 16\dfrac{1}{3}$

5. The magnitude of the size change S with center O and S($\triangle MNO$) = $\triangle PQO$ is $\dfrac{35}{30} = \dfrac{7}{6}$.

6. $\dfrac{x + y}{x} = \dfrac{x}{x} + \dfrac{y}{x} = 1 + \dfrac{y}{x}$ which is choice (b).

7. $\dfrac{z}{z} + \dfrac{y}{z} = \dfrac{z + y}{z}$ which is choice (c).

8. The Side-Splitting Converse is that if a line intersects rays $\overrightarrow{OP}$ and $\overrightarrow{OQ}$ in distinct points X and Y so that $\dfrac{OX}{XP} = \dfrac{OY}{YQ}$, then $\overleftrightarrow{XY} \parallel \overrightarrow{PQ}$.

9. Set up and solve a proportion:

$\dfrac{\text{upper segment}}{\text{entire segment}} = \dfrac{20}{50} = \dfrac{AC}{60}$

$50 \cdot AC = 1200$

$AC = 24$

Then, since $AC + CE = AE,$

$CE = 60 - 24 = 36.$

10. a. Set up and solve a proportion:

$\dfrac{DB}{5} = \dfrac{6}{4}$

$4 \cdot DB = 30$

$DB = 7.5$ units

b. Set up and solve a proportion:

$\dfrac{FA}{6} = \dfrac{6}{4}$

$4 \cdot FA = 36$

$FA = 9$ units

c. $\angle A$ and $\angle AFE$ are interior angles on the same side of a transversal to parallel lines, so they are supplementary.

d. There are two ratios each equal to $\dfrac{BE}{EC}$:

$\dfrac{BE}{EC} = \dfrac{FA}{CF}$ and $\dfrac{BE}{EC} = \dfrac{BD}{DA}$, so $\dfrac{FA}{CF} = \dfrac{BD}{DA}$.

11. If $\dfrac{x}{y} = \dfrac{z}{w}$, then $\dfrac{x}{z} = \dfrac{y}{w}, \dfrac{z}{x} = \dfrac{w}{y}, \dfrac{y}{x} = \dfrac{w}{z},$

$\dfrac{x + y}{y} = \dfrac{z + w}{w}, \dfrac{z + x}{x} = \dfrac{w + y}{y},$ etc.

12. a-b. The justification for each proportion is the Side-Splitting Theorem.

c. The justification for the proportion is the Transitive Property of Equality.

13. Use the Side-Splitting Theorem to set up some proportions, then solve them:

$\dfrac{250}{200} = \dfrac{x}{100} = \dfrac{y}{80}$

So $200x = 25,000$, and $x = 125$ m, and $200y = (250)(80) = 20,000$, so $y = 100$ m.

14. $\overleftrightarrow{BE}$ bisects $\angle ABC$, so $\angle ABD \cong \angle CBD$ by the definition of angle bisector (meaning). The angles at vertices A and C are right angles, so $\triangle ABE \sim \triangle CBD$ by the AA Similarity Theorem.

15. Only one pair of congruent angles is indicated, so you cannot conclude that the triangles are similar.

16. Three pairs of congruent angles are indicated, so the triangles are similar by the AA Similarity Theorem. The corresponding vertices are P and S, R and U, and Q and T.

17. The given information is that three sides of one triangle are proportional to the three sides of the second triangle, so the triangles are similar by the SSS Similarity Theorem. The corresponding vertices are S and X, T and Y, and O and Z.

18. The angle that corresponds to $\angle D$ is $\angle H$, so $m\angle H = 40$, and the angle that corresponds to $\angle F$ is $\angle B$, so $m\angle B = 75$.

Corresponding sides $\overline{BC}$ and $\overline{FG}$ are both given, so set up and solve proportions to find other sides:

$$\frac{BC}{FG} = \frac{140}{28} = \frac{105}{HI} = \frac{AB}{35}$$

$140 \cdot HI = (28)(105) = 2940$, so $HI = 21$, and $28 \cdot AB = (140)(35) = 4900$, so $AB = 175$.

19. Set up and solve a proportion:

$$\frac{\text{map distance}}{\text{actual distance}} = \frac{4}{150} = \frac{2.5}{x}$$

$4x = (150)(2.5) = 375$

$x = 93.75$

The actual distance between them is about 93.75 miles.

20.

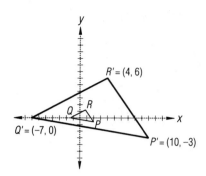

21. Segments $\overline{AD}$ and $\overline{AE}$ do not trisect $\angle BAC$. (On page 145, there is an Exploration question about the impossibility of trisecting an angle using just a straightedge and compass.)

Here is a specific counterexample: Suppose you start with segment $\overline{DE}$, then find vertex A so that $\triangle ADE$ is an equilateral triangle.

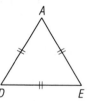

Extend $\overleftrightarrow{DE}$ in both directions, to find points B and C.

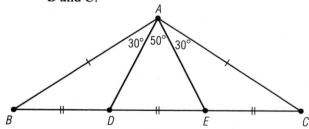

You know that $m\angle DAE = 60$, so the measures of the other two angles at vertex A must each be less than 60, because $\angle BAC$ is not a straight angle.

22. a.

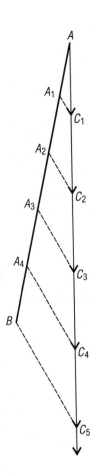

b. By several applications of the Side-Splitting Theorem, the segments of $\overline{AB}$ have the same ratio as the segments $\overline{AC_1}$, $\overline{C_1C_2}$, $\overline{C_2C_3}$, and so on, and that ratio is 1. So the five parts of $\overline{AB}$ are congruent, and each must be $\frac{1}{5}$ of AB.

1.

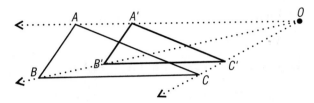

Draw $\overline{OA}$, $\overline{OB}$, and $\overline{OC}$. Then find A', B', and C' so that $AA' = \frac{3}{4}AO$, $BB' = \frac{3}{4}BO$, and $CC' = \frac{3}{4}CO$.

2.

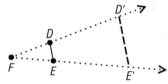

Draw $\overrightarrow{FD}$ and $\overrightarrow{FE}$. Then find D' and E' so that $FD' = 2.8FD$ and $FE' = 2.8FE$.

3. A size change is a similarity transformation. It does not necessarily preserve distance, area, and volume, but it does preserve angle measure (also betweenness, collinearity, and orientation). The answer is choice (a).

4. Under a size change of magnitude $\frac{3}{4}$, the area of the image changes by the square of the ratio of similitude, so Area

$(\Delta A'B'C') = \left(\frac{3}{4}\right)^2$ Area $(\Delta ABC) =$

$\frac{9}{16}$ Area(ΔABC).

5. Two figures are similar if and only if there is a similarity transformation (that is, a composite of size changes and reflections) mapping one onto the other.

6. $\overleftrightarrow{WX} \parallel \overleftrightarrow{YZ}$, so $\overleftrightarrow{WX}$ divides $\overline{YV}$ and $\overline{ZV}$ proportionally. So $\frac{VW}{WY} = \frac{VX}{XZ}$.

7. Using $\frac{VW}{VY} = \frac{VX}{VZ}$ with $VW = 11$, $VY = VW + WY = 11 + 13 = 24$, and $VZ = 30$, then $\frac{11}{24} = \frac{VX}{30}$, so $330 = 24VX$, and $VX = 13.75$ units.

8. Using $\frac{VW}{VY} = \frac{WX}{YZ}$ with $WX = 8$, $YZ = 20$, and $WV = 10$, then $\frac{10}{VY} = \frac{8}{20}$ so $8VY = 200$ and $VY = 25$ units.

9. If $\frac{a}{b} = \frac{c}{d}$, then some other true proportions are $\frac{a}{c} = \frac{b}{d}$, $\frac{d}{b} = \frac{c}{a}$, $\frac{b}{a} = \frac{d}{c}$, $\frac{c}{a} = \frac{d}{b}$. (To check, the means-extremes product should be $ad = bc$.)

10. $\triangle ACB \sim \triangle ECD$ ($\angle BAC \cong \angle DEC$ by $\parallel$ lines $\Rightarrow$ AIA $=$; $\angle ACB \cong \angle ECD$ by the Vertical Angle Theorem), so $\frac{AC}{EC} = \frac{BC}{DC}$. Using $AC = 32$, $CE = 24$, and $DC = 20$, then $\frac{32}{24} = \frac{BC}{20}$ so $640 = 24BC$ and $BC = 26.\overline{6} = 26\frac{2}{3}$ units.

11. $\angle AUQ$ corresponds to $\angle O$, so m$\angle AUQ =$ m$\angle O = 37$. The ratio of similitude can be found using $\frac{DQ}{RF} = \frac{6}{8} = \frac{3}{4}$. So $DA = \frac{3}{4}RU = \frac{3}{4}(27) = \frac{81}{4} = 20.25$ units, and $AU = \frac{3}{4}UO$ or $24 = \frac{3}{4}UO$, $UO = \frac{4}{3}(24) = 4(8) = 32$ units.

12. The ratio of volumes is the cube of the ratio of sides, so the ratio of volumes is $5^3{:}1^3 = 125{:}1$.

13. Using the proportion $\frac{w_1}{w_2} = \left(\frac{h_1}{h_2}\right)^3$, where w represents weight and h represents height, $\frac{5}{w_2} = \left(\frac{4}{12}\right)^3 = \frac{64}{1728}$. So $64w_2 = 8640$ and $w_2 = 135$ lb.

14. The ratios of side lengths can be written as $\frac{8}{12} = \frac{2}{3}$, $\frac{12}{18} = \frac{2}{3}$, and $\frac{18}{27} = \frac{2}{3}$. Since all 3 ratios are equal, the two triangles are similar by the SSS Similarity Theorem.

15. $\angle A \cong \angle E$ and $\angle B \cong \angle D$ because $\parallel$ lines $\Rightarrow$ AIA $=$ (also, $\angle BCA \cong \angle DCE$ by the Vertical Angle Theorem). So the triangles are similar by the AA Similarity Theorem.

16. The parallel streets, Washington, Adams, and Jefferson, divide Martha Lane and Abigail Avenue proportionally. So $\frac{200}{150} = \frac{x}{165}$ and $150x = 33{,}000$, so $x = 220$ m.

17. The slides are similar figures, so $\frac{5}{3} = \frac{x}{25}$ (note that both shorter sides, 3 cm and 25 cm, appear in corresponding positions in the fractions). Then $3x = 125$ and $x = 41.\overline{6} = 41\frac{2}{3}$ cm.

18. The ratio of the lengths of feet equals the ratio of heights, because each is a linear measurement. So $\frac{2}{30} = \frac{0.4}{x}$ (note that both numerators are in meters, while both denominators are in centimeters). Then $2x = 12$ and $x = 6$ cm.

19. The ratio of weights is the cube of the ratio of heights, and the ratio of (foot) areas is the square of the ratio of heights. So the weight would be $6^3 = 216$ times as much and corresponding areas would differ by a factor of $6^2 = 36$.

20.

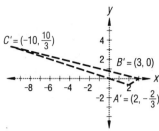

Under a size change of magnitude $\frac{1}{3}$, centered on the origin,

$A = (6, -2)$ so $A' = \left(2, -\frac{2}{3}\right)$;

$B = (9, 0)$ so $B' = (3, 0)$;

$C = (-30, 10)$ so $C' = \left(-10, 3\frac{1}{3}\right)$.

CHAPTER 12 REVIEW   (pp. 624–627)

1.

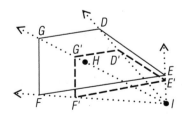

2.

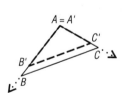

3.

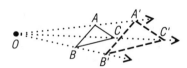

4.

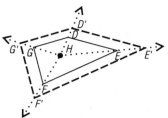

5. For any preimage under a size change with magnitude 1, the image coincides with the preimage, no matter where the center is.

6. The length of each image segment is the product of the magnitude of the size change and the length of the preimage. Using preimage length $JK = 4$ and image length $JM = 4 + 2 = 6$, the magnitude of the size change is $\frac{6}{4} = 1.5$.

Then, to find LN, first find JN, which is $(5)(1.5) = 7.5$. So $LN = JN - JL = 7.5 - 5 = 2.5$ units.

7. Set up and solve a proportion:

$\frac{MP}{PS} = \frac{QR}{RS}$ so $\frac{30}{120} = \frac{25}{RS}$

$30 \cdot RS = (120)(25) = 3000$

$RS = 100$

8. Set up and solve a proportion:

$\frac{MN}{MQ} = \frac{MP}{MS}$ so $\frac{MN}{90} = \frac{30}{150}$

Then $150 \cdot MN = 2700$

$MN = \frac{2700}{150} = 18.$

9. Set up and solve a proportion:

$\frac{AB}{CD} = \frac{BE}{DE}$ so $\frac{42}{12} = \frac{20 + DE}{DE}$

$42 \cdot DE = (12)(20 + DE) = 240 + 12 \cdot DE$

$30 \cdot DE = 240$

$DE = 8$

10. Set up and solve a proportion:

$\frac{SW}{SU} = \frac{WV}{UT}$ so $\frac{SW}{SW + 18} = \frac{11}{20}$

$20 \cdot SW = (11)(SW + 18) = 11 \cdot SW + 198$

$9 \cdot SW = 198$

$SW = 22$

11. Set up and solve a proportion:
$\frac{TV}{WV} = \frac{UV}{XV}$ so $\frac{10}{5} = \frac{UV}{6}$
$5 \cdot UV = 60$
$UV = 12$

12. Set up and solve a proportion:
$\frac{TV}{WV} = \frac{TU}{WX}$ so $\frac{112.5}{WV} = \frac{70}{42}$
$70 \cdot WV = (112.5)(42) = 4725$
$WV = 67.5$

13. The angle that corresponds to $\angle P$ is $\angle H$, so $m\angle H = 100$.
Two corresponding sides with given lengths are $\overline{RS}$ and $\overline{TA}$ so the ratio of proportion is $\frac{6.6}{5} = 1.32$.
The side that corresponds with $\overline{EN}$ is $\overline{OU}$, so $OU = 1.32 \cdot EN = (1.32)(6) = 7.92$; the side that corresponds with $\overline{HO}$ is $\overline{PE}$, so $PE = \frac{HO}{1.32} = \frac{5.5}{1.32} = 4.167$.

14. The ratio of similitude is $\frac{8}{6} = \frac{4}{3}$, so the area of the larger hexagon is $\left(\frac{4}{3}\right)^2$ times the area of the smaller hexagon, or $\left(\frac{4}{3}\right)^2(20) = \left(\frac{16}{9}\right)(20) = \frac{320}{9} \approx 35.56$ cm².

15. If the triangles are similar, then the angles will be congruent. So the measures of the angles in the similar triangle are 57, 33, and 90.

16. The ratio of similitude is the same as the ratio of heights (because height is a linear dimension), so the ratio of similitude is $\frac{3}{4}$.
The volume of the smaller prism is the product of the cube of the ratio of similitude and the volume of the larger prism, or $\left(\frac{3}{4}\right)^3(64) = \left(\frac{27}{64}\right)(64) = 27$ cubic meters.

17. The size change is the same as the ratio of similitude, so the ratio of similitude is 2.5. The area of the image is the product of the square of the ratio of similitude and the area of the preimage, or $(2.5)^2(100) = (6.25)(100) = 625$ units².

18. The area of the image is the product of the square of the ratio of similitude and the area of the preimage. The ratio of similitude is the same as the magnitude of the size change, or 1.5, so the ratio of the areas is $(1.5)^2 = 2.25$.

19. **a.** In a size change, a point which is its own image is the center of the size change, so the center of the size change is point J.
b. The size change takes $JK = 4$ to $JM = 6$, so the magnitude of size change is $\frac{6}{4} = 1.5$.
c. By the Side-Splitting Converse, $\overleftrightarrow{MN} \parallel \overleftrightarrow{KL}$, so the statement is *true*.

20. Size changes preserve angle measure, betweenness, and collinearity, but do not preserve distance; that is choice (d).

21. The ratio of the volumes of similar figures is the cube of the ratio of similitude.

22. **a.**

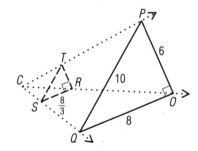

b. The size change takes $OQ = 8$ to $RS = \frac{8}{3}$, so the magnitude of the size change is $\frac{1}{3}$.

c. $\overline{RT}$ is the image of $\overline{PO}$ under a size change of $\frac{1}{3}$.

$PO = 6$, so $RT = \left(\frac{1}{3}\right)(6) = 2$ units.

$\overline{ST}$ is the image of $\overline{PQ}$. $PQ = 10$, so

$ST = \left(\frac{1}{3}\right)(10) = \frac{10}{3}$ units.

23. The ratio of corresponding lengths for similar figures is the same as the ratio of similitude, and the ratio of areas is the square of the ratio of similitude. Given that the ratio of areas is 4:1, then the ratio of similitude (and hence the ratio of lengths) is 2:1.

24. a-b. The two kites do not have to be similar; here is a counterexample:

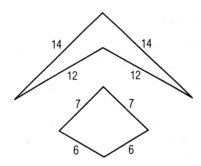

(On page 608, there was an Exploration question dealing with the result that there is no SSSS Similarity Theorem for quadrilaterals.)

25. Some other true proportions that can be derived from $\frac{m}{a} = \frac{t}{e}$ are $\frac{m}{t} = \frac{a}{e}$, $\frac{a}{m} = \frac{e}{t}$,

$\frac{m + a}{a} = \frac{t + e}{e}$, etc.

26. If $\frac{u}{v} = \frac{w}{x}$, then

$\frac{u}{v} + 1 = \frac{w}{x} + 1$

$\frac{u}{v} + \frac{v}{v} = \frac{w}{x} + \frac{x}{x}$

$\frac{u + v}{v} = \frac{w + x}{x}$; that choice is (c).

27. Some true proportions involving the numbers 8, 12, 24, and 16 are $\frac{8}{12} = \frac{16}{24}$, $\frac{8}{16} = \frac{12}{24}$,

$\frac{16}{8} = \frac{24}{12}$, $\frac{8 + 12}{12} = \frac{16 + 24}{24}$, etc.

28. If the Means Exchange Property is applied to $\frac{3}{x} = \frac{4}{5}$, the resulting proportion is $\frac{3}{4} = \frac{x}{5}$.

29. a-b. The numbers 40, 45, and 50 can be expressed as:

$40 = (5)(8)$
$45 = (5)(9)$
$50 = (5)(10)$,

so the sides of the 40, 45, and 50 triangle are proportional to the sides of a 10, 9, 8 triangle, and the triangles are similar by the SSS Similarity Theorem.

30. The third angle in the triangle at the left has measure $180 - (60 + 59) = 180 - 119 = 61$, so the two triangles are similar by the AA Similarity Theorem.

31. The ratios of the sides can be written as $\frac{8}{6}$ and $\frac{12}{9}$, and those two ratios are equal (each equals $\frac{4}{3}$). Since the angles included by those sides are equal, the triangles are similar by the SAS Similarity Theorem.

32. $\overleftrightarrow{AB} \parallel \overleftrightarrow{CD}$, so $\angle BAE \cong \angle CDE$ and $\angle ABE \cong \angle DCE$ because $\parallel$ lines $\Rightarrow$ AIA $=$. So $\triangle ABE \sim \triangle DCE$ by the AA Similarity Theorem.

33. For right triangles ABC and DAC, the shorter legs are in the ratio $x:2x = 1:2$, and the longer legs are in the ratio $2x:4x = 1:2$. The right angles are congruent, so $\triangle ABC \sim \triangle DAC$ by the SAS Similarity Theorem.

34. Use the Side-Splitting Theorem to set up and solve a proportion (use the decimal equivalents for the fractions):

$$\frac{2000}{x} = \frac{.25}{.375}$$

$$.25x = (2000)(.375) = 750$$

$$x = \frac{750}{.25} = 3000$$

There is 3000 feet of frontage on Slant Street between Maple and Pine.

35. Set up and solve a proportion:

$$\frac{\text{shorter dimension}}{\text{longer dimension}} = \frac{5}{8} = \frac{x}{10}$$

$$8x = 50$$

$$x = 6.25$$

The shorter dimension of the similar photograph is 6.25 inches.

36. Set up and solve a proportion:

$$\frac{\text{vertical distance}}{\text{horizontal distance}} = \frac{1.3}{1.5} = \frac{x}{4}$$

$$1.5x = (4)(1.3) = 5.2$$

$$x = \frac{5.2}{1.5} = 3.4667 \approx 3.5 \text{ m}$$

37. Set up and solve a proportion (convert all measurements to meters):

$$\frac{\text{vertical distance}}{\text{horizontal distance}} = \frac{t}{9} = \frac{1}{.6}$$

$$.6t = 9$$

$$t = \frac{9}{.6} = 15$$

The tree is 15 m tall.

38. Set up and solve a proportion:

$$\frac{\text{weight}}{\text{cost}} = \frac{4}{1.89} = \frac{5}{x}$$

$$4x = (5)(1.89) = 9.45$$

$$n = 2.3625 \text{ or } \$2.37$$

39. Set up and solve a proportion:

$$\frac{\text{diagonal length}}{\text{width}} = \frac{9}{7} = \frac{26}{x}$$

$$9x = (7)(26) = 182$$

$$x = 20.22$$

The width of a 26″ screen is about 20″.

40. The ratio of similitude for the two figurines is the same as the ratio of the heights, or

$\frac{32}{20} = 1.6$. The weight of the heavier figurine is the product of the cube of the ratio of similitude and the weight of the smaller figurine, or $(1.6)^3(3) = (4.096)(3) = 12.288$ or about 12.3 kg.

41. The ratio of costs is the same as the ratio of the surface areas of the pizzas, which is the square of the ratio of corresponding linear dimensions, such as the diameter. The ratio of similitude is $\frac{16}{10} = 1.6$, so the larger pizza should be about $(1.6)^2(5.89) = (2.56)(5.89) = 15.0784$ or about $15.

42. The amount of material needed for clothes is related to the surface area of the dolls, which is related to the square of the ratio of similitude. So the amount of material that will make one real coat would make about $12^2 = 144$ coats for dolls.

43. The ratio of similitude, from the ratio of heights, is $\frac{1}{16}$. The weight of the tiny elephant would be the product of the cube of the ratio of similitude and the weight of the full-sized elephant, or $\left(\frac{1}{16}\right)^3(14,000) = (.0625)^3(14,000) \approx 3.42$ pounds.

44. The ratio of similitude, from the heights, is 8. The weight of the taller person would be $8^3 = 512$ times as much as you, and the foot area would be $8^2 = 64$ times as much as yours.

45. As the size of animals increases, the weight grows proportionally faster than the cross-sectional area of the leg. So larger animals need thicker legs (proportionally) to hold their weight than smaller animals; the statement is *true*.

46.

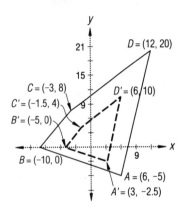

47.

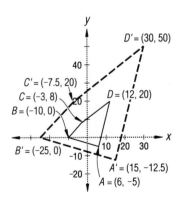

48. $A' = S_k(A) = S_k(6, -5) = (6k, -5k)$;
$B' = S_k(B) = S_k(-10, 0) = (-10k, 0)$;
$C' = S_k(C) = S_k(-3, 8) = (-3k, 8k)$;
$D' = S_k(D) = S_k(12, 20) = (12k, 20k)$;

49. a. $P' = S_4(P) = S_4(-5, -8, 11) = (-20, -32, 44)$

b. $OP = \sqrt{(-5)^2 + (-8)^2 + (11)^2} = \sqrt{25 + 64 + 121} = \sqrt{210}$
$OP' = \sqrt{(-20)^2 + (-32)^2 + 44^2} = \sqrt{400 + 1024 + 1936} = \sqrt{3360} = \sqrt{(16)(210)} = 4\sqrt{210}$
So $OP' = 4 \cdot OP$.

50. a. $S(P) = S_5(1, 4) = (5, 20)$
$S(Q) = S_5(2, -1) = (10, -5)$
$S(R) = S_5(3, -6) = (15, -30)$

b. The question asks to prove that the distance between $S(P)$ and $S(Q)$ is 5 times the distance between P and Q.
$PQ = \sqrt{(1 - 2)^2 + (4 - -1)^2} = \sqrt{(-1)^2 + 5^2} = \sqrt{1 + 25} = \sqrt{26}$
The distance between $S(P)$ and $S(Q)$ is
$\sqrt{(5 - 10)^2 + (20 - -5)^2} = \sqrt{(-5)^2 + 25^2} = \sqrt{25 + 625} = \sqrt{650} = \sqrt{(25)(26)} = 5\sqrt{26}$.

c. slope of $\overline{PQ}$: $\dfrac{y_2 - y_1}{x_2 - x_1} = \dfrac{-1 - 4}{2 - 1} = \dfrac{-5}{1} = -5$
slope of line through $S(P)$ and $S(Q)$:
$\dfrac{y_2 - y_1}{x_2 - x_1} = \dfrac{-5 - 20}{10 - 5} = \dfrac{-25}{5} = -5$
By the Parallel Lines and Slopes Theorem, the two lines are parallel.

d. The slope of the line through $S(P)$ and $S(R)$ is

$$\frac{y_2 - y_1}{x_2 - x_1} = \frac{-30 - 20}{15 - 5} = \frac{-50}{10} = -5.$$

With the result from part c, the lines through $S(P)$ and $S(Q)$ and between $S(P)$ and $S(R)$ have the same slope, and both contain $S(P)$. So the three points $S(P)$, $S(Q)$, and $S(R)$ are collinear.

e. The distance from $S(P)$ to $S(Q)$ is $5\sqrt{26}$ (part b); the distance from $S(Q)$ to $S(R)$ is

$$\sqrt{(10 - 15)^2 + (-5 - -30)^2} = \sqrt{(-5)^2 + 25^2} = \sqrt{25 + 625} = \sqrt{650} = 5\sqrt{26}.$$

The distance from $S(P)$ to $S(R)$ is

$$\sqrt{(5 - 15)^2 + (20 - -30)^2} = \sqrt{(-10)^2 + 50^2} = \sqrt{100 + 2500} = \sqrt{2600} = 10\sqrt{26}.$$

So $S(Q)$ is between $S(P)$ and $S(R)$ by the definition of betweenness.

CHAPTER 13 LOGIC AND INDIRECT REASONING

LESSON 13-1 (pp. 628–634)

1. The puzzle is famous partially because nothing in the clue seems to have anything to do with water or zebras.

2. The two kinds of proofs in mathematics are direct proofs and indirect proofs.

3. The two logical principles in the proof which begins this lesson are the Law of Detachment and the Law of Transitivity.

4. If p is given and $p \Rightarrow q$ is true, then (by the Law of Detachment) q can be concluded.

5. The first statement is $s \Rightarrow r$, and the second statement is $r \Rightarrow p$; you can conclude, by the Law of Transitivity, that $s \Rightarrow p$, or every square is a parallelogram.

6. The second sentence is "isosceles $\Rightarrow$ 2 congruent sides" and the first sentence states that "2 congruent sides $\Rightarrow$ 2 congruent angles." By the Law of Transitivity, you can conclude that if a triangle is isosceles, then it has at least two congruent angles.

7. The first sentence states that "Toothdazzle $\Rightarrow$ whiter teeth," and the second sentence states that "whiter teeth $\Rightarrow$ popularity." By the Law of Transitivity, you can conclude that "If you use Toothdazzle, you will be more popular."
   (Note: While the *validity* of the argument depends on the logic, the *truth* of the conclusion depends on the truth of the premises.)

8. Both statements have the same conclusion: If a figure is something, then it is a polyhedron. No further conclusions are possible.

9. From the given statement you can conclude that "if $7(x - 12) < 70$, then $(x - 12) < 10$," and from that statement you can conclude that "if $x - 12 < 10$, then $x < 22$."
   Using the Law of Transitivity, you can state that "if $7(x - 12) < 70$, then $x < 22$."

10. The statement about Martina Navratilova satisfies the antecedent of the assumed-true statement, so by the Law of Detachment, you can conclude that Martina Navratilova is world class.

11. The statement about Boris Becker satisfies the antecedent of the assumed-true statement, so by the Law of Detachment, you can conclude that Boris Becker is world class.

12. The statement about Gabriela Sabatini does not satisfy the antecedent of the assumed-true statement, so you can make no conclusions based on the Law of Detachment.

13. The statement about Arthur Ashe does not satisfy the antecedent of the assumed-true statement, so you can make no conclusions based on the Law of Detachment.

14. The second statement satisfies the consequent of the first sentence, not its antecedent, so no conclusion is possible based on the Law of Detachment.

15. The statement about Joe satisfies the antecedent of the statement, "If a person has a driver's license, then the person's age is at least 16." So by the Law of Detachement, you can conclude that Joe is at least 16.

16. The statement about Jamie satisfies the antecedent of the statement, "If a person has a driver's license, then the person's age is at least 16." So by the Law of Detachment, you can conclude that Jamie is at least 16.

17. The statement about Florence satisfies the consequent not the antecedent, of the statement, "If a person has a driver's license, then the person's age is at least 16." So no conclusion can be made.

18. The statement about Isabel is not related to the statement, "If a person has a driver's license, then the person's age is at least 16." (She could have a license, for identification purposes, but not drive a car.) So no conclusion can be made.

19. **a.** Some of the conditional statements related to the diagram are:

    If a ray divides an angle into two congruent angles, then the ray bisects that angle.

    If two angles form a linear pair, then they are supplementary.

    The diagram satisfies the antecedents in these sentences, so possible conclusions based on the Law of Detachment are $\overrightarrow{BC}$ bisects $\angle ABD$ or that $\angle EBA$ is supplementary to $\angle ABC$ (or $\angle EBD$ is supplementary to $\angle DBC$).

    b. We know that $x + m\angle ABC = 180$ and that $m\angle EBD + m\angle DBC = 180$, so a conclusion based on the Law of Transitivity is that $x + m\angle ABC = m\angle EBD + m\angle DBC$.

20. Statement 1 is "If D, then U" and statement 2 is "If U, then V." By the Law of Transitivity, a conclusion is "If D, then V" or "a dictionary is valuable"; the reasoning is correct.

21. **a.** $\overline{FI}$ is the hypotenuse of a right triangle with legs 6 and 8, so $FI = 10$.

    b. $\overline{FH}$ is the hypotenuse of a right triangle with legs 4 and 10, so $FI = \sqrt{4^2 + 10^2} = \sqrt{16 + 100} = \sqrt{116}$.

    c. $\overline{GH}$ is the hypotenuse of a right triangle with legs 10 and $\sqrt{116}$, so $GH = \sqrt{(\sqrt{116})^2 + 10^2} = \sqrt{116 + 100} = \sqrt{216}$.

    d. In each part, the Law of Detachment is used to apply the Pythagorean Theorem, as is the Law of Transitivity. So all three properties are used; that is choice (iv).

22. In $\triangle GFH$, $GH^2 = FG^2 + HF^2$; in $\triangle FIH$, $HF^2 = HI^2 + IF^2$; in $\triangle FEI$, $IF^2 = IE^2 + EF^2$. Substituting,
$$GH^2 = FG^2 + HF^2$$
$$= FG^2 + HI^2 + IF^2$$
$$= FG^2 + HI^2 + IE^2 + EF^2.$$

23. The dimensions of the base are tripled, so the area of the new base is $3^2 = 9$ times the area of the old base. The height of the pyramid is doubled, so the volume of the new pyramid is $(9)(2) = 18$ times the volume of the old pyramid.

24. The diameter of the base is tripled, so the area of the base is multiplied by $3^2 = 9$. The height of the cylinder is doubled, so the volume of the new cylinder is $(9)(2) = 18$ times the volume of the old cylinder.

25.

The pentagon can be triangulated into 3 triangles, and the sum of the measures of each triangle is 180. So the sum of the measures for the pentagon is $(3)(180) = 540$. This is equivalent to using the Polygon-Sum Theorem:
$$S = (n - 2)(180) = (5 - 2)(180) = 3(180) = 540.$$

26. A figure is a trapezoid if and only if it is a quadrilateral with at least one pair of parallel sides.

27.

28. a.

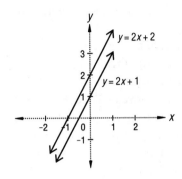

b. The lines have the same slope and do not intersect; they are parallel.

c. The lines are neither horizontal nor vertical; they are oblique.

29. a. $(x - y)^2 = (x - y)(x - y)$
$$= x^2 - xy - xy + y^2$$
$$= x^2 - 2xy + y^2$$

b. $(a - (-a))^2 = (a - -a)^2$
$$= (a + a)^2$$
$$= (2a)^2$$
$$= (2a)(2a)$$
$$= 4a^2$$

30. Here is rectangle $ABCD$.

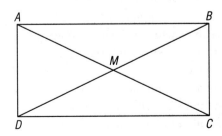

Some theorems are:
If a figure is a rectangle, then it is a parallelogram. ($ABCD$) is a parallelogram.)
If a figure is a rectangle, then its diagonals are congruent. ($AC = BD$)
If a figure is a rectangle, then its diagonals bisect each other. ($\overline{AC}$ and $\overline{BD}$ bisect each other, or M is the midpoint of $\overline{AC}$ and $\overline{BD}$, or $AM = MC$ and $BM = MD$.)
If a figure is a rectangle, then it has four right angles. ($\angle$s A, B, C, and D are right angles.)
If a figure is a rectangle, then its opposite sides are parallel. ($\overline{AB} \parallel \overline{DC}$ and $\overline{AD} \parallel \overline{BC}$.)
If a figure is a rectangle, then its opposite sides are congruent. ($\overline{AB} \cong \overline{DC}$ and $\overline{AD} \cong \overline{BC}$.)

31. From clue 10 (The Norwegian lives in the first house on the left.) and clue 15 (The Norwegian lives next to the blue house.), some conclusions are:
The blue house is the second house from the left.
The Norwegian does not live in the blue house.

LESSON 13–2 (pp. 635–639)

1. The negation is "It is not the case that the perimeter of an n-gon with side s is ns" or "The perimeter of an n-gon with side s is not ns."

2. The negation is "It is not the case that $\angle A$ is acute," or "$\angle A$ is not acute" or "$\angle A$ is either right or obtuse."

3. The negation is "It is not the case that you were not late for school today" or "You were late for school today."

4. The negation is "It is not the case that $\triangle GHI$ is scalene," or "$\triangle GHI$ is not scalene," or "$\triangle GHI$ is either isosceles or equilateral."

5. The negation of a statement p is written *not-p.*

6. The statement is "If $m\angle T = 45$, then $\angle T$ is acute."
   a. The converse is "If $\angle T$ is acute, then $m\angle T = 45$."
   b. The contrapositive is "If $\angle T$ is not acute, then $m\angle T \neq 45$."
   c. The inverse is "If $m\angle T \neq 45$, then $\angle T$ is not acute."

7. The statement is $p \Rightarrow q$.
   a. The converse is $q \Rightarrow p$.
   b. The contrapositive is $not\text{-}q \Rightarrow not\text{-}p$.
   c. The inverse is $not\text{-}p \Rightarrow not\text{-}q$.

8. The statement is "If $ax + by = c$, then $ax = c - by$."
   a. The converse is "If $ax = c - by$, then $ax + by = c$."
   b. The contrapositive is "If $ax \neq c - by$, then $ax + by \neq c$."
   c. The inverse is "If $ax + by \neq c$, then $ax \neq c - by$."

9. The statement is "If you bring in that tape recorder on Saturday, then you will get $10."
   a. The converse is "If you got $10, then you brought in that tape recorder on Saturday."
   b. The contrapositive is "If you did not get $10, then you did not bring in that tape recorder on Saturday."
   c. The inverse is "If you do not bring in that tape recorder on Saturday, then you will not get $10."

10. By the Law of the Contrapositive, if a statement is true, its contrapositive must be true. (Choice d)

11. By the definition of negation, if a statement is true, its negation is false. (Choice a)

12. By the Law of the Contrapositive, if a statement is false, its contrapositive must be false. (Choice d)

13. Statement:
    If $\triangle ABC$ is not a right triangle, then the Pythagorean Theorem does not hold for $\triangle ABC$.
    Negation of consequent:
    The Pythagorean Theorem does hold for $\triangle ABC$.
    Negation of antecedent:
    $\triangle ABC$ is a right triangle.
    Contrapositive:
    If the Pythagorean Theorem does hold for $\triangle ABC$, then $\triangle ABC$ is a right triangle.

14. The contrapositive of the first statement is that if a network is not traversable, then it does not have only even vertices (that is, it has at least one odd vertex).
    The second statement satisfies the antecedent of that contrapositive, so by the Law of Detachment, the network below has at least one odd vertex. (In fact, it has 4 odd vertices.)
    (Note that while the first given statement is true, it is "stronger" than absolutely necessary—a network can have up to two odd vertices and still be traversable.)

15. a. The first statement can be expressed as "If p, then q," and its contrapositive is "If $not\text{-}q$, then $not\text{-}p$." The second statement can be expressed as "$not\text{-}q$." By the Law of Detachment, a conclusion is "$not\text{-}p$" or "x is not equal to 3."
    b. The conclusion used the Law of the Contrapositive and the Law of Detachment.

16. From $not\text{-}r$ and the contrapositive of statement 2, $not\text{-}r \Rightarrow not\text{-}q$, the Law of Detachment lets you conclude $not\text{-}q$. Then, from $not\text{-}q$ and the contrapositive of statement 1, $not\text{-}q \Rightarrow not\text{-}p$, the Law of Detachment lets you conclude $not\text{-}p$.

17. The contrapositive of her mother's statement is "If you go out tonight, then you apologize to your brother." Joanne went out, which satisfied the antecedent of that statement, so by the Law of Detachment, she apologized to her brother.

18. Jose was not sorry, which satisfies the consequent of the ad, not its antecedent. Nothing can be concluded.

19. From statement 2, and the contrapositive of statement 1, you can conclude that these apples are wholesome, so they are ripe. Statement 3 can be restated as "If fruit is grown in the shade, it is not ripe"; from the contrapositive of this statement, and your ripe apples from the first conclusion, you can conclude that these apples were not grown in the shade.

20. From statement 2, that $m\angle ABC$ is not 60, and from the contrapositive of statement 1, that triangles that do not have three 60-degree angles are not equilateral, you can conclude that $\triangle ABC$ is not an equilateral triangle.

21. The Law of Detachment states that if you have a statement or given information p and a justification of the form $p \Rightarrow q$, you may conclude q.

22. The second statement is "If a figure is a rhombus, then it is a parallelogram." Statement 1 satisfies the antecedent of statement 2, so by the Law of Detachment, $ABCD$ is a parallelogram.
Then, restating the third statement as "If a figure is a parallelogram, then its opposite sides are parallel," and noting that our conclusion that $ABCD$ is a parallelogram satisfies the antecedent of statement 3, you can conclude (by the Law of Detachment) that the opposite sides of $ABCD$ are parallel.

23. It is given that the opposite sides of $ABCD$ are parallel, so $ABCD$ is a parallelogram by the definition of parallelogram (sufficient condition). Then you can conclude that $\overline{AB} \cong \overline{CD}$ by the Properties of a Parallelogram Theorem (part b).

24. The antecedent is that the figure is a parallelogram, and the consequent is that opposite sides are congruent, so you have proved the statement that in a parallelogram, opposite sides are congruent; that is choice (b).

25. $$5x - 13 = 19x + 15$$
$$-14x - 13 = 15$$
$$-14x = 28$$
$$x = -2$$

26. $$8(y - 3) = 7(3y + 1)$$
$$8y - 24 = 21y + 7$$
$$-13y - 24 = 7$$
$$-13y = 31$$
$$y = \frac{-31}{13} \approx -2.38$$

27. $$6z^2 = 150$$
$$z^2 = 25$$
$$z = \pm 5$$

28. $$(w + 5)^2 = 289$$
$$w + 5 = \pm 17$$
So $w = 17 - 5 = 12$ or $w = -17 - 5 = -22$.

29. Puzzles and conclusions will vary.

LESSON 13-3 (pp. 640–644)

1. When a coin is tossed, there are only two possibilities. If the face that shows is not "heads," you can conclude that it is "tails" by the Law of Ruling Out Possibilities.

2. If either m or n is true, and m is not true, then by the Law of Ruling Out Possibilities, you can conclude that n is true.

3. Two different lines in a plane are either parallel or they intersect. If they are not parallel, then you can conclude, by the Law of Ruling Out Possibilities, that they intersect.

4. Clue 3 is "The secretary is either Catherine or Ms. Landis." So the secretary is not a man; the secretary is not Mr. Farmer or Mr. Guinness (or redundantly, not Edgar or Wilbur).

5. Clue 1 is "Neither Catherine nor Marjorie is the teller and neither is Ms. Edwards."
   From that clue you can conclude:
   Ms. Edwards' first name is Shirley.
   The teller is a male.

6. Clue 5 is "Mr. Farmer, Edgar, and the bookkeeper have all worked at the bank for more than 5 years."
   From that clue you can conclude:
   Edgar is not the bookkeeper.
   Mr. Farmer is not the bookkeeper.
   Mr. Farmer's first name is not Edgar (so it must be Wilbur, and Edgar's last name is Guinness).
   The bookkeeper is a woman.

7.

	Clarinet	Cornet	Flute	Trombone	Tuba
Carol	O	X	X_1	X_1	X
Sue	X	X	X_2	O	X
Jill	X	X	O	X	X
Dave	X_3	X_3	X_3	X_3	O
Jim	X	O	X	X	X

Carol—Clarinet; Sue—Trombone;
Jill—Flute; Dave—Tuba; Jim—Cornet.

8. A line is either parallel to a plane, in the plane, or it intersects the plane in a single point. It is given that m is not parallel to plane X, and m is not in plane X. So, by the Law of Ruling Out Possibilities, m intersects plane X and m and X have exactly one point in common.

9. If trapezoid $ABCD$ is not a parallelogram, then one pair of opposite sides must be not parallel. Since it is given that $\overline{AB} \parallel \overline{CD}$, you can conclude that $\overline{AD}$ is not parallel to $\overline{BC}$.

10. By the Trichotomy Law and the Law of Ruling Out Possibilities, if $\sqrt{2} \neq \frac{41}{29}$, then either $\sqrt{2} < \frac{41}{29}$ or $\sqrt{2} > \frac{41}{29}$.
    (In fact, $\sqrt{2} \approx 1.414$ and $\frac{41}{29} \approx 1.41379$, so $\sqrt{2} > \frac{41}{29}$.)

11.

	lawyer	farmer	teacher	doctor	dentist	car dealer	chemist
Joyce	O	X	X	X_1	X	X_1	X_1
Mike	X	X	X	X_2	X	X_2	O
Darlene	X_6	X_6	X_6	X_6	O_6	X_6	X_6
Gary	X_3	X	O	X_3	X	X_3	X_3
Wanda	X	X	X	X	X	O	X
Ken	X_4	O	X_4	X_4	X	X_4	X_4
Brad	X	X	X	O	X	X_5	X

Joyce—lawyer; Mike—chemist;
Darlene—dentist; Gary—teacher; Wanda—car
dealer; Ken—farmer; Brad—doctor

12.

	Ms. Lardis	Mr. Farmer	Mr. Guinness	Ms. Voila	Ms. Edwards	Teller	Secretary	Bookkeeper	Guard	Manager
Catherine	X_3	X	X	O	X_1	X_1	O	X	X	X
Edgar	X	X_5	O	X_4	X	X_4	X_3	X_5	X_4	O
Wilbur	X	O	X	X	X	O	X_3	X	X	X
Marjorie	O	X	X	X	X_1	X_1	X	X	O	X
Shirley	X	X	X	X	O	X	X	O	X_2	X
Teller	O	X	X	X_4	X_1					
Secretary	X	X_3	X_3	O	X_4					
Bookkeeper	X	X_5	X	X	O					
Guard	O	X	X	X_4	X					
Manager	X	X	O	X	X					

Catherine Voila—Secretary;
Edgar Guinness—Manager;
Wilbur Farmer—Teller;
Marjorie Lardis—Guard;
Shirley Edwards—Bookkeeper

13. The statement is "If Jackie is a good cook,
I'll eat my hat!"

   a. The converse is "If I eat my hat, Jackie is
(will become) a good cook!"

   b. The inverse if "If Jackie is not a good
cook, I will not eat my hat."

   c. The contrapositive is "If I do not eat my
hat, Jackie is not a good cook."

14. From the second statement and then the first, by the Law of Transitivity, every natural number is a real number. Then, using that statement with the contrapositive of statement 3, you can conclude that every natural number is not the complex number i.

15. From the first and third statement and the Law of Transitivity, you can conclude that every square is a kite. Then, using that statement and statement 2, you can conclude that every square has diagonals that are perpendicular.

16. The negation of "$\triangle ABC$ is isosceles" can be written as:
It is not the case that $\triangle ABC$ is isosceles.
$\triangle ABC$ is not isosceles.
$\triangle ABC$ is scalene.
(Note: the statement "$\triangle ABC$ is equilateral" is **not** a negation of "$\triangle ABC$ is isosceles," because every equilateral triangle is also isosceles.)

17. $\triangle CAB$ and $\triangle CDE$ are isosceles, with vertex angle C, so $AC = BC$ and $DC = EC$ by the definition of isosceles triangle (meaning). Also, $\angle ACD \cong \angle BCE$ by the Vertical Angle Theorem. So $\triangle ACD \cong \triangle BCE$ by the SAS Congruence Theorem.

18. a.

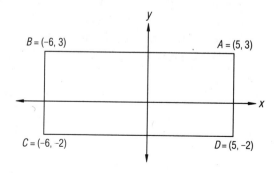

The four angles of $ABCD$ are right angles, so $ABCD$ is a rectangle.

b. Using the distance formula,
$$AC = \sqrt{(5 - \text{-}6)^2 + (3 - \text{-}2)^2}$$
$$= \sqrt{11^2 + 5^2}$$
$$= \sqrt{121 + 25}$$
$$= \sqrt{146}$$
$$BD = \sqrt{(\text{-}6 - 5)^2 + (3 - \text{-}2)^2}$$
$$= \sqrt{(\text{-}11)^2 + 5^2}$$
$$= \sqrt{121 + 25}$$
$$= \sqrt{146}.$$
So $AC = BD$.

19. Examples of logic puzzles will vary.

LESSON 13-4 (pp. 645–650)

1. In this lesson, the lawyer used indirect reasoning.

2. The student used valid logic and came to a contradiction. The student should conclude that the original premise is impossible; in this case, that it cannot be that $2 + 5x = 5x - 8$ for any value of x.

3. Valid reasoning from the statement $\sqrt{2400} = 49$ led to the false conclusion $2400 = 2401$. So, by the Law of Indirect Reasoning, the original statement $\sqrt{2400} = 49$ is false, or $\sqrt{2400} \neq 49$.

4. The Law of Indirect Reasoning states that if valid reasoning from a statement p leads to a false conclusion, then p is false.

5. $3(x - 2) = 3x - 2$
$3x - 6 = 3x - 2$
$-6 = -2$
Valid reasoning from the statement $3(x - 2) = 3x - 2$ led to the false conclusion $-6 = -2$. So, by the Law of Indirect Reasoning, the original statement $3(x - 2) = 3x - 2$ is false, and the equation is never true; that is choice (a).

6. Two statements p and q are contradictory if and only if they cannot both be true at the same time.

7. Start with the (temporary) assumption that $\sqrt{9800} = 99$. Squaring both sides, you can deduce that $9800 = 99^2 = 9801$. But the statement that $9800 = 9801$ is a contradiction. So, by the Law of Indirect Reasoning, the original assumption that $\sqrt{9800} = 99$ is false, so $\sqrt{9800} \neq 99$.

8. a.

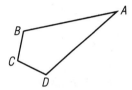

   b. Start with the (temporary) assumption that a quadrilateral has all four angles obtuse; that is, that all four angle measures are greater than 90. Adding those angle measures, you can conclude that the sum of the angles of the quadrilateral is greater than 360. But, by the Quadrilateral-Sum Theorem, the sum of the measures of a quadrilateral equals 360, which is a contradiction of your previous conclusion. So, by the Law of Indirect Reasoning, the original assumption that a quadrilateral can have four obtuse angles is impossible, and a quadrilateral cannot have all four angles obtuse.

9. Statements contradictory to "$\triangle ABC$ is isosceles" are "$\triangle ABC$ is not isosceles" and "$\triangle ABC$ is scalene."
(Note: The statement "$\triangle ABC$ is equilateral" is not contradictory to "$\triangle ABC$ is isosceles" because they are both true for equilateral triangle ABC.)

10. A statement contradictory to "Coplanar lines m and n are parallel" is "lines m and n intersect in exactly one point."
(Note: The definition of parallel lines (p. 36) allows identical lines to be parallel. So the phrase "in exactly one point" is needed to assure a contradictory statement to the given statement.)

11. Yes; $m\angle A$ cannot be both equal to 85 and greater than 90, so the statements are contradictory.

12. Not contradictory; a square has two pairs of parallel sides, and any quadrilateral with at least one pair of parallel sides is a trapezoid. So every square is a trapezoid.

13. Not contradictory; many people older than 25 attend and graduate high school.

14. a-b. Assume (temporarily) that a right triangle has two right angles. Then the sum of the measures of the three angles of the triangle must be greater than 180. But this contradicts the Triangle-Sum Theorem. So the original assumption is false, and, by the Law of Ruling Out Possibilities, you can conclude that a triangle cannot have two right angles. Another way to state that conclusion is that a triangle can have no more than one right angle.

15. a. $-12x > 252$
$0 > 12x + 252$
$-252 > 12x$
$-21 > x$
(Note: If you divided both sides of the first inequality by -12, remember that multiplying or dividing an inequality by a negative number **reverses** the sense of the inequality.)

   b. Each of the three steps in part a uses direct reasoning.

16. Assume (temporarily) that it is false that $\triangle ABC$ is scalene; that would mean that $\triangle ABC$ is isoceles (or equilateral, but an equilateral triangle is also isosceles). But if $\triangle ABC$ is isosceles, then two sides have equal length by the definition of isosceles triangle (meaning), and so you can conclude that two angles are congruent by the Isosceles Triangle Theorem. But it is given that no two angles are congruent, which contradicts your prior conclusion. So your original assumption, that $\triangle ABC$ is isosceles, is false, and so by the Law of Ruling Out Possibilities, $\triangle ABC$ is scalene.

17.

	5′6″	5′7″	5′8″	5′10″	5′11″	blond	red	auburn	black	brunette
Mary	X_3	X	X	O_1	X_3	X	X_1	X	O	X
Isobel	X_5	X	X	X	O	X_5	X	X	X	O
Marcia	X_3	O	X	X	X_3	O	X	X	X	X
Grace	O_5	X	X_5	X	X_5	X_5	O	X	X	X
Ruth	X	X	O_1	X	X	X	X_1	O	X	X
blond	X	O_5	X	X	X					
red	O_1	X_1	X	X_1	X_1					
auburn	X	X	O	X	X					
black	X	X	X	O_4	X					
brunette	X	X	X_2	X	O					

Isobel—5′11″—brunette;
Mary—5′10″—black; Ruth—5′8″—auburn;
Marcia—5′7″—blond; Grace—5′6″—red

18. The negation of the statement "$\triangle ABC \sim \triangle DEF$" is that "$\triangle ABC$ is not similar to $\triangle DEF$." (Another way to indicate this same conclusion is m$\angle A \neq$ m$\angle D$.)

19. The statement is "If $\triangle ABC \sim \triangle DEF$, then $\angle A \cong \angle D$."

a. The contrapositive is "If $\angle A$ is not congruent to $\angle D$, then $\triangle ABC$ is not similar to $\triangle DEF$."

b. The converse is "If $\angle A \cong \angle D$, then $\triangle ABC \sim \triangle DEF$."

c. The inverse is "If $\triangle ABC$ is not similar to $\triangle DEF$, then $\angle A$ is not congruent to $\angle D$."

d. The contrapositive is *true*.

20. Use the Side-Splitting Theorem to set up a proportion:
$$\frac{XW}{WZ} = \frac{XV}{VY} \text{ so } \frac{7}{WZ} = \frac{9}{11}$$
$$9 \cdot WZ = 77$$
$$WZ = \frac{77}{9} \approx 8.556 \text{ units}$$

21. Use the Side-Splitting Theorem to set up a proportion:
$$\frac{XW}{XZ} = \frac{WV}{YZ} \text{ so } \frac{6}{9} = \frac{8}{YZ}$$
$$6 \cdot YZ = 72$$
$$YZ = 12 \text{ units}$$

22. Using the given coordinates,
$$RC = \sqrt{(0-a)^2 + (b-0)^2}$$
$$= \sqrt{(-a)^2 + b^2}$$
$$= \sqrt{a^2 + b^2}$$
$$TE = \sqrt{(0-a)^2 + (0-b)^2}$$
$$= \sqrt{(-a)^2 + (-b)^2}$$
$$= \sqrt{a^2 + b^2}$$

So $RC = TE$, and in a rectangle, the diagonals have the same length.

23. Examples will vary. Some samples are
A: You drive too fast.
B: You have a serious accident.

A: You exercise without stretching first.
B: You injure a muscle.

LESSON 13-5 (pp. 651–657)

1. **a.** By definition, a line and a circle, in the same plane, are tangent if and only if the line intersects the circle in exactly one point.
   b. Another condition sufficient for a line to be tangent to a circle is a theorem: If a line is perpendicular to a radius of a circle at the radius's endpoint on the circle, then the line is tangent to the circle.

2. Yes. The second theorem in this lesson states that if a line is tangent to a circle, then it is perpendicular to the radius drawn to the point of tangency. The situation with line ℓ and the circle satisfies the antecedent of that theorem, so by the Law of Detachment you can conclude that ℓ is perpendicular to $\overline{OP}$.

3. In the proof of the first theorem of this lesson, a conclusion is reached that $OQ > OP$ and $OQ = OP$; that is a contradiction.

4. Abbreviate the first two theorems in this lesson:

   If the line is perpendicular, then it's a tangent.
   If a line is tangent, then it's perpendicular.

   These two theorems are converses; that is choice (a).

5. In order to prove the second theorem:

   If a line is tangent to a circle, then it is perpendicular to the radius drawn to the point of tangency,

   the following statement was proved:

   If a line is not perpendicular to the radius drawn to the point of tangency, then the line is not tangent to the circle.

The second statement is the contrapositive of the first, and, by the Law of the Contrapositive, a statement is equivalent to its contrapositive; that is, they are either both true or both false.

6. **a.** For linear dimensions, the ratio of the size of the sun to the moon is

   $$\frac{\text{radius of sun}}{\text{radius of moon}} = \frac{432{,}000}{1080} = \frac{400}{1}$$

   The linear dimensions of the sun are about 400 times larger than those of the moon.
   b. The ratio of distances is

   $$\frac{\text{earth to sun}}{\text{earth to moon}} = \frac{93{,}000{,}000}{240{,}000} = \frac{387.5}{1}$$

   The sun is about 387.5 times further from the earth than the moon is from the earth.

7. Lines $\overleftrightarrow{PA}$ and $\overleftrightarrow{QB}$ are both perpendicular to $\overleftrightarrow{AC}$, so they are parallel by the Two Perpendiculars Theorem. So you can use the Side-Splitting Theorem to set up a proportion:

   $$\frac{PA}{AC} = \frac{QB}{BC} \text{ so } \frac{PA}{15} = \frac{3}{5}$$
   $$5 \cdot PA = 45$$
   $$PA = 9 \text{ units}$$

8. A real-world example of a line tangent to a circle is in a circus, with a unicycle on a "high wire."

9. A real-world example of a plane tangent to a sphere is a basketball resting on a basketball court.

10. A real-world example of a line tangent to a sphere would be a ball just balanced on a telephone wire.

11. $\triangle PAC$ and $\triangle QBC$ are right triangles, so $QC = \sqrt{3^2 + 5^2} = \sqrt{9 + 25} = \sqrt{34}$, and $PC = \sqrt{PA^2 + AC^2} = \sqrt{9^2 + 15^2} = \sqrt{81 + 225} = \sqrt{306} = \sqrt{(9)(34)} = 3\sqrt{34}$. So $PQ = 3\sqrt{34} - \sqrt{34} = 2\sqrt{34} \approx 11.66$.

12. a. A Radius-Tangent Theorem for a sphere would be that a line or plane is tangent to a sphere if and only if that line or plane is perpendicular to a radius of the sphere at the radius's endpoint on the sphere.

b. The statement in part a is true.

13. a. Yes; according to the extension in Question 12a, if $\overleftrightarrow{IZ}$ is tangent to sphere P at point I, then $\overline{ZI} \perp \overline{IP}$.

b.

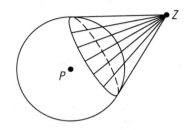

There are an infinite number of tangents from point Z to sphere P; they form a cone with vertex P such that the lateral surface of the cone is tangent to the sphere.

14. Draw segment $\overline{NP}$. Then $\angle X$ and $\angle Y$ are right angles, because they are the intersections of tangents and radii, so ΔXNP and ΔYNP are right triangles. $XN = YN$ by the definition of circle (meaning), and $NP = NP$ by the Reflexive Property of Equality, so $\Delta XNP \cong \Delta YNP$ by the HL Congruence Theorem, and $XP = YP$ by the CPCF Theorem. So $PXNY$ is a kite by the definition of kite (sufficient condition).

15.

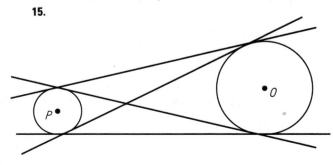

16. a. $\overline{PT}$ is tangent to the circle, so ΔOTP is a right triangle and $\overline{OT}$ is a leg of a right triangle with hypotenuse 15 and other leg 12. The triangle is a multiple of a 3-4-5 right triangle, so the sides are 9, 12, and 15, and so the radius is $OT = 9$ and the area is $A = \pi r^2 = \pi(9)^2 = 81\pi \approx$ 254.5 units^2.

b. $PN = PO - ON$
$= PO - OT$
$= 15 - 9$
$= 6$

17. The ratio of volumes of two spheres is the cube of the ratio of similitude. Using the information that the radius of the sun is 432,000 and the radius of the earth is 3960 miles, the cube of the ratio of similitude is $\left(\frac{432,000}{3960}\right)^3 = (109.09)^3 \approx 1,298,240$.
The volume of the sun is about 1.3 million times that of the earth; that is closest to choice (b).

18. Assume (temporarily) that $\sqrt{39,600} = 199$. Then square both sides to conclude $39,600 = 199^2 = 39,601$. This is a contradiction, so the orginal assumption must be false. Then, by the Law of Ruling Out Possibilities, $\sqrt{39,600} \neq 199$.

19. a. If statement 1 is true, then the second part of it is false by statement 2. So the first part must be true: Julie walks to school.

b. The reasoning law used was the Law of Ruling Out Possibilities.

20. a. First step: The contrapositive of the first statement is, "If you do not have a southern accent, then you did not grow up in Mississippi."

Second step: The third statement satisfies the antecedent of that statement, so you can conclude "Murray did not grow up in Mississippi."

Third step: With that conclusion and the second statement, you can conclude "Murray does not know the Ole Miss fight song."

b. The reasoning laws used are the Law of the Contrapositive (first step) and the Law of Detachment (second and third steps).

21. a. The contrapositive of the statement "If a figure is a rectangle, then its diagonals are congruent is

"If the diagonals of a figure are not congruent, then the figure is not a rectangle."

b. Yes; the original statement is true, so by the Law of the Contrapositive, the contrapositive is also true.

22.

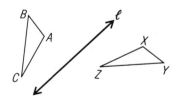

23. a.

Earth

1 in. ≈ 41,400 mi   moon

b. Using the given circle (which has a diameter of $\frac{5}{16}$″) as the earth (which has a diameter of about 7920 miles), the scale is that 1 inch represents about 25,000 miles. So the sun would be a circle with a diameter of about 35 inches, and the distance between the centers of the earth and the sun would be about 310 feet.

24.

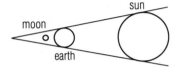

25. An annular eclipse occurs when the moon comes between the sun and the earth so that from the earth you see only a ring of the sun all the way around the moon.

LESSON 13–6 (pp. 658–664)

1. By the first postulate of Euclid, two points determine a line segment, so a line through two points is uniquely determined.

2. By the Uniqueness of Parallels Theorem, a line parallel to a given line through a point not on it is uniquely determined.

333

3.

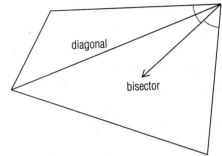

A diagonal of a quadrilateral does not always bisect the angle(s) of the quadrilateral, so the situation is **not** uniquely determined. (It is sometimes said that this situation is "overdetermined".)

4.

5.

6. Playfair's Parallel Postulate (or the Uniqueness of Parallels Theorem) states that through a point not on a line, there is exactly one parallel to the line.

7. Euclid's first book of geometry had 10 postulates.

8. Of the 10 postulates, 5 were specifically geometric in nature.

9. Euclid's fifth postulate (If two lines are cut by a transversal, and the interior angles on the same side of the transversal have a total measure of less than 180, then the lines will intersect on that side of the transversal) was the one that most troubled mathematicians.

10. Playfair's Parallel Postulate is equivalent to Euclid's fifth postulate; it cannot be proved from Euclid's first four postulates.

11. Geometries in which Playfair's Parallel Postulate is not true are called non-Euclidean geometries.

12. Since the discovery of non-Euclidean geometries, postulates have been viewed as *statements assumed to be true* rather than as statements which are definitely true.

13.

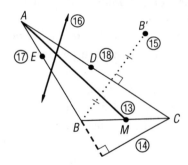

Point A and the midpoint of $\overline{BC}$ are both uniquely determined, so the segment connecting those two points is uniquely determined.

14. There is exactly one line perpendicular to a given line through a given point, so the desired line is uniquely determined.

15. A point has exactly one reflection over a given line, so the situation is uniquely determined.

16. A bisector of segment $\overline{AB}$ is any line, segment, ray, or point through the midpoint of $\overline{AB}$. There are many such lines, segments, and rays, so the situation is not uniquely determined.

17. There are many points between A and B, so point E is not uniquely determined.

18. AD is a unique distance, and there is exactly one point on ray $\overrightarrow{AC}$ that is that specific distance from A. So point D is uniquely determined.

19.

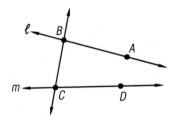

Antecedent:
$m\angle ABC + m\angle BCD < 180$
Consequent:
Lines ℓ and m will meet on the same side of $\overleftrightarrow{BC}$ as A and D are.

20. Euclid's first postulate (Two points determine a line segment) is like the Unique line assumption of the Point-Line-Plane Postulate.

21. Euclid's third postulate (A circle can be drawn with any center and any radius) is like the Compass Rule property of constructions.

22. The lines parallel to $3x + 2y = 5$ have the same x- and y-coefficients; those are choices (a) and (c). Check which one contains the point (10, 13):
(a) Does $3(10) + 2(13) = 23$?
   Does $30 + 26 = 23$? No.
(c) Does $3(10) + 2(13) = 56$?
   Does $30 + 26 = 56$? Yes.
So the line that satisfies the condition is choice (c).

23. The radius and the tangent are perpendicular, so $\overline{TO}$ is the leg of a right triangle with hypotenuse 20 and other leg 16. The lengths 20 and 16 are multiples of 4 and 5, so the unknown leg is the same multiple of 3; $TO = (4)(3) = 12$ units.

24. Assume (temporarily) that a quadrilateral has four acute angles. By the definition of acute angle (meaning), each angle has a measure less than 90, so you can conclude that the sum of the four measures is less than 360. But this conclusion contradicts the Quadrilateral-Sum Theorem. So the original assumption must be false, and a quadrilateral cannot have four acute angles.

25. The second statement satisfies the antecedent of the contrapositive of the first statement. So by the Law of Detachment, the consequent of the contrapositive of the first statement must be true: Richard Nixon did not win the majority of electoral votes in 1960.

26. The first statement says that Miami had 6 points, and that satisfies the antecedent of the second statement. So, by the Law of Detachment, Miami scored either three safeties, two field goals, or one touchdown. By the second and third statements, and the Law of Ruling Out Possibilities, Miami scored only on field goals, so they scored two field goals.

27. "The diagonals are congruent" is true for rectangles (and isosceles trapezoids, but not all trapezoids).

28. "There is a pair of congruent sides" is true for kites, parallelograms, rhombuses, and rectangles (and isosceles trapezoids, but not all trapezoids).

29. Outside of mathematics, the term *auxiliary* means assisting or supplementing.

30. **a.** Some examples of things that are unique are a person's date of birth (unless it is February 29), the mayor of a city, the current speed limit for a section of a highway, or the winner of a tennis tournament.

   b. Some things that are not unique are speed limits and players in tournaments.

31. To follow along with the reasoning, draw 5 houses (numbered 1 through 5, from left to right), with room to label the appropriate colors, nationalities, pets, drinks, and cigarettes.

To start, the Norwegian lives in house 1, (clue 10) and house 2 is blue (clue 15). House 1 is not ivory or green (clue 6) nor red (clue 2); it must be yellow by elimination. So Kools are smoked in house 1 (clue 8). Then house 2 has the horse (clue 12). Also, house 3 has milk (clue 9).

From here on, you have to use the Law of Ruling Out Possibilities to make your decisions. Some of the possibilities, though, take many steps to rule out.

From clue 5, the red house cannot be between the ivory and green houses, so either house 3 or house 5 is red. Suppose the red house is house 5. Then:

House 5 has the Englishman (clue 2). House 3 is ivory and house 4 is green (clue 6), and house 4 has coffee (clue 4). The Ukrainian and tea go together (clue 5); that is house 2 by elimination. Lucky Strikes and orange juice go together (clue 13); that is house 5 by elimination. The Spaniard owns the dog (clue 3), and they can either be in house 3 or house 4.

If they are in house 3, then the Japanese and Parliaments (clue 14) are in house 4. But this leaves no house for Old Golds and snails (clue 7); so the assumption that the Spaniard and the dog are in house 3 is incorrect. If the Spaniard and the dog are in house 4, then the Japanese and Parliaments (clue 14) are in house 3. But Old Golds and snails go together (clue 7), and no house is available; the Spaniard and the dog cannot be in house 4. So the supposition that the red house is house 5 leads only to impossible situations; the red house must be house 3.

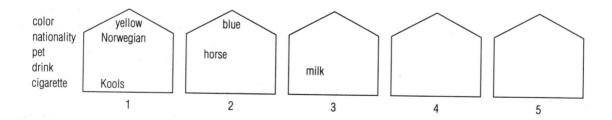

color	yellow	blue			
nationality	Norwegian				
pet		horse			
drink			milk		
cigarette	Kools				
	1	2	3	4	5

House 3 then has the Englishman (clue 2), and house 4 is ivory and house 5 is green (clue 6). Then house 5 has coffee (clue 4). The Spaniard and the dog are together (clue 3); they are either in house 4 or house 5. If they were in house 5, then the Lucky Strikes and orange juice are either in house 2 or house 4. Neither is possible:

If they were in house 2, then the Ukrainian and the tea (clue 5) would be in house 4, and the Japanese would be in house 2 (with the Lucky Strikes); that would contradict clue 14. If the Lucky Strikes and orange juice were in house 4, then the Ukrainian and the tea (clue 5) would be in house 2, and the Japanese would be in house 4; that would also contradict clue 14. So the Spaniard and the dog can't be in house 5; they must be in house 4.

Then the Ukrainian and the tea (clue 5) can only be in house 2; the Japanese must be in house 5 with Parliaments (clue 14); the Lucky Strikes and orange juice (clue 13) can only be in house 4; the Old Golds and snails (clue 7) can only be in house 3. By elimination, Chesterfields must be in house 2, and so the fox is in house 1 (clue 11).

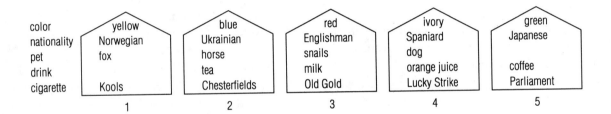

color	yellow	blue	red	ivory	green
nationality	Norwegian	Ukrainian	Englishman	Spaniard	Japanese
pet	fox	horse	snails	dog	
drink		tea	milk	orange juice	coffee
cigarette	Kools	Chesterfields	Old Gold	Lucky Strike	Parliament
	1	2	3	4	5

That puts the zebra in house 5 (with the Japanese) and water in house 1 (with the Norwegian).

LESSON 13–7 (pp. 665–670)

1. a. $x + m\angle C + m\angle D = 180$

$x + 50 + 90 = 180$

$x + 140 = 180$

$x = 40$

b. $x + y = 180$

$40 + y = 180$

$y = 140$

c. $z = x$

$z = 40$

2. $\angle ABD$ is an exterior angle of $\triangle BCD$, so by the Exterior Angle Theorem, $m\angle ABD = m\angle C + m\angle D$.

3. $\angle 4$, an exterior angle, is greater than either nonadjacent interior angle, so two angles with less measure are $\angle 1$ and $\angle 2$.

4. $\angle 5$, an exterior angle, is greater than either nonadjacent interior angle, so two angles with less measure are $\angle 1$ and $\angle 3$.

5. $\angle 6$, an exterior angle, is greater than either nonadjacent interior angle, so two angles with less measure are $\angle 2$ and $\angle 3$.

6. a. The Exterior Angle Theorem states that in a triangle, the measure of an exterior angle is equal to the sum of the measures of the two nonadjacent interior angles.

b. The Exterior Angle Inequality states that in a triangle, the measure of an exterior angle is greater than the measure of either nonadjacent interior angle.

7. The largest angle of $\triangle ABC$ is opposite the longest side, which is $\overline{AC}$, so the largest angle is $\angle B$.

8. The smallest angle of $\triangle ABC$ is opposite the shortest side, which is $\overline{AB}$, so the smallest angle is $\angle C$.

9. The longest side of $\triangle DEF$ is opposite the largest angle. $m\angle F = 59$, so the largest angle is $\angle D$ and the longest side is $\overline{EF}$.

10. The shortest side of $\triangle DEF$ is opposite the smallest angle, which is $\angle F$. So the shortest side is $\overline{DE}$.

11. A triangle can have at most one obtuse angle (otherwise the sum of the measures of the angles will contradict the Triangle-Sum Theorem), so any obtuse angle in a triangle must be the largest angle in the triangle. So, in an obtuse triangle, the obtuse angle is the largest angle, and the longest side in the triangle will be opposite that obtuse angle; the statement is *true*.

12. The given information indicates that the triangle is scalene, so no angles have the same measure. If the largest angle has measure 60, then the sum of the 3 angles must be less than 180. Similarly, if the smallest angle has measure 60, then the sum of the 3 angles must be greater than 180. Neither of these is possible, so by the Law of Ruling Out Possibilities, the angle with measure 60 is the middle-sized angle, which must be opposite the middle-length side. The middle-length side is $\overline{UV}$, and the angle oppposite that side is $\angle L$.

13. Fill in additional angle measures:

$m\angle JHI = 180 - (18 + 15) = 147$;

$m\angle GHJ = 180 - 147 = 33$;

$m\angle G = 180 - (40 + 33) = 107$.

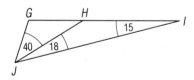

In $\triangle HIJ$, the smallest angle is $\angle I$, so the shortest side in that triangle is $\overline{HJ}$. But in $\triangle HJG$, the smallest angle is $\angle GHJ$, so $GJ < HJ$. So the shortest segment (in an accurately-drawn diagram) is $\overline{GJ}$.

14. By the Exterior Angle Inequality,
m∠3 > m∠2 and m∠2 > m∠1. So by the
Transitive Property of Inequality,
m∠3 > m∠1.

15. $\triangle PSQ$ is a right triangle, so $PQ^2 + SQ^2 = PS^2$. Then, by the Equation to Inequality Property, $PQ^2 < PS^2$, and since all measurements are positive lengths, you can take the square root of each side to conclude $PQ < PS$.

16. **a.**

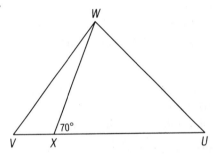

∠WXU is an exterior angle and ∠V is a nonadjacent interior angle, so m∠V < 70.

b. ∠U and ∠WXU are in the same triangle, so m∠U < 110.

c. Similarly to ∠U, m∠UWX < 110.

17. **a.** Ray $\overrightarrow{CB}$ bisects ∠ACD, so m∠ACB = x by the definition of angle bisector (meaning).

b. ∠CBD is an exterior angle of $\triangle ABC$, so by the Exterior Angle Theorem, m∠CBD = y + x.

c. Applying the Triangle-Sum Theorem to $\triangle CBD$, m∠D = 180 − (y + x + x) = 180 − (2x + y) = 180 − 2x − y.

18. **a-b.**

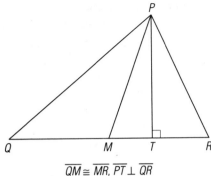

$\overline{QM} \cong \overline{MR}, \overline{PT} \perp \overline{QR}$

In an isosceles triangle, the line from the vertex that is perpendicular to the opposite side contains the midpoint of that opposite side, but this is not possible in other triangles (or from other vertices in an isosceles triangle). The segment is not uniquely determined.

19. Playfair's Parallel Postulate (the Uniqueness of Parallels Theorem) states that through a point not on a line, there is exactly one parallel to the given line.

20. No; postulates are statements that are assumed to be true, rather than statements that are definitely true.

21. Of Euclid's first 10 postulates, 5 were specifically geometric.

22.

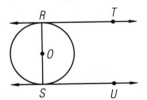

Given that $\overline{RS}$ is a diameter and that $\overline{RT}$ and $\overline{SU}$ are tangents, then $\overline{RT}$ and $\overline{SU}$ is each perpendicular to $\overline{RS}$, by the Radius-Tangent Theorem. So $\overline{RT} \parallel \overline{SU}$ by the Two Perpendiculars Theorem.

23. $\overline{BO}$ and $\overline{CP}$ are radii, so each is perpendicular to $\overline{AC}$. So $\overline{BO} \parallel \overline{CP}$ by the Two Perpendiculars Theorem, and you can use the Side-Splitting Theorem to set up a proportion:

$\dfrac{AB}{AC} = \dfrac{BO}{CP}$ so $\dfrac{12}{AC} = \dfrac{3}{8}$

$3 \cdot AC = 96$

$\quad AC = 32$ cm

24. $15(x - 7) = 3(19 + 5x)$

$15x - 105 = 57 + 15x$

$\quad\ \ 0 - 105 = 57$

$\qquad\quad 0 = 162$

This is a contradiction, so the original statement that $15(x - 7) = 3(19 + 5x)$ must be false; the original equation has no solution.

25. a.

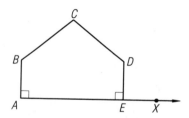

The exterior angle $\angle DEX$ is not greater than the interior angles $\angle A$, $\angle B$, or $\angle D$.

b. No. Consider any rectangle. Each exterior angle is equal to each interior angle, so there is no Exterior Angle Inequality for quadrilaterals.

LESSON 13-8 (pp. 671–674)

1. a. $a + 95 = 180$

$\qquad\quad a = 85$

b. $a + b + c + d + e$ represents the sum of the exterior angles of a polygon, one at each vertex, so $a + b + c + d + e = 360$.

2. a. Using the Polygon-Sum Theorem,

$S = (n - 2)180$ for a hexagon, $n = 6$ and

$S = (4)(180) = 720$.

b. For any polygon, the Exterior Angles of a Polygon Sum Theorem states that the sum of the measures of the exterior angles is 360.

3. a. Using the Polygon-Sum Theorem,

$S = (n - 2)180$, for an n-gon,

$S = (n - 2)180$.

b. For any polygon, the Exterior Angles of a Polygon-Sum Theorem states that the sum of the measures of the exterior angles is 360.

4. a. Polygon *CONSIDERABLY* is a regular 12-gon, so the measure of each exterior angle is $\dfrac{360}{12} = 30$.

b. $\angle SID$ and $\angle SIX$ are supplementary, so $m\angle SID = 180 - 30 = 150$.

5. For a regular octagon, the measure of each exterior angle is $\dfrac{360}{8} = 45$. So write a program that will draw a side of length 12 (that is [FORWARD 12]) and then rotate clockwise through the exterior angle ([RIGHT 45]):

TO OCT

   REPEAT 8 [FORWARD 12 RIGHT 45]

END

6. For a regular decagon (a 10-gon), the measure of each exterior angle is $\dfrac{360}{10} = 36$.

So write a program that will draw a side of length 5 (that is [FORWARD 5]) and then rotate clockwise through the exterior angle ([RIGHT 36]):

TO DEC

   REPEAT 10 [FORWARD 5 RIGHT 36]

END

7. The Logo program draws a line of length 4, then rotates clockwise through an (exterior) angle of measure 12; it performs this 30 times. It rotates through a total exterior angle of (12)(30) = 360, so the program constructs a regular 30-gon with side length 4.

8. The smaller pentagon at the center of the diagram is also a regular pentagon. Since each exterior angle of any regular pentagon has measure $\frac{360}{5} = 72$, then each interior angle of a regular pentagon has measure 180 − 72 = 108. The 5 marked angles are each vertical angles to the interior angles of the pentagon, so each one has measure 108 and the sum of the 5 measures is (5)(108) = 540.

9. Assume (temporarily) that a convex decagon has four right interior angles. Then the exterior angle at each of those vertices is also a right angle, and the sum of those 4 exterior angles is (4)(90) = 360. So you can conclude that the sum of those 4 exterior angles and the other 6 exterior angles is greater than 360. But this contradicts the Exterior Angles of a Polygon-Sum Theorem, which states that in any convex polygon, the sum of the measures of the exterior angles, one at each vertex, is 360. So the original assumption must be incorrect, and no convex decagon can have 4 right interior angles.

10. a. ∠CBD and ∠ABD form a linear pair, so they are supplementary by the Linear Pair Theorem. So m∠ABD = 180 − m∠CBD = 180 − 71 = 109.

b. ∠C is a nonadjacent interior angle for exterior angle ∠ABD, so m∠C < 109 by the Exterior Angle Inequality.

c. ∠D is a nonadjacent interior angle for exterior angle ∠ABD, so m∠D < 109 by the Exterior Angle Inequality.

11. By the Exterior Angle Inequality, m∠1 < m∠2 and m∠2 < m∠3. So by the Transitive Property of Inequality, m∠1 < m∠3 and ∠1 is the smallest angle.

12.

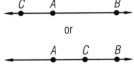

Point C is not uniquely determined; there are two possible locations for C. (The point C can be uniquely determined if you are told whether or not C is between A and B.)

13.

Point C is not uniquely determined. (Point C can be any point on the perpendicular bisector of segment $\overline{AB}$, or can even be any point on the plane which is the perpendicular bisector of segment $\overline{AB}$.)

14.

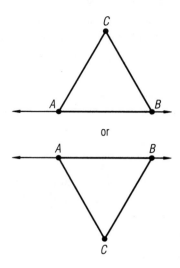

Point C is not uniquely determined; in a single plane, there are two possible locations for C, while in space, C can be any point on a circle whose center is the midpoint of $\overline{AB}$ and whose radius is the altitude of equilateral triangle ABC.

15. For the square, using the formula $A = s^2$ with $A = 400$, then $s = 20$ m and $p = 4s = 80$ m.

For the circle, using the formula $A = \pi r^2$ with $A = 400$, then $r^2 = \dfrac{400}{\pi}$ and $r = \sqrt{\dfrac{400}{\pi}}$.

Then using $C = 2\pi r$, $C = 2\pi \sqrt{\dfrac{400}{\pi}} \approx$ $(2)(3.1416)(11.28) = 70.87$ m.

So for the given area 400 m², the square has the larger perimeter.

16.

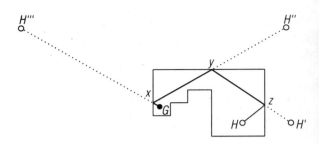

17. There are several similar triangles in the diagram.

The two large triangles, $\triangle ADC$ and $\triangle CBA$, are congruent, so they are also similar.

$\triangle ACB$ and $\triangle BCP$ both contain $\angle PCB$ and a right angle, so they are similar by the AA Similarity Theorem.

So $\triangle ACB$ is similar to each of the other two triangles, and hence all three are similar.

So $m\angle CAB = m\angle ACD = m\angle CBP$.

(Also, $\triangle ACB$ and $\triangle ABP$ both contain $\angle BAP$ and a right angle, so they are similar by the AA Similarity Theorem, but this similarity is not needed to talk about the angles congruent to $\angle CAB$.)

18. a. Student printout of the REGGON program may vary; the 18-gon should look like the one on page 672.

b. Student Logo programs will vary.

CHAPTER 13 PROGRESS SELF-TEST (p. 676–677)

1. a. A hexagon is a specific kind of polygon, so the statement is true.

b. Inverse: If a figure is not a hexagon, then it is not a polygon.

c. counterexamples:

Any *n*-gon, where $n \neq 6$, is not a hexagon (so the antecedent of the inverse is satisfied), but it is a polygon (so the consequent is not satisfied).

2. a. If two angles do not form a linear pair, then they are not adjacent angles.

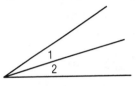

b. counterexample:
Angles 1 and 2 do not form a linear pair (so the antecedent of the contrapositive is satisfied), but they are adjacent (so the consequent is not satisfied).

3. a. An angle may be acute, right, or obtuse. If it is neither acute nor obtuse, then it must be a right angle.
b. The conclusion in part **a** is based on the Law of Ruling Out Possibilities.

4. If all three angles of a triangle are less than 50°, then the sum of the measures of the angles of the triangle must be under 150. This is a contradiction, since the sum of the measures of the three angles in a triangle must be 180. Therefore the original assumption, that the measures of the three angles in a triangle can all be under 50°, must be false.

5. Suppose $\sqrt{80} = 40$. Then $80 = (\sqrt{80})^2 = 40^2 = 1600$. But $80 \neq 1600$. So the original assumption, that $\sqrt{80} = 40$, is false, and $\sqrt{80} \neq 40$.

6.

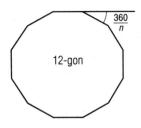

12-gon

The measure of the exterior angle of a regular duodecagon (12-gon) is $\frac{360}{12} = 30$.

7. Sample:
TO REGOCT
    REPEAT 8 [FORWARD 6 RIGHT 45]
END
This program draws a side of length 6, then moves through an exterior angle of 45° (because $\frac{360}{8} = 45$). The program does this 8 times.

8. Assign letters to statements:
$b \Rightarrow h$ (All babies are happy.)
$t \Rightarrow b$ (If someone is teething, that person is a baby.)
$n \Rightarrow$ *not-h*   (Nate is sad.)
Then starting with *n*, the fourth statement lets you conclude *not-h*. From the contrapositive of the first conditional, you can conclude *not-b*. From the contrapositive of the second conditional, you can conclude *not-t*. Thus you can state $n \Rightarrow$ *not-t*, or "Nate is not teething."

9.

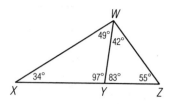

Find the measures of the angles: m∠XWY = 180 − (34 + 97) = 49, m∠WYZ = 180 − 97 = 83; m∠YWZ = 180 − (83 + 55) = 42. Then, in ΔXYW, $\overline{WY}$ is opposite the smallest angle, so it is the shortest of the three segments. Then, in ΔWYZ, $\overline{YZ}$ is shorter than $\overline{WY}$ because $\overline{YZ}$ is opposite the smaller angle. So $\overline{YZ}$ is the shortest segment; that is choice (f).

10. **a.** ∠ABD and ∠CBD form a linear pair, so they are supplementary. So if m∠ABD = 120, then m∠CBD = 60.

b-c. In ΔBCD, ∠ABD is an exterior angle and ∠C and ∠D are the nonadjacent interior angles. So m∠C < 120 and m∠D < 120 by the Exterior Angle Inequality.

11. Until the discovery of non-Euclidean geometries, postulates were thought to be *definitely* true. Now it is realized that they are only *assumed* true.

12.

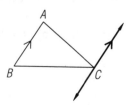

There is a unique line through C parallel to $\overleftrightarrow{AB}$; that is the Uniqueness of Parallels Theorem.

13.

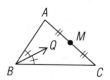

The bisector $\overrightarrow{BQ}$ of ∠B does not necessarily contain the midpoint M of $\overline{AC}$. ($\overrightarrow{BQ}$ does contain M if AB = BC.)

14. $\overline{PT}$ and $\overline{PU}$ are tangents to ⊙O, so $\overline{PT} \perp \overline{OT}$ and $\overline{PU} \perp \overline{OU}$. ∠P is given to be a right angle, and ∠O is a right angle because the sum of the four angles in quadrilateral OUPT is 360°. So OUPT is a rectangle by the definition of rectangle (sufficient condition). Moreover, PT = PU because two tangents to a circle from an external point have the same length. So OUPT is a square by the definition of square (sufficient condition).

15. Drawing $\overline{AE}$ and $\overline{DB}$, each is ⊥ to the common tangent $\overleftrightarrow{CE}$. So ΔCDB ∼ ΔCEA by the AA Similarity Theorem (each triangle contains ∠C, and ∠CDB and ∠CEA are right angles). Then $\frac{CD}{CE} = \frac{DB}{EA}$. Using BD = 9, CD = 20, and CE = 50, $\frac{20}{50} = \frac{9}{EA}$ or 20EA = 450 and EA = 22.5. So the radius of ⊙A is 22.5 units.

16.

	20th	19th	18th	17th
Jack	X_2	X_2	O	X_3
Queen	X_1	O		
King	O			X_1
Ace	X_3			O

From clue 1, the Queen is not from the 20th century, and the King is not from the 17th century. From clue 2, the Jack is not from the 20th century and is not from the 19th century. From clue 3, the Jack is not from the 17th century, and the Ace is not from the 20th century. That means that the Jack must be from the 18th century, which makes the Queen from the 19th century, the King from the 20th century, and the Ace from the 17th century.

CHAPTER 13 REVIEW (pp. 678–681)

1. For a regular hexagon, the measure of each exterior angle is $\frac{360}{6} = 60$:

```
TO HEXAGON
    REPEAT 6 [FORWARD 10 RIGHT 60]
END
```

2. For a regular 360-gon, the measure of each exterior angle is 1 degree:

```
TO 360-GON
    REPEAT 360 [FORWARD .5 RIGHT 1]
END
```

3. **a.** The measure of the interior angle at vertex Z is $180 - 138 = 42$, so the sum of the three interior angles is

$$q + 2q + 42 = 180$$
$$3q = 138$$
$$q = 46$$

So $m\angle X = 46$.

b. $m\angle Y = 2q = 2(46) = 92$

4. **a.** The sum of the measures of the exterior angles in a regular octagon is the same as for any polygon; that is 360.

b. To find the measure of each interior angle in a regular octagon, first calculate the measure of each exterior angle $\left(\frac{360}{8} = 45\right)$ and then find the supplement to that measure; it is $180 - 45 = 135$.

5. The statement is "If $x = 3$, then $x^2 = 9$."

a. The converse is "If $x^2 = 9$, then $x = 3$."

b. The inverse is "If $x \neq 3$, then $x^2 \neq 9$."

c. The contrapositive is "If $x^2 \neq 9$, then $x \neq 3$."

d. The converse and the inverse are not true (a counterexample for each is $x = -3$); the statement is true, so its contrapositive (part c) is also true.

6. The statement is "If a figure is a rectangle, then it is a square."

a. The converse is "If a figure is a square, then it is a rectangle."

b. The inverse is "If a figure is not a rectangle, then it is not a square."

c. The contrapositive is "If a figure is not a square, then it is not a rectangle."

d. The statement is not true (a counterexample is any non-square rectangle), so its contrapositive is also not true. The converse is true (if a figure is a square, then it has 4 right angles, which is sufficient for it to be a rectangle) and the inverse is also true (if a figure is not a rectangle, then it cannot have four right angles, so it cannot be a square).

7. The statement, "All New Yorkers live in the U.S.," can be written in if-then form: "If a person is a New Yorker, then that person lives in the U.S."

   a. The converse is "If a person lives in the U.S., then that person is a New Yorker."

   b. The inverse is "If a person is not a New Yorker, then that person does not live in the U.S."

   c. The contrapositive is "If a person does not live in the U.S., then that person is not a New Yorker."

   d. Assuming that the original statement is true, then the converse and inverse are false (a counterexample is any person who lives in the U.S. but not in New York) and the contrapositive is true. (However, the original statement is not necessarily true; many people who have lived for a while in New York still consider themselves to be New Yorkers, while some people who live in New York do not like to call themselves "New Yorkers." So from this point of view, none of the statements is necessarily true.)

8. The statement, for the given diagram, is: "If $m\angle ABC = 40$, then $m\angle DBC = 140$."

   a. The converse is "If $m\angle DBC = 140$, then $m\angle ABC = 40$."

   b. The inverse is "If $m\angle ABC \neq 40$, then $m\angle DBC \neq 140$."

   c. The contrapositive is "If $m\angle DBC \neq 140$, then $m\angle ABC \neq 40$."

   d. $\angle DBC$ and $\angle ABC$ are supplementary, so the statement, its converse, inverse, and contrapositive are all true.

9. a-b. The second statement satisfies the antecedent of the first statement, so *LOVE* is a trapezoid by the Law of Detachment.

10. a-b. The second sentence is of the form $p \Rightarrow q$, and the first sentence is of the form $q \Rightarrow r$. So, by the Law of Transitivity, you can conclude $p \Rightarrow r$, or "If alternate interior angles formed by a transversal are congruent, then two lines are parallel."

11. a-b. The second statement negates the consequent of the first statement, so by the Law of Detachment and the Law of the Contrapositive, the negation of the first statement must be true, or $x \neq 11$.

12. a-b. By the Law of Ruling Out Possibilities, the first part of the first sentence must be true, or $x = 11$.

13. a-b. The second statement negates the consequent of the first statement, so by the Law of Detachment and the Law of the Contrapositive, the negation of the first statement must be true, or ℓ is not perpendicular to m.

14. a-b. The first statement can be written "If correct, then I feel good" and the second statement can be written "If I feel good, then I hug." So, by the Law of Transitivity, a valid conclusion is "If correct, then I hug."
The third statement satisfies the antecedent of this conclusion, so by the Law of Detachment you can further conclude that "I will give you a hug."

15. a-b. Rewrite the three premises:

(1) All names on the list are suitable.

(2) If a name begins with a vowel, then it is melodious.

(3) If it begins with a consonant, then it is not suitable.

Statement 1 negates the consequent of statement 3, so by the Laws of the Contrapositive and Detachment, you can conclude the negation of the antecedent of statement 3, that all names (on the list) do not begin with consonants; that is, they begin with vowels. That satisfies the antecedent of statement 2, so by the Law of Detachment, all the names (on the list) are melodious.

16. a-b. The Law of Indirect Reasoning states that if valid reasoning from a statement p leads to a false conclusion, then p is false. Nella came to the conclusion that $-20 = 1$, which is false, so by the Law of Indirect Reasoning she should conclude that there is no solution to the original equation.

17. a-b. If the teacher's claim, that the perimeter of the square is 144 mm, is correct, then the side of the square is $\frac{144}{4} = 36$ mm, and the area of the square must be $36^2 = 1296$ mm². But this contradicts the given information that the area is 48 mm². So, by the Law of Indirect Reasoning, the teacher's claim is not correct.

18.

	1	2	3	4	5
a					
b		X_3	X_3		X_3
c		X_3	X_3		X_2
d	X_1		X_1		X_1
e	X_2				

If $b = 4$, then $c = 1$ and $d = 2$. But this contradicts clue 4. So $b = 1$, $c = 4$, and $d = 2$. That leaves $e = 5$ from clue 2 and $a = 3$.

19. Assume (temporarily) that a quadrilateral has 4 acute angles. Then the measure of each of those angles is less than 90, and so the sum of those 4 measures is less than 360. But this contradicts the Quadrilateral-Sum Theorem. So our original assumption must be false, and a quadrilateral cannot have 4 acute angles.

20. Assume (temporarily) that $\sqrt{2400} = 49$. Then, squaring both sides, $2400 = 49^2 = 2401$. But this is a contradiction, so the original assumption is incorrect, and $\sqrt{2400} \neq 49$.

21. Assume (temporarily) that $\sqrt{2} = \frac{239}{169}$. Then, squaring both sides, $2 = \left(\frac{239}{169}\right)^2 = \frac{239^2}{169^2} = \frac{57,121}{28,561} = 1.99996499$. While close, this is not a true statement, so the original assumption is incorrect, and $\sqrt{2} \neq \frac{249}{169}$.

22. **a.** $\triangle ADB$ and $\triangle ADC$ are right triangles (because the tangents are perpendicular to the radii) with congruent legs $\overline{DB}$ and $\overline{DC}$ and congruent hypotenuses $\overline{AD}$. So the triangles are congruent by the HL Congruence Theorem, and $AB = AC$ by the CPCF Theorem. So $ABDC$ is a kite by the definition of kite (sufficient condition).

   b. $\triangle ABD$ is a right triangle because tangent $\overleftrightarrow{AB}$ is perpendicular to radii $\overline{BD}$.

23. First find CD, the leg of a right triangle with hypotenuse 41 and other leg 40:
    $CD^2 = 41^2 - 40^2 = 1681 - 1600 = 81$, so $CD = 9$ (the triangle is a 9-40-41 right triangle). So the circumference of $\odot D$ is
    $C = 2\pi r = 2\pi 9 = 18\pi \approx 56.55$ units.

24. Radii $\overline{OZ}$ and $\overline{PY}$, each perpendicular to tangent $\overline{ZX}$, are parallel by the Two Perpendiculars Theorem, so you can use the Side-Splitting Theorem to set up a proportion:
    $\frac{OZ}{PY} = \frac{ZX}{YX}$ so $\frac{8}{4} = \frac{ZY + 10}{10}$
    $4(ZY + 10) = 80$
    $4 \cdot ZY + 40 = 80$
    $4 \cdot ZY = 40$
    $ZY = 10$ units

25. Radii $\overline{OZ}$ and $\overline{PY}$, each perpendicular to tangent $\overline{ZX}$, are parallel by the Two Perpendiculars Theorem, so you can use the Side-Splitting Theorem to set up a proportion:
    $\frac{OZ}{PY} = \frac{XZ}{XY}$ so $\frac{OZ}{15} = \frac{165}{45}$
    $45 \cdot OZ = (15)(165) = 2475$
    $OZ = \frac{2475}{45} = 55$
    So the radius of $\odot O$ is 55, and the area is
    $A = \pi r^2 = \pi (55)^2 = 3025\pi \approx 9503$ mm².

26. Diagonal $\overline{AC}$ is uniquely determined by the Point-Line-Plane Postulate, so it can be drawn.

27. Line $\overleftrightarrow{CE}$ is a line through C parallel to $\overleftrightarrow{AD}$, so it is unique by the Uniqueness of Parallels Theorem and it can be drawn.

28. An angle has a unique bisector by the Angle Measure Postulate, so it can be drawn.

29. Each of segments $\overline{AB}$ and $\overline{CD}$ has a unique perpendicular bisector, but they may not be the same line. So the $\perp$ bisector of $\overline{AB}$ and $\overline{CD}$ cannot be drawn.

30. By the Unequal Sides Theorem, the largest angle is opposite the longest side. The longest side is $\overline{BC}$, so the largest angle is $\angle A$.

31. By the Unequal Sides Theorem, the smallest angle is opposite the shortest side. The shortest side is $\overline{AB}$, so the smallest angle is $\angle C$.

32. By the Triangle-Sum Theorem,
    $m\angle F = 180 - (68 + 47) = 180 - 115 = 65$.
    So the angles, from smallest to largest, are $\angle D < \angle F < \angle E$. That is the same as the order of the sides opposite those angles, so the order of sides, from shortest to longest, is $EF < DE < DF$.

33. In $\triangle HJG$, the smallest angle is $\angle G$, so by the Unequal Angles Theorem, the shortest side in $\triangle HJG$ is opposite $\angle G$; that is $\overline{HJ}$. In $\triangle HIJ$, the smallest angle is $\angle HJI$, so by the Unequal Angles Theorem, the shortest side in $\triangle HIJ$ is $\overline{HI}$. So $\overline{HI}$ is the shortest segment in the figure.

34. a. $\angle QSR$ is supplementary to $\angle QST$, because they form a linear pair, so $m\angle QSR = 180 - 132 = 48$.
   b. $\angle Q$ is a nonadjacent interior angle to exterior angle QST, so by the Exterior Angle Inequality, $m\angle Q < 132$.
   c. $\angle R$ is a nonadjacent interior angle to exterior angle QST, so by the Exterior Angle Inequality, $m\angle R < 132$.

35. By the Exterior Angle Inequality, $m\angle 1 > m\angle 2$, $m\angle 2 > m\angle 3$, and $m\angle 3 > m\angle 4$.
   So by the Transitivity of Inequality, $m\angle 1 > m\angle 2 > m\angle 3 > m\angle 4$; or $\angle 1$ is the largest of the 4 angles.

36. Statement 2 is the negation of the consequent of statement 1, so by the Laws of the Contrapositive and Detachment, the negation of the antecedent of statement 1 must be true—I did not finish my homework.

37. By the Law of Ruling Out Possibilities, the first part of the first statement must be true—Mary is too old for camp.

38. By the second and third statements, and the Law of Transitivity, no mammal can live on the moon. By that conclusion, the first statement, and the Law of Detachment, you can conclude that no bat can live on the moon.

39. a. Ted assumed that the homework paper was either in his notebook, in his school locker, or at home. Then he used the Law of Ruling Out Possibilities to conclude that it must be at his home.

   b. His reasoning is valid, but his original assumption is false. There may be other possibilities for the location of the lost homework paper, such as the dog ate it, his little brother ripped it up, it fell into a puddle on the way to school, or even some other fate.

40. Of the ten postulates in the first book of Euclid's *Elements*, five were geometric in nature.

41. Playfair's Parallel Postulate states that through a point not on a line, there is exactly one parallel to the given line.

42. One result of the development of non-Euclidean geometries (that through a point not on a line, there may be more than one line parallel to the given line, or there may be no lines parallel to the given line) was that postulates were viewed as statements that are assumed to be true (to see what conclusions can be reached from those statements), rather than statements that are definitely true.

LESSON 14–1   (pp. 682–689)

1. In an isosceles right triangle, the sum of the measures of the acute angles is 90 and the two acute angles are congruent, so each acute angle measures 45.

2.

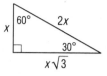

In a right triangle with sides x, $x\sqrt{3}$, and $2x$, the acute angles have measures 30 and 60.

3. In the drawing of regular hexagon $DEFGHI$, the diagonals drawn are $\overline{DG}$, $\overline{DH}$, $\overline{EG}$, $\overline{EH}$, and $\overline{IF}$ (the others, not drawn, are $\overline{DF}$, $\overline{EI}$, $\overline{FH}$, and $\overline{GI}$).
   The 30-60-90 triangles drawn are DJI, DJL, EKL, EKF, GKF, GKL, HJI, HJL, EHG, DHG, HED, and GED.

4. **a.** A 30-60-90 right triangle is not similar to a 45-45-90 right triangle (or to a 40-50-90 right triangle), so not all right triangles are similar; the statement is *false*.

   b. All right triangles with a 60 degree angle have two other angles with measures 30 and 90, so they are similar by the AA Similarity Theorem; the statement is *true*.

   c. All isosceles right triangles have angles with measures 45, 45, and 90, so they are similar by the AA Similarity Theorem; the statement is *true*.

5. In Example 3,
$$m\angle ZXY = m\angle ZXW + m\angle WXY$$
$$= 45 + 60$$
$$= 105$$
Another way:
The sum of the measures of the angles of $\triangle XYZ$ is 180, so $m\angle ZXY = 180 - (45 + 30) = 180 - 75 = 105$.

6. In Example 3, the perimeter of $\triangle XYZ$ is
$$ZX + XY + ZW + WY$$
$$= 4\sqrt{2} + 8 + 4 + 4\sqrt{3}$$
$$= 4\sqrt{2} + 12 + 4\sqrt{3}$$
$$\approx 5.66 + 12 + 6.93$$
$$= 24.59 \text{ units}$$

7. If one leg of an isosceles right triangle has length 10 cm, the hypotenuse is the leg times $\sqrt{2}$, so the hypotenuse has length $10\sqrt{2} \approx 14.14$ cm.

8. If the side of a square is s, then the diagonal is the hypotenuse of an isosceles right triangle with leg s, so the length of the diagonal is $s\sqrt{2}$.

9. If the shortest side is 6 cm, then the hypotenuse is twice that length, or 12 cm, and the other leg is the short leg times $\sqrt{3}$, or $6\sqrt{3} \approx 10.4$ cm.

10. The distance from first base to third base is the length of the diagonal of a square whose side is 90 feet (the distance between bases); the length of that diagonal is $90\sqrt{2} \approx 127.28$ feet.

11. If the side of the equilateral triangle is E units, then half the side is $\frac{E}{2}$ units (that is the short side of a 30-60-90 triangle) and the length of the altitude of the equilateral triangle is the short side times $\sqrt{3}$, or $\frac{E\sqrt{3}}{2}$.

12.

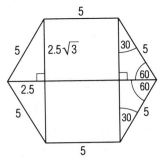

For each of the 30-60-90 triangles, the vertical side is half the hypotenuse, or 2.5 mm, and the length of the horizontal side is $(2.5)(\sqrt{3})$ mm. So the width of the cell is $(2)(2.5)(\sqrt{3}) \approx 8.66$ mm.

13. In general, if the leg of an isosceles right triangle is given, then the length of the hypotenuse is that length times $\sqrt{2}$, while if the length of the hypotenuse is given, then the length of the leg is that length divided by $\sqrt{2}$.

The length of the hypotenuse of an isosceles right triangle is given as 100 feet, so the length of each of the legs is $\frac{100}{\sqrt{2}} \approx \frac{100}{1.414} \approx$ 70.7 feet.

14. $\triangle LOT$ is a 45-45-90 triangle, so the lengths of the sides are $OT = h$ and $LT = h\sqrt{2}$.
$\triangle LOB$ is a 30-60-90 triangle, so the lengths of the sides are $BL = 2h$ and $BO = h\sqrt{3}$.
The perimeter of $\triangle BLT$ is
$BO + OT + TL + BL$
$= h\sqrt{3} + h + h\sqrt{2} + 2h$
$= 3h + h\sqrt{2} + h\sqrt{3}$
$\approx 3h + 1.414h + 1.732h$
$= 6.146h$.

15. All the triangles are similar to $\triangle BCA$ because they all have a right angle, an angle that is congruent to $\angle BAC$, and an angle that is congruent to $\angle BCA$. Listing the vertices in the order "right angle, vertex at smaller acute angle, vertex at larger acute angle," the similar triangles are:
$\triangle BAC \sim \triangle DCA \sim \triangle PAB \sim \triangle PBC$.

16. The triangle at the left is a 6-8-10 right triangle, so $a = 10$ miles.
The middle triangle is similar to the one at the left by the AA Similarity Theorem (they both have angles of measure 90 and x), so $\frac{b}{6} = \frac{3}{8}$, and $b = \frac{18}{8} = 2\frac{1}{4}$ miles.
For the triangle at the right, the two acute angles are complementary so the other acute angle must have measure x, and that triangle is similar to the other two. So $\frac{c}{10} = \frac{4}{6}$, and
$c = \frac{40}{6} = 6\frac{2}{3}$ yards.

17. $\frac{30}{DE} = \frac{DE}{5}$
$DE^2 = 150$
$DE = \sqrt{150} = \sqrt{(25)(6)} = 5\sqrt{6}$
(DE must be positive since it is a length.)

18. a. $\frac{5}{\sqrt{3}} = \frac{5\sqrt{3}}{\sqrt{3}\sqrt{3}} = \frac{5\sqrt{3}}{3}$

b. $\frac{1}{\sqrt{2}} = \frac{1\sqrt{2}}{\sqrt{2}\sqrt{2}} = \frac{\sqrt{2}}{2}$

c. $\frac{3}{\sqrt{6}} = \frac{3\sqrt{6}}{\sqrt{6}\sqrt{6}} = \frac{3\sqrt{6}}{6} = \frac{\sqrt{6}}{2}$

19. $\sqrt{75} = \sqrt{(25)(3)} = (\sqrt{25})(\sqrt{3}) = 5\sqrt{3}$; that is choice (a).

20. $\sqrt{16 + 16} = \sqrt{32} = \sqrt{(16)(2)} = 4\sqrt{2}$; that is choice (c).

21. For the square :
If the area is 400 square meters, then using the formula $A = s^2$, the side has length 20 meters, and using the formula $p = 4s$, the perimeter is 80 meters.

For the circle:
If the area is 400 square meters, then from the formula $A = \pi r^2$, $r^2 = \dfrac{400}{\pi}$ and

$r = \sqrt{\dfrac{400}{\pi}} = \dfrac{20}{\sqrt{\pi}}$.

Then, using the formula $C = 2\pi r$, the

perimeter (circumference) is $C = 2\pi\dfrac{20}{\sqrt{\pi}} =$

$40\dfrac{\pi}{\sqrt{\pi}} = 40\sqrt{\pi} \approx 70.898$.

So the square has the larger perimeter.

22. **a.**

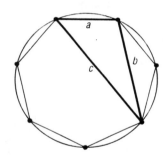

(An accurate way to draw a regular heptagon (7-gon) is to use a protractor at the center of a circle and draw 7 radii that form congruent central angles. For the heptagon, each central angle would be $\dfrac{360}{7} \approx 51.4°$.)

b. Specific values of a, b, and c will vary, but the sum of the squares of the three ratios should be close to 6.

c. All students' triangles should be similar. The angle measures should be about 25.7, 51.4, and 102.9. Actually, the angles are in the ratio 1:2:4; using the Triangle-Sum Theorem, $x + 2x + 4x = 180$, so $x = \dfrac{180}{7}$.

LESSON 14-2 (pp. 690–695)

1. For the geometric mean of 2 and 50, $\dfrac{2}{x} = \dfrac{x}{50}$, so $x^2 = 100$ and $x = 10$.
(The geometric mean is positive.)

2. For the geometric mean of 9 and 12, $\dfrac{9}{x} = \dfrac{x}{12}$, so $x^2 = 108$ and $x = \sqrt{108} \approx 10.39$.

3. The geometric mean of a and b is always closer to the smaller of a or b, so the geometric mean is closer to a; the statement is *true*.

4. **a.** $\angle P$ is complementary to $\angle Q$; another angle complementary to $\angle Q$ is $\angle QRS$, so $m\angle P = m\angle QRS$.

   b. All three triangles have a right angle; two triangles both have $\angle P$; and two triangles both have $\angle Q$. So all three triangles are similar. Use the order of vertices "smaller acute angle, right angle, larger acute angle":
   $\triangle PRQ \sim \triangle PSR \sim \triangle RSQ$.

   c. Using part b of the Right Triangle Altitude Theorem, that each leg is the geometric mean of the hypotenuse and the segment of the hypotenuse adjacent to the leg, then $\dfrac{QS}{RQ} = \dfrac{RQ}{QP}$.

   d. Using part a of the Right Triangle Altitude Theorem, that the altitude to the hypotenuse is the geometric mean of the segments into which it divides the hypotenuse, then $\dfrac{QS}{RS} = \dfrac{RS}{PS}$.

   e. Using part b of the Right Triangle Altitude Theorem, that each leg is the geometric mean of the hypotenuse and the segment of the hypotenuse adjacent to the leg, then RP is the geometric mean of PS and PQ.

f. Using part a of the Right Triangle Altitude Theorem, that the altitude to the hypotenuse is the geometric mean of the segments into which it divides the hypotenuse, then RS is the geometric mean of PS and SQ.

g. Using part b of the Right Triangle Altitude Theorem, that each leg is the geometric mean of the hypotenuse and the segment of the hypotenuse adjacent to the leg, then RQ is the geometric mean of QS and QP.

5. Using part a of the Right Triangle Altitude Theorem, that the altitude to the hypotenuse is the geometric mean of the segments into which it divides the hypotenuse, then RS is the geometric mean of PS and SQ.

So $\dfrac{PS}{RS} = \dfrac{RS}{SQ}$ so $\dfrac{9}{6} = \dfrac{6}{SQ}$

$9 \cdot SQ = 36$

$SQ = 4$ units.

6. $\overline{QR}$ is the hypotenuse of a right triangle with legs 6 and 4, so use the Pythagorean Theorem: $QR = \sqrt{6^2 + 4^2} = \sqrt{36 + 16} = \sqrt{52} \approx 7.21$ units.

7. a. $\overline{NS}$ is the hypotenuse of a right triangle with legs 5 and 12. Since (5, 12, 13) is a Pythagorean triple, then $NS = 13$ units. Or: $NS = \sqrt{5^2 + 12^2} = \sqrt{25 + 144} = \sqrt{169} = 13$.

b. Using part b of the Right Triangle Altitude Theorem, that each leg is the geometric mean of the hypotenuse and the segment of the hypotenuse adjacent to the leg, then

$\dfrac{NS}{SI} = \dfrac{SI}{SE}$ so $\dfrac{13}{5} = \dfrac{5}{SE}$

$13 \cdot SE = 25$

$SE = \dfrac{25}{13} \approx 1.923$ units.

c. Using part a of the Right Triangle Altitude Theorem, that the altitude to the hypotenuse is the geometric mean of the segments into which it divides the hypotenuse, then $\dfrac{NE}{IE} = \dfrac{IE}{ES}$

so $\dfrac{13 - 1.932}{IE} = \dfrac{IE}{1.932}$

$IE^2 = (11.068)(1.932) = 21.38$

$IE \approx 4.62$

Another way: In right triangle ESI, $IE =$

$$\sqrt{SI^2 - ES^2} = \sqrt{5^2 - \left(\dfrac{25}{13}\right)^2}$$

$$= \sqrt{25 - \dfrac{625}{169}}$$

$$= \sqrt{\dfrac{(4225 - 625)}{169}}$$

$$= \sqrt{\dfrac{3600}{169}}$$

$$= \dfrac{60}{13}$$

$$\approx 4.615 \text{ units.}$$

8. Using part b of the Right Triangle Altitude Theorem, that each leg is the geometric mean of the hypotenuse and the segment of the hypotenuse adjacent to the leg, then

$\dfrac{5}{4} = \dfrac{4}{x}$ and $\dfrac{5}{3} = \dfrac{3}{y}$

Then $5x = 16$ and $x = \dfrac{16}{5}$, and $5y = 9$ so

$y = \dfrac{9}{5}$. Using part a of the Right Triangle Altitude Theorem, that the altitude to the hypotenuse is the geometric mean of the segments into which it divides the hypotenuse, then

$\dfrac{y}{h} = \dfrac{h}{x}$ so $\dfrac{1.8}{h} = \dfrac{h}{3.2}$

Then $h^2 = (1.8)(3.2) = 5.76$, so

$h = \sqrt{5.76} = 2.4$.

9. **a.** For $\triangle QRT$ and $\triangle RST$, the ratio of short leg to short leg is $3:6 = 1:2$, and the ratio of long leg to long leg is $6:12 = 1:2$. Also, both triangles have a right angle. So the triangles are similar by the SAS Similarity Theorem.

   b. Using the Pythagorean Theorem in $\triangle QRT$ and $\triangle SRT$,
   $QR^2 = 3^2 + 6^2 = 9 + 36 = 45$, and
   $SR^2 = 6^2 + 12^2 = 36 + 144 = 180$.
   Then looking at $\triangle QRS$,
   $QR^2 + RS^2 = 45 + 180 = 225 = 15^2 = QS^2$.
   So, by the Pythagorean Converse Theorem, $\triangle QRS$ is a right triangle and $m\angle QRS = 90$; the statement is *true*.

10. **a.** The distance from Nancy to the tower is the length of the altitude of the right triangle determined by the square corner of the notebook, the height of Nancy's eye is one segment of the hypotenuse, and the distance from Nancy's eye level to the top of the lifeguard tower is the other segment of the hypotenuse. So Nancy was using part a of the Right Triangle Altitude Theorem, that the altitude to the hypotenuse is the geometric mean of the segments into which it divides the hypotenuse.

   b. Using x as the distance from Nancy's eye level to the top of the lifeguard tower:
   $$\frac{x}{8} = \frac{8}{5}$$
   $$5x = 64$$
   $$x = \frac{64}{5} = 12.8 \text{ feet}$$
   So the height of the lifeguard tower is $12.8 + 5 = 17.8$ feet.

11. **a.** The justification that a is the geometric mean of c and x and that b is the geometric mean of c and y is part b of the Right Triangle Altitude Theorem, that each leg is the geometric mean of the hypotenuse and the segment of the hypotenuse adjacent to the leg.

   b. The justification that $a = \sqrt{cx}$ and that $b = \sqrt{cy}$ is the Geometric Mean Theorem.

   c-d. From $a^2 = cx$ and $b^2 = cy$, the justifications that $a^2 + b^2 = cx + cy = c(x + y)$ are the Additive Property of Equality and the Distributive Property.

   e. From $a^2 + b^2 = c(x + y)$ and $(x + y) = c$, the justification that $a^2 + b^2 = (c)(c) = c^2$ is Substitution.

12. Question 11 is a proof of the Pythagorean Theorem; so it would be an example of circularity or circular reasoning to use the Pythagorean Theorem as a justification.

13. **a.** An altitude in an equilateral triangle forms two 30-60-90 triangles. If the side of the triangle is 5, then the smaller leg of the 30-60-90 triangle has length 2.5, and the longer leg (which is the altitude of the original triangle) has length $\frac{5\sqrt{3}}{2} \approx 4.33$ units.

   b. Using the formula for the area of any triangle, $A = \frac{1}{2}bh$, $b = 5$ and $h = 2.5\sqrt{3}$, so $A = \frac{1}{2} \frac{(5)(5\sqrt{3})}{2} = \frac{25\sqrt{3}}{4}$.
   (This can be generalized: If an equilateral triangle has side s, then the altitude has length $\frac{s\sqrt{3}}{2}$ and the area of the triangle is $\frac{s^2\sqrt{3}}{4}$.)

14. For any isosceles right triangle, if the hypotenuse is x then the leg is x divided by $\sqrt{2}$. So if the diagonal of a square field has length 50 m, then the side of the field is $\frac{50}{\sqrt{2}} \approx \frac{50}{1.414} \approx 35.36$ m.

15. The volume of a prism with base B and height h is $V = \frac{1}{3}Bh$ and the volume of a pyramid with the same base and height $2h$ is $V = B(2h) = 2Bh$. The ratio of these two volumes, prism to pyramid, is $\frac{2Bh}{\frac{1}{3}Bh} = \frac{2}{\frac{1}{3}} = 6$; the prism has 6 times the volume of the pyramid.

16. **a.** There are two rectangular faces congruent to face $ABCD$, and each has two congruent diagonals, so there are three other segments with the same length as segment $\overline{AC}$, or 4 segments altogether; they are $\overline{AC}$, $\overline{BD}$, $\overline{GE}$, and $\overline{FH}$.

    b. There is a diagonal congruent to segment $\overline{AG}$ from each vertex of face $FDCG$. They are $\overline{GA}$, $\overline{FB}$, $\overline{DH}$, and $\overline{CE}$, so there are 4 of them.

17. M is the midpoint of $\overline{DE}$, so $DM = EM$ by the definition of midpoint (meaning). Then, with the given, $\Delta DMB \cong \Delta EMC$ by the SSS Congruence Theorem, and $m\angle D = m\angle E$ by the CPCF Theorem. So in ΔADE, $AD = AE$ by the Isosceles Triangle Converse Theorem. Then, using the Betweenness Theorem and the Addition Property of Equality to justify that $AB = AD - DB$ and $AC = AE - CE$, you can conclude that $AB = AC$ by substitution and the Transitive Property of Equality. So $ABMC$ is a kite by the definition of kite (sufficient condition).

18. **a.** $\frac{1}{\sqrt{3}} = \frac{1\sqrt{3}}{\sqrt{3}\sqrt{3}} = \frac{\sqrt{3}}{3}$

    b. Using a calculator, $\frac{1}{\sqrt{3}}$ $= 3$ $\boxed{\sqrt{x}}$ $\boxed{1/x}$; the display shows 0.577350.

19. $3y - 2 = y^2$
    $0 = y^2 - 3y + 2$
    $0 = (y - 2)(y - 1)$
    So $0 = y - 2$ which means $y = 2$, or $0 = y - 1$ which means $y = 1$.
    So $y = 1$ or $y = 2$.

20. **a.** The harmonic mean of two numbers x and y is defined as the reciprocal of the mean of the reciprocals:
    $$\frac{1}{\frac{\frac{1}{x} + \frac{1}{y}}{2}} = \frac{1}{\frac{\frac{y}{xy} + \frac{x}{xy}}{2}}$$
    $$= \frac{1}{\frac{\frac{1}{x+y}}{xy}}$$

    $$= \frac{1}{\frac{x+y}{2xy}}$$
    $$= \frac{2xy}{x+y}$$

    So another way to describe the harmonic mean is that it is twice the product, divided by the sum.

355

b. If the two numbers are 1 and 4, their (positive) geometric mean is $\sqrt{4} = 2$.

Their harmonic mean is $\frac{2(1)(4)}{1 + 4} = \frac{8}{5} = 1.6$.

So the geometric mean is greater than the harmonic mean.

In general, for $0 < a < b$, the geometric mean is $\sqrt{ab}$. Start with the next-to-last step in the derivation of Question 21:

$2\sqrt{ab} < a + b$

$\dfrac{2\sqrt{ab}}{2ab} < \dfrac{a + b}{2ab}$ Divide both sides by $2ab$.

$\dfrac{\sqrt{ab}}{ab} < \dfrac{a + b}{2ab}$ $\dfrac{2}{2} = 1$

$\dfrac{1}{\sqrt{ab}} < \dfrac{a + b}{2ab}$ Divide numerator and denominator by $\sqrt{ab}$.

$\sqrt{ab} > \dfrac{2ab}{a + b}$ For x, $y > 0$, if $x < y$ then $\dfrac{1}{x} > \dfrac{1}{y}$.

So the geometric mean is greater than the harmonic mean.

21. For numbers $0 < a < b$, the geometric mean is $\sqrt{ab}$ and the arithmetic mean is $\frac{a + b}{2}$. The following steps show that $\sqrt{ab} < \frac{a + b}{2}$.

$a < b$	given
$0 < b - a$	Addition Property of Inequality
$0 < (b - a)^2$	Mult. Prop. of Inequali
$0 < b^2 - 2ab + a^2$	FOIL pattern
$4ab < b^2 + 2ab + a^2$	Addition Property of Inequality
$4ab < (a + b)^2$	Substitution: $(a + b)^2$ for $a^2 + 2ab + b^2$
$2\sqrt{ab} < a + b$	Square roots of positive numbers
$\sqrt{ab} < \dfrac{a + b}{2}$	Mult. Property of Inequality

So the geometric mean is less than the arithmetic mean.

LESSON 14–3 (pp. 696–701)

1.

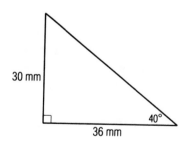

Example: if the length of the leg adjacent to the 40-degree angle is 36 mm, then the length of the other leg will be about 30 mm, and the ratio will be $\tan 40 \approx \frac{30}{36} = .833$. (The actual value of tan 40 is about .839.)

2. Using a ruler, $BC \approx 14$ mm and $AC \approx 30$ mm, so $\tan A = \frac{14}{30} \approx .466$; reasonable estimates are between .4 and .5.

3. Using a calculator, enter 73 $\boxed{\text{TAN}}$ to display 3.270852618 or about 3.271.

4. $\tan 32° = \frac{w}{25}$, so $w = 25 \tan 32° \approx$

(25)(.6249) = 15.62 m.

5. $\tan E = \frac{7}{24} \approx .292$

6. $\tan F = \frac{24}{7} \approx 3.43$

7.

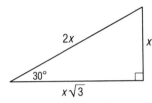

$\tan 30° = \frac{x}{x\sqrt{3}} = \frac{1}{\sqrt{3}} = \frac{\sqrt{3}}{3}$

8.

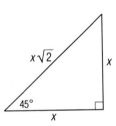

$\tan 45° = \frac{x}{x} = 1$

9.

a. If $\tan A = \frac{2}{3}$, then m$\angle A$ is between 30 and 35. (Using a calculator, 2 $\boxed{\div}$ 3 $\boxed{=}$ $\boxed{\text{INV}}$ $\boxed{\text{TAN}}$ displays 33.69007.)

b. If $\tan A = \frac{3}{2}$, then m$\angle A$ is between 55 and 60. (Using a calculator, 3 $\boxed{\div}$ 2 $\boxed{=}$ $\boxed{\text{INV}}$ $\boxed{\text{TAN}}$ displays 56.30993.)

10. Use the tangent ratio to find the height x of the portion of the pole that is above eye level:

$\tan 40° = \frac{x}{20}$, so $x = 20 \tan 40° \approx$

(20)(.839) = 16.78.
So the total height of the pole is about 16.78 + 5 = 21.78 ft.

11. a-b. The value of the tangent is the ratio $\frac{\text{vertical leg}}{\text{horizontal leg}}$. The length of the vertical leg is constant, so as the length of the horizontal leg increases, the value of the ratio decreases. The largest tangent ratio occurs when the denominator is smallest, so $\angle 4$ has the largest tangent ratio. The smallest tangent ratio occurs when the denominator is largest, so $\angle 1$ has the smallest tangent ratio.

12.

For the definition of tangent as a ratio of lengths of sides in a right triangle, Question 11 can be interpreted as the tangent ratio increases as the size of an angle increases. So $\tan 75° > \tan 74°$ because an angle of 75 degrees is larger than an angle of 74 degrees.

13. a. $\tan BCD = \frac{x}{h}$

b. $\tan A = \frac{h}{y}$

c. From the equality $\tan BCD = \tan A$, you can substitute the values from parts a and b to get $\frac{x}{h} = \frac{h}{y}$.

d. The result from part c is part a of the Right Triangle Altitude Theorem, that the altitude to the hypotenuse is the geometric mean of the segments into which it divides the hypotenuse.

14. Using part a of the Right Triangle Altitude Theorem, that the altitude to the hypotenuse is the geometric mean of the segments into which it divides the hypotenuse, $\frac{AD}{CD} = \frac{CD}{DB}$

so $\frac{9}{CD} = \frac{CD}{6}$

$CD^2 = 54$

$CD = \sqrt{54} \approx 7.35$ units.

Using part b of the Right Triangle Altitude Theorem, that each leg is the geometric mean of the hypotenuse and the segment of the hypotenuse adjacent to the leg, $\frac{15}{a} = \frac{a}{6}$

and $\frac{15}{b} = \frac{b}{9}$ so $a^2 = 90$ or

$a = \sqrt{90} \approx 9.487$ units, and

$b^2 = 135$ or $b = \sqrt{135} \approx 11.619$ units.

15. $\triangle ABC$ and $\triangle ACD$ each have a right angle and $\angle A$, and $\triangle ABC$ and $\triangle CBD$ each have a right angle and $\angle B$, so all three triangles are similar by the AA Similarity Theorem. So $\triangle ABC \sim \triangle ACD \sim \triangle CBD$.

16.

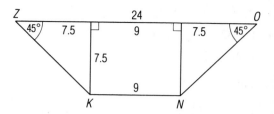

Side $\overline{ZO}$ can be divided into 3 segments of lengths 7.5, 9, and 7.5. So the altitude is 7.5. Using the formula for the area of a trapezoid, $A = \frac{1}{2}h(b_1 + b_2)$, the area is

$\frac{1}{2}(7.5)(9 + 24) = \frac{1}{2}(7.5)(33) = $ 123.75 units^2.

17. The diagonal of a box with dimensions 3", 4", and 8" is $\sqrt{3^2 + 4^2 + 8^2} = \sqrt{9 + 16 + 64} = \sqrt{89} \approx 9.434"$.

18. a.

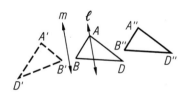

b. The result of the composite of the two reflections is a translation of $\triangle ABD$, in the direction perpendicular to ℓ and m, from m to ℓ, with a magnitude twice that between m and ℓ.

19. a. Using a calculator and the numbers 25, 97, and 58,

$\tan 25° + \tan 97° + \tan 58° \approx .466 + -8.144 + 1.600$
≈ -6.078

b. $(\tan 25°)(\tan 97°)(\tan 58°) \approx (.466)(-8.144)(1.600)$
≈ -6.077

c. With three other angle measures whose sum is 180, you will again find that the sum of the tangents is equal to the product of the tangents.

d. In general, if three angle measures add up to 180 (no angle can have measure 90), then the sum of the tangents of those measures is equal to the product of the tangents of those measures.

LESSON 14-4 (pp. 702–707)

1. a. $\sin \angle A$ is defined as a ratio of sides in a right triangle; it is the length of the leg opposite $\angle A$ divided by the length of the hypotenuse.

b. $\cos \angle A$ is defined as a ratio of sides in a right triangle; it is the length of the leg adjacent to $\angle A$ divided by the length of the hypotenuse.

2. a. The leg opposite $\angle N$ is $\overline{MO}$.

b. The hypotenuse is $\overline{MN}$.

c. The leg adjacent to $\angle M$ is $\overline{MO}$.

d. The leg adjacent to $\angle N$ is $\overline{NO}$.

3. a. $\sin F = \dfrac{GH}{GF} = \dfrac{2}{2\sqrt{5}} = \dfrac{1}{\sqrt{5}} \approx \dfrac{1}{2.236} \approx .447$

b. $\cos F = \dfrac{FH}{GF} = \dfrac{4}{2\sqrt{5}} = \dfrac{2}{\sqrt{5}} \approx \dfrac{2}{2.236} \approx .894$

c. $\tan G = \dfrac{FH}{GH} = \dfrac{4}{2} = 2$

d. $\sin G = \dfrac{FH}{FG} = \dfrac{4}{2\sqrt{5}} \approx \dfrac{4}{4.472} \approx .894$

4.

a. $\sin 60° = \dfrac{\sqrt{3}}{2}$

b. $\cos 60° = \dfrac{1}{2}$

c. $\tan 60° = \dfrac{\sqrt{3}}{1} = \sqrt{3}$

5.

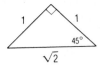

a. $\sin 45° = \dfrac{1}{\sqrt{2}} = \dfrac{\sqrt{2}}{2}$

b. $\cos 45° = \dfrac{1}{\sqrt{2}} = \dfrac{\sqrt{2}}{2}$

c. $\tan 45° = \dfrac{1}{1} = 1$

6. a. $\sin 48° \approx \dfrac{11}{15} \approx .733$

b. $\cos 48° \approx \dfrac{10}{15} \approx .667$

c. $\tan 42° \approx \dfrac{10}{11} \approx .909$

d. $\cos 42° \approx \dfrac{11}{15} \approx .733$

7. a. $\sin 13.2° \approx .22835 \approx .228$

b. $\cos 13.2° \approx .97358 \approx .974$

8. a.

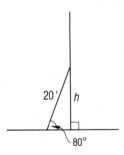

Using the maximum angle of 80 degrees,

$\sin 80° = \dfrac{h}{20}$,

so $h = 20 \sin 80°$

$\approx (20)(.985)$

$= 19.7$ feet.

b. Using the maximum angle to minimize the distance from the foot of the ladder to the wall, $\cos 80° = \dfrac{d}{20}$, so

$d = 20 \cos 80°$
$\approx (20)(.174)$
$= 3.48$ feet.

9.

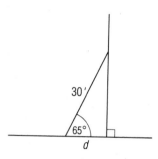

Using the minimum angle to maximize the distance from the foot of the ladder to the wall, $\cos 65° = \dfrac{d}{30}$, so

$d = 30 \cos 65°$
$\approx (30)(.4226)$
≈ 12.7 feet.

10. a. Using a calculator, 89 $\boxed{\text{SIN}}$ displays .999847 ≈ .9998.

b. For an angle of 89 degrees, the lengths of the opposite side and hypotenuse are nearly the same, so the ratio of the two lengths will be close to 1.

11. a. Using measurements, $\sin B \approx \dfrac{25}{46} \approx .543$,

and $\sin B' \approx \dfrac{17}{32} \approx .531$.

b. Since $m\angle B = m\angle B'$, it is expected that their sine ratios will be equal. Within the limits of measurement error, the results from part a agree with that expectation.

12. a. If the length of the opposite side in the sine ratio remains constant, then the length of the hypotenuse will decrease as the angle increases, so the sine ratio will increase as the angle increases. So $\angle 5$ has the largest sine ratio.

b.

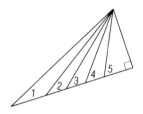

Using the extreme values for the cosine ratio, for a very small angle the adjacent side is almost equal to the hypotenuse, so the cosine ratio is close to 1, while for an angle close to 90 degrees, the adjacent side is very small, so the cosine ratio is close to zero. So the cosine ratio decreases as the angle ranges between zero and 90 degrees. The smallest angle in the figure is $\angle 1$, so the angles with the largest cosine is $\angle 1$.

13. The diagram refers to the side opposite the 85-degree angle and the hypotenuse.

$\sin 85° = \dfrac{20}{h}$

$h \sin 85° = 20$

$h = \dfrac{20}{\sin 85°} \approx \dfrac{20}{.996} \approx 20.076 \approx 20.1$ ft

14. The diagram refers to the side adjacent to the 40-degree angle and the hypotenuse.

$$\cos 40° = \frac{55}{h}$$

$$h \cos 40° = 55$$

$$h = \frac{55}{\cos 40°} \approx \frac{55}{.766} \approx 71.797 \approx 72 \text{ ft}$$

It is usual to use the value of the angle of depression in such problems, because there is an angle in the triangle with that same measure (it is called the angle of elevation):

$$\sin 50° = \frac{55}{h}, \text{ so } h = \frac{55}{\sin 50°} \approx \frac{55}{.766} \approx 72 \text{ ft.}$$

15. The diagram refers to the sides opposite and adjacent to the given angle.

$$\tan 40° = \frac{h}{800}$$

$$h = 800 \tan 40° \approx (800)(.839) \approx 671.33 \approx 670 \text{ feet.}$$

16. Using the measurements $LM = 14$ mm and $LN = 26$ mm, then $\tan N = \frac{ML}{LN} = \frac{14}{26}$

$$\approx .538.$$

17. $\frac{75}{x} = \frac{x}{100}$

$$x^2 = 7500$$

$$x = \sqrt{7500} \approx 86.6025 \approx 86.60$$

18. a. From part b of the Right Triangle Altitude Theorem, each leg is the geometric mean of the hypotenuse and the segment of the hypotenuse adjacent to the leg, so RQ is the geometric mean of QS and QT.

  b. From part a of the Right Triangle Altitude Theorem, the altitude to the hypotenuse is the geometric mean of the segments into which it divides the hypotenuse, so RT is the geometric mean of QT and TS.

  c. From part b of the Right Triangle Altitude Theorem, each leg is the geometric mean of the hypotenuse and the segment of the hypotenuse adjacent to the leg, so RS is the geometric mean of QS and TS.

19. a. The statement is
  "If M is between P and Q, then
  $PM + MQ = PQ$."
  The converse is
  "If $PM + MQ = PQ$, then M is between P and Q."
  The inverse is
  "If M is not between P and Q, then
  $PM + MQ \neq PQ$."
  The contrapositive is
  "If $PM + MQ \neq PQ$, then M is not between P and Q."

  b. All are true.
  The statement is a definition. In general, the contrapositive of any true statement is true. Also, the converse of a definition is true because it is the sufficient condition for the defined term. Then by the Law of the Contrapositive, the inverse is true, because the inverse is the contrapositive of the converse.

20.

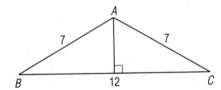

The two parts of the base of the isosceles triangle have length 6. Applying the Pythagorean Theorem, the altitude $= \sqrt{7^2 - 6^2} = \sqrt{49 - 36} = \sqrt{13} \approx 3.606$ units.

21. a. $\frac{100}{\sqrt{2}} = \frac{100\sqrt{2}}{2} = 50\sqrt{2}$

  b. $\frac{100}{\sqrt{2}} + 8\sqrt{2} = 50\sqrt{2} + 8\sqrt{2} = 58\sqrt{2}$

22. a.

x	$\sin x$	$\cos x$
0	0.0	1.0
5	.087	.996
10	.174	.985
15	.259	.966
20	.342	.940
25	.423	.906

x	$\sin x$	$\cos x$
30	.5	.866
35	.574	.819
40	.643	.766
45	.707	.707
50	.766	.643
55	.819	.574

x	$\sin x$	$\cos x$
60	.866	.5
65	.906	.423
70	.940	.342
75	.966	.259
80	.985	.174
85	.996	.087
90	1.0	0.0

b. $(\sin x)^2 + (\cos x)^2 = 1$ for all the values in the table.

$$\sin x = \frac{b}{c} \text{ and } \cos x = \frac{a}{c} \text{ so}$$

$$(\sin x)^2 + (\cos x)^2 = \left(\frac{b}{c}\right)^2 + \left(\frac{a}{c}\right)^2$$

$$= \frac{b^2}{c^2} + \frac{a^2}{c^2}$$

$$= \frac{a^2 + b^2}{c^2}$$

$$= \frac{c^2}{c^2}$$

$$= 1$$

LESSON 14–5 (pp. 708–713)

1. **a-b.** The time scheduled for east-to-west flights is not the same as the time scheduled for west-to-east flights because winds in the upper atmosphere either increase the plane's speed (for west-to-east flights) or decrease the plane's speed (for east-to-west flights). So the east-to-west flights usually take longer.

2. **a.** Subtracting the 4 mph current from the 20 mph water speed, the maximum ground speed against the current is $20 - 4 = 16$ mph.

   b. Adding the 5 mph current to the 20 mph water speed the maximum ground speed with the current is $20 + 5 = 25$ mph.

3. The initial point is the opposite end from the arrow; that is point O. The terminal point is the end with the arrow; that is point A. The direction is 20 degrees south of east (or 70 degrees east of south). The magnitude is 400.

4.

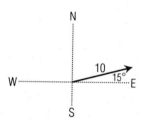

5. By the definition, two vectors are equal if and only if they have the same direction and the same magnitude.

6.

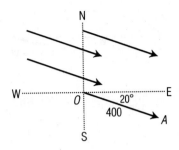

10.

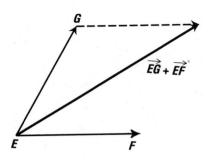

7. The diagram shows the two vectors -4 and -2; the resultant is -6, so the diagram shows the sum -4 + -2 = -6.

8.

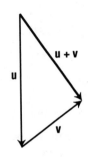

11.

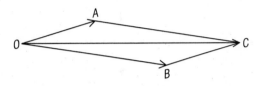

The parallelogram rule for adding two noncollinear vectors is that the sum of vectors $\overrightarrow{OA}$ and $\overrightarrow{OB}$ is the vector $\overrightarrow{OC}$ such that $OACB$ is a parallelogram.

12.

9.

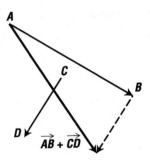

13.

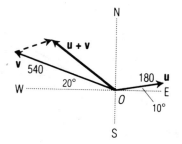

14.

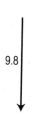

15.

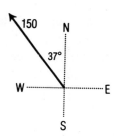

16.

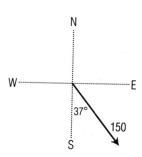

17.

18. a. $\sin X = \dfrac{\text{opp}}{\text{hyp}} = \dfrac{YZ}{XZ} = \dfrac{56}{65} \approx .862$

   b. $\tan X = \dfrac{\text{opp}}{\text{adj}} = \dfrac{YZ}{XY} = \dfrac{56}{33} \approx 1.697$

   c. $\cos Z = \dfrac{\text{adj}}{\text{hyp}} = \dfrac{YZ}{XZ} = \dfrac{56}{65} \approx .862$

19. Using the measurements $r = 35$ mm, $p = 15$ mm, and $q = 38$ mm, then

$\tan R = \dfrac{35}{15} \approx 2.3333$; $\sin R = \dfrac{35}{38} \approx .9211$;

and $\cos R = \dfrac{15}{38} \approx .3947$.

20. In terms of $\angle P$, two ratios involve p:

$\sin P = \dfrac{p}{q}$, so $p = q \sin P$, and

$\tan P = \dfrac{p}{r}$, so $p = r \tan P$.

The second value for p does not appear among the choices, but the first does; that is choice (a).

21. The problem involves the side opposite the 43-degree angle and the hypotenuse, which is the sine ratio.

$\sin 43° = \dfrac{8}{h}$, so $h \sin 43° = 8$ and

$h = \dfrac{8}{\sin 43}$

   $\approx \dfrac{8}{.682}$

   $= 11.7302$

The rope is about 11.7 m long.

22.

The ratio of adjacent:hypotenuse for a 30-degree angle is $\sqrt{3}$:2, so $\cos 30 = \dfrac{\sqrt{3}}{2}$.

23. Using the formula for the surface area of a sphere, S.A. $= 4\pi r^2$, with $r = 12$, then
S.A. $= 4\pi(12)^2$
$= 4\pi(144)$
$= 576\pi$
≈ 1809.557
$\approx 1810 \text{ units}^2$.

24. Using the formula for the volume of a sphere, $V = \dfrac{4}{3}\pi r^3$, with $r = 12$, then

$V = \dfrac{4}{3}\pi(12)^3$

$= \dfrac{4}{3}\pi(1728)$

$= 2304\pi$

≈ 7238.229

$\approx 7238 \text{ units}^3$.

25. **a-b.** Students' data for flight times, flight speeds, and wind assumptions will vary.

LESSON 14–6 (pp. 714–719)

1. For the vector $(2, 3)$, the horizontal component is the x-coordinate, which is 2, and the vertical component is the y-coordinate, which is 3.

2. Add the x-components and add the y-components:
$(300, 15) + (100, 212) = (300 + 100, 15 + 212)$
$= (400, 227)$.

3. Add the x-components and add the y-components:
$(a, b) + (c, d) = (a + c, b + d)$.

4. Add the x-components and add the y-components:
$(-9, 6) + (9, -6) = (-9 + 9, 6 + -6)$
$= (0, 0)$.

5. Add the x-components and add the y-components:
$(0, 0) + \left(\dfrac{1}{2}, \dfrac{-\sqrt{3}}{2}\right) = \left(\dfrac{1}{2}, \dfrac{-\sqrt{3}}{2}\right)$

6. Opposite vectors are vectors whose sum is the zero vector, $(0, 0)$; in Question 4 the sum is the zero vector, so $(-9, 6)$ and $(9, -6)$ are opposite vectors.

7. The additive identity vector is the vector that, when added to a second vector, results in that same second vector. That is the situation in Question 5, so $(0, 0)$ is the identity vector.

8. **a.** The effect of gravity is to have no horizontal change and to have a vertical change of -10; the vector that describes this is $(0, -10)$.

b. If the plane were standing still, after one second the location of the bullet would have changed by -10 in the vertical direction, due to gravity, and by -175 in the horizontal direction (it is negative, since the bullet was fired backwards); the vector that describes this is $(-175, -10)$.

c. The vector that describes the location of the plane after one second is $(250, 0)$; and
$(250, 0) + (-175, -10) = (250 + -175, 0 + -10)$
$= (75, -10)$.

9. a.

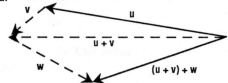

b.

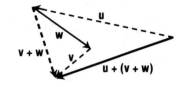

c. The first vector sum first "associates" vectors **u** and **v**, and the second vector sum first "associates" vectors **v** and **w**. The resultants are equal, so the property that is verified is that vector addition is associative.

10. Using the definition of scalar multiple that $k(a, b) = (ka, kb)$, then $2(-9, 5) = (-18, 10)$.

11.

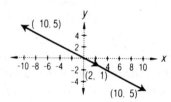

12. The result, that $k(a, b) = (ka, kb)$, is called scalar multiplication.

13.

14. a. To show that vectors $\overrightarrow{MP}$ and $\overrightarrow{ON}$ are parallel, you need to show that they have the same slope:

slope of $\overrightarrow{MP} = \dfrac{(b + d) - b}{(a + c) - a} = \dfrac{d}{c}$;

slope of $\overrightarrow{ON} = \dfrac{d - 0}{c - 0} = \dfrac{d}{c}$.

So $\overrightarrow{MP} \parallel \overrightarrow{ON}$.

b. To show that vectors $\overrightarrow{MP}$ and $\overrightarrow{ON}$ have the same length, use the distance formula:

$MP = \sqrt{(a + c - a)^2 + (b + d - b)^2}$
$\quad = \sqrt{c^2 + d^2}$;

$ON = \sqrt{(c - 0)^2 + (d - 0)^2}$
$\quad = \sqrt{c^2 + d^2}$.

So $MP = ON$.

15. Start with the sum of two vectors:

$(a, b) + (c, d)$
$= (a + c, b + d)$ by the Vector Addition Theorem,
$= (c + a, d + b)$ because addition is commutative,
$= (c, d) + (a, b)$ by the Vector Addition Theorem.

So vector addition is commutative.

16. $(a, b) + (-a, -b)$
$= (a + -a, b + -b)$ by the Vector Addition Theorem,
$= (0, 0)$ by addition of real numbers.

So the sum of two vectors is the zero vector; those two vectors must be opposite vectors by the definition of opposite vectors (sufficient condition).

17. $\dfrac{350 \text{ mi}}{1 \text{ hr}} \times \dfrac{5280 \text{ ft}}{1 \text{ mi}} \times \dfrac{1 \text{ hr}}{60 \text{ min}} = \dfrac{30{,}800 \text{ ft}}{1 \text{ min}}$

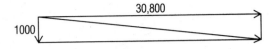

The slope is

$\dfrac{\text{change in } y\text{-values}}{\text{change in } x\text{-values}} = \dfrac{-1000}{30{,}800} \approx -.032.$

Converting 1000 feet per minute to miles per hour:

$\dfrac{1000 \text{ ft}}{1 \text{ min}} \times \dfrac{60 \text{ min}}{1 \text{ hr}} \times \dfrac{1 \text{ mi}}{5280 \text{ ft}} \approx \dfrac{11.364 \text{ mi}}{1 \text{ hr}}$

Then the slope would be $\dfrac{-11.364}{350} \approx -.032.$

18. a. $k[(a, b) + (c, d)]$

$\quad = k(a+c, b+d)$ vector addition

$\quad = (k(a+c), k(b+d))$ scalar multiplication

$\quad = (ka+kc, kb+kd)$ distributive property

$\quad = (ka, kb)+(kc, kd)$ vector addition

$\quad = k(a, b)+k(c, d)$ scalar multiplication

So the statement is *true*.

b. The result that $k[(a, b) + (c, d)] = k(a, b) + k(c, d)$ is the statement (in symbols) that scalar multiplication is distributive over vector addition.

19.

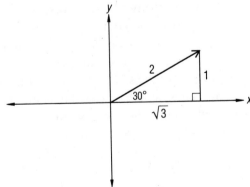

The triangle is a 30-60-90 right triangle, so the vertical component is half the hypotenuse, or 1, and the horizontal component is half the hypotenuse times $\sqrt{3}$, or $1\sqrt{3} = \sqrt{3}.$

20.

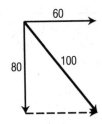

21.

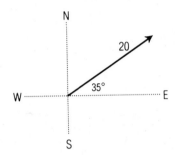

22. a. $\cos A = \dfrac{\text{adj}}{\text{hyp}} = \dfrac{42}{58} = \dfrac{21}{29}$

b. $\tan B = \dfrac{\text{opp}}{\text{hyp}} = \dfrac{42}{40} = \dfrac{21}{20} = 1.05$

c. $\sin A = \dfrac{\text{opp}}{\text{hyp}} = \dfrac{40}{58} = \dfrac{20}{29}$

23. By the Unequal Sides Theorem, the larger angle is opposite the longer side. Since $AC > CB$, then $m\angle B > m\angle A$; the statement is *false*.

24. Using the measurements $DE = 17$ mm, $EF = 31$ mm, and $DF = 35$ mm, then:

a. $\cos D = \dfrac{\text{adj}}{\text{hyp}} = \dfrac{DE}{DF} = \dfrac{17}{35} \approx .4857 \approx .5$

b. $\tan D = \dfrac{\text{opp}}{\text{adj}} = \dfrac{EF}{DE} = \dfrac{31}{17} \approx 1.8235 \approx 1.8$

25.

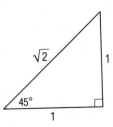

$\tan 45° = \dfrac{1}{1} = 1$

26. The area of square $ABCD$ is $36^2 = 1296$ units^2. Drawing the altitude from E to $\overline{DC}$ forms two 30-60-90 triangles. Half the base is 18, and the altitude is $18\sqrt{3}$. So the area of the triangle is $\frac{1}{2}bh = \frac{1}{2}(36)(18\sqrt{3}) = 324\sqrt{3}$ units^2.

The difference between the areas of the square and the triangle is $1296 - 324\sqrt{3} \approx 1296 - 561.18 \approx 734.8$ units^2.

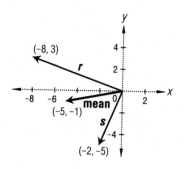

27. a.

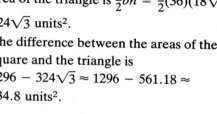

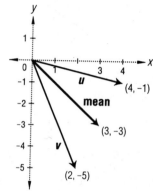

If $\mathbf{u} = (a, b)$ and $\mathbf{v} = (c, d)$, then the mean of the two vectors is $\frac{1}{2}(\mathbf{u} + \mathbf{v}) = \frac{1}{2}[(a, b) + (c, d)]$.

Using the result from Question 18 (or going through the steps again for these vectors), $\frac{1}{2}(\mathbf{u} + \mathbf{v}) = \frac{1}{2}\mathbf{u} + \frac{1}{2}\mathbf{v}$.

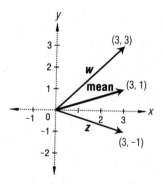

b. Geometrically, the mean of two vectors is either half the resultant vector or the resultant of the two half-vectors.

28. Extend the definition of the sum of two vectors so that the x-coordinate of the sum is the sum of the two x-coordinates, the y-coordinate of the sum is the sum of the two y-coordinates, and the z-coordinate of the sum is the sum of the two z-coordinates: $(a, b, c) + (d, e, f) = (a + d, b + e, c + f)$.

LESSON 14-7   (pp. 720–724)

1. Two ways of describing vectors are as directed segments and as ordered pairs.

2.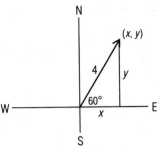

$\cos 60° = \frac{x}{4}$, so $x = 4 \cos 60° = (4)(.5) =$ 2 units.

$\sin 60° = \frac{y}{4}$, so $y = 4 \sin 60° \approx$ (4)(.866) = 3.464.

3.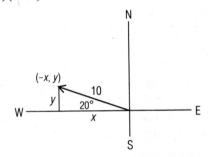

$\cos 20° = \frac{-x}{10}$, so $-x = 10 \cos 20°$ and $x \approx (-10)(.9397) = -9.397$.

$\sin 20° = \frac{y}{10}$, so $y = 10 \sin 20°$ $\approx (10)(.342) = 3.42$.

4.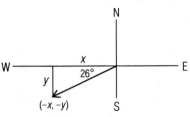

$\cos 26° = \frac{-x}{150}$, so $-x = 150 \cos 26°$ and $x \approx (-150)(.8988) = -134.82$.

$\sin 26° = \frac{-y}{150}$, so $-y = 150 \sin 26°$ and $y \approx (-150)(.438) = -65.76$.

5. The directed segment from the origin with length 3 can be described using the ordered pair (0, -3), so $x = 0$ and $y = -3$.

6. Using a calculator, .532 $\boxed{\text{INV}}\,\boxed{\text{TAN}}$ displays 28.012977, so m$\angle A \approx 28$.

7. Use the Pythagorean Theorem to find the magnitude:
$r = \sqrt{6^2 + 2^2} = \sqrt{36 + 4} = \sqrt{40} \approx 6.32$.
Use the tangent ratio to find the direction:
2 $\boxed{\div}$ 6 $\boxed{=}$ $\boxed{\text{INV}}\,\boxed{\text{TAN}}$ displays 18.4349, so the direction is about 18 degrees north of east (or $90 - 18 = 72$ degrees east of north).

8. Use the Pythagorean Theorem to find the magnitude:
$r = \sqrt{3^2 + (-4)^2} = \sqrt{9 + 16} = \sqrt{25} = 5$.
Use the tangent ratio to find the direction:
4 $\boxed{+/-}$ $\boxed{\div}$ 3 $\boxed{=}$ $\boxed{\text{INV}}\,\boxed{\text{TAN}}$ displays -53.130, so the direction is about 53 degrees south of east (or $90 - 53 = 37$ degrees east of south).

9.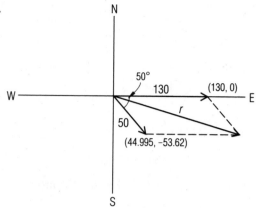

10.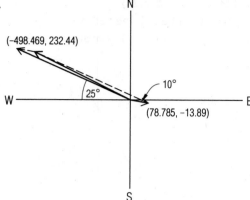

Convert the vectors to ordered pairs: for the east force, the vector is (130, 0). For the other, the coordinates are (70 cos 50°, -70 sin 50°) = (44.995, -53.62). The resultant is the sum of the vectors: (130, 0) + (44.995, -53.62) = (174.995, -53.62).

Use the Pythagorean Theorem to find the magnitude of the resultant:

$r = \sqrt{174.995^2 + (-53.62)^2} = \sqrt{33498} \approx 183$.

Use the tangent ratio of the resultant to find its direction:

53.62 $\boxed{+/-}$ $\boxed{\div}$ 174.995 $\boxed{=}$ $\boxed{INV}$ $\boxed{TAN}$ displays 17.0355.

So the resultant force acting on the crate is about 183 pounds, in the direction that is about 17 degrees south of east (or 90 − 17 = 73 degrees east of south).

Convert the vectors to ordered pairs: For the 550 mph air speed, the coordinates are (-550 cos 25°, 550 sin 25°) = (-498.469, 232.44), and for the 80 mph wind speed, the coordinates are (80 cos 10°, -80 sin 10°) = (78.785, -13.89). The resultant is the sum of the vectors: (-498.469, 232.44) + (78.785, -13.89) = (-419.684, 218.55).

Use the Pythagorean Theorem to find the magnitude of the resultant:

$r = \sqrt{(-419.684)^2 + 218.55^2} = \sqrt{223899} = 473$.

Use the tangent ratio of the resultant to find its direction:

218.55 $\boxed{\div}$ 419.684 $\boxed{+/-}$ $\boxed{=}$ $\boxed{INV}$ $\boxed{TAN}$ displays -27.508.

So the ground speed of the plane is about 473 mph and the direction is about 27.5 degrees north of west (or 90 − 27.5 = 62.5 degrees west of north).

11. Use the Pythagorean Theorem to find the length of the resultant after one second: $r = \sqrt{88^2 + (-32)^2} = \sqrt{8768} = 93.6376$. Use the tangent ratio to find the direction from the person after one second: 32 $\boxed{+/-}$ $\boxed{\div}$ 88 $\boxed{=}$ $\boxed{\text{INV}}$ $\boxed{\text{TAN}}$ displays $-19.983 \approx -20$. The ball will be about 93.7 feet from the person, and the line of sight from the person to the ball will be 20 degrees below the horizontal.

12. If $(-7, 13) + (x, y) = (0, 0)$, then $-7 + x = 0$, or $x = 7$, and $13 + y = 0$, or $y = -13$. So the inverse of $(-7, 13)$ is $(7, -13)$.

13.

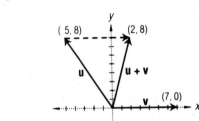

14.

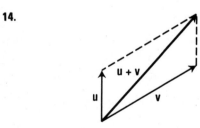

15.

16. Using part b of the Right Triangle Altitude Theorem, that each leg is the geometric mean of the hypotenuse and the segment of the hypotenuse adjacent to the leg, then
$$\frac{13}{12} = \frac{12}{x} \text{ and } \frac{13}{5} = \frac{5}{y}, \text{ then}$$
$13x = 144$, so $x = \frac{144}{13}$, and
$13y = 25$, so $y = \frac{25}{13}$.
The segments of the hypotenuse are $\frac{144}{13}$ and $\frac{25}{13}$.

Using part a of the Right Triangle Altitude Theorem, that the altitude to the hypotenuse is the geometric mean of the segments into which it divides the hypotenuse, then
$$\frac{\frac{144}{13}}{x} = \frac{x}{\frac{25}{13}} \text{ then } x^2 = \frac{144}{13} \cdot \frac{25}{13} = \frac{3600}{169}$$
so $x = \frac{60}{13}$.

17. Drawing the altitude from U forms two 30-60-90 triangles. So the altitude from U is half 15 or 7.5, and half of the base $\overline{ST}$ is $7.5\sqrt{3}$.
So the area of $\triangle STU$ is $\frac{1}{2}(15\sqrt{3})(7.5) = 56.35\sqrt{3} \approx 97.43$ units^2.

18. Statement 3 satisfies the negation of the consequent of statement 2, so by the Laws of the Contrapositive and Detachment, it must satisfy the negation of the antecedent of statement 2, and you can conclude that "Rudolf is a y." Rewriting statement 1 as "If an animal is an x, then it is not a y," your previous conclusion satisfies the negation of the rewritten statement 1, so by the Laws of the Contrapositive and Detachment it must satisfy the negation of the antecedent of that statement, or "Rudolf is not an x."

19. The ratio of the volumes of two similar figures is the cube of the ratio of heights (because height is a linear dimension, the ratio of heights is the same as the ratio of similitude).

So if the ratio of volumes is 1:8, then the ratio of heights is $\sqrt[3]{1}:\sqrt[3]{8} = 1:2$; the height of the $\frac{1}{8}$-size cello is half the height of the full-sized cello.

20. **a.**

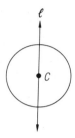

The figure is a sphere with center and radius the same as circle C.

b.

The figure has the shape of a doughnut (it is called a "torus"). The width of the torus is the same as the diameter of circle A, and the radius of the "hole" of the figure is the distance from line ℓ to point A, less the radius of circle A.

21. The dot product of two vectors is a real number. For the two vectors (a, b) and (c, d), the dot product $(a, b) \cdot (c, d) = ac + bd$.

CHAPTER 14 PROGRESS SELF-TEST (p. 726–727)

1. The three sides have lengths $XY \approx 5.5$ cm, $XZ \approx 1.6$ cm, and $YZ \approx 5.3$ cm. So cos $Y = \dfrac{\text{side adjacent to } \angle Y}{\text{hypotenuse}} = \dfrac{YZ}{XY} \approx \dfrac{5.3}{5.5} \approx 0.96$.

2. The tangent ratio is $\dfrac{\text{opposite side}}{\text{adjacent side}}$. For the three numbered angles, the opposite side is constant, so the smallest tangent will be associated with longest adjacent side; $\angle 3$ will have the smallest tangent.

3. Sin $B = \dfrac{\text{side opposite } \angle B}{\text{hypotenuse}} = \dfrac{AC}{AB} = \dfrac{\text{side adjacent to } \angle A}{\text{hypotenuse}} = \cos A$. So if $\sin B = \dfrac{9}{11}$, then $\cos A = \dfrac{9}{11}$.

4–5. To find WZ and WY, use the property that each leg is the mean proportional between the hypotenuse and its segment adjacent to the leg. For WZ, $\dfrac{YZ}{XZ} = \dfrac{XZ}{WZ}$ or $\dfrac{75}{45} = \dfrac{45}{WZ}$. So $75WZ = 2025$, or $WZ = 27$ units. For WY, $\dfrac{YZ}{XY} = \dfrac{XY}{WY}$ or $\dfrac{75}{60} = \dfrac{60}{WY}$. So $75WY = 3600$, or $WY = 48$ units.

6. In right triangle CDB, $CD^2 = \sqrt{CB^2 - DB^2} = \sqrt{6^2 - 2^2} = \sqrt{36 - 4} = \sqrt{32}$. Then, since the altitude is the mean proportional to the segments of the hypotenuse, $\dfrac{AD}{CD} = \dfrac{CD}{DB}$ or $\dfrac{AD}{\sqrt{32}} = \dfrac{\sqrt{32}}{2}$. So $2AD = 32$ and $AD = 16$. Since $AB = AD + DB$, then $AB = 16 + 2 = 18$ units.

7. CD, the altitude to the hypotenuse of a right triangle, is the mean proportional to the lengths of the segments of the hypotenuse which are the distances AD and DB.

8. $\triangle ABC$ is an isosceles triangle with legs $\overline{AB}$ and $\overline{BC}$. Since AB is given to be 7 units, then $BC = 7$ units.

9. $\triangle ABC$ is a 45-45-90 triangle, so its hypotenuse is $\sqrt{2}$ times the length of a leg. So $AC = 7\sqrt{2}$ ≈ 9.9 units.

10. $\triangle ACD$ is a 30-60-90 triangle so AD is twice the length of the side $\overline{AC}$ opposite the 30° angle. Since $AC = 7\sqrt{2}$ (from Question 9), then $AD = 2(7\sqrt{2}) = 14\sqrt{2} \approx 19.8$ units.

11. Tan $D = \dfrac{\text{side opposite } \angle D}{\text{side adjacent to } \angle D} = \dfrac{EF}{DF} = \dfrac{48}{14}$
≈ 3.43.

12. Cos $E = \dfrac{\text{side adjacent to } \angle E}{\text{hypotenuse}} = \dfrac{EF}{DE} = \dfrac{48}{50}$
$= .96$.

13.

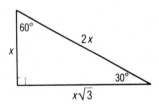

In a 30-60-90 triangle, the lengths of the sides are x, $x\sqrt{3}$, and $2x$,

so $\sin 60° = \dfrac{x\sqrt{3}}{2x} = \dfrac{\sqrt{3}}{2}$.

14.

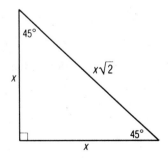

In a 45-45-90 triangle, the lengths of the sides are x, x, and $x\sqrt{2}$. So $\tan 45° = \dfrac{x}{x} = 1$.

15. $\dfrac{18}{x} = \dfrac{x}{30}$, so $x^2 = (18)(30) = 540$ and
$x = \sqrt{540} \approx 23.2379 \approx 23.24$.

16. To find the height of the tree above eye level, use $\tan 35° = \dfrac{h}{40}$. Using a calculator (in degree mode), 35 $\boxed{\text{TAN}}$ $\boxed{\times}$ 40 $\boxed{=}$ 28.0083 $\approx$ 28 feet. Adding the five feet for eye level, the height of the tree is about 33 feet.

17.

$\sin 80° = \dfrac{h}{15}$

$h = 15 \sin 80$

$= 80 \boxed{\text{SIN}} \boxed{\times} 15 \boxed{=}$

≈ 14.772116

≈ 14.77 ft

18.

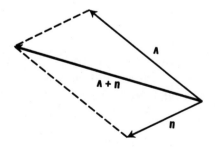

Use the parallelogram rule:

19. Use equal vectors such that the endpoint of one vector is the initial point of the next.

a.

For the sum 2**v** + **u**, its initial point is the initial point of the starting vector **v**, and its terminal point is the terminal point of vector **u**.

b.

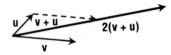

Find **v** + **u** using the parallelogram method. Then find 2(**v** + **u**) by starting another vector **v** + **u** at the terminal point of **v** + **u**.

20.

The opposite of a vector has the same length but opposite direction. Below are vectors $\overrightarrow{AB}$ and several opposite vectors $\overrightarrow{CD}$ and $\overrightarrow{EF}$.

21.

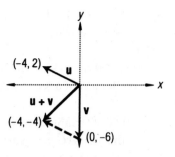

Find **u** + **v** either by the parallelogram rule or by adding the *x*- and *y*-coordinates:
u + **v** = (-4 + 0, 2 + -6) = (-4, -4).

22. For the horizontal component, $\cos 35° = \frac{x}{50}$, so $x = 50 \cos 35 \approx 40.958 \approx 41$; since the horizontal component is in the negative direction, it is $\approx$ -41. For the vertical component: $\sin 35° = \frac{y}{50}$ so $y = 50 \sin 35 \approx 28.6788 \approx 28.7$; it is in the negative direction, so it is about -28.7.

23.

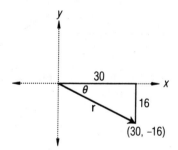

$\tan \theta = \frac{16}{30}$, so $\theta = 16$ [÷] 30 [=] [INV] [TAN] $\approx 28°$. $r = \sqrt{16^2 + 30^2} = \sqrt{256 + 900} = \sqrt{1156} = 34$. The direction of the vector is about 28° south of east (or 62° east of south) and its magnitude is 34.

24.

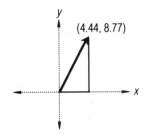

700 km/hr → 150 km/hr ←

The resultant speed is $700 - 150 =$ 550 km/hr. In $3\frac{1}{2}$ hours, the plane could travel $(550)(3.5) = 1925$ km.

25.

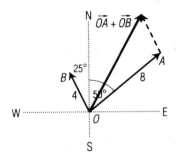

Using the Parallelogram Rule, the kayaker will be moving in a direction east of north. Trigonometry can give a more exact answer.

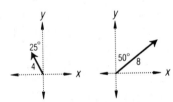

For the current vector, horizontal component is $-4 \sin 25° \approx -1.69$ and the vertical component is $4 \cos 25° = 3.63$, so its terminal point is $(-1.69, 3.63)$. For the kayaker, the horizontal component is $8 \sin 50 \approx 6.13$ and the vertical component is $8 \cos 50 \approx 5.14$, so its terminal point is $(6.13, 5.14)$. The components of the sum of the vectors are $(-1.69 + 6.13, 3.63 + 5.14) = (4.44, 8.77)$.

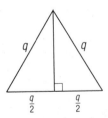

(4.44, 8.77)

The direction of the resultant vector is 8.77 $\boxed{÷}$ 4.44 $\boxed{=}$ $\boxed{INV}$ $\boxed{TAN}$ $\approx 63.15°$ north of east, and its magnitude is $\sqrt{4.44^2 + 8.77^2} = \sqrt{96.6265} \approx 9.83$ mph.

CHAPTER 14 REVIEW (pp. 728–731)

1. $\triangle ABC$ is a 30-60-90 triangle, so the length of $\overline{AC}$ is $\sqrt{3}$ times the length of $\overline{AB}$, or $4\sqrt{3} \approx 6.928$ units, and the length of $\overline{BC}$ is twice the length of $\overline{AB}$, or 8 units.

2. $\triangle DEF$ is a 45-45-90 triangle, so $DE = DF = 16x$, and the length EF is DE times $\sqrt{2}$, or $(16x)(\sqrt{2}) \approx 22.627x$.

3. A diagonal of a square forms two 45-45-90 triangles, so the length of the diagonal of a square is $\sqrt{2}$ times the side of the square. If the side has length 12, then the length of the diagonal is $12\sqrt{2} \approx 16.97$ units.

4.

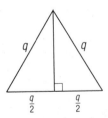

The altitude of an equilateral triangle forms 30-60-90 triangles. If the side of the original triangle is q, then the short leg of the 30-60-90 triangle is $\frac{q}{2}$, and the altitude of the original triangle is $\frac{q\sqrt{3}}{2}$.

5. a. $\triangle TSU$ is a 45-45-90 triangle, so
$$TU = TS\sqrt{2} = 7\sqrt{2} \approx 9.899 \text{ units.}$$
b. $\triangle TSU$ is a 45-45-90 triangle, so
$$US = TS = 7 \text{ units.}$$
c. $\triangle TSK$ is a 30-60-90 triangle, so
$$SK = TS\sqrt{3} = 7\sqrt{3} \approx 12.124 \text{ units.}$$
d. $\triangle TSK$ is 30-60-90 triangle, so
$$TK = 2 \cdot TS = (2)(7) = 14 \text{ units.}$$

6. $\triangle TSK$ is a 30-60-90 triangle and $\triangle TSU$ is a 45-45-90 triangle, so

a. $ST = \dfrac{SK}{\sqrt{3}} = \dfrac{13}{\sqrt{3}} = \dfrac{13\sqrt{3}}{3} \approx$
7.50555 units.

b. $SU = ST = \dfrac{13}{\sqrt{3}} = \dfrac{13\sqrt{3}}{3} \approx$
7.50555 units.

c. $TK = 2 \cdot ST = \dfrac{26}{\sqrt{3}} = \dfrac{26\sqrt{3}}{3} \approx$
15.01 units.

7.

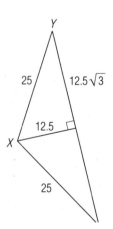

$\triangle XYZ$ is an isosceles triangle, so by the theorem that the altitude from the vertex of an isosceles triangle bisects the vertex angle, then the altitude forms two 30-60-90 triangles. So the altitude from X has length 12.5. Then half of YZ is $12.5\sqrt{3}$, so $YZ = 25\sqrt{3} \approx 43.301$ units.

8. Using measurements, approximate values are $m\angle A = 33$, $\tan A = .65$, $\sin A = .54$, and $\cos A = .84$.

9. Using measurements, approximate values are $m\angle E = 76$, $\sin E = .97$, $\cos E = .24$, and $\tan E = 4$.

10.

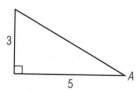

From the diagram, an approximate value is $m\angle A = 30$.
Using a calculator,
3 [÷] 5 [=] [INV][TAN] displays 30.96376. So $m\angle A \approx 31$.

11. In the tangent ratio, $\dfrac{\text{opp}}{\text{adj}}$, if the opposite side is constant then the value of the tangent decreases as the length of the adjacent side increases. So the angle with the largest tangent is the one with smallest adjacent side; that is $\angle 1$.

12. In the sine ratio, $\dfrac{\text{opp}}{\text{hyp}}$, if the opposite side is constant then the value of the sine decreases as the length of the hypotenuse increases. So the angle with the largest sine is the one with the smallest hypotenuse; that is $\angle 1$.

13. $\sin A = \dfrac{\text{opp}}{\text{hyp}} = \dfrac{24}{26} = \dfrac{12}{13}$

14. $\cos B = \dfrac{\text{adj}}{\text{hyp}} = \dfrac{24}{26} = \dfrac{12}{13}$

15. $\tan B = \dfrac{\text{opp}}{\text{adj}} = \dfrac{10}{24} = \dfrac{5}{12}$

16. $\cos A = \dfrac{\text{adj}}{\text{hyp}} = \dfrac{10}{26} = \dfrac{5}{13}$

17. 57.5 [SIN] displays .8343391, so $\sin 57.5° \approx 0.843$.

18. 22.1 [TAN] displays .4060579, so $\tan 22.1° \approx 0.406$.

19. 1 [COS] displays .9998477, so $\cos 1° \approx 1.000$.

20. In a 30-60-90 triangle, $\sin 30° = \dfrac{\text{opp}}{\text{hyp}} = \dfrac{1}{2} = 0.5$.

21. In a 30-60-90 triangle,

$$\tan 60° = \frac{\text{opp}}{\text{adj}} = \frac{\sqrt{3}}{1} = \sqrt{3}.$$

22. In a 45-45-90 triangle,

$$\tan 45° = \frac{\text{opp}}{\text{adj}} = \frac{1}{1} = 1.$$

23. In a 45-45-90 triangle,

$$\cos 45° = \frac{\text{opp}}{\text{hyp}} = \frac{1}{\sqrt{2}} = \frac{\sqrt{2}}{2}.$$

24. Using part a of the Right Triangle Altitude Theorem, that the altitude to the hypotenuse is the geometric mean of the segments into which it divides the hypotenuse, then

$$\frac{AD}{CD} = \frac{CD}{DB} \text{ so } \frac{9}{CD} = \frac{CD}{4}$$

$$CD^2 = 36$$

$$CD = 6.$$

25. Using part b of the Right Triangle Altitude Theorem, that each leg is the geometric mean of the hypotenuse and the segment of the hypotenuse adjacent to the leg, then

$$\frac{AD}{AC} = \frac{AC}{AB} \text{ so } \frac{AD}{7} = \frac{7}{12}$$

$$12AD = 49$$

$$AD = \frac{49}{12} \approx 4.08 \text{ units.}$$

26. First use part a of the Right Triangle Altitude Theorem, that the altitude to the hypotenuse is the geometric mean of the segments into which it divides the hypotenuse, to find DB:

$$\frac{AD}{CD} = \frac{CD}{DB} \text{ so } \frac{18}{12} = \frac{12}{DB}$$

$$18 \cdot DB = 144$$

$$DB = 8$$

Then use the Pythagorean Theorem to find CB:

$$CB = \sqrt{CD^2 + DB^2}$$
$$= \sqrt{12^2 + 8^2}$$
$$= \sqrt{144 + 64}$$
$$= \sqrt{208}$$
$$\approx 14.42 \text{ units.}$$

27. Using part b of the Right Triangle Altitude Theorem, that each leg is the geometric mean of the hypotenuse and the segment of the hypotenuse adjacent to the leg, then

$$\frac{25}{7} = \frac{7}{x} \text{ and } \frac{25}{24} = \frac{24}{z}, \text{ so}$$

$$25x = 49, \text{ and } x = \frac{49}{25} = 1.96 \text{ units, and}$$

$$25z = 576, \text{ so } z = \frac{576}{25} = 23.04 \text{ units.}$$

Then, using part a of the Right Triangle Altitude Theorem, that the altitude to the hypotenuse is the geometric mean of the segments into which it divides the hypotenuse,

$$\frac{1.96}{y} = \frac{y}{23.04}$$
$$y^2 = (1.96)(23.04) = 45.1584$$
$$y = \sqrt{45.1584} = 6.72 \text{ units.}$$

28. a. Using part a of the Right Triangle Altitude Theorem, that the altitude to the hypotenuse is the geometric mean of the segments into which it divides the hypotenuse, then

$$\frac{QT}{RT} = \frac{RT}{TS} \text{ so } \frac{QT}{4} = \frac{4}{8}$$

$$8 \cdot QT = 16$$
$$QT = 2 \text{ units.}$$

b. Using part b of the Right Triangle Altitude Theorem, that each leg is the geometric mean of the hypotenuse and the segment of the hypotenuse adjacent to the leg, then

$$\frac{QS}{QR} = \frac{QR}{QT}. \ QS = QT + TS = 10,$$

$$\text{so } \frac{10}{QR} = \frac{QR}{2}$$

$$QR^2 = 20$$
$$QR = \sqrt{20} = \sqrt{(4)(5)} = 2\sqrt{5} \approx$$
$$4.472 \text{ units.}$$

c. Using the Pythagorean Theorem in $\triangle RTS$,
$$RS = \sqrt{RT^2 + TS^2}$$
$$= \sqrt{4^2 + 8^2}$$
$$\sqrt{16 + 64}$$
$$\sqrt{80}$$
$$\approx 8.9443 \text{ units.}$$
d. $QS = QT + TS$
$$= 2 + 8$$
$$= 10 \text{ units}$$

29.

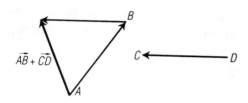

30.

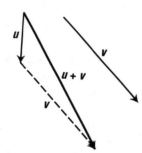

31.

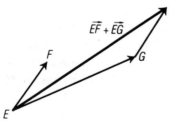

32.

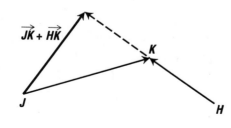

33.

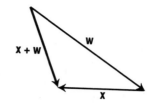

34.

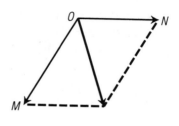

35.

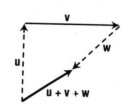

36. a.

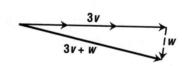

b.

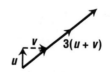

37. In a right triangle ABC with right angle C,
$$\cos A = \frac{\text{adj}}{\text{hyp}} = \frac{AC}{AB}.$$

38. In a right triangle ABC with right angle C,
$$\sin A = \frac{\text{opp}}{\text{hyp}} = \frac{BC}{AB}.$$

39. In a right triangle ABC with right angle C,
$\tan A = \frac{\text{opp}}{\text{hyp}} = \frac{BC}{AC}$.

40. $\overline{MP}$ is opposite $\angle Q$ and $\overline{MQ}$ is adjacent to $\angle Q$, so $\frac{MP}{MQ}$ is the tangent of $\angle Q$.

41. $\overline{MQ}$ is the side opposite $\angle P$, and $\overline{PQ}$ is the hypotenuse, so $\frac{MQ}{PQ}$ is the sine of $\angle P$.

42. $\tan B = \frac{\text{opp}}{\text{adj}} = \frac{AC}{BC}$.

43.

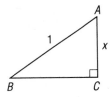

If $\cos A = x = \frac{x}{1}$, then $\sin A = \frac{x}{1} = x$.

44. According to part b of the Right Triangle Altitude Theorem, that each leg is the geometric mean of the hypotenuse and the segment of the hypotenuse adjacent to the leg, so AB is the geometric mean of BC and BD.

45. According to part a of the Right Triangle Altitude Theorem, that the altitude to the hypotenuse is the geometric mean of the segments into which it divides the hypotenuse, then AD is the geometric mean of BD and DC.

46. According to part b of the Right Triangle Altitude Theorem, that each leg is the geometric mean of the hypotenuse and the segment of the hypotenuse adjacent to the leg, so AC is the geometric mean of BC and DC.

47. Two triangles have a right angle and $\angle B$, and two triangles have a right angle and $\angle C$, so all three triangles are similar by the AA Similarity Theorem. Using the order "right angle, angle similar to B, and angle similar to C," the similarity statement is $\triangle ABC \sim \triangle DBA \sim \triangle DAC$.

48. For any vector (a, b), $(a, b) + (0, 0) = (a, b)$, so the identity vector is $(0, 0)$.

49.

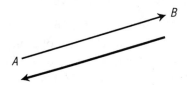

50. The sum of two inverse vectors is the zero vector, $(0, 0)$. So $(2, 9) + (a, b) = (0,0)$, and $2 + a = 0$, so $a = -2$, and $9 + b = 0$, so $b = -9$. So the inverse vector for $(2, 9)$ is $(-2, -9)$.

51.

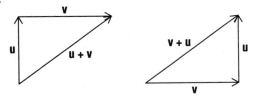

Yes $\mathbf{u} + \mathbf{v} = \mathbf{v} + \mathbf{u}$. In general, vector addition is commutative, so $\mathbf{u} + \mathbf{v} = \mathbf{v} + \mathbf{u}$ for any two vectors $\mathbf{u}$ and $\mathbf{v}$.

52.

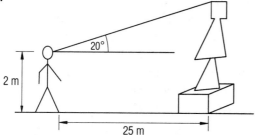

Using the tangent ratio to find the height h of the sculpture above eye level, $\tan 20° = \frac{h}{25}$, so $h = 25 \tan 20° \approx (25)(.36397) \approx 9.099$ m. Adding the eye-level height of 2 m, the total height of the sculpture is $9.099 + 2 = 11.099 \approx 11.1$ m.

53. Using the tangent ratio to find the height h of the tree, $\tan 57° = \frac{h}{14}$ so $h = 14 \tan 57° \approx (14)(1.53986) \approx 21.6$ yards.

54.

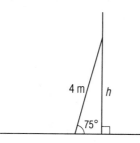

Using the sine ratio to find the height h on the wall reached by the ladder, $\sin 75° = \frac{h}{4}$, so $h = 4 \sin 75° \approx (4)(.9659) \approx 3.86$ m.

55. Using the cosine ratio to find the distance d to the clown, $\cos 25° = \frac{60}{d}$, so $d \cos 25° = 60$ and $d = \frac{60}{\cos 25} \approx \frac{60}{.9063} \approx 66$ feet.

56. The motorboat is traveling directly against the current, so subtract the rate of the current from the still-water rate of the boat. So the traveling rate of the boat is $30 - 10 = 20$ mph. In 15 minutes, or one-quarter of an hour, the boat travels $(20)(.25) = 5$ miles.

57. The airplane is traveling directly with the wind, so add the rate of the plane in still air to the tail wind to get the traveling rate of the plane: $600 + 100 = 700$ kilometers per hour. So in 2.5 hours, the plane would travel $(700)(2.5) = 1750$ kilometers.

58.

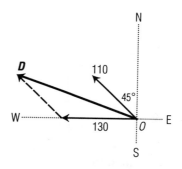

59.

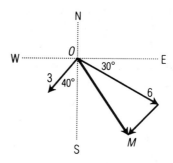

60.

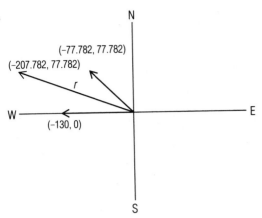

First write the vectors as ordered pairs:
The 130-pound, westerly vector can be written as (-130, 0).

For the 110-pound vector, the coordinates are (-110 cos 45°, 110 sin 45°) = (-77.782, 77.782).

Use the vector addition to find the resultant: (-130, 0) + (-77.782, 77.782) = (-207.782, 77,782).

Use the Pythagorean Theorem to find the magnitude r of the resultant:
$r = \sqrt{(-207.782)^2 + 77.782^2} = \sqrt{49223} \approx 221.86$.

Then use the tangent ratio to find the direction of the resultant:
77.782 $\boxed{\div}$ 207.782 $\boxed{+/-}$ $\boxed{=}$ $\boxed{INV}$ $\boxed{TAN}$ displays -20.523.

So the magnitude of the combined force is about 221.86 pounds, and it acts in the direction 20.5 degrees north of west (or 90 − 20.5 = 69.5 degrees west of north).

61. For consistency, express the direction "40 degrees west of south" as "50 degrees south of west."

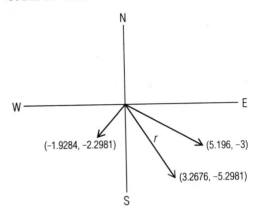

First write the vectors as ordered pairs:
The current vector can be written as (6 cos 30°, -6 sin 30°) = (5.196, -3), and the rowers' vector can be written as (-3 cos 50°, -3 sin 50°) = (-1.9284, -2.2981).

Use vector addition to find the resultant: (5.196, -3) + (-1.9284, -2.2981) = (3.2676, -5.2981).

Then use the Pythagorean Theorem to find the magnitude r of the resultant:
$r = \sqrt{3.2676^2 + (-5.2981)^2} = \sqrt{38.7470} \approx 6.2247$.

Then use the tangent ratio to find the direction of the resultant:
5.2981 $\boxed{+/-}$ $\boxed{\div}$ 3.2676 $\boxed{=}$ $\boxed{INV}$ $\boxed{TAN}$ displays -58.3358.

So the magnitude of the combined force is about 6.2 mph, and the direction is about 58 degrees south of east (or 32 degrees east of south).

62.

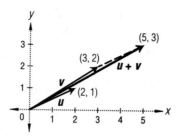

63.

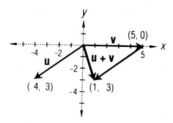

64.

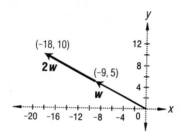

65.

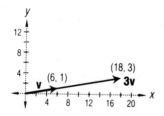

66. $\cos 18° = \frac{x}{100}$, so the horizontal component
of vector $\overrightarrow{OA}$ is $x = 100 \cos 18° \approx$
$(100)(.951) = 95.1$;

$\sin 18° = \frac{y}{100}$, so the vertical component of
the vector is $y = 100 \sin 18° \approx$
$(100)(.309) = 30.9$.

67. As an ordered pair, vector $\overrightarrow{OB}$ can be written
as $(-25 \cos 60°, 25 \sin 60°) = (-12.5, 21.65)$.

68.

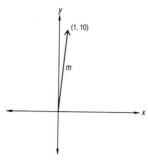

Use the Pythagorean Theorem to find the
magnitude m of the vector:
$m = \sqrt{1^2 + 10^2} = \sqrt{1 + 100} =$
$\sqrt{101} \approx 10.05.$
Use the tangent ratio to find the direction of
the vector:
$10 \boxed{÷} 1 \boxed{=} \boxed{\text{INV}} \boxed{\text{TAN}}$ displays 84.2894.
So the magnitude of the vector is about
10.05 units, and its direction is 84.3 degrees
north of east (or $90 - 84.3 = 5.7$ degrees
east of north).

69.

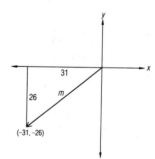

Use the Pythagorean Theorem to find the
magnitude m of the vector:
$m = \sqrt{(-31)^2 + (-26)^2} = \sqrt{1637} \approx 40.4599.$
Use the tangent ratio to find the direction of
the vector:
$26 \boxed{+/-} \boxed{÷} 31 \boxed{+/-} \boxed{=} \boxed{\text{INV}} \boxed{\text{TAN}}$ displays
39.9869.
So the magnitude of the vector is about
40.5 units, and its direction is about
40 degrees south of west (or $90 - 40 =$
50 degrees west of south).

1. A minor arc corresponds to a central angle of less than 180 degrees, so the measure of a minor arc is between 0° and 180°.

2. A major arc corresponds to a central angle of greater than 180 degrees, so the measure of a major arc is between 180° and 360°.

3. If m∠*POQ* = 98, then its intercepted arc has the same measure, so m $\widehat{PQ}$ = 98°.

4. Radii $\overline{OP}$ and $\overline{OQ}$ have the same length, by the definition of circle (meaning), so △*OPQ* is isosceles by the definition of isosceles triangle (sufficient condition).

5. If $\overleftrightarrow{OM}$, the line containing the center of the circle, is perpendicular to chord $\overline{PQ}$ then, by part a of the Chord-Center Theorem, $\overline{OM}$ bisects $\overline{PQ}$.

6. If $\overleftrightarrow{OM}$, the line containing the center of the circle, bisects central angle *POQ* then, by part c of the Chord-Center Theorem, $\overline{OM}$ is the perpendicular bisector of $\overline{PQ}$.

7. Part b: "the midpoint of the chord" refers to the median to the base, so the median to the base is also the bisector of the vertex angle.
    Part c: "perpendicular to and bisecting the chord" is the altitude and perpendicular bisector, so the bisector of the vertex angle is also the altitude to and the perpendicular bisector of the base.
    Part d: "containing the center of the circle" means the line passes through the vertex angle, so the perpendicular bisector of the base is the altitude from the vertex.

8. Two circles are congruent if their radii have the same length or are congruent; that is choice (c).

9. If m∠*Z* = m∠*A*, then two arc measures are equal, namely $\widehat{BC}$ = $\widehat{XY}$. But the circles are not necessarily congruent, so $BC \neq XY$; the statement is *false*.

10.

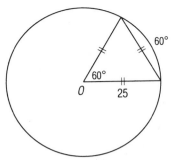

The measure of the central angle is also 60, so the triangle is equilateral. Then the chord has length 25 m.

11.

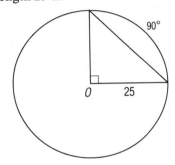

The central angle has measure 90, so the chord is the hypotenuse of a 45-45-90 triangle, and its measure is $25\sqrt{2} \approx 35.355$ m.

12.

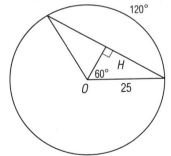

From parts a and b of the Chord-Center Theorem, the ⊥ from the center to the chord bisects the chord and the central angle. So if H is half the length of the chord, H is the long leg in a 30-60-90 triangle, and H = $12.5\sqrt{3}$. So the length of the chord is $25\sqrt{3} \approx 43.3$ m.

13.

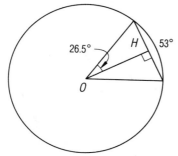

If H is half the chord, then $\sin 26.5° = \frac{H}{25}$, so
$H = 25 \sin 26.5°$ and the length of the chord
is $50 \sin 26.5° \approx (50)(.4462) \approx 22.3$ m.

14. It is given that $AB = CD$; also, $AO = BO = CO = DO$ by the definition of circle (meaning). So $\triangle AOB \cong \triangle COD$ by the SSS Congruence Theorem, and $m\angle AOB = m\angle COD$ by the CPCF Theorem. Then, by the definition of arc measure, $m\overset{\frown}{AB} = m\angle AOB$ and $m\overset{\frown}{CD} = m\angle COD$, so $m\overset{\frown}{AB} = m\overset{\frown}{CD}$ by the Transitive Property of Equality.

15.

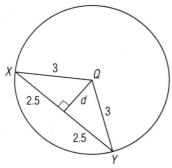

The distance d from Q to the board is the length of the leg of a right triangle with hypotenuse 2.5 (by part a of the Chord-Center Theorem: a line through the center of a circle, perpendicular to a chord, bisects the chord) and other leg 3 (definition of circle—meaning). Using the Pythagorean Theorem: $d = \sqrt{3^2 - 2.5^2} = \sqrt{9 - 6.25} = \sqrt{2.75} = 1.658$ ft.

16. a. All 6 sides of $ABCDEF$ have the same length, by the definition of regular polygon (meaning), so all 6 minor arcs ($\overset{\frown}{AB}$, $\overset{\frown}{BC}$, $\overset{\frown}{CD}$, $\overset{\frown}{DE}$, $\overset{\frown}{EF}$, and $\overset{\frown}{FA}$) have the same length by part b of the Arc-Chord Congruence Theorem. The arc measure of the entire circle is 360 degrees, so $m\overset{\frown}{AB} = \frac{360}{6} = 60°$. Then, by the definition of arc measure, the measure of central angle $AHB = 60$.

b. First show that $\triangle HAB$ is an equilateral triangle:
It is isosceles, with vertex H, by the definition of circle (meaning) and the definition of isosceles triangle (sufficient condition). So its base angles are congruent, by the Isosceles Triangle Theorem, and $m\angle AHB = 60$ from part a, so using the Triangle-Sum Theorem, each of the base angles is 60. So $\triangle HAB$ is equilateral, by the definition of equilateral triangle (sufficient condition).
Then, since $AB = HA$, then $AB = 13$, and the perimeter of $ABCDEF = (6)(13) = 78$ units.

17. Each of the four small triangles is a 45-45-90 triangle, so the hypotenuse is the radius of the circle times $\sqrt{2}$. So the length of the side of the square is $(6\sqrt{2})(\sqrt{2}) = (6)(2) = 12$ units.

18. Draw radii $\overline{QA}$, $\overline{QB}$, and $\overline{QC}$ and use the relation that minor arcs and central angles have the same measure. Then $m\angle AQB + m\angle BQC = m\angle AQC$ by the Angle Addition Property of the Angle Measure Postulate, and $m\angle AQB = m\angle AQC - m\angle BQC$. So $m\overset{\frown}{AB} = m\overset{\frown}{ABC} - m\overset{\frown}{BC} = 178° - 94° = 84°$.

19. Arcs $\overset{\frown}{AB}$, $\overset{\frown}{BC}$, $\overset{\frown}{CD}$, and $\overset{\frown}{DA}$ form a complete circle, so the sum of the 4 arc measures is 360°.

20. ∠ACD is an exterior angle and ∠A and ∠B are the nonadjacent interior angles, so by the Exterior Angle Theorem,

$$x + 2x = 141$$
$$3x = 141$$
$$x = 47$$

Then m∠A = 2x = (2)(47) = 94.

21. Using the formula for the volume of a pyramid, $V = \frac{1}{3}Bh$, with $B = 2^2 = 4$ and $h = 1.4$, then $V = \frac{1}{3}(4)(1.4) = \frac{5.6}{3} \approx$ 1.8667 m³.

22. By the Two Reflection Theorem for rotations, to rotate a figure -120°, the acute angle between the lines should have half that measure, or 60°.

23. **a.** For a regular n-gon, the measure of each exterior angle is $\frac{360}{n}$, so the measure of each interior angle is the supplement of that:

$$180 - \frac{360}{n} = \frac{180n}{n} - \frac{360}{n} = \frac{180n - 360}{n}$$
$$= \frac{180(n - 2)}{n}.$$

b. Substituting $n = 8$, the measure of each interior angle of an octagon is

$$\frac{180(8 - 2)}{8} = \frac{(180)(6)}{8} = \frac{1080}{8} = 135.$$

24. Answers may vary. Parts a, c, and d are false and b is true; here are counterexamples and a proof:

a.

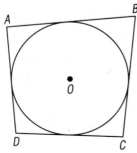

ABCD is circumscribed around ⊙O; $AB \neq BC \neq CD \neq DA$.

b.

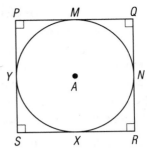

PQRS is a rectangle, so PQ = SR and PS = QR. But MX = YM, so all four sides are equal and the figure is a square.

c.

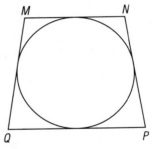

MNPQ is an isosceles trapezoid, but MNPQ is not a rectangle.

d.

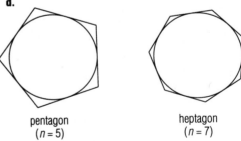

pentagon ($n = 5$)   heptagon ($n = 7$)

Here are regular polygons having odd numbers of sides (greater than 3) circumscribed about a circle.

LESSON 15-2 (pp. 740–744)

1. Team 1 has played everybody, team 2 has played every team except 7, team 3 has played every team except 5, and team 4 has played every team except 6. So the pairings are 2 plays 7, 3 plays 5, 4 plays 6, and 1 bye.

2. The game between 4 and 6 is pictured as a chord connecting 4 and 6.

3. To find the pairings for the first week, the chord connecting teams 2 and 7 is drawn, then all chords parallel to it are drawn.

4. There are 7 points located as the vertices of a regular heptagon around the circle. For each subsequent week, the chords are rotated $\frac{1}{7}$ of a revolution.

5.

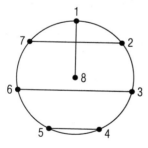

The pairings are 6-1, 5-2, 3-4, and 7-bye.

6. For an even number of teams, the last team is located at the center of the circle.

7.

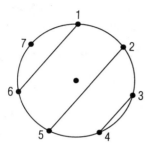

Team 8 replaces the bye in the pairings for 7 teams.

first week:	7-2, 6-3, 5-4, 1-8
second week:	1-3, 7-4, 6-5, 2-8
third week:	2-4, 1-5, 7-6, 3-8
fourth week:	3-5, 2-6, 1-7, 4-8
fifth week:	4-6, 3-7, 2-1, 5-8
sixth week:	5-7, 4-1, 3-2, 6-8
seventh week:	6-1, 5-2, 3-4, 7-8

8.

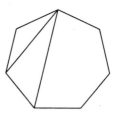

The diagonals of a regular heptagon are either separated by one vertex or by two vertices. So the diagonals can be of 2 lengths.

9. A schedule of 9 teams, uses a regular 9-gon, is rotated 9 times, so it needs 9 rounds. A schedule for 10 teams uses a regular 9-gon and its center, so it also needs 9 rounds. So both schedules need 9 rounds; the statement is *true*.

10. a. To schedule 9 teams, start with the 9 teams as the vertices of a regular 9-gon.

b-c.

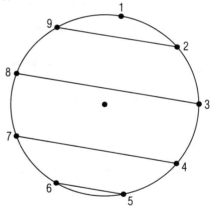

round 1:	9-2, 8-3, 7-4, 6-5, 1-bye
round 2:	1-3, 9-4, 8-5, 7-6, 2-bye
round 3:	2-4, 1-5, 9-6, 8-7, 3-bye
round 4:	3-5, 2-6, 1-7, 9-8, 4-bye
round 5:	4-6, 3-7, 2-8, 1-9, 5-bye
round 6:	5-7, 4-8, 3-9, 2-1, 6-bye
round 7:	6-8, 5-9, 4-1, 3-2, 7-bye
round 8:	7-9, 6-1, 5-2, 4-3, 8-bye
round 9:	8-1, 7-2, 6-3, 5-4, 9-bye

d. Each of the 9 vertices is connected to 6 other vertices, for 54 segments. This counts each diagonal twice, so the number of diagonals in a nonagon is 27.

e. For a 10-team schedule, replace the "bye" in each round with team 10.

11.

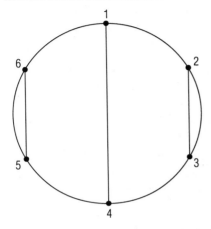

Two chords have the same length, and no chords connect vertices that are separated by 1 vertex. So after 2 rounds, pairings will be repeated (for example, 5 and 6 will again be paired up), and some pairings cannot be made (for example, 5 cannot be paired with 1 or 3).

12.

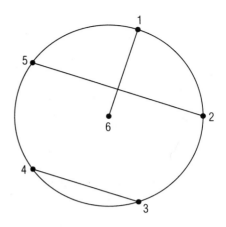

round 1:   2-5, 3-4, 1-6
round 2:   3-1, 4-5, 2-6
round 3:   4-2, 5-1, 3-6
round 4:   5-3, 1-2, 4-6
round 5:   1-4, 2-3, 5-6

13. The idea of scheduling uses locations around a circle (choice c) and connects two points with chords (choice d). It does not use graphs and ordered pairs (choice b) or points with size (choice a); the answer is (c) and (d).

14.

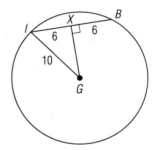

The distance from G to $\overline{IB}$ is the length of the perpendicular $\overline{GX}$ from G to $\overline{IB}$. By part a of the Chord-Center Theorem, X is the midpoint of $\overline{IB}$, so $IX = 6$. So $\triangle IXG$ is a 6-8-10 right triangle, and the distance from G to $\overline{IB}$ is 8 units.

15.

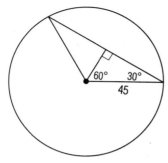

Half the chord is the side opposite a 60-degree angle in a 30-60-90 triangle with hypotenuse 45 mm. That is $\frac{45\sqrt{3}}{2}$. So the length of the entire chord is $45\sqrt{3} \approx 77.942 \approx 77.9$ mm.

16.

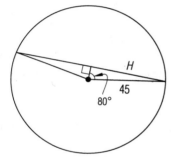

To find H, the length of half the chord, use the sine ratio for the central angle of 80 degrees:

$\sin 80° = \frac{H}{45}$, so $H = 45 \sin 80°$. So the whole chord has length $(2)(45 \sin 80°) = 90 \sin 80° \approx 88.6$ units.

17. It is given that ℓ is tangent to $\odot E$, so $\ell \perp \overline{CE}$ because if a line is tangent to a circle then it is perpendicular to the radius drawn to the point of tangency. Then, since $AD = DB$, $\overline{AB} \perp \overline{CE}$ by parts b and c of the Chord-Center Theorem (the line containing the center of a circle and the midpoint of a chord bisects the central angle determined by the chord; then the bisector of the central angle of a chord is perpendicular to the chord). So $\overline{AB} \parallel \ell$ by the Two Perpendiculars Theorem.

18. Each side of the square is the hypotenuse of a 45-45-90 triangle whose side is the radius of the circle. So the side of the square is $\sqrt{13}\sqrt{2} = \sqrt{26}$, and the perimeter of the square is $4\sqrt{26} \approx 20.396 \approx 20.4$ cm.

19. The east-west streets are parallel, so use the Side-Splitting Theorem to set up a proportion:

$$\frac{\text{top distance}}{\text{total distance}} = \frac{x}{3} = \frac{1.5}{2.5}$$
$$2.5x = 4.5$$
$$x = 1.8 \text{ mi}$$

The distance between Willow and Lake is 1.8 miles.

20.

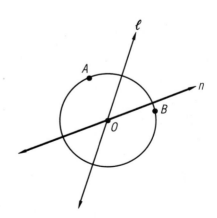

21.

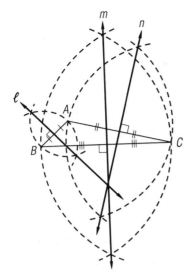

22. $100n - 200 + x = 100n$
$-200 + x = 0$
$x = 200$

23. a-b. Schedules may vary. Some of the factors that affect schedules are where the game is played; whether it is a school day or weekend; amount of travel time needed; and certain pairings may be reserved for the final game of the season.

LESSON 15-3 (pp. 745–751)

1. The picture angle of a camera lens is a measure of how wide a field of vision can be captured in one photo.

2. The diagram shows that the house fills a picture angle of 40 degrees.

a. Yes; a normal camera lens has a picture angle of 46 degrees, so the entire front of the house will fit.

b. No; a telephoto lens has a picture angle of about 18 degrees, so the entire front will not fit.

c. Yes; a wide-angle lens has a picture angle of up to 118 degrees, so the entire front will fit.

3. The measure of inscribed angle ABC is half the intercepted arc. Since m $\overset{\frown}{AC} = 97$, then
m$\angle ABC = \frac{1}{2}(97) = 48.5$.

4. The measure of inscribed angle DEF is half the intercepted arc. Since m$\angle DEF = 108$, then m $\overset{\frown}{DGF} = (2)(108) = 216°$.

5. A semicircle has arc measure 180°; an angle inscribed in that arc has half the measure of the arc, so the angle inscribed in a semicircle has measure 90.

6. a. Arc $\overset{\frown}{MLN}$ is a semicircle, so m $\overset{\frown}{ML}$ $= 180° - $ m $\overset{\frown}{LN} = 180° - 50° = 130°$.

b. Arc $\overset{\frown}{MPN}$ is a semicircle, so m $\overset{\frown}{MPN} = 180°$.

7. a. $\angle M$ is inscribed in an arc whose measure is 50°, so m$\angle M = \frac{1}{2}(50) = 25$.

b. $\angle N$ is inscribed in $\overset{\frown}{ML}$, and m $\overset{\frown}{ML} = 130°$, so m$\angle N = \frac{1}{2}(130) = 65$.

c. $\angle L$ is inscribed in a semicircle, so $\angle L$ is a right angle and m$\angle L = 90$.

d. $\angle L$ is a right angle, so $\triangle LMN$ is a right triangle.

8. a. The three vertices of $\triangle TUV$ are points on the circle, so $\triangle TUV$ is inscribed in the circle.

b. m$\overset{\frown}{VUT} = $ m $\overset{\frown}{VU} + $ m $\overset{\frown}{UT} = 45° + 60° = 105°$, so m $\overset{\frown}{VWT} = 360° - 105° = 255°$. $\angle U$ is inscribed in $\overset{\frown}{VWT}$, so m$\angle U = \frac{1}{2}(255) = 127.5$.

9. a. $\angle WOZ$ is a central angle, so its measure is equal to its intercepted arc. So m$\angle WOZ = n$.

b. $\angle Y$ is inscribed in arc $\overset{\frown}{WZ}$, so its measure is half the measure of its intercepted arc. So m$\angle Y = \frac{n}{2}$.

10. The difference in the three cases is the location of the center of the circle in relation to the inscribed angle. The center of the circle is either on (a side of) the angle, in the interior of the angle, or not in the interior of the angle (that is, in the exterior of the angle).

11. For Case III of the Inscribed Angle Theorem, the center of the circle is not in the interior of the angle. Draw diameter $\overline{BOD}$. From the Angle Addition Postulate, $m\angle ABD = m\angle ABC + m\angle CBD$, so by the Addition Property of Equality, $m\angle ABC = m\angle ABD - m\angle CBD$.
Then, from the Arc Addition Property and the Addition Property of Equality, $m\widehat{AC} = m\widehat{AD} - m\widehat{CD}$. Both $\angle ABD$ and $\angle CBD$ are inscribed angles with one side containing the center of the circle, so they satisfy the conditions of Case I, and

$$m\angle ABC = \tfrac{1}{2}m\widehat{AD} - \tfrac{1}{2}m\widehat{CD}$$
$$= \tfrac{1}{2}(m\widehat{AD} - m\widehat{CD})$$
$$= \tfrac{1}{2}m\widehat{AC}$$

12. $m\angle A = \tfrac{1}{2}(m\,\widehat{DC} + m\,\widehat{CB})$
$$= \tfrac{1}{2}(60 + 120)$$
$$= \tfrac{1}{2}(180)$$
$$= 90$$

$m\angle B = \tfrac{1}{2}(m\,\widehat{AD} + m\,\widehat{DC})$
$$= \tfrac{1}{2}(80 + 60)$$
$$= \tfrac{1}{2}(140)$$
$$= 70$$

$m\angle C = \tfrac{1}{2}(m\,\widehat{DA} + m\,\widehat{AB})$
$$= \tfrac{1}{2}(80 + 100)$$
$$= \tfrac{1}{2}(180)$$
$$= 90$$

$\angle D = \tfrac{1}{2}(m\,\widehat{AB} + m\,\widehat{BC})$
$$= \tfrac{1}{2}(100 + 120)$$
$$= \tfrac{1}{2}(220)$$
$$= 110$$

13. $\overline{AC}$ is a diameter of the circle, so $\triangle ADC$ is a right triangle with $m\angle DAC = 30$, and $m\angle D = 90$ and $m\angle DCA = 60$.
$\triangle ABC$ is an isosceles right triangle, so $m\angle B = 90$ and $m\angle BAC = m\angle BCA = 45$. Finally, $m\angle DAB = m\angle DAC + m\angle BAC = 30 + 45 = 75$, and $m\angle DCB = m\angle DCA + m\angle BCA = 60 + 45 = 105$.

14. The measure of inscribed angle P is 92, so the measure of major arc $\widehat{MN}$ is twice that, or 184°, and m$\angle M = 35$ so m$\widehat{PQ} = 70°$. $MP = NQ$, so m$\widehat{MP} = $ m$\widehat{NQ}$. Then, substitute into

$360° = $ m$\widehat{MN} + $ m$\widehat{NQ} + $ m$\widehat{QP} + $ m$\widehat{PM}$

$360° = 184° + $ m$\widehat{MP} + 70° + $ m$\widehat{MP}$

$360° = 254° + 2$m$\widehat{MP}$

$106° = 2$m$\widehat{MP}$

m$\widehat{MP} = 53°$.

15. **a-b.** The justification that the measure of the two inscribed angles, $\angle AMB$ and $\angle ANB$, is half its intercepted arc is the Inscribed Angle Theorem.

c. The justification that m$\angle AMB = $ m$\angle ANB$ is the Transitive Property of Equality (in steps 1 and 2).

16. m$\angle M = $ m$\angle N$ and m$\angle A = $ m$\angle B$ because two inscribed angles that intercept the same arc have the same measure. (This is the theorem that was proved as question 15.) Then $\triangle AXM \sim \triangle BXN$ by the AA Similarity Theorem.

17.

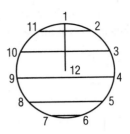

week 1:	11-2, 10-3, 9-4, 8-5, 7-6, 1-12
week 2:	1-3, 11-4, 10-5, 9-6, 8-7, 2-12
week 3:	2-4, 1-5, 11-6, 10-7, 9-8, 3-12
week 4:	3-5, 2-6, 1-7, 11-8, 10-9, 4-12
week 5:	4-6, 3-7, 2-8, 1-9, 11-10, 5-12
week 6:	5-7, 4-8, 3-9, 2-10, 11-1, 6-12
week 7:	6-8, 9-5, 10-4, 11-3, 1-2, 7-12
week 8:	7-9, 10-6, 11-5, 1-4, 2-3, 8-12
week 9:	8-10, 11-7, 1-6, 2-5, 3-4, 9-12
week 10:	9-11, 1-8, 2-7, 3-6, 4-5, 10-12
week 11:	10-1, 2-9, 3-8, 4-7, 5-6, 11-12

18.

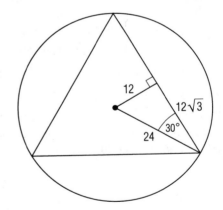

Drawing perpendiculars from the center of the circle to the sides of the triangle forms 30-60-90 triangles. The short leg in each right triangle is half the radius of the circle, or 12, and so the side of the original triangle is $(2)(12\sqrt{3}) = 24\sqrt{3}$. So the perimeter of the original triangle is $(3)(24\sqrt{3}) = 72\sqrt{3} \approx 124.71$ units.

19. a. Each side of the regular pentagon determines a central angle with measure $\frac{360}{5} = 72$, so m $\widehat{WX} = 72°$.

b.

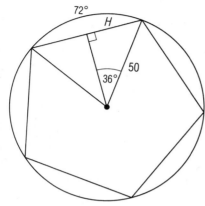

The central angle determined by each side of the pentagon has measure 72, so a perpendicular from the center to the side forms a right triangle with a 36-degree angle. If H represents half the side of the pentagon, which is the side opposite that 36-degree angle, then $\sin 36° = \frac{H}{50}$ and $H = 50 \sin 36°$ and each side of the pentagon is twice that, or $100 \sin 36°$. So the perimeter of the entire pentagon is $500 \sin 36° \approx 293.89 \approx 294$ units.

20.

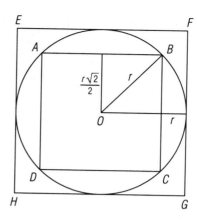

The radius of the circle is r, so a side of the large square is $2r$ and its area is $(2r)^2 = 4r^2$. In the small isosceles right triangle, the side is $\frac{r}{\sqrt{2}} = \frac{r\sqrt{2}}{2}$, so the side of the small square is $r\sqrt{2}$ and the area of the small square is $(r\sqrt{2})^2 = 2r^2$.

a. The area between the circle and the large square is
$$4r^2 - \pi r^2 = (4 - \pi)r^2 \approx .858r^2.$$

b. The area between the small square and the circle is
$$\pi r^2 - 2r^2 = (\pi - 2)r^2 \approx 1.14159r^2.$$

c. The area from part b is larger than the area from part a.

21. If the dimensions are x and $2x$, then
$$(x)(2x) = 280$$
$$2x^2 = 280$$
$$x^2 = 140$$
$$x = \sqrt{140}.$$
Then the dimensions are $\sqrt{140}$ and $2\sqrt{140}$. Use the Pythagorean Theorem to find the length of d of the diagonal of the ballroom:
$$d^2 = (\sqrt{140})^2 + (2\sqrt{140})^2$$
$$= 140 + (4)(140)$$
$$= 140 + 560$$
$$= 700$$
So $d = \sqrt{700} \approx 26.4575 \approx 26.46$ yards.

22. $\angle PSN$ is an exterior angle of the nonagon, so its measure is $\frac{360}{9} = 40$.

23. The exact value of the normal picture angle of a camera may vary; many are around 45 degrees.

LESSON 15–4 (pp. 752–757)

1.

2.

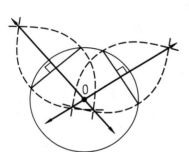

3.

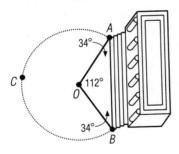

You could stand anywhere on $\overparen{ACB}$.

4.

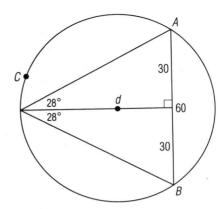

$\tan 28° = \frac{30}{d}$, so $d = \frac{30}{\tan 28°} \approx 56.4$ yd.

5. a.

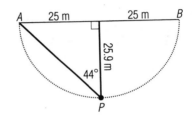

$\tan 44° = \frac{25}{d}$

$d = \frac{25}{\tan 44°} \approx 25.9$ m

b. They can stand anywhere on $\overparen{APB}$, since every point determines an inscribed angle with the same arc.

6.

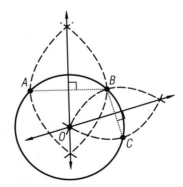

7.

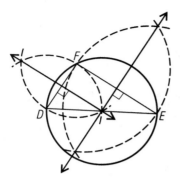

8.

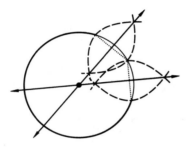

9.

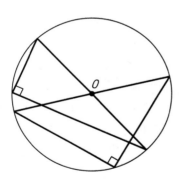

10. a. $m\angle L = x$, so the arc determined by $\angle L$ has measure $2x°$; that is $\overarc{IJK}$.

b. $m\angle J = y$, so the arc determined by $\angle J$ has measure $2y°$; that is $\overarc{ILK}$.

c. $m\overarc{IJK} + m\overarc{ILK} = 360°$, so $2x + 2y = 360$.

d. The sum of the measures of $\angle ILK$ and $\angle IJK$ is half of the sum of the measures of the intercepted arcs. Since the sum of the measures of the intercepted arcs is 360 degrees, the sum of the measure of the two angles is 180.

e. In quadrilateral *IJKL*, the sum of the measures of the four angles is 360 by the Quadrilateral-Sum Theorem. The sum of the measures of two of the angles ($\angle ILK$ and $\angle IJK$) is 180, so the sum of the other two must be also 180.

f. This proves that for opposite angles in an inscribed quadrilateral, the measures of those angles add to 180, or opposite angles in an inscribed quadrilateral are supplementary.

11. a. *BEHIVS* is a regular hexagon, so each of its sides is congruent and each congruent side determines congruent arcs. There are six congruent arcs, so each one has measure 60 degrees.

Each of angles 1, 2, 3, and 4 is an inscribed angle whose intercepted arc is 60 degrees, so the measure of each angle is $\frac{1}{2}(60)$ = 30.

b. $\overarc{VSBE} = \overarc{VIHE}$, and $m\overarc{VSBE} + m\overarc{VIHE} = 360°$, so $m\overarc{VIHE} = 180°$ and $m\angle VBE = 90$. So $\triangle VBE$ is a right triangle; the statement is *true*.

12. a. If *M* is the midpoint of $\overline{PQ}$, then by part b of the Chord-Center Theorem, $\overrightarrow{OM}$ bisects $\angle POQ$; then by part c of the same theorem, $\overline{OM} \perp \overline{PQ}$.

b. If $\overline{OM} \perp \overline{PQ}$, then by part a of the Chord-Center Theorem, *M* is the midpoint of $\overline{PQ}$ or $PM = MQ$.

c. If $\overrightarrow{OM}$ bisects $\angle POQ$, then by part c of the Chord-Center Theorem, $\overline{OM}$ is the $\perp$ bisector of $\overline{PQ}$, or $\overline{OM} \perp \overline{PQ}$ and $PM = MQ$.

13. By part d of the Chord-Center Theorem, the perpendicular bisector of a chord of a circle contains the center of the circle.

14. By part a of the Chord-Center Theorem, the chord $\overline{PQ}$ is bisected. So the two small right triangles have legs of 6 and 8, which means the hypotenuse is 10; $OQ = 10$ units.

15. **a.** $\triangle BCD$ is equilateral, so m$\angle B$ = m$\angle BCD$ = m$\angle BDC$ = 60. $\overline{AB}$ is a diameter, so $\triangle ABD$ is a right triangle. Then m$\angle BDA$ = 90, and m$\angle CDA$ = $90 - 60 = 30$.
    Also in $\triangle ABD$,
    m$\angle A = 180 - ($m$\angle B + m\angle ADB) = 180 - (60 + 90) = 180 - 150 = 30$.
    Finally, in $\triangle ACD$, m$\angle ACD = 180 - ($m$\angle A + m\angle ADC) = 180 - (30 + 30) = 180 - 60 = 120$.

    b. $\triangle BCD$ is equilateral, so $CB = x$. Also, $AC = CB$ (they are both radii), so $AC = x$.

    c. If $BD = 7$, then $AB = AC + CB = 7 + 7 = 14$. Then use the Pythagorean Theorem to find AD:
    $AD = \sqrt{14^2 - 7^2} = \sqrt{196 - 49} = \sqrt{147} = \sqrt{(49)(3)} = 7\sqrt{3} \approx 12.12$.

16. **a.** Statement:
    If a figure is a rectangle, then its diagonals are congruent.
    Contrapositive:
    If the diagonals of a quadrilateral are not congruent, then the figure is not a rectangle.

    b. The Law of the Contrapositive states that a statement and its contrapositive are either both true or both false. The original statement is true, so the contrapositive is also true.

17. If the diameter is 50′, then the radius is 25′. Using the formula for the area of a circle, $A = \pi r^2$, then $A = \pi 25^2 = 625\pi \approx 1963.4954 \approx 1963.5$ ft^2.

18. Answers may vary, but the common chords are always concurrent; the conjecture always holds.

LESSON 15–5 (pp. 758–762)

1. **a.** $\angle 1$ is an inscribed angle; so
    m$\angle 1 = \frac{1}{2}$m$\widehat{AB} = \frac{1}{2}(25) = 12.5$.

    b. $\angle 2$ is an inscribed angle, so
    m$\angle 2 = \frac{1}{2}$m$\widehat{CD} = \frac{1}{2}(96) = 48$.

    c. $\angle 3$ is formed by two chords, so
    m$\angle 3 = \frac{1}{2}($m$\widehat{AB} + m\widehat{CD})$
    $= \frac{1}{2}(25 + 96)$
    $= \frac{1}{2}(121)$
    $= 60.5$.

    d. $\angle 4$ is supplementary to $\angle 3$, so
    m$\angle 4 = 180 - m\angle 3$
    $= 180 - 60.5$
    $= 119.5$.

2. $\angle 1$ is formed by two chords, and its intercepted arcs are $\widehat{WZ}$ and $\widehat{XY}$. m$\widehat{WZ}$ is given, so m$\widehat{XY}$ needs to be found. However, since all arc measures except m$\widehat{WX}$ and m$\widehat{XY}$ are given, then you can calculate m$\widehat{XY}$ if m$\widehat{WX}$ is given. So you need either m$\widehat{XY}$ or m$\widehat{WX}$.

3. If $\overline{XZ}$ is a diameter, then
    m$\widehat{XY} = 180° - 120° = 60°$, and
    m$\angle 1 = \frac{1}{2}(140 + 60) = \frac{1}{2}(200) = 100$.

4. **a-b.** Yes, $\angle F$ is formed by two secants, and both intercepted arc measures are given.
    m$\angle F = \frac{1}{2}($m$\widehat{JK} - m\widehat{HG})$
    $= \frac{1}{2}(82 - 30)$
    $= \frac{1}{2}(52)$
    $= 26$.

5. a. $\angle MQO$ is formed by two chords, so

$$m\angle MQO = \tfrac{1}{2}(m\widehat{MO} + m\widehat{LP})$$

$$= \tfrac{1}{2}(50 + 80)$$

$$= \tfrac{1}{2}(130)$$

$$= 65.$$

b. $\angle N$ is formed by two secants, so

$$m\angle N = \tfrac{1}{2}(m\widehat{LP} - m\widehat{MO})$$

$$= \tfrac{1}{2}(80 - 50)$$

$$= \tfrac{1}{2}(30)$$

$$= 15.$$

6. A line is a secant if and only if it is a line that intersects a circle in two distinct points.

7.

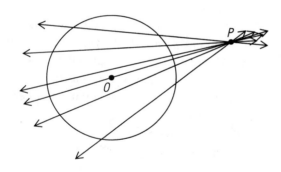

There are an infinite number of secants of the circle that contain the given point external to the circle.

8. $\angle RVU$ is formed by two chords, so its measure is half the sum of its intercepted arcs.

$$m\angle RVU = \tfrac{1}{2}(m\widehat{RU} + m\widehat{ST})$$

$$90 = \tfrac{1}{2}(101 + m\widehat{ST})$$

$$180 = 101 + m\widehat{ST}$$

$$79° = m\widehat{ST}$$

9. a. Opposite sides of the rectangle are congruent, so $m\widehat{VY} = m\widehat{WX} = 40$, and the measure of the acute angle between the diagonals is half the sum of $m\widehat{VY}$ plus

$$m\widehat{WX} = \tfrac{1}{2}(40 + 40) = \tfrac{1}{2}(80) = 40.$$

b. $\angle VYX$ is a right angle, so the measure of its arc $\widehat{VWX}$ is 180°. Then $m\widehat{VW} = 180° - 40° = 140°$, and the measure of $\angle VYW$, the angle inscribed in $\widehat{VW}$, is 70.

10. $\angle C$ is formed by two secants, so

$$m\angle C = \tfrac{1}{2}(m\widehat{AE} - m\widehat{BD})$$

$$45 = \tfrac{1}{2}(m\widehat{AE} - 53)$$

$$90 = m\widehat{AE} - 53$$

$$143 = m\widehat{AE}.$$

11.

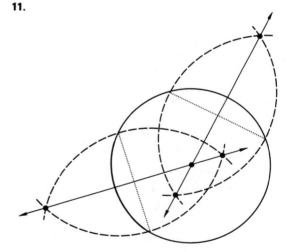

396

12.

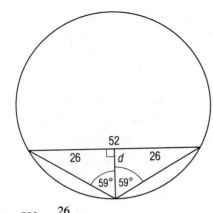

$$\tan 59° = \frac{26}{d}$$

$$d = \frac{26}{\tan 59°} \approx 15.6 \text{ ft}$$

13. $m\angle A = \frac{1}{2}(m\widehat{BC} + m\widehat{CD} + m\widehat{ED})$

$\qquad = \frac{1}{2}(90 + 80 + 75)$

$\qquad = \frac{1}{2}(245)$

$\qquad = 122.5$

$m\angle B = \frac{1}{2}(m\widehat{CD} + m\widehat{ED} + m\widehat{AE})$

$\qquad = \frac{1}{2}(80 + 75 + 15)$

$\qquad = \frac{1}{2}(170)$

$\qquad = 85$

$m\angle C = \frac{1}{2}(m\widehat{AB} + m\widehat{AE} + m\widehat{ED})$

$\qquad = \frac{1}{2}(100 + 15 + 75)$

$\qquad = \frac{1}{2}(190)$

$\qquad = 95$

$m\angle D = \frac{1}{2}(m\widehat{AE} + m\widehat{AB} + m\widehat{BC})$

$\qquad = \frac{1}{2}(15 + 100 + 90)$

$\qquad = \frac{1}{2}(205)$

$\qquad = 102.5$

$m\angle E = \frac{1}{2}(m\widehat{AB} + m\widehat{BC} + m\widehat{CD})$

$\qquad = \frac{1}{2}(100 + 90 + 80)$

$\qquad = \frac{1}{2}(270)$

$\qquad = 135$

14.

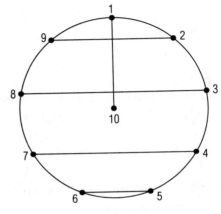

round 1:   2-9, 3-8, 4-7, 5-6, 1-10
round 2:   3-1, 4-9, 5-8, 6-7, 2-10
round 3:   4-2, 5-1, 6-9, 7-8, 3-10
round 4:   5-3, 6-2, 7-1, 8-9, 4-10
round 5:   6-4, 7-3, 8-2, 9-1, 5-10
round 6:   7-5, 8-4, 9-3, 1-2, 6-10
round 7:   8-6, 9-5, 1-4, 2-3, 7-10
round 8:   9-7, 1-6, 2-5, 3-4, 8-10
round 9:   1-8, 2-7, 3-6, 4-5, 9-10

15.

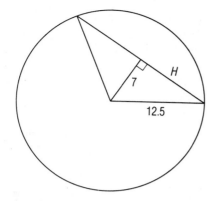

If H represents half the length of the chord, then H is the leg of a right triangle with hypotenuse 12.5 and other leg 7, so
$H = \sqrt{12.5^2 - 7^2} = \sqrt{156.25 - 49} = \sqrt{107.25}$,
and the length of the chord is $2\sqrt{107.25} \approx 20.7123 \approx 20.71$ inches.

16. a. If $ax^2 + bx + c = 0$, for real numbers a, b, and c, then $x = \dfrac{-b \pm \sqrt{b^2 - 4ac}}{2a}$.

b. If $2x^2 + 5x - 1 = 0$, then $a = 2$, $b = 5$, and $c = -1$,

so $x = \dfrac{-5 \pm \sqrt{5^2 - (4)(2)(-1)}}{(2)(2)}$

$= \dfrac{-5 \pm \sqrt{25 - -8}}{4}$

$= \dfrac{-5 \pm \sqrt{33}}{4}$

or $x = \dfrac{-5 + \sqrt{33}}{4} \approx .186$

or $x = \dfrac{-5 - \sqrt{33}}{4} \approx -2.686$.

17. $x^2 - 30 = 34$
$x^2 = 64$
$x = \pm 8$

18. $y + 12 \qquad > 21$
$y + 12 - 12 > 21 - 12$
$y > 9$

19. a. The sides of the original pentagon $ABCDE$ are congruent, so each of the arcs formed by a side of the pentagon has measure $\dfrac{360}{5} = 72°$.

Each of the angles F, G, H, I, and J has the same measure. For $\angle F$, it is an angle formed by two secants, so

$m\angle F = \frac{1}{2}(m\widehat{EDC} - m\widehat{AB})$

$= \frac{1}{2}((2)(72) - 72)$

$= \frac{1}{2}(72)$

$= 36$.

So the sum of the five measures is $(5)(36) = 180$.

b. If $ABCDE$ is not regular, then add the measures of the angles at the points in terms of their intercepted arcs:

$m\angle F = \frac{1}{2}(m\widehat{DE} + m\widehat{CD} - m\widehat{AB})$

$m\angle G = \frac{1}{2}(m\widehat{AE} + m\widehat{DE} - m\widehat{BC})$

$m\angle H = \frac{1}{2}(m\widehat{AE} + m\widehat{AB} - m\widehat{CD})$

$m\angle I = \frac{1}{2}(m\widehat{AB} + m\widehat{BC} - m\widehat{DE})$

$m\angle J = \frac{1}{2}(m\widehat{BC} + m\widehat{CD} - m\widehat{AE})$

Multiply each equation by 2 (to rid the fractions), and add them. On the left, you will have twice the sum of the five angle measures.
Rearranging the terms on the right,
$m\widehat{AB} + m\widehat{AB} - m\widehat{AB}$
$+ \, m\widehat{BC} + m\widehat{BC} - m\widehat{BC}$
$+ \, m\widehat{CD} + m\widehat{CD} - m\widehat{CD}$
$+ \, m\widehat{DE} + m\widehat{DE} - m\widehat{DE}$
$+ \, m\widehat{EA} + m\widehat{EA} - m\widehat{EA}$
which is the sum of the five arcs, or 360 degrees. So the sum of the five angle measures is $\dfrac{360}{2} = 180$.

LESSON 15-6 (pp. 763–768)

1. a. Tangent $\overleftrightarrow{BC}$ is perpendicular to diameter $\overline{EB}$, so m$\angle ABC = 90$.

b. $\angle DBC$ is formed by a tangent and a chord, so m$\angle DBC = \frac{1}{2}$m$\widehat{DB} = \frac{1}{2}(110) = 55$.

2. $\angle P$ is formed by a tangent and a secant, so

$$\text{m}\angle P = \frac{1}{2}(\text{m }\widehat{RS} - \text{m }\widehat{SQ})$$

$$= \frac{1}{2}(108 - 68)$$

$$= \frac{1}{2}(40)$$

$$= 20.$$

3. $\angle TSR$ is formed by a tangent and a chord, so

$$\text{m}\angle TSR = \frac{1}{2}\text{m }\widehat{RS} = \frac{1}{2}(108) = 54.$$

4. $\angle RSP$ is formed by a tangent and a chord, so its measure is $\frac{1}{2}$ its intercepted arc, or $\frac{1}{2}$m $\widehat{RQS}$; the statement is *true*.

5. a. $\angle ABD$ is formed by a tangent and a chord, so m$\angle ABD = \frac{1}{2}$m $\widehat{DCB} = \frac{1}{2}(360 - 75) = \frac{1}{2}(285) = 142.5$.

b. $\angle CAB$ is formed by two tangents. m $\widehat{BDC} = 75° + 165° = 240°$, and m $\widehat{BEC} = 360° - \text{m }\widehat{BDC} = 360° - 240° = 120°$. So:

$$\text{m}\angle CAB = \frac{1}{2}(\text{m }\widehat{BDC} - \text{m }\widehat{BEC})$$

$$= \frac{1}{2}(240 - 120)$$

$$= \frac{1}{2}(120)$$

$$= 60.$$

c. $\angle ACD$ is formed by a tangent and a chord, so

$$\text{m}\angle ACD = \frac{1}{2}\text{m }\widehat{DBC}$$

$$= \frac{1}{2}(360 - 165)$$

$$= \frac{1}{2}(195)$$

$$= 97.5.$$

6.

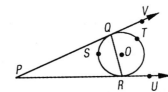

Draw $\overline{QR}$. Then $\angle VQR$ is an exterior angle of $\triangle QPR$, so m$\angle VQR = \text{m}\angle P + \text{m}\angle PRQ$ by the Exterior Angle Theorem, so m$\angle P = \text{m}\angle VQR - \text{m}\angle PRQ$ by the Addition Property of Equality.

$\angle VQR$ and $\angle PRS$ are each formed by a tangent and a chord, so m$\angle VQR = \frac{1}{2}\text{m}\widehat{QTR}$ and m$\angle PRQ = \frac{1}{2}\text{m}\widehat{QSR}$ by the Tangent-Chord Theorem. So, by substitution,

$$\text{m}\angle P = \frac{1}{2}\text{m}\widehat{QTR} - \frac{1}{2}\text{m}\widehat{QSR};$$ then, by the Distributive Property,

$$\text{m}\angle P = \frac{1}{2}(\text{m }\widehat{QTR} - \text{m }\widehat{QSR}).$$

7. m$\widehat{QSR}$ + m$\widehat{QTR} = 360°$, so m$\widehat{QTR} = 360° - \text{m }\widehat{QSR}$. $\angle P$ is formed by two tangents, so

m$\angle P = \frac{1}{2}(\text{m}\widehat{QTR} - \text{m}\widehat{QSR})$. Substituting:

$$25 = \frac{1}{2}(360 - \text{m}\widehat{QSR} - \text{m}\widehat{QSR})$$

$$50 = 360 - 2\text{m}\widehat{QSR}$$

$$-310 = -2\text{m}\widehat{QSR}$$

$$155 = \text{m}\widehat{QSR}$$

Then m$\widehat{QTR} = 360° - 155° = 205°$.

8. a. The angle between two chords is measured by half the sum of the intercepted arcs; that is choice (iii).

b. The angle between two secants is measured by half the difference of the intercepted arcs; that is choice (iv).

c. The angle between two tangents is measured by half the difference of the intercepted arcs; that is choice (iv).

d. The angle between a secant and a tangent is measured by half the difference of the intercepted arcs; that is choice (iv).

e. The angle between a chord and a tangent is measured by half the intercepted arc; that is choice (ii).

f. An inscribed angle is measured by half the intercepted arc; that is choice (ii).

g. A central angle is measured by the intercepted arc; that is choice (i).

9.

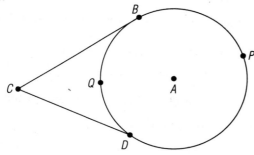

$\overrightarrow{CD}$ and $\overrightarrow{CB}$ are tangents. Then
$m\angle C = \frac{1}{2}(m\,\widehat{BPD} - m\,\widehat{BD})$, so
$2m\angle C = m\,\widehat{BPD} - m\,\widehat{BD}$ or $m\,\widehat{BD} =$
$m\,\widehat{BPD} - 2m\angle C$.
$m\,\widehat{BPD} = 360° - m\,\widehat{BD}$, so substituting for
$m\,\widehat{BPD}$, $m\,\widehat{BD} = 360° - m\,\widehat{BD} - 2m\angle C$ or
$2m\,\widehat{BD} = 360° - 2m\angle C$. Multiplying both
sides by $\frac{1}{2}$, $m\,\widehat{BD} = 180 - m\angle C$.

10.

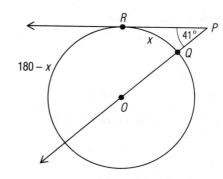

O is the center of the circle, so the two arcs above the secant have measure $180 - x$ and x. Then $m\angle P = 41 = \frac{1}{2}(180 - x - x)$ or $82 = 180 - 2x$. So $-98 = -2x$, and $x = 49$. So $m\,\widehat{QR} = 49°$.

11. Major arc $\widehat{RT}$ + minor arc $\widehat{RT} = 360°$, so major arc $\widehat{RT} = 360° - m\widehat{RT}$. Then
$m\angle RTS = 125 = \frac{1}{2}(360 - m\widehat{RT})$
$250 = 360 - m\widehat{RT}$
$-110 = -m\widehat{RT}$
$110° = m\widehat{RT}.$

12.

13. a. $m\angle 2 = \frac{1}{2}(m\,\widehat{FD} + m\,\widehat{DC})$

$= \frac{1}{2}(100 + 30) = 65$

b. $m\angle 3 = \frac{1}{2}(m\,\widehat{GF} + m\,\widehat{DC} + m\,\widehat{CB})$

$= \frac{1}{2}(50 + 30 + 105)$

$= \frac{1}{2}(185)$

$= 92.5$

c. $m\angle 4 = \frac{1}{2}(m\,\widehat{FD} + m\,\widehat{GB})$

$= \frac{1}{2}(100 + 75) = 87.5$

d. $m\angle E = \frac{1}{2}(m\overset{\frown}{GB} - m\overset{\frown}{DC}) = \frac{1}{2}(75 - 30)$

$\quad = 22.5$

14. $m\angle S = \frac{1}{2}(m\overset{\frown}{CN} - m\overset{\frown}{EA})$

$\quad 23 = \frac{1}{2}(85 - m\overset{\frown}{AE})$

$\quad 46 = 85 - m\overset{\frown}{AE}$

$\quad -39 = -m\overset{\frown}{AE}$

$\quad m\overset{\frown}{AE} = 39°$

15. a. Yes; $\angle N$ and $\angle C$ is each measured by half of $m\overset{\frown}{EA}$, and $\angle ETC$ and $\angle ATN$ are vertical angles, so the triangles are similar by the AA Similarity Theorem.

b. No, the triangles are not necessarily congruent. Here is a counterexample:

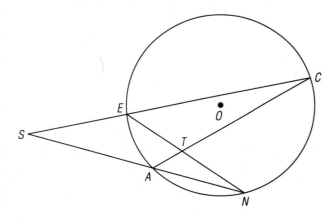

$\triangle ANT$ is not congruent to $\triangle ECT$.

16.

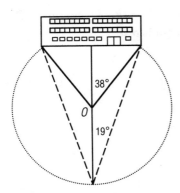

17. By part a of the Chord-Center Theorem, the segment from the center of the circle bisects the chord, so each part of the chord is 4″. So the radius is 5″ (it is the hypotenuse of a 3-4-5 right triangle), and the area of the circle is $\pi r^2 = \pi 5^2 = 25\pi \approx 78.5398 \approx 78.5$ in.²

18. a. The sum of the measures of the exterior angles of any polygon is 360, so

$$(4x) + (8x - 23)$$
$$+ (9x + 7) + (5x - 40) = 360$$
$$26x - 56 = 360$$
$$26x = 416$$
$$x = 16.$$

b. The measures of the exterior angles are:

$4x = (4)(16) = 64;$

$8x - 23 = (8)(16) - 23 =$
$128 - 23 = 105;$

$9x + 7 = (9)(16) + 7 = 144 + 7 = 151;$
and
$5x - 40 = (5)(16) - 40 = 80 - 40 = 40;$
so the interior angles are:

$180 - 64 = 116;$

$180 - 105 = 75;$

$180 - 151 = 29;$ and

$180 - 40 = 140.$

19. The ratio of similitude, from larger to smaller, is $\frac{12}{8} = \frac{3}{2} = 1.5$. So $JG = \frac{24}{1.5} = 16,$ and $BC = (10)(1.5) = 15$. Also, $m\angle G = m\angle D = 81.$

20. If $\frac{4}{x} = \frac{q}{10}$, then some other true proportions are $\frac{4}{q} = \frac{x}{10}, \frac{10}{q} = \frac{x}{4}, \frac{4 + x}{x} = \frac{q + 10}{10}$, etc.

21. If the diameter of a sphere is 24 mm, then its radius is 12 mm.

a. The volume is $V = \frac{4}{3}\pi r^3 = \frac{4}{3}\pi(12)^3 =$

$\frac{4}{3}\pi 1728 = 2304\pi \approx 7238.229 \approx$

7238.2 mm³.

b. The surface area is $4\pi r^2 = 4\pi(12)^2 =$
$4\pi(144) = 576\pi \approx 1809.557 \approx$
1809.6 mm^2.

22.

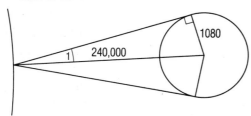

$\sin \angle 1 = \dfrac{1080}{240,000}$

Using a calculator:
$1080 \boxed{\div} 240,000 \boxed{=} \boxed{\text{INV}}\boxed{\text{SIN}}$ displays
0.25783, and the angle between the tangents
is twice that, or about 0.51° (about half of 1
degree).

LESSON 15-7 (pp. 769–774)

1. By the Secant Length Theorem,
$DP \cdot DT = DU \cdot DV$.

2. By the Secant Length Theorem,
$AT \cdot TQ = PT \cdot TR$.

3. Substituting $AT = 6$, $TQ = 4$, and $TR = 3$
into the results from Question 2, then
$(6)(4) = (PT)(3)$
$3 \cdot PT = 24$
$PT = 8$.

4. a.

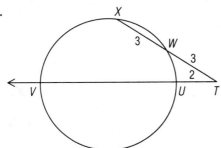

From the Secant Length Theorem,
$TW \cdot TX = TU \cdot TV$, so
$(3)(6) = (2)(TV)$
$18 = 2 \cdot TV$
$TV = 9$ units.

b. The power of a point for a circle is the
product of the lengths of the two segments
from the point to the circle. For point T,
the power of T is $(3)(6) = (2)(9) = 18$.

c. $UV = TV - TU = 9 - 2 = 7$ units.

5. In Example 1, the power of point P for the
circle is $(5)(6) = (3)(10) = 30$.

6. By the Tangent Square Theorem, $JQ^2 =$
$(JY)(JX)$, which can be written as $\dfrac{JY}{JQ} = \dfrac{JQ}{JX}$.
So JQ is the geometric mean of JX and JY.

7. From the Tangent Square Theorem, $JQ^2 =$
$(JY)(JX)$, so $JQ^2 = (8)(2) = 16$, so $JQ = 4$.

8. a. By the Secant Length Theorem,
$(3)(6) = 2x$, so $2x = 18$, and $x = 9$ units.

b. The power of P in this circle is
$(3)(6) = (2)(9) = 18$.

9. By the Secant Length Theorem, $(JI)(JH) =$
$(JA)(JE)$ or $(10)(10 + HI) = (8)(20)$. So
$100 + 10 \cdot HI = 160$
$10 \cdot HI = 60$
$HI = 6$.

10. From part a of the Chord-Center Theorem,
Z is the midpoint of $\overline{XY}$ and so $XZ = 5$. So
$\overline{ZO}$ is the leg of a right triangle with
hypotenuse 8 and other leg 5, so
$ZO = \sqrt{8^2 - 5^2} = \sqrt{64 - 25} = \sqrt{39}$.
Then WZ is the radius of the circle, less ZO;
that is, $WZ = 8 - \sqrt{39} \approx 1.76$.

11. From the Secant Length Theorem,
$PD \cdot PB = PA \cdot PC$. If $PA = PD = k$,
then $k \cdot PB = k \cdot PC$ or $PB = PC$; the
statement is *true*.

12.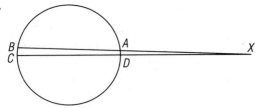

True; $\frac{1}{2}(\text{m}\overset{\frown}{BC} - \text{m}\overset{\frown}{AD}) = \text{m}\angle AXD$. If $\text{m}\overset{\frown}{BC} = \text{m}\overset{\frown}{AD}$, then $\text{m}\angle AXD = 0$, and then $\overleftrightarrow{BX}$ and $\overleftrightarrow{CX}$ are not different lines.

13. Intersecting lines $\overleftrightarrow{PC}$ and $\overleftrightarrow{PA}$ determine a single plane, and the intersection of that plane and the sphere is a circle containing points A, B, C, and D. For those points, the Secant Length Theorem states that $PC \cdot PD = PA \cdot PB$, so the result is also true for the original sphere.

14. $\text{m}\overset{\frown}{CD} = 360° - 230° = 130°$, so

$\text{m}\angle B = \frac{1}{2}(\text{m}\overset{\frown}{CD} - \text{m}\overset{\frown}{CE}) =$

$\frac{1}{2}(130 - 80) = 25;$

$\text{m}\angle D = \frac{1}{2}\text{m}\overset{\frown}{CE} = \frac{1}{2}(80) = 40;$ and

$\text{m}\angle BCD = \frac{1}{2}\text{m}\overset{\frown}{CED} = \frac{1}{2}(230) = 115.$

15. Major arc $\overset{\frown}{YZ} = 360° -$ minor arc $\overset{\frown}{YZ}$, so

$\text{m}\angle X = 45 = \frac{1}{2}(360 - \text{m}\overset{\frown}{YZ} - \text{m}\overset{\frown}{YZ})$

$90 = 360 - 2\text{m}\overset{\frown}{YZ}$

$-270 = -2\text{m}\overset{\frown}{YZ}$

$\text{m}\overset{\frown}{YZ} = 135°.$

16. $\text{m}\overset{\frown}{RT} = 360° - (140° + 15° + 105°) = 360° - 260° = 100°$, so $\text{m}\angle A =$

$\frac{1}{2}(\text{m}\overset{\frown}{RT} - \text{m}\overset{\frown}{QV}) =$

$\frac{1}{2}(100 - 15) = \frac{1}{2}(85) = 42.5.$

17.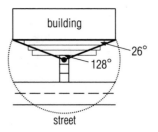

18.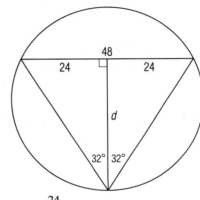

$\tan 32° = \frac{24}{d}$

$d = \frac{24}{\tan 32°} \approx 38.4 \text{ m}$

19. **a.** Using the Pythagorean Theorem,

$AC = \sqrt{29^2 - 21^2} = \sqrt{841 - 441} = \sqrt{400} = 20.$

b. $\tan B = \frac{\text{opp}}{\text{adj}} = \frac{20}{21} \approx .952$

c. $\sin A = \frac{\text{opp}}{\text{hyp}} = \frac{21}{29} \approx .724$

d. $\cos B = \frac{\text{adj}}{\text{hyp}} = \frac{21}{29} \approx .724$

20. a-b.

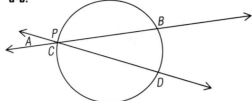

If the secants intersect at point P on the circle, then points $A, B,$ and P coincide, and $PA = PC = 0$. The question is, does $PA \cdot PB = PC \cdot PD$? Since $PA = PC = 0$, then the value on each side of the equal sign is zero, and the equation is true. So the Secant Length Theorem is true (in a trivial way) if the secants intersect *on* the circle.

21.

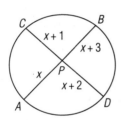

Use an indirect proof.
Suppose the lengths of the 4 segments are consecutive integers, say $x, x + 1, x + 2,$ and $x + 3$. Then the Secant Length Theorem states that $(x)(x + 3) = (x + 1)(x + 2)$ or $x^2 + 3x = x^2 + 3x + 2$.
This would mean that $0 = 2$, which is impossible; so the original assumption is false, and the lengths of the 4 segments cannot be consecutive integers.

LESSON 15-8 (pp. 775–779)

1. Suppose the figure is a rectangle, with length $10 + x$ feet. Then the width would be $10 - x$ feet (so the perimeter would be 100 feet). Then the area would be $(10 + x)(10 - x) = 100 - x^2$ ft². That is x^2 ft² <u>less</u> than the area of a square with side 10 ft. So of all rectangles with perimeter 100 ft, the one with the most area is the square with side 10 ft.

2. **a.** According to the Isoperimetric Theorem, of all figures with a given perimeter, the one with the most area is a circle.

   b. If $C = 2\pi r = 100$, then $\pi r = 50$ and $r = \frac{50}{\pi}$. Then the area of that circle is
   $$A = \pi r^2 = \pi(\frac{50}{\pi})^2 = \frac{\pi 2500}{\pi^2} =$$
   $$\frac{2500}{\pi} \approx 796 \text{ ft}^2.$$

3.

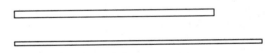

equal perimeters
decreasing areas

The minimum area is as close to zero as you like.

4. According to the Isoperimetric Theorem, of all figures with a given area, the one with the least perimeter is the circle.

5.

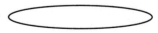

6.

7. Using the formula $A = \pi r^2$ with $A = 9\pi$ cm², then $9\pi = \pi r^2$ and $r = 3$ cm. Then the circumference is $C = 2\pi r = 2\pi(3) = 6\pi \approx 18.8$ cm.

8. Using the formula $A = s^2$ with $A = 9\pi$ cm^2, then $9\pi = s^2$ and $s = \sqrt{9\pi} = 3\sqrt{\pi}$. So the perimeter is $4s = 12\sqrt{\pi} \approx 21.3$ cm.

9. For a given area, the Isoperimetric Theorem states that a circle should have the smallest perimeter. So the perimeter in Question 8 should be larger, which it is.

10. According to different statements of the Isoperimetric Theorem,

   a. Of all figures with the same area, the circle has the least perimeter.

   b. Of all figures with the same perimeter, the circle has the most area.

11. **a.** The lower rectangle has dimensions $20'$ and $24'$; its area is $(20)(24) = 480$ ft^2. For the triangle at the top, the altitude is $5'$ and the base is $24'$, so the area is

   $$\tfrac{1}{2}bh = \tfrac{1}{2}(24)(5) = 60 \text{ ft}^2.$$

   So the area of the pentagonal region is $480 + 60 = 540$ ft^2.

   b. Each of segments $\overline{AB}$ and $\overline{BC}$ is the hypotenuse of a right triangle with legs 5 and half of 24:

   $$AB = \sqrt{5^2 + 12^2} = \sqrt{25 + 144} = \sqrt{169} = 13'.$$

   So the perimeter of the pentagonal region is $13 + 13 + 20 + 24 + 20 = 90$ feet. By the Isoperimetric Theorem, the largest region that could be enclosed by a fixed perimeter is a circle. That circle would have circumference 90 feet, so using the formula $C = 2\pi r$, then $90 = 2\pi r$ and $r = \dfrac{45}{\pi}$. Then the area of that circle would be

$$A = \pi r^2$$
$$= \pi\left(\frac{45}{\pi}\right)^2$$
$$= \pi\frac{2025}{\pi^2}$$
$$= \frac{2025}{\pi}$$
$$\approx 645 \text{ ft}^2.$$

12. **a.** The area of the rectangle is the product of its length and width:
$$(s - t)(s + t) = s^2 + st - st - t^2$$
$$= s^2 - t^2.$$

   b. Using the result generalized from Question 1, for all rectangles with a given perimeter, the square has the greatest area. So if the length equals the width, then

$$s - t = s + t$$
$$\text{-}t = t$$
$$\text{-}2t = 0$$
$$t = 0.$$

   So the value of t for which the area is the largest is $t = 0$.

   (Another way: the area of the rectangle is $s^2 - t^2$, and that value is maximized when $t^2 = 0$; that is when $t = 0$.)

13. **a.** By the Secant Length Theorem,
$$XY \cdot XZ = XW \cdot XV.$$
   So $(8)(28) = (10)(10 + WV)$
$$224 = 100 + 10 \cdot WV$$
$$124 = 10 \cdot WV$$
$$WV = 12.4 \text{ units.}$$

   b. The power of point X for circle O is
   $$(8)(28) = (10)(22.4) = 224.$$

14. By the Secant Length Theorem,
$$AE \cdot BE = CE \cdot DE, \text{ so}$$
$$(16)(14) = 18 \cdot DE$$
$$224 = 18 \cdot DE$$
$$DE = \frac{224}{18} = \frac{112}{9} \approx 12.4 \text{ units.}$$

15. a-b. $\overline{CD}$ is a diameter, so
$m\widehat{BD} = 180° - m\widehat{BC}.$ So
$$m\angle A = \tfrac{1}{2}(m\widehat{BD} - m\widehat{BC})$$
$$40 = \tfrac{1}{2}(180 - m\widehat{BC} - m\widehat{BC})$$
$$80 = 180 - 2m\widehat{BC}$$
$$-100 = -2m\widehat{BC}$$
$$m\widehat{BC} = 50°.$$
So $m\widehat{BD} = 180° - m\widehat{BC} =$
$180° - 50° = 130°.$

16. $\angle CBD$ is inscribed in semicircle $\widehat{CBD}$, so
$m\angle CBD = 90.$

17. The measure of an angle formed by two chords is half the measure of its intercepted arcs, so $x = \tfrac{1}{2}(27 + 101) = \tfrac{1}{2}(128) = 64.$

18. For a regular decagon (10-gon), the sum of the exterior angles is 360, so each exterior angle has measure 36. Each interior angle is supplementary to that, so the measure of each interior angle is $180 - 36 = 144.$

19. Statement:

If we finish the next lesson, our class will have done every lesson in the book.

a. converse:

If our class has done every lesson in the book, then we will have finished the next lesson.

b. inverse:

If we do not finish the next lesson, our class will not have done every lesson in the book.

c. contrapositive:

If our class will not have done every lesson in the book, then we will not have finished the next lesson.

20. $\boxed{\pi}\,\boxed{y^x}\,3\,\boxed{1/x}\,\boxed{=}$ displays 1.4645919; to the nearest hundredth, that is 1.46.

21.

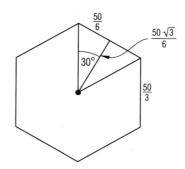

For a regular hexagon, if the perimeter is 100 ft then the length of each side is $\frac{100}{6} = \frac{50}{3}$ ft. The altitude of each equilateral triangle is $\frac{50\sqrt{3}}{6}$, so the area of the hexagon is $6\left(\frac{1}{2} \cdot \frac{50}{3} \cdot \frac{50\sqrt{3}}{6}\right) = \frac{2500\sqrt{3}}{6} \approx 721.69$ ft^2, which is greater than 625 ft^2. In fact, any regular polygon having more than 4 sides will satisfy the condition.

LESSON 15–9 (pp. 780–784)

1. By the Isoperimetric Theorem (space version), of all the figures with the same surface area, the sphere has the most volume.

2. By the Isoperimetric Theorem (space version), of all the figures with the same volume, the sphere has the least surface area.

3. A soap bubble represents a fixed amount of air trapped within soap film. For the bubble's current altitude, that amount of air translates to a fixed volume. That is the antecedent for the statement in Question 2, so the version of the Isoperimetric Theorem (space version) that explains the shape of a soap bubble is that of all the figures with the same volume, the sphere has the least surface area.

4. For the fixed surface area of 600 m², the figure with the largest possible volume is a sphere. To find the volume of the sphere, use the formula for the surface area of a sphere:

$$\text{S.A.} = 4\pi r^2$$
$$600 = 4\pi r^2$$
$$150 = \pi r^2$$
$$r = \sqrt{\frac{150}{\pi}}.$$

So the volume of the sphere is

$$V = \frac{4}{3}\pi r^3$$
$$= \frac{4}{3}\pi \left(\sqrt{\frac{150}{\pi}}\right)^3$$
$$= \frac{4}{3}\pi \frac{150}{\pi}\sqrt{\frac{150}{\pi}}$$
$$= 200\sqrt{\frac{150}{\pi}}$$
$$\approx 1381.977$$
$$\approx 1400 \text{ m}^3.$$

5.

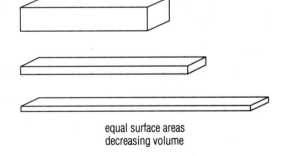

equal surface areas
decreasing volume

For any given surface area, the minimum volume is as close to zero as you like.

6. If the volume of a cube is 8 units³, then $V = s^3$, so $8 = s^3$ and $s = 2$ units. The surface area of a cube with side s is $6s^2$, so the surface area of a cube with side 2 is $6(2)^2 = (6)(4) = 24$ units².

7. Sponges hold water because some water has sponge surface area under it; other water clings to the sponge's surface area by surface tension.

8. a. Yes; by slicing a small object very, very thinly, the surface area of that sliced-up object can be made very large.

b. If the degree of filtering depends on the surface area of the filter, then you would want the filter to have a large surface area in order to filter out the maximum amount of smoke.

9. a. Using the formula for the volume of a sphere, $V = \frac{4}{3}\pi r^3$, with $V = 36\pi$, then

$$36\pi = \frac{4}{3}\pi r^3$$
$$36 = \frac{4}{3}r^3$$
$$27 = r^3$$
$$r = 3.$$

So the surface area of that sphere is
$$\text{S.A.} = 4\pi r^2$$
$$= 4\pi 3^2$$
$$= 4\pi 9$$
$$= 36\pi$$
$$\approx 113 \text{ m}^2.$$

b.

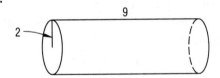

Sample:
$r = 2$ and $h = 9$, so
$$\text{S.A.} = 2B + 2\pi rh$$
$$= 2(\pi 2^2) + 2\pi(2)(9)$$
$$= 8\pi + 36\pi$$
$$= 44\pi$$
$$\approx 138 \text{ m}^2$$

c.

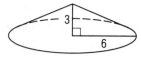

If $r = 6$ and $h = 3$, then

$$V = \frac{1}{3}\pi r^2 h = \frac{1}{3}\pi(6^2)(3)$$

$$= \frac{1}{3}\pi(108)$$

$$= 36\pi.$$

Then $\ell = \sqrt{3^2 + 6^2} = \sqrt{45}$,

and S.A. $= \pi r^2 + \frac{1}{2}\ell p$

$$= \pi 6^2 + \frac{1}{2}(2\pi 6)(\sqrt{45})$$

$$= 36\pi + 6\pi\sqrt{45}$$

$$\approx 240 \text{ m}^2.$$

d. According to the Isoperimetric Inequality, for a given volume (in this case, $36\pi \text{ m}^3$), the sphere has the least surface area. So the surface area in part a, which was for a sphere, must be less than the surface area in parts b or c.

10. Spherical containers would be the most efficient in terms of the amount they would contain for the amount of material in the container, but they would be inefficient in terms of fitting them into shipping crates and keeping them from rolling off the shelves.

11. If a sphere has surface area $x \cdot \pi$, then

$$x\pi = 4\pi r^2$$

$$x = 4r^2$$

$$r^2 = \frac{x}{4}$$

$$r = \frac{\sqrt{x}}{2}.$$

So the volume is

$$V = \frac{4}{3}\pi r^3$$

$$= \frac{4\pi(\sqrt{x})^3}{3(2)^3}$$

$$= \frac{4\pi x\sqrt{x}}{24}$$

$$= \frac{\pi x\sqrt{x}}{6}.$$

12. a. According to the Isoperimetric Theorem (plane version), of all figures with a given area, the one with the smallest perimeter is the circle.

b. If the area of a circle is 12 m^2,

Then $A = \pi r^2$

$$12 = \pi r^2$$

$$r = \sqrt{\frac{12}{\pi}}.$$

So the perimeter (circumference) is

$$C = 2\pi r$$

$$= 2\pi\sqrt{\frac{12}{\pi}}$$

$$\approx 12.3 \text{ m}.$$

13. a. For the square:

$p = 96$, so $s = \dfrac{96}{4} = 24$, and

$A = S^2 = 576$ in.²

For the circle:

$C = 2\pi r$

$96 = 2\pi r$

$r = \dfrac{48}{\pi}$

So $A = \pi r^2$

$= \pi\left(\dfrac{48}{\pi}\right)^2$

$= \dfrac{2304}{\pi}$

≈ 733 in.²

b. The square has the smaller area.

14. By the Tangent Square Theorem,
$QL^2 = QN \cdot QP$, so $QL^2 = (6)(18) = 108$,
and $QL = \sqrt{108} \approx 10.39$ units.

15. By the Secant Length Theorem, $CD \cdot CE = AC \cdot CB$, which can be written as a proportion by dividing both sides by $CD \cdot CB$:

$\dfrac{CD \cdot CE}{CD \cdot CB} = \dfrac{AC \cdot CB}{CD \cdot CB}$ so $\dfrac{CE}{CB} = \dfrac{AC}{CD}$.

But by part a of the Chord-Center Theorem, C is the midpoint of $\overline{AB}$ or $AC = CB$. So substituting AC for CB:

$\dfrac{CE}{AC} = \dfrac{AC}{CD}$; or AC is the geometric mean of CD and CE.

16. $m\angle A = \frac{1}{2}m\,\overset{\frown}{BC} = \frac{1}{2}(79) = 39.5$;

$m\angle C = \frac{1}{2}m\,\overset{\frown}{AB} = \frac{1}{2}(85) = 42.5$; and

$m\angle B = 180 - (39.5 + 42.5) = 180 - 82 = 98$.

17. By the Unequal Angles Theorem, the shortest side is opposite the smallest angle. The smallest angle (from Question 16) is $\angle A$, so the shortest side is $\overline{BC}$.

18.

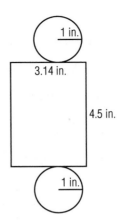

19. If Buffalo were between New York City and Boston (it is not), then the distance between New York City and Boston would be maximized as the sum of the two distances, or $457 + 436 = 893$ miles.

If New York City were between Boston and Buffalo (it is not), then the distance between New York City and Boston would be minimized as the difference between those distances, or $457 - 436 = 21$ miles.

So you can conclude that the distance between Boston and New York City is between 21 and 893 miles. (Actually, the distance is around 212 miles.)

20. a. Carthage was a city on the north coast of Africa, on the Bay of Tunis.

b. Dido was granted all the land that could be surrounded by a piece of cowhide. She sliced the cowhide into very thin strips, and used them to encircle land; that land became Carthage.

21. Suppose a space figure has a surface area of S.A. If that figure is a sphere, then

S.A. $= 4\pi r^2$ and $V = \dfrac{4}{3}\pi r^3$.

Solving each formula for r, $r = \sqrt{\dfrac{S.A.}{4\pi}}$ and

$r = \sqrt[3]{\dfrac{3V}{4\pi}}$. Thus $\sqrt{\dfrac{S.A.}{4\pi}} = \sqrt[3]{\dfrac{3V}{4\pi}}$. Cubing

both sides, $\dfrac{3V}{4\pi} = \left(\sqrt{\dfrac{S.A.}{4\pi}}\right)^3 = \dfrac{S.A.}{4\pi}\sqrt{\dfrac{S.A.}{4\pi}}$.

So, $V = \dfrac{S.A.}{3}\sqrt{\dfrac{S.A.}{4\pi}} = \dfrac{S.A.}{6}\sqrt{\dfrac{S.A.}{\pi}}$. Now the

sphere has the most volume for a given surface area, so for any figure,

$V \le \dfrac{S.A.}{6}\sqrt{\dfrac{S.A.}{\pi}}$.

CHAPTER 15 PROGRESS SELF-TEST (p. 786–787)

1.

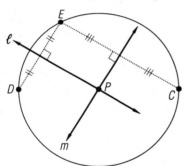

Construct the ⊥ bisectors of $\overline{DE}$ and $\overline{EC}$. They meet at P, the center of the circle. Use point D, E, or C to draw the circle.

2. Start with 5 points equally spaced around a circle:
Draw chords connecting 5-2 and 4-3. This gives the first week's pairings:
Round 1: 2-5, 3-4, 1 bye.
Rotate the chords around the circle for the next 4 rounds:
round 2: 1-3, 4-5, 2 bye
round 3: 2-4, 1-5, 3 bye
round 4: 3-5, 1-2, 4 bye
round 5: 1-4, 2-3, 5 bye.

3. Points O and M are equidistant from points X and Y, so $\overleftrightarrow{OM}$ is the ⊥ bisector of $\overline{XY}$. Line ℓ is a tangent line, so $\ell \perp \overleftrightarrow{OQ}$. So $\ell \parallel \overleftrightarrow{XY}$ by the Two Parallels Theorem.

4. Draw segments $\overline{JL}$ and $\overline{KM}$. In each of the four small right isosceles triangles, the side is 30 (the radius of the circle) so the hypotenuse is $30\sqrt{2}$. So the perimeter of $JKLM$ is $4(30\sqrt{2}) = 120\sqrt{2} \approx 169.7$ units.

5. $\angle B$, an inscribed angle, is measured by half its intercepted arc. So $m\angle B = \frac{1}{2}(\overset{\frown}{DC}) = \frac{1}{2}(80) = 40$.

6. To find $m\overset{\frown}{AB}$, use the property that $\angle DEC$ is measured by half the sum of the intercepted arcs. So $m\angle DEC = \frac{1}{2}(m\overset{\frown}{DC} + m\overset{\frown}{AB})$ or $110 = \frac{1}{2}(80 + m\overset{\frown}{AB})$. Then $220 = 80 + m\overset{\frown}{AB}$ and $m\overset{\frown}{AB} = 140°$

7. To find $m\angle R$, first find $m\overset{\frown}{VT}$: $m\overset{\frown}{VT} = 360° - m\overset{\frown}{VUT} = 360° - (80° + 30° + 140°) - 360° - 250° = 110°$. Then $m\angle R = \frac{1}{2}(m\overset{\frown}{VT} - m\overset{\frown}{US}) = \frac{1}{2}(110 - 30) = \frac{1}{2}(80) = 40$.

8. $\overrightarrow{PT}$ and $\overrightarrow{PU}$ are tangents to $\odot O$, so $\overline{PT} \perp \overline{OT}$ and $\overline{PU} \perp \overline{OU}$. Given that $m\overset{\frown}{UT} = 90$, then $m\angle O = 90$ and $\angle P$ is a right angle because the sum of the four angles in quadrilateral $OUPT$ is 360°. So $OUPT$ is a rectangle by the definition of rectangle (sufficient condition). Moreover, $PT = PU$ because two tangents to a circle from an external point have the same length. So $OUPT$ is a square by the definition of square (sufficient condition).

9. For the two chords $\overline{BC}$ and $\overline{AD}$, $(AQ)(DQ) = (CQ)(BQ)$. Using $AQ = 19$, $BQ = 40$, and $CQ = 38$, then $(19)(DQ) = (38)(40)$ so $19(DQ) = 1520$ and $DQ = 80$ units.

10. For the two secants $\overline{WY}$ and $\overline{WV}$, $(WX)(WY)$ $= (WZ)(WV)$. Using $WX = 12$, $XY = 16$, and $WZ = 10$, then $(12)(12 + 16) =$ $(10)(10 + ZV)$ so $(12)(28) = 100 + 10(ZV)$ or $336 = 100 + 10(ZV)$ and $236 = 10(ZV)$ so $ZV = 23.6$ units.

11. a. The figure with the greatest area for a fixed perimeter is a circle.

    b. Using $C = 2\pi r$ with $C = 30$ cm, $30 = 2\pi r$ and $r = \frac{15}{\pi}$. Then using $A = \pi r^2$,

$$A = \pi\left(\frac{15}{\pi}\right)^2 = \frac{225\pi}{\pi^2} = \frac{225}{\pi} \approx 71.6 \text{ cm}^2.$$

12. For a given volume, a sphere has the smallest surface area. So if a cube and sphere have the same volume, the cube will have the larger surface area.

13.

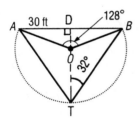

To find point T on the $\perp$ bisector of $\overline{AB}$:
$\tan 32° = \frac{30}{TD}$, so $TD = 30$ ⌷÷⌷ 32 ⌷TAN⌷ ⌷=⌷
≈ 48.
Find the circle through A, B, and T; then at any point on $\overset{\frown}{ATB}$ the entire stage will fit and fill the camera angle.

14. From Question 13, you can stand 48 feet from the center of the stage.

1. The figure is a regular hexagon, so each arc has measure $\frac{360}{6} = 60°$. Draw two radii to consecutive vertices of the hexagon, and show that the triangle is equilateral: The central angle has the same measure as its arc, so its measure is 60, and the radii are congruent, so the other two angles are congruent by the Isosceles Triangle Theorem, and their sum is 120 by the Triangle-Sum Theorem. So each angle of the triangle has measure 60, and the triangle is equilateral. Then, since the radius is 12 units, each side of the hexagon is 12 units.

2.

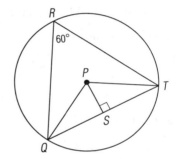

Draw radii $\overline{PQ}$ and $\overline{PT}$. $\triangle QRT$ is equilateral, so m$\angle R = 60$ and then m$\overset{\frown}{QT} = 120$ (because an inscribed angle is measured by half its arc). $\angle QPT$ is a central angle, so m$\angle QPT = $ m$\overset{\frown}{QT} = 120$. Draw $\overline{PS}$, the perpendicular from P to $\overline{QT}$. By the Chord-Center Theorem, $\overline{PS}$ bisects $\overline{QT}$ (part a) and so $\overline{PS}$ bisects $\angle QPT$ (part b); hence m$\angle QPS = 60$. So $\triangle QPS$ is a 30-60-90 triangle with hypotenuse 15; then $QS = 7.5\sqrt{3}$ and $QT = 15\sqrt{3}$. So the perimeter of $\triangle QRT$ is $(3)(15\sqrt{3}) = 45\sqrt{3} \approx$ 77.9 units.

3. $\overline{OB}$ is leg of a 45-45-90 triangle whose hypotenuse is $12\sqrt{2}$, so its length is 12 units.

4. The radius of the circle is 12, so its area is
$A = \pi r^2 = \pi(12)^2 = 144\pi.$
The side of the square is $12\sqrt{2}$, so the area of
the square is $A = s^2 = (12\sqrt{2})^2 = (144)(2)$
$= 288.$
So the area of the shaded region is
$144\pi - 288 \approx 164.4$ units^2.

5.

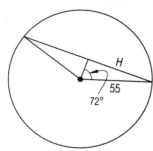

If H represents the length of half the chord,
then $\sin 72° = \dfrac{H}{55}$ and $H = 55 \sin 72°$. So the
length of the chord is $110 \sin 72° \approx$
104.6 mm.

6. a. The figure is a regular octagon, so the
measure of each arc is $\dfrac{360}{8} = 45°$; in
particular, $\text{m}\,\widehat{IZ} = 45°$.

  b. Draw radii $\overline{QT}$ and $\overline{QO}$, and draw the
perpendicular $\overline{QA}$ from Q to $\overline{TO}$. Then
from parts a and b of the Chord-Center
Theorem, $\overline{QA}$ bisects $\angle TQO$, and
$\text{m}\angle TQA = 22.5.$
So $\sin 22.5° = \dfrac{TA}{15}$, and $TA = 15 \sin 22.5°$.
The perimeter of the octagon is 16 times
the length TA, so the perimeter is
$(16)(15 \sin 22.5°) = 240 \sin 22.5° \approx$
91.8 units.

7. $\text{m}\angle CAB = \frac{1}{2}\text{m}\,\widehat{CB}$

  $53 = \frac{1}{2}\text{m}\,\widehat{CB}$

  $106° = \text{m}\,\widehat{CB}$

8. $\text{m}\angle B = \frac{1}{2}\text{m}\,\widehat{ADC}$

  $89 = \frac{1}{2}\text{m}\,\widehat{ADC}$

  $178° = \text{m}\,\widehat{ADC}$

9. $\angle D$ is inscribed in an arc that is the sum of
$\widehat{AB}$ and $\widehat{BC}$, and $\text{m}\,\widehat{BC}$ was found in
Question 7. So find $\text{m}\,\widehat{AB}$.
$\text{m}\angle ACB = 180 - (53 + 89) =$
$180 - 142 = 38$
So $\frac{1}{2}\text{m}\,\widehat{AB} = 38°$, and $\text{m}\,\widehat{AB} = 76°$.
So $\text{m}\angle D = \frac{1}{2}(\text{m}\,\widehat{AB} + \text{m}\,\widehat{BC})$

  $= \frac{1}{2}(76 + 106)$

  $= \frac{1}{2}(182)$

  $= 91.$

10. $\angle Q$ is inscribed in $\widehat{PR}$, so
$\text{m}\angle Q = \frac{1}{2}\text{m}\,\widehat{PR}$

  $= \frac{1}{2}(162)$

  $= 81.$

11. $\angle P$ is inscribed in $\widehat{QR}$, and $\text{m}\,\widehat{QR} =$
$360 - (94 + 162) = 360 - 256 = 104.$
So $\text{m}\angle P = \frac{1}{2}\text{m}\,\widehat{QR} = \frac{1}{2}(104) = 52.$

12. $\angle EHF$ is formed by two chords, so
$\text{m}\angle EHF = \frac{1}{2}(\text{m}\,\widehat{DG} + \text{m}\,\widehat{EF})$

  $= \frac{1}{2}(100 + 140)$

  $= \frac{1}{2}(240)$

  $= 120.$

13. $\angle EHD$ is formed by two chords, so its measure is half the sum of its intercepted arcs, $\overset{\frown}{GF}$ and $\overset{\frown}{DE}$. Since $m\angle EHD$ and $m\overset{\frown}{GF}$ are given, you can find $m\overset{\frown}{DE}$:

$$m\angle EHD = \tfrac{1}{2}(m\overset{\frown}{GF} + m\overset{\frown}{DE})$$
$$51 = \tfrac{1}{2}(37 + m\overset{\frown}{DE})$$
$$102 = 37 + m\overset{\frown}{DE}$$
$$m\overset{\frown}{DE} = 65°.$$

14. $\angle A$ is formed by two secants, so $m\angle A = \tfrac{1}{2}(m\overset{\frown}{ED} - m\overset{\frown}{BC}) = \tfrac{1}{2}(125 - 30) = 47.5$;

$\angle E$ and $\angle D$ are both measured by half the measure of $\overset{\frown}{BC}$, so $m\angle E = m\angle D = \tfrac{1}{2}m\overset{\frown}{BC}$

$= \tfrac{1}{2}(30) = 15$;

$\angle EBD$ and $\angle ECD$ are both measured by half the measure of $\overset{\frown}{ED}$, so $m\angle EBD =$

$m\angle ECD = \tfrac{1}{2}(125) = 62.5$.

$\angle ACE$ and $\angle ABD$ are each supplementary to angles of measure 62.5, so $m\angle ACE = m\angle ABD = 180 - 62.5 = 117.5$.

$\angle BFC$ and its vertical angle EFD are formed by two chords, so each measure is half the sum of the intercepted arcs, so $m\angle BFC =$

$m\angle EFD = \tfrac{1}{2}(m\overset{\frown}{BC} + m\overset{\frown}{ED}) =$

$\tfrac{1}{2}(30 + 125) = \tfrac{1}{2}(155) = 77.5$.

$\angle BFE$ and $\angle CFD$ are each supplementary to angles of measure 77.5, so $m\angle BFE = m\angle CFD = 180 - 77.5 = 102.5$.

15. $\angle PJQ$ is formed by a tangent and a secant, so its measure is half the difference of the intercepted arcs, or $m\angle PJQ =$

$\tfrac{1}{2}(60 - 32) = \tfrac{1}{2}(28) = 14.$

16. First, $\angle L$ is a central angle, so its arc has the same measure as $\angle L$, and so $m\overset{\frown}{QR} = 80°$. Then use $\angle QJR$ to find $m\overset{\frown}{ON}$:

$$m\angle QJR = \tfrac{1}{2}(m\overset{\frown}{QR} - m\overset{\frown}{ON})$$
$$20 = \tfrac{1}{2}(80 - m\overset{\frown}{ON})$$
$$40 = 80 - m\overset{\frown}{ON}$$
$$-40 = -m\overset{\frown}{ON}$$
$$m\overset{\frown}{ON} = 40.$$

17. Use the values found in Questions 15 and 16 to find $m\overset{\frown}{MR}$:

$$m\overset{\frown}{MR} = 360 - (m\overset{\frown}{MN} + m\overset{\frown}{ON} + m\overset{\frown}{OP} + m\overset{\frown}{PQ} + m\overset{\frown}{QR})$$
$$= 360 - (30 + 40 + 32 + 60 + 80)$$
$$= 360 - 242$$
$$= 118.$$

So $m\angle PJM = \tfrac{1}{2}(m\overset{\frown}{PQM} - m\overset{\frown}{POM})$

$$= \tfrac{1}{2}(60 + 80 + 118 - (32 + 40 + 30))$$
$$= \tfrac{1}{2}(258 - 102)$$
$$= \tfrac{1}{2}(156)$$
$$= 78.$$

18.

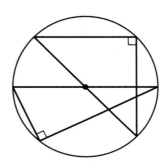

19.

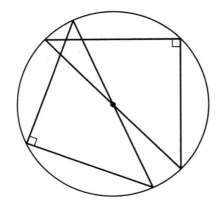

20.

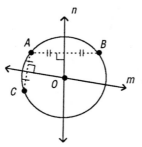

21.

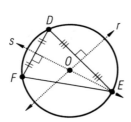

22.

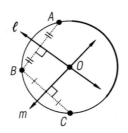

23.

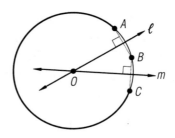

24. By the Secant Length Theorem,
$AX \cdot XB = DX \cdot XC$.
So $(12)(40) = (48)(CX)$
$$480 = 48 \cdot CX$$
$$CX = 10 \text{ units.}$$

25. By the Secant Length Theorem,
$LM \cdot LN = LK \cdot LJ$. Note that $LM = LN - MN = 20 - 15 = 5$.
So $(5)(20) = (25 - KJ)(25)$
$$100 = 625 - 25 \cdot KJ$$
$$-525 = -25 \cdot KJ$$
$$KJ = 21 \text{ units.}$$

26. As in Question 25, $LM \cdot LN = LK \cdot LJ$. So
$(6)(13) = (LK)(LK + 8)$
$78 = LK^2 + 8 \cdot LK$
$LK^2 + 8 \cdot LK - 78 = 0$.
Using the Quadratic Formula with $a = 1$, $b = 8$, and $c = -78$, then
$$LK = \frac{-8 \pm \sqrt{8^2 - (4)(1)(-78)}}{(2)(1)}$$
$$= \frac{-8 \pm \sqrt{64 + 312}}{2}$$
$$= \frac{-8 \pm \sqrt{376}}{2}$$
$$= \frac{-8 \pm 2\sqrt{94}}{2}$$
$$= -4 \pm \sqrt{94}.$$
Eliminate $-4 - \sqrt{94}$, because it is negative, and the length LK cannot be less than zero.
So $LK = -4 + \sqrt{94} \approx 5.7$ units.

27. By the Tangent Square Theorem,
$$QR^2 = QX \cdot QY.$$
So $8^2 = (4)(YX + 4)$
$$64 = 4 \cdot YX + 16$$
$$48 = 4 \cdot YX$$
$$YX = 12 \text{ units.}$$

28. By part a of the Chord-Center Theorem, $\overline{AB}$ bisects $\overline{DC}$ and so $DE = EC$.

29. $\overline{DC}$ can be translated anywhere along $\overline{AB}$, as long as $\overline{DC} \perp \overline{AB}$. So E is not necessarily the midpoint of $\overline{OB}$, and the statement cannot be justified.

30. ℓ and $\overline{DC}$ are both perpendicular to $\overline{AB}$, so $\ell \parallel \overline{DC}$ by the Two Perpendiculars Theorem.

31. W is the midpoint of $\overline{YX}$, so by parts b and c of the Chord-Center Theorem, $\overline{ZW}$ is the $\perp$ bisector of $\overline{YX}$. Z is equidistant from Y and X (that is, $ZY = ZX$) by the Perpendicular Bisector Theorem (page 183), and so ΔZYX is isosceles by the definition of isosceles triangle (sufficient condition).

32. $\angle A$ (or $\angle D$) is a right angle, by the definition of rectangle. It is also an inscribed angle, so its intercepted arc is a semicircle and $\overline{BC}$ is a diameter.

33. $m\angle ACB$ is half of its intercepted arc, so if $m\overset{\frown}{AB} = x$, then $m\angle ACB = \frac{x}{2}$.

34. $\angle ABD$ is formed by a tangent and a chord, so its measure is half its intercepted arc, and
$$m\angle ABD = \frac{1}{2}m\overset{\frown}{BD}.$$
$\angle C$ is an inscribed angle, so its measure is half its intercepted arc, so $m\angle C = \frac{1}{2}m\overset{\frown}{BD}$.
So $m\angle ABD = m\angle C$ by the Transitive Property of Equality.

35. **a.** By the Isoperimetric Theorem, of all plane figures with a given area, the one with the least perimeter is the circle.
b. If the area of a circle is 800 ft², then use the formula for the area of a circle to find its radius:
$$A = \pi r^2$$
$$800 = \pi r^2$$
$$r^2 = \frac{800}{\pi}$$
$$r = \sqrt{\frac{800}{\pi}}.$$
Then use the formula for the circumference of a circle:
$$C = 2\pi r$$
$$= 2\pi\sqrt{\frac{800}{\pi}}$$
$$\approx 100.3 \text{ ft}$$

36. **a.** Of all rectangles with a given perimeter, the one with the most area is a square.
b. If the perimeter is 2000 cm, then the length of each side is $\frac{2000}{4} = 500$ cm, so the area is $500^2 = 250{,}000$ cm².

37. **a.** If the perimeter of a square is 32 inches, then each side is 8 inches and the area is 64 in.²
If the circumference of a circle is 32 inches, then
$$C = 2\pi r$$
$$32 = 2\pi r$$
$$r = \frac{16}{\pi}.$$
Then $A = \pi r^2 = \pi\left(\frac{16}{\pi}\right)^2 = \frac{256}{\pi} \approx 81.5$ in.²
b. In accord with the Isoperimetric Theorem, the circle has the larger area.

38. By the Isoperimetric Theorem (space version), of all the solids with a given surface area, the one with the largest volume is the sphere.

(You can also calculate the volume of the sphere. S.A. $= 10,000 = 4\pi r^2$, so

$r = \sqrt{\dfrac{2500}{\pi}}$. Then $V = \dfrac{4}{3}\pi r^3 = \dfrac{4}{3}\pi\left(\sqrt{\dfrac{2500}{\pi}}\right)^3$

$\approx (1.33)(3.14)(22448) \approx 94,000$ m³.)

39. a. Of all boxes with a given surface area, the one with the most volume is the cube.

  b. If the surface area of a cube is 48 ft², then use the formula for the surface area of a cube to find its side:

  S.A. $= 6s^2$
  $48 = 6s^2$
  $8 = s^2$
  $s = \sqrt{8}$.

  So the volume of the cube is $(\sqrt{8})^3 = 8\sqrt{8} \approx (8)(2.83) \approx 22.6$ ft³.

40. a-b. By the Isoperimetric Theorem (space version), of all figures with a given volume, the sphere has the smallest surface area. So if a sphere and a cylinder have the same volume, the one which must have the <u>larger</u> surface area is the cylinder.

41. a.

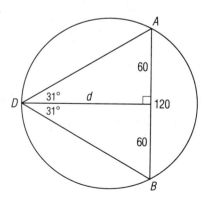

anywhere on arc $\overset{\frown}{ADB}$

b. $\tan 31° = \dfrac{60}{d}$

$d = \dfrac{60}{\tan 31°} \approx 99.9$ yd

The photographer must stand about 100 yards away from C.

42. a.

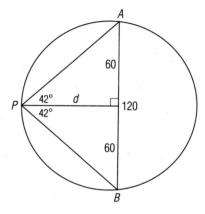

anywhere on arc $\overset{\frown}{APB}$

b. $\tan 42° = \dfrac{60}{d}$

$d = \dfrac{60}{\tan 42°} \approx 66.6$ yd

The photographer must stand about 66.6 yards away from C.

43. a. By the Isoperimetric Theorem (space version), of all figures with a given volume, the sphere has the smallest surface area.

  b. Spherical containers are rarely used because they would not be efficiently packaged into boxes, and they would roll off shelves and displays.

44. a. For a given perimeter, the most efficient rectangle (that is, the one that encloses the most area) is a square. So if the perimeter is 60 feet, then each side of the square is 15 feet and the area is $15^2 = 225$ square feet.

b. The circle with circumference 60 would be the most efficient shape. To find its area, first find its radius:

$$C = 2\pi r$$
$$60 = 2\pi r$$
$$r = \frac{30}{\pi}.$$

Then $A = \pi r^2 = \pi\left(\frac{30}{\pi}\right)^2 = \frac{900}{\pi} \approx 286 \text{ ft}^2$.

45.

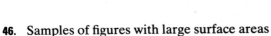

46. Samples of figures with large surface areas for their volume are sheets of notebook paper or newsprint, and perfume bottles or other containers of expensive ingredients.

47.

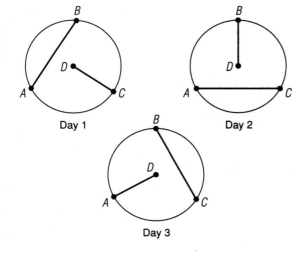

Day 1

Day 2

Day 3

round 1: A-B, C-D
round 2: A-C, B-D
round 3: A-D, B-C

48.

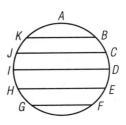

round 1:	K-B	J-C	I-D	H-E	G-F	A-bye
round 2:	A-C	K-D	J-E	I-F	H-G	B-bye
round 3:	B-D	A-E	K-F	J-G	I-H	C-bye
round 4:	C-E	B-F	A-G	K-H	J-I	D-bye
round 5:	D-F	C-G	B-H	A-I	K-J	E-bye
round 6:	E-G	D-H	C-I	B-J	A-K	F-bye
rounc 7:	F-H	E-I	D-J	C-K	B-A	G-bye
round 8:	G-I	F-J	E-K	D-A	C-B	H-bye
round 9:	H-J	G-K	F-A	E-B	D-C	I-bye
round 10:	I-K	H-A	G-B	F-C	E-D	J-bye
round 11:	J-A	I-B	H-C	G-D	F-E	K-bye

49.

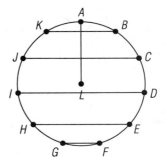

Use the same pairings as for Question 48, but replace the "bye" with the 12th team L.